What's That Job

and How the Hell Do I Get It?

Go Put Your Strengths to Work
Marcus Buckingham
list activities
I feel

Strong   weak
        when

Strong
special
unique

how does it
make you
feel you

focus

Also by David J. Rosen

I Just Want My Pants Back: A Novel

David J. Rosen

What's That Job

and How the Hell Do I Get It?

The Inside Scoop
on More Than
50 Cool Jobs
from People
Who Actually
Have Them

Broadway Books
New York

BROADWAY

PUBLISHED BY BROADWAY BOOKS

Copyright © 2008 by David J. Rosen

Published in the United States by Broadway Books, an imprint of The Doubleday
Broadway Publishing Group, a division of Random House, Inc., New York.
www.broadwaybooks.com

BROADWAY BOOKS and its logo, a letter B bisected on the diagonal, are trademarks
of Random House, Inc.

Library of Congress Cataloging-in-Publication Data
Rosen, David J.
    What's that job and how the hell do I get it? : the inside scoop on more than 50 cool
jobs from people who actually have them / By David J. Rosen. — 1st ed.
        p. cm.
    1. Occupations. 2. Professions. 3. Job descriptions. 4. Vocational guidance.
5. Self-evaluation. I. Title. II. Title: The inside scoop on more than 50 cool jobs from
people who actually have them.
    HF5381R7615   2008
    331.702—dc22

                                                                    2007032346

ISBN 978-0-7679-2612-6

PRINTED IN THE UNITED STATES OF AMERICA

10 9 8 7 6 5 4 3 2 1

First Edition

Contents

Introduction   vii

A&R Executive   1

Actor   7

Advertising Creative   15
Copywriter/Art Director

Alternative-Medicine Practitioner   24
Chiropractor/Acupuncturist

Architect   31

Author   40

Band Manager   48

Blogger   54

Boutique Owner   60

Chef   67

Clergy   73

Composer   79

Designer   87

Doula   93

Entrepreneur   99

Event Planner   105

Fashion Designer   112

Film Director   119

Flash Developer/
Multimedia Designer   128

Gallerist   134

Headhunter   141

Information Architect   148

Investment Banker   153

Jewelry Designer   160

Life Coach   165

Magazine Writer/Magazine Editor   171

Management Consultant   179

Mediator   186

Personal Trainer   195

Pharmaceutical Salesperson   201

Photographer   208

Physical Therapist   216

get a good feel for exactly what each job is, whether you want to pursue it, and what the hell it's going to take to get it.

Hopefully, without any paper cuts.

But before We Begin . . . Two Pieces of Advice

Regardless of his or her profession, interviewee after interviewee uttered the same two suggestions for breaking into their exciting, competitive fields:

One, be willing to intern or work for free to get your foot in the door. As you shall see, it's important to show you're willing to "do whatever it takes" to gain an entry-level position. And that often involves, for a little while, working for nothing.

Two, get to know people in the field, any way you can. Yep, it really *is* who you know. Ask everyone and anyone if they have any connections to a kind soul in the industry you seek. Your brother's girlfriend's cousin's sister with the Beanie Baby collection might just be the hookup you've been searching for. Don't be shy: network.

Sure, you may have already known those things. But as you'll see across a wide swath of professions, it turns out they are even more important than most people believe. If you walk away with only those two things from this mighty tome, those are the ones to carry.

And One Quick Note on the Money

Salary is always a tricky subject. In this book, compensation is reported two ways. First, whenever possible, salary figures are quoted from a respected statistical survey. The preferred reportage is from the government's Bureau of Labor Statistics (bls.gov), followed by sites like salary.com or industry-specific salary surveys.

Several careers in this book, however, are either so new or so specialized that statistical data do not yet exist. Don't fret, because for each job, "anecdotal" salary figures are also provided. These are the salaries quoted by interviewees and then backed up by more than one source in the profession. Often the anecdotal salaries are higher than the ones in surveys like the BLS's, as those tend to come from a more generic sample. For example, the BLS's mean salary figures for the profession of jewelry designer averages in the jobs of stone setter and gem polisher, which are lower-paying positions.

Thus endeth the preamble. Onward to the main event . . .

What's That Job

and How the Hell Do I Get It?

A&R Executive

A&R executives don't make music—but without them, you probably wouldn't have heard your favorite song. They're the folks at record labels who discover bands and musicians, get them record deals, and then shepherd them through the music industry bureaucracy until their albums are in stores. It's an amazing career where you can meet unknown, talented musicians and—if you really believe in them—help make their wildest dreams come true.

You just got a little misty-eyed, didn't you?

My job is first to help decide what artists are signed to the label, and then, on an album-by-album basis, to help them continue on a progressive journey toward full artistdom, so to speak.
—**Mark Jowett, head of A&R, Nettwerk**

What's A&R?

A stands for *artists,* the actual human musicians, and *R* stands for their *repertoire,* or their songs. So the A&R department is the part of a record label that first scouts and discovers the Artists, and then develops their musical talent, Repertoire, with the goal of eventually making albums that earn millions. To do this, they not only find the musicians, but then help handle everything including the contractual negotiations involved in signing a band, hiring songwriters and record producers to improve the band's sound, and scheduling the actual recording sessions.

Sometimes A&R people toil to make important records, sometimes mediocre records, but either way, records that everyone hopes will make money. It's not just about art—the A&R people's job is to find and develop moneymakers. And if they don't, well, generally they get about eighteen to twenty-four months' leeway before it's time to pack up their crap and wave buh-bye.

And What's It Like to Work at a Label?

Rockin'. Well, it's not a used-record store, and colleagues don't hold lighters in the air when you make a good presentation, but as you'd imagine, it's pretty damn casual. Every label has its own culture, but it's the music world and it's open to letting you be the person you want to be. You need not hide the piercings or tattoos here; feel free to let your inner Goth, rocker, or diva show. Some labels focus on indie rock and their vibe is very jeans and T-shirts; others are more hip-hop oriented and the gold rope chains are in effect. There are large labels housed in shiny office towers and small ones in makeshift lofts. They are all places where (just about) every employee chose to work because they loved music and wanted to be close to it, from the marketers to the receptionists to the accountants.

A&R folks' jobs are entirely performance based—everyone sees what you do and what bands you sign. In fact, the whole business starts with you. You find the band, sign them, get their record made, and then feed it into the company machine. The rest of the label—marketing folks, online promotions people, and so on—then works feverishly on it. They may love the album, or they might grumble, "Why are we working on this piece of crap?"

But You Won't Always Be in the Office

As an A&R person, you'll travel a lot. Sometimes you'll go see bands across the country (or world), and sometimes you'll literally be chasing them around because other labels want to sign them as well. There are a lot of frequent-flyer miles to be had.

If one of your bands is recording their record away from where you live, you'll go join them. You need to be at the studio for support, to help them make the best record they can, and to make sure they are using their expensive studio time wisely. Soup to nuts, recording and getting out a record (promotion, artwork, and so on) at a major label costs a minimum of a million bucks. And the label is doing it all because they believe in your taste, that you picked a winner. Yeah, you'll be at the recording session.

Where You Start and Where You Go

So you're getting excited—you love music and this job sounds pretty cool, huh? Well, hear this now and digest it: you are not going to start working at a label in the A&R department. There is no job there for you; they simply do not hire entry-level anyone. So how do you get started in A&R? The first step is getting in the door of a record label any way you can. Then once inside, do your best to network. Go meet people in A&R, and then, somehow, migrate over. So the first job you take at a label could be in marketing or accounting, you might be the receptionist even, but it's all a means to an end, your first job in A&R. How long that migration takes—weeks, months, years—really depends on you, and how well you work it. More advice on breaking in shortly.

Once you are working in A&R, the job pretty much stays the same, even as you climb the ladder (and you ascend strictly based on your track record of

Even if your last band went to the top of the charts, that was then, what's happening now? The saying in A&R goes, "You are only as good as your last hit."
—Jared Sheer, A&R manager, Epic

successful records). Sure, there are bigger titles and money and added managerial duties, and you'll be able to tell someone beneath you, "Hey, go check these guys out in Philly and tell me if they're any good live," but the major responsibilities will remain the same: find good musicians, sign them, and help them make a great record that will earn the label gobs of cash.

That said, rising in the organization requires a lot of luck. Everyone in the industry knows it—the best bands just don't always make it big. And behind every "almost" band is an A&R guy holding an economy-sized jug of Pepto.

What Kind of Person Fits the Bill?

First off, surprise, surprise, you should love music. Sure, in the end it's about money, but if you are just about money, there are easier ways to get rich. But even though you have the love, you also need to exercise some level of emotional detachment. You have to separate yourself from the dreams of the musicians you work with; otherwise, you'll be a mess when things don't work out, which is frequently. The band will be wrecks, but you need to be clearheaded and able to see the next move.

If you're to be good at A&R, you must be a somewhat creative person yourself. You have to be able to think abstractly and understand the band's vision. And then you need to be willing to do what it takes to make this vision a reality. Self-starters and go-getters tend to do well. With the long hours, energy and stamina are another must, so if you poop out before Conan comes on, you're probably not going to make it. Also, you must be patient; the odds are always against your making the next big album, so you have to persevere and try, try again.

Last and most important, to be successful in A&R you need to have a quality that can't be learned: the ability to identify music that will appeal to a wide audience. It's hard to define, yet it's critical to your success.

Hours?

A job in A&R is truly a twenty-four-hour gig. Any time could be work time. You'll leave the office and go out to see a bunch of shows. You'll travel on the weekends to see bands playing out of town. Musicians record when they feel the muse, so your sessions are frequently late-night, early-morning affairs. And all the while, you'll be rocking the Blackberry, doing the two-thumb shuffle on one of the other projects you're developing.

However, even though you might be working all night, c'mon, it's music. It's got to be one of the most social jobs in the world. You will be hanging out

So much is out of your control. You could find a great band, get them through the nightmare of signing, booking studios, and finally making an actual album, a great album . . . and it could flop. The public may just "not be ready for it." Or the timing could be wrong on the release date, or the record comes out opposite some huge hit from someone else.
—Jared Sheer, A&R manager, Epic

Good A&R people can actually make a huge indent on pop culture; that's what makes the job so exciting. They can literally define the modern music scene by the musicians they discover, develop, and then vigorously promote and defend.
—Jared Sheer, A&R manager, Epic

with people who, like you, love music. People who would pay to go out and see bands, find ones they dig, and help them make an album. When it's midnight and you're drinking a beer in the VIP section, it's hard to complain about it being a tough job. At the same time, it's sometimes hard to maintain a social life outside the industry. You'll go to a friend's birthday party and inevitably look at your watch and say, "Shit, gotta jet and catch this band downtown." You will always, always have a pair of earplugs somewhere on your person. (When you see loud shows five nights a week, you aren't ashamed to rock the earplugs. Otherwise you end up with tinnitus, Pete Townshend style.)

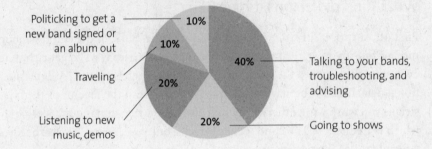

Politicking to get a new band signed or an album out — 10%

10%

Traveling

20%

Listening to new music, demos

10%

40% — Talking to your bands, troubleshooting, and advising

20% — Going to shows

How Much Cheddar?

A&R folks make a salary, plus there is a point system, meaning they get a percentage of the sales of the records on which they've worked. There really haven't been any surveys of A&R salaries, nor is it a career covered by the fine people at the Bureau of Labor Statistics.

Your first job in A&R will probably pay somewhere between $20,000 and $25,000. However, discover a few bands that make it big, and you will see the Benjamins. Pay of between $150,000 and $200,000 is not out of the ordinary. And at the top, the money is fantastic. Yacht-riffic.

1   10

Stress-o-Meter: 6 (1 being a hand model, 10 being a hand surgeon)

But on occasion, it peaks to 10. It's always fun to be making records. But remember, for every band you sign and album you make, you are basically asking the label to spend at least $1,000,000. And with that expenditure comes the pressure to perform. You'll be dealing with lots of egos and maybe even people with drug and alcohol problems. However, it's music, not heart surgery—although bands' careers may be just as hard to resuscitate.

Pros

It's a glamorous job.

You'll see bands all night, and listen to music all day.

You work with cool people who, like you, love music.

There are expense accounts.

You get to go to sick parties, and get free stuff in abundance, like music, movies, DVDs, and video games.

Cons

You may have to deal with some nasty celebrity egos.

Long, long hours and being on the road can make the gig quite tiring.

Breaking in isn't a cakewalk, and once you do, there's pressure to succeed.

You get caught up in a lot of "pop culture bullshit."

The music industry is not doing so well these days.

Congratulations, You Work in A&R. You Wake Up And . . .

9:00 AM: You brush your teeth and swallow a couple of Advil. You were out until three last night at a showcase you booked so executives at the label could see the bands you're currently interested in.

10:30 AM: You arrive at the office. You drink a pint-sized iced coffee and check your voice mail. Good news, one of your bands impressed last night; you have a few messages about them from the heads of the label.

11:00 AM: You have a lot of projects going on, all in different stages of development. In a whirlwind of activity, you set up one of your bands to be interviewed by a music writer from *CMJ (College Music Journal)*, find studio time for another band to record an EP, and coordinate the travel arrangements for a third band.

5:30 PM: You head out with a colleague. Every night there's something to do; you might see a show, meet a band's manager, go to a movie premiere that one of your band's songs is in, you name it. Tonight you have a dinner meeting with a band you are on the verge of signing; they are considering your label and one other. You pocket your corporate credit card and hit the street.

8:00 PM: After the fried calamari is served, you get serious for a minute. You tell the band that if they sign with you, you'll kill yourself to make their record the best it can be. You know your label is bigger than some of the others they've been talking to, but you give them your oath they will never get lost there.

10:00 PM: Last night was a late one, so after dinner you make a beeline for your couch, lie down, and watch TV.

I've Got the Music in Me. How the Hell Do I Get This Job?

Okay, brace yourself for another annoying nugget of truth. You are going to have a hard time getting a job in A&R if you don't live in New York City or Los Angeles. There are music labels elsewhere, but the majority are in those two cities (in America, that is; of course there are heaps of labels in London, Tokyo, Rio, and so on).

The way into a label, in any capacity, is to get an internship, or several internships year after year, and get them as early as possible. If you can get one while you're still in high school even, bravo. (If you live outside New York or L.A., consider spending a summer in one of those cities and getting a summer internship.) If you do get an interview for an internship, don't ever, ever say you want to intern in A&R. Everybody wants that, and odds are you will be rejected (since you've shown no interest in the other departments that actually have openings). Just get in, in any department, and start absorbing how a label works. And then, schmooze it up. Make friends with the A&R people; find out what floor they're on and somehow ingratiate yourself. Think of something. For example, everyone loves donuts. And once you've gotten to know them, toward the end of the current internship, ask them if you could intern in their department next semester or summer. Sounds crazy, right? It works.

There's really no other experience that will help you land an A&R job. You could be a DJ for your college radio station, write music reviews for a Web site, or book bands for a local club, but only in the craziest, rarest of circumstances would that get you directly into A&R. But they are worthwhile activities, because they will help you get a different entry-level job or an internship. No matter how padded your résumé, you still will need to go that route. Truth is, A&R jobs really don't exist. They are created for individuals who the label thinks might know something that will eventually land a great band. That's why you first need to get in the door and make the relationships with the decision makers. And show them how awesome you are.

Resources, or What Helps You Be the Kind of Person Labels Want to Create a Job For?

You should be immersed in pop culture. You should see shows and look for new bands constantly, be versed in who is playing and drawing people. Information can be found anywhere—there are a billion music blogs, such as pitchforkmedia.com and stereogum.com, but you have to take everything you read with a grain of salt until you see or hear the bands for yourself. The label is paying for your opinion. Talking to friends whose opinions you trust is just as important as learning about bands from the press or scouts; talk to bartenders and bouncers and sound engineers at the cool clubs, the folks who are there every night. Just go up to them and ask who sounds good, who have they seen lately who has promise?

And you should be browsing sites like myspace.com. These have become a vital place for new bands to start; set aside some time every day and go on a treasure hunt. When you find bands you love, champion them. Be one of the voices in the crowd that turns on the people who are already working in A&R.

You could try to find one or two bands that you really love and start a tiny label on your own. It doesn't cost very much to put music on the Net. The reality is that the music industry these days is a bit like the Wild West, because it's so much easier for artists to reach fans directly through the Internet with MySpace and BandSpace and many other sites. If you make some noise, well, labels will be more inclined to meet you.
—Mark Jowett, head of A&R, Nettwerk

Actor

"Are you talking to me? Because there's no one else here. Are you talking to me?" As just words in a script, the lines are innocuous. It is the actor's job to interpret these words and bring them to life. Like Robert De Niro did, when he took those words in *Taxi Driver,* and through his character, made them absolutely sinister and foreboding. The Mohawk didn't hurt either.

Professional actors work in theater, television, radio, Web films, commercials, and even video games. Those who pursue it can't picture themselves doing anything else. It's not a choice; it's who they are. And you may well understand that feeling. Perhaps you were belting out "Tomorrow" as Little Orphan Annie in elementary school, or putting on your best English accent to say "Please sir, can I have some more?" as Oliver. Did you ever "act sick" to stay home from school? Did you successfully act out the "I'm getting tired" yawn to put your arm around a date? Or "cry on cue" to get out of your first speeding ticket? If so, then you just might have the acting bug. Read on, young thespian.

The Big But

As you must know, making a living solely through acting is a long shot. It is a business filled with rejection. To work as an actor, and only an actor, you pretty much have to live in Los Angeles for TV and film, or New York City for theater as well as TV and film, albeit on a lesser scale. You can be an actor in other cities, but rarely is there enough paying work for you to do nothing else.

In fact, most actors have a secondary source of income, especially starting out. And most roles are for actors between ages twenty and forty, which means you'll probably need that secondary income toward the latter part of your career as well.

If you want to be an actor, take solace in the fact that plenty of little-known working actors make decent salaries and are living their dreams. And of course, there are the lucky few who've made it big and live lives of mansions, personal assistants, and stables filled with giraffes.

My goal as an actor is to make the audience emotionally go through what my character is going through.
—Melonie Diaz, actor, *Raising Victor Vargas*

As an actor you're constantly looking for work, and even if you're auditioning all the time, you're not necessarily booking the job. So as much as you know it's not about you personally, it starts to creep into your mind—"Am I in the right business? What am I doing wrong that's preventing me from getting this gig?"
—Gibson Frazier, actor, co-writer, and producer, *Man of the Century*

Auditions, Auditions, Auditions

The biggest part of the job of actor, as well as the largest frustration, is actually looking for work. This unpaid hunt for roles will take up far more time than the paid performing part. Actors' working lives can basically be split in two: life when you're looking for a role, and life when you have one.

To get a part in any sort of production, you must audition for it, unless you happen to be Meryl Streep. Auditions are like job interviews; they don't pay. You'll be called to the studio or casting director's office along with a lot of other actors, and one by one, you will each perform some of the script. You will be videotaped for later review by the director (who generally doesn't attend the first round of casting), and the whole thing will usually be over in about five to ten minutes. However, you may well be sitting on your butt in an overcrowded room full of actors with coffee breath for up to an hour, until you're called into the actual audition. It's a bit like waiting for the doctor during flu season.

Auditions are pretty rough. First, you will spend a lot of time and effort running around town to different ones. You could have two or three in a day, in different parts of town. Second, many times you walk into them cold, are handed a script, and then are asked on the spot to act it out. You won't get a lot of direction, and you can leave feeling very defeated. It's a hard thing to constantly do to your ego. You really have to believe in yourself and develop thick skin.

If you nail an audition—yee-ha!—two things can happen. One is boom, you get the part. The other is you are invited to a *callback,* basically a second audition, which will be attended by the decision makers—the director and producers. Only a few actors are called back for a given role, so you'll be directed more closely and spend more time acting than waiting. Then after performing, you'll leave, and hope the call you get later from your agent is a happy one.

Speaking of Agents . . .

To be invited to auditions, you generally need an agent. Sure, there are *open calls,* meaning auditions anyone can show up at, but for most of the better roles, only actors with agents are asked to try out.

Agents can also get you into auditions for which casting directors may not have thought of you. Your agent can say, "I know you want a statuesque blonde, but you should really look at this actress, she has a quality I think might be perfect." If your agent has a good track record, you very well may be

On stage, we talk about being "in the moment." That's what is appealing for an audience to watch—two actors that seem as if they are talking for real. And that's the experience you want in the audition, regardless of the material. I mean, you obviously want your read to be good and make sense, but you also want to have some magic, some spark going on between you and the rest of the room, separate from that.
—Gibson Frazier, actor, co-writer, and producer, *Man of the Century*

invited. Plus, as you get more successful, an agent will really guide your career. They help you move up, one role at a time, with an eye on building you as an actor. They're pretty much a necessity.

Of course, it's hard to get an agent if you haven't had a role. And it's hard to get an audition to get a role if you don't have an agent. It's the first of many wonderful Catch-22s you'll find in the acting game.

The Union

Here's the second. Acting is a union gig. There are three main unions: the Actors' Equity Association (AEA), which is the union for the theater; the Screen Actors Guild (SAG), which is for films and TV; and the American Federation of Television and Radio Artists (AFTRA), which is for radio, recordings, and some television. To work as a professional actor, you have to be in the appropriate union. You can't get a job until you join. However, you cannot join any of the unions until you have a job. Figure that one out.

Actually, somehow, you will. Perhaps you'll have been given extra work on a Nike commercial, and suddenly are needed to do a speaking part. Boom, that one line—"Boy, he's fast!"—is your first official "role," and your ticket into the Screen Actors Guild.

Although getting in the union seems an insurmountable hurdle at first, once you are a member, you're a member for life (assuming you pay your dues, which are based on your yearly earnings). It's sort of like being "made" in the Mafia. The unions protect actors from being taken advantage of and ensure they are paid at least the legal minimums, which are amounts they've negotiated. In addition, if you make over a certain amount of money acting, you can get health insurance and other benefits through the unions.

Life When You Have a Part

When you're working as an actor, life is pretty damn fun. You're part of a group of people with a common goal: making the production—be it a play, film, or commercial—the best it can be. You'll be around other actors, as well as set designers, wardrobe stylists, producers, and directors, who share your passion. You're being treated with respect; you're one of the most important people on the set or backstage. It's like you've finally found your home, and the spirit and energy of it are addictive. Actors say that there's just something magical about the camaraderie.

If you're working on film sets of any kind (TV, features, commercials), you'll find there's a lot of downtime and hanging out. You may be on the set for ten hours, but spend only twenty minutes actually acting. Even less if your role is a small one. Lighting, blocking camerawork, shooting scenes you aren't in, and so on all take time. A day on a film set as an actor can best be described as hours of boredom interrupted by minutes of exhilaration.

As an actor, you'll see that every director's approach is different. Sometimes you'll do a lot of rehearsal before a production begins, learning and tweaking your part. On other projects you'll literally meet your co-actors on the set the morning of the first day and begin filming hours later. It all depends.

In the theater, there is far less free time. Before a play opens to the public, there are weeks of rehearsals. When the show finally does open, actors arrive at the theater around an hour before the curtain rises. Then it's showtime! And once it's over, after some hanging out backstage, the actors leave. Sure, there will be a few nights out with the cast and crew, tipping back glasses of champagne and all that, but Broadway shows have eight performances a week. You can't go out for celebratory drinks after each one. Not unless you're Peter O'Toole.

What It Takes to Be an Actor

A lot of people dream of being professional actors. A lot of them have the charisma and charm to be entertaining on the stage or screen. And a lot of them don't make it. Those who do are incredibly hardworking; they've made personal sacrifices and have been damn lucky. "Right place, right time" stories abound. Start looking for a four leaf clover on eBay.

The odds of being lucky increase if you are diligent. You probably aren't going to nail your first audition, or your fiftieth. You just have to hang in there, though, and believe in yourself. Take nonpaying parts in plays in crappy little theaters, and roles in short, independent films that only a few people will ever see at festivals. But hey, you'll go to that festival, and you'll feel like a star—you can wear sunglasses at night and everything. One day, the right person just may be in the audience.

It sounds a little corny, but what makes you a great actor is really knowing yourself. It's having had life experiences that you can bring to a character and then share with the world in a way that truly connects. It comes from your own unique personal background, your self-education.

A formal acting education is another tool you can use to help increase your self-awareness. While there are a few "naturals" out there in the world, you probably will want to take acting classes. This doesn't mean you need to go the whole hog and major in drama, or even get an MFA (although if you do, you can always teach as your "day job"), but most actors will tell you the acting workshops they've attended and training they've received are invaluable. Just watch any episode of *Inside the Actors Studio;* all the actors always give props to their teachers and mentors. With education, you'll understand how to take direction and what a director may want from you. Sure, none of these can give you that magical "star" quality, but they will make you a more intelligent actor.

When you go to an audition, no one is going to ask to see a résumé or your GPA. But although your college major and extracurricular activities don't really count in terms of "getting a job," they may help you better understand yourself, and thus be a better actor.

Hours?

When you are working on a film, TV show, or commercial, you'll probably need to be on set ten to twelve hours a day. And it might actually be during the day, or it could be a night shoot. In the theater, before a show opens you will rehearse from 10 AM to 5 PM, five days a week. Once it does, you'll be at the theater an hour before the curtains go up, and you'll leave when the play ends, so you're working three to five hours a day, tops.

When you don't have a part, it depends how many auditions you have scheduled, what scripts you are reading, and really, what you define as "work." It might be zero hours; it might be three or four. If you are secure and feel another job is coming, you can really enjoy these days off. You can plan extended trips; you live outside the normal system the rest of the working world follows. You get to go to the gym during off hours; when everyone else is stuck in their office, you, my friend, will be king or queen of the treadmills. However, if you're more neurotic, these downtimes can give you the shakes.

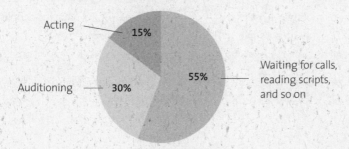

Acting — 15%
Auditioning — 30%
55% Waiting for calls, reading scripts, and so on

Play Money?

You could make nothing, but there's always the chance you could be the next Tom Cruise and have hand-tailored suits made of endangered species. Until

As an actor, you use your body and mind as tools. Training helps you get the most out of them. The education really helps you learn more about yourself as well, and how to take different experiences and bring them to a role.
—Melonie Diaz, actor, *Raising Victor Vargas*

I was a waitress for a long time. When *Raising Victor Vargas* came out and I was starting to really get noticed, I was still waitressing. That's just how it is. Most actors have to support themselves with another job.

— **Melonie Diaz, actor,**
  Raising Victor Vargas

you start booking jobs consistently enough to feed yourself and your cats, you'll need a "real" job that's flexible enough that you can run out to auditions.

Once you are working, how much you're paid is based on minimums set by the different unions. Your agent may be able to get more for you, depending on how hot you are. Union guidelines are fairly complex, really splicing and dissecting out every possibility of performance. (You can download all the possibilities from each union's site, listed in the Resources section.) As complex as they are, looking at the unions' salary guidelines is really the best way to go, because salary surveys are a bit spotty for this profession.

Salary.com reports that actors' and performers' salaries range from $30,737 to $65,843 nationally. The Bureau of Labor Statistics reports an hourly salary for this field instead of an annual, $23.37 being the mean hourly wage—with the following caveat: "There is wide variation in the number of hours worked by those employed as actors, dancers, musicians, and singers. Many jobs are for a duration of 1 day or 1 week and it is extremely rare for a performer to have guaranteed employment for a period that exceeds 3 to 6 months."

1   10

Stress-o-Meter: 5 (1 being a crossing guard, 10 being a prison guard)

It's an average; actors will tell you that when they're working, it's around a 3. And when they aren't working, it's around 9.5. The constant fear of never working again, of nobody liking you, is the hard part. Performing is the joy. And of course, there are the reviews. Some actors never read them; some can't wait to. Either way, being judged is never a stress-free activity.

Pros

You love to act. You'd do it for free.

Making films or theater is a collaborative artistic project where you meet amazing, talented people.

You live a life different from all the other "suckers" out there.

Cons

The inconsistency of work is stressful.

A lot of creepy, fake, parasitic people are attached to the entertainment world.

You may be somewhat poor. Ramen noodles could be a staple in your life.

Break a Leg, Kid. You're an Actor. You Wake Up And . . .

10:00 AM: Last night was the final performance of an off-Broadway play you've been performing in for the past three months. You give yourself permission to "act lazy" and lounge in bed for a little while.

11:15 AM: Now showered and dressed, you check your e-mail and then flip through a few scripts your agent has sent over. These are projects that will be casting in the next several weeks, and you want to dig in to the material.

11:30 AM: Your agent calls. It's last minute, but he's been able to squeeze you in to an audition for a laundry detergent commercial. Do you think you can be a suburban dad by 1 PM?

12:45 PM: You walk into the waiting room of the audition at a midtown casting company. Ten other actors are there, each of them dressed to look like the Father of the Year. You sign in with the receptionist, who lets you know they are running a bit behind.

1:25 PM: You're called in and told the plot of the commercial: you've just come home from work and discovered that the kids have been playing "grown-up" in your dress shirts—and now they are filthy. Instead of being upset, though, you are nonchalant, because you can count on this fantastic laundry detergent. They ask you to ad-lib the scene, using a paper towel to represent your dirty dress shirt.

1:35 PM: You have no idea how that went, but you didn't bomb. As you exit the building, you have a slight shiver as you remember saying something like, "That's okay, Sally, Daddy knows just what to do." Aaaargh.

3:30 PM: You try to finish one of the scripts from earlier in the day.

5:00 PM: Your agent calls. You have been asked to a callback, tomorrow at noon, for the laundry detergent!

6:00 PM: You have an early dinner and then go out to see a friend in a small production downtown, which starts at eight. You haven't been able to see many plays lately as you've been in one yourself, and you're looking forward to being part of the audience. But only for a little while, please!

Bravo, I Love It. So How the Hell Do I Become an Actor?

Get an audition and nail it. Or be discovered serving coffee when a famous director's hybrid breaks down in your hometown. Or write your own movie, cast yourself in the lead role, get it into Sundance, and let the star-studded industry audience see your amazing chops. There's no one surefire way to break in. The most traveled path, though, is the path of training, and then dedication. Take any role you can get, salaried or not, until you start to land more steady work.

What helps on this journey? Well, as mentioned, living in L.A. or NYC. Next, a positive attitude. You have to believe, deep down, that it is going to happen for you.

You have little control in this profession, as ultimately whether you get a role is someone else's decision. So when you finally get into that audition room, control the one thing at your mercy—the vibe in the room. That doesn't mean coming up with a joke beforehand and telling it as you walk in the door. It's the true sense of improvisation, feeling out the people in front of you, and truly engaging them. Finally, don't put so much pressure on every audition. You will have bad ones and good ones. And there's always another coming up.

Just like in every other profession, who you know means a lot. So whenever you see a play or a film premiere or just attend a party, network. Don't be slimy or desperate, of course, but when you talk with other people you may hear about auditions or even end up in a conversation with a director who will remember your face in six months' time. You never know.

Resources

Look at the acting union Web sites, which have advice for actors just starting out, casting call information, union salary minimums, and more:

Screen Actors Guild: sag.org

American Federation of Television and Radio Artists: aftra.com

Actors' Equity Association: actorsequity.org

A subscription to IMDbPro.com will keep you up-to-date with everything happening in the film and TV world. It's pretty amazing, and only around $12 a month. Also check out actors-network.com for tons of great info on all things thespian.

The industry magazines are *Backstage, Variety,* and *The Hollywood Reporter.* These all have useful Web sites as well: backstage.com, variety.com, and hollywoodreporter.com. *Backstage* is really tailored to actors more than the other two and offers a wealth of info, especially online.

There are many great books on acting. Two recommended ones are by Stephen Book: *The Actor Takes a Meeting* and *Book on Acting: Improvisation Technique for the Professional Actor in Film, Theater, and Television.*

The most famous acting schools, workshops, and teachers, such as Stella Adler (stellaadler.com), Lee Strasberg (strasberg.com), HB Studio (hbstudio .org) and the Actors Studio (theactorsstudio.org), are all based in New York City or Los Angeles. To find a school near you, go to hollywoodauditions .com/schools.htm. It has a search engine that allows you to find acting schools by location.

Advertising Creative
Copywriter/Art Director

Advertising creatives, whose titles include *copywriter, art director,* and, as they are promoted, *creative director,* are the people at advertising agencies who actually come up with the TV commercials, print ads, billboards, Web sites, and viral videos that you see every day. They can create ideas for something as epic as a new Levi's TV campaign set in Antarctica, or as tactical as what it will say on the tags that hang off the jeans—and everything in between. America has a love/hate relationship with advertising. When it's good, a commercial can be better than anything else on TV. When it's bad, like a pharmaceutical commercial that reminds us, repeatedly, "This medication may have serious side effects. If you find yourself bleeding from the mouth, nose, or genitals, consult your doctor," we want to throw a shoe at our flatscreens.

Some agencies, and the creatives who work at them, specialize in a certain type of advertising. For example, healthcare agencies do mostly pharmaceutical advertising; other agencies do only fashion ads. Although agencies may be known for creating ads for luxury goods over packaged goods, as far as media (print, radio, TV, and so on) is concerned, the trend in the business is for agencies to be able to work across the entire spectrum. Yes, some agencies focus on interactive or online work, but that is beginning to change. People who create TV commercials must also be able to come up with ideas for the Web, mobile phones, ads written on the sand at the beach, anything.

The Ad Agency in Two Little Paragraphs

Before we get to the creatives, a little background on the ol' ad game. Advertising agencies are in the business of developing corporate communication, that is, ads, for paying clients. Their main task is to create communications that build brands, build relationships, and, most important, build sales. Creatives are the heart and soul of the advertising agency, but not the only people who work there.

Almost all agencies have the same structure, although in the inevitable advertising way, they may try to differentiate themselves by giving departments

> As a creative, you have to be able to see through the eyes of people who may not be exactly like you. You put yourself in their shoes and figure out what interesting creative message would resonate with them, excite them, make them like the brand, and compel them to buy.
> —**Gary Resch, associate creative director, DraftFCB, New York**

> Nowadays, a good advertising idea needs to be bigger than any one piece of media. It's not the TV business or the Web business, it's the idea business.
> —**Noah Davis, associate creative director, DraftFCB, New York**

new names. Basically there are four main departments: *creative*, the people who write and make the ideas; *account management*, who aren't accountants, but businesspeople who manage the agency's clients; *media*, who figure out where the target market is—for example, for Pepsi, college students watch *South Park*, let's put an ad on during that show; and *production*, the folks who actually help physically produce the artwork, film, video, and so on, needed to make the ads. Large agencies have support departments as well, such as human resources. But for now, let's keep it simple.

The Creative Department

The creative department is based on teams. Writers and art directors work together (one of each) as a single unit to come up with ideas. Of course, there are anomalies at every agency: the threesome team, or the one person who works alone (really smart or serial killer). Being in these partnerships is a bit like being in a marriage. Partners are parents, and their ideas are their children, who must be constantly protected from bad suggestions from clients, account people, and so on. Partners rely on each other to grow and advance not only their ideas, but also each other's careers. That's why when a partnership is working, it usually lasts many years, broken only when one of the partners moves, changes careers, or is party to an unfortunate fishing accident.

You can be only one or the other, writer or art director, by the way. Before you go for your first job, you'll need to make the choice. Chances are you already know which one better suits you. Still, there is a lot of crossover between writers and art directors. The writer may come up with a visual solution, the art director with a great headline. The writer may do all the drawing to present the team's concepts; the art director might be great with dialogue and write radio scripts. But basically, when push comes to shove, the writer must be able to write, interestingly, insightfully. The art director must be able to art direct and design, to make things look perfect. Photos of food must look mouthwatering, headlines and type expertly kerned and spaced. Art directors must know all the major design programs: Adobe InDesign or Quark, Adobe Photoshop, and Adobe Illustrator. And it helps if they can draw.

Here's (Roughly) How an Ad Is Born:

The creatives get an assignment; let's say Nike needs a TV spot to sell a new running shoe. They lock themselves in their office and brainstorm ideas based on the research and insight provided by the client and the account people, until they come up with what they think are "killer" ideas. They may have a day,

You can look at an agency like it's a restaurant. The client is the customer who comes in looking for sustenance. An account manager is the waiter, who makes suggestions and consults with the client, and then brings their order into the kitchen. The account manager tells the creatives, the chefs, the client wants "something spicy, something different." The creatives whip together an ad, a meal, they think will fulfill the client's needs. It may or may not get sent back into the kitchen after it's served.
—**Scott Bassen, associate creative director, Taxi**

Most people are on their own when they get a job out of college. Creatives are joined at the hip with their partners; it's you two against the world. You really work together all day, every day. You'll probably end up spending more time with your partner than you will with your girlfriend or boyfriend. You get to know all their habits, what they like to eat for lunch, their allergies, what foods disagree with them, everything.
—**Scott Bassen, associate creative director, Taxi**

they may have two weeks; advertising timelines are always unpredictable. They then present these ideas to their boss, the creative director. Creative directors (CDs), as their title says, direct and manage writers and art directors. Before the client or anyone else at the agency gets a peek, the CDs see the work of the creative teams and help shape and focus them. Good CDs are mentors who will do anything to help make ideas the best they can be and to sell them down the line. However, advertising is infamous for the occasional bad CDs, ones who are spiteful, paranoid, and in competition with smart young juniors. But such is life—a few great human beings on a planet teeming with jerks.

Usually the CD will have some comments to make; he or she will kill a couple of the weaker ideas and have thoughts on how the survivors could be stronger or funnier. Once these changes are made, the creatives will show the account management team, who may also have suggestions. There may be some friction at this point; the creatives think the account management "suits" have no creative vision, and the account management team thinks the creatives are being "too wacky for wacky's sake." (Or they may call it "too edgy.") After some back-and-forth, the work is blessed by all, and it's the client's turn to see it, generally in a meeting in a nice big conference room. If the project is a TV commercial, scripts will be read by the writer, and the art director may show a full storyboard or just some key visuals to help the client better understand the idea. Hopefully the client likes one of the ideas (three is generally the magic number to show: two to be killed, one to live), and then the team (with the help of a director, producer, and so on) goes forth and makes the commercial. If not, back to square one.

Once an idea has been "sold" to the client, creatives are then responsible for the idea's production. They make sure the vision they've presented develops into the vision the public sees. If it is a TV commercial like the preceding example, creatives will select the director, go to the shoot, pick the casting, oversee the edit, music, and so on, shepherding the idea until it is finished. This often means travel to L.A. and fancy hotels with Jacuzzis.

What Are Creatives Like?

Creatives are supposed to be fun loving and off the wall. They are stereotypically hip and stylish and rock 'n' roll, the coolest, artiest people in the agency. If you walk around the average creative department, it will look like Urban Outfitters styled the younger members, and Marc Jacobs the older, more senior ones. (There are a lot fewer older creatives than younger ones, by the way. Very few gray heads on the creative floor.) But there are, of course, all kinds of creatives, from the kind who rarely shave and play foosball at every opportu-

Here's a reality of the job: you will have thousands of ideas die in order to sell one. Some ideas your partner won't like, some your creative director will kill, or your CEO, or your client, or your client's CEO. You just have to roll with it and just keep coming up with even better ideas in order to survive.
—Tim Roan, copywriter, DraftFCB, New York

The trick is to have LOTS of ideas. So what I usually do to stave off the panic is to give myself a quota for each session. Say, four ideas I know are on strategy. Doesn't matter if they're good or bad. Then I have four the next session. And the next. After a week, I have twenty ideas. Usually there's one in there that is the seed for a really great concept. It takes some practice, but to be a really good idea person, you have to learn to stop worrying whether you're a really good idea person.
—Tom Christmann, creative director, Taxi

nity to the ones who wear a suit and are day traders on the side. They are hard workers, thinking about ideas all the time: in the shower, while walking the dog, and so on. They definitely all share an immense curiosity, a slightly off-center way of viewing the world, and an ability to communicate in a way that connects and resonates with other people. That, or they get laid off. Seriously.

It's one thing to come up with a funny ad. It's a whole other ball game to convince a nervous client that the target market for his product will indeed find this idea cool and funny and drop tons of money into his lap. Selling an idea takes presentation skills and the nerve to stand in front of a room—often a rather large room with up to twenty people in it—and explain what you did and why it will work fabulously. In other words, if you are shy, better make sure your partner is an extrovert.

The Office

Ad agencies strive to be funky, or at least modern and well designed. When the clients walk in, the feeling the agency wants them to have is, "Wow, these guys are up on popular culture, and they seem way smart too." Agencies are very casual places, especially creative departments. Expect all the clichés—Nerf footballs being tossed about, music playing, people laughing. But also expect times of quiet and intense working. There is a definite camaraderie and a sense of gallows humor; creatives like to pull pranks on one another and to go out for drinks after hours. And although they are supposed to be businesspeople, they are also expected to be a little out there; frankly, it's their job. Agencies should nurture this "outside the box" thinking and off-center individualism.

But beyond all that, creative folks work long and hard. Advertising is a deadline business, and there's nothing quite as intimidating as being a creative and staring at a blank sheet of paper with a deadline looming.

How Many Hours Does One Toil?

Most creatives get in around ten in the morning and leave around seven at night. That's a typical, things-aren't-going-haywire day. Thing is, there are a lot of madcap panic-filled ones. Let's say your company is trying to win a new piece of business. The work you do on that "pitch" will be in addition to your regular workload; thus, those weeks or months will be busy, and especially busy right before the big new business meeting. And expect the occasional weekend work as well; it's part of the game. On the plus side, being a creative is about coming up with ideas. For some people that takes every minute of

We're lucky; we're surrounded by people who spend their days trying to outdo and one-up each other with wit. When things are good, there's a lot of laughter.
—Noah Davis, associate creative director, DraftFCB, New York

And we get to sit in Aeron chairs.
—Tim Roan, copywriter, DraftFCB, New York

every day. Other creatives can screw around most of the day and then the idea comes to them between 4:30 and 5:00.

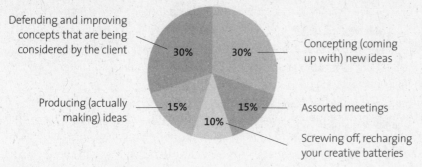

Defending and improving concepts that are being considered by the client — 30%

Concepting (coming up with) new ideas — 30%

Producing (actually making) ideas — 15%

10%

Assorted meetings — 15%

Screwing off, recharging your creative batteries

You can work in the office, or you can spend twenty hours a week in a café, it doesn't matter. As long as when it's time to see your creative director you bring in a great idea, you're a hero. The hours are different for different people. You work until the ideas come.
—Gary Resch, associate creative director, DraftFCB, New York

How Much Cheddar?

Salaries vary depending on company size and geography, but an entry-level East Coast creative can expect to make $35,000 to $50,000. From there the sky is the limit; big CDs who run important brands at large agencies can make more than $500,000; a midlevel creative with a title like senior copywriter can expect to make around $90,000 to $125,000. Raises and bonuses are based on what you accomplish, and unlike other jobs, people will really know what you do, because they'll see the ads you've created.

Talentzoo.com, a well-known advertising recruitment specialist, has an on-line "Salary Monitor" based on its own surveys. You provide where you live and what position you are interested in, and it supplies the salary range.

Stress-o-Meter: 6.5 (1 being a bikini waxer, 10 being a bikini waxee)

Walk into any ad agency and you will see a stressed-out creative crying out, "The client is ruining everything!" Although they feel tremendous pressure to do good work and the stress can hit a 10 sometimes, most creatives tend to be fairly laid back, thus the lower score. Plus, many creatives can step back at the end of the day and say, "It's only advertising."

Pros

You get paid for your personality.

Your friends and family will see all the cool stuff you make.

You'll travel for shoots and meet all kinds of other creative people like directors and actors.

Your co-workers will be hilarious.

You can wear jeans every damn day.

Cons

Some long hours, and during certain periods, many weekends.

Any whim of a client can take the account you work on to another agency, leaving you unemployed.

You will have ideas die because someone just doesn't "get it."

There aren't many people in advertising over fifty; this seems cool at first, until you realize that someday you will be fifty and have kids who need braces.

Okay, You're a Creative. You Wake Up And . . .

9:00 AM: The agency opens. By 9:30, all of the account and media people arrive and settle in. You are still in the shower.

10:15 AM: You roll in. You have one new voice mail and ten e-mails. You begin answering them and await your partner's arrival.

10:30 AM: Your partner shows up. You both spend the next half hour eating breakfast and catching up.

11:00 AM: You have a meeting in the conference room. You and your partner get briefed on a new TV campaign for Mitchum deodorant. The good news—it's a sweet assignment, three television commercials. The bad news—the ideas are due in three days.

12:05 PM: You prepare for a 6 PM Snapple meeting where you'll be presenting a new print campaign. Your partner, an art director, prints everything out in color and mounts the ads on black boards.

1:30 PM: You grab lunch with your partner and begin talking about Mitchum. Your partner mentions that he was in such a rush this morning, he forgot to wear deodorant, but he doesn't think he smells. He is mistaken. You work on this direction for a bit—how to tell people that sometimes, they smell.

4:00 PM: Another creative comes in to chat. He asks you if you think an idea he has for one of his assignments is funny, and you critique it.

4:10 PM: You continue to work on Mitchum. You talk about animation, how that might make the idea less gross. You write a very simple line, "For a deodorant that won't fail you, switch to Mitchum." You dub it campaign number one, and keep thinking.

6:00 PM: You greet your Snapple clients in the conference room and get ready to present three print campaigns of three ads each. First the account people set up what these ads are trying to achieve, and then you launch in, showing each campaign. You sell a little bit, saying how these are different from what everyone else is doing, and how they'll really "jump" from magazines.

6:40 PM: Your clients give you feedback on what they like and what they don't. They agree with your favorite but want you to increase the "appetite appeal." Your partner offers that the product can be shot next to slices of glistening fruit. That suggestion seems to work for everyone.

7:15 PM: You and your partner decide you're too burned to work on Mitchum any more. You promise to REALLY start at 9:30 tomorrow morning. Then you both split.

This Sounds Ad-Tastic!
How the Hell Do I Become a Creative?

Becoming a creative all comes down to one thing: The Portfolio.

An advertising portfolio is made up of *spec* ads one makes to show the kind of ideas he or she can create. Basically you have to come up with your own ads for existing products and show how creative you are. (Note that spec ads are for entry-level jobs; as you work in the industry, the work you put in your portfolio and on your reel will be real produced ideas.) Portfolios usually contain about fifteen to twenty examples, generally print or outdoor (billboards, bus shelters). With the emergence of the Web and new media (meaning how these days, anything can become an ad: a matchbook, a trash can, a stencil on the sidewalk, you name it) as powerful advertising tools, these thoughts are expected as well. But use your judgment. Creative directors and creative recruiters are incredibly busy. They want to flip through your book, not read or have to try to figure things out.

What makes for a great ad? That's a book in itself. Briefly, an idea that is surprising, yet really gets to the point of why this product or service merits attention from the viewer. It can take six months to a year to make your first portfolio, and then you'll probably still need to tweak it as you get people's feedback. And, over the course of your career, you will continuously upgrade it; your portfolio, and as you get more senior, your TV reel, will always be the way you get work. A sketch of a good idea is better than a slick-looking bad ad someone else has photographed and retouched. Still, with computers, agencies expect things to look pretty "finished."

Although it is not mandatory, these days many new junior creatives have attended graduate-level portfolio schools, like the Miami Ad School or the Portfolio Center in Atlanta. (A list of some of the best schools follows.) There is no degree from these schools, and they don't guarantee you will be hired. You will leave with a very professional-looking book, however. For those look-

I see books these days where out of twenty pieces, only five are print ads and the rest are new media concepts. New media is very in vogue these days, but you really still must have print, because it's the hardest media to do, and it really shows you know your stuff.
—Tim Roan, copywriter, DraftFCB, New York

ing for structure and guidance in creating a portfolio, they are worth checking out. If you are a writer with few art skills, it is best to try to hook up with a budding art director who can help polish your layouts if you help tighten his headlines. Another reason school is a good idea.

Once you have a good portfolio, whom do you call? Most big agencies have creative recruiters; call the main number and ask who they are and how you can contact them. E-mail is always best (these types don't answer the phone much). Even better, when you see an ad you like, do some research online (or use the resources that follow) and see if you can find out who the creatives were on it. Write or call them, compliment the work, and ask if they wouldn't mind seeing your portfolio. This is a great way in. But the best way? Know somebody. So network, network, network. If you went to portfolio school, you'll probably be all hooked up with alumni across the country. If not, attend any advertising functions you can and meet folks. Search online for your local ad club, by Googling or at the American Advertising Federation's site, aaf.org, which has chapters nationwide. When you meet creatives at these events, don't be shy. Anyone under thirty will remember their struggles getting their first job and, if they have a soul at all, will hear you out. (There are some soulless creatives, mind you.) No one has a "piece of cake" first-job story in the creative department; getting in has always been a bitch. Just don't be overly aggressive; make contact, and then follow up the next day.

Some agencies also offer internships. Most of these don't really involve learning or doing much creative work, unfortunately. Sadly, most creative departments are too busy to train interns. However, these internships do help you meet people. If you can get one at one of the hot agencies, jump on it. But if the internship is at a huge agency, in, say, the media department, know that you may well never see the creatives. You might be on a separate floor, if not in a different building. Make sure you know what you are getting into.

Resources

To stay current on what's happening in the ad world (especially who is winning accounts and might be hiring), check out adage.com and adweek.com. To stay current on new creative and general industry gossip, look at adrants.com and adpulp.com, both of which will have links to many other ad blogs worth investigating.

To find work you might admire and want to emulate, *Communication Arts* and *Archive* magazine showcase the best worldwide ad work and the names and agencies of who created each piece. They are expensive, though, so you may want to leaf through them at the store. Also look at *The One Show*, an award annual you can find in most bookstores. You can join the One Club (yes, the group that organizes *The One Show*), it has lots of helpful portfolio reviews and guidance, it's a great place to start, actually: oneclub.org. Another similar association is the Art Directors Club: adcglobal.org. And as mentioned earlier, the American Advertising Federation, aaf.org, has chapters nationwide. Many offer programs to help people network, or at least learn about the business. Check under the College Connection link.

There are many books on the topic of creativity in advertising. Two worth checking out: although getting a little long in the tooth, David Ogilvy's excellent *Ogilvy on Advertising* is a classic. A more recent book creatives find insightful is *Hey, Whipple, Squeeze This: A Guide to Creating Great Ads* by Luke Sullivan.

A selection of portfolio schools:

Miami Ad School: miamiadschool.com

Virginia Commonwealth University, VCU Adcenter: adcenter.vcu.edu

Portfolio Center: portfoliocenter.com

The Creative Circus: creativecircus.com

School of Visual Arts: schoolofvisualarts.edu

Brainco: Minneapolis School of Advertising, Design, and Interactive Studies: adschool.com

Alternative-Medicine Practitioner
Chiropractor/Acupuncturist

W estern medicine doesn't have the cure for everything. For ailments like allergies and bad backs, some patients just cannot find an acceptable answer in modern medicine. They may have been prescribed so many pills that they rattle when they walk. Or they've visited multiple specialists and spent hours in waiting rooms flipping through germ-covered *National Geographic* magazines, but still they don't feel any better. Perhaps that's why alternative medicine is gaining in popularity.

Alternative medicine, also known as complementary medicine (used in conjunction with conventional treatments), is becoming more and more accepted in the United States. In fact, some of these practices are now pretty much mainstream. There are many different kinds of alternative practitioners—acupuncturists, herbalists, chiropractors, aromatherapists, meditation experts, massage therapists, and on and on—and although their treatments might vary, much of their working lives are the same. This chapter will attempt to address the generalities of the field, using acupuncture and chiropractic, two of the most popular alternative practices, as the focus. Hopefully you'll find them a healthy read.

How Do You First Learn about This Stuff?

Most practitioners of alternative treatments have had a personal incident or encounter that opened their eyes to the healing possibilities outside Western medicine. Maybe they were sick and nothing helped until they tried "something crazy," like acupuncture. Or they had a parent or sibling who had trouble with pharmaceuticals but were cured with herbs. American society is very skeptical of outside medical practices, but those who have been helped or healed by alternative means become believers, dedicated to learning more.

Many people who get into alternative medicine are a little "alternative" themselves. They seek out different answers to questions in life. It differs by field, of course—chiropractors are way less alternative than, say, tonal healers.

> More and more people are looking for alternative ways to deal with their health. Many people feel bombarded with all the pharmaceutical ads on TV and are looking for other ways to improve their well-being. They've usually gone to other places first—a medical doctor or a physical therapist, for example—and have not been getting the results they wanted.
> —Dr. Chad Weinstein, doctor of chiropractic

They are all people who want to help others with their ailments and who choose to not take the conventional path.

Just like there is a rigid and structured path to becoming a conventional doctor, so too is there one for each different type of alternative medical field. Chiropractors must go to chiropractic school, an intense three-year program. Acupuncturists go to school for four years. Generally, part of the studying involves clinical work (just like in Western medicine). For Eastern medicine, some people even spend time in China. These alternative medical schools aren't cheap; in fact, tuition is roughly the same cost as traditional medical school. Mmm, loans and debt, the signs of true adulthood.

Every state is different, but in whatever state you choose to practice, you'll need to become licensed. In some states, that license will give you the title of "Dr." In others it won't. More on how to become a practitioner in a minute.

So What Do You Do after School?

There are a few entry-level options. Some graduates work as an associate for another doctor, meaning you are her employee. A slightly different choice is to be an independent doctor, which means you work at a doctor's office in your own space. You aren't part of his practice, your clients compensate you, and that's your salary. In this case, you may be paying rent or the doctor may take a percentage of your earnings. Another option is to start your own practice. This is many people's goal; some go for it straight out of school. They take out (more) loans, get an office space, lease equipment, and slowly start to build a patient list.

The Office, and What Happens in It

Just like conventional doctors, most alternative-medicine practitioners have office space where people make appointments and come in to be treated. There are the typical waiting rooms, receptionists, and bad magazines. If you take insurance, your receptionist might double as an assistant; paperwork for insurance companies tends to be time consuming and frustrating. (Yes, alternative medicine has become so widely accepted that most insurance companies compensate for it.) The vibe is generally business-casual; with the scrutiny still given to alternative practices, it's best to look and act professional. You're not a quack or a guru, you're not going to wear tie-dye or hemp—you are a trained professional, helping people. At the same time, you don't need to be wearing a suit or tie or anything like that.

Our décor and dress is very professional. We also try to have a "warm" feeling in our practice. It's not a cold, quiet, insensitive office.
—**Dr. Chad Weinstein, doctor of chiropractic**

The alternative-medicine experience is not much different from going to a traditional physician, but some distinctions stand out. First off, most Western doctors spend approximately two minutes learning a patient's symptoms and history, the ol' quick look at the chart. Alternative-medicine practitioners tend to spend way more time than that, a half hour or forty minutes on average. They'll go over a lot of things doctors skip—diet, exercise, and life habits— just to get a bigger overall sense of the patient's health. Alternative medicine, for the most part, believes in getting one's body back in balance, so it treats more than just the symptom. A bad back might not be from jogging; it might come from, say, anxiety.

After that, treatment begins. In a nutshell, chiropractors will usually first X-ray their patients so they can get a good look at the spine. Chiropractors don't just "crack your back" like your buddy Bubba might do for you; they are expertly trained to precisely move the vertebrae just so. The basic idea is that spinal joint misalignment, which chiropractors call *vertebral subluxation,* can result in all kinds of health issues. After examining the spinal X ray, on subsequent visits, chiropractors will manipulate and adjust the patient's spine and vertebrae, aiming to correct this vertebral subluxation. Many patients come in seeking relief from lower back or neck pain. The goal is that after adjustments and corrections, this pain will subside.

Acupuncturists insert needles into acupuncture points on the body, hopefully resulting in restored health and lessening of whatever malady was afflicting the patient. For example, let's say someone comes in to the office with a migraine headache. An acupuncturist might place small needles into the fleshy area between the patient's thumb and forefinger (one of the points treated for headaches). This does not result in cries of "Ow!" Most folks actually feel quite relaxed while the needles are in, believe it or not. After fifteen minutes or so, the needles are removed and, hopefully, the headache is gone.

Many patients who use alternative medicine become repeat patients (a lot have chronic pain); they'll go once a week or once a month, until they see improvement. For more in-depth descriptions of either practice, please check out the Resources section.

What Kind of Person Is Good at This?

Like any medical practitioner, you have to be compassionate and caring. If people irk you, helping them is probably not the best career direction. A good "bedside manner" and a charming personality do wonders for patients. You should also be confident, the type of person who doesn't need another's approval. You will get a lot of questions such as, "Why didn't you just become a

Western medicine is successful with emergency care, like a broken arm. Chinese medicine deals more with "Why is this person getting this constant rash? Why does this person have chronic yeast infections or irritable bowel syndrome?" It looks past the symptoms, to the cause.
—Gabriel Sher, licensed acupuncturist and herbalist

regular doctor? Why didn't you go to medical school?" It's inevitable; your parents' friends will quiz you. Try not to tear your hair out.

Then there is also the business side. Confidence, initiative, and personality play a huge role there as well. Having a successful practice, or at least one that stays in business, involves building up a clientele. You can't just hang up a sign and expect a line of patients to begin forming. You have to go out and meet and network with conventional doctors and other types of practitioners (if you are an acupuncturist, you might meet with chiropractors or massage therapists—anyone who might refer a patient to you) and try to build the practice. It involves lunches and networking associations and conventions, like any other business. As most practitioners eventually go out on their own, it's a point that can't be emphasized enough.

Up All Night or Nine-to-Five?

Just like doctors, alternative-medicine practitioners work normal business hours, which are somewhere from 10 AM to 8 PM. Unlike doctors, they rarely get emergency calls or have night shifts at the hospital. The appointments in the mornings and evenings are the busiest, while two in the afternoon can be slow. It all depends on the practice, but you may see between thirty-five and sixty patients a week. If you are a single-person operation, as many practices are, with the paperwork and scheduling (and even going out to buy your own herbs, medical supplies, toilet paper, you name it), the hours can be fairly long. But on the upside, a lot of practices are open only four days a week. Still, you may be taking care of paperwork and other tasks on that fifth day.

Ninety percent of alternative medical practices fail because ninety percent of people who do alternative medicine know zero about business. Asking people who are "alternative" to run a business, charge fees, all the things that many have been running from . . . it's difficult. They want to help people because they are all heart.
—**Gabriel Sher, licensed acupuncturist and herbalist**

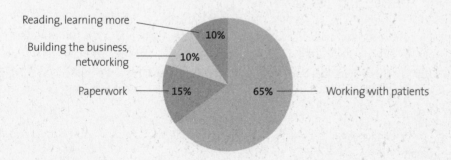

Reading, learning more — 10%

Building the business, networking — 10%

Paperwork — 15%

65% — Working with patients

Money?

In the beginning, you can expect to make between $20,000 and $35,000. And if you choose to open your own office, there are those additional expenses—rent, equipment—to float.

But if you are a decent businessperson and networker, after three or so years you can do pretty well. The possibility of $100,000-plus is definitely possible. Salary.com reports that chiropractors' salaries nationally average between $51,091 and $113,568. Payscale.com's national salary survey shows acupuncturists with one to four years of experience earning $42,000, topping out with more than twenty years' experience at $84,000.

Stress-o-Meter: 4.5 (1 being a glass blower, 10 being a whistleblower)

It's not the job itself that's stressful; it feels amazing to help people. No, it's the "running a business" part, the paying the bills part, the money part; in other words, the part that isn't any fun.

Pros

The satisfaction you get from helping people. They walk in one way and leave another.

The freedom of being your own boss.

Working in a field you believe in.

Cons

The financial aspects of running your own business.

Occasionally seeing people whom you may not like—the "crazies."

People being skeptical of your field.

Congratulations, You Are an Alternative-Medicine Practitioner. You Wake Up And . . .

9:15 AM: After a cup of green tea, you leave the house and ride your bike to work. When you arrive at your office, you change into your business-casual attire.

9:45 AM: Before the first patient arrives, you check e-mails, make some phone calls, and try to firm up any scheduling conflicts.

10:00 AM: Your first appointment of the day, an older man. This is his first time coming in, so you sit down and not only find out what is immediately troubling him, but also ask him for a full health history. Any prior injuries, or surgeries? Nope. But his back has been "killing him" for months now, and he says he has tried "almost everything." You don't have your own X-ray machine on premise, so you send him down the road to have one done. You want to look inside this gentleman before choosing any treatment course.

11:00 AM: Your next patient arrives. Regular patients are seen in half-hour shifts throughout the day; new ones are seen for a full hour.

2:00 PM: You have a half-hour break. You grab some lunch while ordering some new supplies online.

2:30 PM: A patient comes in grinning. His back pain has decreased significantly. You treat him for a half hour and then shake his hand. Hopefully this will be his last visit for a while. And hopefully, he'll tell his friends of the magic you worked.

3:00 PM: You continue to see patients until 7:30 PM, when you lock the door. You spend a half hour getting everything into shape for the morning, and then split.

8:30 PM: You go to a local gym, where you are giving a free clinic. It's a good way to meet prospective patients and build the practice.

Let the Healing Begin.
How the Hell Do I Become a Practitioner?

Every field of alternative medicine has its own path, but as stated previously, in general they are all well-worn and fairly rigid paths involving schooling and licensing. You don't just fall into these fields like you do in some other professions. There are no shortcuts. Prepare yourself to go through a fairly long and challenging program, the alternative take to medical school.

Most of these schools require a bachelor's degree. They have three-to-four-year programs, which are very similar to medical school if you actually compare the classes. Likewise, they also have residency programs, where you work directly with patients. Beyond medical training, many alternative-medicine practitioners recommend studying business. A lot wish they had taken more business classes when they were undergrads.

If you are interested in alternative medicine, the best advice is to talk to different practitioners and learn about what they do. Many are quite friendly and want to talk about their fields; people get into this because they truly believe in the healing powers outside conventional medicine. See who's local and make a few phone calls, or send a few e-mails, and see if you can meet with them. It sounds forward, but it works.

Resources

There's this thing called the Internet, and it's totally awesome. There are a ton of informational sites; you can easily check out whichever specific alternative field excites you. Perhaps the best place to start is at the National Centers for Complementary and Alternative Medicine, which is a division of the National Institutes of Health. Go to nccam.nih.gov for information on a wide swath of alternative treatments.

For acupuncture, these associations and journals are a great start:

American Association of Acupuncture and Oriental Medicine: aaaomonline.org

National Acupuncture and Oriental Medicine Alliance: acuall.org

American Journal of Acupuncture: acupuncturejournal.com

TCM Student: tcmstudent.com

The TCM Student site also lists its picks for the top five acupuncture schools:

Oregon College of Oriental Medicine, Portland, OR

Southwest Acupuncture College, Santa Fe, NM

New England School of Acupuncture, Watertown, MA

American College of Acupuncture and Oriental Medicine, Houston, TX

Bastyr University, Kenmore, WA

For chiropractic information and schools, the following links are quite useful: *Chiropractic Economics* offers a list of, and links to, local and state chiropractic associations at its site, chiroeco.com/chiroshopper/assoc.php. The Association of Chiropractic Colleges, www.chirocolleges.org/collegest.html (Note: this one needs the "www"), contains links to each college. World Chiropractic Alliance, worldchiropracticalliance.org, is another popular site filled with information and advice.

Architect

Long before construction crews start digging earth, or real estate agents tout exclusive listings of houses, apartments, or office buildings, architects labor. Architects plan, design, and then shepherd through construction every type of edifice imaginable, from churches and university buildings to cheap motels and International Houses of Pancakes. Yes, somewhere an architect pounded his fist on a conference room table and said, "A house of pancakes must have a slanted blue roof!" The rest, as they say, is flapjack history.

Architecture is a challenging career that requires painstaking attention to detail and the patience of several saints. It's one of those rare jobs that takes both sides of the brain to be successful: the creative "designy" side and the logical, scientific "how will this work?" side. Those who toil in the field consider it a labor of love, and most of society considers it a profession as respected as law or medicine. And well it should, because architecture is important to how we view ourselves. The pyramids defined ancient Egypt, skyscrapers the modern metropolis. Plus, TV's Mike Brady was an architect; how much more legitimate can you get?

Projects, from Birth to Adulthood

Architects are involved in every phase of a project's construction. How each phase comes together differs according to the specifics of the project; obviously the approach to designing the next SeaWorld will be slightly different from a simple bathroom remodel. Still, most projects share distinct phases. In the broadest terms, there is a time when you are planning, designing, and drawing, using both a computer and pencil and paper, and a time when you are at the "job site," supervising the physical construction of your design.

Say you are designing a large new building for a state university, meant to house the biology department. The building will need classrooms, plus complex labs that may require ventilation systems and other safety precautions, lest nasty pathogens escape and become the premise for a campus horror movie. The entire process from start to finish for a building this large and multifaceted can take four years or more. Some buildings take less than one. Some take a decade.

An architect is someone who imagines and designs environments, and then helps them get built. And helping them get built can be eight million things. You're coordinating all the work of the other professional trades, like the structural, mechanical, and electrical engineers; the plumbing; the fire protection; and so on. You're sort of the orchestra leader.
—Andrew Bernheimer and Jared Della Valle, partners, Della Valle Bernheimer Architects

Architecture is something that has a longevity to it. It's something that can outlast the architect's life, something that can transcend their whole existence. Every architect gets off on that, at least a little bit. There's sort of a civic responsibility to create beautiful, uplifting places. First you have to believe there's the possibility of creating a space someone will be moved by. And then, you try to achieve it.
—Evan Ripley, architect, Tod Williams Billy Tsien Architects

The initial phase is what some call the *programming phase,* or *pre-design.* This is a learning and information-gathering stage; it's when you will be figuring out where things really should go and the relationship between various components. Where should the researchers' offices and labs be, where should the administrative offices lie, and why? You don't want to make two groups who need to be near one another climb three flights of stairs to meet; that would be bad, frustrating design. For this reason, the pre-design/ programming phase requires a lot of communication with the clients. You have to really understand their needs, how they will ultimately use the space. All of your thinking will come out of this knowledge. The ability to interact with clients, to hear what they are saying and to explain clearly what you intend and how it will work for them, is key to being a successful architect.

Moving on, the pre-design/programming phase morphs into the designing of actual building concepts, which are called *schematic designs.* These are the big-picture ideas of how the building may look and function; for example, will it be a round building with a hole in the center inspired by a donut, or a tall, skinny tower inspired by a supermodel? This stage is followed by *design development,* which is basically a further refinement of the agreed-on schematic design. It's a time to get into the details and nitty-gritty.

Construction documents come next. These highly detailed drawings and specifications define exactly how the project is going to be built. The creation of the construction documents is the most intense phase for architects, as it's the final stage before actual construction is set to start. These documents are used to assess the construction price of the building. Basically, you, the architect, give this set of drawings to a contractor, the person or company that does the physical construction; he or she looks at them and says, "Okay, I'll build this sucker for X dollars, as long as there are no changes." So there's pressure to get the construction documents as tight as possible, because any changes later on are where you start to break the budget. And clients don't like broken budgets. They can only be fixed with more money.

After that, the rest of the time is *construction administration,* which is supervising the physical building of the building. Usually you will visit job sites once a week to see how things are progressing, and to deal with any issues that arise.

When the project is finally completed, and you walk through the university and see the fully functioning building you birthed—a building filled with biologists hopefully furthering the health of humanity—it's an incredible thrill. Something you dreamed up is now a physical presence. Pretty amazing.

Construction almost always takes forever. You hardly ever hear anyone say, "My project is finished early, and it was under budget." People think architects care only about design, but if your project is executed incorrectly, all that gets thrown away. The project is like your child. Basically, you have to work hard to create the child, and then construction is like child rearing, and you definitely spend a lot of time rearing the child. Because if you stop monitoring that phase, well, your child ends up a mess.
—Andrew Bernheimer and Jared Della Valle, partners, Della Valle Bernheimer Architects

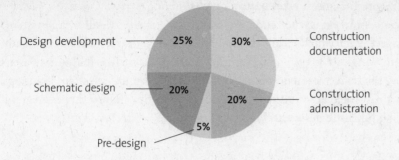

Design development — 25%   30% — Construction documentation

Schematic design — 20%   20% — Construction administration

5% — Pre-design

Do I Do All That When I First Start?

Hell no! That's too much responsibility to start; would you want to be in a building some snot-nosed kid fresh out of school designed and presided over? Yikes. Beginning architects spend a lot of time doing things like researching zoning and building codes, or drafting their bosses' designs and helping build their models. You'll be expected to be up to speed on all the latest design programs, especially AutoCAD for drafting. In addition, a program called BIM (Building Information Modeling) is a popular one for the bigger firms; it's technical drawing in 3D. It's being used to help build the Freedom Tower in New York City, and the industry seems to be embracing it and employing it more and more. Finally, there are several 3D visualization programs, including 3D Studio Max, Maya, and Form Z; you should be familiar with at least one of them.

As a new architect, you'll be working your ass off and learning from mentors all the way. It can be pretty grueling. A number of people switch careers at this point if they aren't loving it. Because guess what: they aren't truly architects yet.

See, when you graduate from architecture school, even when you accept your first job at an architecture firm, you aren't officially an architect yet. It's a bit confusing, because you can work at an architecture firm in the role of an architect, but technically you aren't one until you fulfill a series of requirements. Basically, these involve three elements: education (which you'll already have gotten; more on that later), work experience, and passing the Architect Registration Examination (ARE). For the experience requirement, each architect-to-be needs to complete 700 training units across sixteen categories; each unit equals eight hours of experience working under the direct supervision of a licensed architect. This simply means you'll need to be working for a few years.

The ARE isn't a test to be sneezed at. It's nine tests actually, administered by the National Council of Architectural Registration Boards (NCARB). As

> Good computer skills on all the popular design programs are really a must. You can't survive without them.
> —Sung Kim, design director, Studio Red at Rockwell Group

you might imagine, it takes quite a bit of studying to pass. Once you have the education and experience and have passed the exam, you will be a Registered Architect (RA), which means you can practice on your own without being under the wing of a firm. The reason people drop out early is that if they aren't loving the field, there's no need to jump through all the requirement hoops. Plus, there are loads of other fun jobs for people with architecture degrees, including furniture design and interior design.

Senioritis

Architects say the most exciting part of their job is coming up with killer designs and then seeing those designs come to life. Unfortunately, most of the days aren't spent on the designs alone, but on menial tasks in the service of them. There'll be tons of meetings, phone calls, and e-mails. Clients will change their minds, and altered plans will need to be filed with the state. As you become more senior, you'll be doing more presenting and selling of ideas, more hand holding and managing of clients. You'll be in your client's conference room in a meeting while other architects are back at the firm, designing. The biggest complaint of successful architects is that they wish they could spend more time designing instead of problem solving.

What Makes for a Good Architect?

Are you an utter and total control freak? Because that's not a bad place to start. Although architecture is a collaborative field, where you'll work with all kinds of vendors and clients, you are ultimately in charge of building something, and that's quite a responsibility. So you have to care deeply, nay, profoundly, about every last detail. You have to be passionate about design, you have to be passionate about space, and you have to be passionate about functionality. That's a lot of passion, friend. And this may sound strange, but you have to care about people, because you'll spend your days designing projects you'll never inhabit. Say you are designing a house for someone; you have to want it to bring them some level of joy. And the same mindset goes into larger projects—for example, a public building where you're trying to create a space that should—here comes something corny—elevate people's souls in some way. Think about great public places you've been—Grand Central Station, the Louvre; there's something awe inspiring about them.

As an architect, you have to be imaginative, but you have to be disciplined. Again, it's a both-sides-of-the-brain profession. And you also need to be good with people. You have to be able to present your ideas to clients, and defend them—without seeming defensive. Salesmanship is part of the job, especially if you own your own firm. Finally, you need to be able to manage people. Everyone involved in building this project reports to you. It's a skill you can learn, but it helps if you have had some experience doing it in any kind of previous or summer job. Babysitting quintuplets, perhaps?

The Offices Must Be Awesome, Right?

You'd be surprised. Most architects spend their time making their clients' projects look good, and so their own offices can be in need of a tune-up. This is true of many architects' homes as well. Their own domestic projects are the ones that always get pushed to the bottom of the "to-do" list. That said, some firms are gorgeous, airy places filled with light and custom furniture.

Architecture firms can be large corporations, medium to small companies, and even single-person proprietorships. Some architects are entrepreneurial and long to have their own firm with their name on the door; others really don't want to deal with the headaches of business ownership.

Regardless of size, some offices are laid back, the kind where you can walk around in whatever you want and play music at your desk, while others are pretty corporate. It all depends on the principals and the type of clients they service. Generally you won't have to wear a suit, though, except perhaps to certain client meetings. A lot of architects make bold choices in their eyeglass frames, for some reason. A little modern design right on the bridge of their nose, perhaps.

The stereotype of most architecture firms is that they are pressure-packed, hardworking places. It fits. The offices are never really "mellow" and the hours can be long, as you will read in a momentito. But architects also like to have fun. These are people who are into design, and it's hard to design with any whimsy if you are miserable. If you want to be a painter or a writer, however, misery can be a nice plus.

So, the Hours Are Long?

Yes, for the most part. Not ridiculous hours by any means (the definition of ridiculous hours keeps evolving in our modern world, mind you), but figure on average you'll work a ten-hour day, and there will be some weekend work. Architecture is so detail oriented that there's always more to do, more to refine. You care deeply how your projects turn out; you want to keep tweaking and improving them. It's addictive.

One of the most important things is to be assertive, because you are constantly negotiating with contractors. There's a lot of management in architecture. If you are a wallflower, it can be hard.
 —Andrew Bernheimer and Jared Della Valle, partners, Della Valle Bernheimer Architects

The hours can be pretty long. In a creative job, long hours sort of come with the territory. I get in around 9:15; I leave at 7:00 on light days, and 11:00 or even 12:00 on busy ones.
 —Sung Kim, design director, Studio Red at Rockwell Group

Wallet-Sized, Rectangular Sheets of Green Paper?

For the amount of work they do, the years of training required, and the esteem in which society holds them, architects' paychecks aren't as large as you might expect. That said, if you start your own firm and it does well, you'll certainly be able to afford that midcentury modern house of your dreams. The Bureau of Labor Statistics reports the mean salary as $68,560, with a range from $39,130 to $105,500. In urban areas, the numbers are considerably higher than that for senior-level architects. A great place to keep abreast of such information is the architectural Web site DesignIntelligence, di.net. Simply search on "salary" for the latest compensation news.

Stress-o-Meter: 8 (1 being a member of the fraternity AEPi, 10 being a member of the American FBI)

Being an architect is pretty stressful. Besides the long hours and deadlines that always breed stress, you'll care deeply about the outcome of your projects. You'll be juggling infinite details and managing many personalities along the way, and any mistake you make can cost thousands or even millions of dollars. And architecture is in the public eye; people will see your projects and critique them. A high-profile building can be vilified in the newspaper or on a blog, just like a bomb of a movie.

Pros

Seeing a finished project is an incredible high.

Creating spaces people will enjoy and find uplifting is a satisfying way to make money.

It's a very well-respected profession.

Cons

There's lots o' stress.

There's an incredible amount of liability; yes, it's quite easy to get sued.

Some clients can be frustratingly difficult.

Huzzh! You Are an Architect. You Wake Up And . . .

8:00 AM: You go into your kitchen and make yourself a coffee with your sleek Italian espresso machine.

9:30 AM: You arrive at the office, a medium-sized firm of about thirty people. You don't have an actual office, but share an "area" with a colleague, which is an alcove with a couple of desks. You check your e-mail and see if there are any emergencies.

10:00 AM: You've been working with a more senior architect on the design of an advertising agency's new office space. You've met with them several times, and are going to show them your initial design concepts later today. You print out some 3D renderings to see if they need any last-second tweaks.

11:00 AM: You take a call from a contractor on another project you're helping out on. You were supposed to go to the job site tomorrow, but the contractor would like to push the visit back a few days. So far it's been on schedule, so you say "Okay."

12:00 PM: You run out and grab an early bite.

1:30 PM: Five folks from the ad agency arrive. You and the senior architect meet with them in the "nice" conference room, which has a Saarinen table and chairs.

1:45 PM: After some pleasantries, the senior architect talks about what you've created. She is a very good presenter, very articulate. She explains how you've taken the agency's "holistic" approach and tried to create an office with no boundaries that still gives employees personal space.

2:00 PM: You unveil the models. You walk the clients through your thoughts, step by step. Although they are creative, clients often find it hard to envision what you intend. Plus, they are nervous. This won't be cheap.

3:00 PM: They like one of the designs. But they have a million questions. How long will it take? How much will it cost? Can we incorporate the agency's shade of blue into some of the conference rooms. Still, it's all moving forward. You breathe a sigh of relief and escort them to the elevator.

3:30 PM: You deserve a candy bar. You get a candy bar.

4:00 PM: You have "the meeting after the meeting" with the senior architect. She's pleased; she was worried they would be even more difficult. She wants to make the changes discussed ASAP so you can get the project rolling. She sends you back to your desk with a bunch of things to try.

7:30 PM: You've been pointing and clicking in AutoCAD for three hours, working on the tweaks. It's time to call it a night. And so you do.

I Want to Design a Skyscraper.
How the Hell Do I Become an Architect?

You, sir or ma'am, need to go to architecture school. There are a couple of ways to do this. You can go to a regular college as an undergrad, and then go to graduate architecture school to get your master's in architecture. You can also go to an architecture school as an undergrad and then continue on there, or go to a different graduate school, to get your master's. Both of these are six years of education. Some architecture programs combine undergrad and grad and give you the whole ball of wax in five years, saving a year of school (and tuition). Instead of the master's, these five-year programs give you a BArch, a bachelor's degree in architecture. Plus, a few other programs not only educate you, but also provide the experience requirement so that you can take the ARE exam without having to work first. Drexel University and Boston Architectural College are two that have this unique plan.

Architecture school, undergrad or grad, is a competitive atmosphere. You'll quickly learn that in order to be an architect you need to verbalize your ideas, defend them, and accept criticism. A lot of criticism. Having your subjective ideas picked at and shot with arrows takes some getting used to, but you'll soon see that there is validity in all the criticism.

Architecture graduate schools often have a mix of different-aged students. It's one of those careers that seems an unattainable dream for young people, who later in life come back to it. For example, a successful designer or engineer may decide that he or she is ready for a new challenge and a career change.

You will leave grad school with a portfolio, a collection of architectural designs that you'll be judged on when applying for a job. Some students make clever or fancy presentations, but many architects seem to think it's best to keep it simple. Just let the work speak for itself, and avoid getting too wrapped up in fancy graphics. Your portfolio is the single most important thing that will help you land a job. Some firms will want you to send yours ahead of time; others don't have a spare minute to look through portfolios and instead recommend that applicants send an e-mail with a PDF attachment containing a few images.

Although we live in the digital age and everything (including our sex lives) is becoming cyber, many firms still want to see a physical portfolio. Architects live in a very tangible world; they like to touch and feel and poke. Still, a Web site portfolio is a good idea, too, because although you should keep your physical portfolio fairly limited, you can put extra information online. And then you can say, "If you want to see more, just go to my Web site." (You can also say that to someone you are flirting with in a bar; it's a flexible line.)

Finally, to get a job, it always helps to know people. Many architects suggest contacting alumni from your school; lots of firms end up hiring people from the same universities the more senior staff attended. It makes sense, as they have common backgrounds, mentors, and professors.

Resources

DesignIntelligence has a great site: di.net. It also publishes *America's Best Architecture & Design Schools*, which is a guide to, well, America's best architecture and design schools.

The American Institute of Architects is a professional organization repre-

Half of architecture school is defending your ideas. You'll have to present your ideas to a jury of your peers, and they may or may not like them.
—Andrew Bernheimer and Jared Della Valle, partners, Della Valle Bernheimer Architects

The best portfolios, in our opinion, are teasers; they'll show maybe five or six projects, but not in their entirety; they'll leave us wanting more. If you show everything in your portfolio, then prospective employers are going to draw their own conclusions, without the architect explaining his or her intentions, and you don't want that. Too much info is bad; a few really sexy images are good. The best way to get our attention is to know someone here, or to have amazing images in your portfolio that you send to us as a teaser.
—Andrew Bernheimer and Jared Della Valle, partners, Della Valle Bernheimer Architects

senting architects licensed in the United States. The site has loads of information, including a section on careers: aia.org.

The National Council of Architectural Registration Boards site has information about the ARE, as well as a wealth of other information, including a section on careers: ncarb.org.

The Society of American Registered Architects Web site is sara-national.org, and if you surf to psa-publishers.com, you can find profiles of architecture firms worldwide.

Finally, some insightful resources to help keep you up-to-date on all the latest news, trends, highlights, and gossip in the architecture world:

Architect Magazine: architectmagazine.com

Architectural Record: archrecord.construction.com

Metropolis: metropolismag.com

Author

Authors have one of the most revered professions in the world. Say you're at your high school reunion, and someone asks, "So, what do you do for a living?" If you can answer, "I'm an author," well, my friend, you've just trumped pretty much every other profession in the room. People will ask excitedly, "What have you written; do I know it?" If your published work is a novel, a circle will form around you. Ex-girlfriends will second-guess their sophomore-year decision to break up with you for that JV quarterback. However, if your tome was a small travel guide, or say, a book on careers—however riveting and genre-busting a career book it might be—it will garner you much less regard. Sigh.

An Honest Introduction

There are two basic genres of books: fiction and nonfiction. To make a living as an author of either, you must get published. If you don't get published, then you don't get paid. And if you don't get paid, then writing is really a hobby, not a job. Not that there's anything wrong with that, but being an author is many people's dream. For most though, it only partially comes true; yes, they publish every few years, but they also support themselves by doing other things writing related, like teaching, freelance editing, or writing for magazines. Only a small percentage write books and do nothing else.

Why? Well, the audience for books continues to diminish. And not because people have suddenly stopped reading; there are simply more and more alternatives for society's smaller and smaller amounts of free time. Books are up against films, TV shows, video games, iPods, the Internet, and porn. And the truth is, there are only so many publishing houses. Each of these houses puts out X number of books a year. And of these, they only put their publicity muscle behind a tiny percentage. There are just so many slots on the *Today* show to fill, only so many books they can get reviewed in *The New York Times* or *People*. Without that publicity muscle, the odds of a book becoming a huge seller, and a big moneymaker for the author, are slim. Thus, the need for additional income. Plus, writing a book takes a long time. Very few authors can pump a book out every year. Except Danielle Steel. Damn, girl!

My job? I make up stuff and put it down on paper. Putting it on paper is the hard part. It's funny, but being an author is one of those careers you have to constantly convince friends is actually a job, since you don't have an actual workplace or boss. It may not seem like it, but I work all the time—I can't come over and watch your cats.
—**Darin Strauss, author of** *Chang and Eng* **and** *The Real McCoy*

But don't be pessimistic. It's never been as easy as getting a job as a shoe salesman. Despite the odds, you can be successful if you are committed. Why not you?

Writing Must Become Your Primary Job

So the odds are, especially before your first book is published, you will be toiling at a "real" job while also working on your writing. Writing is taxing and takes a lot of energy; it's very difficult to give your all in two different areas and be successful at both.

If after a few years you don't get published, well, then you have to be honest with yourself and see if it's time to put more effort in or find another job you might like better. It can be a soul-searching moment.

On the plus side, it's incredibly satisfying to quit your job because you just sold your book.

So Like, You Just Sit in a Room by Yourself and Write?

Writing is, as advertised, mostly a solitary sport. This is not a job that needs a whole lot of defining; authors sit down and write books. Each has his or her own process; some write longhand, some dictate, some use a fancy new Mac, and others use an old Smith Corona. Some labor at nonfiction books that require extensive research; some write novels that are completely made up. But at the end of the day, or at the end of several years, if they want to make money, they produce a work of words.

Many authors work at home. In major urban areas, community writing spaces, like the Writer's Room and Paragraph in New York City, rent out small spaces to writers who don't want to be alone all day. Other folks work in diners and coffee shops. Still, it's not like you are talking to anyone. There's no real "on-the-job" camaraderie. There are readings and get-togethers where authors socialize, but when you are writing, it's just you, writing.

What Hours Are You Alone, Writing?

The hours authors work is a completely individual choice. Some are night owls, some are morning people, some are obsessive and write twelve hours a day, and others are regimented—they write only from noon until six, five days a week.

Most writers also believe you have to allow yourself breaks and be forgiv-

That's a great thing I learned from E. L. Doctorow. It's okay to take another job if you need it; you aren't giving up, you just have to eat. But do the minimum, just enough so you won't get fired. I used to have my novel open in one computer window, and my work in another, and flip back and forth. As a writer with a day job, it's fun to think of yourself as a bit of a con man; no one knows what you are really doing.
—Darin Strauss, author of *Chang and Eng* and *The Real McCoy*

For me, the best place to work is at home. You can't control the music at Starbucks.
—Nicola Kraus, co-author of *The Nanny Diaries*, *Citizen Girl*, and *Dedication*

ing. It's pretty much impossible to write for eight hours a day, five days a week. But once you make a schedule, it's best to stick to it like any other job, and do the best you can during those hours to get quality writing done.

Authors are ruled by deadlines. Once sold, your book, finished, will be due on a specific date to the publisher. Publishers generally give you a healthy amount of time to write, so in the beginning, it might seem like you have forever. As much as you mean to work hard, you might slack. But when the deadline's looming, it gets hectic. (Ed. note: Trust me. *Hectic.*) You might hole up in a motel room, drink coffee, and stay awake for five straight days trying to get the book done. Authors are often granted extensions, but the goal is always to make the deadline.

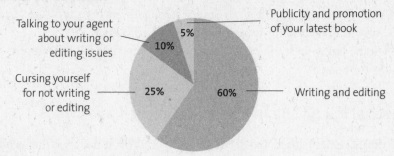

Talking to your agent about writing or editing issues — 10%

Publicity and promotion of your latest book — 5%

Cursing yourself for not writing or editing — 25%

Writing and editing — 60%

Your Team

The writing part of an author's life may be solitary, but once you are in the process of being published, you become part of a team. On your team will be business folks and creative folks.

The business side is your agent, your lawyer, and the marketing and publicity department at the publisher. Although they often do more, technically agents facilitate your "getting a deal" with a publisher. They "shop" your manuscript to editors they know and think it will be a good fit. Many are great readers who'll provide invaluable criticism that will improve your work. You pretty much need an agent in order to get published. And lawyers, briefly—well, they check your contracts and make sure you aren't getting screwed.

The marketing department markets your book. They decide if there will be an advertising campaign or a book tour, how much money will be put behind the book, and how it will be spent. Publishing is a business, and your book is a product. It needs to be well marketed to sell. And if it doesn't sell well, it might be your last book. That's no joke: disappointing book sales will make it very difficult for you to get a publisher to put out your next tome, no matter how groundbreaking it might be. Your bad track record sticks with you.

On the creative side, you have the editor and art department. Editors work with your book to improve it. They are the people who have literally "bought" your book and made your dreams come true. Your agent will have sent the manuscript to several editors. One read it, loved it, brought it to an editorial meeting, and said to the company, "We should publish this." He or she will shepherd your book through all the steps, including guiding the cover design, pulling quotes to put on the back cover, and shielding it from bad opinions along the way. You will spend a lot of time working closely with your editor.

The art department designs the book, inside and out. Your opinion will be asked for, but generally the art department has the final word. Covers make a huge impact on book sales—plus, you just don't want to hate your own cover.

What Does It Take to Get Published?

Skill and luck. Many people wonder, do you need to write the whole book to get published? Sometimes yes, sometimes no. Some books, like the one you hold in your hot little hands, are sold by writing a proposal. A proposal, in general, explains the concept of the book and provides some sample writing, perhaps several chapters. Generally, books sold on proposals are nonfiction. If you're interested, many books instruct you on how to write nonfiction proposals.

Some fiction books are sold based on a premise and fifty or a hundred pages of writing. The bigger-name author you are, the less you need to have written. But more novels (especially first novels) are sold as complete pieces, the entire book crafted and finished.

Here's how it often works: assuming you're an author with an agent, you tell them what you're working on, checking in with them (or vice versa) along the way. When the work is finished (or at a place where you both decide it's time to show publishers), your agent will craft a letter and sales pitch and send your baby out into the world. If an editor is interested, he or she will make an offer. After some negotiating and hand wringing, you have a deal.

Platform and Promotion

Not as sexy as a Pulitzer, but important for sales, are platforms and promotion. An author's platform is what, other than his writing, he brings to the party to help the book sell. Maybe he is a famous musician, and he has a fan base. Maybe he was a writer at a magazine, and he's guaranteed coverage by his former colleagues. Publishers weigh these platforms in their dollars-and-cents publishing decisions; all things being equal, a good platform definitely helps tilt a decision toward your getting a deal.

> Editors are crucial to your book's success for reasons beyond their editing skills. Basically, your editor is the nanny of your book. He or she is your advocate inside the publishing house.
> —Nicola Kraus, co-author of *The Nanny Diaries*, *Citizen Girl*, and *Dedication*

Before the book launches, as well as after, you, the author, will have to promote your book. Although it is the publisher's job to market it and publicize it, the individual author must get out there and hustle as well. Using your platform, building a Web site and a MySpace page, giving readings, telling friends, pulling PR stunts, you name it, authors will try it. Your own efforts at promotion are key to book sales, and sales are key in your getting to publish another book.

Book Money?

There's no telling. You could be a starving artist or a bestseller.

You are paid as an author in two main ways: the advance and royalties. The advance is an advance payment, made to you by the publisher, before your book is actually published. You generally will be paid the bulk of it on signing the contract with the publisher, a bit more when the finished book is actually turned in, and the last of it on book publication. Advances could be six figures, they could be in the millions, but they could also be $5,000 or $10,000.

Royalties are payments you receive based on the sales of your book. However, you don't start earning these royalties until you've "paid back" your advance. So if you get an advance of $75,000, you won't see any royalties until the percentage of sales you're entitled to tops $75,000. Let's say your book is a paperback; a 7.5 percent royalty (pretty standard for paperbacks) on a sales price of $13 (again, standard) is $0.98. So you'll have to sell almost 77,000 copies of your book to pay back your advance. After that, you'll start seeing royalties on all the subsequent sales. However, if your book never sells enough copies to pay back the advance, well, you'll never get any royalties, but you get to keep the advance.

Your book may be able to generate other income. A foreign sale, meaning the book has been purchased by a publisher in another country for distribution there, earns you an advance and royalties all over again. You can also possibly sell the film rights to your book. These can vary from a paltry $2,000 to millions if you have a bestselling story.

> The thing to remember is this: a publisher may put out 200 books a year. They'll only spend the money to publicize five to ten of these. And those are the books that will probably sell the most and make the most money. Odds are, your book won't be one of the five to ten. In that case, in order for your book to sell and for you to make more money, a lot falls on your shoulders to get out there and promote it.
> —**Nicola Kraus, co-author of** *The Nanny Diaries,* *Citizen Girl,* **and** *Dedication*

> Writing is not a career you go into for the money. It's a gamble to spend three or so years writing a book which may never be published, or which may have poor sales.
> —**Darin Strauss, author of** *Chang and Eng* **and** *The Real McCoy*

 Stress-o-Meter: 6 (1 being an air conditioner repairer in December, 10 being an air conditioner repairer in August)

There are long stretches of peaceful writing, and the lifestyle, making your own hours, is wonderful. But earning a living being creative, on deadline, is stressful. You work for years on one thing—what if it doesn't sell? And being critiqued in the public eye is scary. A bad review could be the end of a career.

Pros

Making your living doing what you'd do for free.

Flexible time.

Possible celebrity (if you consider that a pro).

Cons

It's not the romantic life of living in castles and writing you've seen in movies.

Having your work critiqued by people who may be having a bad day, which can affect your entire career.

You are alone a lot. You might actually see your social skills decline.

Well Done! You Are an Author. You Wake Up And . . .

7:00 AM: You are very structured; when you are not writing you are not writing, and mornings, you don't write. You get up and walk your dogs before you head to the gym.

12:00 PM: You begin to write. No phone, no IM, no e-mail, just writing. You work from 12:00 to 6:00 like this, each day.

6:00 PM: You hit Save one last time and then send a backup copy to your e-mail. You clock out and check messages. Then you walk the dog again.

7:00 PM: Since you spend the day alone, you make sure you get out at night. Tonight it's dinner with your agent. She'd better be buying.

I Rather Like This Profession.
How the Hell Can I Become an Author?

If you want to be an author, start by thinking of yourself as a writer all the time. When you read, ask yourself, "Why does this seem to work so well?" Or, "Why doesn't this work, and what would I do to fix it?" For every interesting thing you experience, ponder how you would tell it as a story on the written page.

Then, write something. Write something good. Then make it very good. Show it to friends and family, teachers and professors. Revise it. Revise it again. Repeat a dozen times. Then send it out to every agent and editor with whom you are friendly. Okay, odds are, you're not friendly with any. Look at the books you love, look at the acknowledgments, and you'll see who the editors and agents are. Write to them, send them your work, and tell them why it's good.

And get out of your house, stop writing for a minute, and mingle and network at writing conferences, even just at bars and family events. You never know whom you might meet who is connected to publishing. Anything helps.

> Leave your apartment sometimes. Someone's brother's stepsister's roommate's cousin might date an agent. Meet people at book readings and events; knowing people is invaluable.
> —Nicola Kraus, co-author of *The Nanny Diaries, Citizen Girl,* and *Dedication*

To Get an MFA or Not to Get an MFA?

There are plenty of opinions among authors as to the value of an MFA in creative writing. It's really not the most practical degree; it's not as if there are creative-writing corporations out there looking to hire graduates. Many will say it's an unnecessary expense if you already have connections, and it represents a large debt that will take you a long time to pay back. However, if you don't know anyone in the publishing world, an MFA program will certainly help you meet other writers as well as agents and editors. And if you need structure, an MFA program will provide that. They'll constantly improve your writing as well—but how much they do is debatable.

Many people choose MFA programs in New York City, as that's where most publishing houses reside, so you'll definitely have encounters with agents and editors. If you decide to get an MFA, try to go to one of the best schools, the ones agents are circling like hawks. There are books that rank the programs; do your research. Here are two you can check out: *The Creative Writing MFA Handbook: A Guide for Prospective Graduate Students* by Tom Kealey and *An Insider's Guide to Creative Writing Programs: Choosing the Right MFA or MA Program, Colony, Residency, Grant or Fellowship* by Amy Holman. Another way to approach an MFA program is to find out who is teaching where, and try to study under an author you respect.

An enticing trend is just starting to develop in the MFA world: free programs. Yes, free. Each school has its own way of offering these; some are fellowships you must be awarded. Ohio State offers a free MFA, as does Stanford (through a difficult-to-get fellowship). As this trend grows in popularity, it's certainly worth investigating which schools are offering it and what the requirements are.

Beyond the MFA, many writers find weekly workshops and writing groups helpful to provide feedback and deadlines. There are also weeklong and monthlong writers' retreats.

Resources

To find agents (beyond the methods described earlier), check the publishing section of your local bookstore. There are reference books with names and addresses of literary agencies, such as *Guide to Literary Agents* by Joanna Masterson. Also worth checking out, and always a wealth of information on where to try to get published, is *Writer's Market* by Robert Lee Brewer. Both of these are constantly updated; make sure you get the latest version. Another way to find literary journals to submit stories to (which may be read by agents and pub-

A good writing teacher can train into a student a capacity and passion for vigilant revision, in which the literary work can gradually come into its own, transcend the limits of subjectivity (which is riddled with blind spots), and emerge more and more clearly into the light of day.
—Christopher Noel, faculty, Vermont College MFA in Writing Program, and author of *In the Unlikely Event of a Water Landing: A Geography of Grief*

Philip Roth went to a friend's funeral once, and he was thinking about how he would write the experience if it were a scene. He said afterward, "That's the problem with this profession, it even fucks up grief." A good writer will always be looking at the world and wondering how it could be described in an interesting way.
—Darin Strauss, author of *Chang and Eng* and *The Real McCoy*

lishers) is to look inside the annual *Best American Short Stories* volumes, which always include a list of highly regarded journals.

Also, visit publisherslunch.com, and sign up for their free e-mail newsletter. It's a good place to follow what agents are doing, what they are selling (and in general, what's selling in the marketplace), and maybe which of them handles material similar to yours.

A sampling of some of the more notable books about writing:

Writing Down the Bones: Freeing the Writer Within by Natalie Goldberg

The Art of Fiction: Notes on Craft for Young Writers by John Gardner

Reading as a Writer: A Guide for People Who Love Books and for Those Who Want to Write Them by Francine Prose

A Writing Life by Annie Dillard

Burning Down the House: Essays on Fiction by Charles Baxter

Band Manager

anaging bands. It's not all babysitting Jim Morrison types and keeping them from choking on their own vomit. Although sure, there's a fair bit of that. Band managers guide and oversee the careers of musicians. Every aspect—tour dates, business dealings, coordinating schedules—falls under their supervision. They are the point person on everything the artist does.

Band managers get paid whenever the artists they represent get paid. So as one, you're constantly trying to find streams of income and opportunities for the band to make money. Managers make a commission on every piece of income an artist gets: touring, merchandise, record sales, contracts, appearances, songs used in films or TV shows, music in video games, ringtones, you name it. But unfortunately, not every artist is Christina Aguilera or the Rolling Stones; it can be a hard road. You work with musical artists because you're passionate about it, not to become rich. Sure, you'll always hope your bands make it big and you can finally buy a castle and stock it with models, but you go into it knowing the odds are not in your favor. A decent wage and the chance to live a rock 'n' roll (or hip-hop, or jazz, or country) lifestyle, however, is conceivable.

> My primary job is to make sure everyone involved with my artists is doing their job.
> —Seth Friedman, manager of the Black Eyed Peas, and John Legend, DAS Communication

What Does Managing a Band Mean?

Think of a band like any business—its goal is to make money. Now, no band wants to sell out (well, maybe some do)—they are in the music world because they're artists with something to say. Your job as manager is to keep the business side away from the art side, shield the artists from having to deal with the day-to-day dollars and cents, so they can create the kind of music that will make the dollars and cents.

Without getting too nitty-gritty, here are some of the duties you have as a manager. You will help your band get gigs by calling venues and sending out MP3s. Planning tours, finding the right used van to take them around, even making sure they all have working cell phones falls on your shoulders. For a tour, you'll book the hotel rooms. You'll help with the T-shirt designs, so they can sell the most merchandise. You will try to get them deals with equipment suppliers, so they pay less for amps and guitars and you all make more. And as the tour generates buzz, you'll help them land a record deal, the right record deal with the right label that will support them. You'll sit with the accountants after a long tour and wrap up the final tallies. You'll meet with music supervisors from TV shows and try to get your band's song on the air. You'll do everything you can to make your band the next big thing, without anyone feeling like they sold out. It's a balancing act, and there's no set way to go about it.

What Kind of Backgrounds Do Band Managers Have?

Varied, but pretty much everyone is a "music person." Many started at record labels, as either talent scouts or disgruntled A&R executives (see the chapter on A&R executives). Some were fans or friends who were simply helping out their favorite local band, and then as the band grew, they organically became its manager. Some were club promoters and booked bands, some were bouncers who got to know everyone. It's rock 'n' roll, dude, and pretty much anything goes.

How Do You Even Find a Band to Manage?

Usually at first by seeing them at a local club and approaching them. Since you're passionate about music, after a show you like, you go over to the band and talk. You'll see if they need help getting gigs and so on. Do they even have a manager? It won't all happen in that one conversation, of course, but you open a dialogue.

Now once you manage that first band, the word, at least at the local level, will be on the street. Other bands that play with your band might approach you. You'll start to find unsolicited MP3s and CDs coming your way. You'll research artists on the Web, especially (right now, anyway) on sites like garage band.com and myspace.com. Once you have one successful-ish band under your banner, it becomes far easier to find others: "Do for us what you did for them."

Adjectives That Describe Good Band Managers

Instinctive, gutsy, crafty, and *ambitious.* This is a job where you have to hustle and try to make all the right moves as the opportunities present themselves.

Two other characteristics you should have are charm and a thick skin. You will be at your client's beck and call, so you have to be the sort of person who can deal with that, someone who realizes that even the small, stupid things (Madonna wants only candlelight in her hotel room) add up. You have to be

I got a job right out of college at a label doing Internet marketing, but I was unhappy with the distance between me and the music. I knew an underground hip-hop music producer and I approached him: "Listen, I don't know what I'm doing but I want to be your manager. I've never been a manager before but I don't get paid unless you get paid 'cause it's strictly commission, you have nothing to lose." He agreed and then I got him a record contract and a publishing deal; his career and mine started taking off.
—Gabe Hilfer, music manager, GDH Media

The band that got me started as a manager I had just been just a fan of. I was able to get them some gigs, and I sent their CD, which hadn't been released outside Canada, to some people I knew. I was just doing this purely as a fan, making use of my connections. When they realized all of the stuff that was happening for them as a result, they asked me to manage them. And I was suddenly a band manager.
—Nadine Gelineau, president and founder, The Musebox

someone who likes helping people, and someone who can at times swallow his or her pride.

You're the band's partner in this whole crazy entertainment business they are trying to navigate. They need to be able to trust you, respect you, and frankly, like being with you.

Do You Work out of the Back of a Van?

Yup, sometimes, if you are on tour. You actually may spend up to 50 percent of your time on the road if your artists are successful, which, though allowing you to see the world in style, can put a crimp on long-term relationships.

Usually you will have a proper office, though, although this might be a home office. Most band management companies are small operations with one or two managers, maybe an assistant and an intern or two. Offices are laid-back affairs, as you'd imagine. This is the music industry, so really, anything goes. There are no dress codes or formalities, dude; let your freak flag fly. Of course, when you have big meetings at a label or with a music supervisor for a film, you probably shouldn't walk in wearing your "I [heart] Meth" T-shirt. But you won't exactly don the three-piece suit, either.

Hours?

You are on call 24/7. There's no average day, and you're dealing with artists who often tend to be night owls. Not to mention you may well be doing business with Europe and Asia during their work hours. You can't really put up barriers or hang up "Out to Lunch" signs; these are your clients and they count on you. A good manager is always on, with cell phone and Blackberry charged, ready at a moment's notice. A band could call in at any hour from the road, or they're writing songs and they want to bounce them off you, or they want to talk about the "next step" for them, or even if they just want a sounding board . . . you are their professional sounding board.

That doesn't mean you are working all day long, it just means that the day is never officially done, the phone can always ring. On the flip side, there are days when your phone won't ring at all. That's equally frustrating, though, because if your phone isn't ringing, well, then the band probably isn't out there making money.

A person who is somewhat fearless and really sociable is the best sort of personality to be a band manager. Somebody who has a lot of backbone, a lot of social skills, is very diplomatic, and clearly can relate to those in the arts. You know, a person who doesn't see everything in black and white, who can understand the nuances. It's not a great job for people who need a map or a "how-to" list. You have to think on your feet.
—Nadine Gelineau, president and founder, the Musebox

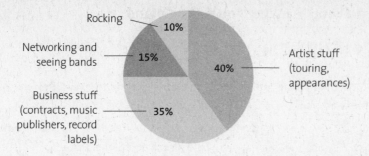

Rocking — 10%

Networking and seeing bands — 15%

Business stuff (contracts, music publishers, record labels) — 35%

Artist stuff (touring, appearances) — 40%

Dumptrucks Filled with Money?

Not at first. The money is actually terrible when you begin. (This career isn't covered by the Bureau of Labor Statistics, nor are any of its ilk.) Band managers typically make between 10 and 20 percent of the band's net. So at first, as you will probably be starting out with unknown bands, you're making a percentage of very little. But if your band hits it big and has a multiplatinum record followed by another followed by a sold-out world tour, you are going to be, dare we say, rich. You'll start flying only in private jets, and you might even own a white suit. Yeah.

But those band managers are few and far between. This is a job you do for the love of it, and the lifestyle of being part of pop culture and the music business.

Stress-o-Meter: 7 (1 being an opera soprano, 10 being Tony Soprano)

Surprisingly stressful. Managing relationships always has its tense moments, and artists are notoriously difficult. You're dealing with a lot of sensitive people with big egos, and when you manage several bands (one may be in the studio, another on tour), you'll be juggling lots of different tasks. And of course, doing it all 24/7. Plus, it's the music world, where no artist wants to be responsible ("We're blowing off the show tomorrow, we're tired"), and you have to be the one to get them to be ("No, you're playing; I'm coming over right now.") Add to that the fact that it's not a steady paycheck and yeah, you've got yourself a decent amount of stress.

Pros

Working with what you love—bands and music.

Getting to see the world on tour.

Meeting and befriending incredibly talented people.

If your band blows up, you really will be living the dream.

Cons

No steady paycheck.

Occasionally dealing with tremendous jerks.

Being on the road constantly can be tiring and difficult.

Bands break up, albums flop, lots of heartbreak.

You Are Ready to Rock. You're a Band Manager. You Wake Up And . . .

9:00 AM: Last night was a late one, the final date on your band's tour, luckily in your hometown. You take a much-needed shower and eat breakfast.

11:00 AM: You stop in to your office, which you share with one other manager. You start to go over the final tour numbers and see how the band (and you) did. You dive headfirst into the merchandise sales.

1:00 PM: You meet the band for lunch. They live in another town, and this is the last time you'll see them in person for a while. Everyone is hung over, but happy. You promise them numbers soon.

3:00 PM: You leave lunch and begin a marathon phone session with another artist who can't decide whether to let a *Fortune* 500 company use one of his songs in a commercial. He's basically broke and they are offering $75,000, but he doesn't want people to think he supports the company.

5:00 PM: You finally come to closure. He's not going to sell the song. You don't 100 percent agree, but you're supportive.

8:00 PM: You head out to see some band a bouncer friend told you "rips."

10:00 PM: They did rip. They shouldn't be some opening act at a tiny club. You talk to the band after the show and vow to stay in touch.

> I think something people don't realize is how important it is to be well liked. And I don't mean that in the vapid way it sounds! But in order to command respect and get all of the many players on the team to do what you want, there are two paths. One is fear, and the other is to get people to like you, to be someone who it's "great to work with." It sounds silly, but in this business, being well liked is almost as important as being smart.
> —Seth Friedman, manager of the Black Eyed Peas, and John Legend, DAS Communication

I'm Down. How the Hell Do I Become a Band Manager?

This is not the kind of job your uncle can get you. (Unless, of course, your uncle is Rick Rubin.) And there's really no degree or formal training. Some music-business extension classes are offered at universities, but the jury is out on their value. A basic business background, whether a degree or not, will be helpful, since you'll be doing all the marketing, sales, contracts, and so on, for the band, at least at first.

The first thing you should be doing is getting out of your house and out to wherever live bands play. It definitely helps if you live somewhere that's a hotbed of music. Sure, you can manage bands in Peoria, but there are a lot more bands in Brooklyn, and better odds of one of them making it with record labels based in Manhattan. Most major cities have a scene.

Without music industry knowledge, you'll be lost. As stated earlier, many managers come from having worked at labels. That's one way to further your music industry knowledge. But probably the best way to break into this field is to work for an established manager. As is the case in so many fields, this probably means interning, or volunteering your services. Don't know any band managers to approach? Open up the CDs of your favorite artists, and in the liner notes you'll see who their management team is. Be ballsy, show your moxie; call them and try to intern. But know that just like any internship in an exciting field, it's really not going to be glamorous to start. You'll have to swallow your pride and work really hard on silly crap. But work hard you must. If they want you to make photocopies, make the cleanest copies you can. If they ask you to make coffee, make goddamn delicious coffee. Sounds a little stupid, right? Well, managing a band is a client-service business. If you can prove yourself on those small tasks, then you'll move on to bigger responsibilities.

Any experience you can get on your own will help land these internships. If you were a college DJ, or worked at a club, or were on your school's entertainment board, let folks know. It's not the be-all and end-all, but it shows some commitment to the music game.

Once you are inside, use your youth. You can still stay up until four and see the late-night bands your older bosses might blow off. Bring that cutting-edge knowledge to the table. You have to know the current music scene, and the Internet, in a way a member of the older generation might not. Most bosses will listen to "the kids" and the bands they think are hot. Become their go-to person.

Keep meeting people every time you go to shows. Networking is huge; it's eventually how you will find a band or a job at a management firm. Get to know all the younger people like yourself trying to break into the music world—the ones coming up, the people who want to be the players in five or ten years. The industry is all about relationships—if not for today, then for tomorrow.

Resources

The best resource is just to get out there, see bands, and get involved.

Some industry trade magazines will help you keep track of the latest music world developments: *Billboard, Music Connection, CMJ,* plus all the ones you probably already read, such as *Blender, Fader, Rolling Stone,* and *Spin.*

Music conventions are great places to see new bands and to meet industry folks. Some of the hottest right now are South by Southwest in Austin, CMJ in New York, North by Northeast in Toronto, and Coachella in Palm Springs. There's probably one in your region. Go with some friends; cram into a hotel room if it's expensive. You can really network and learn your region too—make sure you're an expert in your area before jumping into a bigger pond.

There are many books on the music game, but one that is recommended over and over again is *All You Need to Know about the Music Business* by Donald Passman.

There are Harvard MBAs who are managers, and there are managers who are high school dropouts who are extremely smart and aggressive and have good instincts. There's no specific path of study for this at all.
—Peter Cohen, music and artist manager, Special Teams Music

It's very important that you know the vernacular and the lay of the land in the music world. No one expects you to know contract specifics, but you need to know the difference between an agent and a lawyer, the basics of the business. Be on the concert committee of your school, keep meeting people, get that knowledge, and be tenacious about it. Oh, and if you are going to intern, try to be an intern who's available 24/7. Many places have no need for someone available only three days a week. That's not the reality of the business.
—Seth Friedman, manager of the Black Eyed Peas, and John Legend, DAS Communication

Blogger

Getting paid for journal entries. That's the dream of the blogger. But to turn your blogging hobby into a blogging career, those journal entries are probably going to have to be a whole lot more interesting than "Brian looked at me in calculus today, I totally think he's cute but he needs a mint."

When blogs first appeared, they really were nothing more than online diaries and scrapbooks. Today, they could be described as pithy content that often links to separate sites where users can dig deeper into the subject matter. That short content could be anything from a technology blog detailing the latest gadgets coming our way to a gossip site following the lives of celebrities. The key to success for any of these is as simple and as difficult as the personality of the writer. If people love what you say and how you say it, they'll come back to your site, and hopefully bring even more visitors. If not, you're just another voice crying out in the darkness of the cyber world. Which is both bleak and nerdy.

> You have to have a unique angle. We take newsworthy stuff and we put our own sort of funny, nasty, irreverent spin on it. We position ourselves as the antidote to the old Hollywood bullshit machine.
> —Seth Abramovitch, associate editor, Defamer.com

How Do People Make Any Money from Their "Journals"?

Advertising, advertising, advertising. The way blogs make money is the same way TV stations and magazines do. The more people who view them, the more they can charge for the advertising on the site. (Ed. note: Blogging is a rapidly developing field; any minute now some genius may have cracked another way to monetize it.) Getting views and clicks is a complicated business, but if you can field a steady stream, you can make a decent living.

Not many can, though. While there are millions of bloggers out there, at this point only a small percentage blog full time. But as people turn away from the mainstream media to the Web for news, entertainment, and information, and as advertisers recognize that and pour more money into their online media buys, that number will continue to grow.

There Are Two Types of Bloggers

The first type is simply a writer. Writers don't own, or publish, their blog; they work as a writer for it, the same way a reporter writes for *Newsweek*. Blog writers are paid a salary if they are officially on staff, or they may be freelance and get paid per submission. Both are low dollar figures.

The second type is a blog publisher. Here, you are the owner of the blog, which you probably also write. This doesn't necessarily mean you make more money or are more successful, it just means you own the damn thing. And if it grows, so do your revenues.

Blogs Are Kind of Like Online Magazines, Right? So How Does This Differ from a Job as a Magazine Writer?

Wow, good question. You are really paying attention. A lot of current bloggers do come from the magazine world. But other than the "writing" part, the jobs are quite different.

At a magazine, an established one anyway, there is a big office with a lot of different departments. Anything you write is generally an assignment that comes to you through an editor. And once written, your little piece will go through fact checking, copyediting, and the art department. (See the chapter on magazine writers, it's a page-turner.)

Blogs are smaller, one- or two- (occasionally ten-) people operations. Because of the timeliness of the Internet, you don't bother to go too deep with the copyediting and fact checking—you just get the post up damn fast. If you make a factual mistake, you correct it a few posts later. You get all the credit, but if something's wrong, you get all the blame. Remember, the Internet invites conversation, and those who read blogs aren't shy. As a magazine writer, you won't often receive a letter chiding or lauding you personally. As a blogger, you'll get comments on nearly every piece you post. And part of the job of continuing to build your audience is the skill with which you respond and react to comments and keep the dialogue open. There's nothing like that in the magazine world. It can be like broadcasting live on a call-in radio show.

So Like, You Just Blog All Day?

Sorta. Meaning you research and write posts throughout the day on whatever subject the blog is about, to fill up the site. If you are the publisher, there are, of course, added responsibilities. There's marketing the site (perhaps doing interviews with other blogs, buying small ads on other sites, etc.), dealing with ad sales, and the assorted accounting and legal issues that come with being an independent business.

Trust me, I've learned the hard way that if you don't check your facts quickly, the blogosphere will quickly correct you with much finger pointing and laughing. The same goes for typos and spelling errors, all that stuff. It's made me better because I am always on the lookout.
—Seth Abramovitch, associate editor, Defamer.com

What Makes for a Good Blogger?

Well, you should be able to write. What type of writing depends on what type of blog, but you need to be able to communicate. A charming, humorous tone, although not necessary everywhere, tends to go a long way online.

You need to be fast. People are waiting for content, and you need to get it to them. And on that note, you need to be committed. There are a lot of other sites people can go to, and if you don't post for a while . . . they will. You could understand, then, that obsessiveness is a fairly common trait among bloggers.

Most important, you need to have a vast knowledge of your subject, because your readers will. If you write about pop culture, you need to be on top of all the breaking stories. If you write about gadgets, you need to know the technology. You have to have authority and credibility in the arena you are blogging about. Plus, you need to be okay with spending a lot of your day alone. Blogging is a very social job online, but it's done by individuals chained to computers.

Other than that—you need basic computing skills. And of course, a computer.

Office?

Sometimes. But often your home computer is your office. This can be a pro or a con, depending on whether you like to stay home. If you live somewhere warm and your Wi-Fi reaches the backyard—definitely consider a laptop. Some people go to coffee shops to blog or find small spaces they can rent just to change their environments. The bottom line is if there is an office, it's completely, totally casual. Unless you are an in-house blogger for a large corporation—jobs like this are just starting to surface, the newfangled company newsletter. In that case, well, it depends on your office's specific corporate culture, natch.

What Hours Are You Blogging?

Obviously the Internet is a twenty-four-hour institution, so all hours are possible. If you're awake and online, you're sort of working. Even if you're not posting, you're surfing around, always considering what might be your next post.
—Josh Rubin, editor in chief, coolhunting.com

The hours just totally depend. You could be addicted to posting, pasty white from being indoors all the time, logging insane hours online—or you might post a few times a day and that's it. If you're a publisher you are probably a little more vested than if you are a hired writer, and are online more. Some sites are known for constant updating; others seem to be updated around certain hours. Viewers of the site will get used to a certain schedule, and you'll be expected to stick to it.

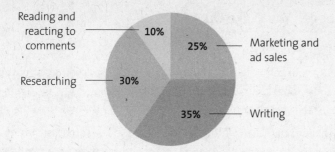

Reading and reacting to comments — 10%

Marketing and ad sales — 25%

Researching — 30%

Writing — 35%

Bread for Blogging?

Not much. It's hard to quantify exactly what bloggers make, as the career is such a new one. Neither the Bureau of Labor Statistics, nor any of the other usual suspects, covers bloggers yet. But for the most part the salaries (if you are a salaried writer) are low, even at established sites—between $200 and $3,000 per month. And if you're freelance, the pay is even lower.

If you are a publisher and your site is getting a lot of hits, you can definitely do pretty well. At this point in time, a million page views a month is worth, at minimum, $2,500 a month in small ad placements, and up to $20,000 if the ads are larger, multiplacement jobs. And hey, maybe you become so popular that some mainstream site, say Yahoo!, wants to buy you. It happens. You could blog from your Bentley.

Stress-o-Meter: 6 (1 being a paraglider, 10 being a paramedic)

There is a certain thrill in writing quickly, posting, and seeing the responses of your readers. But it does all have to happen at a quick pace. And it has to happen constantly, or your viewers (and your ad dollars) are off to another site.

Pros

You're a writer building your own audience, and if you are a publisher too, there are no bosses or editors getting in the way.

You'll be considered "press" and get all kinds of fun invites to events and parties.

Flexible hours, work from home.

Instant feedback on your writing.

Cons

Some days you don't want to write.

Some days you don't want to go online.

Money ain't great.

Instant feedback on your writing.

Ctrl Alt Awesome. You Are a Blogger. You Wake Up And . . .

This assumes you are the publisher and it is a one-person operation.

9:30 AM: You roll out of bed and over to your computer. It's a little late for you; usually you try to post before normal people get to work and go online, but you were writing until three last night and damn it, you needed the sleep. You start to read your personal e-mail as well as feedback e-mail from the site.

10:15 AM: You put up a quick post explaining why you're off to a late start. Then you do some fast surfing to see what's happening out there in the cyber world. You see a topic of interest and start writing a piece.

11:00 AM: You post it. You have the speed of a puma.

11:30 AM: With only a quick break for lunch, you spend the next few hours writing and posting two more stories. Then you take a walk around the block to keep your retinas from burning out from staring at the monitor.

3:30 PM: You are interviewed by a blog similar to yours. You agreed to this a few days ago. It's good quid pro quo. They'll write about you, and someday soon you'll write about them, hopefully increasing both audiences.

4:30 PM: You spend an hour on the phone—the first half with your accountant going over how you're doing, the second with an advertiser trying to up his ad buy to better how you're doing.

5:30 PM: You get back to surfing and surfing, looking for more ideas. You find a few and start writing up posts.

7:30 PM: The new posts are up. You take a break and go out to meet some friends. But you can't wait to get back to your computer later. It's sick but true.

I Am Wired. How the Hell Do I Become a Blogger?

Start a blog. Bam, you're a blogger. You're not a blogger who makes money, but you're a blogger all the same.

Seriously, the best way to get started is to start. You'll learn a ton and also have your own portfolio of writing samples with which to impress larger blogs that might actually hire you. And their hiring you doesn't mean you have to give up your own blog either, so it's, as they say in boardrooms across our fine country, a "win-win."

Let people know you are doing this blog. Blogs feed off blogs. Post comments on like-minded blogs, ask them if you may link to their site, if they'll link to yours. And to the bigger blogs, do the same—just don't be annoying. Give them tips, point them in directions, make it known you are out there without being a stalker. Perhaps they'll want you to write, or perhaps they'll point some of their readership toward you once you've proven yourself. It's

Anybody who has gotten a job at Gawker has had their own blog first, a blog that garnered attention of its own accord.
—Seth Abramovitch, associate editor, Defamer.com

hard to get started, but once you build some momentum, readership can grow exponentially.

As far as your site design goes, it really pays to give it a distinct look and not use a template that comes from blogger.com, Movable Type, Mac, and so on. If you can't do it yourself it's worth tossing a friend a few bucks.

Resources

Thousands of sites give advice on how to become a blogger. But most successful bloggers don't recommend these, since a distinctive voice is the most important thing. Therefore, none is recommended here. If you are interested, a Google search will find oodles, though. One thing you should definitely do is read all the help sections on sixapart.com; it's a site from the owners of blogging software that will help you through all kinds of technical issues. Which blogging software should you go with? Recommending one program would be futile; every blogger has a favorite. A fairly complete list of services for you to choose from, with links, can be found at en.wikipedia.org/wiki/Weblog_software.

The other piece of advice bloggers give is not to identify yourself as a blogger. It's limiting. You're a writer. You're a journalist or an editorialist. This will help you get interviews with people who may not yet recognize blogging as an important part of the media tapestry. But they will. Soon.

A custom-designed site brings credibility. It says this is for real, not just a hobby. The writing of course must be engaging, but a distinctive look really helps.
—Josh Rubin,
  editor in chief,
  coolhunting.com

Boutique Owner

Owning one's own boutique—ah, it's the dream of many a young shopper. Having customers squeal, "Oh my gawd I want it!" and then spend their hard-earned ducats on items you've discovered and marked way the hell up is pretty fun. Of course, there's a tad more to it than that. But if you're the type of person who loves finding something new and turning people on to it, and if you are pretty confident in your own exquisite taste, maybe owning a boutique will fit you. Get it, *fit?* Never mind.

A Quick Definition

A boutique is a small store (well, some are less small than others) that sells fashion. Fashion can be more than strictly clothes, of course; many boutiques sell a lifestyle—music, items for the home, even food. The wares for sale can be profoundly high end or they can be inexpensive vintage, but the thing that all boutiques have in common, what separates them from chain stores like the Gap, is that there is a personality who is buying the items for sale, who makes the store a seemingly one-of-a-kind, special place. Here it is then, the key to success for a small shoppe in rhyme form—unique, boutique.

Wait—What Exactly Makes a Boutique Unique?

The only way you can distinguish yourself and turn a bit of a profit is by creating a niche and being really, really damn good at it.
—Joseph Quartana, co-owner and buyer, Seven New York

Something better. Because if a boutique doesn't have a differentiating quality, it won't stay in business long. What makes a boutique special is the person or people running it. Their vision of fashion, their take on the latest trends, is paramount. Otherwise, why would customers visit them instead of, say, Urban Outfitters? You have to have something different, even if it's not your wares, but just the vibe in the store. This can't be said enough, and it should reverberate throughout this chapter: when it comes to successful boutiques—differentiate or die.

What Do Boutique Owners Do All Day?

More than sit by the register reading magazines. The first and most important task is buying—finding the items with which you want to stock your store.

This involves going to showrooms and fashion shows, and becoming friendly with the types of designers you love and will want to continually showcase. Of course, it's more sophisticated than simply buying what you like. You can't just have pants and no blouses, unless your boutique is called The Pants Emporium. Assuming that's not your niche, the blouses and pants you buy will need to go together to create outfits, and the accessories you stock will need to work with these, and so on. This ritual of buying happens several times a year, in concert with the fashion seasons and shows.

Once the stock is bought, it needs to be priced—that is, marked up. How much do you think you can ask for it? And then, it needs to be put out on "the floor" in a way that is appealing. You can't have any poorly dressed mannequins. There are window displays to make and change. There's music to choose and crank up or down. There's the general feel of the place, what you wear, and what your employees wear, to consider. Again, this is your boutique, right? How is it different, special, a place where customers want to come?

Then there is the part that almost all boutique owners, even the ones who were economics majors, call their least favorite: the accounting. Paying the bills, figuring out if you are up or down, knowing how to price things properly, what should be put "on sale" and for how much less, opening up accounts with Visa and AMEX, and so on. This money stuff can get complicated. Some seasons you're up, others you're down, and you have to plan ahead so you can pay the rent and be able to buy what you want. It doesn't hurt to be decent at math. Especially when you're buying items from Europe and the price is in euros, which you need to convert to dollars, and then factor in the shipping costs to figure out if the price you're quoted is expensive or cheap. Fun, fun, snore. But if you're not smart with the money, you don't get to do any of the other enjoyable parts. Ain't that America?

What Kind of Person Opens a Successful Boutique?

Lots of folks with lots of varied backgrounds. There are people who took business classes, as well as people who never went to college. But they share certain qualities that you'll need.

First off, you must have an innate understanding of trends and fashion. Obnoxious as it sounds, taste is one of those things that can't really be taught. If you don't love, live, and breathe fashion, this job may not be for you. Can you put yourself together? Can you put someone else together? You have to be able to employ current trends and see the emerging ones.

You have to be a hard worker. You can't be averse to rolling up your sleeves and cleaning fingerprints off the window. You have to persevere; there will be

> It's important to be honest with customers. I don't want my employees selling a garment to someone who clearly does not look good in it, because you'll lose a customer that way. We want our customers to walk out, see their friends, and hear, "You look incredible." If someone comes out of the fitting room wearing things that don't fit properly, I'll say, "Don't get that." I'd rather be honest, have them trust us and come back next time, than make a sale for a few hundred dollars right then and there.
> —Joseph Quartana, co-owner and buyer, Seven New York

high seasons and low seasons, and you have to learn to roll with the punches, emotionally and financially.

And this is yet another job where you really need to be a people person. And not only a people person, but also a diplomat, because, hey, morons come into the store. You'll get morons by the truckloads sometimes, and you'll need to make even them feel welcome. And you'll always have to walk the fine line between being a helpful salesperson and being pushy.

And What Is a Successful Boutique?

Good question. Most boutique owners aren't out to get rich. They are happy to "do well." Some do spectacularly and sell out to a major chain for big bucks. The main thing to realize if you are opening your own boutique is that success comes very, very slowly. You can't expect to see a real profit for two to five years, and most have a five-year, basic business plan. A business plan is necessary; if you weren't a business major and don't really understand those, you'll need to either buy some books or talk to some people who are in the know. Because without one, you'll never really know where you stand. By the way, not turning a profit doesn't mean you aren't paying yourself a nice salary, along with the salaries of every one else in your employ. It just means there isn't that additional big money. Yet.

You'll need to figure out a plan. How long can you stay in business if you do X amount of sales? Are you going to pay yourself a salary and build that into your business expenses, or are you going to live on peanut butter and put everything into the store to start? It truly helps to have a nice little financial cushion when opening a boutique.

So What Kind of Money Are We Talking?

It depends. There are no official numbers or estimates, because it's a total gamble: you could go out of business, or you could become a retail giant. There's no way to know or assign a dollar figure to what you can expect to take home. And will you even pay yourself a salary to begin, or will you sink it all back into the boutique? It's all individual choice.

How about the Hours?

Most boutiques are open six days a week, with hours like eleven to seven or noon to eight. A lot of the nonsales parts of the job can be done during the slow parts of the day. For example, if the store is slow, you can do some billing or research designers online; there's no real reason to arrive too early or stay too late. Conceivably, you could lock up the store at eight and consider the day done. But for many, the boutique is their baby and they are working every waking hour. They'll be online first thing in the morning e-mailing suppliers in Europe, and going out with magazine editors in the evenings, trying to get items from their stores placed in articles. The hours aren't too bad, and when you do kill yourself, no one is forcing you but you.

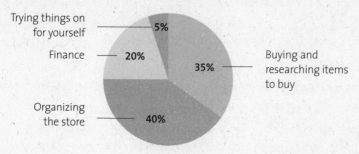

Stress-o-Meter: 5 (1 being a trend hunter, 10 being a bounty hunter)

The stress comes from owning your own business and being responsible for bills, employees, orders, unhappy customers, the music playing in the store—everything, really. But if you love your store, if it's your special place, none of this will bother you.

Pros

Owning your own business, answering to no one.
Spending your days around cool people you've hired, and customers who like your taste.
Hearing people say, "This is my favorite store!"
Wholesale clothing for you!

Cons

Dealing with accounting and bills and invoices and ugh.
Anything that isn't working, you have to fix.
Money. You can make a killing in the fall, and nothing in the winter. You have to plan.
Refolding clothes after others unfold them.

Congratulations, You Own a Boutique. You Wake Up And . . .

Of course, it all depends on what exactly you sell, and on the season, but basically . . .

12:00 PM: After breakfast at home followed by a Pilates class, you arrive to the store at noon on the nose and unlock the door. You put on some music and make sure everything looks just so. Then you sit at the desk and begin going through some receipts.

12:15 PM: Two of your employees arrive. You send them to the back to start unpacking boxes of new jeans, affixing the store's price tags, and putting some on the floor.

12:30 PM: The store is officially open.

1:30 PM: As your employees help the first few shoppers, you surf online and look at some fashions from Japan. You're starting to think about next season. You click on a travel site and book a hotel in Paris; you're going to the shows this year to do a little buying. You can't wait.

2:30 PM: You fold some clothes. You are quite an accomplished folder.

3:00 PM: Weekday afternoons are always slow. You leave the store in your employees' hands and walk around the neighborhood, window shopping, looking at stylish people. It's important to know what other people are doing, what looks good, what's going on.

4:00 PM: One of your favorite customers arrives, a local celebrity. You personally help her out. She answers her cell phone: "I can't talk, I'm in the *best* shop." You beam.

5:00 PM: You take a call from your accountant. She bugs you to put more money into your IRA. You are once again reminded that there's no pension or 401(k) (or health insurance) that comes with owning your own store.

6:00 PM: An old Cure song comes over the sound system: "Boys Don't Cry." Spontaneous dancing between you and your employees begins. A customer walks in and laughs. Business usually starts picking up after normal work hours are over, but still the store is pretty quiet.

7:00 PM: You start going through some more dreaded invoices and pay some bills. You can't believe how expensive your electric is.

7:30 PM: It was a fairly slow day, but you made a few sales. You and the employees sweep and mop the store, refold clothing, and get the place into shape so you're ready to open tomorrow without any hassles. They split at eight. You hang out and do a bit more research for your Paris trip.

I Wish to Birth a Unique Boutique. How the Hell Do I Do It?

There's no real prerequisite; you can be from any background, any major, anywhere. But you will need some money. Money to get a lease, to stock items, to design and decorate; it takes quite a serious investment. So yes, anyone with these means can open a boutique. Not just anyone can open a successful boutique, however.

The first thing you should do to prepare is to get a job in a boutique as a salesperson. Try to be a salesperson in the kind of place that's similar to the one you may one day want to open. If you want to get into the designer market, being a salesperson at Abercrombie and Fitch isn't going to help you all that much, other than learning general sales stuff. The fashion world is snobby, so if designer is your goal, know that you can't really ever go from being a salesperson at the Gap to one at Dior; of course, you can go the opposite way.

But at places like Dior or Gucci (or Saks, Barney's, and the like), you're much more likely to be an intern first than to actually be a salesperson. And, yup, intern you should. Getting to know the fashion business, how it works, what sells and why, is crucial.

Another way to gain knowledge of the designer world is to intern (or work) at one of the magazines that cover the fashion world, such as *Elle, Vogue,* or *V.* From that side, you'll learn the trends and how they ebb and flow, and you could take that experience and go to a sales job, or right to boutique ownership, if you like. The most common backgrounds are sales jobs at other boutiques, jobs in fashion, or jobs at the magazines.

It's important to be realistic, though, in terms of the top magazines and designer boutiques. Believe it or not, a lot of people who score internships or entry-level positions come from Ivy League schools, and a lot of times these places *want* that, or a Duke, or a USC . . . but only with like a 4.0.

Lastly, you could get some practical business experience. Take accounting classes and learn about all the things that keep businesses afloat. If you have great natural taste and are a born fashionista, the business stuff is more important to learn.

Finally, when you do get interviews, don't be arrogant. It's a turnoff to the owners. If anyone gets to be arrogant it's them, not you. And obviously, dress fashionably for your interview. Show that you have style and taste that is going to make the store an even better place to be. But don't just wear the style of the store if it's not for you; your look has to be "convincing."

> A sales job is important. Selling is the flip side to buying, and buying, what you actually decide to have in your store, is what makes a boutique. .
> —Joseph Quartana, co-owner and buyer, Seven New York

Resources

It's important, obviously, to stay on top of the fashion world. Some fashion magazines (a small sampling, there are cubic tons) that will help are *ID, V, V Man, Soma* (New York), *Surface* (L.A.), *Self Service* (France), *Kirkel* (France), *Crash* (France), *Ryuko Tsuihsin* (Japan), *Vogue, Elle, Bazaar,* and *Lucky Magazine.*

There are also many fashion Web sites, of course, such as style.com and hintmag.com. You can keep track of different designers and their fashion shows at their individual sites. Plus, you can travel. If you don't live in a fashion capital (such as New York, Milan, or Paris), try to visit one at least once, or a few times, a year. Walk around and see what the other boutiques are showing, and why.

Owning a boutique is an entrepreneurial venture. Perhaps it's worth reading the chapter on entrepreneurs. Some resources that might be handy in opening a new business include the U.S. Small Business Administration, which has "programs and services to help you start, grow and succeed." It's at sba.gov.

The IRS has some helpful advice. Yes, *that* IRS; sheesh, don't be so cynical. Surf over to irs.gov, click on the "businesses" tab, and you'll see information on starting and operating a business.

Chef

The greatest pleasures in life, arguably, are sex and food. And sadly, as you get older, eating starts to trump sex. Well, it's not that sad really, as most of us would take a perfectly cooked *steak-frites* over a lousy lay any day of the week.

So it's no wonder that many people dream of becoming chefs, making their living creating dishes that will have diners licking their chops. Is it an easy career? No. Does it pay a lot? Not really. Might you pile on pounds being around food all day? It's a definite possibility. And not everyone can pull off the puffy hat without looking like a Muppet. But to most chefs, there's no other job in the world they'd rather have.

The most common venue where chefs work is, of course, in restaurants. However, there are other places where chefs roast, grill, and poach. There are catering companies that provide the food at all sorts of affairs; private chefs who work for wealthy individuals or at companies like Google that believe an expertly cooked lunch is a worthy employee pleaser; and even chefs who work exclusively on yachts, sailing around the world with the mega-rich and feeding them and the crew. With that in mind, however, this chapter will focus on chefs who work in restaurant kitchens. Even if you do choose to be a chef in a different setting, you'll most likely work in a restaurant at some point; restaurant experience is invaluable.

What's Up in the Kitchen?

If you're a chef, you cook, right? Right, but it's not like there's one chef in the back of the restaurant cooking everyone's meals. There is a hierarchy of chefs in the kitchen, the same way there is a management hierarchy in a marketing department. On the top of the food pyramid is the *head chef, executive chef,* or *chef owner.* This person is the lead dog, the CEO: he or she has designed the menu, decided on the ingredients, and basically created the blueprint that the other cooks will follow to help construct the meal. Just like a CEO, he or she may or may not be in on the daily action, and may not do a lot of the actual cooking. Right below the head chef is the *chef du cuisine,* who is in the kitchen pretty much five days a week, running the show. The chef du cuisine is second in command but the boss of the kitchen, making sure everything comes out

This is a job where you feel you can learn something new every day. I think that's one of the main reasons I got into it; with food you can always learn more, a different way to cook, a different way to put something on the plate, ways to change the appearance of certain vegetables.
—Marc Johnson, line cook, Blue Hill, New York City

just right. Next in line is the *sous chef,* who is the right hand of the chef du cuisine, sort of a vice president. The sous chef sometimes also plays the role of "expeditor," meaning he or she is the liaison between the wait staff and the kitchen, helps make sure all dishes ordered by a table arrive simultaneously, and so on. (If you've ever traveled abroad, you know that some cultures don't believe in the expeditor.) Under the sous chef comes the *chef de partie,* or line cook. These do most of the actual cooking. In a larger restaurant they specialize, so there will be a fish cook, a meat cook, a vegetable cook. Finally, there are cooks and assistants, who help out the line cooks and do slicing, chopping, and more grunt-type work.

There are two parts of the day in the kitchen: prep and service. Prep is the time before customers come in, when chefs get everything ready to go. They make stocks and sauces, do the butchering, get all their ducks in a row. Service is meal time, when people arrive and order, and the sautéing, roasting, and searing begins in earnest.

And What's It Like in the Kitchen? Calm? Chaos?

It ranges. But there's always pressure. Different days of the week have different vibes. Some nights the restaurant can be packed, yet everything is humming smoothly in the kitchen; another night it could be a mess. If the restaurant is fairly successful, the scene in the kitchen is constantly intense. No one wants to wait for a meal, and every meal has to come out perfect and delicious, plated beautifully.

While kitchens are infamous for having uptight chefs and cooks, there is also a great camaraderie. It's like going into an impossible battle with a group of friends, and pulling off miracles night after night. It's addictive, and a high.

What Ingredients Do You Need to Be a Good Chef?

It goes without saying that you need a passion for food and flavor, but what the heck, let's just say it anyway: you need a passion for food and flavor. You have to be extremely flexible, because you never know if the head chef ordered something different, wants to try a new variation tonight, or just wants to change the menu. And you have to be a good multitasker; you'll be cooking three, four, five things at once.

You also have to realize that being a chef is a physical job. You pretty much stand for hours on end, cutting and chopping in a small, hot environment. Every chef has an "and it kept bleeding and bleeding" finger-slicing story. It's

At 5:00, when customers come in and start ordering, the kitchen begins to become very, very intense. You're just cooking and cooking. We'll have nights with like seventy customers and you think it will be the easiest night, but it's the most harrowing. And then we'll have nights with one hundred forty people, we're packed the whole night, but everything runs smoothly. You can't predict it.
—Marc Johnson,
line cook, Blue Hill,
New York City

That's what's nice about working in kitchens. It's all about teamwork, and everybody works together to accomplish the task of making the guests happy. You spend a lot of time in really small places and so people make more of an effort.
—Cristina Topham,
private chef

dangerous in the kitchen sometimes. Every one is moving fast, and accidents—burns, cuts—happen.

Hours?

The hours are long, and often late. Most chefs work from noon to around midnight, five days a week. Sixty hours.

And the hours you work the hardest are the hours most everyone else has off. Forget having dinner with your friends and family, especially on weekends and holidays, which are the busiest times for restaurants. While everyone else is playing, you are working. That's just the job.

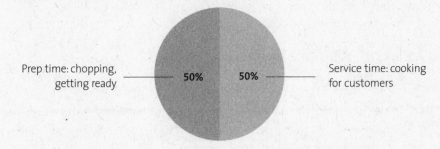

Prep time: chopping, getting ready — 50%   50% — Service time: cooking for customers

What Do You Get Paid for That Sixty-Hour Week?

Not much. And the better the restaurant, the more it's considered an honor to work there, a résumé builder, and thus the pay is less. The average starting salary in a city like New York is around $400 a week, or about $21,000 a year. And most jobs aren't staff jobs with benefits, except at larger, corporate restaurants. A chef du cuisine, second in command, might make only around $60,000. The Bureau of Labor Statistics reports a mean salary of $35,840, with a range from $18,890 to $57,420.

It takes a little while to move up the ladder, although if you work at a heralded restaurant you can jump levels by going to a less well-known one. If you want to stay in fine dining, you have to put in at least a few years as a line chef before getting the opportunity to become a sous chef, and so on. But just like any other job, moving up depends on who you know and your personality as much as on your cooking and dedication.

Stress-o-Meter: 9 (1 being a bikini inspector, 10 being an atomic weapons inspector)

As has been stated multiple times, it gets hairy in the kitchen. There can be screaming and crying, even the rare fight. You love every second; food gives you a thrill and is of huge importance in your life. But it's rough. It's one of the more stressful jobs in this book.

Pros

You get paid for what you love to do: cook.

Amazing camaraderie with colleagues.

It's gratifying when people enjoy what you've made for them.

Cons

The money.

The hours.

Sometimes you're just so tired and stressed it's hard to cook.

Bon Appétit. You Are a Chef. You Wake Up And . . .

This assumes you are at the level of line cook, and your specialty is meat, marvelous meat.

10:00 AM: You do some sit-ups. You're about to spend the rest of your day around food and don't want to end up looking like Paul Prudhomme. Then you do your e-mailing for the day—there's no computer in the kitchen, and you'll take only the occasional cell phone break.

12:00 PM: You arrive at the restaurant in your kitchen whites. You begin by making some sauces, starting with beurre blanc.

1:00 PM: The meat arrives. And it arrives as almost-whole animals, not cuts of meat like in ShopRite. No, *you* cut the meat. With almost-whole animals, you get a lot of scrap meat, from which more sauces are prepared. While the sauces and stocks cook, you do some vacuum sealing. You put poultry into vacuum-seal bags with different aromatics and herbs, then seal those and cook them in a combination steamer.

2:00 PM: Now that things are bubbling, you get to the special projects of the day. There's quail to wrap and pork bellies to trim. You're fairly busy, but you remind yourself it's the calm before the storm.

3:00 PM: You continue trimming other meats for the evening. You and the pastry chef step outside for a quick breath of air.

4:00 PM: You start preparing the "family meal," the meal for all the staff, chefs, waiters, and bussers, about twenty people at your restaurant. You make macaroni and cheese with pork belly scraps.

5:00 PM: The restaurant opens. People place orders and you begin to cook the cuts of meat you've prepared.

6:00 PM: You cook . . .

7:00 PM: and cook . . .

8:00 PM: and cook . . .

9:00 PM: Cooking, cooking, cooking.

10:00 PM: The maitre d' has "screwed up again" with reservations, and suddenly the kitchen is in a tizzy. You are cooking six different meals at once, and sweating. The kitchen has gone from a busy, whistle-while-you-work vibe to "Holy crap!" You hear a lot of cussing in French from the Parisian sous chef.

11:00 PM: You survive. You clean up and have a glass of wine. You chat with a couple of line cooks outside while they smoke.

12:00 AM: You bolt.

Food Completes Me. How the Hell Do I Become a Chef?

Well, if you can cook (however you've acquired the skill; information on culinary schools follows) and are hardworking, you can get a job in a kitchen. But it's not that easy; you can't just walk in the door of a hot French bistro and start roasting things up.

So here's what you do: go to several restaurants you admire and tell them you'd like to *trail*. Trailing is the equivalent of an interview or a tryout for chefs. You'll go in and spend the day in the kitchen doing stuff, mostly menial tasks like peeling shrimp and doing certain knife cuts. The chefs working there will watch how persistent you are, how you interact with others, and whether you listen and follow through.

Anyone can trail. And no one gets paid. It's a nonpaying working interview. You will need to have basic kitchen gear, like one or two chef knives. All chefs own their own knives—pretty fancy, crazy-sharp ones. Good knives start at around $35; chefs usually own a range. For example, in a three-knife set they might own an $80, a $100, and a $200 knife.

But just because anyone can trail doesn't mean any one gets to. While it's true you don't need to go to culinary school, you do need to know your way around a professional kitchen. Plus, just like any other job, who you know opens doors. Culinary school helps on both fronts, providing training and great networking opportunities. There are several different-length programs, from six months to two years. The two-year program is the equivalent of an associate degree, so you also have courses like mathematics; it's probably not for you if you've already gone to college. The six- and nine-month degrees offer more of a basic foundation in culinary training. In the competitive world of cooking, especially in the larger cities, you realistically need to attend a culinary school to trail at the better restaurants, even if you've held jobs in lesser kitchens since you were fourteen.

> When people come in and trail, we are judging, thinking, "Do they take direction, do they ask questions, do they seem interested in what the kitchen is doing?"
> —Marc Johnson,
> line cook, Blue Hill,
> New York City

> Every industry has its own language, and culinary school will give you an understanding of our language. I notice that chefs who haven't gone to school don't seem to have the verbiage down.
> —Cristina Topham,
> private chef

Tips for the Budding Chef

Before you commit to this field just because you love your new crock pot, do yourself a favor. If you haven't yet, work in a restaurant, even if it is in a nonkitchen position. Learn what it is like to be on your feet for long hours, serving others, and see if you can deal.

Also, be honest with yourself. Make sure you can swallow the fact that no matter how smart or gifted you might be in the kitchen, your first jobs will probably require your labor on the most menial tasks. As you develop and further your education, you'll advance. But it doesn't come quickly or easily. Becoming a successful chef in a major city takes years and years of commitment, hands-on experience, and training. Make sure you love it before you leap.

Resources

To stay current on what's happening in the food world, read. *Food and Wine* is recommended, as is *Savoir*. The dining-out section of the *New York Times* on Wednesdays is insightful. Also keep up with local magazines, read restaurant reviews, and see which chefs are moving to different places and may need fresh blood, or what interesting new restaurants are opening. New food Web sites pop up every day, some aimed directly at chefs. A great New York–based one is chowhound.com.

There are culinary schools throughout the country. Some good ones are the Institute of Culinary Education on 23rd Street in New York, iceculinary.com, as well as the famed French Culinary Institute, frenchculinary.com, which has its own critically acclaimed "on-campus" restaurant, manned by students. See the American Culinary Federation Web site, acfchefs.org, for information about other accredited culinary schools, apprenticeships, certification, jobs, and related organizations. The Culinary Institute of America has similar information available on its site, ciachef.edu.

Two books that do a great job of detailing the life of a chef are *Kitchen Confidential* by Anthony Bourdain, and *Heat* by Bill Buford.

I can always tell who's worked in restaurants and who hasn't. It gives you a really good foundation for understanding portion size, plating, and prepping, as well as working clean and working quickly. You're forced to understand timing and all these other tiny elements. Even if you decide to go into catering or something else, I think that a year in a restaurant kitchen is time well spent.
—Cristina Topham, private chef

Clergy

Although serving God and the community is far more than a mere job, it does pay the mortgage and the cable bill. With small differences based on denomination, professional clergy are responsible for spiritual guidance, education, and counseling of their congregations. And while the profession is a calling, most clergy go to college and get their BA before deciding to move on to graduate-level divinity schooling. In our capitalist society where you need fistfuls of green paper to survive, there's nothing quite as fulfilling as a career that allows you to selflessly help humanity and be true to your spiritual side. And it's probably the only job where you will always respect your boss.

The First Question

The first question to ponder when considering whether to become clergy is, "Whoa, how do I know I am qualified to be a spiritual mouthpiece?" The answer is, at some point, you just do. And that doesn't mean you were born always thinking that you were meant to speak for God; that's a myth. You don't have to be "the golden child." Many rabbis and pastors of different faiths come to the decision later in life; for some it's a second career. Some former attorneys and doctors are now clergy. Of course, in the case of Catholic clergy with its strict celibacy rules, decisions need to happen earlier (in most cases). At the same time, it's not as simple as, "Yeah, I like horses, I think I'll quit my marketing job and do some jockeying." One does it because one feels a profound pull toward it.

So, Do You, Like, Pray All Day?

Not really. If you are clergy, then you are one of the leaders of a religious congregation. For small congregations, there may be only one clergy member, a pastor or priest or rabbi or imam who runs the show. For larger ones there will be a staff, a senior clergy member with others beneath him or her. In other words, you are sort of like the president or CEO (or SVP or VP, depending on size) of the temple, church, mosque, and so on. Most religious organizations also have an elected board of officials made up of members of the congrega-

This is very hard to explain to other people, but as clergy, you get to talk about God all the time and you get to talk to God all the time. People want to know, "How does God allow war?" I get to talk about that, and I get to research that. And you get to tell people what you think God wants. Now that's a very weird thing to say. But if you don't like doing that, you shouldn't have this job.
—the reverend
    Dr. Daniel Meeter,
    pastor, Old First
    Reformed Church

If you're thinking about being a rabbi, you need to consider your motivation. You have to really want to serve other people and want to help out other people. You can't just do it because you want to fulfill your own spiritual journey.
—Rabbi Dan Bronstein,
    Congregational
    scholar, Beth Elohim

tion, with whom you'll interact closely. With that in mind, beyond the daily spiritual matters, a lot of your day is actually taken up with organizational ones. There will be meetings on everything including construction in the lobby, raising dues, meeting a new organist, and getting different educational and charitable programs together. You'll work very closely with lay members of the congregation on all types of issues. There's a lot more administrative work than one would think.

Of course, as a clergy member, you'll toil on religious matters. Depending on the religion, you'll write sermons, read texts for further learning, and, of course, perform prayer ceremonies. At every important juncture of human existence, organized religion tends to play a role, and as clergy so will you. On both happy occasions, like births and marriages, and sad ones, such as funerals and divorces, you will counsel the families. And you will spend one-on-one time with members of your congregation who are in crisis and need your help.

Beyond the roles just described, there are also clergy positions outside the traditional. For example, military chaplains are members of the armed forces and work with the troops. Hospital chaplains are clergy who work full time in hospitals, providing solace to the sick and their families. These also work in retirement communities and hospices. And some clergy become professors of theology who teach religious studies at universities and divinity schools.

And What Qualities Make for a Good Clergy Member?

Nearly all of your duties call for talking to people. Clergy is not a career for the introverted. Whether organizing a field trip for Sunday school students or counseling a couple on their marriage, clergy are called on to have the right words and to lead. Being a hard-line, iron-fist clergy member doesn't work that well these days, although back during the Spanish Inquisition, you might have been a hit. Clergy tend to be nonthreatening and "safe" to talk to. *Empathetic, sympathetic, caring, trustworthy:* these are all good clergylike adjectives. You must be a good listener, someone who wants to hear others' stories, because you will be the person your congregation longs to talk to, seek counsel from, connect with. And you have to accept that this job is all about helping other people, and very little about helping yourself.

To be a good clergymember you also have to love learning. You will constantly be reinterpreting texts and will be asked philosophical questions that you may need to research to answer. Since a lot of time is your own, you also must self-discipline. You have to make time for prayer, study, and self-reflection.

You will be going against some modern-day norms. You will be choosing a

If I were to wear my collar and sit in a café, by the end of the night I would have talked to at least four people. When they see the collar, they really want to talk. You constantly get invited into people's lives. You have to be open to that.
—the reverend Dr. Daniel Meeter, pastor, Old First Reformed Church

You should always be prepared to think critically. You need to be able to challenge yourself to be self-critical and thoughtful and to work on yourself. Intellectually, morally, and psychologically. And last, but certainly not least, you should always have a sense of humor.
—Rabbi Dan Bronstein, Congregational scholar, Beth Elohim

field that few of your peers choose, most of whom may have lucrative, capitalistic jobs. You have to be okay knowing you will do fine financially, but that's not your goal in life. And, well, you have to be willing to let people think you are just a bit strange. When you go to a gathering or party (yes, clergy attend parties—not *Girls Gone Wild* parties, mind you) and say you're a pastor or a rabbi (you won't wear the "uniform" all the time), the reactions will be different than if you said "accountant." You'll be respected, but outside the house of worship, in a restaurant or the supermarket, people will always look at you slightly differently. It's not a bad thing at all. But it's there.

Education and Getting Started

Clergy in almost all denominations first get a bachelor of arts degree and then continue on to divinity school for their religious training. The BA may be attained at a religious school or at a regular university. It need not be in theology; you can be an English or history major, anything really. Basically, you need to emerge from undergraduate education knowing how to think critically, read and decipher a text, and present and refute arguments. Of course, if you aim to be a rabbi, for example, you'll need to know some Hebrew.

The next step, divinity school or seminary, isn't cheap. It's less expensive than, say, medical school, but it is in the ballpark of graduate school prices. How long the schooling takes varies by religion, but three to five years is the norm. Usually you will attempt to get a master's degree in divinity, Hebrew letters, or whatever your faith requires. Schooling will include religious training, but also practical training, like how to counsel people and how to organize services and groups.

Once you finish school, how you get your first job is, again, based on what religion you are. Catholic, Methodist, and Episcopal priests get appointed by a bishop. Presbyterian, Baptist, and Reformed clergy "present" themselves. In a way, it's similar to getting a teaching job. You send a résumé, you interview, a search committee from the house of worship debates your merits, and you may give a trial sermon. Then they make their decision. Your divinity school will be hugely helpful in your placement.

Hours?

If you are congregational clergy, the most common type, the hours are 24/7. That doesn't mean you are pulling all-nighters, just that there's really no line between your working life and your nonworking life. And if there is a line, it's porous. When you are out shopping, perhaps looking for a ripe melon, you

One of the things my father told me (also a rabbi) a long time ago is yes, it's very anxiety provoking at certain points, but you're never bored. And I think that's true. That's been my experience.
—Rabbi Dan Bronstein, Congregational scholar, Beth Elohim

may see someone from your congregation who wants to talk, right then and there. You'll get phone calls at night. Births and deaths aren't scheduled. The job is a life choice, and once you choose it, it defines you. Of course, you will take vacation and sabbaticals. You will probably try to go away to a quiet place to think and reflect a few times a year. But when you are on, you are on, and there are no real boundaries. And you, and the congregation who count on you, wouldn't have it any other way.

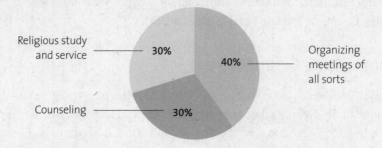

Spiritual Space?

Your working space will be the house of worship itself. Inside, or attached to it, will be some kind of office space and meeting rooms. A big church with a congregation of a thousand or more may have offices that look like, well, offices. There might be cubicles, even. Smaller houses of worship may have an administrative wing with a makeshift office or two, tops. The feeling inside is surprisingly friendly and congenial. There can be lots of joking; perhaps that's because tasks like funerals and counseling can be so heavy. Outside services, dress codes tend to be relaxed. Most clergy don't dress formally every day, although depending on the religion, traditional garb—collars, robes, and the like, may be worn. In general, business-casual tends to be the look.

Also, believe it or not, a lot of the business of clergy gets done electronically these days. Yes, many clergy carry Blackberries and the like, because a tremendous amount of e-mailing takes place. Scheduling weddings that you will officiate, or times for counseling, is just easier electronically. Still, these are no substitute for in-person meetings. But it is somewhat fascinating to think of spiritual counsel via text message: "u r ok."

Pennies from Heaven?

You shouldn't be in it for the money, but you won't be broke. Depending on where you live in the country, you'll either be middle class or upper middle class. But you will have to scrimp and save for retirement if your house of wor-

I usually try to look nice, but I wouldn't say I wear business suits. This totally varies according to the culture of each community. This community is a pretty casual one in terms of clothing, but at the same time, I wouldn't dress Goth.
—**Rabbi Dan Bronstein, Congregational scholar, Beth Elohim**

ship doesn't provide for that. Different religions offer different benefits on top of salary, such as sending clergy on retreats, providing housing, or paying all or part of housing costs. These benefits, plus your pay, are figured out differently for different religions, and within each religion, different houses of worship do things their own way. Generally the lay leadership are involved in sorting out the compensation, since it will come from dues or donations.

The fine folks at the Bureau of Labor Statistics report the mean salary of clergy to be $41,700, ranging from $20,480 to $67,980.

Stress-o-Meter: 8 (1 being an underground poet, 10 being an undercover policeman)

Being a clergy member is surprisingly stressful. Although there are times of peaceful meditation, clergy are involved in the most stressful times in people's lives. Divorce. Tragedy. Funerals. There can be a funeral for a 103-year-old man who has lived a good life, but there are also funerals for small children, and the community is looking to you for words of wisdom, to help answer the "why?" That's no picnic, and it never gets easier. And as mentioned earlier, it is a 24/7 job. Plus, there are no personal boundaries. If you are a member of a congregation, the clergy's private life is something you want to know about.

Pros

There's a huge sense of fulfillment from helping others.

If you like people, there's no job that gives you as much intimate interaction.

You are serving God (this should appeal to you).

Cons

There's a complete lack of privacy, which can be hard on you and your family.

It can be exhausting.

You're never really "off stage."

You tend to get a lot of criticism, but not that much positive feedback from the congregation.

Mazel Tov, You Are Clergy. You Wake Up And . . .

Obviously it depends on your religion. This assumes you are a pastor at a Reformed church.

6:30 AM: You pray for an hour to start the day.

8:45 AM: You arrive at the church and do some religious reading and study that corresponds to the holy days on the horizon.

10:00 AM: You sit down in the conference room with some members of the church administration and discuss plans for building an addition on the church. It's a lot of money, but the congregation continues to grow. You all agree it's time to start meeting with architects.

12:30 PM: You go to lunch with a parishioner, a recent widower. You do more listening than talking.

2:00 PM:	You meet with a few other local pastors to discuss a group service you are planning in honor of Martin Luther King.
3:30 PM:	You spend the rest of the afternoon meeting with different parishioners, some who want your counsel, others who want to complain about goings-on at the church.
6:30 PM:	You've been invited to dinner at a parishioner's home. This happens often; the congregation wants to know you personally, and you want to know them.
9:45 PM:	You head home, full but tired. You see your wife and children for a short time before it's bedtime for all.

I Hear the Call. How the Heck Do I Get This Job?

No secrets here. Depending on your religion, after graduating from college you go on to divinity school or the equivalent. Then you take the appropriate steps from there. There really aren't any shortcuts.

Once you get through divinity school, how you find an actual job differs by religion. If yours is the kind that has you take interviews, as you might guess, personality is key. You can be the world's foremost scholar in your religion, but if you are a lousy people person, not too many houses of worship are going to be interested.

Resources

The appropriate resources naturally depend on your religion. And, of course, the basic texts of those religions—the Bible, Torah, Qur'an, and so on—are pretty much the top resources out there. Your best bet is to talk to clergy members of your faith whom you respect. They're very open to being approached with questions; it's part of the job. Each religion has its own organizations, such as the Rabbinical Council of America (rabbis.org) or the National Conference of Diocesan Vocation Directors (ncdvd.org). Google your faith (how modern!) to easily find your own. Beyond that, beliefnet.com is the largest spiritual Web site. It's independent and not affiliated with any spiritual organization or movement. And some of the following periodicals and news organizations might be of interest: *Lilith Magazine* (which calls itself "independent, Jewish and frankly feminist"), *Biblical Review, Cross Currents Magazine* ("the best of major world religions"), the Jewish Telegraphic Agency (basically the UPI or AP for Jewish news), *Tricycle* (Buddhist), *Theology Today* (a journal from Princeton University), and *Books and Religion,* which is kind of like *The New York Review of Books,* but from a Christian point of view.

Composer

et's start this chapter with some old-school parlance, shall we? In the world of composing, music can be separated into two types: "serious music" and "practical music." These terms aren't used very often today, but they're helpful for our purposes. Serious music is music made for art's sake, an opera, a symphony; even a Weird Al Yankovic album, although recorded essentially to make money, is serious music in that it is not a commissioned piece of work.

Practical music, on the other hand, is music for hire. It serves a purpose larger than the songs and melodies themselves. It's the music in films, TV commercials, TV shows, and even theater productions. Here the soundtrack is simply one part of an overall piece, helping set the emotional tone of the greater whole. What would *Rocky* be without the theme song? Or *The Godfather?* Or the "Plop plop fizz fizz" Alka Seltzer commercials, for that matter? This chapter is about a career composing such practical music, which is better known these days as "commercial music" (but don't be thrown, that doesn't mean music just for advertisements, it means music that has been commissioned). Are you a good musician who never really thought of writing pop songs or fronting a band as a realistic career? Well, perhaps you'll find this path a bit more, er, practical.

Composing 101

Here's how it works: you, the composer, are commissioned by music supervisors for films, producers for TV shows, or advertising agencies for commercials to write original music. Generally, you've been chosen for the job based on work you've done in the past. Often there can be what's called a round of *demos,* which is when a few different composers have been approached and asked to "mock up" a track, which means roughly compose and record a piece of music. It's basically an audition, or shootout, for the job, and quite common in the commercial world. This "getting the gig" part shouldn't be overlooked. Although the most important skill is composing, networking, making phone calls, and finding the next paying job or invitation to submit a demo are also an important part of what composers do.

By the time the composer is hired and joins the team, most of the visual

One of the key things about our job is that we aren't on our own, writing music for music's sake. We are one part of a collaborative creative process that started with the writer, then went to the director and art department, etc. All of our efforts go to make one cohesive, evocative piece. A good composer understands they are helping fulfill a vision, and that sometimes the best piece of music they may have ever written might be wrong for that vision, and needs to be replaced by something simple.
—Pete Nashel, composer, music producer, and principal, Duotone

work has been completed. It's very rare that composers get involved before filming and editing. Once you're officially on board and receive this edited film or video, you'll view the footage and meet with the director or producer in charge to discuss what feeling they're going for, what they want you to help them achieve. And then . . . you'll actually start composing.

It's Time to Score

Yes, it's time to retreat to your studio. You may be trying to help scare the audience if it's a horror film, or give them goose bumps in an emotional AT&T ad. Using various samplers, synthesizers, and computers, you will not only compose the music, but create a replica, a *synth track,* or mock-up of the music you think will best fit the film. The computer is a hugely important composing tool, because you need to be able to create something inexpensively so the rest of the team, be they the filmmakers or advertising agency, can listen to and comment on it. Also, you are trying to score exact moments in the film, and the computer helps you be incredibly accurate. So the surge of string instruments hits the precise moment when the ninja's head is lopped off. (You need to be a bit of a nerdlinger to compose commercial music.) Every day these computer-generated instruments sound better and better, yet they're still nowhere near the real thing. Hiring actual musicians, though (which is what happens next if the piece is liked and you move forward), is just too expensive for a piece that might get rejected.

For a thirty-second commercial, this process can happen over the course of a few days or a week. On a feature film, the time period is longer, and you will probably be sending in a few scenes you've scored each week. Comments will come in and be addressed along the way, until you've written music for the entire film.

> At this stage in scoring the piece, the music needs to be very malleable. We can all listen to it, collaborate, and change things without having to scrap the whole piece.
> —Pete Nashel, composer, music producer, and principal, Duotone

They Like It, They Really Like It! Now for Phase Two

You've presented and made some adjustments. Now everyone agrees, they love the music. The next step is to take the computer score and make it real. This is where the composing part of the job ends, and the music production, done by a music producer, begins. A lot of composers are also music producers, although some strictly compose and then hand off the music they've written to others.

As a music producer, you make the music. You hire the musicians needed for the piece. For example, you may need two French horn players, a drummer, and an oboist. You bring them into a proper recording studio and record them. Of course, it's far more complicated than that. Other specific people may get involved at this point, like mixers and arrangers and orchestrators.

It breaks down like this: a composer writes the song "Happy Birthday." An arranger takes that song and says, let's do a jazz version; they interpret the song and "rearrange" it in other styles. An orchestrator takes "Happy Birthday" and sets it up for a hundred-piece orchestra to play, writing melody lines for the violins and harmony for the violas. A mixer takes anything that's recorded and "tweaks the levels" to perfect them; in other words, in a much more professional way, he or she adjusts the bass, treble, and so on, like one does on a home stereo equalizer. Once the music is finished, it's given to the music supervisor or advertising agency, who "locks it to the picture," or digitally puts the visual and audio together. And you are off to the next job.

So What Do I Need to Know to Be a Composer?

Naturally, you need to be a pretty accomplished musician. But it's also imperative that you have computer skills. Knowledge of software like Logic, Pro Tools, Reaktor, Sibelius, and a host of other digital plug-ins is compulsory if you want to be a composer of practical music.

Beyond those, it's important to note that just being good at writing songs is not enough. You have to be someone who can play well with others, who's a good listener; this is a collaborative process. You have to be someone who wants to work with other people—and many songwriters really just want to work alone. Some are just sooooo moody. That may work for serious music, but not commercial.

Finally, a good composer has some of the same skills as a good psychologist. If it's an action-adventure scene, how do people want to feel? Should they feel tension and then a little bit of relief and then boom, crazy tension again? What musical notes make people feel that way?

Where Does All This Composing Happen?

A studio, which is a room with a computer, some instruments, and usually four walls and a door so you don't drive the neighbors bonkers. Most composers have a studio space, be it a separate one they work out of or a home studio. With all of the technological advancements these days, home studios have become pretty powerful. All you really need is a fast computer and a bunch of software, and off you go. These small studios are for composing and for mocking up the replica tracks. When it comes to actual recording, a proper studio with a recording booth, a mixing board, and space for a few (at least) musi-

You need to be someone who appreciates narrative, someone who is visual as well as aural. Sometimes the best music almost disappears if you aren't listening specifically for it, it just sucks you even deeper into the story and characters.
—Jack Livesey, composer, music producer, and principal, Duotone

cians to play is required. For some lucky composers, their day-to-day studio can also be a recording studio; most others rent the space only when they need it.

As you might guess, each composer's studio reflects his or her own personal taste. There could be a coffee table with a built-in bong, life-size posters of Thelonious Monk, or an austere temple-like setting. They are laid-back, creative spaces, usually filled with cables of various lengths and pretty good speakers, where the business of writing and playing music can be accomplished.

What Do You Do in the Studio When You Are Not Composing?

Listen to music, hang out, drink tea. What you will really be doing, and what is the lifeblood of your career, is networking—making phone calls, sending out demos, trying to get meetings with music supervisors or advertising agency producers. You may do this on your own, or you may have a manager or agent who helps you; it all depends on your level of success.

On top of that, you'll always be upgrading your studio and your abilities. You'll be tweaking the sound of your equipment, working on your composing skills, listening to music you love and trying to figure out how they got it to sound a certain way—just constantly trying to improve your craft, every day in every way.

1, 2, 3, 4 . . . How Many Hours?

The hours are really all or nothing. Composing is a deadline-based business: you'll work full tilt on a project until it's done. So either you're in some phase of composing or producing, racing toward making a deadline, or you're in the noncomposing phase, e-mailing and making calls. It's either long days and weekends, or an easy ten to four.

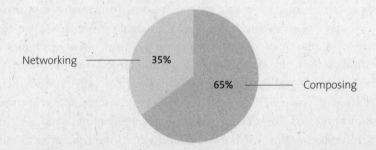

Networking ——— 35%

65% ——— Composing

Golden Tones?

One of the most interesting, or perhaps better put, *crazy* parts of the job of selling music is figuring out what music is worth. Can you charge $1,000 for a track? Is scoring this film worth $100,000? Lots of times you'll be offered an amount based on precedent, which means you'll be making different amounts from different people for essentially the same job. There are market forces and going rates, but the range is as wide as a four-lane highway.

There are two ways composers get paid: *front end* and *back end*. Front end is the money you get paid up front for composing. Most employees get paid front end. In the world of advertising, almost all payment comes from this fee. Back-end payments are royalty money. Royalties are based on the number of times the music is played. It's a fairly complicated system involving ASCAP and BMI that almost no one completely understands, but basically you get a percentage based on popularity and income derived from the project. In the world of TV and film, the front end and the back end are negotiated on every deal. The back end is where the potentially huge payday lies. Score the opening song on *Law & Order* that gets played every damn week in perpetuity, and if you have a good back-end deal, you're going to have not only one good year, but many good years. Those royalty checks keep coming in.

With that in mind, in a solid year, a composer can make between $150,000 and $250,000—much more, of course, if you are the next John Williams (he scored *Star Wars,* among many other films.) The Bureau of Labor Statistics reports the mean salary for music composers in the motion picture and video industries to be $78,030.

Stress-o-Meter: 6.5 (1 being an aromatherapist, 10 being a prison therapist)

The stress level when you are looking for work is a bit higher ("I'll never work again!") and the stress level when actually composing is a bit lower ("Check this out, it sounds awesome"). Except when people hate a track you've written and a deadline's looming. Then, of course, the stress rockets off the charts.

Pros

You get paid to make music, which is what you love to do.

You have complete control over which jobs you decide to take.

Since you work project to project, if you have a crappy boss, soon they will be gone.

Cons

There's no real security, or guarantees that jobs will keep coming in.

You start from zero on every job. No one cares how great your last score was: what is there to listen to today?

Everybody and their brother has a comment to make on the music.

Thank You, Cleveland! You Are a Composer. You Wake Up And . . .

This assumes you are a composer on a film, and you are in the middle of the project, still far from the deadline.

9:00 AM: Your alarm clock radio is blaring "Thong Song" by Sisqo. Not an auspicious start to the day, you think, sleepily.

10:00 AM: You arrive at your studio, which you share with a partner. You check your e-mail to see if there are any comments from the filmmakers on cues you submitted yesterday. Nothing. No news is good news.

10:30 AM: You sit back in your chair, and watch, listen to, and review what you have scored so far, in a manner similar to an author rereading a chapter. It helps you get a good feel for what is needed next and overall.

12:30 PM: Like a lot of artists, you don't chug along at a constant pace, but instead have one juicy creative moment in the day where you do a lot of writing. Then you spend the rest of the day tweaking that juiciness. This is such a moment for you. You don't work linearly, and as you were scrolling through the film, making notes for a bit more cello over a sailboat sequence, you had an idea for the big emotional apex. You begin to score it.

5:00 PM: A solid day of composing will yield two to three minutes of music. You've done that and more. You've reaffirmed how the music was moving with the film and have set yourself up to go further tomorrow. You save all your work and back it up.

6:00 PM: You return a couple of calls that you ignored during your hours of power. A music supervisor left you a message about a new ninja film she'd like to talk to you about. You want in on it. You leave a voice mail saying so on her cell.

7:00 PM: You hit the lights and head toward the homestead.

I Plan to Write a Song about How Badly I Want This Job. So How the Hell Do I Get It?

First, you'll need to know how to compose. There's no entry-level position where that basic, all-important skill is taught. It will be nourished and sharpened by a mentor, sure, but you can't walk in cold. That probably doesn't need to be said, but just in case you were daydreaming of learning it all from scratch from some hippie guitarist shaman, consider this your reality check. So to begin, you'll need to study music. You can do this privately, or you can go to a world-renowned music school; it doesn't really matter as long as you learn. This isn't the kind of field where you'll ever be asked to show a degree or GPA. What your musical compositions sound like is what matters.

What you're aiming to get with this musical education is an apprenticeship with a composer or a music production house (which is essentially a place where several composers have banded together to both write and produce tracks). As an apprentice, you'll study underneath someone who's actually doing the job. You'll improve your computing skills, you'll help write and tweak tracks, and you'll be pushed pretty hard, but it will be worth it. Impress them, and you'll start to be thrown a real job or two. And then all of a sudden, you'll be composing for real.

How do you get the apprenticeship? First, find the kind of composers for whom you might want to apprentice. Research all the films, TV shows, and commercials that have scores you like, and find out who the composers, studios, and music producers on them were. If it's film or TV, sites like imdb.com have the names (look at the project's full credits). For commercials, creativity-online.com lets you view recent spots for free; but to see older ones you'll need an expensive membership. However, with some creative Googling (the brand, the subject of the commercial, etc.), you should be able to track down who did what sans fee.

Okay, you've got some names, now you need to show these folks what you can do. Send them your music, whatever you've composed. If you've written some "music for picture" and have that, great, send it. If you just have a CD of tracks you've written, that's totally fine, too. The whole thing needs to sound, and look, amazing. Of course the sound needs to be professional, as close to real as can be, you could've guessed that. But even the sheer packaging itself—the CD case and the envelope, needs to be slick. Composers get stacks and stacks of demo CDs, and they are way more likely to play the ones that look cool than some blank CD case from Staples with a name and phone number written in black marker. Spend the time, or get help from a designer friend,

There's a famous quote, "Everybody knows their job...and music." There will be a lot of comments on your work, so you need to have thick skin. Honestly, it's not always bad, though. We collaborate with some really talented people, and we get notes that often improve the piece.
—Jack Livesey

If you apprentice, be passionate about what you're doing. Sheer composing skill isn't enough. People who are internally motivated move up; you have to want to make it work. You have to fix and tweak things that need fixing and tweaking, without having to be told. Show that you are a perfectionist, obsessed with getting all the details right.
—Pete Nashel, composer, music producer, and principal, Duotone

and make your identity sharp. It will really help distinguish you before any-one's heard a single note.

Resources

The first resource is films, TV shows, and commercials with great scores. Study them and see what makes them work so well. Rent all the Oscar and Emmy winners for soundtracks and see what you can learn, what you may want to try to emulate.

There are a few good books on the art of composing. Two recommended ones are *On the Track* by Fred Karlin, Rayburn Wright, and John Williams, which is a comprehensive guide to scoring for film and television; and *Knowing the Score: Film Composers Talk about the Art, Craft, Blood, Sweat, and Tears of Writing for Cinema* by David Morgan, which is a collection of insightful interviews with Hollywood composers.

Recommended magazines to help keep you on the cutting edge of composing today are *Mix Magazine* and *Electronic Musician.* Another Web site worth checking out is ampnow.com, which is the home of the Association of Music Producers. It has lots of great information on the world of commercial composing, as does the American Society of Composers, Authors and Publishers site: ascap.com.

Watch films and shows with an analytical ear. Listen to when and how music is used, and when its absence is even more powerful than its presence.
—Jack Livesey, composer, music producer, and principal, Duotone

Designer

Do you make your own birthday cards to give to friends? Do certain combinations of colors make you weak in the knees? Have you ever named a pet Sans Serif? You, sir or ma'am, are designy. The truth is, you probably already have an inkling that the job of designer might suit you. And if you're looking at this page and thinking, "Hmm, I'd have tightened up the margins and gone for more negative space," well, this may just be your chapter.

But first, a quick note. Designers can specialize. There are people who are solely book jacket designers, or magazine designers, or Web designers, or package designers, and so on. It's a field where you can be employed at a general design agency and work on many different kinds of projects, or you can be a highly specialized designer and spend your career solely designing perfume bottles. This chapter aims to give you an overview of the general field.

Who Are Designers?

Designers are the people who take the essence of a product, essay, book, or what have you and visually tell the story through shape, color, photography, illustration, typefaces, and other graphic means. They use all of these tools to communicate what the item is about. Elegant type and a photo of the perfect beach on the cover of *Travel + Leisure:* the designer wanted us to know that the magazine is about upscale holidays. Intricate old-world design on the label of Classico marinara sauce: the designer wanted the product to say, "Hey, look at me, I come from Naples." Whether book, magazine, or even prescription drug packaging, the first thing a consumer sees is the design. People say, "Don't judge a book by its cover," but let's face it—we all do.

What Does a Designer Actually Do?

Here's how it basically works. Somewhere, be it at a design agency or a record label, something needs to be designed. Designers go to a meeting where they are given a *brief,* or a description of the project from those requesting the design. Designers then go back to their offices and enter the first stage of a designer's job, conceptualization. This is the most important part of designing,

If you're the sort of person who constantly rearranges the table until it looks pretty, you're in the ballpark.
— Sandra Garcia, associate art director, *Travel + Leisure*

I design book covers. I try to find a conceptual way, a beautiful way, to say what's inside. The design should showcase the personality and the story of the manuscript. It should tell people, visually, "what this is."
— Gabriele Wilson, senior designer, Knopf

where they brainstorm all the different ideas and ways to solve the design issue. They'll use pen and paper or the computer. They'll look anywhere and everywhere for inspiration—museums, old movies, foreign magazines, you name it.

Once they have three or so ideas they love, they'll return to the people who briefed them and present their concepts. This can often be a sticky time because everyone fancies himself or herself as having good taste.

Once a concept is agreed on and given the green light to go from idea to reality, the designers take it to the next stage, preproduction. They'll work out exact typefaces and look for photographers or illustrators to hire if necessary. When everything is lined up, they then go into actual production, staying with the project from the photo shoot to the printing press, ensuring that the piece comes out the way they envisioned it. A great idea can end up a crappy design if it isn't watched carefully every step of the way.

You'll Need More Than a Sense of Color

Being a designer requires a certain amount of true artistic skill. However, these days, you can fudge a lot. Computers, digital cameras, and scanners have allowed people with great taste and good eyes but no real illustration skills to become designers. Before such inventions, designers were truly artists; they could all draw quite well. It still helps to be able to draw, at least a little.

Beyond the artistic, designers need to be good communicators. There are a lot of people to interact with, and successful designers must convey their ideas to their clients and then to all the people involved in production. And during these interactions, good designers must be flexible; hell, they have to be like a yoga instructor, because there will be challenges at every turn. A competitor launches something using the typeface you planned to use. Someone decides they hate the color green. Suddenly the CEO demands you put a picture of a kitten on the package.

You must know, especially as a junior employee, the design computer programs, the mighty triumvirate of Adobe Photoshop, Illustrator, and InDesign. When you begin as a designer, you will be doing less of your own conceptual work; more of your labor will be spent working your superiors' ideas on the computer. They will expect your computer skills to be fast and accurate. As you move up, you'll still need these skills, but the conceptual part and overall look will become more what you are paid to do.

Finally, you need to care about the details, and you need to be quite precise when projects go into production. You can't be one decimal point off in your x- or y-axis or suddenly the piece will look funny. But not "ha-ha" funny.

Designers all have horror stories about the client who said, "I designed our rec room, I have a good eye," and proceeded to make some awful suggestions.
—Noel Claro,
design director/
creative director

Lots of fingers will touch your work; that's just the way it is once you leave school and get paid to design. So the ability to hear people out, absorb what needs to be done, and then somehow, craftily, succeed in doing it without losing the integrity of the piece, is the recipe for success.
—Noel Claro,
design director/
creative director

The Designer Vibe

Design departments in any corporation are always the "cool" part of the company, set up to foster creativity. Even in the most cubicled office, the design area is usually an open space where people can talk freely and bounce ideas off each other. Everyone else at the company is a little jealous of it, or at least designers feel that way. For the most part, you can wear what you want to wear and be who you want to be, even when others are dressed up. As long as your designs look good, you can get away with a lot.

Design agencies are even more artsy and funky. Most tend to be small, and their owners' or founders' personal tastes dictate the space. There will be the occasional foosball table or PlayStation set up and music being played (or a lot of people wearing headphones). In either case, there will be plenty of tricked-out Apple computers (90 percent of the design world runs on Macs) and oversized flatscreen monitors.

How Many Hours Am I Clicking and Dragging?

Designers work hard. They're perfectionists; they want their projects to be designed beautifully, right down to the legal type. A typical day for most is around ten to seven, but it is an industry of deadlines. And when you are up against one, all bets are off. Sixty-hour weeks are not out of the norm for many designers. On the other hand, as you are creative and goofy, slipping out to catch a midday movie on the rare occasion or stopping by a gallery for a few hours for inspiration is not unheard of, and often encouraged. Designers tend to be social; there are a lot of after-work activities, be they field trips or parties, that happen as well.

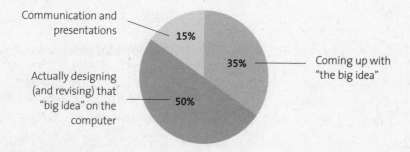

Communication and presentations — 15%

Coming up with "the big idea" — 35%

Actually designing (and revising) that "big idea" on the computer — 50%

Dollars for Designing?

You've heard this song before: a lot of people want to be designers and the competition is fairly tough, so for entry-level positions, "the man" is able to keep the pay low. As you reach the midlevels, though, the salary becomes much more fair, and for someone at a higher level, $150,000 to $200,000 is not impossible. But it all depends on the specific field. For example, magazine designers generally make more than book designers. Who knows why?

Here are some figures from the Bureau of Labor Statistics. For graphic designers (anything nonWeb), the median entry-level salary is $32,000, the median for senior designers is $56,000, and the median for design directors is $90,000.

Salary.com reports the salaries of Web designers to range from $30,846 to $99,814. Senior-level Web designers, who are in high demand at this point, tend to make even more than those figures, well over $100,000.

Stress-o-Meter: 6 (1 being a koi pond tender, 10 being an Alaskan king crab fisherman)

There are a lot of different personalities to deal with, and if you're designing the cover of a book someone's written, for example, it's as if you are handling their baby. When deadlines come, and come in bunches (as they often do), things can get hairy, and the stress number can spike. At the same time, you're not exactly handling nuclear waste. You're just designing the "Hey, watch out, you're handling nuclear waste!" logo.

Pros

You spend your day making things with art and type, which is something you love.

You work with great people and all kinds of artists.

You (and your friends and family) get to see your work out in the world.

Cons

Everyone thinks they know design and has suggestions, which can be frustrating.

Constant judging of your ideas, especially when people dislike them, is a bit of a bummer.

Staring intently at a computer screen all day can take its toll.

Okay, You're a Designer. You Wake Up, Fix Your Stylish but Complicated Haircut, And . . .

10:00 AM: You arrive at work and check your e-mail. You generally have about four to six projects you're juggling, all in different stages of completion. You put out a few fires and then do a quick eBay search, looking for vintage drinking glasses with the Ghostbusters on them. You like kitsch.

11:00 AM: You look through images from yesterday's photo shoot to go into a magazine spread. You choose a few selects, and then create a rough layout in InDesign.

1:00 PM: You pick at a salad while sketching out ideas for a new project you're starting: packaging for condoms.

2:00 PM: You run out to supervise a small shoot of some jewelry. You eat two handfuls of M&Ms while making sure the photographer's lighting enhances the diamonds' sparkle.

4:30 PM: You begin carefully designing the project you began the day with, the layout. You play with lots of different fonts; nothing is sacred and you want to just keep playing until it feels perfect. You print out a few variations that you can look at with fresh eyes in the morning.

7:00 PM: You put your Mac to sleep and head out with a co-worker for a few cold, fermented beverages.

I Like Making Things Pretty. How the Hell Do I Get This Job?

There's really just one way to get a job as a designer, and that's by having a kick-ass portfolio (or portfolio Web site, the electronic version). Résumés and GPAs don't help all that much; many people skip down to your computer skills at the bottom.

A portfolio (or *book)* is your visual identity; it's a physical book or virtual site filled with examples of things you have designed, about fifteen to twenty different pieces that represent your sensibility and skills. Odds are you won't get an interview until after your portfolio has been reviewed—first companies will have you drop it off so they can judge your design sense. Then, if they like it, they'll have you come in person to make sure you're not an ax murderer. Your portfolio should be filled with designs for the sort of field you want a job in, although it can have samples from other design areas as well. But if you want a job at Random House designing book covers, obviously you should have examples of book cover designs in your portfolio. And if you want a job as a Web designer, you'll have a portfolio Web site that shows or links to all of your online designs: sites, banner ads, what have you.

And how do you go about creating a jobworthy portfolio? Well, any undergrad BFA program will help you design one; by the time you graduate you will probably have made and remade your book a few times. If you majored in something else, you can take classes at night at a local design school, like the Art Center in California, or SVA or Parsons in New York. You can even get an MFA in design. In the end, though, you are only as good as your book.

If you manage to get an interview, don't explain your work if the interviewer flips through your book in front of you. It needs to stand on its own, and you can show your confidence by keeping quiet. Don't dress self-consciously arty or grungy, even though the person who is interviewing you might; you need to be somewhat respectful. You haven't earned the right to be a mess just yet. Don't wear a suit; be yourself, but don't roll up in a baseball hat, either. And as always, go to the firm's Web site and know the work they've done. Even better, do a bit of research on the designers you'll be meeting with. Have they won any awards? Do you like their designs? Start with Google.

Portfolios need to look slick, swanky, tight, and real. You should know how to use the computer well enough to make the pieces look finished, and amazing. There's no excuse for sloppiness.
—Noel Claro,
design director/
creative director

The world of design is a meritocracy. The guy who sits next to me used to be a concert pianist. It's all about how good you are at design, how good your portfolio is, not some PhD design background.
—Sandra Garcia,
associate art director,
Travel + Leisure

Finally, design school is great for learning skills and the history of design and for building a book, but most projects there tend to be "dream assignments." To see the real day-to-day, it's highly recommended that you intern, and, luckily, internships are available at many firms (check your college's career center or the AIGA; more info on that follows). These also allow you to network, and maybe even, like a tick, burrow your way into a full-time gig.

Resources

There are a lot of great design magazines for inspiration, such as *Communication Arts, Eye, Print, Blind Spot,* and *I.D.* Go to a good news agent and flip through all of those, plus the crazy foreign magazines.

There are many, many fabulous design books. Take a look at some from the masters, like Eames, Rand, Brodovitch, and Lustig, as well as some of the newer icons: Chip Kidd, Tibor Kalman, and Stefan Sagmeister. You'll find titles by all of these on display in the design section of good bookstores.

Core77.com and coroflot.com are great design Web sites that have everything including creative showcases and job listings. They cover all kinds of design, such as graphic, Web, and industrial, and they even allow you to upload your portfolio to share with recruiters and other designers (if you want criticism).

The AIGA is an association of graphic artists (it is just AIGA—it used to stand for the American Institute of Graphic Arts, but no longer). The site, aiga.org, is filled with job opportunities, internships, discounts, and advice, as well as a link to an archive of award-winning designs. Make it your first stop.

Doula

Making babies. Sure, the conceiving part is good times, but the actual delivery and birthing can be traumatic, especially for first-time mothers. Delivery rooms can be filled with pain, confusion, and the mother-to-be's hate-filled screams of "I can't believe you did this to me!" That's when a doula can be quite helpful.

Doulas are women (yes, this job is 99.9 percent female—sorry, gents) who provide physical, emotional, and informational support to women before, during, and sometimes after their births. They are usually privately hired, trained, experienced guides who help couples through one of life's most intense moments. As doctors and nurses have become overburdened in hospitals, the demand for doulas has increased, and today the career is growing rapidly. The term *doula,* in case you are ever on *Jeopardy,* comes from the ancient Greek, and it means "woman's servant." Just remember to phrase your answer in the form of a question.

According to some research, a doula's presence at birth can be more than a comforting presence. Studies show that working with a doula tends to result in shorter labors, reduces the patients' need for pain medication, and helps new parents feel more secure and have less postpartum depression, among other statistics. Granted, these studies come courtesy of the Doulas of North America (dona.org). But they are a respected organization, and a great resource for all things doula.

The doula is there to work with the patient and provide this necessary tender, loving care. She explains everything the doctor is doing, she can be the patient's advocate, she can comfort the patient with reflexology or massage or anything else that supports and helps her with the pushing process.
—Ms. Anonymous, doula

So a Doula Takes the Place of a Doctor?

Nope. Doulas don't replace doctors, nurses, or any medically trained staff. In fact, doulas are not medically trained, nor do they give medical advice. They are simply there for support. It sounds small when stated like that, but go into a delivery room sometime and you'll see how much support is needed. It's trippy in there. Doulas like to say they provide care, not pharmaceuticals. Training for doulas is far shorter and simpler than for medical practitioners. A midwife, on the other hand, though not a replacement for a doctor, is someone who actually delivers babies and is medically trained, generally as an RN.

So what do doulas actually do then? Pretty much anything and everything outside the medical to increase the mother-to-be's comfort. This process begins long before the 3:00 AM ninety-mile-an-hour drive to the hospital for the actual birth, when the doula first meets with the mother- and father-to-be. This is generally a two-to-three-hour consultation where the doula answers any and all questions about childbirth, offers advice and information about what to expect, and helps the couple make their "birth plan." The doula will also make herself available to the couple via call times, when they can call her with any questions, as well as update her with any new developments.

While the due date may be circled on the calendar with a big ol' fat marker, part of being a doula is being available to answer that bat phone at any time, since very few women give birth on their actual due date. That means you'll get calls in the middle of the night, with the "Am I going into labor?" question. If the answer is yes, you need to get up and hightail it over to the hospital to meet the mother-to-be. You can't go to sleep without having an outfit picked out and ready to go and the car filled up with gas. You're kind of like a fire-fighter. Sans pole.

Once in the delivery room, doulas explain every single thing that's happening in plain English to the patient (assuming English is her native tongue), so she understands what the doctor is doing and why. If you've ever been in a hospital (or watched *ER*), you know there's a lot of jargon tossed around by doctors and nurses, who occasionally don't always have time to fully explain what they are about to do. Doulas are the patients' advocate, someone who has been through the process before and looks out for them.

As the contractions intensify, the doula is there to help soothe the patient in any way she can. Doulas will use massage and breathing techniques to help the mother get through the labor as easily and comfortably as possible. The goal is to stay out of the way of the medical caregivers, but stay emotionally close to the mother-to-be. At the same time, they try not to take the husband's place in the "Breathe! Breathe!" coaching role, but instead to make sure he is as involved as possible and isn't fainting or otherwise freaking out.

Once the baby is born, the doula makes sure the recovery room is set up and the new mom gets there safely. The doula will usually visit and answer any newborn questions the mother might have. And then, like some sort of caped birth superhero, she is on to the next delivery. However, sometimes doulas continue on with their families in the role of postpartum doula, helping them transition to their role of new parents, a.k.a. the sleepless ones.

Doulas really are down with the whole business of babies. Some doulas work full time and that's all they do, but many also dabble in other fields, like prenatal yoga, childbirth education classes, or pregnant massage therapy.

The most important part of being a doula is having a connection with the people that you're working with. The birth is the most intimate of all life experiences, an incredible time when couples are connecting deeply with each other. It's very important that the doula helps to facilitate this process, to support them and to allow the partner to be the primary birth support. And she can do this helping by taking the edge off and giving the couple confidence and a sense of security that everything is okay.
—Rachel Yellin, doula

What Type of Person Makes for a Dyn-o-Mite Doula?

You can't be a cold fish, that's for sure. It takes someone who can be intimate, caring, compassionate, and kind. A sense of humor is helpful, as being able to get people to chuckle relaxes them. You must be able to communicate well, verbally and physically, to gain your patients' confidence and help them get through the pushing process.

You'll need to have training in different techniques to help soothe the mother-to-be, such as massage and reflexology, and you'll of course need to be fully informed about how the labor process works, and what the mother will be feeling physically and emotionally.

Speaking of emotion, you need to be a strong, confident person. You can't be a shrieker or a crier; leave that to the family. You'll be in the thick of some intense situations, and your job is to be calming and focused. It can get hairy in the delivery room at times, like if a doctor wants to perform a cesarean and the mother doesn't want him to. Your job in these situations is to inform the mother, but not to advise her. She'll make her own choice; you'll give her the information to be able to do so.

Where Do You Doula?

Most doulas don't have an office per se. They field calls and answer e-mails from home, and then they work at their clients' homes or in delivery rooms. And delivery rooms differ, markedly. Some are simply hospital rooms; others can be kind of swanky, like hotel rooms, or new agey even, like anything but a delivery room. It all depends on the hospital. And while on the job, doulas try to create a vibe of warmth, confidence, and professionalism. They don't wear suits, but they don't wear tie-dyes, either. A comfortable look, slightly more casual than business-casual, is the norm.

Doulas don't really work with colleagues, so there is a bit of a sense of being a lone wolf. You connect emotionally with your clients, but after they have the child, you are usually off to the next family. You may befriend nurses and doctors if you frequent the same hospitals, but there's not much, if any, water cooler chitchat or sending your officemates goofy JPGs. There's no intraoffice dating. It's not a social gig. Still, it is, of course, an extremely personality-driven job with clients. You just have to be okay with being on your own a lot.

Hours?

It's not a nine-to-five job. You'll have anywhere from three to seven clients each month, and you're pretty much on call 24/7 two weeks from the due date until baby time. Generally this means you're spending around forty hours a week working, which means speaking to current, potential, and former clients on the phone; meeting with new clients and couples; attending births, and following up with new parents. Some weeks could be more; some weeks could be substantially less. It all depends on the stork. Attending births could be at any given time, day or night; labor lengths can be marathon or sprint.

> It does get hard to make plans in advance or do anything that requires a reservation or deposit. If I get tickets to a show or a concert, there's always a risk that I won't be able to go and lose the money.
> —Rachel Yellin, doula

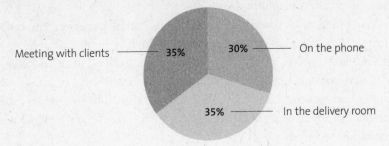

Meeting with clients — 35%   30% — On the phone

35% — In the delivery room

Salary?

There are no set salaries or fees for doulas; they work freelance, and every doula charges differently. It's not a profession you go into to get rich, but doulas can make a comfortable living if they are popular. A doula can usually command between $1,000 and $1,500 per laboring patient. That includes the interview prior to labor, being on call for questions, being in labor with them, recovery time (which can sometimes be a long time), and then a postpartum visit at their home. If you have three patients a month at $1,000 per, that's $36,000 a year. If you have seven at $1,500, it's $126,000. And a lot of babies—that's eighty-four babies a year!

1   10

Stress-o-Meter: 7 (1 being a stamp collector, 10 being a rent collector)

Though magical, being in the delivery room can be stressful. Most of the time all is well, but something can go wrong, and if it does, it's crushing. Occasionally there can be some tension between you and the doctors and nurses as well.

Pros

You are involved in the most magical time of a couple's life.

Every birth is heartwarming.

Cons

It can be impossible to make plans.

There's the occasional bitchy patient.

If something does go wrong, it's heartbreaking.

Congratulations, You Are a Doula. You Wake Up And . . .

4:30 AM: You hear the *ring ring ring* of your phone. It's one of your clients. Her water has broken and her husband is putting her in the car. You get into your doula gear and hit the road.

5:10 AM: You beat them to the hospital. As they arrive, you make sure everything is being set up for them.

6:30 AM: You are in the delivery room. Everything is fairly calm; the patient is not in pain. You put on a mellow jazz CD, then rub the patient's arm and try to keep her relaxed. You explain to her and her husband what is going to happen next.

8:00 AM: It happens just like that. The husband is yelling, "Push, push!" and you're working to keep the patient comfortable as the contractions become intense. The doctor thinks it can be any minute now.

8:47 AM: Well, forty-seven minutes, anyway, and then a healthy, bouncing baby boy arrives. You hug the mom and the husband. There are waterfalls of joyful tears.

9:30 AM: You make sure the new parents are all set up in the postpartum room. You talk to them about what to expect over the next days, until they leave the hospital, and answer any questions they may have.

10:30 AM: You plan a call tomorrow to check in, and make plans for a visit once they get home. Then you head to your own home for a nap, hoping the phone won't ring again today!

I Was Born to Birth. How Do I Get This Job?

Becoming a doula is fairly straightforward. You take a course, generally twenty-five to forty hours of training, and you emerge a doula. It's actually not very hard to become one. Your best bet is to go with the Doulas of North America (DONA) training, which you can learn more about at dona.org. They will point you to recommended training courses somewhere near where you live. The courses are taught by other doulas and midwives, and they're pretty similar to the birthing classes couples take before having a baby, in that they teach all about the process and what to expect. Doula classes go a bit further, of course, instructing on topics such as how to comfort and soothe patients, assisting with their emotional needs, what to do during a cesarean, beginning massage, acupressure, patterned breathing, and maternal positioning.

While becoming a doula is fairly easy, getting paying work as a new one isn't. Most work comes through referrals, so getting the first gig is the hardest. If you are already part of the world of babies—perhaps you work in prenatal yoga or massage—it will make breaking in a little easier as you are among the pregnant. If not, you'll need to get out there and do some networking. Go to childbirth education classes and seminars and meet people. Or help out a friend who is pregnant for free, and when you do a good job, she can refer you to others. You have to be a bit creative to start, and then success will feed off itself. May your clients be fruitful and multiply.

Resources

Dona.org has everything you need. It's the hub of the doula world; explore it fully. Another great site is childbirth.org. Click around and you'll see a variety of articles and information on doulas.

Entrepreneur

Maybe you sold T-shirts in college, or hell, were the dude selling handmade bongs. In your own small, possibly illegal way, you started a business, and were captain of your own destiny. Perhaps that's the way you'd like to live your life from now on, as an entrepreneur, earning a living out of a business you conceive and build on your own. It's the dream of many, but it's a dream that requires a lot of blood, sweat, and tears. Maybe even saliva. It's a massive undertaking, but the payoff, if successful, is total control of your life and the potential for lots of money.

In some ways, entrepreneurs are control freaks who don't want to work for anyone but themselves. Which is not to say they don't want to work with other people—they just don't want to work *for* other people. There are all kinds of entrepreneurs, of course, from the person who opens her own specialty furniture store, to the gentlemen who founded YouTube (lucky bastards). With that in mind, this chapter will focus on the commonalities that run across the majority of different ways to be an entrepreneur and will attempt to help you understand what life's actually like, should you choose to be one.

> Entrepreneurs are starters. They don't take things over in the middle, or come in and clean up messes at the end. They are people who have a business idea, a seed they want to plant themselves, and grow.
> —**Craig Kanarick, co-founder, Razorfish and Studio Red at Rockwell Group**

So What Do Entrepreneurs Do?

The more accurate question, as you'll see, is what *don't* they do? Well, first, of course, by definition, they start some kind of business venture and aim to build it from the ground up. In the beginning, regardless of the field, most of the time will be spent hustling for money. If you make a microbrew, your time will be spent brewing it and then trying to find bars to buy it. If you've started a design firm, you will be pitching prospective clients while staying up all night doing work for the current ones. It takes money to start a business. And that cushion lasts only so long. So the first order of business for any new business is: Get Cash Now. Cash equals survival.

In the beginning, you will be lean. Your office won't be teeming with assistants; no, you'll be wearing all the hats. You'll do everything, even the things you don't know how to do, or frankly, realize you aren't very good at. You might be a baker, but you'll also do the billing and empty the trash. Graphic designer who is, hooray, finally moving out of the home office and getting real office space? Guess who's going out with the broker and negotiating the lease?

Think of it like this: working for someone else is like renting an apartment. If something breaks, no big deal; you call the super or the landlord, and they hire the right person to fix it. Running your own company is like owning a home: you care deeply about everything, and if it runs down, it's up to you to make it right.

Live It. Love It.

You won't even know how many hours you are working; your regular life and your work life will meld into one. Which, while overwhelming, if you love what you do, can be invigorating.
—Craig Kanarick, co-founder, Razorfish and Studio Red at Rockwell Group

Most entrepreneurs will tell you that until you *"make it* make it," the hours are insane. Underline the word *insane,* and maybe add an exclamation point. This entity you've started is your baby, and no one can keep it alive but you, Mommy. The company is your life, and your life is the company. Let's say you're a baker again. If a restaurant stops ordering your pies, they didn't just reject some delicious baked goods, they rejected you. You'll take it personally. It's a very emotional thing, and it takes thick skin to handle the inevitable lows.

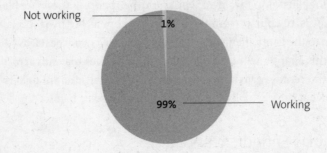

Not working — 1%

99% — Working

Sacrificial CEO

When I first started the company it was always an issue of cash flow. You know, 99 percent of entrepreneurial ventures fail. So I didn't sleep for the first five years. Now, it's much better.
—Christiane Lemieux, founder and CEO, Dwell

When you first try the entrepreneurial life, you'll find you have to make sacrifices. When it's your company and your dime, you might just find out, "Hey, I'm kind of a cheapskate." Say you're the graphic designer. If you were at a design agency and had to travel to cover a shoot in L.A., they'd probably put you up at a swanky hotel. (Ed. note: Go for the Sunset Marquis; there's a hidden pool in the back, where you can often see celebrities—celebrities in bathing suits!) But when it's your company, you might forgo the $300-a-night rooms for the $100 Comfort Inn near the airport. You'll rent the cheapest cars and grimace when it's time to expense a meal.

There are other sacrifices as well. You may watch as colleagues who work at large companies outearn you. You may not be able to take any vacation time the first few years. You may fail. Remember, it's a risky, gutsy thing to start your own business.

Dinero?

It all depends. The goal, of course, and one of the reasons you do it, is to be successful and have enough money for private islands and personal fire trucks and a pet chimp named Mr. Cuddles D. Moneyman. When you start, though, you may well make nothing. Hell, you may, and probably will, lose money or owe the bank. It's good to have some sort of cushion, a bit of money saved up for ramen noodles and peanut butter and jelly, or a significant other who can hold down the fort. Now, since you do own it, if it's successful . . . well, you can make oodles of cash. A lot of people fail, some people do pretty well, and a very few make gobs. Gobs is good.

How Do I Even Know If I'm Entrepreneurial?

The short answer is, you just sort of know that you don't want to be working for anyone else. Some people try lots of different jobs, but feel dissatisfied at all of them. There were no jobs they wanted—or the ones they wanted, they just couldn't get. Others were experts in their fields and suddenly realized, "Hey, why the hell am I working with these schnooks—I can do this on my own." And then there are those who just always dreamed of owning their own company, and have never, in their adult lives, worked for anyone else. But as you can hopefully tell by now, the level of commitment required to be successful is off the charts. So before you leap, make sure you love what you're planning to do.

Well Then, What Kind of Person Makes for a Successful Entrepreneur?

Actually, the person most likely to be a success is someone really rich who has the money to start things off right. Short of that, well, it takes a person with an enormous amount of confidence. You'll be selling yourself a lot, and that's not easy for the shy or self-deprecating.

Patience is a trait you'll need as well. You need to be the sort of person who won't run at the first sign of trouble and realizes that empires are not built overnight. Yet at the same time it helps to be a little impatient—"Why *aren't* empires built overnight? I can do it!" You have to be willing to do a lot by yourself, yes, but you also can't be so pigheaded that you don't know when it's time to ask, or spend money, for help. Speaking of money, you also need to be willing to ask for it. It's not always an easy thing to do, but clients must pay you the right amount and pay it on time. And finally, you need to be able to

To be a successful entrepreneur, you need a tremendous amount of courage. You have to go out there and try to convince the world that your idea, whatever it may be, makes sense.
  —Craig Kanarick,
    co-founder, Razorfish
    and Studio Red at
    Rockwell Group

"helicopter up" and take the long view, the "Where will we be in three years?" view, while at the same time being able to focus on one line item on a contract and see what's right or wrong about it. Macro, micro, you need to have all kinds of vision. While multitasking, naturally.

Stress-o-Meter: 11 (1 being captain of the spirit squad, 10 being captain of the search-and-rescue squad)

Even if what you've chosen to start is the most Zen job in the world—opening a yoga studio—the truth is you are putting your well-being on the line. There's no stability at first, and you'll constantly find yourself making huge decisions (which lawyer to use, which insurance company, is this too much per square foot?) outside your sweet spot (downward facing dog). And it never ends. There is no home and office separation, not for years.

Pros	Cons
It's all you.	It's all you.

You've Made the Leap. You're an Entrepreneur. You Wake Up And . . .

This is assuming the hardest, but most exciting time, the beginning, and that you are a software entrepreneur. So you're the young, poor, nerdy Bill Gates. Not the modern, filthy rich, nerdy Bill Gates.

8:00 AM: You're still in bed, but your bed is a sea of invoices. You've been up for a while, installing new tax software on your computer. It keeps beeping at you and you kind of want to punch it.

10:00 AM: You go to the bank. They've been charging weird fees on your account and you do not abide weird fees. You wait in line and use your Blackberry to answer some e-mails at the same time.

11:30 AM: You walk out of a different bank, where you just opened an account. Forget the first guys. You hustle back to the home office to print out a few things before a meeting.

12:30 PM: You meet your clients at their office. They don't know that yours doesn't exist yet. The plan is to have office space in a year. You always go to their offices or meet in hotel lobbies, whatever it takes. No one shall see your Garfield sheets.

2:00 PM: It was a great meeting. You landed a nice new chunk of business from them, so you look online at possible office spaces for a few minutes. To you, it's like looking at porn.

3:00 PM: You're a great programmer but a lousy businessperson, you're discovering. You've decided to take on a partner, an old friend you used to work with who has an MBA. The idea is, she will be good at the things you're bad at, and vice versa. You call your lawyer and ask him how the hell this is done and what it's going to cost.

5:00 PM: Time to finally start doing actual work. You sit down at the kitchen table with your laptop and hit it.

11:00 PM: You're back in bed, back trying to reinstall the tax software. You wonder where the day went. Tomorrow you will go to the lawyer and soon the partner will be on board. Then you will proceed to conquer the world.

I Want to Be an Entrepreneur. How the Hell Do I Become One?

Start by answering the following questions: What's your idea? Is it good? Has it been done? Is it marketable? Are you going to lose all your money, your spouse's money, your parents' money? The first advice successful entrepreneurs give: don't just dive in. Do some research, make a business plan, and see what cards you hold.

Is this a business that exists? If you're not an inventor, the answer is probably yes. Try to get all the practical experience you can working in the field. If you want to open a bakery, work for a baker for a while. If you want to start a Web site dedicated to video, work for another site to learn the daily ins and outs. Intern. Work cheap. Learn.

Next, remember, you are starting a business. This is important, let's repeat it. You are starting a business. You'll need to run it like one and do the things you'd never think you'd do. Time sheets are stupid, right? Wrong; you'll need to do them if you want your company to succeed. You can't run everything on gut; you need to formalize. So although anyone can be an entrepreneur, having business school training or an MBA that teaches you these formal business practices certainly helps. Outside an MBA, loads of college classes and continuing-education classes may be worth attending. Myriad sites online can also help you, or, if you can't be bothered, you can outsource to get this knowledge—hire a consultant. And at the bookstore, you'll find even more advice on starting your own business; there are tons of advice books on the subject. There's no reason to fly by the seat of your pants.

Owning one's own business is a dream for many. It's your creation; it's great for the ego, and when successful, great for cocktail party conversation. It's a ton of work, but those who have done it could never, ever see themselves working for anyone else again.

If you want to be an entrepreneur, the first thing you should do is to write a business plan, do the research, look at what already exists in your field. You are going to know pretty quickly if your idea is out there, whether it's oversaturated, whether there's room in the marketplace. You can be the best designer, banker, whatever, but if the idea is out there and already done in a big way, it is really hard to trump that.

—Christiane Lemieux, founder and CEO, Dwell

Resources

Keep abreast of the business world with magazines like *Inc., The Wall Street Journal, Fast Company, Barron's, Business 2.0,* and *Forbes.* There's even *Entrepreneur Magazine.* Check it out online at entrepreneur.com/magazine.

The U.S. Small Business Administration has "programs and services to help you start, grow and succeed." Check out the informative Web site at sba.gov.

The IRS has some helpful information. See, they're not your enemy. Information and resources can be found at irs.gov—click on the "Businesses" tab. Finally, the Entrepreneurs' Organization (EO) is a global community of business owners who share advice and experiences: eonetwork.org.

Event Planner

All you do is party. You live to go to different fun events; you love to plan your friends' celebrations and make them outrageous and different. Like that Eddie Murphy song from the eighties, you want to "party all the time, party all the time, party all the time." Well, you, my friend, might want to consider the career of event planner.

Event planning encompasses more than mere partying. Planners organize and coordinate all kinds of affairs: conferences, conventions, exhibitions, trade shows, celebrity brunches, and every kind of celebration under the sun and/or moon. Some event planners focus on corporate clients, some on individuals; some do a mixture of both. They are responsible for the whole enchilada: finding the location, coming up with creative themes, hiring caterers and floral designers, making sure there are enough bathrooms, you name it. There's a lot of budgeting, hand holding, and cell phone calling, and it's all in the service of creating a singular, killer gathering.

Event Planning in the House, Y'all

Event planners can work on their own or at event-planning companies. Some work in-house at organizations that hold so many events, like museums and magazines, that they have their own event-planning staff. There are lots of different opportunities to get into event planning nowadays; it's amazing how important it's become in the corporate world. And whether you work in events at a fashion label or at a two-person event-planning company, the basic job is pretty much the same. You help plan and put together an affair, from initial concept to final details.

Here's how it works: Chanel (let's assume they have no in-house event-planning department) calls you up. They are releasing a new perfume, Chanel Number 6, and they want to launch it with the party of the century, something that every celebrity will want to attend, that will be written about in every newspaper. They give you a budget, a date for the event (six months off, in the spring), and some parameters (it needs to be in New York City, no sushi, make it splashy).

You—and on an event this large, your staff—begin to conceptualize different themes for the party. You look everywhere for inspiration: spring in New

York, the number 6, even the history of Chanel. Once you come up with a few different directions, you'll meet with Chanel again and present the concepts. Luckily, they "luuuuve!" your "6th Sense" idea, which involves creating a large maze on a pier in the Hudson, which partygoers will wind their way through. At every turn, they'll experience one of the five senses, until they reach the end of the maze, which leads them aboard a yacht appropriately named *The 6th Sense.* There the new scent will be unveiled as the yacht takes them on an all-night party cruise around Manhattan.

Now you just need to execute the idea, that's all. Every last detail is on your shoulders. You need to find a big yacht. And the people who can transform a gritty pier into a wonderland, and who can build a maze. (Are there "maze experts" in New York? You get an assistant on it.) Caterers and staff for food and drink, and security, must be found. As must transportation for when people get off the boat late at night and there are no cabs around. You even have to obtain some beautiful, gleaming portable toilets for the pier, so celebrities can relieve themselves stylishly. You'll be coordinating all this and more, along with managing the guest lists and making sure, with all the staff and decorations, that you don't break the budget. And then, when the night finally arrives, you will be there, on site, making sure everything runs smoothly. There will be snafus—the yacht bar might run out of vodka and you'll need to improvise (you have some hustled out via rented speedboat), or a starlet will be given something with carbohydrates in it and you will need to find a way to calm the ensuing freakout (you give gentle hugs and tell her how thin she looks).

What Kind of Person Is an Event Person?

The social kind, for starters. This is a career where you'll be a so-called point person, meaning everyone involved will be talking to you, and you'll be talking to everyone involved. You'll have to be confident interacting with all sorts of people: the pissed-off bathroom attendant and the pissed-off socialite, the drunk waiter and the drunk A-list celebrity. You need to be able to handle yourself in any situation.

A certain level of creativity is a must. Not every affair requires you to come up with some never-before-seen concept, but you still need to have a good eye and sense of design. It's your job to make sure every disparate element from all the different vendors gels, and oh-so-tastefully.

You also have to understand the flip side of creativity—the business side. Because there's a good chance many of the events you will be doing, à la the Chanel example, are corporate, it's imperative that you comprehend their

> You need to be able to see every detail through from start to finish and imagine how they will all come together. You should be able to visualize things in their totality.
> —Rachel Kash, founder, Icing

> Every day and project are different. You have to enjoy change, or at least embrace it because with events it all changes, even on the day of. You also have to be able to get along with people, because you have to deal with people all day long.
> —Mark Testa, owner, Mark Steven Enterprises

marketing objectives. Chanel wants PR. Another event might be a fund-raiser, with a different goal. And so on.

It helps to be detail oriented, a good manager of people and processes, organized, and able to think on your feet. If you're not inherently like that, you will become a list maker and checker-offer; it's the only way to stay on top of it all. You should also be a leader, able to instill confidence in the people around you. They're looking to you to solve problems and to be the calm, cool, and collected one amid the chaos.

Where Do You Do All This Planning?

If you're on staff with an organization, you'll have a cubicle or office in their office. The vibe of these offices depends on what kind of organization you're at. A record label tends to be laid back; a museum tends to be professional but artsy. Event-planning firms' offices, on the other hand, all tend to be casual and very creative; think of a nice loft with some bamboo. You won't see any suits.

Occasionally, you'll have to travel for events. If you work in New York but are planning an event in the tropics, you'll need to get your butt to the tropics, at least a few times, before the event (when you will be there again). You can do only so much remotely.

Hours?

It depends what stage of planning you're in, but event planners on the whole tend to work long hours and weekends. Why? Well, for starters, events often go late into the night, on weekends. There are definite event seasons, and the work can ebb and flow. But the job can eat up a lot of socializing time, since while your friends are out at their own smaller parties, you are running a separate big one. A rule of thumb is, the closer you get to the event, the longer and harder you'll need to work. It's the nature of the beast. You'll probably work a standard forty-hour week until the date of the event nears. Then all bets are off. You could work twelve or fourteen hours on the days preceding.

People think event planners get to hang out at these great parties, but really you spend all of your time behind the scenes, working. So while yes, you're at the party, you're not "at the party." You have to enjoy helping others have a good time, while you yourself are working hard.
 —Lauren Kash Smetana, manager of special events, Whitney Museum

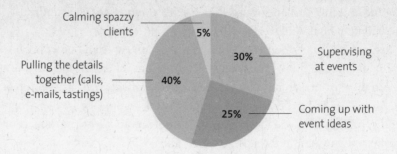

Calming spazzy clients — 5%

Supervising at events — 30%

Coming up with event ideas — 25%

Pulling the details together (calls, e-mails, tastings) — 40%

The most stressful moment of the job is the day of the event. That's when all of the disparate elements must come together perfectly. You need to make sure all of the vendors you have hired are doing their jobs, and that the host is able to relax and enjoy their event. There are always hiccups and things that go wrong, and your job is not only to right them, but to make sure all the drama remains behind the scenes, unknown to the attendees.
—Rachel Kash, founder, Icing

Money

How much you make really depends on where you work. If you are in special events for a nonprofit, you aren't going to make as much if you are in special events at a for-profit. If you have your own firm and you specialize in weddings and bar mitzvahs, you aren't going to make as much as if you have your own firm and you handle corporate clients and celebrities.

Starting salaries, just like in all "fun fields," tend to be low, between $20,000 and $30,000. Salary.com reports the median salary of an event planner to be $51,474. Assuming you have your own company, a lot of good clients, and repeat business, you can probably expect between $100,000 and $150,000. And if you are the SVP of special events at a big, privately held company like Donna Karan, you'll make even more than that, $200,000 or more.

Stress-o-Meter: 7 (1 being a tour guide at a museum, 10 being a tour guide in the Sudan)

On the day of the event the stress is higher (especially if there are any "issues"), and on other days it's lower. You have to be a person who can manage stress and stay calm even when it seems the sky is falling. You need a brave face and quick feet. A strong bladder doesn't hurt either. Sometimes you are so busy at events it's hard to run to the restroom.

Pros

Your job is different event to event; you never get bored.

Great sense of accomplishment when you pull off a large event.

You work with some really fun people.

Your workplace is the party.

Cons

Demanding clients who don't understand the constraints of their own budgets.

Constant phone calling and e-mailing to stay on top of the details.

You miss out on social opportunities because of event times.

Money could be better for how much effort you put in.

Cheers. You're an Event Planner. You Wake Up And . . .

This assumes it's the day of the event, a sit-down dinner.

7:00 AM: It's going to be a long day. You arrive at the event location and oversee the vendors who are beginning to load in tables, chairs, sound equipment, and other supplies. You make sure nothing's missing and everything, at least to start, is going as planned.

9:00 AM: You check your e-mail, and the RSVP voice mail, to see if there are last-minute attendee additions or cancellations. You will check these constantly throughout the day, as table seating needs to be finalized.

11:00 AM: You meet with the co-chairs of the event and go through the table seating. You scramble to rearrange a few tables of dignitaries so there are no empty chairs. Then it's back to supervising the setting up of the room. The table centerpieces look amazing, but they are a little tall. They can't be fixed, though, you're told, so you learn to love them.

2:00 PM: The caterers arrive. Mmm, food you won't get to eat! You go through a checklist with them, and make sure everything is there. You then talk about the schedule of the evening, when food should be served, and when honorees will be speaking.

4:00 PM: Seating is finalized. You print out the seating cards and place them on a table near the entrance, then supervise final touches on the room's decorations.

6:00 PM: Check one, two. Check one, two. It's the sound check, and it's working fine.

6:45 PM: Doors open. The staff is in place. Your adrenalin is pumping. Smiles, everyone, smiles!

7:00 PM: Guests begin to arrive. You greet the first fifty or so, and then for the rest of the event, you work behind the scenes to make sure everything is choreographed correctly, from the serving of appetizers to the speeches to the gift bags attendees get on departure.

12:00 AM: The party is over and you're wiped. It was a huge success. You head home and dive under the covers.

I Will Fight for My Right to Party.
How the Hell Do I Get This Job?

What I'd recommend would be to have a creative college education. I have a graphics background. A knowledge of theater, sets, and architecture is also going to be helpful.
—**Mark Testa, owner, Mark Steven Enterprises**

The good news is there's really no special education or experience necessary to become an event planner, although any large organization is going to want to see a bachelor's degree. Along the way, if you took courses in business administration, marketing, hotel management, hospitality administration, or even tourism, it couldn't hurt. Another area of schooling that some event planners look for in their candidates is design. Since the overall look and feel of an event is paramount, a trained eye for design is certainly a nice attribute to be able to trumpet in an interview.

Internships are available in event planning and special events, and you should definitely try to get them. Since so many different organizations have event planning, think about both the types of companies, and the kinds of events, you'd like to work on. A magazine doing tie-ins with advertisers, say a raunchy Maxim party sponsored by Red Bull? A museum fund-raiser held in a private collector's townhouse? If you have the time, consider doing a few internships and trying different avenues.

And how do you get these internships? Research, my friends. Write the people working in event planning, or special events at magazines, museums, event companies, you name it, and ask. Go to bizbash.com, an event-planning site, and search for organizations as well as internships and entry-level jobs. The other thing to try is getting freelance work as an event production person. You could help string lights or be a bartender or part of a wait staff. Not only will you meet people and learn how things are run, but it will show that you have been to events and know what it takes to make them shine. Experience like that will help you stand out.

The truth is the industry runs on word of mouth and referrals. The key thing is to be reliable and come through with what you've promised, or more than what you've promised. Once you've proven yourself to others, they will go to bat for you, be it for an entry-level job or even to refer a whole event to you.
—**Rachel Kash, founder, Icing**

If you happen to throw any parties for friends, or maybe a special anniversary soirée for your folks, why not document the event? Take photographs of the table settings, any pieces that show the event theme. Be able to talk about how you put the whole thing together on a shoestring. Be careful; if it's too amateur, don't show it. But if it's pretty cool . . . you can have it with you, and pull out the photos only if it seems like they might help. (But don't just have a stack of photos. Put together a nice little presentation; remember, you are all about presentation.)

Beyond event planning, if you get a job in retail merchandising, say, helping design window displays, it will show your ability to take a space and make it interesting to a large group of people. And some graduate programs and additional training, like certificate courses, are available, but most event planners are hesitant to recommend these as "necessary." Your boss probably won't have done these, so keep 'em in mind as you measure their value.

Now, with your nice experience, it's time to find that entry-level position. Be prepared to be paid peanuts, and to learn. Since the pay is low, be picky about where you are going to work. Try to get a job at the most reputable, fun, or coolest place you can. In the interview, show your personality. You're fun, unflappable, and willing to do what it takes to make this job, and any event, work. Party on.

Resources

Bizbash.com is your mecca. It's a magazine as well as a Web site, and has everything—everything—to do with event planning in and on it. Party rentals, venues, you name it, it's there. There's even a great job search area, which will come in pretty handy. Other sites worth checking out: eventdesign.com, ises.com.

Event Solutions is an industry magazine worth leafing through; you can also visit it online at event-solutions.com. Another similar magazine is *Special Events;* its home on the Web is specialevents.com.

Also, simply keep your eyes open. If you go to a Japanese restaurant and like an appetizer, hmm, maybe that's something you can re-create and serve at an event. Or if you go to a gallery to look at art, you may also walk around and think, "Wow, great space. Maybe they'll rent it." Inspiration can happen anywhere.

Fashion Designer

D id you like to play dress-up when you were little? Did you go through a phase in high school when you were making your own clothes, creating original outfits for your dog, generally just bedazzling the hell out of everything? Well, if you have the drive and the determination to, as *Project Runway*'s Tim Gunn says, "make it work," perhaps you could do this for a living, as a fashion designer.

Fashion design is a highly competitive field. It's hot, it's now, it's sexy, it's awesome, and therefore, a lot of people want to be part of it. And once in, designers are under constant pressure to make clothing that excites the public. In fact, part of a designer's job is to help evolve consumers' tastes with new and tempting looks, each season. It's more than just making fabulous frocks, though; it's making fabulous frocks that sell, consistently.

What Do Fashion Designers Do All Day?

They design clothes, accessories, shoes, anything that falls under the mantle of "fashion." It's one of those job titles that's also a definition.

What steps does this involve? The design process starts with a designer sketching and daydreaming up different kinds of garments. Let's say he works for a small company that makes men's suits. He'll sketch out different cuts and fits, maybe a three-button blazer that fits snugly, and maybe a four-button suit. For each design, he'll search for fabric patterns and swatches that show the material he'd like to use. He'll show his design and materials to others at the company, and if they like it, they'll take it to the next step, production of the actual garment. Very few fashion designers fabricate their own clothes. It gets complicated here and depending on where one works, either out-of-house vendors are contracted or in-house pattern making and preproduction departments communicate with factories and help get clothes made, sewn, and shipped.

Fashion designers can work in-house, at large, corporate labels like Banana Republic, or for higher-end designers like Gucci. They can even start their own labels, although this really is a different job with different responsibilities. A designer with his or her own label is also an entrepreneur (see the chapter on entrepreneurs), and running one's own business adds new elements of

> It's a really exciting thing when something you thought about, designed and truly like, actually does sell.
> —Kate Spade, designer

> I design women's clothing, specifically women's tops, skirts, and dresses. I do sketches, work on the fabrics, the fit, everything that goes into making a garment.
> —Sarah Herr, fashion designer

work, stress, and possible reward. It is the dream of many young designers, but rarely a first job.

Where Do You Design?

At a fashion company. Some are giant conglomerates; some are sole proprietorships operating out of the back of a boutique. In a big company, like J. Crew or Abercrombie & Fitch, you might start off as an intern or design assistant, helping one or a group of designers with small tasks and learning along the way. After a while, if you prove yourself, you'll be promoted to associate designer; you'll begin to actually design. From there you progress to designer, then senior designer, then director, then senior director. You could one day become VP of a certain division, like women's, where you'll approve and influence the creative direction of all the label's women's garments.

At smaller companies, the career path is much less formal. You can be hired as an assistant and in one promotion become a full-fledged designer. There sometimes isn't a next step after that, because the owner of the company is the name on the label, *the* designer of the company. Larger companies offer more structure; smaller ones often offer more opportunities, just because of sheer need. And of course, smaller companies tend to be more creative, so if you start out at one, it's usually easier to later jump to a larger house.

What's It Like Inside a Fashion House?

The vibe at most houses, whether large or small, is pretty loose and casual. It's fashion, after all, and everyone there loves it. There's lots of laughing and hanging out; it's quite social. And of course, on occasion, it can get catty. But don't make the mistake of thinking there's a bunch of folks sitting at sewing machines, being artsy. Designers work long and hard.

As far as dress code is concerned, designers do dress stylishly, but few come to work in over-the-top couture. It's way more casual than that. How relaxed, of course, is a firm-to-firm thing.

As a designer, you won't always be in the office. You may travel to fashion shows, and you'll even visit the factories that make your clothes, to ensure they're coming out as you envisioned. This might mean trips to India, China, Hong Kong, Bahrain, all over the globe. Unfortunately, in those exotic lands, the factories aren't exactly located in the most wonderful spots.

I get e-mails from girls all the time who say, "I want to be a fashion designer; what do I do?" Or "I want to own my own business; what do I do?" I say, "Go to business school if you want your own business." And, "If you want to be a fashion designer, go to fashion design school and then intern for somebody." But if you want to do both, well, there's no easy path. It takes a lot of work.
— Wendy Mullin, designer and owner, Built by Wendy

I dress casual. I get sick of all the clothes I already have in my store because I designed them a year ago. And I can't go shopping and wear other people's stuff because it doesn't feel right. I think that's why people who make clothes often wear all black, or dress in jeans and a T-shirt.
— Wendy Mullin, designer and owner, Built by Wendy

What Skills Do I Need? What Does It Take to Be Good at It?

First, of course, you'll need to be artistically creative. A sensibility for colors, styles, and shapes can be sharpened in school, an entry-level job, or an internship. But if you don't have it to begin with, it can't really be taught.

You'll need to know the basics of design, including computer design programs. Sketching well and being able to sketch flats (which are very technical drawings) are important skills to hone. You'll need to understand how garments are constructed, which includes the basics of pattern making and sewing. And if you want to be a fashion designer, c'mon, you really must know how to sew. You don't have to be a savant, as you'll work with technical experts. But you must at least comprehend how things get made, so you'll have the knowledge and vocabulary to explain to colleagues how you want your garment produced.

An understanding of the fashion world, of textiles, and of different fabrics is going to be necessary. Much of this can be learned in undergraduate or graduate fashion programs, as will be explained shortly.

Beyond these fashion skills, you'll need to be motivated and hardworking. A career in fashion design is highly sought after; you need more than good taste to "make it." And even though this is a fun job full of quirky individuals, it's crucial that you act professionally, recognize deadlines and budgets, and respect them. Finally, a friendly outgoing personality is always a plus, because you're constantly presenting ideas and designs. Under the catch-more-flies-with-honey rationale, it's far better to be likeable than "a bitch" when trying to sell a design.

Finally, to get a job as a fashion designer, you'll need a killer portfolio. A portfolio is a book filled with pages of your ideas, a compilation of sketches and photos of garments you've designed. Beyond the standard résumé, it's what you show potential employers in order for them to consider you. You'll need one to get your first job, and you'll have to continually improve it to get the job after that, and the one after that.

What Are the Hours? Will I Be a Slave to Fashion?

You'll work hard, that's for sure. Especially at first, when you're trying to prove yourself and build your portfolio. There are always deadlines, be they upcoming fashion shows or seasonal clothing that needs to get out the door. Ten-to-twelve-hour days are not out of the norm during busy seasons, and as deadlines approach, all bets are off. Since smaller companies have less infrastructure than larger ones, that often translates into more to do for everyone.

> Sometimes young designers think it's expected of them to be cool and aloof, to have attitude, like that's just the way you're supposed to act in fashion. It's not. People who are more fun and enthusiastic and less jaded are the ones I'd rather work with.
> —Kate Spade, designer

More opportunities, yes, but also increased work hours. And if you own or are starting your very own line, well, you'll need two watches to count all the hours you will be working, at least until you become the next Karl Lagerfeld. Sans little fan, hopefully.

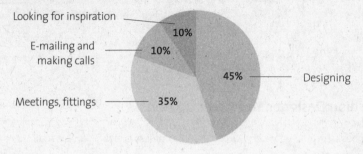

Couture Money?

This is a sought-after job, so just like other sought-after jobs, in the beginning, there isn't much. Starting salaries average around $25,000, more at larger corporate firms, less at smaller ones. You have to weigh the experience you'll get at one versus the money you'll get at the other, especially early on when you're building the foundation of your career.

How high can salaries go? Very, very high. If you have your own label and it sells well, you'll have a villa in Italy. Or you could be a very successful designer at a large corporation and become so valued that you're given shares in the company. Most people in mid-to-high-salary positions end up between $100,000 and $125,000.

The Bureau of Labor Statistics reports the mean salary for fashion designers as $67,370. Salaries range from $30,600 to $112,930.

Stress-o-Meter: 6 (1 being Vanilla Ice's bodyguard, 10 being 50 Cent's bodyguard)

You're just designing clothes, but deadlines are deadlines, and long hours are always stressful. And your clothes had better sell, or after a few bad seasons you just might get the boot. If you have your own label, the stress is exponentially higher.

Pros

Working with creative people who, like you, love fashion.

A fun, flexible atmosphere.

Getting paid for your artistic outlet.

Being part of a field everyone talks about.

Cons

Long hours and crazy schedules.

Stores or consumers sometimes don't like your designs.

It takes a lot of work to break in.

Air Kisses! You Are a Fashion Designer. You Wake Up And . . .

9:00 AM: You arrive at your desk, turn on your computer, and do a cursory check of your e-mail.

10:00 AM: You are currently dreaming up next fall's collection. You look at some of your sketches from the past few days. You take one you love and "ink it up."

11:00 AM: You have a meeting with your boss where you show, for the first time, a few of your preliminary designs. She talks about what she does—and doesn't—like. Overall it goes well, and you leave her office with a grin.

12:00 PM: You attend a meeting with the preproduction team, the folks in charge of getting the clothing actually made and dealing with any factory issues that arise during the process.

1:00 PM: You grab a salad from a place around the corner and eat it at a colleague's desk, where you catch up on his love life. Sadly for him, it's a short conversation.

2:00 PM: You put on your headphones and hole up at your desk. You have a lot of brainstorming and sketching left to do for the fall line. You hunker down and don't look up for a while.

7:00 PM: That *was* a while! But you got tons done. You don't review it, though; you put the new thoughts and sketches on your desk, so you can look at them fresh first thing in the morning. Then you grab your fashionable coat and beat it.

I Am Fashion, Hear Me Roar. How the Hell Do I Get This Job?

To get an entry-level job in fashion design, you'll need the knowledge and skills outlined earlier, and a great portfolio. Most people go to fashion school to gain these, but it's not entirely necessary. You may have been sewing since you were thirteen, or maybe you had a job in a different part of the fashion industry, where you learned the ins and outs on your own.

That said, most designers did go to fashion school, and this is probably the first step for you. You can get an undergraduate fashion education, or, if it's too late for that, you can also get an MFA in fashion. Either way, while you are in school, one of the most important things to do is to intern. Many fashion companies have internships, and guess what? Most don't pay. Still, they are invaluable. They sharpen your fashion skills, add to your résumé, and get you started on the golden path of networking your way into the fashion world. Let's put it this way: you won't meet a designer who doesn't recommend internships.

You can do some other things to help sharpen your eye, skills, and résumé before going for a fashion design job. You could work at a fashion boutique and surround yourself with some of the best designs. See what sells, and what doesn't, and why. Or you could work at a fashion magazine; these magazines are arguably the tastemakers of the popular fashion world; they can literally make or break designers by what they decide to feature on their glossy pages. While working there, you'll see what the fashion editors like and don't like, which pitches succeed in getting designers covered and which ones don't, and why. This is amazing inside knowledge, because soon, if you are a designer, you'll be pitching these very same magazines.

The All-Important Portfolio

Okay, so you're in school, you're interning, you're doing all the right things. Now what you need is an amazing portfolio, filled with photographs and sketches of garments and accessories you've designed. (You may even need to show said portfolio to get certain internships.) These pieces may have come from fashion school assignments, or they could be things you designed on your own, but either way, they need to look sharp. Do not show anything that isn't your best work; it's better to show fewer good pieces than throw a few questionable ones in there. Remember, you are being judged on your taste and sensibility.

It depends on the company, but many times your portfolio gets examined before you do. Which means only after the company has flipped through your portfolio and liked your work will they bother to call you in for an interview. It goes to show you how all-important the book is.

Huzzah! Your book is good enough to get you an interview. What should you say? What should you wear? Well, as mentioned earlier, be friendly. Don't be all, "Well, what can you guys do for me?" And please, learn about the company where you're trying to get a job. You don't have to be able to write a thesis; just get on the computer, see their designs, their philosophy, and understand it. There's no excuse for walking into any interview unprepared.

And if you are prepared, you'll know what to wear. The interview outfit definitely counts for a fashion designer. You don't want to fake it, but it helps if

> I would encourage people to intern, even if what you're doing is pulling together the archives. And if possible, I'd go to the most creative company. If you're not getting paid either way, why not get the most out of it? I never interned, but if I were able to do it again, I'd definitely take an internship, and I would want to get one at the craziest of creative companies.
> —Kate Spade, designer

> I worked as an editor at *Mademoiselle*. It was invaluable experience once I became a designer, because I had already learned how to appeal to editors. Like, I understood I couldn't have some strung-out, all-over-the-place collection. I knew it had to be tight and focused and have a point of view if it was going to interest them.
> —Kate Spade, designer

you are dressed in the same sensibility as the fashion house where you are trying to get hired.

If your book is good enough—yee-ha!—you'll get an entry-level job, most likely at a large fashion house. (Hey, that's where most of the jobs are, not at the smaller, hipper labels.) But whatever you do, don't stop working on your portfolio. If you get a job designing boxer shorts for Hanes, in a couple of years the only "real" designs in your book are going to be boxers. That's fine if designing underwear is your dream job, but if you hope to someday be at a cooler label, say, designing cocktail dresses, you'll need to keep creating spec pieces and evolving your portfolio.

Resources

In the world of fashion magazines, *Women's Wear Daily* (WWD) is the bible. You should get a subscription, although if you go to fashion school a lot of free copies are often lying around. The online version is limited without a subscription but is still worth checking out: wwd.com. And flip through all the other major, glossy fashion magazines—*Vogue, Bazaar,* and so on—to keep up with the latest fashions.

Style.com follows all the major fashion trends, players, and runway shows. Almost every label has its own Web site where you can see its new lines. Many of these sites are getting pretty sophisticated, even showing videos of their runway shows, so go to the Web sites of all your favorite designers and see what they're currently doing. There's also an online service that showcases upcoming trends: wgsn.com. Unfortunately, it's a fairly pricey subscription, but some fashion schools subscribe, and anywhere you intern may as well. You can also go to the "lite" version, wgsn-edu.com, which is specifically for students. It has much of the same info as wgsn.com, but it's not quite as up to date, or as deep. Fashion Group International's site, fgi.org, is filled with all kinds of industry information and has a dedicated student section as well. No subscription needed, either.

Many major universities have fashion programs, and some schools are strictly for fashion design. Two of the most famous are FIT, the Fashion Institute of Technology, and Parsons the New School of Design (the *Project Runway* place.)

Film Director

If you daydream of becoming a Hollywood film director, you might picture yourself doing things like sitting in a director's chair with your name embroidered on the back, or eating Cobb salad at the Ivy with scantily clad international superstars, or talking about stunts and thematic threads via your Bluetooth-enabled earpiece while driving your eco-friendly hybrid back to your Malibu mansion. Sure, those stereotypes hold true, if you hit the big time, but they are just the sprinkles on the large ice cream sundae of hard work and sacrifice that is the life of the film director. Helming films is not as glamorous as it seems; moviemaking is a slow, tedious practice that works in painstaking detail. But when it all comes together and your film is everything you hoped and fought for . . . goose bumps.

Directors helm movies, TV shows, commercials, music videos, corporate videos, and Web films. ("Films" can actually be shot on video these days, of course.) Regardless of type, the job of a director is to read a script and then have "the vision" of how that script should come to life and become an even larger and stronger story as a moving image. This chapter is going to focus on the brass ring: directing feature films. But it should be noted that work in music videos, Web videos, and commercials is often the entrée into features. Imagine these as smaller productions on smaller budgets; they are the same game, but in a sense, the minor leagues, or training camp. Independent films, while offering greater creative freedom, can also in a sense be seen as the minors, leading up to the bigger budgets, paydays, and popularity of studio films.

Most films are made, or at least bought and financed, in Los Angeles (primarily) or New York City (a distant second). If you are aiming to make features, you probably should consider living in L.A. or NYC. Or at least plan on flying out to L.A. pretty often.

> You toil to make the movie; you finally put it together in your little edit room and sit back and think, "Okay, well, we think this is pretty good, pretty funny." And then you take it out of that protective bubble and show it to the world. There's just nothing like the moment you go sit in a theater of six hundred strangers, and the first comedic scene of your movie plays, and then . . . they all laugh together. It's the ultimate reward. And the ultimate drug.
> —Jonathan Dayton and Valerie Faris, directors, *Little Miss Sunshine*

What Does the Director Really Do?

The work it takes to put any kind of filmed production together is surprisingly enormous to anyone unacquainted with the film game. Directors work their bottoms off. (Look at Spielberg, Scorsese, Wes Anderson, John Waters, or Quentin Tarantino; each of them has a pretty small behind. Coincidence?) Directors are responsible for the images audiences see flickering before them, and about a million details are involved in making those images.

Nearly all filmed productions start with a script, which the director reads and begins to translate how the story could best come off the paper and onto the screen. The director really takes over where the writer left off. Which actors will play these different roles; should some of the scenes be changed; what is the overall vision; how should the whole thing look, sound, and feel?

Making this vision real can't be done alone. Filmmaking is a collaborative sport, and directors will bring in many, many creative minds to help them. Think about it this way: when a feature film is "green-lit," it's like the opening of a multimillion-dollar company. Hundreds of people will be employed to make the company a success. And directors have (or should have; sometimes the studios do) the final say on all the members of the cast and crew who are hired. They will need a DP, or director of photography (or cinematographer), the person who actually works the camera and shoots the film; a production designer, who supervises the building of sets and gives the film an overall style; a costume designer and a wardrobe stylist (see the chapter on wardrobe stylists); hair and makeup people; stunt people; animal trainers; you name it. The importance of this team cannot be overemphasized. The director declares what he or she wants; these people figure out how to physically execute his or her ideas so they end up on film.

In addition, directors choose the cast in their films. Yes, studios can demand use of a certain actor, or sometimes actors are attached to the project before a director comes on board, but for the most part, directors pick 'em. The process happens through a series of auditions and callbacks, and with the help of a casting director, another member of the team whose specialty is matching actors to roles.

Let's Shoot

Once the team is in place and you've figured out what you want to achieve and how, it's shooting time, and you'll go to work on a set. If you are on a big studio *back lot*, there will be a trailer on the set that has an office just for you, not to mention your very own toilet. Sets are crazy places. They are like little cities that move from location to location. They bring everything—power, delicious food (there will be a cook for the 50 to 500 or more members of the cast and crew), you name it. Sets are hectic places where time and money are constantly butting up against each other. Every minute is worth hundreds or thousands of dollars, and you'll spend the entire day making rapid-fire decisions. Wardrobe asks, "Should we use the red shirt or the blue shirt?" Props and stunts want to know, "Are we going dagger to the throat or ice pick to the groin?" The DP wonders, "Dolly shot or Steadicam on this one?" Directors are the generals on set, and their crews are the army, waiting for marching orders.

With all the cast and crew, you must deal with a lot of personalities, politics, and opinions. To get your team to perform, you have to inspire them. Or you have to instill fear. You have two tools: one's the carrot, and the other's the stick. You'll probably use both.

This is especially true when directing the talent. The actors are the faces of your story, and more than anyone, they need to understand your vision. Directors do this in many ways, but being a good communicator and a bit of a psychologist are key. Some actors can be divalike and flighty, others grounded and professional. You'll work with all types.

Time and Money

Managing people is one big part of your day. The other is managing time. The studio has financed your picture, and they don't want to spend a dime more than they have budgeted. When a film is green-lit and set to shoot, a plan is put in place. For example, the budget may be $10,000,000 and you will shoot the film in twenty-one days. Everyone will know exactly what shots are planned for each day; it will be all laid out and scheduled. The trick is, you have to "make your days." In other words, each day, you have to get everything you scheduled/promised you'd get done, done. As much as you can try to micromanage, a lot is out of your control. The plan is to shoot at the beach, and it rains all week. An actor gets drunk the night before a tender love scene, gets in a fight, and has his nose broken. Anything can, and will, happen. All you can do is adapt on the fly. There's not much room for excuses. If you fall behind, the studio will be nervous that you are going to break the budget. They'll be up your butt. Have you ever had anything as large as a studio up your bottom? It's disconcerting. Seriously, though, you can even be fired if you're way off schedule. It happens.

Directors are known to complain about studios interfering with their work. Films are expensive to make, and as much as they are art, they are for-profit art pieces. You have to be a grown-up and realize that this is a business, and the studios are going to treat it as such. At the end of each day, directors look at the "dailies" from the previous day. You want to make sure you've gotten everything you need, and that there weren't any technical glitches that will require a reshoot. And at the same time you're looking, the studio also has a set of dailies. Nothing has been edited; you haven't yet tossed all the crappy takes and kept that one jewel that worked. They see all your dirty laundry. And in

Some of the best training I got was when I was a counselor at Meadowbrook Day Camp, supervising thirty-five ten-year-olds. Those skills of babysitting and problem-solving are far more important on set than framing a shot. Everyone has an ego, and actors can be so temperamental.
—Eli Roth, director, *Cabin Fever, Hostel, Hostel: Part II*

some cases, you have to get on the phone and defend your dirty laundry, mid-wash.

After the Shoot

After the craziness of the set, there is a methodical calm in the edit room. These generally feel like living rooms; you'll be sitting on a couch watching as an editor and an assistant splice your story together on a computer. Many days the editor will work alone, but many you will be sitting with him or her, putting together scenes. These are long, eye-melting hours spent staring at footage. The edit is where you can hide or fix any mistakes you might have made while filming, and it's the place where the story truly comes together. After the edit comes a sequence of other postproduction stops, such as audio mixes and special effects, until the film is finished.

Then the studios will want to test-screen your movie. They'll show it to focus groups and make sure it's not a *bomb* or a *dud,* terms which, although usually antonyms, stand for failure in the film world. While this process can be valuable, it can also be soul crushing. The fate of your film is in the hands of a group of strangers who, had they seen the trailer, might not be the type of people who would've bought a ticket in the first place. They're viewing it while there's still time to re-edit and tweak it before release, and you may be forced to make changes you loathe.

Still, These Are Exciting Times

Despite the hard work and frustration that come with the business, the most fun you'll have as a director is when you are actually making a movie. Because film directors aren't constantly directing, or even in preproduction, preparing to go shoot. On average, feature directors shoot only around forty days, every three years. Most often they are reading scripts, looking for projects, or pitching ideas to studios and hoping for financing. Although they're technically "working," these tasks are unpaid. And not as much fun as filming a car crash. It's hard to get a big-budget, or small-budget, movie made. In fact, it's considered one of the hardest things to accomplish in the totality of the commercial art world. Which is why you may notice that many feature directors these days are taking a crack at commercials, episodes of TV shows, and music videos; they love to direct and don't want to wait until they can get back out on the feature set again.

What Makes for a Good Director?

Well, naturally, you have to have artistic storytelling skills. These can be en-hanced and sharpened in film school and by practice, but either you are a good storyteller or you aren't. And you have to be a visual person; the script exists, and you have to take it to the next level.

Personality is a key in the film business. You need to have chutzpah, be able to put yourself out there and pursue work. And you must be confident that you can pull it all off. Imagine yourself leading a team of a hundred people: you have to know, or at least bluff, that you can do it. If you are really, really talented, you can get away with being a butthead and still work. If you are marginally talented but "user-friendly," easy for the studios to deal with (this doesn't mean bending over necessarily), you can also work and do quite well. Remember, for every *Citizen Kane* there are a thousand *Giglis*.

Hours?

Ever notice that many male directors have beards? When you work eighteen hours a day, shaving becomes less of a priority. Most shooting days for the cast and crew, because of many union rules, are capped between ten and fourteen hours (they can go longer, but overtime can be exorbitant and most studios try to stay away from it). But for the director, all waking hours become work time. There's always something to fix, tweak, or work out, if not for that day's shoot, then for the big stunt next week.

Look at making a film as having four phases: the writing time (when you are reinterpreting the script), the prepping time (hiring and creating with your team), the shoot, and postproduction. During all four, something will keep your mind racing at all hours. Before you shoot, you will be carrying around your ideas with you everywhere you go, just adding and adding to them until you are armed and ready to make the film.

There's a fifth phase as well: promoting your film—going on the morning shows, flying around, shaking hands, doing whatever is on the promotional calendar. These can be some grueling weeks of forcing yourself to smile. But, c'mon, no complaining. It's cool.

Sometimes it's all you think about. Even when you are not "on a job" you are looking around, picking up ideas, always on alert. If I weren't a di-rector, I'd hate to be mar-ried to a director. *(Ed. note: The directing team of Dayton and Faris are husband and wife.)* We, luckily, can indulge each other's obsessions. Other spouses may have to pretend to be interested a lot.
—Jonathan Dayton and Valerie Faris, directors, *Little Miss Sunshine*

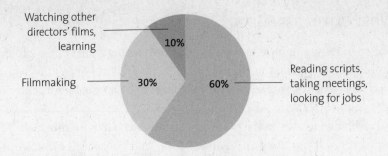

Watching other directors' films, learning — 10%

Filmmaking — 30%

Reading scripts, taking meetings, looking for jobs — 60%

Money?

Directors can go hungry, or they can make a killing. It all depends what sort of projects you're working on, or if you're working at all. Independent short films really don't pay; in fact, you may be financing them yourself. Big-budget blockbusters send dump trucks filled with money to your house, literally millions. Commercials pay better than music videos. You'll make anywhere from $2,000 to $20,000 a day for commercials (and that's not just shoot days; you'll get paid for a day or two of "prep" as well), whereas music videos, unless you are a big-time director, are more like $500 to $8,000 total.

In the feature world, a union called the Directors Guild of America (DGA) regulates industry minimums. It would take pages to detail all the possible pay permutations; it's fairly complex and changes year to year and contract to contract; you can see the current DGA minimums for both film and TV by going to dga.org and clicking on the "Rate Card" tab. To give you an idea, on a high-budget (over $7,000,000) full-length feature, the minimum weekly salary is $14,597. You are guaranteed a minimum of thirteen weeks of that pay (two for prep, ten for shooting, one for editing). That's almost $190,000. Not bad for a minimum. And of course there are "back-end" deals and all sorts of negotiations that will raise your compensation.

1   10

Stress-o-Meter: 7.5 (1 being a Girl Scout, 10 being a Green Beret)

Like many jobs, the stress ebbs and flows, but it generally stays on the high side. When you first start out, so much is riding on the success of your production (like, if you'll ever get to do another one) that it's a 10. Some features begin to shoot before a film is completely figured out (because of an actor's availability, for example), so you'll be shooting during the day and writing scenes for a few days down the line at night. Oh yeah, that's a 10 on the ol' stress-o-meter. And then there are the bright sunny days when you're filming and everything is coming together just how you dreamed it, plus you are making fistfuls of cash. Although you'll be busy, that's not an overwhelmingly stressful day. The truth is, you are really aiming to please yourself.

Pros

You are being paid to do something you love, something people dream of being able to do.

Working with other artists on the set, collaboratively, is very rewarding.

Seeing an idea you had in your head actually come to fruition.

Cons

You'll have to deal with some difficult personalities.

Trying to make art that makes money can make you frustrated.

When you're not working, you wonder if you ever will again.

And . . . Action. You Are a Director. You Wake Up And . . .

This assumes it's a shoot day.

6:00 AM: You arrive on set and sit down with your DP, who's been there since 5:30. The first scene you are shooting today is of a man and his teenage daughter fishing in the early morning hours. Your DP points to the sky, which looks cloudy. You talk about solutions if the sun doesn't break through. Sunrise is at 7:03.

6:20 AM: You talk with both actors, briefly. You don't want to overprepare them. You just want them to act natural. "Hey, try to actually catch a fish, why not!"

7:00 AM: Everyone is in place by the side of the lake. The sun is burning through the cloud cover. You let the assistant director yell "Action," and you shoot the first take. Then you do three more, until you get it right.

8:00 AM: You head to craft services, where you are served a delicious breakfast burrito. While cramming it in your mouth, you have to pick a prop for the next scene, a rake. The prop department has four different ones to choose from.

9:00 AM: You start to shoot the rake scene when a car alarm goes off. It takes a good fifteen minutes to locate the owner and shut the damn thing off—fifteen minutes you know you're going to want later.

10:00 AM: You "push in" for close-ups of the actors in the same scene.

11:00 AM: You break for lunch. Most of the crew has been working since 5 AM. Union rules. While everyone eats, you and the producer have a conference call with the studio. Everyone loved the dailies from yesterday. You mime "Phew!" as the conference call continues.

12:00 PM: For the rest of the day you'll be shooting a dialogue scene between father and daughter in a moving pickup truck. This takes very careful rigging of the camera on the truck, which will be towed behind another vehicle. The rigging takes a while.

2:20 PM: Holy crap, that took a while! You need to finish this scene by 5 PM to make your day. You discuss it with your DP. He decides to use a zoom lens so he can shoot a wide and zoom in for a tight without changing lenses. It will save a good ten minutes with the complicated rig.

5:00 PM: You hustled but you made it. The day is wrapped.

6:00 PM:	You, the DP, and the producers go over the plan for mañana. You'll be shooting in the lake, using an underwater camera. It's a complicated sequence, and you try to troubleshoot.
8:00 PM:	You are exhausted. You're like a zombie but with a better tan. Still, your producers want to talk about the day after tomorrow, since you may not get a chance to tomorrow. You groan and pull out your script.
10:00 PM:	You're home, in bed with your new best friends, two slices of pizza. You set your alarm for 5 AM again, eat your friends, and then go to sleep.

Becoming a feature director requires taking a lot of baby steps. You have to be willing to work incredibly hard. While I was a film school student, I also interned full time on real films. You do what you have to do.

—Eli Roth, director, *Cabin Fever, Hostel, Hostel: Part II*

A lot of people say, "Oh, but Quentin Tarentino never went to film school, he just worked in a video store and than made *Reservoir Dogs.*" What they don't know is Quentin spent two years making a movie before that which he never finished, because he knew he had made a lot of mistakes. That was basically his version of film school, his student film. *Reservoir Dogs* came after that.

—Eli Roth, director, *Cabin Fever, Hostel, Hostel: Part II*

Brilliant! How the Hell Do I Become a Director?

You start making your own films. Somehow you get Hollywood to notice, perhaps at a festival, perhaps through a friend of a friend. And then someone in Hollywood takes a chance on you. Sounds straightforward, right? It's not.

You can take a few paths, and as you can probably guess, none of them is primrose. You may well want to try all of them. The first path is to go to film school. There are many great schools; for example, on the East Coast there's NYU, and out west there's UCLA. Film school not only teaches you technique and surrounds you with students who will help you make your film if you help them make theirs, but it gives you a place to experiment. No one has to see your bad student film, except maybe your parents. There is a lot of talk these days about taking the money you would've spent on film school and using it to shoot your first movie, but most directors advise against it. Film school is a safe place to learn and, if you make a good student film, a place that will help you get Hollywood to notice. They have connections to studios, agents, and festivals. Connections are, of course, everything.

Okay, let's say you do go to film school and graduate, and no one wants you. Or maybe you never went at all. But you have a great script. Well, with production costs dropping, you might consider maxing out credit cards, holding bake sales, and financing it yourself. This is around a 15 on the stress-o-meter, by the way, and a gamble, but it certainly has paid off for some people. Make your film, enter it in festivals, cross your fingers, and remember, you can always declare bankruptcy. That's not a joke, sadly.

Next, this is the age of the Internet. Perhaps you may have heard of it, it's like the whole world is in your computer? The Internet is a democracy, meaning any film you make you can post on sites like youtube.com and all of humankind can see it. Though it's no substitute for film school or festivals, it is a place where if you make something people like, it can get noticed. More and more agents and studios are looking for talent on the Web. If your online short blows up, will you get noticed? Maybe. It's a long shot. Better to think of it as salt and pepper on a meatier plan of film school or festivals.

Another thing to do is work on movie sets. First, it simply gives you a sense of how features are made and whether you really love it or were just in love with the idea of it. Plus, you'll meet people who might help you get a gig someday, or maybe will help you on a student film. Maybe you'll slip a script to an actor you befriend, who agrees to a cameo in your film. It happens. Get the *Hollywood Reporter* magazine, or go to hollywoodreporter.com; it lists what is being made and where, as well as, often, who to contact. Offer to work for free if you have to. Consider it an internship. You'll be a PA, a production assistant, and will do all kinds of grunt work. You'll learn a ton.

Finally, find a director you can identify with, and follow her path. Research her online; what did she do, what were the steps she took to break in? Every one has a different story; learn from hers.

Resources

There are film schools nationwide, but the best ones, arguably, are in New York and California. Some of the more notable ones are University of California—Los Angeles (UCLA), www.tft.ucla.edu; University of Southern California (USC), www-cntv.usc.edu; California Institute of Technology (Caltech), caltech.edu; New York University (NYU), filmtv.tisch.nyu.edu; and American Film Institute (AFI), afi.com.

Variety.com, hollywoodreporter.com, and imdb.com report on the day-to-day Hollywood scene. They also talk about what is being shot where, if you are looking to get a job on the set.

Many sites support filmmakers. Here are a few of the most popular: filmmaker.com, filmmakermagazine.com, indiewire.com, filmmakersalliance .com.

These filmmaking organizations offer advice and information: American Film Institute (yes, same as before), afi.com; Motion Picture Association of America, mpaa.org; and Directors Guild of America, dga.org.

You should read original screenplays and think about how you would interpret them. Download them gratis at script-o-rama.com. Then watch the films and see what the director did, and why. Rent DVDs—the better films, not *Porky's*—and watch them while listening to the director's commentary; you'd be surprised how educational they are.

Finally, check out the DVDs of the shows *Project Greenlight* and *Film School,* two shows that depict the highs and lows of the filmmaking process.

Flash Developer/ Multimedia Designer

What's Flash, you ask? Well, if you were down with the computer science crew, you'd know Flash is the dope new technology used in most funky fresh Web design today. All the phat coders think it's the bomb.

Okay, no more passé hip-hop-speak. Sorry. Let's get more technical.

Flash is a multimedia program created specifically for Web design. What makes Flash so popular is that it allows developers to work with video, audio, animation, text, stills, editing, you name it. In effect, a Flash developer (also known as Flash designers or multimedia designers, as they often work in other programs besides Flash) is to multimedia what a film director is to film. Whether they write their own "screenplay" or work off others' ideas, Flash designers bring two-dimensional concepts into animated, moving life online. As the Internet continues to grow and dominate our lives, Flash developers are a hot commodity. And just like there are well-known directors, famous for certain styles and genres, so too are there a growing number of respected Flash developers. It's a field growing by leaps and bounds. That said, if you are considering this job, you probably have (or will need to have) a strong grasp of the ways of the Web, how sites basically work, and maybe even some HTML skills before getting started.

> I mostly do the animation, the building and the user interface design. I generally get another person, a strict designer, to do the site look and feel for me, because it takes too much time to do that and try to program at the same time.
> —Ming Thompson, owner, Ming Media

Keep Explaining, Please

As you well know, there are all kinds of Web sites, from the cruddy ones built at home by novices to the slickest, most sophisticated million-dollar ones. Teams of people build the professional sites. The overall site concept is dreamed up by designers (or art directors) and writers. These work with an information architect (see the chapter on information architects) who figures out the blueprint of the site's structure, how it flows, and where the navigation takes you. Once the big idea is cracked and the structure sorted, a production team is needed to bring the site to life. The more complicated the site, the bigger the team. The Flash developer is brought on board to help design and program all the moving pieces.

What's that mean? Well, as a Flash developer, you will create interactive "movies" on the Web. Sometimes these are literally short films with music and video. Other times they are neat effects, or transitions, like when you click on a Web page and it changes via a cool (or subtle) animation—that's Flash. But you won't be so compartmentalized that you work only on things that "move." Everything is connected, so your Flash skills will also affect the user interface, or how users interact with the site, and basic usability.

Flash is a program. Meaning, if you use it, you will be programming, or coding. This is different from other designer programs, like Photoshop or Illustrator (or if you are not familiar with those, Microsoft Word), where you are simply working within the program, not creating wholly new scripts. Although everything you work on is visual and needs to be well designed, you also need to be able to do the technical part. They go hand in hand.

Coding can be time consuming. You may love a design idea, but to get it to work the way you want, you may have to overcome programming bugs or glitches. These can become nerve racking, because Web sites are generally built on deadlines. They need to be up and running by a certain date, and as that date approacheth, the pressure riseth. And the pressure on the Flash developer with a programming bug can be pretty intenseth.

What Kind of Person Is a Flash Person?

Since this is a relatively new field, the answer is still evolving. Obviously, though, creative skills are a must. You must be passionate about art and design, but at the same time, you can't just be a flaky creative type. Flash is not just painting, it is coding, and so you have to be very organized, detail oriented, and meticulous.

This may sound silly, but you can't be a Flash developer until you know the program Flash. But beyond that, you need to have mastery of the other common design programs, like Photoshop and Illustrator, as well as digital video programs, like Final Cut Pro. And you'll need to be familiar with other common programming languages, like HTML.

There is no formal educational requirement to get the job. Most places don't care where you went to school or if you have a master's, a bachelor's, or a high school equivalency diploma. But as you can see from the preceding quote, you'll need to have a lot of knowledge under your belt, so however you decide to get it—get it. The bottom line is, you are hired based on the quality of your portfolio. A Flash portfolio is a compilation of sites you've created that shows your best work.

You have to be able to see the big picture, the goal of the overall site, and not get lost in the details. You need to persevere, because when there are lots of bugs you will be working late into the night. You need to be able to perform under pressure and be able to meet deadlines. You'll also collaborate with a lot of different people to create the site, so you need the ability to work well with others.
—Alfredo Tadiar, creative director, Nurun

I would say people need to know all the design elements: Photoshop, Illustrator, Dreamweaver helps a lot if you don't know HTML, and you also need to know the back end, how to do a database and how to pass variables. JavaScript will take you everywhere. Once you learn JavaScript or any programming language, everything is the same and you can pick up other languages easily.
—Ming Thompson, owner, Ming Media

Where Do You Flash?

Wherever a Web site cries out for animation, a Flash developer is there. They're employed at advertising and interactive agencies who build sites, at corporations that have their own sites, and of course at dot-coms, which are themselves sites. In all of these places, the vibe of the interative department is almost always casual and laid back. Video games will be played, music will be heard, and jeans will be worn. Flash designers are half in the art world, half in the technology world. That allows them to wear black Converses as well as *Star Trek* shirts (original ones, not *Next Generation*), if that is their wont.

Flash developers are in high demand. Their skills are needed for the most cutting-edge sites, and who wants to have a site with a noncutting edge? Certainly not any large company, music artist, Hollywood film promotion site, you name it. Flash designers have been able to go freelance, to become animation mercenaries. They work on the premises sometimes, bouncing from office to office, but often they can work remotely. All it takes is an Internet connection and a dream.

Cyber Hours?

Flash developers work on deadlines, and as anyone who has ever written a college paper knows, an approaching deadline means longer hours. One strange bug that you can't seem to fix can turn into an all-nighter. Interactive departments as a whole tend to work fairly long hours. You are definitely looking at solid forty- to sixty-hour weeks, toward the lower end if you are in a large company where there is more help, toward the higher end if you work someplace small and the load is on your shoulders. The good news is, you can't really be working when you aren't in front of a computer. The bad news is you have a computer at home.

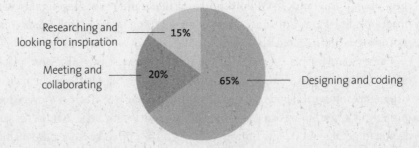

Researching and looking for inspiration — 15%

Meeting and collaborating — 20%

Designing and coding — 65%

Flashy Salary?

Fairly flashy, yes. This is a relatively new field, so salary levels are still adjusting; in fact, salary reference sites like the BLS and even salary.com currently lump this in under Web designer. (For reference though, salary.com says that salaries for senior Web designers in New York City range from $88,855 to $121,045.)

Currently there is a dearth of good Flash people, so starting salaries seem to be quite high, sometimes even in the $50,000 range. As you become more senior, you will definitely break the $100,000 range, and quite easily too. And if you become a star, you'll go well beyond that.

> Sometimes it's easy and sometimes you're just so stressed out. Sometimes you have to work two days straight and burn the midnight oil, and sometimes you have better timelines and you don't have to worry about it too much.
> —**Ming Thompson, owner, Ming Media**

Stress-o-Meter: 6 (1 being a candle maker, 10 being a firefighter)

But at first, until you get used to the fast pace and deadlines, it might be a 9.

Pros	Cons
Creative and interesting projects.	You're often asked to work extra hours for no extra money.
You'll work with a lot of like-minded people who are interested in things you are: movies, animation, art, and music.	Deadlines add a lot of pressure.
The salary is nice and the technology is cool.	Any kind of coding means there will be software bugs; these can be mind-numbing to fix.
You can garner a little bit of fame in the Flash community.	Staring at a computer screen twelve hours a day can give you a headache.

Ta-Da—You're a Flash Designer. You Wake Up And . . .

This assumes you work at a company and are not a remote freelancer.

9:15 AM: You arrive at work and shake off the cobwebs with some coffee. You check your e-mail and the status of your projects.

10:00 AM: You attend a kickoff meeting for a new project with the entire team: a writer, art director, information architect, and businessperson. The project is for an e-commerce site selling jewelry. Even though your part won't come until the site idea is ready for production, it's good for you, when possible, to understand the goals of the project.

10:45 AM: You have an IM freakout with a friend who just dumped her boyfriend.

11:00 AM: You quit out of IM so you can get to work, designing/coding a Web site that is in its fourth week of production. It's a pretty deep site and an intense project.

1:45 PM: Another meeting. This is an internal review of a site you've been working on for a fishing rod company. You all sit in a conference room and look at the site projected on a large screen. As a team, you scroll around and brainstorm ways for it to be even more creative.

3:00 PM: One idea that comes out of the meeting is to change some of the transition animations, the way one click brings you to a new part of the site. The initial animations were slow fades of fish in a pond. The new ones will be assorted: fish will jump from the water and wipe the screen, schools will swim by. All sorts of fish things will happen. It's a lot to do, but it might just be awesome.

4:45 PM: You finish up the transitions and then go back and do some work on the initial project from the morning. It's nice to be able to switch gears.

7:00 PM: Your retinas are starting to glow. You work for another fifteen minutes, shoot out a few e-mails, and then start to pedal home.

I Dig Art and Technology.
How the Hell Do I Become a Flash Developer?

This is one of those new jobs where you can pretty much carve your own path. The only thing needed to get hired, as mentioned earlier, is a portfolio. A portfolio is simply (or maybe not so simply) a compilation of sites you've made using Flash and any other designing or programming skills you want to show off. Generally it lives as a portfolio Web site, a link you can send around that houses all of the different animations, designs, and sites you've built. You can also burn a bunch of DVDs.

How do you build a portfolio? Well, most Flash developers will tell you that they are self-taught. But they obviously had creative skills of some sort to start. They purchased the Flash program, took tutorials, bought books, did research online, and started to make stuff. If you're considering this as a career, there's probably a good chance you've been fiddling around and have tried a few experiments of your own. Take those and sharpen them. Offer to help friends and family with their own sites, and use them as guinea pigs for designs and codes you want to try. Schools are out there as well, for both continuing education and full-blown graduate degrees. But most Flash designers dismiss those as unnecessary and costly.

That said, school works for some people who may not be as self-motivated as others. See what's available locally and try taking a class or two before committing to any sort of graduate degree. Like filmmaking, this is a skill you really need to come to on your own and learn your own style and way of doing things. Now if you happen to still be an undergraduate, definitely see what classes are available in the art school and/or the computer science department.

Finally, as always, never put anything you aren't absolutely proud of in your portfolio. Part of this job is taste, and it's better to have fewer great things than more questionable things. You'll send your portfolio in to companies before they grant you an interview, which they'll grant only if they like your stuff. So if you get asked in, your skills have already passed judgment. The interview now is really just for them to meet you and see if your personality will fit in with the current team. Be confident about what you've created, and be able to talk about the programming you did and why you did it. And even though it's a creative environment, look professional. Don't show up in a suit—you won't fit in—but you might want to wear something a tad (just a tad, though) nicer than jeans. It's just respectful and shows you are serious.

Resources

Check out actionscripts.org. It's a learning resource and a highly recommended user group forum; plus, it also has job postings. Macromedia was the original maker of Flash; now it's owned by Adobe, whose site, adobe.com, is an excellent resource as well. A good place to network with other professionals is at the annual Flash Forward Conference. Their site, flashforwardconference.com, is filled with loads of information. Flashmagazine.com is a great way to keep up on all the latest and greatest tricks of the trade. And finally, Flash Kit, a Flash developer's resource guide, is available at flashkit.com. Another group forum, tutorials, tools, and even galleries of others' work also are housed on the site.

For inspiration, look at interactive awards annuals and Web sites. Some of the good ones include the *Communication Arts* Interactive Annual, *ID Magazine,* and the Webby awards, webbyawards.com. New interactive awards sprout up each year, so do a search for them and check out the winners.

I suggest you build your own Web site that showcases everything you can do; it's the first thing that potential employers will look at. It should showcase your ability to design and to create a good user interface, your animation skills, and any knowledge you have of audio and video.
—**Alfredo Tadiar, creative director, Nurun**

Gallerist

So you like art, huh? You've read that Jansen book cover to cover, and whenever you go with your friends to a museum, they always end up waiting for you in the café because "You're like, so friggin' slow." Well then, a job in art could be in your future.

A gallerist is a person who works in an art gallery and helps the artists handled by that gallery sell their works to collectors. Collectors count on the galleries, and the gallerists who work there, to show them the most exciting artists. Galleries aren't museums; they're businesses. Hence, though you're no auctioneer, a big part of being a gallerist is being a salesperson.

A quick word on the word *gallerist*. The art world, as you might expect, defies easy categorization. So more than one title defines the people who work at galleries, or who own them. *Gallery director, gallerist, gallery manager*—each of these titles basically stands for the same gig.

Galleries, in General

Although there are many well-known, large art galleries, most are small, employing anywhere from two to twenty people. Galleries typically have eight new art shows a year, and it is important that each is successful—galleries, unlike museums, are funded solely by the art sales. Four or five unsuccessful shows in a row, and a gallery might be gone.

Galleries are spaces that are open to the public. Given this, a lot of the job of gallerist will be making this space a nice place for people to come look at art and, hopefully, buy some.

What Do Gallerists Do?

Assuming the job is at a small gallery, gallerists have several responsibilities. (Large galleries often have administrative staff, as well as staff who are on the gallery floor selling and informing; responsibilities are doled out a bit more rigidly.) Boring as it seems, one of the main tasks is keeping the business moving. A good chunk of the day will be spent invoicing, following up on sales, making sure art is hung correctly, adjusting lights so they are hitting the work properly, working with a designer to make invitations to the next show, updating the Web site, talking to the gallery's publicist, and so on. The rest of the day will be spent actually curating, meeting with collectors and trying to make sales. Most of the time will be spent at the gallery itself, but there are studio visits and art fairs when you will travel. And yes, even assistants travel to art fairs and local artists' studios.

The more senior you become as a gallerist, the less time you'll spend in the gallery. More of your time will be spent networking; it's a very social job as you ascend.

Art Dealing with Art People

So who are these people you'll be networking with? Artists and buyers, and it is your job to merge their very different worlds.

First, the artists. Galleries actually represent artists, whom they promote via shows at their gallery space or shows they may set up in other spaces. Gallerists are like agents; they work to build up the artist—the bigger the artist gets, the more expensive the work, the more money for the gallery. Yet note that there are no clear rules in the art world. There are often no contracts, so you could lose an artist to a bigger, more powerful gallery at any time. People are cutthroat. The art world can be a little shady that way. Check out the film *Basquiat*.

The flip side is, artists rely on you financially. Galleries represent anywhere from fifteen to fifty artists who generally have their own show once every two years. It's your job to help them get their art ready for that show. Some artists will want you to be a coach and a therapist, others need a mother, and still others are incredibly savvy and will pepper you with ideas on how to "market" them. Some really will value your opinion. Some just want you to act as their personal assistant. But no matter what, the art must be exciting, it must go up in time for the show, and it must sell. Otherwise it's bad for them, bad for you, and bad for the gallery.

Now to the client, or collectors, who in some ways are even trickier to deal with than the artists. Because of the expense, and the fact that art is a luxury item, buying art really has to be a pleasant experience for collectors in every single way; it can't be a hassle. That is why many gallerists will not hand off even small pieces of their sales to assistants or interns; from framing to shipping, they want everything to go extra smoothly.

Last point on art people: it's a small world, and it's a who-you-know world. That's why it's important to meet everyone you can, and go out as often as you can to events and network.

As a gallerist, you bounce between the abstract of the art itself and the concrete day-to-day business of it. You'll go from visiting an artist at their studio and remarking, "Wow, what a great conceptual piece" to trying to solve, "How am I going to get that fifteen-hundred-pound concrete sculpture to the gallery?"
—Josee Bienvenu, Josee Bienvenu Gallery

You can have a billionaire in your gallery and a literally starving artist on the phone, and it can be fascinating to find yourself there, in the crossroads of society.
—Josee Bienvenu, Josee Bienvenu Gallery

Art is a luxury good; no one really needs art to live, like they might need prescription medication. People who purchase such luxury items are used to being catered to; they are quite demanding, and you must be quite accommodating.
—Josee Bienvenu, Josee Bienvenu Gallery

What Skills Do You Need?

Gallerists should be detail-oriented perfectionists. The space and exhibitions can't ever look sloppy. You must be demanding but also diplomatic with artists, and smooth as silk with rich clients. Gallerists must be sort of intellectual—this is the art world, and there will be conversations about classic art, references to cinema and literature, and you need to be able to feel at least somewhat comfortable in the give and take of such cultured talk. And you must feel comfortable initiating conversations and approaching people, as well as following up. This is yet another job that isn't particularly good for the shy.

Last but not least, you have to understand art. Yes, the history and the current scene both, which you can learn and keep up on, but you must also have an eye for art. It's hard to describe, but as gallerist, you are a tastemaker. You decide what is "good" in a world that is completely subjective, and then you hang that "good" art on your walls and try to sell it to others who have their own opinions. It is a quality that can be sharpened, but not really taught.

> You need to be honest and trustworthy. You want people to have a good experience, to feel they can trust your expertise. That way, they'll be happy to deal with you again.
> —**Steven Sergiovanni,
> Mixed Greens Gallery**

Art Hours?

Galleries are open, for the most part, from ten to six, Tuesday to Saturday. Working in a gallery is more of an afternoon job than a morning job; even though the gallery may be open, most don't get crowded until later in the day. There isn't a lot of the "I'm working late" or "I had to come in on Sunday" of other jobs, but of course, these things do happen occasionally. At the same time, the day isn't quite over when the gallery closes. This is America and even in the art world, we find new and exciting ways to work. To stay up-to-date with the art scene, it's imperative to go to the myriad benefits, openings, and other events that happen in the evenings. This is when you get to see many different artists' work and people's reactions to it. And you'll network, which, besides the "good cause" aspect, is why benefits exist.

> These events are all very social and exciting, and quite fun, but they're still technically work. Even with a glass of wine in your hand, you need to be aware you are in a workplace and are repping your gallery.
> —**Steven Sergiovanni,
> Mixed Greens Gallery**

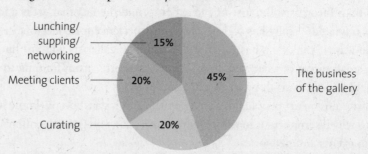

- Lunching/supping/networking — 15%
- Meeting clients — 20%
- Curating — 20%
- The business of the gallery — 45%

Your Office Is Nicer Than Your Apartment

One of the great things about working in a gallery is the physical space itself. Almost all galleries are large, airy, loftlike spaces, with yes, nice art on the walls. Since there are so many shows a year, the art is constantly changing and there's always something new and, hopefully, brilliant, with which to spend your day. You'll meet lots of nice people who come in and want to talk about your favorite subject, art. There just aren't much more pleasant places to be employed.

Galleries are also very personal spaces, which is why most are named after their owners. When you work at one, you need to understand the taste of the owner, because it will be the taste of the gallery. It will inform the art on the walls and the clothes on your back. Some galleries are very funky, and pink hair and T-shirts with Smurfette flipping the bird go over well. Others are a little more "corporate," and a smarter, artsy look is required, more of a Prada all-black thing. Bottom line, your look counts. There is an aesthetic to each gallery and to the people who work within them.

I Start as What for How Much?

You'll probably start as a . . . wait for it . . . intern. The unpaid kind. Soon after, hopefully, you'll move up to a paid position, something called Front Desk. Then, depending on the exact titles, which, as mentioned, differ at different galleries, you'll become an assistant director, and then a director.

No official salary statistics are available for gallerists. Anecdotally, salaries for starting jobs, like Front Desk, are low, around $25,000. Up until recently, working in a gallery was sort of considered a "rich kid" job, a trust fund job, meaning a gig for people for whom salaries didn't mean much. This has changed in recent years. Now it's truly a job for art lovers, but still, the salaries haven't exactly started soaring. At some galleries, you may make a small commission, about 3 to 5 percent of the sales price of the piece. However small that sounds, the sky is the limit on what you could earn. If you happen to own your own gallery and it's mildly successful, you could be earning in excess of $100,000 a year.

Although salaries may not be sky high, gallery jobs offer some nice perks. Like time off. Almost all galleries are closed the entire month of August, for the two weeks around Christmas, and offer regular vacation packages in between. Perhaps you'll visit some museums?

The rest of the world calls it "receptionist," but in galleries it's Front Desk.
—**Steven Sergiovanni, Mixed Greens Gallery**

Stress-o-Meter: 5 (1 being a bearded lady, 10 being the First Lady)

Hey, it's art. Still, dealing with artists and clients can get frustrating at times. And the art market is fickle (this week everyone loves "sweet" portraits painted with maple syrup; next week sugar is out, gravy portraiture is in). Still, this stress isn't the kind that makes you tear your hair out.

Pros

You work with interesting people, both artists and clients.

Your office is beautiful.

It's a very special, laid-back lifestyle.

You sell a product you strongly believe in.

Cons

You're dealing with people all day. People can be annoying.

The late nights of networking and drinking can get tiring after a while.

Working on the weekend makes going away with friends and family difficult.

Magnifico! You're a Gallerist. You Wake Up And . . .

9:00 AM: You take an extra-long shower. You were at an opening last night and are still woozy from all the champagne you shared with an influential collector you're courting.

10:00 AM: You arrive at the gallery. You turn on the lights, make sure the art is hung straight, get the espresso machine working, and check your messages.

11:00 AM: The gallery opens at eleven to the public. A few early birds walk around, and you answer questions from a German tourist. You never know who is a big collector; you are polite to everyone. An art advisor (a person who helps wealthy people choose artwork) and her client arrive. You take a meeting with them, explaining why one of your artists would be great to add to their collection.

1:00 PM: You go to lunch with one of your artists and talk about all that he's been working on.

3:00 PM: Another one of your artists arrives at the gallery, and she shows you new work. You really like it; her work has really evolved. You discuss how it could be a cornerstone of a new show and encourage her to "do more."

5:00 PM: A framer delivers some pieces you sold. You inspect them and then package them and ship them out to the buyer. Then you fix yourself, and a few people browsing, some late-afternoon espressos.

6:00 PM: You close. There's an opening at a nearby gallery, so even though you're tired, you suck it up and go. You see a few of your artists there, and you keep your eye on them as they talk to the gallery owner.

8:30 PM: You're invited to the post-opening dinner. You go, meet a few new young collectors, and network.

I Am One with Art. How the Hell Do I Get into the Gallery Game?

To get in, first you have to know the art scene and learn the lingo. There are lots of different ways to do that, but that is what needs to be done.

Schools like FIT and NYU have graduate programs for gallerists. The biggest benefit of the graduate school experience, according to gallerists, is the opportunity to "meet the right people." But it's possible to accomplish this without spending the tuition. Try getting into the art world as early as you can, through the previously mentioned internships. The experience you'll acquire is key, not to mention the networking opportunities. Of course, this assumes you already have a deep understanding of art. If not, or if you don't live in a big art city where you can intern, then grad school may make a good deal of sense.

Gallerists can come from many different backgrounds, and other than art, a general wealth of knowledge and strong cultural background is important. So although being an art history major is helpful, it's not mandatory, as long as somewhere along the way you learned about art. For example, many gallerists come from families that are collectors, which is where they developed their arts background. Some are artists who also work in galleries as their "day job" to support themselves.

The Art of the Interview

Since being a gallerist is such a people job, it's important to have a good overall presentation when trying to get into a gallery as an intern or for an entry-level job. Dress in a style that fits the gallery, showing them just by how you look that you know their vibe. Also, your résumé should be well designed; it needn't be an art piece in itself, but a bit of flair beyond the regular goldenrod paper and Helvetica is probably a good move.

You should absolutely learn about the artists of any gallery where you'll be interviewing. As is true with breaking into any field, it's important to do your homework, and it's amazing how many people don't. Also, be familiar with all the art world terminology; you really don't want to sound like a phony. Try to see shows in nearby galleries before you interview, so you can also be knowledgeable on what is happening locally. You should be able to answer this question: what artists would you choose to be in your dream gallery, and why? It's silly, but it's a question that comes up—so don't be stumped. And finally, know your magazines. Know the difference between *Frieze* and *Art in America*—and what's in each this month.

Resources

If you're considering the field, reading and monitoring the following Web sites and periodicals will keep you up to date on the art world.

Sites:

Artnet.com—An online art magazine and auction, a good place to find out what's hot.

Nyfa.org—This site often has job and internship listings.

Artforum.com—Read the gossip column; it's a good way to follow the movers and shakers in the art world.

Periodicals:
(In all the following, make sure you pay attention to the ads—these will inform you on the artists who are showing currently.)

The New York Times Friday Arts and Leisure section—It contains the recent "important" openings and their reviews.

Art in America, Art News—These two art magazines are both classic and American in style.

The Art Newspaper—A British monthly that follows the art world.

Headhunter

Headhunters hunt heads. Often corporate heads, perhaps the most dangerous of all prey. Headhunters thrive in urban centers and use telephones and computers in lieu of witchcraft and blow darts.

Headhunters help people find jobs—or, more accurately, they help their clients, companies and corporations, fill job openings with people, or candidates. It is truly part "hunting heads," or poaching—finding a likely candidate who may be at a client's competitor and wooing her away. But more so, it's matchmaking—finding the right person with the right skill set and personality to fit seamlessly into a client's culture. It's like setting two people up on a date (the interview) and hoping for a love match (a job offer). Sans goodnight kiss, naturally.

> We look for the perfect coupling of client and candidate in the world of employment. It's the other type of marriage.
> —Lori Habas Miller, co-president, Sam and Lori

Tell Me More, Por Favor

Headhunters are sometimes known as recruiters, although at larger headhunting firms there is a difference between a recruiter and a sales manager. Briefly, at these, recruiters are the ones who screen the people looking for new employment to see if they are strong candidates. The recruiters rarely talk to the clients, the companies with jobs to fill. The sales managers do that, "managing" the accounts. This division of labor does not exist at every firm, and certainly not at smaller ones, where as a headhunter you'll both recruit and manage. And we will not focus on it in this chapter. But it's worth pointing out early on, since the role or duties of recruiter are entry-level ones at larger companies.

The Business of Relationships

Headhunters tend to specialize. Some firms work solely in the legal field, or medical, or advertising, or technology. Larger headhunters might have a different division for each one of these. Other firms, or divisions within firms, work primarily in the "temp" world, or unskilled world, meaning receptionists, assistants, and the like.

Whatever niche you might be in, the basics are the same. It's a business of relationships. You will have clients who have open jobs. You find the right candidates to fill these jobs and send them to clients to be interviewed. If they get along and the candidate is hired, your company gets a commission, anywhere from 15 to 25 percent. And on top of a base salary, you get a percentage of that commission, generally 40 percent. You make a match and you make some money. Cha-ching. Of course, the employee needs to stay at the job (not quit or be fired) for a certain minimum amount of time (a few months or so) before you see that commission.

So what's the key to making the magic happen? Knowing both clients and candidates, really, really well. First there are the clients; your contacts at these may be in the human resources department of a larger company, or you might be speaking directly with the president of a midsized firm. You will learn their vibe; are they buttoned down and corporate, or fun loving? Do they like risk takers as employees, or more conservative types? Do they expect seventy-five-hour weeks, or are they nine to five? You'll have visited them many times, gone out to lunch, and spent hours on the phone. Because of this, you won't waste their time with the wrong candidate.

And to find them the right candidate, you will have to know those people well too. Whether they have come on their own to your firm, or whether you have sought them out, you'll meet each and every one. You'll join them for a coffee near their offices, or they'll swing by your place surreptitiously, before or after work. You'll know what they want out of life—whether they hope to take over the world and are willing to make sacrifices to do it, or whether they just had a second child and are looking for a more balanced existence. It can't be stressed enough: the only way to be successful as a headhunter is to know whom you are setting up with whom. Because if you recommend a candidate who ends up getting hired, and then leaves or is canned in a short amount of time, you and your company don't get any commission. And sometimes a bad recommendation may lose you a client as well.

So at the end of the day, the career is all about how well you know your clients and candidates. When you have solid relationships, you have repeat business and referrals. And repeat business and referrals make more money. And with more money comes better toys. And toys are fun.

Maybe 40 percent of a successful placement comes from the chemistry between client and candidate. You can have a great person on paper, but if it's like oil and water with the manager they'll be working with, you don't have a shot of placing them. So you've really got to know who the clients are, their environments, and what types will thrive in their environments. Otherwise you're out of it.
—Michael Goldstein, manager, Quantum Management Services

OK. But What Exactly Do You Do All Day?

Build those relationships. Do you like making phone calls? As a headhunter, you will spend an inordinate amount of time on the phone. You will make teenage girls seem phone phobic with all the chitchat you'll be chitchatting. You'll be on one call explaining to Candidate A why a position's right for them with Client B, and then be on the next call telling Client B why Candidate A is perfect for their organization. You'll help schedule the interview. If it goes well between the two, you'll negotiate the money, benefits, and titles upon the job offer. And you'll be at one stage or another of this process on several projects at once, constantly multitasking.

How do you find the right candidate? Sometimes you'll find a likely one working at another firm. Other times you just "know the right person." Plus, every headhunting firm keeps an easily searchable database of candidates, with notes on their skills, job history, and so on.

Before and after office hours, you'll spend time interviewing new candidates who are currently working at other jobs. And once or twice a week you'll go to lunch with a client, trying to solidify or expand your relationship. You're constantly building relationships and closing deals. It's a commission business, and you are always hustling.

Know the Game

It's paramount that you understand the dynamics of the specific field in which you headhunt. You'll need to learn what the companies in it do, how they make money, and what makes them successful. So it really helps to have a background in the field in which you are headhunting. To stay up to date, you'll read the same newspaper columns, trade magazines, and Web sites as your candidates and clients. You'll know about the big deals and the layoffs. Because in truth, you too are in the industry, and as it fares, so too do you fare.

What Kind of Person Is Good at This Job?

A self-starter. This isn't the kind of business where you're "an employee," waiting for a task from your boss. No, this is a game that rewards motivated individuals who carve their own path. The bulk of your salary is based on commission; you have to perform in order to earn. You have to be motivated by money—well, at least to some extent. It's sales. Human sales. You're sort of a pimp, really.

What else? Well, you need to be gregarious. A people person. A good talker. You can't ever be afraid to pick up the phone and make a call. "I know you are happy at your current job, but would you consider . . ." And some of the calls are going to go badly. And some candidates are not going to work out. But you must persevere.

And when you do talk to these people, you need to be genuine; this is someone's career. You have to counsel people not to take a certain job when the match is going to be a train wreck. So although you may be a pimp, it's impor-

I'm on the phone all the time; I go from one call to the next call to the next call. So yeah, I wear one of those headsets. I was resistant to it at first because I always thought they were so cheesy, but it really makes life easier, because you can talk and do other things at the same time.
—Lori Habas Miller, co-president, Sam and Lori

If you want to recruit in an industry, you have to know it really quite well. You can't fudge it. That's why many headhunters have at one time worked in the industry they recruit in. They know the playing field and all of the players. You can't really advise a candidate on a career decision if you know nothing about their career. Why should they listen to you?
—Lori Habas Miller, co-president, Sam and Lori

tant to be ethical and not just go for the score. If you screw people, they won't come back. And if they do, they may be carrying a hammer.

Finally, you must be discreet. You're going to know secrets. Candidates will come in who have jobs, but hate them and want to leave. Employers may be about to fire someone and want to fill the position. Hell, you could have a client on the line looking to hire a counterpart for one of his employees, and a second later that employee could call saying she wants to move on. You have to keep it all on the inside. Loose lips sink careers.

What's the Office Like?

There are huge firms and two-person boutique firms, and naturally the offices differ. Beyond that, they're similar: fast-paced environments, with phones ringing and constant chatter. The smell of money is in the air. Ahh, that motivating money smell, equal parts fear and lobster. Breathe it in.

Whether the vibe of these offices is casual or formal depends on whether the firm headhunts for a casual or professional field. If you're a headhunter who works in the design field, you'll probably dress like a designer and your firm's walls will be adorned with interesting artwork. If you hunt heads for the legal profession, you will wear a suit and the place will feel not unlike a law firm.

But even when the vibe is casual, you will still be somewhat professional. Candidates are coming to you for career help, and corporations are coming to you to fill their ranks with top-quality employees. You can't wear short-shorts and a muscle shirt.

You can also leave the office and still be working. Ninety percent of this job happens on the phone or over e-mail, so you can be anywhere and still be working, thanks to our good pal technology. That flexibility is a nice bonus.

Hours?

How hard you work each day is based on how motivated you are. Obviously, though, you have to perform up to some basic numbers or you'll be replaced. Some headhunters work sixty-hour weeks, some work forty. For the most part, you can't do much work when your clients aren't open, and there's hardly ever any weekend work. So for even the most aggressive headhunter, the hours aren't overwhelming.

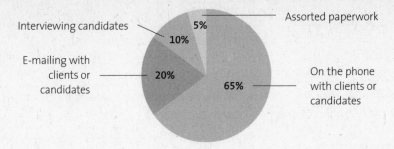

Interviewing candidates — 10%

Assorted paperwork — 5%

E-mailing with clients or candidates — 20%

On the phone with clients or candidates — 65%

Salary?

It's good. As a headhunter you get a small base salary, plus commission on your placements. The company gets paid anywhere from 15 to 25 percent of the candidate's salary by the client, and you get about 40 percent of that 15 to 25 percent. So let's say you place a candidate for $100,000 at a pharmaceutical company. Your company gets 20 percent, or $20,000. And you get a commission of $8,000.

In your first year as a headhunter, you can expect to make around $30,000 in base salary, and another $20,000 to $30,000 in commission. In the second year, that commission total can often double. And the third year, it may well double again. This doesn't go on forever, but damn . . . Salary.com lists the national average salary of recruiters with five to eight years' experience as being between $30,527 and $93,074. The Bureau of Labor Statistics reports the mean salary as $48,470. These figures are for all recruiters; in the world of executive recruiting, the numbers are much higher.

Keep in mind, in any commission-based job—especially recruiting, which is strongly tied to the economy—there will inevitably be some down years.

Stress-o-Meter: 5 (1 being a windsurfer, 10 being a storm chaser)

The days are fairly hectic; you could have six positions you are trying to fill and be juggling all sorts of details and candidates for each. If you aren't very good at the multitasking, you could become flustered. But assuming you have skills, you'll be more energized than overwhelmed; hey, you're looking at six possible commissions. And you're not a surgeon; you don't have anyone's life in your hands. Although you do have their careers.

Pros

Good money, honey.

It's a social job; you'll be talking to people all day.

It's gratifying to help people get a new job.

Cons

You're on the phone, all damn day.

The nagging feeling you could always be doing more, making one more placement.

If the industry you specialize in is doing badly, you're doing badly. It's out of your hands.

Boom, You're a Headhunter. You Wake Up And . . .

This assumes you're a headhunter in the legal field.

9:15 AM: You arrive at the office and sit at your desk. You delight in the sugary goodness of a donut as you check your e-mail and try to organize the day.

9:30 AM: Well, there's no organizing the day today. You've already gotten two calls in a row from clients looking for senior-level paralegals. You go through your database of candidates and create a list of people you think might fit. And then call them.

12:00 PM: You've found two people so far who might be interested and left a few messages. In the meantime, you got a call from a civil lawyer candidate of yours who is sick of his firm and wants out.

12:30 PM: You have lunch with an environmental lawyer who is looking to leave his firm. This is the first time you've met, and frankly, you're quite impressed.

1:45 PM: When you get back to your office, what the heck, you call a firm you work with that does environmental law. "I know you aren't looking," you tell them, "but I have a great candidate you might just want to meet." Just like that, they want to meet him. You send an e-mail to the lawyer's personal account and tell him the news. If that dude isn't blown away by that . . .

3:00 PM: You schedule interviews for a couple of paralegals at both of the firms from the morning. You have some other people who have called in, but these are the best fits, and you don't want to overwhelm or waste anyone's time.

5:00 PM: You get a call from a client where your candidate had a second interview earlier in the week. They want to hire her! You call her cell phone and catch her as she's leaving her office.

6:00 PM: You pack up and head out. It's been a good day.

I Want to Hunt Heads. How the Hell Do I Get This Job?

There are a few ways folks get into the business. First, you can graduate from college, go to a large headhunting firm, and interview for an entry-level job. If hired, you'll become a recruiter, someone who is on the phone all day talking to possible candidates. You'll slowly learn the ropes, and learn about the industry the firm (or the division you're in) specializes in, and then move up the ladder. But be aware, you are not going to start off advising candidates or clients on career moves or good potential matches. No one is going to take career advice from a twenty-two-year-old with no experience or working knowledge of the field.

Another way, and generally the recommended one, is to get some real experience in a field, and then move over into the headhunting world and help staff it. You start already knowing the industry, and, more important, people in the industry. And knowing people is what it's all about. Let's say you were an engineering major, and when you left school you worked as an engineer. After a few years, you might realize that although you like engineering, well, you don't really love working as an engineer. But you can stay in the field and leverage your experience as an engineering headhunter.

When you get an interview for a position at a headhunting firm, you want to be seen as someone who is incredibly motivated to be successful. Not just by the cold hard cash, but by filling positions with the right people. Which of course leads to cold hard cash, but there's an important distinction. You're not working just in your own interest, but in your clients' and candidates' interests as well. Many headhunting firms have a mission statement that says something ethical to that effect, and they take it seriously. Be careful you don't come off as someone in it just for the Benjamins. No one wants to hire a used-car salesman. Except a used-car dealer, of course.

Resources

Whatever field you may wish to become a recruiter for, you should read all of the industry magazines and sites associated with it. In terms of recruitment, itzbigblog.com is an amazing resource. It bills itself as a blog "serving the unserved, recruiters, job-seekers and quiet working professionals." There you'll find posts, articles, and a ton of links about all things headhunter. Another site to check out is A Recruiter's View, recruitersview.blogspot.com. More of a traditional blog than itzbigblog, it still offers some vital information and another great list of recruitment links.

> Nobody really goes to school to be a headhunter. What happens quite a lot is someone comes in to a headhunter to interview for a position in his or her field, and next thing you know, the interview turns into an interview for a headhunting job.
> —**Michael Goldstein, manager, Quantum Management Services**

Information Architect

A hh, the Internet. Friend, confidant, secret lover. And who makes sure all your favorite Internet sites are organized and built so that they are intuitive to you, the user, as you go through them? Information architects. And just like their name says, they are the architects of Web sites, the ones who make sense of the site's cyberspace to visitors, much the same way a traditional architect (see the chapter on architects) makes sense of physical space in a building. A bathroom here, a kitchen there for architects; a navigation bar here, a Back button there for those in IA. Information architects, however, don't wear hard hats while constructing a site. Although they do sometimes wear those carpal tunnel wrist supports.

That Sounds Like a Lot

It *is* a lot. The best way to understand what IAs do is to consider them the people in charge of a Web site's "usability." They don't design the site's look; they don't write the words on the site; they don't create interesting animations that might transport you from one place to the next. Think back to the building metaphor. An architect doesn't pick the couch, but she does decide what part of the space is the living room and that you enter the living room from the hallway.

IAs' jobs are much the same, but in cyberspace. They are responsible for planning out every page of the Web site they are helping create—what the navigation is between pages (click on a button? rollover?), how the navigation will be structured (from where to where makes sense), what are all the things the user can do and what's the result of those actions, how much information there will be on each page, how users know where they are, and so on.

IAs spend a lot of time working with other key members of the team responsible for building a site—technologists who program; designers who shape the look and feel; and writers who, um, write the words. There are lots of meetings and brainstorming sessions that happen before and during the planning process; it's not an isolated field.

An information architect is responsible for planning out every page, answering questions like what is the navigation, how will the navigation be structured, where do all the links go, what are all the things the user can do and what's the result of those actions?
—Jeremy Bernstein, vice president, director of information architecture, Deutsch, New York

IA is the bridge between graphics and technology, responsible for creating user experience.
—Ronni Kimm, freelance information architect

Where Do IAs Work?

Wherever a professional-level Web site is needed and is being built, an IA person is there. So IAs can work on staff at advertising agencies helping build marketing sites for clients, or at all kinds of corporations—from record labels and movie studios to pharmaceutical companies and big retailers.

IAs can also be freelancers. They may hop from project to project; they may even do consulting from home. At the time of writing, IA is a highly sought position for many firms; there are simply not enough trained people around. Right now, freelancers are making a killing.

Wherever IAs do work, though, for the most part, the office setting is casual. It's a holdover from the Internet boom of the nineties, but even in the most conservative of firms, usually the interactive division is allowed some dress code and behavioral leeway. They're "the wacky Internet guys." You won't need to really own any suits, although you will occasionally need to wear some khakis or a skirt.

What Attributes Make for a Good IA?

First off, you have to love the Web, surfing around, and dissecting how sites are built. New user experiences should make you feel warm and tingly. IAs are often the "pretty creative, but also pretty analytical" types. They must be organized, able to break complex problems down and see many steps ahead, as a single click on a site can set off twenty-five different reactions on the back end.

But IAs needn't be completely logical, like Spock. They are analytical people who use systematic thinking to evaluate different situations, but they can also develop creative solutions that make sense to regular folks. As with any job where you understand the subject matter more than the person who is paying you to do the job, it's important to be a good communicator. Once you have ideas, they're no good if you can't convince other people.

Hours?

As an IA, you'll work fairly hard. Fifty-hour weeks and the occasional weekend tend to be the norm, but these amounts differ with each firm. Unfortunately, you'll find that sweatshops abound in the Internet field. Many times you'll be working toward a deadline (most sites need to be up and operational by a certain date), and as the time ticks down, the long nights begin. You'll also spend a lot, a *lot* of time on e-mail and IM, plus you'll have some sort of wire-

Developing a site is a collaborative process, but in general, information architects essentially are responsible for creating a site's blueprint. Then, usually an art director, a graphic designer, and a copywriter from the team will follow the blueprint to build the site, as well as the technology people, who program and set up the inner workings.
> —Jeremy Bernstein, vice president, director of information architecture, Deutsch, New York

It's important to understand what's possible, but even more than really understanding technical details is understanding consumers and users, and what makes sense to them and what doesn't. That's foremost. There are always technology people who you can turn to and say, "Hey I want to do this, or what's the problem with this?" But what you're really supposed to be the expert on is, "Will visitors be able to understand this?"
> —Jeremy Bernstein, vice president, director of information architecture, Deutsch, New York

less device so that you can be found whenever and wherever to deal with site issues and problems.

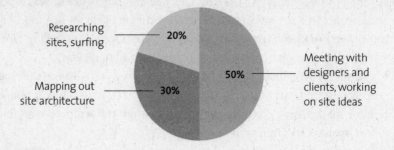

Salary?

This is a relatively new field, and thus there are no statistics from the Bureau of Labor Statistics or the like yet. But there have been some surveys: according to a 2005 salary survey by the Information Architecture Institute (iainsti tute.org), the average salary for IAs is around $80,000. Starting salaries are usually in the high $40,000s, while 25 percent of respondents made more than $100,000.

And if you are a freelancer who's proven himself or herself and works constantly, you could even make in the neighborhood of $250,000. That's a nice neighborhood; very few rusty cars on front lawns.

Stress-o-Meter: 6.5 (1 being a shepherd, 10 being a sheriff)

In general, the stress of the job comes from working on too many projects at once. That comes from the lack of qualified IAs around at this time, as well as the "thriftiness" of Internet firms still figuring out how to monetize certain services. Couple that with deadlines on each project, and there can be a fair bit of stress as the clock winds down.

Pros

Great opportunity to be creative.

Exposes you to lots of businesses and types of people, both internally and externally.

It's always changing; you are helping pioneer a new field.

Cons:

It's always changing, which can make it hard to keep up.

Clients may not respect what it takes to come up with a good Web site or a good interactive product.

Sitting in front of a computer for so many hours mushes the mind.

Ta-Da! You Are an Information Architect. You Wake Up And . . .

10:00 AM: You arrive at work. As you suck down some OJ, you check your e-mail and surf some new sites you heard were cool.

10:30 AM: You meet with a designer and a writer to talk about a site you are creating for a retail company. They want it to be fun, but also easy for people to buy stuff. You brainstorm simple ways to accomplish both, as they have a small budget.

12:00 PM: Back in your office, you begin to map out a different project. This one is a video-sharing site. You plan how people will be able to search out videos, and then save them to a favorites page in the fewest clicks.

3:00 PM: The designer on the retail project IMs you to check out a few sites he likes the look of, for reference. You surf to them and discuss the pros and cons of each.

3:50 PM: You chain-chew some gum and head to a 4:00 meeting to present your ideas on the video-sharing site to your boss.

4:30 PM: After waiting for your boss, who is always late, you receive some good constructive criticism. She offers a few additional insights. You head back to your desk and incorporate them into your schematic.

6:00 PM: You have a bit more thinking to do, but you head home. You'll do it on your laptop from your couch.

This Seems Architecturally Sound. How the Hell Do I Become an IA?

The first thing you need to understand is that the current crop of IAs never intended to become IAs. It just sort of happened during the Internet boom. They come from all kinds of backgrounds, including industrial design, architecture, and, most commonly, liberal arts. Each employer, then, has slightly different criteria as to what they are looking for in an entry-level candidate. But they *are* looking for candidates; this is not the most difficult field to get into if you fit the basic profile.

One thing everyone wants is a love of the Web. Perhaps you've built some Web sites—for yourself, or for friends or family. Great. Show those sites and the thinking and schematics that led to the completed project. Demonstrate that you have those abilities. Some IA departments don't hire entry-level positions. In that case, get into the interactive department where you can, and then befriend some IAs.

Seek out headhunters. Headhunters place a lot of IA jobs and will know IAs personally and what they may be looking for in a candidate. Many times IA jobs get split to two different types of headhunters: "creative" ones and "tech-

> When I hire an information architect, I look for design training, whether it's a design degree or classes, that shows that you've made an effort to know design, especially functional design.
> —Jeremy Bernstein, vice president, director of information architecture, Deutsch, New York

nological" ones. Creative ones tend to have IA jobs in the advertising and design worlds, whereas the tech ones tend to have jobs building internal training
systems for JPMorgan and the like. You can find these headhunters on job sites
like monster.com or even craigslist.com.

Once you do get an interview, if asked, be able to make a strong argument
about why you built a site a certain way. It's not just that they want to see the
strength of your convictions, but more that you've considered alternatives and
then picked the best route to accomplish something for a reason.

Finally, when you start your search, remember that this is an industry in
transition, and new, different-sounding job titles are being introduced and redefined. At their core, though, these still are information architect gigs. Some
new titles are *interaction designer, user interface designer, usability specialist/en-
gineer, experience designer, experience lead,* and *business analyst,* to name a few.
Don't let 'em throw you.

Resources

Some schools are starting to offer IA training, and these will continue to grow
in number. It's not required; most working IAs don't have this schooling (nor
did it exist when they started), but it could give you a leg up. If you're interested in formal training, try these for starters: the ITP program at NYU, Illi-
nois Institute of Technology in Chicago, the Carnegie Mellon Interaction
Program, and the UCLA Media and Design Program.

To stay on top of Web trends, well-built sites, and technology, check out the
following sites, magazines, and hey, a book too:

Slashdot.com

Newstoday.com

Iaslash.org

Boxesandarrows.com

Goodexperience.com (also has job postings)

Information Architecture Institute: iainstitute.org

Communication Arts magazine

Information Architecture for the World Wide Web by Peter Morville and
Louis Rosenfeld

Investment Banker

When you need money, say, for college tuition or to buy a home, you probably borrow it from a bank. But when large corporations need to bum a half billion dollars or so, they can't go down to the corner Chase. For vast amounts of capital, investment banks, and the investment bankers who work at them, are the answer. Investment bankers specialize in helping corporations, or even governments, raise hundreds of millions, even billions of dollars, through a variety of financial markets and instruments. Just a bit more dough than you need for tuition, even if you're attending private school.

Investment banking is a storied career, probably because of the large amounts of money one can make doing it, and the occasional Wall Street scandal where the term *investment banker* is bandied about. It's an incredibly competitive field to try to enter; in fact, let's start with a rough little fact: if you are a senior in college, it's almost too late for you to begin thinking about an entry-level job in investment banking. Top-tier candidates begin seeking internships as sophomores and juniors. Fear not, though; you can still get into the game a different way, as a post-MBA associate.

One other note: with all of the SEC regulations, corporate policies, and simply the sheer amount of money being handled discreetly, all investment bankers interviewed for this chapter asked to be anonymous.

So What Do You Do at the Bank?

Investment bankers are the "front end," meaning they're the ones at the firm who interact with the bank's clients and help them strategically figure out their banking needs. Once they help clients sort out their goals, bankers then turn to others in the firm—capital markets people who specialize in different financial instruments, like bonds, for example—to help best execute and implement them. These goals can be things other than raising capital. Investment bankers also deal with other strategic-planning decisions, like mergers and acquisitions. For example, let's say you have a client that is a smaller company looking to be acquired for a ton of cash by a larger one. Or maybe they don't want to be bought outright, but instead want to merge with a competitor and become stronger. Investment bankers act as advisors or "go-betweens"

My client, Company A, calls and says "Hey, we're looking at doing an acquisition of a company, so we need to raise $500 million, where can we get it?" And my job as investment banker is to know enough about all the markets that are available to them so I can bring in the right expert at the firm who can help them get the money in the optimal way. Ultimately then, the investment bank acts as the middleman between the company that wants to raise the capital and pools of investors who have capital to invest.
—Mr. Anonymous
I-Banker

to bring the two sides together. And investment bankers don't just sit around and wait passively for the call. They actively "call on" their clients and offer strategic advice, with the goal of becoming their close and trusted advisors for the long haul.

Investment banking is a broadly used term these days, but can pretty much be divided into three main areas: corporate finance, sales and trading, and research analysis. Corporate finance basically means raising money for corporate clients, which is the bread and butter of traditional investment banking. Sales and trading is where salespeople and traders buy and sell securities and commodities. And research analysts (different from the entry-level *analyst* title) are bankers who publish research pieces that recommend buys, sells, and holds of various fixed-income and equity instruments. Many traders and clients of the firm rely on their judgments; if their recommendations perform well, theirs can be one of the higher compensated positions. Within each of these groups are different industry focuses. So you could be solely covering a field like technology, healthcare, or retail.

When you first start, of course, you aren't exactly golfing with the client, discussing billion-dollar moves. The entry-level, straight-out-of-undergrad investment banker position is called *analyst*. It's a 24/7 job, and that is not much of an exaggeration. You are on call, like a medical resident or fraternity pledge, and there are no real excuses. Analysts are often told to purchase travel insurance for vacations, because they may have to reschedule them if they get staffed last minute on a deal. You'll work in a group, led by a managing director; underneath him or her are directors, then vice presidents, then associates, and then finally you. The higher-level bankers will be working closely with the client, as well as trying to land prospective clients. No matter what is needed, it's up to the group to pull off. So at the lowest levels, this means a lot of research and analysis. You could be asked to find industry reports, fill in complicated and tedious forms, work on financial models, prepare and proofread presentation materials, even simply make printouts—whatever is requested of you. And lots will be asked.

The next level up, *associate,* is generally a post-MBA position. Perhaps 10 to 15 percent of associates don't hold an MBA degree, but were promoted after three years' service as an analyst. Some associates worked as analysts and then went back to school for their MBAs before returning to the field. For others, the associate position is their first toehold in the investment banking world. Since getting the analyst job, as you'll see, is incredibly competitive, this post-MBA associate position is a good possible entryway to consider.

What Makes for a Good Investment Banker?

Being a masochist, for starters. To be an investment banker, you have to be a profoundly hardworking individual. You need to have thick skin, as the office is a high-stress area. A lot will be thrown at you, not always softly, and sometimes when you're not looking. You'll need to be, or quickly become, highly proficient at Excel and PowerPoint. And when working in these, or on anything, you have to have an eye for minute and mundane detail, like whether the font on a footnote is the same font that is used throughout a presentation. Even though that's not what makes or breaks a deal, when incorrect, it *is* what drives senior management crazy. Seriously, you will get a talking to for something as seemingly small as the wrong use of quotation marks. It takes a high level of discipline to proofread an analysis when it's three in the morning, and you know you have to be back at you desk, fresh as a daisy, in just six hours. The person who takes that extra hour to double check his or her work is the kind of person who succeeds in investment banking. Finally, you have to be willing to put aside short-term pleasures, like getting a beer with friends, for long-term gain, like being able to afford to fly to Germany first class on a whim for Heffenweiser.

A Busy Office Filled with Power Suits?

Investment banks are hectic places. So although there is a collegial, almost fraternity-like atmosphere with plenty of overworked gallows humor, it's not a place where gadflies and office clowns are really admired.

Most major investment banks are professional, suit-and-tie establishments. The technology division, which deals with the most laid-back clients, the dot-coms, might be slightly—and only slightly—more laid back. But for the most part, you'll be dressed up.

How Many Hours Must You Invest?

To start, it's insanity. Eighteen-hour days plus weekends are not considered unreasonable. Of course there will be lighter times, but those are few and far between. As you get higher up in the bank, time does become more manageable; it's still a lot of hours, you just have more control over when you work them. You really have to love the investment game, and get sucked into and enjoy the grind; otherwise you won't want to keep at it, even with the great compensation.

This assumes you are an analyst:

Let's put it this way—you do not want to be the analyst who's always chatting or hanging out in someone else's cube. Because what are you really doing? Clearly not what you are supposed to, and if you don't have stuff to do there's always someone who needs help.
  —Mr. Anonymous
    I-Banker

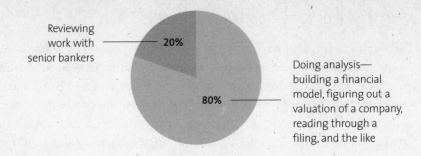

Reviewing work with senior bankers — 20%

Doing analysis—building a financial model, figuring out a valuation of a company, reading through a filing, and the like — 80%

I'm the staffer for my group, which means I'm in charge of allocating analysts and associates to help pull together whatever is required. Last night I got an e-mail from a first-year analyst giving me an update of what she was expecting her week to look like, and she reported that last week she had worked 110 hours, and that this week looked like it would be 115. So the long hours you hear about are not hyperbole.

—Mr. Other Anonymous I-Banker

You're Going to Need a Bigger Wallet

Investment bankers make bank. Their actual salaries aren't really that outrageously high; it's the bonuses that bring in the Lamborghini money. Take a managing director. He could easily make $1,000,000, $2,000,000, or $3,000,000 a year, but his actual salary is probably around $200,000. The rest is bonus.

Coming in as a first-year analyst, you can expect to make around $60,000, with close to a 100 percent bonus, meaning you'll make more than $100,000 as a twenty-three-year-old. Not bad. You'll have no time to spend it, of course. Associates can make between $300,000 and $500,000, and vice presidents between $500,000 and $1,000,000! Payscale.com reports a New York associate-level investment banker's median wage to be $82,007, with a median bonus of $61,804.

Stress-o-Meter: 9.5 (1 being a blimp pilot, 10 being an air force bombardier)

It's pretty stressful, especially at first. There's a lot on the line and you are just working, working, working. Some people leave after being an analyst and don't come back. High compensation for high stress.

Pros	Cons
You'll make a lot of money.	All you do is work. Your social life is kaput for a while.
You are working with smart, quick-witted people.	It's a rough business; there's no room for error.
If you like the business world, you're working in the engine room.	

Cha-Ching. You Are an Investment Banker. You Wake Up And . . .

This assumes you are an analyst.

8:15 AM: You arrive at the office. You (and the rest of the analysts) always aim to get in before your superiors; they like it that way. You check your voice mail and your e-mail immediately. You don't expect anything pressing, as you checked before you went to sleep last night at 3 AM.

8:30 AM: The rest of the office starts trickling in. Before any new work lands on your desk, you try to finish up the research project you've been slaving away on all week.

9:00 AM: You get an e-mail from one of the VPs. Looks like you'll definitely be finishing it, as she'd like to see that research project by lunch. Your adrenalin kicks in, and your fingers fly.

11:00 AM: You e-mail it to her, then attend a status meeting with the rest of the team.

1:00 PM: You eat a ham sandwich in front of your computer while you get started on your next project, creating a financial model. You also have a stack of pitch books to work on. It's going to be another late one.

2:00 PM: When you are an analyst, anyone can walk up to you anytime and give you more work to do. It happens right now. An associate wants you to do some research, and he needs the research tomorrow first thing. You try not to hyperventilate as he takes you through what he'd like done.

6:30 PM: You order dinner, for which you can put in a receipt. The company is happy to buy you dinner, knowing that you will be working for many more hours. You eat with two other analysts and talk about sports. It's a nice reprieve.

7:30 PM: You are jamming on the research when you get a call about more work coming your way. Weekend work. Work your firm has promised to a client by Monday. You cancel plans for brunch with your folks.

12:00 AM: You print out your first pass on the research report due in the morning and discover tons of grammatical errors. You begin to fix them.

3:00 AM: You think you're done, but to be honest, you're so tired you can hardly read. You plan to get in extra early tomorrow and double-check it before turning it in.

I Love the Smell of Money in the Morning.
How the Hell Do I Get This Job?

There are really two ways to break in. One is as an analyst. On-campus interviews can start as early as first semester of your sophomore or junior year, for a very difficult-to-score summer internship. If you get one, assuming you don't do something ridiculous during your internship like photocopy your bottom or spill a Diet Coke into the company server, you are in the fabled catbird seat in terms of landing the actual analyst position come graduation.

If you don't get an internship, it's not impossible to get an analyst position, but it's a little harder. Most banks recruit only on the top campuses, so you're competing against kids who are studying finance at Wharton, Columbia, and the University of Michigan business school, for example. The ideal background is a finance major, followed by accounting and economics, but non-business majors with very high GPAs and some economics education are always hired each year. Remember, the higher you go in investment banking, the more client relationship work, and thus the more personable you need to be. And sometimes the most interesting people don't major in business. Usually, investment banks will interview at campuses near them; banks out of Chicago will recruit in the Midwest, for example.

The second way into a career in investment banking is to get an MBA and then start as an associate. As an MBA candidate you will primarily get a job through an on-campus interview with visiting recruiters from the firm, followed by interviews on site at the investment bank. Pretty straightforward and—assuming you had a business job before attending graduate school and the program you are in is one of the better ones—easier to get than an analyst position. Not a piece of cake, mind you, but comparatively easier. So it's not the end of the world if you don't get past the hurdles to an analyst job. One thing that will help you, though, is if the business job you had before the MBA program was at a large, well-respected corporation, an IBM or a Verizon, for example.

So if you do get the analyst interview, what will you be asked? Well, you'll be quizzed on your background; if you were an accounting major, expect accounting questions. And if you are a non-business major, you will be asked some basic finance questions, just to make sure you at least have an idea of the field. A routine one is, "How much would you value Company X at?" The interviewers aren't looking for an accurate dollar figure, they just want to know if you understand how to figure valuations. You should be able to discuss all three basic ways: comparables, precedent transactions, and discounted cash flow analysis.

What investment banks really want to confirm, on top of all this, is that prospective candidates know what they are getting themselves into. That the stress and long hours will not be a surprise, that they will not be unhappy and quit. Show them that you understand and are ready, willing, and able to make the commitment.

Resources

Keep up to date on the Wall Street world with *The Wall Street Journal* (wsj.com), *Barron's* (barrons.com), the *Financial Times* (ft.com), *The Economist* (economist.com), and *Institutional Investor* (institutionalinvestor.com). Watch CNBC and visit cnbc.com. These are really the staples. Investment bankers are too busy to read much else.

Jewelry Designer

Who among us doesn't love bling? Jewelry has always been an important part of fashion, and today jewelry designers, or jewelers, are out from behind the scenes and sometimes celebrities in their own right. Do you have a good eye for detail? Were you the kind of kid who went crazy with the beads and lanyard in arts and crafts? Is "Rhinestone Cowboy" the ringtone on your cell phone? Do read on, dear reader.

What Do Jewelry Designers Actually Do?

First and foremost, they design jewelry, sometimes completely original pieces, other times reproductions. Rings, earrings, necklaces, brooches, assorted pieces for new and exotic piercings, you name it. Some manufacture their own jewelry from their designs; they have an anvil, hammers, and other tools that look like they might belong in an S&M dungeon. Most others, especially at the mass-market level, outsource the production to commercial vendors who do that work—some as far away as China.

Jewelry designers may sell their creations in their own store or on their own Web site. Or they may not even have a store; they might sell their wares to buyers from large stores, like Kay or Macy's or Barney's. Some do all of the above. Or they may design a line of jewelry that doesn't have their name on it at all. For example, a company like Banana Republic might contract them to design their spring line of jewelry. Or they can even take a full-time job at Banana Republic and work in the accessories department.

If a jeweler does sell to the larger stores, a lot of that selling happens at trade shows.

What Kind of Person Is Good at This Job?

First, naturally, you have to be fashionable and have a good sense of aesthetics—jewelry is, after all, fashion. You have to be someone who can design, someone who could easily be designing something else if it weren't jewelry. Also, you must be meticulous.

You have to be artful, but you can't be a flaky artist. You'll be working with valuable materials; you can't exactly lose any, let alone over- or under-order

My store has a boutique in front and my workshop in the back. You can see my bench and all of my tools out in the open. It's kind of taking that old-school idea about what a trade is really supposed to be. So I'm selling not only the jewelry, but I'm also selling the experience that I made the jewelry and it's not mass-produced. There is a person there who can adjust it and fix whatever's not working.
—Hannah Clark, jewelry designer and owner, Hannah Clark

160

gold or diamonds. And like in any business, it also helps to be extroverted. A little bit of a sales personality, especially if you are representing your own work and trying to get boutiques and individuals to pay you for it, is indispensable.

Fashion is an oversaturated, competitive business, and jewelry design is no exception. With a few designs and a Web site, there really isn't that much of a barrier to saying you're a jewelry designer. Thus, loads of failed ones are scattered around the fashion world. Know going in that you will have to work hard and be persistent and, frankly, a little lucky to be successful.

So Where Do You Work Every Day?

It depends. Some jewelers are part of a large company, some work in the back of large stores, some do everything in their single-employee boutiques/workshops, and some have their own studios with no retail space at all. Almost all of the working situations are laid back and artsy. Jewelry is supposed to be beautiful, but also, well, spiritual in a way—these are pieces designed to have meaning. The workspaces, although filled with design equipment and possibly cluttered, reflect that. It is still a "trade." Large jewelers' offices are divided between the industrial and the "office" office.

Even if you are a single-person entity, you'll still work with others, such as suppliers of gold and precious metals, and specialists like stone setters (so that the diamond doesn't fall out of the ring you designed). You might buy crystal from the Czech Republic and resin from Europe, and you'll deal with the vendors of these items. Plus, if you outsource the actual production (you design one set of earrings, someone else produces a thousand more), you'll be coordinating all of that manufacturing. And hopefully, you'll be talking with the fashion media—magazines and Web sites—that want to use your jewelry for shoots and fashion stories, maybe even on a celebrity.

Hours?

If you are one of ten jewelry designers at a large place, you may work traditional nine-to-five or ten-to-six type hours. If you own your own store and design in a studio in the back, you might work the store's hours, say twelve to seven, plus some extra hours for design, six days a week. You also may spend some time traveling to trade shows and the like. If you own a larger business, then you will be managing others, traveling, and working the longer hours of anyone who owns a bigger business. You'll probably have a smartphone and be on your wireless carrier's unlimited data plan. On the other hand, you'll probably be making more money and buying fancier sneakers.

You have to be interested in the finest details because if, for example, you don't get a clasp just right on a necklace, then it's not a good piece of jewelry. If you're going to be great at it, you can't be detail-oriented enough.
—Hannah Clark, jewelry designer and owner, Hannah Clark

We show at trade shows, which are similar to fashion shows in the clothing business. These are really, really high-end boutique trade shows and everyone has a booth, like a super-upscale science fair. The buyers come and shop your booth. Then they buy in quantity. If they are a small boutique they might only buy fifty pieces, if they are a department store, they may buy five thousand pieces. We also have a retail Web site.
—Tracy Kahn, jewelry designer and president, Paste by Tracy Kahn

Magazine editors will come to us and say that they are doing a fall story, and it's on the beach and the theme is salsa, can they borrow some jewelry for that photo shoot? It's a symbiotic relationship, because we get our name in the magazine with our jewelry, and they get to pick from whatever they want to style a great editorial piece.

—Tracy Kahn, jewelry designer and president, Paste by Tracy Kahn

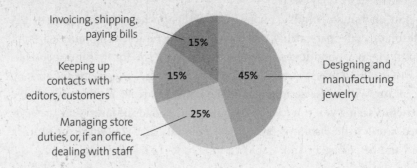

- Invoicing, shipping, paying bills — 15%
- Keeping up contacts with editors, customers — 15%
- Managing store duties, or, if an office, dealing with staff — 25%
- Designing and manufacturing jewelry — 45%

Salary?

Jewelry designers say, "This is the type of career you get into because you love it." That sentiment is usually code for, "It's not easy to make a lot of money." There's a huge range of salaries, from people who struggle to pay the rent (the majority) to those who sell their designs on the Home Shopping Network and, yes, make a killing.

According to the Bureau of Labor Statistics, the mean annual wage for those who work with jewelry and precious stones is $32,830, with a range from $17,590 to $53,240. These numbers may be a bit low, because included are lower-paying jobs in the field, such as stone setters and diamond polishers.

Stress-o-Meter: 5 (1 being a secret Santa, 10 being a Secret Service member)

It's not too bad. But for many jewelry designers, it's their name on the door, their reputation on the line, their own (and possibly) their employees' salaries to pay, and with that comes a fair amount of stress. Jewelry designing itself is a treat. It's the business part that adds the stress.

Pros

Getting paid for creative self-expression.
Having people love what you make, and pay money for it.
Seeing your designs in magazines.
Being an important part of the fashion world.

Cons

Fashion is a tough business; it's extremely competitive.
A lot of luck is involved.
You always have to come up with something new, even if you don't feel like it.
If it's your small business, tasks like bookkeeping and sweeping up take time away from designing.

Congratulations, You're a Jewelry Designer. You Wake Up And . . .

This assumes you own your own jewelry store and work in the back.

8:00 AM: You drink coffee and flip through a few fashion magazines that arrived yesterday, checking out the accessory trends.

10:00 AM: Freshly showered, you arrive at the store two hours before you officially open. You do some bookkeeping and answer e-mails in a fury. You order some 18K gold for an engagement ring you are custom-making for a client.

12:00 PM: You open the store. Your lone employee arrives and runs the sales area, while you go to the back and sketch some designs. After a while, you drop the pen and pick up some wax, working on sculpting the engagement ring prototype.

2:00 PM: A retail buyer comes in, and together you eat the light takeout lunch you've brought in. You show her some of your latest designs, and she places a juicy order on one particular set of earrings.

4:00 PM: You join the salesperson in the sales area. You like to see people as they look at, and hopefully purchase, your stuff. You answer some questions about one particular necklace. And then the customer buys it!

5:00 PM: More designing. There's a trade show coming up and you'd like to have one or two more pieces to bring to it.

7:30 PM: You close the store, say good-bye to your salesperson, and head out to a dinner that you are having with an editor of a fashion magazine. You bring some photos of your latest designs, and make sure to wear a few nice pieces.

I Want People Dripping in My Jewels.
How the Hell Do I Get Started?

First, and maybe this goes without saying, you need to be able to make jewelry. Not just design it, but also physically make it. At least the basics. There are a lot of paths to becoming a jewelry designer, but somewhere along the way you'll want to pick up these skills. Yes, there are jewelers who never learn how to make actual jewelry, who simply design on a computer and then send the designs overseas and have them made. But many jewelry designers frown at this approach, because some design ideas may not work when made tangible.

Where do you learn both design and manufacturing? Some art schools have jewelry programs, but sadly, a lot have done away with them and offer only a class or two. Both Parsons and FIT in New York City, near the fashion and jewelry districts, have such classes. And even if the classes are limited, they

I can't say that you can expect to make a lot of money, but there's potential. Sky's the limit, really, I mean it's jewelry. There's a huge range. You could struggle. You could end up making a setting for the Hope Diamond. You never know.
—Hannah Clark, jewelry designer and owner, Hannah Clark

may be worth taking just to meet the teacher and to possibly make connections toward internships (discussed shortly). Craft schools also teach how to make jewelry, but there, a lot of people are doing it as more of a hobby. Some jewelry designers went to art school and majored in product design or industrial design, which is pretty closely related and teaches you a lot of skills that will help in creating jewelry.

Even if you do take classes, most jewelry designers will tell you that although such experiences may help with design, they leave out important things like how to create a production line and get it sold, how to get into a store, and how to get insurance. The truth is, it's not the easiest path to find and follow in school. In this old field, most knowledge has been handed down within it, rather than taught. (This is not to say you shouldn't get a university education or a general art education that will inform your every design.) One highly recommended way to learn is to work for a jeweler, to apprentice. Or intern. (As it is a trade, the word *apprentice* often trumps *intern*.) It's totally old world; you'll be learning from the person you want to become.

The other place you can intern is at a *label*—a fashion house that also does jewelry, in its accessories department. There you'll see jewelry designers at work as well. It's a whole different world from an apprenticeship at a jeweler's; if you can do both, though, you'll walk away with more understanding than you could ever get in class.

Finally, as much fun as it is to express yourself creatively, this is a business, not just an outlet for you to make pretty, sparkly things. It comes down to how much does it cost to make the piece, and how much can you sell it for. Reality. What a bummer.

> The best thing to do is if you see a jewelry shop and you like the vibe, you go in and politely say that you want to learn how to make jewelry; can you possibly help clean castings or apprentice? Then after helping with the grunt work, you can look over the jeweler's shoulders and absorb.
> —Hannah Clark, jewelry designer and owner, Hannah Clark

Resources

To keep current on jewelry trends, you should read all the fashion magazines and see what they're showcasing. The most important of these is the bible, *Women's Wear Daily.* These are some more crafty magazines that are also helpful: *Beadwork, Ornament, Metalsmith, Crafts Report,* and *Art Jeweler.* Plus, a myriad of craft books are out there. And keep your eyes open in used bookstores for vintage jewelry-making books; these contain how-to techniques that have since lost popularity with publishers but many jewelers still know and love.

Online, for inspiration, check in daily at style.com. Jewelrydesigners guild.com is an online community for those working in the "jewelry arts." Ganoksin.com has forums where you can ask burning questions like, "Does anyone know a great opal supplier?" and get answers from other wired jewelers.

Life Coach

The saying "Get a life," seems to have been replaced these days by the kinder, gentler "Get a life coach." Life coaches help people gain perspective, solve problems, achieve goals, and overcome obstacles, mostly in their professional lives, but also sometimes in their personal lives. However, they don't do any psychoanalyzing; there's no delving into the past about issues one might have had with his or her mother. If you're not sure what you want to do, or have tried several different careers but haven't yet found one you love, congratulations! You already have one of the most common backgrounds of life coaches.

Sometimes there are just too many choices and not enough guidance. When it comes to careers, things are changing so fast and there's so much information that it can get overwhelming. People in search of life goals can get caught up in all this information and lose sight of the right path to take. That's where coaches come in.

Coaching involves facets of psychology, sociology, and career counseling and mentoring. The type and level of help is different from coach to coach and according to client need. A writing coach may help one client tangibly understand and take all the steps toward getting published: getting an agent, weighing the pros and cons of a publicist, and so on. He might help another simply become more organized in her life, so she can *get to* writing. It varies.

Coaches are perhaps best known for their career and business advice, but you could look at Dr. Phil as an example of a life coach who helps people with all different aspects of their lives. Yes, Dr. Phil is a life coach. You see, you do learn something new every day. The career is becoming more and more popular, and with that popularity has come a little bit of controversy.

Use Your Life Experience. Carve a Niche.

Coaches often specialize. There are coaches for teachers and coaches for artists. People in the field often find niches where they are uniquely qualified to assist; for example, a former professor would make an excellent coach for anyone in academia.

There are all kinds of niches. Pick a field—retail, entertainment, academic;

> Basically, a life coach helps people figure stuff out. I guess you could say I'm a stand-in for the role that a family member or clergy used to play. I'm an objective person who has expertise in careers and building self-confidence.
> —Marta Kagan, CEO and president, Lifeline Coaching

> Coaching is different from therapy, which deals more with the past. Coaching is more about achieving very clear and concrete present and future goals. Pathology should be absent from it. A coach should give an objective perspective on choices, not so much family relations or childhood traumas, like a therapist.
> —Marta Kagan, CEO and president, Lifeline Coaching

there's even a life coaching niche, coaches who help other coaches. Yep. The key is to use your own life lessons to help others. Once you are doing well in one area, it becomes easier to expand to related areas. Specialists also tend to make more money than generalists, and the networking to find new clients becomes easier as well.

Let Me Get This Straight.
There's No Entry-Level Position in Coaching?

No, there's pretty much not. You can't really get a junior-level gig in this job. Most coaches were already part of the workforce for a few years when they decided, "To hell with this," and got into coaching. It makes sense that many of these people have had several unfulfilling jobs and have become experts in dissatisfaction with many different career paths. Their goal as coaches is to help others not go down those roads. In fact, many life coaches got into the field themselves by having visited a life coach. Also, most coaches work on their own. There aren't really any life-coaching firms, although you could perhaps become a busy coach's administrative assistant.

So coaching is probably not going to be your first job out of college. A forty-year-old man with two kids contemplating a career change is going to have a hard time taking life advice from a twenty-two-year-old. But, this doesn't mean that just a few years down the road it wouldn't make sense. Or, if you were life coaching kids on attending certain schools, what to major in, or about joining certain clubs or frats, sort of like a peer-level guidance counselor, there might just be a niche for you. Hey, that's a pretty good job idea, actually. Hmmm.

Whose Lives Are You Coaching?

A typical client is someone who has been wrestling with a problem. He or she wants to make a change or accomplish a goal, but can't figure out the best way to go about it, or, sometimes, how to just get up and do it. A coach should give an objective perspective on choices that face the client, not delve into family relations or childhood traumas. These aren't people in need of intensive therapy. (If they are, you need to print them out Mapquest directions and get them to a therapist.) These are people with dreams and desires who need guidance to achieve them.

What Makes for a Good Coach?

Well, if you find people annoying, it's probably not for you. You have to be interested in helping people change and in expanding their thinking. You need to be insightful, so you can help clearly articulate what may seem foggy.

As far as educational background goes, a degree in psychology or social work is helpful, but really, you could have studied anything. There are no prerequisites. But as stated earlier, most life coaches have had some kind of professional experience that they use as a "platform."

Where Do Coaches Work?

A lot of coaches work from home. They often work alone; maybe they have a part-time assistant or, on occasion, a partner. The look of these offices is almost always business-casual, comfortable but not messy or shabby. And when seeing clients, coaches dress professionally, not in jeans and flip-flops.

A lot of coaching happens over the phone—a surprising amount, almost 70 percent of some coaches' workload. Many coaches even have "call-in classes," which are group sessions via conference call. And some of the life coach training programs, as you'll see shortly, are phone courses. It pays to invest in a serious speakerphone or headset. Coaches also have Web sites where they promote themselves and may sell informational DVDs, books, and recordings.

Hours?

They're not too hairy. Like any sort of professional who takes appointments, as a life coach you'll have fairly structured days and a schedule to abide by. As in the case of personal trainers, many appointments take place before work or after work. It's a flexible day, though, and you'll make your own calendar. Odds are you'll max out at forty hours a week, rather than start there as in some professions.

Because of the need to network to find clients, many life coaches find that they are even more social than they would normally be. And since the boundaries of coach/client relationships are not as strict as those of therapist/patient, you may actually become friends and socialize with your clients.

I was a coach before I even knew that "coaching" could be an actual career. [As a magazine writer] I had done an interview years before, and at the end of the interview, the person said to me, "Wow, that felt amazing. I feel like I should have paid you for that." And more than one person had said that to me and I never understood what that meant. But as I started learning about coaching, it was all crystal clear. I knew this was what I was going to do, and that I was going to be good at it.
—**Sophfronia Scott, author and owner, Creative Coaching Plans**

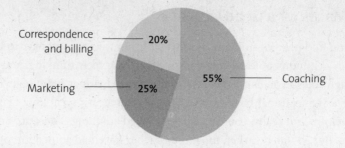

Cash for Coaching?

You're basically opening up your own business, so you can expect to make very little your first year; we're talking $20,000 or less. In fact, it's really a part-time job at this point. Thus, a lot of coaches don't recommend that you leap right into it and quit your job; it's better to ease in and go full time only once you start to build a client base. Also, you can do only so many one-on-one sessions in a day; you'll need to eventually branch out into Web sites, DVDs, and so on to continue to build your income. It takes some marketing know-how, but if you can make yourself a coaching commodity, you can be making six figures and up. On the flip side, how many Dr. Phils are out there?

There aren't many hard statistics on life coach salaries. *Entrepreneur Magazine* reported in 2002 that life coaches generally charge $300 to $500 per month for a weekly thirty-minute conversation (entrepreneur.com/magazine/home officemagcom/2002/january/47770-11.html). So if you made the top end of that, you'd need sixteen solid clients to make six figures.

> It's totally not stressful. The only time the number would go higher is let's say business is slow, and I start feeling financial pressure.
> —**Marta Kagan, CEO and president, Lifeline Coaching**

Stress-o-Meter: 4 (1 being a cat-sitter, 10 being a lion tamer)

It's not very stressful at all. You are helping solve others' problems, and they are not problems like anorexia or anything life-threatening, usually. What *is* a bit stressful is running your own business, finding new clients and income.

Pros

It's fun to help people get more out of their lives and see the results of your work.

Hours and days are flexible.

Opportunity to be creative and specialize and establish yourself as an expert.

It's all you.

Cons

Some people don't "get it" and associate you with an infomercial quack.

The money can be inconsistent.

Sometimes you have unlikable clients.

It's all you.

Okay, You Are a Life Coach. You Wake Up And . . .

8:00 AM: You spend about fifteen minutes practicing what you preach. You write out three goals for the day, three things you are grateful for, and three successes from the day before. These help put you in the right frame of mind.

8:30 AM: Your first client session, on the phone, lasts about forty-five minutes. This gentleman wants to open his own B&B, but has a lot of hurdles he needs to overcome. He's currently a lawyer with a successful practice; it's a big leap. Today you discuss some of the very first steps he needs to make. Afterward, you take fifteen minutes to write some additional notes.

9:30 AM: Your second session of the day, again on the phone. You have two more consecutively, until it's . . .

1:00 PM: Lunchtime. You wolf down a tuna sandwich you make in your kitchen. Homemade deliciousness.

1:50 PM: Your first appointment of the afternoon is in person. You sit in the living room together and discuss your client's plans to fulfill his lifelong dream to move his family to the South Pacific. He's nervous but becoming more and more confident as you help him realize he's doing all the right things.

5:30 PM: You work on your newsletter, which you want to send out early next week, for a half hour. Then you send out a few e-mails and call it a day.

Um, What Was That You Mentioned Earlier About "Controversy"?

It's a touchy subject, but there *have* been some quacks and gurus who have cast a shadow over the life-coaching industry. Some complain that life coaches are acting as therapists without being licensed. Life coaches can get certified and credentialed, but they don't actually need to in order to practice. However, self-policing governing bodies, like the International Association for Coaches and the International Coach Federation (ICF), try to keep the industry on the up-and-up. Bottom line, some people question coaching, which is not uncommon for new fields. If you go into it, know that there are some doubters.

Coach Me on Becoming a Coach. How the Hell Do I Get This Job?

You really, really want to be a life coach? Okay, boom, you're a life coach. That's the odd (and as already stated, somewhat controversial) thing about this field; anybody can be a coach. That doesn't mean you'll have any clients, be of any help, or make any money, of course.

To become a coach, the first thing you should do is get some coaching yourself. Find a coach you can trust who can be a mentor, and let him or her help you. This will offer you invaluable experience, both as someone being coached and as someone learning what coaches do. Most will also tell you it's imperative that you have real-life and workplace experience to tap into, so if you're not already out there in the working world, get out there.

There are lots of training courses you can take and certificates and credentials you can earn. For example, NYU has a coaching certificate program; check it out at scps.nyu.edu/areas-of-study/human-resource-management/professional-certificates/personal-and-life-coaching.html. Three great sites that will lead you in the right direction are coachville.com (run by Thomas Leonard, one of the first to realize that coaching had become its own industry); coachinc.com, which offers tools and training; and the site of the International Coach Federation, coachfederation.org. The ICF site will also inform you of some pure coaching schools it has accredited, which aren't affiliated with any universities.

There's not much more to offer than that. First, get a life. Second, find a niche in that life. Third, be a life coach.

Resources

These sites all offer loads of information and advice:

Coachville.com

Coaching.com

Coachfederation.org

Two books on coaching:

Take Yourself to the Top: The Secrets of America's #1 Career Coach by Laura Berman Fortgang

Co-active Coaching by Laura Whitworth

Magazine Writer/Magazine Editor

Magazines. Even the Internet can't kill them. There's just nothing like the tactile and often guilty pleasure of flipping through your favorite magazine. Plus, it's not easy to bring even the most lightweight laptop into the bathroom. There are a million different flavors of magazines, from tabloid celebrity rags to monthlies that focus on all things bow hunting, from bitchy fashion glossies to niche trade papers like *Convenience Store Daily*. The stories that fill these pages are written by people who in some cases can be classified as journalists or reporters, but most are really their own breed: magazine writers.

Magazine writing is often not the hard-core, researched stories one identifies as "news." For example, see *Cat Fancy*'s latest cover story, "How to Make Fluffy Pretty!" Of course, many articles involve reporting, researching, and interviewing, and there are more than a few strict newsmagazines like *Time* and *U.S. News & World Report*. Still, the job of magazine writer is broader and separate from the factual, unbiased world of "the news," which also exists in other media like newspapers, radio, TV, and the Web. This chapter will focus on that broader job, the one that defines most stories and writers at magazines like *Cosmo, Details, GQ,* and *Us Weekly*. (If you want to learn about the news business, investigate the chapter on news reporters.)

Some magazine writers are on staff and go in to the office every day; many others are freelance and e-mail their pieces in from home. Either way, writing for magazines is a cool job, the kind of career the hip characters have on TV shows. And that stereotype holds true: if you are at a fun, sexy magazine, it can be a fun, sexy job. And therefore, it can be a challenging one to procure.

Writers and Editors

First off, under the "magazine writer" career heading, there are writers and there are editors. This can be a tad confusing. Some folks with *editor* in their title never really edit; they are strictly writers, and the title is in a way an honorific to show that they are experienced. This applies to a lot of people with the *contributing editor* title. Editors who are in fact editors have a lot of additional responsibilities; some may write all the time, some only occasionally, and some very, very rarely or even not at all.

It's a fun job, especially if you're writing for a glossy magazine. You get to travel around a lot and interview interesting people, you meet celebrities or people who are excelling in their field, or maybe you're parachuting into worlds that you would otherwise never see. A lot of people want these jobs, and unfortunately there aren't that many of them.
—Mark Binelli,
contributing editor,
Rolling Stone

Here's sort of how it works: before anything can be written, writers need to know what to write about. A big part of editors' jobs is assigning stories. They can go to people on staff—"Hey, Joey, go write an article on Scientology"—as well as to freelance writers whom they pay per assignment or by the word. How do editors know what stories to assign? Sometimes it's easy: the White Stripes have a new album coming out, and the magazine has arranged with their publicist for someone to sit in the studio with them as they do the final mix. Or an obvious story needs covering, say the Winter Olympics. Regardless of magazine type, there's some sort of angle there, whether it's about the Games themselves or the sex lives of athletes in the Olympic village. Other times, editors will be given a tip by a publicist, or simply have an idea themselves that they think will make a great piece.

There's one other way stories get chosen. Writers may pitch their own story ideas to an editor. In other words, writers might find small news or culture items they think could be dug into more deeply, or they may have completely original ideas they believe readers will be interested in, and they present these to their superiors.

So although having ideas for articles is one big responsibility of an editor, really what they do is coordinate all the articles under their purview. They troubleshoot and shepherd the stories until they are safely printed and in the magazine, from assigning the article through proofreading. Larger magazines have all kinds of editing positions: music editors, lifestyle editors, sports editors, and so on. Editors edit the stories their writers submit, shortening them or punching them up, as well as suggesting changes to the writers who then rework them. These are bigger-picture revisions; the copyediting, which includes checking facts, details, spelling, and grammar, is done by copyeditors and fact checkers. Editors also very often write the articles' headlines.

Editors at smaller magazines do all of the above, plus they may take on additional chores. They may even supervise photo shoots—usually the job of a photo editor, which a small magazine may not have. Working at these smaller magazines can be great experience because you will learn how the entire business works.

And what about the pure writers, what do they do? Take a guess, just give it a wild shot. Yes, they write! What they write exactly depends on the assignments they are working on, and for which magazine. For *Entertainment Weekly*, they might be interviewing Johnny Depp in Paris, on the set of his new film. For *Parenting*, they might be writing an article about the pros and cons of teaching infants sign language, interviewing young mothers both in their homes and on the phone. For *Elle*, they could be typing up a fashion piece: "Burnt Orange, It's The New, New Black." Sometimes there's research and interviewing to be done; sometimes it's completely from the mind of the writer. Either way, when they finish their pieces, they submit them to their editors. There may be radical changes to make after that, or possibly just small tweaks. Then it's on to the next assignment.

What Kind of Person Is Good at This?

Well, for starters, you probably don't use the word *ain't* a lot. Obviously, you must have a facility for words and writing. This doesn't necessarily mean you have to go to journalism school or even be an English major; there are good writers from many different backgrounds. But you do need to be curious and have great observational skills. It's not hard to sit down and do an interview, but what makes for great stories are the little details that writers find in a scene. You need a sharp eye or ear to pick out weird, funny, unexpected moments that will delight the reader.

It helps to have wide-ranging interests; the more you know, the more you can write about, and the more opportunities for jobs. Unless for you, it's writing about rock 'n' roll or nothing. If you want to be that specific, then you have to know your subject like a crazy professor.

You also need to be able to present yourself well. For example, as a freelance writer, sometimes you get assignments, but other times you pitch your ideas for stories to editors. When you do that, you need to be able, whether in an e-mail, in person or on the phone, to be an exciting and enticing salesperson. You have to sell that story, kid.

Editors (the "write less, edit more" types) also need to be adept with language, as they cut away the fat in writers' drafts to get to the heart of a story. A large part of the job of editing, though, is problem solving. For example, let's say you've assigned a writer and a photographer to cover a story in Africa. And while they are there, the writer gets food poisoning. Now what? How will the story get written? Guess who has to figure it out?

As many editors rise through the ranks to their positions, it's important, especially in the beginning, to be eager and efficient. A can-do attitude is prized at magazines. And especially at the more competitive ones, it's really important to be confident in your own abilities. Some people in the business can have egos so huge they need four assistants to carry them. You can't let these types bring you down.

> I don't write out questions for an interview, and for the most part I don't consult notes. I try to be relaxed and get a natural conversational flow going, and for the most part it puts people at ease. You want your subjects to forget that you are actually grilling them.
> —Mark Binelli,
> contributing editor,
> *Rolling Stone*

> When I was a secretary just out of college, I had a woman scream at me, "You'll never make it as an editor! Never! Never!" Later I saw the film *The Devil Wears Prada* with friends, and when we walked out I said to them, "Every single word in that is true."
> —Katy McColl,
> lifestyle editor,
> *Jane Magazine*

Where Do You Write?

Freelance writers work wherever they please; at their homes, a coffee shop, you name it. Sometimes they come in to the magazine office, but many times they work via phone and e-mail, remotely. Staff writers work at the magazines' offices, which are generally laid back. How laid back naturally depends on the kind of magazine—*Fortune* is probably more uptight than *High Times*. Smaller independent magazines tend to have funkier environs, while larger magazines' offices are often traditional offices with cubicles, photocopiers, and ferns. Usually a bit nicer than an accounting firm, but still. Remember, there are more than just writers at magazines.

Some magazine offices are famously catty. À la *The Devil Wears Prada*, glossy fashion magazines can be filled with young women in never-repeating couture outfits. There may be no attitude involved like in the book and film, but depending on the magazine, you may feel some pressure to look "hot."

Editors generally stay in the office, but as a staff writer you may get out of the office to cover stories and do interviews. Sure, some pieces you can research at your desk, and some interviews can be done on the phone, but many are best handled face to face. Hopefully the other face is in Fiji. A lot depends on where you work and what kind of articles you write. If you're at *Rolling Stone*, you'll go to wherever the celebrities are and interview them. If you write for *Advertising Age*, you may visit some ad agencies for interviews, but mostly you'll use the phone.

> I can wear pretty much anything I want. I've noticed that people who love clothes aren't big on dress codes. This is a very glamorous company, though, so regardless of whether dressing well is linked to success in any way, you don't want to go to the cafeteria looking like "Ugly Betty."
> —**Katy McColl,**
> **lifestyle editor,**
> ***Jane Magazine***

Hours?

It varies. If you're a staff writer, at a minimum you'll work office hours, more when you're busy or meeting a deadline. The same is true of an editor. There could be a week of late nights followed by a week when you are out the door every night at six. It's not a nine-to-five job, although some weeks it can be close. Others, you'll be eating late dinners of takeout Chinese in the conference room, night after night.

The busy times ebb and flow for freelance writers. You could get a last-minute call to write a last-minute story and have to jam through two coffee-filled days and nights. You could be completely slow for a week, not working or making money, and then all of a sudden get a ton of assignments. These are the pros and cons of freelancing. The key is to be able to enjoy the slow times, without stressing that you will never work again.

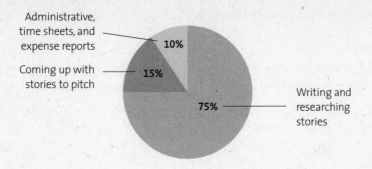

Administrative, time sheets, and expense reports — 10%

Coming up with stories to pitch — 15%

Writing and researching stories — 75%

Ducats?

It's not hedge fund money, but if you are writing for a big magazine, you could do pretty well. To start out, though, the money is very low. Especially when you're an unknown freelance writer, it's hard enough just to find paying jobs.

Editorial assistants at large publications start at around $25,000, and years later when they become seasoned editors they can break $100,000. Not many people go above $150,000, though, without being one of the top names on the masthead.

A great site to keep tabs on what people are actually making as magazine writers and editors is ed2010.com. People anonymously submit actual salaries and the companies and positions that pay them.

1   10

Stress-o-Meter: 5 (1 being a circus clown, 10 being a rodeo clown)

Sure, working on a deadline is always stressful. But if you put your stress into perspective, you'll realize that at the end of the day, as important as it is to you, it's a magazine. That's not to say that some days don't feel like a 10. But stepping back, it's not open-heart surgery. It's supposed to be a little fun.

Pros

You get to write, which you love.

Possible travel and staying in nice hotels.

The chance to meet and hang out with famous people.

The instant gratification of seeing your story in print.

Cons

Working hard with the written word can lead to burnout.

When you're an editor, sometimes writers disappoint you.

Some interviewees and publicists make you jump through hoops to get your story.

You Made It. You're a Magazine Writer. You Wake Up And . . .

This assumes you are a freelance writer.

8:30 AM: After cleaning your body and teeth, you check and return e-mail for an hour and see if any assignments might be pending. You read the *Times* and do a little Internet surfing for inspiration.

10:00 AM: You are working on a story about out-of-work actors and will be interviewing one in an hour. You take your laptop to a café and chip away at the article.

11:00 AM: The out-of-work actor arrives. You engage him in conversation, trying to learn what keeps him going despite the odds.

12:30 PM: After the interview, you leave and go for a walk past the park. You see a couple in the dog park flirting. You wonder how many marriages began with flirting in the dog park and make a note of it as a possible story idea.

1:30 PM: You meet an editor friend for lunch. He says he may have some assignments for you coming up.

3:30 PM: Back home now, you take a break, and catch up on some quality soap operas.

5:00 PM: You start to do a little work on your novel. Your cell phone rings; it's the editor from earlier today. He has an assignment, a different one from those he mentioned at lunch; this is a last-minute one, due tomorrow by five. Can you bust it out in twenty-four hours? Sure you can; all you need is a babbling brook of coffee and the right amount of money. You get a pen and take down the details.

If you can swing it, do an internship while you're in college. It's a good way to get to know people. At *Rolling Stone* several interns have gone on to get staff jobs. You just have to stand out because there are a lot of interns every year, and they can become very faceless. It can be a thankless job where you photocopy articles for writers like me and do a lot of grunt work. But it can be worth it.
—**Mark Binelli,**
    contributing editor,
    Rolling Stone

I Ache to Write. How the Hell Do I Get This Job?

First, a dose or two of reality. Most of these jobs are in New York. Obviously local magazines are scattered all over the country, and certain national magazines are based elsewhere, but for the most part the magazine publishing industry is based in New York City. You may need to move there, at least to start. And, as already mentioned, it is very competitive to break in. A job writing for any magazine, especially a glossy pop culture one, has those buzzwords— Travel! Celebrities!—that get people drooling.

So what do you need to do to get started? Intern. And then intern some more. Start early, your first year of college. If you do, and demonstrate a steadfast commitment to the field, it will make it easier for you to get in the door. Internships lead to jobs—if not at the magazine you're at, than at another where you might be referred. The industry is small like that. But even getting internships is competitive, plus most are unpaid. So if you are coming from outside New York and you are not independently wealthy, it can be hard to get by in the most expensive city in the country.

If you can't get an internship or are unable to come to New York to intern, don't fret. The other thing to do is to start to put clips together. Clips are published articles you've written, a.k.a. press clippings. Write for publications like your college newspaper or magazine, a local alternative weekly, or one of the million sites online that need content. Approach the ones that interest you most and start amassing a file of clips. These will show editors that you can write, you can get the job done, and others have trusted you to do so. Editors have a million things to do; the last thing they want is to assign stories to a totally unknown quantity. Clips that are really solid will help them feel that they can count on you. Even if you do intern, by the way, you should start amassing clips. You want to look like someone who has been dying to be a magazine writer his or her entire life. To that end, you should try to pump up the old résumé by working as an editor on your yearbook, or local literary magazine. Those extracurricular activities show your passion.

Some people go to graduate journalism school before working as magazine writers, but typically journalism school is more for reporters and correspondents. Some schools have magazine programs, like the University of Missouri. If you think you might be interested in the news as well as magazines, it might be worth investigating. If you know you want to write for *Cosmo*, probably not.

When contacting magazines, remember that if you want to work with language professionally, you really shouldn't send lame, boilerplate cover letters and e-mails. You aren't going for a job in accounting; strut your stuff a bit. And when you get an interview, know that you'll be starting at the bottom, and show them that you are willing to kick butt there. Because it is an administrative job in the beginning, magazines are examining you in the interview to make sure you aren't going to quit. Again, you have to show them this is something you've wanted to do forever, even if it really isn't. Finally, at any magazine where you're trying to get a job, make sure you've studied the last ten to twenty issues and can refer to articles in them. (Go online to their sites and check the archives.) Have a bunch of story ideas that will uniquely fit that magazine on the tip of your tongue.

For All the Freelancers in the House

It's a lot easier to find work in the freelance world if you are coming from a staff job. Still, freelancing novice writers also provide a way for magazines to test novices out. But to get work as one, you'll need to be able to pitch stories well. Editors won't just assign you a story until you are a known entity, so for now you have to have such a great idea that they'll want to bring you on.

Here's what to do: first, send an editor (or many editors) a bunch of really

People don't want to hear how you think most magazines are trashy but that you like theirs. It feels condescending. Say you're ready, willing, and able to answer the phone, answer e-mails, and schedule meetings. To get an interview, write a great cover letter and make sure your résumé looks like you've been preparing for this career all of your life. When I see a résumé that indicates that someone is "thinking about" going into magazines, I pretty much set it aside because there's another girl who's been working her tail off at her public school putting out the newspaper/literary magazine who wants it more. And that's the kind of girl who will be able to pull through those first few brutal years.
—Katy McColl,
lifestyle editor,
Jane Magazine

Hit them up front with your qualifications, any publications you've made it into at that point, and keep your story idea short and punchy. Try to pitch ideas that will blow their minds. Don't pitch *Rolling Stone* on a profile of whatever the hot band is, because obviously they'll have already thought of that.
—**Mark Binelli,**
contributing editor,
Rolling Stone

strong clips, along with an e-mail explaining who you are, what you can do, and your story idea. Keep this salvo relatively brief and to the point. And you'll need to be persistent without being overbearing, because editors are busy and most won't respond right away.

If your idea is tempting enough, your clips good enough, and you seem capable, someone will take a bite. And off you go.

Resources

These two Web sites have loads more information on the career, plus internship and job listings, so be sure to check them out: mediabistro.com and ed2010.com, which bills itself as "a group of young editors looking to reach their dream magazine jobs by the year 2010." It's also worth checking out the site of the Magazine Publishers of America, magazine.org. Much of the info on it is "for members only", however, it has a careers section where jobs and internships are listed.

And for inspiration, read the great nonfiction writers. Classic ones include Ian Frazier (wikipedia.org/wiki/Ian_Frazier), Joseph Mitchell (wikipedia.org/wiki/Joseph_Mitchell), and A.J. Liebling (wikipedia.org/wiki/A.J._Liebling). Also check out these notable contemporary writers: Seymour Hersh, Russell Shorto, Ken Auletta, Philip Gourevitch, Mark Bowden, Mark Jacobson, Barbara Ehrenreich, Francine Prose, Anthony Lane, Frank Rich, Paul Krugman, Thomas Friedman, and Nicholas Kristof.

Management Consultant

If you had a bear on your front lawn, you'd probably call animal control instead of trying to tame it with a broomstick. If you were stricken with appendicitis, you'd never perform emergency surgery on yourself. And in much the same way, if you are a large corporation suffering from any number of pressing issues that aren't in your skill set, it's probably best not to try to solve them on your own. Instead you might, like many companies, look for an expert outside opinion from a management consultant.

Management consulting firms are hired by companies to help identify corporate ailments and then prescribe and implement solutions. They provide an objective point of view that makes it easier to pinpoint the problems companies can't seem to see for themselves. Sometimes consultants are brought in for a very specific reason, like "We are having problems with the growth of our computer network." Sometimes it's more general: "How can we improve our presence in the global market?"

Management consultants are born problem solvers. To be one, you need to be willing to work long and hard—and when looking at an issue, you have to be able to see both the forest *and* the trees. Not to mention the leaves on the ground and the clouds in the sky. The whole darn picture.

What Do Consultants Actually Do?

Management consultants don't perform any one particular skill, like accounting, statistics, or magic. The problems they tend to be handed are new and individual, and so are the solutions they tailor. To arrive at these, consultants research and analyze data (sometimes from interviewing people, sometimes from charts and tables) and then strategize based on their findings.

Consultants work in teams. These differ from firm to firm, but generally there will be a very senior staff member who is the team leader, followed by a couple of midlevel consultants and a few lower- to entry-level ones, who usually hold the title *business analyst.* Teams are not permanent, and as a business analyst you will likely work on everything. So if you're a business analyst on one team, when your project ends you will be assigned to another team whose makeup will probably be completely different. One project might be marketing based, the next financial. You really don't begin to specialize on any one

The analysis in the work you do every day is pretty granular, but it would never be just looking at something as small as this week's advertisement or promotion. It would be a much larger-scale look at the client's business: which direction is the boat headed and why, and what does that mean for the bottom line, the constituents the client serves, and how do we quantify that and support that organizationally?
—Susan Munoz, senior project leader, Boston Consulting Group

thing until later in your career. Instead, you'll learn skills that can be applied to almost every corporate issue, across a wide swath of projects.

On the team, every member will be responsible for a different piece of the project. There are usually tremendous amounts of data to sift through, and the business analysts have to rifle through this "data dump," looking for important clues and trends.

An average client assignment might go a little something like this: first, the client's issue needs to be defined. This happens at a high-level meeting with a senior client executive, possibly even the CEO, who will explain the difficulties the organization is facing. Together, your firm and the client will agree what the goal of this project should be. Then you will go off and break the project into several different chunks, with each chunk being assigned to a different team member or members. You will learn as much about your client's business as humanly possible. You'll interview people who work there. You'll work there yourself. You'll be like a method actor and put yourself in their shoes. Plus, you'll do all the normal research, such as investigations of the overall market and competitors. Then it's data time. You'll be gathering and analyzing the stuff, building models and hypotheses, and generally seeing what it all adds up to. And as you do, you'll begin to share these findings with your counterparts at the client. You'll be working closely with them, brainstorming together, and gaining trust, because in the end, you really want to come to the recommended solution together, not just foist one on them. And when you do finally have these recommendations, you help the client implement them. A good idea in the conference room won't change what's going on in the factories and marketplace unless it's well implemented.

Most entry-level business analysts come straight from graduating college. After a couple of years at the firm, they go back to school and get an MBA. You pretty much have to get an MBA if you want to stay in the field long term—a few consultants don't, but very few. Afterward, you can return to the same firm, in a much higher position. In fact, many firms offer incentives for you to do so, such as paying for that expensive MBA. It's a common perk for employees the firm believes in and wants to retain.

What Makes for a Good Consultant?

Consultants like to use fancy buzzwords like *core competency, matrix,* and *vertical integration.* More important, consultants are hardworking, analytical folks who are very good at explaining themselves and getting across what they believe is right and why they believe it. To succeed, you need to be a good lis-

> At the start of every project, there will be an internal kickoff meeting where the manager or partner will present the key issues and major objectives, and the expectations, roles, and responsibilities. And in general, there'll be a bit of "rah-rah, let's get excited" cheerleading, because as you change teams from project to project, there has to be a constant recreation of team spirit. There very well might be a team event where everyone goes out to a restaurant, or some other team-building activity.
> —Agathe Blanchon Ehrsam, director, Vivaldi Partners

tener, a team player, and the sort of person who loves a challenge and lives to solve unexpected problems. A business world MacGyver, if you will. Being a consultant is not a job where you master one thing and repeat, but one where each client's challenges are new to you: new industries, unique circumstances, you name it. You have to enjoy that variety, constantly switching it up. So, as a consultant might say, if any of these attributes describe your core competency, you'll most likely fit into the consulting matrix.

And Where Do You Consult?

Most major consulting firms have large modern airy offices, and sometimes you'll actually work in them. But more often than not, you will work at the client's digs, which means a lot of travel. And as you switch projects (and teams), you'll also switch clients, which means traveling to a whole other place. Consultants can often be based at the client four days out of the week. Clients aren't usually local, so this means hotels, airports, and rental cars. And although travel can be fun, it can also be very trying on personal relationships.

Most large consulting firms are very professional. Suit and tie, professional. However, they aren't stuffy; consultants are social creatures, as you might have guessed from all the teamwork. There is a very big "work hard, party hard" attitude and jocularity around the office. Unlike some working atmospheres, consultants tend to really respect their peers.

Hours

The hours are long, especially when you start. There will be times when, no exaggeration, you will be working until midnight every night, plus weekends. Getting a call on a Saturday to come in on a Sunday is not abnormal. Other times may not be as intense, but still it's never nine to five. As you get higher and higher in the organization, work life becomes more manageable, but consultants joke that if you broke down their pay by the hour, it would be minimum wage. These long days are one of the reasons it's so important that you like your colleagues, and why consulting firms work so hard to ensure that everyone bonds. You are together *a lot*.

All of your co-workers will be very smart people. And I don't mean just book smart, which they all are, but this guy's also a concert pianist, and this woman is a marathoner. You're just surrounded by eclectic, talented, inspiring people.
—Susan Munoz, senior project leader, Boston Consulting Group

When you travel, you're going to be staying at a hotel next to the industrial park of some Midwest city that probably isn't a tourist destination. In very rare cases you might travel to Europe and feel like a jet-setter, but that is very rare.
—Agathe Blanchon Ehrsam, director, Vivaldi Partners

One of the nice things in larger consulting firms is when you are first hired, you enter with a class. It's in the summer, and you all get your training together. It's a continuation of the college spirit. It's all about bonding and sharing your experiences.
—Agathe Blanchon Ehrsam, director, Vivaldi Partners

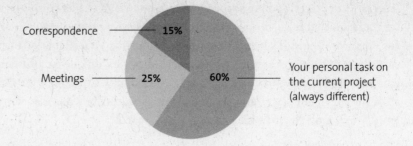

Correspondence — 15%

Meetings — 25%

60% — Your personal task on the current project (always different)

Cash for Consulting?

You can do quite well. You'll start out of college somewhere between $45,000 and $60,000. After you get your MBA, you'll earn, give or take, $120,000. From there, your compensation becomes less about salary and more about bonus. At the highest levels, successful partners are easily making more than a million dollars a year.

The Bureau of Labor Statistics reports the mean annual wage of management consultants (in management and technical consulting services) to be $85,950.

Stress-o-Meter: 8 (1 being an ice cream man, 10 being a repo man)

The hours are long and the expectations are high. It's a client-service business; clients are prone to asking for the almost unachievable, and consulting firms pride themselves on pulling it off. It can get very, very hairy. 1970s porno hairy.

Pros	Cons
You work with incredibly smart people.	You work incredibly long hours.
You get to travel.	You have to travel.
You make a nice salary.	If you divide your salary by the hours you work, it doesn't look as nice.
It's a meritocracy; prove yourself and you'll move up fast.	

Boom—You Are a Management Consultant. You Wake Up And . . .

6:30 AM: You leave the hotel you're staying in while working out of state at the client, a large beverage company in another state, and go for a jog. You try to run every morning, as the rest of the day is spent sitting, working, and drinking soda.

8:15 AM: Showered and dressed in a suit, you gather with your team and discuss last evening's meeting with your client counterparts. You're trying to help them reduce their bloated marketing costs. Your team's theory, based on the analysis to date, is that they have too many different soda brands, and that they should consolidate and focus on only the strongest few.

9:30 AM: Each individual team member gives the status of his or her part of the project. You show the analysis you've done about how advertising dollars could go exponentially further if they were less splintered.

10:30 AM: You disband, planning to meet again for a team lunch. Back at your desk, you double-check your numbers and start on your next responsibility, the public relations implications of dissolving some of the smaller brands.

1:00 PM: Team lunch, off-site. Pizza and, yes, soda. You have been drinking soda twenty-four hours a day on this project. You can easily belch the alphabet.

2:00 PM: The team leader extends lunch to discuss a sensitive issue. If brands are cut, some of the marketing managers on these brands will be shuffled into new positions, but some may be let go. At times, your decisions create new jobs. And at others, the opposite.

4:00 PM: Back to your public relations analysis. And another soda.

6:30 PM: You go to dinner with your counterpart on the client side. You talk a little business, but even more so, you "bond." This is one of many assignments your firm hopes to get from the beverage company, and client relationships are important.

8:30 PM: You work for another three hours, until all the numbers in your Excel spreadsheet blur into one. You hope to finish the PR analysis in the morning and share it with your team leader by lunch.

I'd Kill to Consult. How the Hell Do I Get This Job?

Start by getting good grades. It really doesn't matter so much what you major in; this is one of the few business jobs where being an English or anthropology major might actually be more valuable than being an economics or statistics major. Consulting firms are looking for natural problem solvers whom they then can mold. Almost all of the larger ones have their own intensive training programs, where you'll learn research techniques, accounting, policy, and so on.

Many of these major firms have large on-campus recruitment pushes—if you are in school, check with your career center to see if any might be coming to your campus. Consulting firms' interviews tend to really grill you on your problem-solving skills. They're not looking for you to have the right answers, but want to see more how your brain works and how you attack different conundrums. You'll be asked some pretty offbeat questions, like how many tennis balls fit in a 747 airplane? Or what's your estimate of the number of hairdressers in Chicago? Or how many yards of garden hose are sold each year in America?

As a good group dynamic is so important at consulting firms, there will be several rounds of interviews, and you'll meet many different people. The first is on campus; you could well interview with not one, but several young consultants from the same company. The second set, if you make the cut, will be at the corporate office, where you will make the rounds and meet lots of different people. These second-round interviews can be overwhelming all-day affairs, and one tip consultants offer to help you get through the gauntlet without any missteps is to clarify questions before you answer them. Rephrasing the question is something consultants do every day with their own clients, and it shows a thoughtful demeanor and good listening skills. Try it.

Finally, if you have a business and economics background and know a lot of buzzwords, it's actually best not to flaunt them during your interviews. Every firm has its own way of doing things, and every large firm has a solid training program. They are not looking for people who seem set in their ways. Certainly tout your experience, but not in an "I already know how to do it all" kind of way.

Resources

It's probably no surprise that given the great training offered at consulting firms, many of their Web sites offer incredible insight on a career as a consultant. Be sure not to miss McKinsey's site, which even offers interviews with newly hired consultants. On all, look under the "careers" or "alumni" headings.

Consulting firms' sites:

McKinsey.com

Bcg.com

Bain.com

Monitor.com

Lek.com

Boozallen.com

Deloitte.com

Accenture.com

Ey.com

A few magazines and sites are devoted to the field, most notably Consultant News (consultant-news.com), *Consulting Times* (consulting-times.com), and *Consulting Magazine* (consultingmagazine.com). As well, several books have been written on the subject: *The Pyramid Principle* by Barbara Minto, *The McKinsey Mind* by Ethan M. Rasiel and Paul N. Friga, *The McKinsey Way* by Ethan M. Rasiel, and *Managing the Professional Service Firm* by David H. Maister.

Mediator

Can't we all just get along? Apparently not. Small disputes routinely get out of hand, and suddenly it's time for the lawyers, the courts, and the occasional "Let's settle this ourselves" neighborhood brouhaha. These are adversarial solutions, and all of them are less than ideal. Mediators have a different, nonadversarial point of view on how disputes can be resolved. Perhaps that's why mediation is considered *alternative dispute resolution,* or ADR—although, there is a push to replace *alternative* with *appropriate,* as mediation has become more popular and isn't so alternative anymore, just like certain indie rock bands.

When a dispute is brought into a courtroom, both sides fight it out to prove who's right. There are two different teams of attorneys, one for each party. Eventually, the court makes a judgment based on their arguments; one side wins, one side loses, end of story. When a dispute is brought to a mediator, however, things work quite differently. There's no jury to rule who's officially right or wrong. The mediator is an impartial third party who doesn't make judgments. Instead, he or she sits down with the disputing parties and helps them come to a mutually agreeable solution on their own. Whereas lawyers defend their sides aggressively by pointing out the differences between the parties, mediators look for the commonalities. They believe that both sides want this conflict over with, that both sides want a solution. They start there, by facilitating a conversation between the antagonists. Not that it usually happens so easily.

More on Mediation

An example would be helpful, eh? Okay, let's stick with divorce. Mr. and Mrs. Smith both want one and are arguing about all kinds of details, from alimony to visitation. They show up in court with their respective lawyers, ready to brawl. Before it gets ugly, a judge or court clerk asks if the parties would consider mediation. They both agree. They then meet (with or without their lawyers present) with a mediator in a conference room, most likely at the courthouse. The mediator searches for something both parties agree on; for example, "Hey, I know you both love your daughter, and want to make this separation as easy on her as possible. How can we do that?" He lets the parties

In many court-based cases, everybody loses. By having each party attack the other, the adversarial process doesn't always make good sense as a method for resolving disputes—particularly where there are ongoing relationships. Take divorce, for example. A family is already weakened because of the dynamics of the divorce, and now they have many more problems by virtue of an adversarial legal process. Mediators look for common ground and try to get the parties on a more constructive path.
—Leila Love,
      professor of law,
      Benjamin N. Cardozo
      School of Law

talk and tries to steer the conversation to keep it positive, and to keep it from devolving into bickering. With any luck, through this process a mutually agreed-on settlement will occur. The parties will have avoided court, and—fingers crossed—their relationship won't be damaged any further.

Mediators work on a variety of disputes. Tenant/landlord, merchant/customer, and community disputes; labor negotiations; and even international disputes are settled through mediation. The Oslo and Dayton accords are prime examples of successful mediation.

Hold Up. What's the Difference between Mediation and That Other Term I Hear, Arbitration?

Good question, young scholar. There's a big difference. If you go to a mediator, you and your adversary are basically electing to keep the power of the resolution to yourselves. You'll work out the solution together; nothing will be forced on you by a higher power. The mediator simply helps you collaborate with one another.

If you go to an arbitrator, he or she will hear both sides of the argument and then, just like a judge, render a binding decision. The only real difference between arbitration and public litigation is that arbitration is private; you get to pick and hire your own judge. In court, you're subject to whatever judge the court assigns you.

What Types of Mediators Are There?

There are all kinds. Some volunteer and work in resolving community issues; others are highly paid and work strictly on corporate cases. (Obviously, as this is a career book and most likely you're looking for the type of career that provides pieces of green paper in exchange for your labor, volunteering here is seen as solely a good deed and résumé builder for you, dear reader.) Some mediators have no degree at all; some have a law degree and other specialized conflict resolution training. That's right, no degree is required to become a mediator, although each state has different training requirements you'll need to fulfill. Of course, if you want to handle higher-end disputes, whether they are bigger money cases or legal matters, bachelor's and law degrees, as well as perhaps additional specialized training courses, are going to be necessary.

Most mediators work for themselves, building their own reputations and, as they do so, having cases referred to them. Some work full time for private mediation firms or nonprofit groups. Government officials also work as mediators, resolving all types of national and international disputes.

Mediation allows for you to be a little more creative in resolving the conflict instead of just handing down a win/lose, zero-sum game. Some people say it's win-win, but it doesn't mean that everybody's leaving happy. It means they've at least arrived at a solution where they can say, "All right, I can put this matter behind me."
—**Michael Hurwitz, mediator, social worker, and lawyer**

A lot of retired judges and lawyers become mediators, which they can do on a part-time basis, cashing in on all their old contacts. And some mediators also continue to hold other jobs, such as professorships at law schools. Which leads us to . . .

The Hardest Part

I have some students who got jobs right out of law school—good jobs as court or program administrators. However, parties in a dispute are often looking for someone who is well known and highly experienced. To get "big" cases, a neutral needs a visible track record and a good reputation. So, in that sense, younger people tend not to get the high-end cases unless they are recognized in some field.
—Leila Love,
professor of law,
Benjamin N. Cardozo
School of Law

Might as well get this out in the open early: the hardest part of becoming a mediator is breaking into the field. It's still a relatively new profession, and work can be hard to come by at first.

So it's not as straightforward as earning a degree in accounting and then getting a job as an accountant. For most people it takes some time to work your way up to making money from mediation and from nothing else. The good news is that you can be doing certain kinds of mediation while you are still in school, making contacts and gaining experience along the way.

So How Do You Get Work?

Mediators get jobs in a few ways. Judges often refer cases to mediators before they get entangled in the justice system proper. For instance, if it's an equal employment case, and you are known for having mediated these types of disputes before, a judge may reach out to you as an alternative to court. The courts are overwhelmed in our litigious society. There can be eighty cases slated for a day when only ten can be heard. Instead of just adjourning these for another jam-packed day, court clerks and judges will often ask the parties if they are interested in mediation. If so, the case will be referred to a mediator.

Outside the courts, in community settings, the police will often refer cases to mediators. These referrals often happen after a small altercation; for example, the police know that two neighbors have been filing noise complaints against each other, and they fear that violence might flare as a result. A mediator can help resolve this situation before the fists, or worse, fly. There are also community dispute resolution centers in some cities, where people can come in and have their cases mediated.

Finally, if you are employed full time at a mediation firm or nonprofit, well, that's easy. You get assigned to a conflict just like you get assigned work at any job.

What Makes for a Good Mediator?

To start, you'll need to be incredibly fair and self-confident, comfortable in any situation. You'll work with a wide range of society—people of every ethnic, racial, religious, economic, and sexual orientation. You don't have to have an understanding of everybody's culture, but you must recognize that cultural differences may affect how certain groups communicate and approach one another. People can view the same exact thing in widely divergent ways.

If people are in need of mediation, obviously there's some sort of conflict. That means someone is pissed off, and the situation potentially explosive. You need to be patient, a calming force in the room, the person who makes others confident that an agreement is in sight and will be reached.

It's cliché, but the most important skill you'll need is that of a good listener. That's what you're trying to facilitate—people listening to one another and communicating clearly. Really hearing what the two sides are trying to say will allow you to point out the commonalities, the places where compromise is possible.

Where Do Mediators Do Their Mediating?

In a variety of places. Mediators go where the action is. Depending on the type of case, they can be in a community center, a courthouse conference room, a corporate headquarters, or some other neutral ground. It will be a place where people can be made to feel comfortable to engage in conversation.

The vibe of these places all depends on the type of mediation. If you're in a courthouse conference room, it will feel serious, and you'll be dressed appropriately in a suit. Same for a corporate-type setting. But in a community dispute, you may want things to feel more casual.

Wherever you may be, when you are working, you are working. You are carefully listening to each side, facilitating discussion, not multitasking or daydreaming about the cute new receptionist. There's no IM, e-mail, or giggly conference calls with friends during a mediation.

Money?

According to allcriminaljusticeschools.com, full-time mediators with JDs and some experience make between $82,780 and $130,170. To start, however, you'll probably be making quite a bit less, because most likely you will be on your own (sort of freelance), trying to get cases. And naturally, you get paid only when you're working. The potential for a mediator with conflict resolu-

I think if you're a good listener, then you can help two people listen to one another. It's vital. Another attribute you must have is a commitment to a different type of justice, a kind that doesn't depend on one person winning and one person losing.
   —Michael Hurwitz, mediator, social worker, and lawyer

We typically meet in a conference room. It's a private setting instead of one open to the public, like a courtroom.
   —Leila Love, professor of law, Benjamin N. Cardozo School of Law

I try to present myself in a certain way, an image of, if not authority, then professionalism. I think people, when they go to court, want that. They want to know that this is an official matter, that justice is going to be carried out. A certain way of dressing facilitates that. In a community setting, I think being overly dressy makes it uncomfortable and stiff. People need to feel comfortable to talk openly and freely.
   —Michael Hurwitz, mediator, social worker, and lawyer

tion training and a JD is huge; you could be helping settle an enormous corporate case and the payoff could be very, very high, hundreds of thousands of dollars high.

On the flip side, you may be a nondegree mediator in a nonprofit community setting, helping resolve family and community conflicts. Although lower paying, these are extremely important and gratifying jobs that help curb community and domestic violence. For full-time work within an organization, salaries for candidates with a few years' experience are between $35,000 and $45,000, according to the National Association for Community Mediation, or NAFCM (nafcm.org).

Hours?

If a firm or nonprofit employs you, regular office hours tend to hold. If you get a case from the courts, you'll generally mediate during the same types of hours that the courts operate. Of course, you'll need to take care of other details such as paperwork.

When you are starting out on your own, you'll mediate as often as you can get cases, which, at least to begin, will probably add up to less than forty hours a week. This is why many mediators hold other jobs, such as teaching or social work, as they toil to improve their reputations.

However, if you're on a big, crazy case or an international conflict, there may be some long hours. Multibillion-dollar mediations, or mediations to prevent strikes or wars, can go all night. In these types of cases, all bets are off.

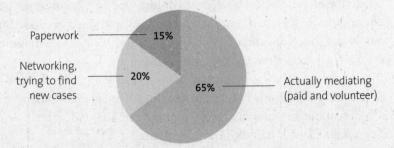

- Paperwork — 15%
- Networking, trying to find new cases — 20%
- Actually mediating (paid and volunteer) — 65%

1   10

Stress-o-Meter: 8.5 (1 being Jack Black's stylist, 10 being J. Lo's stylist)

You're dealing with angry parties in a tense situation. Sometimes they just out-and-out hate each other, and you're being relied on to help them past that. It can be pretty tricky, and pretty stressful.

Pros

It's incredibly satisfying to help people solve disputes.

In a very hands-on way, you facilitate justice.

It's a very well-respected position (by those who know it).

Cons

You're exposed to some tough, nasty situations (especially in family disputes).

It's hard to break in.

The job stays with you long after it's over.

OK, You Are a Mediator. You Wake Up And . . .

This assumes you work on your own.

9:00 AM: You arrive at the courthouse and proceed to a conference room. You were referred a divorce case yesterday, and today you begin. The parties arrive, each with their lawyer in tow. You introduce yourself. Immediately you can tell there's not a lot of love in the room.

10:00 AM: Swear words and insults have been bandied about for the last ten minutes. You finally cajole the parties into moving past that, and you discover the biggest part of the dispute: an apartment they each want to keep.

11:00 AM: After a five-minute break, you start to see some progress. Both parties are discussing what they think they could get for the apartment if they sold it. Everyone loves to talk real estate, thankfully.

12:00 PM: You adjourn until tomorrow. The parties haven't reached a solution, but at least they aren't screaming anymore. You have a feeling that after a good night's sleep, tomorrow might be their day. You run out to get some lunch.

2:00 PM: Now you are in another part of the city, at a community center. You volunteer here, helping mediate neighborhood disputes, three afternoons a week. Off come the jacket and tie. Today you are seeing two sixteen-year-old boys who are in rival gangs. There's a rumor that these two are going to brawl. They show up, tough-guy attitudes in effect.

3:00 PM: The radio is on and you've ordered in some pizza. You are trying to make the setting as relaxed as possible. No one is in trouble here.

4:00 PM: It turns out these two guys have known each other since elementary school. You help get them into a "where are they now?" discussion about some of their former classmates.

5:00 PM: At long last, you bring up the rumor. "So, I heard you two were going to kill each other over some girl." They look at each other and begin to talk about it.

5:30 PM: There's not going to be a fight. They may not be best friends, but they agree it's not worth it. They leave. You eat the last slice, then head home, feeling pretty damn good about the result.

I Burn to Mediate. How the Hell Do I Get This Job?

While, as mentioned, no degree is necessary, there are state requirements before you can actually work. Different states have different standards; these generally involve classroom training (usually a thirty-hour course) as well as a minimum number of cases (around fifteen) mediated under the supervision of a more senior mediator. Again, exact amounts vary by state and program. To find these out, and to find a local program where you can get the training, Google "mediator training" and your city and state, or go to the site of one of the resources listed later.

After you fulfill these requirements, you'll take a test to be an approved mediator; this test almost always involves your being videotaped while resolving a dispute between two role-playing actors. The staff of your program will review the tape; if you "pass," huzzah, you can mediate on your own. And after you mediate approximately twenty cases (again, the number depends on your state), you can become a state-certified mediator.

State certification will enable you to get only so far, though—most likely to work resolving family and community disputes, or to work full time at a community center. If you want more high-profile (and higher-paying) cases, or cases involving rules of law, you'll need to go to law school. Some not only offer certification in mediation, but also will have you mediating cases while you're still in school. So you're not only learning the job, you're also making contacts. Another worthy option on its own account, or to combine with the JD, is a master's degree in conflict resolution.

Network It

The other positive about law school (or the master's) is that when you get a degree from an institution, it has a duty to help you find employment. Every college and law school has a career center and an alumni list, at the very least. Your professors in ADR, who are most likely mediators themselves, will have a network you can tap into. Don't be shy. Tap. You paid for this access, and it is incredibly valuable.

Be aware that the world of mediation is competitive. In law school, a lot of people want to learn mediation skills, even if they don't plan to become full-time mediators. Just getting into some of the classes and programs can be difficult.

And after law school, getting paying jobs is hard. It's still a new enough field that you have to develop the market for yourself. The best way to do that is by

The mediation clinic I teach has approximately 100 applicants each year for sixteen spots.
—Leila Love, professor of law, Benjamin N. Cardozo School of Law

networking, which is why taking training courses and meeting the working mediators who teach them is so helpful, as are volunteering and working pro bono. Meet, meet, meet.

Beyond these, several conferences are worth attending. One is the American Bar Association Section of Dispute Resolution abanet.org/dispute, which has an annual conference. This, of course, focuses more on the law route of mediation. The other big professional conference is the Association for Conflict Resolution, acrnet.org, which has its annual meeting every year in the fall. Its approach is slightly broader.

Finally . . .

If you get an interview for a job at a mediation firm or a nonprofit, or even to get into a highly competitive law school program, remember to be open and honest. They are looking to be able to connect with you, in much the same way you'll need to connect with the parties in a mediation. So stay positive and optimistic. For example, don't be irritated if the interviewer is running late. And whatever you do, do not get defensive in the actual interview. Be calm, open, and flexible. Come up with a mantra if you need one. Be Zen.

Resources

The following sites and associations offer loads of information on mediation, conferences, and mentors:

American Bar Association Section of Dispute Resolution: abanet.org/dispute

Association for Conflict Resolution: acrnet.org

Association of Family and Conciliation Courts: afccnet.org

Southern California Mediation Association: scmediation.org

National Association for Community Mediation: nafcm.org

Benjamin N. Cardozo School of Law, Kukin Program for Conflict Resolution: www.cardozo.yu.edu

Mediate.com

For the best law school mediation programs, look at *U.S. News & World Report*'s ranking of law schools, which ranks all the law schools in terms of conflict resolution. For a master's, two noted programs are Antioch University's Conflict Resolution Program, mcgregor.edu/cr, and the Institute for Conflict Analysis and Resolution at George Mason University, icar.gmu.edu.

The most well-known book on mediation is *Getting to Yes: Negotiating Agreement without Giving In* by Roger Fisher, William L. Ury, and Bruce Patton.

And a bunch of journals cover conflict resolution, none of which are exactly light reading. Still, they are well worth thumbing through:

ACResolution

ABA Journal

National Law Journal

Conflict Resolution Quarterly

The Dispute Resolution Legal Journal

Personal Trainer

Everybody wants to be young and skinny. Or "healthy," which is often code for the same. This is good news for personal trainers, who make their living getting others to feel the burn. If you love to exercise, have a sunny disposition, and enjoy helping others achieve their goals, the lifestyle of a personal trainer might just fit you. And if it doesn't fit, maybe if you work out for a few weeks, you can squeeze into it.

Personal training means one-on-one, or sometimes semiprivate, meaning one-on-a-couple, training. Personal trainers can specialize in a specific type of training, say Pilates or yoga, or they can do a little bit of everything and set different-themed programs for each client. Many personal trainers also teach classes at gyms, not only because it's simply fun to mix it up, but also these classes are a great place to meet future clients for the more lucrative one-on-one training.

As a trainer, you'll help your clients achieve their physical goals through a workout you've specially designed for them. One of your clients may be recently divorced and trying to lose his love handles. Another may be an older woman trying to gain endurance and flexibility. Outside the physical help you'll provide, the intimate nature of one-on-one training means you'll often form strong bonds with clients, becoming a confidant, advisor, and friend to them along the way.

What Do You Do Besides Promoting Rock-Hard Abs?

Personal trainers are on the go a lot. If you don't have your own studio where clients come to you, then you are spending a lot of time going to your clients. Depending on where you live, this is either easy or a pain in the neck. Your cell phone pretty much becomes your office. (Personal trainers, believe it or not, usually carry some pretty advanced smartphones.) People make and break appointments over the phone and over e-mail, and you need to be in the know. You will also spend many small slices of your day killing time between appointments.

If you do have your own studio (which is more common for yoga and Pilates instructors), you'll spend some of the day just doing the business of running your own space—keeping it clean, answering calls, making appoint-

Clients come to the studio for a one-hour session, once or twice, sometimes three times a week. I help them through a customized training session that deals with their specific needs, whether it's strengthening their back, helping overcome an injury, or whatever. They do a series of exercises on different machines, and I both demonstrate and assist them. The best part of my job is seeing a difference in people, seeing the quality of their lives change.
—Dani Parish Rubin, certified Pilates instructor

Some trainers nap during their midday breaks, resting up for nighttime. Downtime comes in small segments; often it's not enough time to actually get stuff done, so you do some shopping, snacking, and hanging out. As a trainer, you get to be great at crosswords.
—Kristi Molinaro, personal trainer and group fitness instructor

ments, even promoting the studio space by designing Web sites or brochures with freelance designers.

Sweatpants and Dreams

Life as a trainer, as you can imagine, is fairly casual. The dress code is gym wear, clothing in which you can work out. You don't want to be showing too much skin, but it certainly doesn't hurt to show that you're in shape.

Gyms and studios are pretty laid back. It's not like you're in an office, with rules of decorum. Raunchy hip-hop can be playing, and people can be very touchy-feely in a way that would have the human resources department at *Fortune* 500 companies running for their sexual harassment policies.

The flip side is there isn't much of a sense of camaraderie in being a personal trainer. You don't really have co-workers. Even if you work at a gym, you aren't hanging and bonding with anyone else who works there, just with your clients. You are in effect running your own business, the business of you.

Beyond Six-Pack Abs, What Makes for a Good Trainer?

I try to make people feel at home, no matter what. For instance, it's silly, but people fart all the time when working out. Well, not all the time, but when it happens, you say, "Oh, don't worry, it happens all the time," to try to make them feel comfortable.
—**Dani Parish Rubin, certified Pilates instructor**

If you're going to be a good personal trainer, you need to like people. You have to empathize, listen, and be able to create an intimate working relationship with your clients. Many of these are not just trying to get in shape, but also to change their lives. You have to understand where they are coming from and where they want to go. These clients are sweating and straining, and if they aren't in shape, it can be a bit embarrassing for them. But like being with a therapist, they need to feel comfortable and know it's okay to be honest and open with you if they are to improve.

Being a personal trainer also requires strong communication skills; this is not a job for an introvert. And not just with current clients; to get new clients you'll need to be outgoing and personable. Basically, whenever you are working with a client, you need to be "on"—there's no free time to IM with your cousin Freddy.

Also, you must continually inspire your clients to really push themselves. Clients expect results, and they can get testy if they feel they aren't reaching them. They'll blame you, not the bucket of snickerdoodles they've been feasting on.

Flexible Hours?

You get paid by the appointment, so when you start off, you will be taking whatever you can get. Personal-training clients tend to be highly paid, high-powered people who are up at the crack of dawn, so many times your first session will be at (gulp) 6 AM. During the middle of the day there are usually a lot of breaks, since most folks are at their jobs. But once it's after five, you'll have appointments up until about 8:30. The hours aren't overwhelming, but they are spread out across a large swath of the day. Keeping your energy up from 6 AM until 9 PM, even with breaks throughout the day, requires pacing yourself.

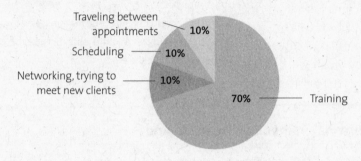

As far as wear and tear on your own body, you have to learn how to teach and not do all day long. It's not about how high you can kick, it's about communication and connecting with clients.
—Kristi Molinaro, personal trainer and group fitness instructor

Money?

The money can really vary. Personal trainers in large urban areas can get anywhere from $70 to $120 an hour. If you work at a gym, you probably have to give $20 to $30 of that back to the gym; if you have your own studio, it's all yours. Of course, lots of other costs are involved with having your own space: rent, machines, upkeep, and so on. Successful trainers aim to have between six and eight appointments a day, and eight appointments can be fairly grueling. What's the best you can do? You could own your own studio, have a very posh clientele, and make more than $200,000 a year. It's pretty rare, but it's possible. The Bureau of Labor Statistics reports the mean salary as $31,060, ranging from $14,540 to $55,020.

Beyond regular training, you can try to make cash in other ways. You can produce and promote your own workout DVDs. Online training—or Web sites with video instruction—is also starting to take off. Obviously, one has to build a bit of a following before venturing into these fields. "Bit of a following" means that you're booked pretty solidly and the gym classes you teach are standing room only.

Stress-o-Meter: 4 (1 being a surfer, 10 being a Navy SEAL)

The only stressful thing is scheduling, and, of course, getting enough clients so that you can pay the mortgage. Once you have steady ones, it's pretty chill. Of course, on the job, you'll work hard to get clients excited, motivated, pumped up. You might be the type who gets in people's faces, yelling, "Push, you maggot!" But still, that's not really stressful.

Pros

You set your own schedule and are your own boss.

You work in a healthy environment with health-conscious people.

People look forward to being with you.

It's fulfilling to see people progress because of your training.

You stay in pretty great shape.

Cons

No sick days, no vacation; if you don't work, you don't get paid.

Same if you are injured, so you need to really take care of your body.

Scheduling conflicts and cancellations are annoying.

Running around to appointments all the time can be hectic and tiresome.

Congrulations, You Are a Personal Trainer. You Wake Up And . . .

6:30 AM: You arrive at the house of your first appointment, a wealthy lawyer who has her own gym. She really wants to tone her arms, which have become "grandmalike." You begin to take her through a rigorous workout.

7:35 AM: You split and drive like a demon to your next appointment at his gym.

8:00 AM: You meet your second appointment and he immediately tells you he is hung over and wants to take it easy. This is the same guy who complains he's lost only two pounds. You coax him onto the treadmill to "sweat out the poison."

9:00 AM: Another appointment at the same gym.

10:00 AM: And another. This one is pregnant, and you guide her through a regimen you specially designed for her.

11:00 AM: One more!

12:00 PM: After the back-to-back morning, you have a big break. You do your own workout quickly and then go get some lunch, followed by a wee bit of shopping. You try not to talk to anyone during your breaks, because of the constant chatter you keep up while working.

4:30 PM: And so begins the first of four more appointments, one every hour on the hour. The last one, at 8:30, is again off site, but just around the corner.

9:30 PM: You go home to some bad TV and a healthy dinner.

I Long to Help Others Obtain Buns of Steel.
How the Hell Do I Get This Job?

Most people follow this route: they become class instructors, and then they become personal trainers. The path for this is defined shortly. Of course, if you are interested in specific disciplines such as Pilates or yoga, there will be additional certification and training.

The first thing to do when thinking about becoming a trainer or instructor is to take lots of workout classes, especially at the gym where you may want to teach someday. Meet everyone and become a fixture there, even as you are observing how to cue and choreograph by watching your instructors. See if you feel that you can do this well enough to lead a class. Now, even though this is an early stage in deciding whether you want to do this, it really helps to pick an exclusive, expensive gym right from the get-go. If you go through the steps outlined here and become a personal trainer, the kind of clients you want (in other words, rich ones) are the kind who attend such exclusive gyms. And it's easier to become a personal trainer there if you have a history with them. It's worth the investment.

But before you can take the first step and become a class instructor at this fancy gym, you'll need to do two things. First, you have to get a certificate that states that you know how to perform CPR. Second, you'll need to take training certification classes in whatever discipline you wish to instruct. You won't be able to take the certification classes without the CPR, so make sure you get that certificate first. When you have it, go online and to see where and when trainer certification courses are being taught in your community. Check the Aerobics and Fitness Association of America (AFAA) Web site, afaa.com, or the American Council on Exercise (ACE) site, acefitness.org. They'll have all the information.

Once you have all your certificates and can officially teach, you need to find a job. Find out about hiring in your area by simply asking at local gyms (especially, of course, your own). If they have an opening, instead of an interview, you usually have to audition. Here's how it works: the gyms will hold large "calls" for instructors, similar to a film casting call for actors. (See the chapter on actors.) Aspiring instructors, like you, will form a class, and then each candidate will take a turn, get up, and teach the class. All the while, the gym director observes. These auditions are pretty competitive; at some of the most prestigious gyms, like Equinox in New York City, they may very well see sixty people in an audition and pick none. This is why it's important, as stated before, to go to the gym you want to work at, even before you go through all of the certifications. Your chances of being picked in an audition are way better

Once you get in the sub rotation, you start to jockey for a permanent spot. So after you teach a class as a sub, you should mention to the class that if they liked you, they should talk to the management or leave a positive comment on a comment card. Let the class know what other locations you'll be at if they're interested in taking your class again. Be outgoing; build a following.
—Kristi Molinaro, personal trainer and group fitness instructor

if you are already friendly with the gym staff. If the gym director likes your audition, he or she will usually put you on a "sub list," which is the same as being a substitute teacher in school. And you'll get called in to teach when the regular instructors are unavailable.

Most people start teaching classes and then later move on to the next step—becoming a full-on personal trainer. Yes, you can skip the teaching-classes step, but it's far harder to build a clientele from scratch. The best way to meet clients is in a gym, and most gyms won't let just anyone show up and try to poach clients. If you're already an instructor there, you're on the inside; it's easier.

To become a personal trainer, you'll need the same CPR certification, plus additional training specific to personal training, which you can also find on the sites previously listed. If you are working as an instructor at a gym, often you can go through the personal training program at that gym.

Once you've gotten the training and are legit, it's time to start building that clientele. If you get hired at a gym, you'll have to pay your dues doing *core work*, which is simply being out on the floor, helping people with machines. (Meanwhile, you can still be teaching classes at the gym; this is the benefit of going in the order of class instructor to personal trainer. You may have clients who love you by now.) You'll start out doing *orientations*, which are the free trials that people get when they sign up for a gym membership, and you'll slowly meet people who want you to train them. Bottom line, the goal is to work at an expensive gym, one with thick towels and fancy showers; make connections; and move upward and onward.

Resources

Fitness magazines are great for new training ideas. Not to mention, your clients will probably read them. So then, should you. Check these: *Self, Fitness, Shape, Muscle and Fitness, Men's Health,* and *Personal Training Professional.*

Lots of different fitness organizations offer advice, training, and additional resources. Here are some of the most respected:

American Council on Exercise: acefitness.org

Aerobics and Fitness Association of America: afaa.com

National Exercise Trainers Association (offers certification, workshops): ndeita.com

National Fitness Trainers Association: naturalfitnesstrainers.com

Pharmaceutical Salesperson

Pharmaceutical salespeople. Technically, they're legitimate drug dealers. The career has long been an attractive one because of the high pay and large expense accounts, although recently new FDA regulations have cut back on some of the fun. These days, salespeople can lavish only so many expensive dinners and golf or spa junkets on doctors. Still, if you are a good salesperson (or *rep,* as they call themselves) who can be likable but aggressive, who is interested in the healthcare industry, and is generally an ethical person, pharmaceutical sales offers a good salary and somewhat flexible hours—which makes it a fairly sought-after job for recent graduates who enjoy both money and flexibility.

Pharma Companies

Pharmaceutical companies make all kinds of drugs, vaccines, medical devices, you name it. And although medicine is technically for the betterment of humanity, this is capitalism, and pills and cures (or hip replacements and artificial heart valves) are the goods from which they make their profits.

Most of these pharma companies are gigantic, huge, gargantuan . . . pick your own large adjective. They have tens of thousands of employees or more, with offices in numerous countries around the world. Some workers are scientists, developing new drugs in labs; others market those drugs, naming them and picking the pill colors (yes!) that will make the drug seem most effective. Still others spread the word about these drugs and try to promote them to doctors and hospitals as safe, effective treatments for their patients. These are the pharmaceutical salespeople.

What Do You Do, as a Salesperson?

Well, basically, once you have obtained the job, the first thing you'll do is go through a very rigorous training program where you will learn all the things you need to know about the company and many of its drugs or medical products. And then you'll be tested on them. These tests are no joke; some last from nine in the morning until five at night. Ouch. A lot of times these programs are about a month long and take place at the company's headquarters, which

There is a lot of competition out there. To be good at this job, you have to be able to talk to anyone; you have to be able to charm them. And you must have a deep knowledge of your product; you're talking to doctors, so you really need to know your stuff. But, when the doctors' offices close, you're pretty much in the clear. Not much happens after 5 PM, other than some paperwork. So the potential of earnings to the hours worked can be really great in this job.
—Brett Reilly, account manager, Dianon Systems (Labcorp)

may mean you are away from home for a month. Diseases, the competition—you'll be cramming it all in. Most important, you'll learn how to sell (or more specifically, how they would like you to sell). It's quite intense.

From training you'll go to starting the job proper, which is different at every company. Usually you will not just be handed a briefcase and asked to call on doctors by your lonesome. To begin, you will "ride along" with someone else on sales calls and learn the ropes.

There are a lot of different fields of medicine to specialize in at large pharma companies, the same way doctors specialize. They may sell meds that help in everything from gynecological issues to asthma. Salespeople generally work in groups whose focus is on just a single area or several interrelated ones. Since you need to be an absolute expert on your drug and get to know the specialists you are selling to, narrowing the field makes sense.

As a sales rep, you will have a list of accounts; these could be in hospitals, nursing homes, or doctors' offices. You'll make appointments with doctors at each, go see them, and explain why they should be prescribing your company's drugs to their patients. You'll give them all the research and studies that detail the drugs' efficacy, as well as free pens and free samples. Many times you'll also be scheduling appointments between the company's scientific people and the physicians, so they can have a direct back-and-forth on data. And you'll be doing a lot of driving; often you'll see ten doctors a day.

When you aren't meeting and greeting or scheduling meet-and-greets, you'll be reviewing new drug studies and data so you'll be up to snuff on your products (and the competitors' drugs you are trying to outsell), and, of course, you'll be filling out expense forms, for the lunches you've bought doctors. But it's not that easy. Doctors are overworked. And many times, they could give a crud about seeing you. Sometimes not even a crud.

What Qualities and Skills Does One Need?

Well, you'll definitely need a four-year degree to get this job, although you needn't necessarily be a premed or science major. Beyond that, just like any good salesperson, you have to be able to talk to anyone, anytime. As Alec Baldwin said in the film *Glengarry Glen Ross:* "ABC—Always. Be. Closing." And it's important to be succinct, to be able to present your message in sixty seconds, because physicians have such little time these days to spend with salespeople—just think how little time doctors spend with you when you're actually sick. Reps will tell you that doctors are really not easy to talk to. They're suspicious of drug companies, and frankly, they don't get paid when they see

Doctors are busy and often they can give you only ten seconds, many times not even that. So basically, you see the receptionists most often and have the best rapport with them. Next are the nurses, because they are the ones who write the requisitions and send things to the laboratory. Lastly would be the doctors; maybe you get to talk with them 10 percent of the time.
—Brett Reilly, account manager, Dianon Systems (Labcorp)

salespeople, so they'd rather squeeze in more patients then "waste" time on a sales call.

Therefore, the key is to build relationships. A primary-care doctor could literally have ten or even twenty reps come to his or her office, all on the same day. He or she certainly doesn't have five minutes for each one, so the more the doctor likes you, the more likely he or she is to talk to you. Seventy percent of the job is really building relationships with these difficult-to-talk-to people. The "gift of gab" cannot be overemphasized.

Office?

All pharma reps have sales territories, or neighborhoods they cover. If your sales territory is near one of your corporate offices, you will have an actual office within the building; if not (more likely), your home will be your office, completely outfitted with everything you need, courtesy of headquarters. Either way, most of your day is spent outside the office, making sales calls and driving to sales calls. It's not the type of job where you'll hang out with your officemates or be able to keep up to date on that eBay auction.

Your car in many ways will really be your office. And for the most part, the company will buy you that car. And give you a gas card. And a laptop. And a mobile phone, and a Blackberry. Nice perks, yes, but all so you can sell, sell, sell!

Hours?

Generally the hours follow doctors' office hours, which are around eight to five daily. Add on top of that reviewing research and doing expenses, plus dinners, speaking events, and seminars to attend, and you are looking at about ten hours a day. Which, given the money you can make, as you'll see shortly, is not bad at all. Keep in mind, though, that most of those hours you will be "on." There won't be a lot of down time; you'll be meeting with people, selling, trying to be charming. Yep, even while driving, you'll be working the phone. So although the number of hours may not be overwhelming, each hour will be somewhat intense.

To be a salesperson you must have thick skin, because sometimes, people can be incredibly rude. Some doctors you approach are really kind, and some are just unbelievable. Like they will just walk away from you. Literally walk away from you and not even say a word.
—Michelle Spitz, account manager, Procter & Gamble

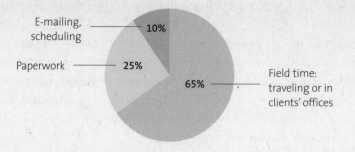

E-mailing, scheduling — 10%

Paperwork — 25%

Field time: traveling or in clients' offices — 65%

Jeans and a T-Shirt or Three-Piece Suit?

Jeans and a T-shirt is for a totally different kind of drug salesperson, sorry. In general, you'll always need to be upbeat and fun (who wants to meet with an angry little salesperson?), and you're expected to look and act professionally. You must be very well spoken and, as mentioned earlier, have expertise on the drug you are peddling. Doctors want to make sure you know the disease profile, how the drug works, what class of drug it is, what the data behind it is, what the efficacy is, how safe the drug is, and so on. You need to exude confidence in all this knowledge; you aren't selling a used car. So for meetings and doctor visits, you'll have to get some nice, crisp suits.

Of course, if your territory is far from a corporate office and you work from home, well, when you're home, you're home. Break out the footie pajamas. And when you are meeting just with your colleagues, even though you'll probably be in a suit, for the most part it's a personable, outgoing crowd. Like you, they were hired for their people skills.

As far as the sales team goes, most everyone is pretty young—most under forty, even under thirty. It's a fun group.
—**Brett Reilly, account manager, Dianon Systems (Labcorp)**

Money?

The money is plentiful and so are the benefits. You can make $40,000 or $50,000 a year right out of school, plus bonus, and in a few years go up to about $120,000 plus bonus. Not too shabby, especially when you consider that the bonuses can be hefty—a large percentage of your income, in fact. You'll also get a car, with the gas and insurance paid for, plus an expense account.

Salary.com places the national median salary, with bonus, for lower-level reps at $72,852. It's not uncommon for experienced reps to make $250,000 or more in a good territory when a new drug or product is launched. Yeah, it's a nice-paying gig.

Stress-o-Meter: 6 (1 being a hot-air balloonist, 10 being a space shuttle astronaut)

Any sales job has pressure. You are expected to make quotas, and bonuses are based on beating those quotas. If you consistently miss your target, there's no bonus, and, well...gulp. If you are a born salesperson, though, this excites you. You thrive on the performance-based compensation model. Plus, the hours are not overwhelming given the payoff.

Pros

Very good pay and benefits.

New drugs are always coming out, so you never get bored.

Freedom to make your own schedule.

When not visiting doctors, you may be able to work from home.

Cons

You have to look good and appear happy all the time.

Lots of overnight travel to conventions, which often means nights and weekends working.

Having to handle problems on the fly (usually on a loud street, on a cell phone).

Often you wait an hour to see a doctor for thirty seconds.

Congratulations, You Are a Pharmaceutical Salesperson. You Wake Up And . . .

8:00 AM: Your territory is far from the corporate office, so you settle down in your home office, wearing just a towel. You get a silly thrill from being able to start the day in total comfort. You check your voice mail and e-mail and make a plan for the day.

9:00 AM: After putting on a suit, you start commuting into the city, eating your breakfast in the car.

9:30 AM: You make your first sales call, or "customer call," of the day. This is the earliest you'd ever make a call, as most offices open at nine. If you get there right when they open, they're usually too busy planning their day.

10:00 AM: You make two other office visits right in the same area.

12:00 PM: You try to take a few different doctors out for lunch, but there are no takers. Everyone is booked up solid with patients. You grab a quick lunch by yourself, and via Blackberry and cell phone, start handling some action items from the morning calls, like making sure the office sends out some additional information one of the doctors asked for.

1:00 PM: You go to the hospital, where you have sales calls for the next two hours. You see two doctors, but the third completely blows you off, leaves you sitting in his office for forty-five minutes and then cancels on you. You grin and tell the receptionist you understand. Inside, though, you are a volcano of curse words.

3:00 PM: You had dinners scheduled with doctors the last two evenings, but tonight you are free and clear. You brave the early rush and commute back to the home office.

4:00 PM:	The suit is on a hanger and you are in shorts and a T-shirt. You get on the computer and deal with a bunch of e-mails. You file a few expense reports and make a plan for tomorrow.
6:00 PM:	You shut the computer down. And go for a jog.

I Want to Sell Drugs. How the Hell Do I Get This Job?

It's all about knowing someone on the inside. Ask around and find someone who works in the industry. Reps cross paths with reps from every side of the industry, so reputation and word of mouth are important. Almost all of our new hires were referred to us by a rep or someone close to that rep.
—**Brett Reilly,**
account manager,
Dianon Systems
(Labcorp)

Because it's a lucrative field with nice perks, it's pretty competitive to get pharmaceutical sales jobs. You can find them a few different ways: through corporate headhunters, on job sites like monster.com and medzilla.com (specializing in jobs in the medical field); through major pharmaceutical companies' own Web sites (look for the employment section to see what's available); or the best way, which is to know someone at one of the companies and hit him or her up to see if there are any openings. In a field where success is based on personality, knowing people and having them like and recommend you is the best way in the door.

Also, many of the big drug companies have internships. If you take one and are at least somewhat impressive, there's a very, very good chance you will be offered a job on graduation. So if you know this is what you want to do while you are in school, definitely intern. Check with your campus career center or with the major drug companies themselves (on their Web sites or by calling their human resources departments) for opportunities.

This is a job where the résumé is quite important, so make sure yours is very professional and corporate. No photos of your cat on these, please. Hundreds of people are applying for these positions, so good grades and success in extracurricular activities will help you get in the door.

Make sure it comes across that you are in this industry to be successful and to make money. Don't come out and say it in those blunt words; finesse it. Just make sure they understand that you are a motivated person who does want to make money.
—**Brett Reilly,**
account manager,
Dianon Systems
(Labcorp)

Once you obtain an interview through one of these methods, keep in mind that you are going for a job in sales. You need to look presentable, confident, and trustworthy. Charm the pants off your interviewer, but don't lie or try to seem smooth. And make sure you ask a ton of questions—not silly ones like, "Hey, where'd you get that tie?"—but questions about which territory you might be working in, the competitors' drugs, and so on. Show them you know something about the field.

But most important, show that you know a lot about their company in your questions and comments. Do your research. Here's a common scenario that happens in interviews: the interviewer will tell you about their drug, and then turn around and say, "Now sell it to me." If you do your homework, you'll be able to "sell it" using some information the interviewer never mentioned. It's a nice move. Also, all of the drug companies are into "values and creeds," and you can find these corporate vision statements on their sites. Make sure you know those as well. They may come up.

Finally, show that you really want it. You are a salesperson, damn it. Close the deal.

Resources

Job listings can be found on Web sites like monster.com and medzilla.com, as well as the major pharmaceutical companies' sites:

Procter & Gamble: pg.com

GlaxoSmithKlien: gsk.com

Pfizer: pfizer.com

Novartis: novartis.com

Johnson & Johnson: jnj.com

And don't miss the National Association of Pharmaceutical Sales Representatives site, napsronline.org. From entry-level training information, to links to just about every pharmaceutical company, NAPSR has it all!

On an interview, you have to be very outgoing and enthusiastic. As the interview is winding down, if you really want the job you should say, "What do I need to do to secure this position? I want this position." You need to let them know you want it.
  —Michelle Spitz, account manager, Procter & Gamble

Photographer

Photographs are everywhere you look. In magazines, on billboards, on juice cartons, in, er, frames. Some are wild dreamscapes with casts of hundreds; others are boring postage stamp–sized shots on coupons—say, a bunch of bananas for fifty cents. Either way, somewhere a professional photographer was paid to take the shot.

There are fine art photographers, who shoot solely for art's sake (hoping that their art sells—see the chapter on gallerists for insight into the art world), photojournalists who work for news agencies like the Associated Press, wedding photographers, forensic crime-scene photographers, and paparazzi. This chapter will focus on what might be the most common working type, and an aspirational one to boot—editorial and commercial photographers, the ones who take pictures for magazines, album covers, and all kinds of products, services, and advertisements.

Freelancin'

Photographers are basically freelance and are hired only by magazines, ad agencies, and designers when they are needed. Here's how it works. Let's say an ad agency is doing a print campaign for a fast-food client, featuring the new giant Rodeo Burger. They've come up with an idea for an ad that features a cowboy on horseback sinking his teeth into the behemoth burger. The next step for them is to hire a photographer to get that shot. The art director on the project (see the chapter on advertising creatives to learn more about art directors and their penchant for fancy fonts) along with, at some agencies, a person known as an *art buyer* will call in several different photographers' portfolios.

How does the agency pick whom to call? A few ways: they may simply know of a particular photographer's work, or they may have seen ads or a promotional piece from the photographer that piqued their interest, or they could have simply called a photographer *rep*, or agent, and asked him or her to recommend someone for the job. These reps represent multiple photographers, and it's their job to promote and sell them. So after hearing about the intended shot, the rep would send over two or three portfolios of photographers they think might fit. Reps get paid by taking a commission of the photographer's fee; they're more common in the higher-paying advertising world than in the editorial. The art director will eventually choose a photographer to shoot with, and if he or she picks you, boom—you're off to capture an image.

Ah, but if only it were that simple. As a professional photographer, you don't just focus and then push the button; in fact, artistic photography skills—understanding composition, lighting, depth of field—are only part of the job. To achieve a shot like this profound hungry cowboy image, there's a lot to be done. And you are in charge of all of it. You need to find a location. You may try to do it yourself, running around all day, but more likely, you'll hire a location scout. Then you'll weigh costs. Is it worth it to go to Wyoming? Or maybe it's more cost effective to do in New Jersey, and then put in a background of mountains and plains via Photoshop? You'll need to cast for the hungry cowboy himself and dress him in the right wardrobe. What is your vision—is he a good cowboy in all white, or a man in black? Then suddenly a question comes from the agency: how can you shoot the image so it is wide enough that we can see our cowboy on horseback, while close enough to show off the burger? Luckily, the thing is 8,000 calories big. Still, it requires thinking about the angle.

You can't do this all yourself. You will build a team, the makeup of which changes according to the needs of each job. For this one, you'll hire assistants to help you lug stuff and set up lights; a stylist for clothes (see the chapter on wardrobe stylists), and another for hair and makeup, to make sure your model looks like a cowboy; plus a food stylist to make the burger look delicious and to keep making new ones throughout the day. You'll even need a horse wrangler to take care of the stallion and, well, get the poop off the set. And, for postproduction (anything that happens after the actual shoot), you'll probably have a retoucher, or Photoshop expert, with whom you'll work. These tweak color and lighting—and even nip and tuck models' bodies—to create an enhanced photo. They are artists in their own right, as poorly done retouching looks fake and cheesy. Some photographers do their own retouching, but most don't, because it can be very time consuming.

Once you've put your team together, you, some folks from the agency, and maybe even a representative from the fast-food client gather at the location. Here you are the leader, the boss, the captain of the ship, exactly like a director on a film shoot. (See the chapter on film directors.) You'll make sure the lighting looks perfect, the model is styled correctly, and the agency is happy with how everything looks. And then . . . you start to take photos. While you snap away, you direct the model. "Show me 'hungry,' like you were a vegetarian for years, and now you can't wait to taste meaty goodness!" until you get the wide-eyed look of craving you envision.

Whether a shoot is as big as this or less complex—say, a simple shot of gum on a white table—the gig is pretty much the same. Put together the team that will get you the best shot. Then get it.

What Do You Do When You're Not Shooting?

Mostly, you'll be doing what it takes to get more jobs. You'll be promoting yourself and networking. You might try to get meetings with photo editors at magazines or art directors at advertising agencies. Or work on your Web site. Or send out promotional mailers with your latest shots inside. You'll constantly be building and rebuilding your portfolio. The number one rule with these is, quality over quantity. If it's not a killer shot, toss it. Show only your best work.

When you're not shooting, there's administrative work to do. You'll be invoicing clients, paying bills, and figuring out budgets for upcoming jobs. You'll be looking through the 300 shots you just took for a magazine to find the best three or four you want to send over. You'll be supervising the color correction a retoucher is doing to one of your images. There's always something—because as a freelancer, you aren't just a photographer; you're also the owner of a small business, the business of you. So if you own your own studio, there are bills to pay. If you rent it out on occasion to other photographers to make extra money, there are those to find and negotiate rates with. You'll be keeping busy.

Is There a Job before I'm the "Captain of the Ship"?

Yes, matey. The natural first step is a job as an assistant to a photographer. As an assistant, generally, you won't be on a photographer's full-time staff, but will be called in when needed. (Very successful photographers may have full-time staff, however.) You will help lug lights, build sets, place props, charge batteries, and move sandbags to steady tripods. There will be a lot of grunt work, and your day rate will be pretty low.

Once they find assistants they can count on, photographers try to keep bringing them back. In that way, assisting is almost an apprenticeship. So you aren't just doing it for the minimal money, you're doing it to learn. Not only will you sharpen all of your photo skills from working with a pro, but you'll hone your expertise in every aspect of what it's like to be on a set and how to conduct yourself there. And you will be setting yourself up to meet, greet, and network when it's time for you to spread your wings and become a full-fledged photographer.

What Does It Take to Be Good at This?

It takes an artistic side and a great eye. You need to be confident when you are running a hectic set and know when to listen to other people and when to trust your gut. Since there is so much self-promotion, you also need to be a good "people" person. It should be fun to work with you, so clients will want to again.

In terms of technical skills, well, you'll need to know everything that's involved with photography, naturally. You also should know Photoshop, even if you plan to hire others to do your retouching work, so you can communicate effectively with the people who'll be doing the tweaking. Also, going through hundreds of photos and cataloging them is time consuming. Software can help, such as iView Media and Photo Mechanic.

Where Do You Work?

When you're shooting, you'll be in one of two places, a studio or a location—which is basically anywhere but a studio. Studios are empty interior spaces set up for the business of photography: the electrical and lighting sources are all controllable; the windows can be "blacked out," and there may be dressing rooms, conference rooms, and "seamless" walls (they curve at the bottom, so there are no edges or seams).

Shooting on location is often the opposite. You've chosen to work at a location for what it intrinsically provides you—for example, it's better to shoot in a real firehouse than try to build and recreate one in a studio. So even though you'll do plenty of tweaking, you'll work with what you have. Location shooting can be fun because you get to travel, but shooting anywhere not "locked down," like a busy street, has its own logistical nightmares.

Wherever you are, the vibe of a shoot—to start, anyway—is relaxed and fun. Even in the service of the most corporate client, you are still creating art. Music might be playing; snacks may abound; the vibe should be cool and arty, comfortable but professional. Of course, if something is not working or the day is running late, things can get a trifle stressful, as money is being spent.

When you aren't shooting, you'll need a small office, which could even be a home office, to e-mail, send out promotional materials, go through digital contact sheets on the computer and "pick selects" (the best shots), and do all sorts of administrative tasks. Thanks to the advent of digital photography, you don't really need access to a darkroom all the time now, just on occasion, so most photographers simply rent these according to need.

When I interact with my clients I want them to feel as comfortable as possible, so I don't put on a different persona around them. I try to keep it laid back. When I'm working I'm usually climbing on things along with my assistants, so I can't wear a ballroom gown. I just wear jeans and a T-shirt. You're not going to be looking hot on the set; you're going to be working hard. I'm a mangled mess by the end. Just the other day we were building a whole office and I was covered in blue paint by the evening.
—Ramona Rosales, photographer

Hours?

As most people who work in "for-hire" jobs will tell you, it depends. When you are working, you're working hard. On a shoot day, you could be working from twelve to eighteen hours. On days between, you'll be looking for work, putting in around six hours. Or if you're just starting out, you may still be assisting on days when you aren't shooting your own projects. Successful photographers tend to average more than the standard forty-hour workweek; it's closer to fifty or sixty.

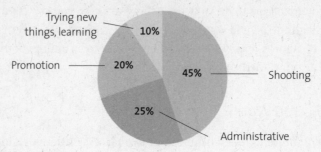

Money?

When you assist, it's low; how low depends on the job and the level of photographer with whom you are working. You could get $100 for the day, you could get $300.

Once you are a full-time photographer, you make money a few different ways. First, you can get a flat fee, what you are paid to take the shot. Then, since you are "producing the shoot," you can potentially mark up your team's services (you had to find them, after all) and make a small amount off that. Increasingly, instead of a flat fee, there's something called *usage*, which refers to how your image will be used and for how long. If you keep ownership and rights to your images, you can license them out again and again and again and collect fees every time they are "used." You're basically letting people borrow or rent the photo for a time period, and they are paying for the rental.

In general, advertising work pays more than editorial. If you get large corporate clients and have a good rep negotiating the right fees, you can make a substantial living. Editorial is more of a struggle. The average fee (including usage) is around $500 a day—not bad if you shoot every day, but no photographer shoots five days a week. Editorial jobs are generally sexier and thus help you promote yourself to advertisers—but remember, with all the equipment you own, repair, and upgrade, it's an expensive career. The goal is to do some of both, the creative and the high-paying, to be fulfilled and make a lot of money at the same time. Oh, and of course, there are no benefits, no medical or dental, when you are freelance.

Cutting to the chase: according to salary.com, the median national salary for a photographer is $47,442. According to the Bureau of Labor Statistics, the salary ranges from $15,240 to $53,900. These probably lump a lot of different types of photographers together, from paparazzi to the people who take "party pix!" at fraternity mixers. Successful photographers who get a decent amount of advertising work will tell you those figures seem very low. You can make in the high six figures if you are a hot photographer in the advertising world.

> It's stressful in the beginning when you first get a good, high-paying job and you have to deliver something great. Then, as you gain experience, it's more the stress of being freelance.
> —Stefano Giovannini, photographer

 ## Stress-o-Meter: 7 (1 being a pharmacist, 10 being a DEA agent)

1   10

A lot is piled on your broad shoulders. First, you're trying to please a client, which is always stressful. And when you're not shooting, you're trying to get jobs, make money, and pay the bills. It's a constant juggle of art and business. And until you are quite successful, the only one who's juggling it all is you.

Pros

Getting paid to do what you love—shoot photos.

Meeting amazing people.

Traveling to far-flung locations on someone else's dime.

Every shoot is at least a little different and interesting.

Cons

Wondering if you can survive until the next job.

Constantly promoting yourself.

The occasional overbearing client.

The occasional overbearing subject.

Congratulations, You Are a Photographer. You Wake Up And . . .

This assumes it's the best kind of day, a shoot day.

7:30 AM: You arrive at the studio, where your crew has already begun setting up. For a magazine article, you're shooting a man sitting at a desk, except everything in the picture is going to be painted pure white: the computer, the chair, the desk, the cubicle, even the model, who will be wearing a white suit and tie.

8:00 AM: The model arrives. You instruct the makeup person on exactly what you want, and she begins to coat the model's face and hands in white.

9:00 AM: You tweak the light a little while the model is painted, then shoot some practice shots using an assistant as a stand-in.

10:00 AM: Your client, the photo editor, arrives. You exchange a hug and go over to the kitchen area, where coffee and pastries await. You show her around the set, and luckily, she loves the way things look.

10:30 AM: The model emerges. He looks pretty good, but you want his hair to look white as well. The makeup person douses it with baby powder—you'll need to do the rest in Photoshop or else subject the poor model to some serious bleaching. You elect Photoshop.

11:00 AM: You start to shoot. You snap multiple exposures of the first angle you want to try, low and wide.

1:15 PM: After a break for lunch, you shoot several more angles. The client seems to really like the profile shot better than the others, so you focus on giving her a wide variety within that angle.

5:30 PM: Just for yuks, you try something different. You have the model sit on top of the desk, Indian-style. Then you have him hold his head in his hands. "Pretend you were just laid off," you tell him.

6:30 PM: You wrap. Your assistants break the set, and one takes the hard drive with the images (you were shooting digital) straight to the retoucher. You head home, tired but happy. You think it's going to look hot.

Let's Shoot. How the Hell Do I Get This Job?

Some rare, headstrong beasts have the drive and the capital to just go out and do it on their own. But most photographers follow the same path. They go to art school to refine their craft and build a portfolio. Then they assist, learn more, and make connections, all the while continuing to take photos and improve their portfolio. And finally they take a chance, send their portfolio around, take some jobs on their own, and suddenly, voilà: they are working photographers.

Let's talk about that all-important portfolio before going any further. Portfolios should show the kind of work you want to do. If you want to shoot portraits, there should be amazing portrait photos in it. If you like landscapes, then landscapes. The whole presentation needs to look slick and professional; you should hit the best art store near you and pick up a nice portfolio case. Don't buy the cheapest one; it will scream "student." It's worth saving up (they can be anywhere from $50 to $500) for a nice one. The container really shouldn't make a difference. But it does.

If you go to art school, obviously you'd want to major in photography. If you went for a regular liberal arts degree (or business) and are suddenly realizing that photography is for you, you might consider an MFA in photography, or at least a battery of continuing-education classes at a respected school. Many photographers feel it's best to look for a school where the instructors, for the most part anyway, are working professionals. First, they are more grounded in the day-to-day, and second, they are going to have lots of connections. While you are in school, hopefully you can use these connections to start assisting; if you have the time, there's no reason to wait until graduation. Show photographers your beginning portfolio, make the presentation as slick as you can, and tell them you are willing to bust your ass to learn. Despite the agony of a busted ass, it's well worth it. Try to assist photographers whose work you admire, and soak everything up like a sponge.

These days, on top of a physical portfolio, you must have a Web site. Sometimes editors and art directors don't even look at a portfolio until after they've narrowed people down by glancing at their sites.
—Stefano Giovannini, photographer

If your instructors aren't as connected as you'd like, go to the Web sites of photographers you admire. Send them an e-mail telling them how much you like their images, where you attended or are attending school, and how much you'd like to assist them. It's not as good as a personal introduction, but it does work.

One thing you may want to consider doing while you are in school, or assisting, is shooting for free. Some well-designed, startup magazines need photos but can't pay. It's a way for you to get published and meet talented folks who will one day hopefully be employed somewhere they can pay you. Plus, the design of many of these magazines is slick; couple that with the lack of pay, and you'll probably be allowed to do fun, edgy, portfolio-caliber work. When you're at that newsstand, see which magazines are only in their first or second issue, check the masthead for the photo editor, and contact him or her. It's a great way to get your foot in the door.

Then, just get out there and keep shooting. Make the killer portfolio. Meet people. And it will all start to fall into place.

> The place you learn the most is on the set. Even now, that's where I continue to learn. You have to assist. There's no class or substitute for that kind of experience; you just have to do it.
> —Ramona Rosales, photographer

Resources

The Web site of the Professional Photographers of America, ppa.com, is chock-full of information, advice, and deals on equipment. Also check out the Web site of the Student Photographic Society, studentphoto.com. It houses articles, information on competitions, and even a forum to meet other photographers and ask all your burning photography questions.

Truckloads of photo books and magazines provide both inspiration and information. *Photo District News* (PDN), *Communication Arts,* and European fashion magazines like Italian *Vogue* are great places to see examples of editorial and commercial photography. The first two compile and highlight creative shots; European fashion magazines tend to hire the best photographers, worldwide. Go to a good local newsagent and just flip through pages and pages, looking for inspiration. In addition, Yahoo! has an excellent compilation of online and traditional photography magazines, complete with links: www.yahoo.com/Arts/Visual_Arts/Photography/Magazines/. Tons to look at.

Finally, many renowned art schools have excellent photography programs. Here are but a few: Art Center College of Design, Rochester Institute of Technology, Yale, School of the Art Institute of Chicago, Rhode Island School of Design, University of New Mexico, and the School of Visual Arts. If you are interested in rankings, *U.S. News & World Report* rates graduate fine arts programs in its "America's Best Graduate Schools" issue.

Physical Therapist

If you've ever suffered an injury and needed rehabilitation, then you know the value of physical therapy. Psychologists help soothe the mind and soul; physical therapists (PTs) work to help people regain their physical independence. Here's the official definition from the American Physical Therapy Association: "Physical therapists are health care professionals who diagnose and treat people of all ages who have medical problems or other health-related conditions that limit their abilities to move and perform functional activities in their daily lives." Like a sonnet, is it not?

The field of physical therapy is a popular one; it's a good choice for folks who enjoy medicine and healing people, but don't want to commit to the rigors of medical school, followed by interning, followed by residency, followed by long hours and pagers buzzing you to the hospital at all hours for emergencies. The goal of physical therapists is simply (or not so simply) to get folks moving again. The goal of occupational therapists, a related field, is to enable injured people to function at work and at home with their injury.

> I work with anyone, from childhood through the geriatric population. I deal mainly with sports and athletic injuries, but also sometimes work-related injuries, deterioration postsurgery, congenital issues, or birth defects.
> —Dr. James Voorhees, physical therapist

So Wait, Physical Therapists Are Doctors?

Some are, and in the future, all will be. But they don't go to medical school, they go to physical therapy school. Basically, for many years, you needed a master's degree to be a physical therapist. Today, the mission of the American Physical Therapy Association is for everyone who is licensed and practicing physical therapy to have a doctorate degree by the year 2020. The shift is happening. In 2007, there were 209 accredited physical therapist programs, meaning you could graduate from any one of these programs and become a physical therapist. Only 46 of these still offer master's degrees; the rest (exactly 163) offer doctoral degrees. They all will be changing over soon, so when choosing schools it makes sense to go for the doctorate over the master's. But more on the schooling later; first, let's see if you are into this job.

Where Do PTs Work?

Physical therapists can practice in a wide variety of settings, including hospitals, clinics, schools, and sports facilities; they can even do home care. You can divide these into two categories: public and private practices.

The major public venues for physical therapy are hospitals. Hospitals, especially those with strong physical therapy facilities, often have more than one department. There is *acute rehab,* whose goal is to get the most severely injured patients in the hospital up and moving; these patients won't be leaving the hospital for a little while. *Inpatient rehab* focuses on getting patients home or to the next part of care. It's for patients who've had strokes, brain injuries, brain surgery, muscular or skeletal surgery like total knee or hip replacement, back surgery, multiple sclerosis, and amputation. Inpatient rehab is where you can sometimes help people take their first steps after an accident or injury. Certain hospitals have *outpatient rehab.* This deals with people who are ambulatory—they go back and forth between their home and the outpatient department. And some hospitals have other specialized services, like a pediatric department or a vestibular department, which works on balance issues stemming from the inner ear.

The vibe of the hospital is, well, hospital-like. But the rehab areas try to be a little more optimistic and upbeat than the rest of the dreary, beige box that is most hospitals.

Private practices can specialize, or they can handle all different types of patients. In private practices, it's professionally casual. But (sigh) no jeans. Generally, PTs' offices are similar to a physician's, but a little less stuffy. Private-practice PTs also aim to make their setting happy, friendly, and optimistic. A lot of rehabilitation is mental; there needs to be hope in the air.

It's a fairly young profession, filled with compassionate individuals. It's very collegial and it's full of a lot of fun and laughter.
—Dr. Stephen Fischer, physical therapist, NYU Medical Center, Rusk Institute

Let's Get Physical. What Do PTs Do?

Let's say a new patient comes in. Most likely, but not necessarily, he has been referred by his physician. People see physical therapists for many different reasons. Some of the most common conditions include arthritis, back and neck pain, sports-related injuries, and children's diseases whose symptoms can be mitigated with therapy, such as cerebral palsy.

As a PT, you'll talk to the patient, ask what makes him go "Ow!" and get a sense of his general medical history. Then you'll make an *objective assessment,* meaning you'll examine the part of the body that's bothering him. This basic process is used to rule out anything serious, guide any forthcoming therapy, and establish a benchmark for monitoring progress.

Actual physical therapy begins after that, and usually continues for a period of time dependent on the injury. Patients may come in one to three times a week for treatment. There are many different kinds of therapy, including electrotherapeutic and mechanical agents (machines!), manual handling (human!), and simple counseling. It all depends on the injury and whether the patient is at the beginning of treatment or toward the end. It doesn't matter if it's a model who's limping because of a sprained toe or a stroke patient who is learning to use a wheelchair; your goal throughout this process is to help this person become as fully functional as he or she can, and frankly, to not need you anymore. To be independent.

Along the way, especially in a hospital setting, you'll interact with other people, too. Depending on the patient and injury, you may be talking with their families, the occupational department, the speech department, the psychology department, the vocational rehab department, and the patient's physician. You are part of the team helping to heal this individual.

What Does It Take to Be a Good PT?

Flexibility. You'll be working with people who are not in the best mood, as they are impaired in some way. You need to be able to empathize with patients' ailments and want to help them overcome their difficulties. You'll be dealing with some sensitive issues, depending on what's causing the physical pain or limitations, so you have to be able to gain patients' trust. The job is mostly one-on-one time with patients. You really just have to like people, warts and all, and enjoy being in their company.

Hours?

If you work in a hospital, there's a good chance you'll be in a union; these will have negotiated your contract, including your hours, benefits, salaries, you name it. Generally union hours total seven (woo-hoo!) per day. Hours vary slightly and there may be shifts, but the normal day is approximately 8:30 AM until 4:00 PM.

Private-practice office hours are from around 7 AM to 8 PM; the before-and-after-work hours accommodate those who have jobs. But don't panic; you won't toil all those hours. You'll work an eight-hour shift; another therapist will overlap with you so that the whole day is covered. You might work three days a week from 7 AM to 3 PM and two days a week from 12 PM to 8 PM.

PTs say that, private or public practice, once you leave work, you are done. Five days a week, seven or eight hours a day. That's it. Although when you are with patients, there's no goofing off and surfing the Web looking for silly JPGs of dogs riding tricycles—it's a solid day of work.

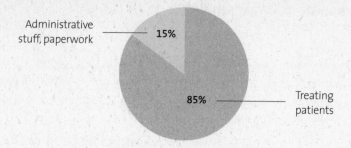

Administrative stuff, paperwork — 15%

85% — Treating patients

Money?

As a staff physical therapist, your starting salary should be around $50,000, whether you work in a hospital or a private practice. From there, if you work at a hospital, your salary, benefits, raises and promotions will most likely be based on the union contract. The highest union salaries tend to be around $100,000, for a PT with a lot of experience and a high title.

As an individual working at a private practice you don't own, the odds are that you'll also cap out around $100,000. If you own the practice and it is going well, you'll bring in other PTs, maybe even expand and open other practices. It's the one way you could potentially make a lot of cash in the field.

Without categorizing for public or private sectors (or location), the Bureau of Labor Statistics reports the mean salary for PTs as $65,350. Salaries range from $42,010 to $88,580.

Stress-o-Meter: 4 (1 being a coin collector, 10 being a debt collector)

The emergency situations that will come are few and far between. Some days you might be overly busy, but generally things are scheduled and under control. There are very few emergencies. The low stress reading is not to say that you won't care deeply for your patients and be concerned about their recovery. You will (if you are any good). But part of the job is to help people, and part of helping them is willing them past their own stresses.

Pros

You'll be working with people who actually want your help.

A feeling of satisfaction from seeing patients improve.

Controllable hours make for a balanced life.

Cons

The occasionally difficult, frustrating patients.

The amount of money you make is about half what physicians make.

Sometimes people don't improve.

You Did It. You're a Physical Therapist. You Wake Up And . . .

This assumes you are a PT in a private practice.

12:00 PM: Your workday officially begins at noon, so after taking care of some personal stuff, you get to the office and take your first appointment, a new patient. Generally appointments are exactly fifty minutes long, but new-patient appointments can run a tad shorter or a tad longer. This one—a football player trying to regain strength in his leg after a ligament strain—goes for an hour.

1:00 PM: A patient you've been treating three times a week comes in for an appointment. He hurt his shoulder at the gym and has now reinjured it twice. You work with him to help him build up its strength and show him some new exercises he can be doing at home between appointments.

1:50 PM: You sign and fill out a few insurance forms. You notice that you are low on quad canes and order some more.

2:00 PM: You hit a local diner for lunch with some of your colleagues, some of whom have become good friends. You check your cell phone messages and make plans for dinner.

3:00 PM: You take a call with the football player's physician, discuss therapy options, and compare notes. You have similar appointments straight through until the end of the day.

8:30 PM: You finish your last appointment and then split for your dinner date.

I Want to Be a PT. How the Hell Do I Become One?

Networking is great for getting a job in this field. Everyone really likes what they do, and so they love to help others get into the profession. Once you know some therapists at different practices, it's much easier for you to find a way in.
—Dr. Stephen Fischer, physical therapist, NYU Medical Center, Rusk Institute

There are no shortcuts or fancy tricks. You need to go to graduate school for two or three years and get your doctorate in physical therapy. However, if you know as an undergrad that physical therapy is the field for you, some programs link college and graduate work, enabling you to get both degrees in five or six years.

Coursework in physical therapy programs is quite serious. You'll be studying movement, which involves muscles, nerves, and the brain. You'll study physiology and anatomy, and here's something to look forward to: you'll probably have to dissect a human cadaver. (Blorf.) As tough as that is, it's necessary to understand the human body. You'll also learn physics concepts like kinesiology, or the way joints move. On top of class work, you'll intern at hospitals or clinics and do rotations. It's a good idea here, if you can, to try to work in as many different environments as possible, to help you decide whether you prefer public or private settings and whether you want to specialize. It's also a great way to meet working PTs.

After you obtain your doctorate, you'll need to pass the state licensing test. And then, my friend, you shall be a PT. But not necessarily a working PT. Unless you jump in and open your own practice (doubtful), you'll need to go on interviews. Networking and word of mouth are always the best ways to see who's hiring and help procure an interview; you can also look on job sites like monster.com. And when you do get the interview, you'll want to make clear that you understand the main facet of the job: working with and helping people. Show that you are sympathetic, flexible, and the type of person who can go with the flow. Questions like, "What's your growth plan?" "Are you looking to specialize?" and "Is this a long-term move or short-term?" are common. Be prepared to answer these, and realize that most facilities are searching for someone who wants a career and wants to stick around for a while—not a person who's looking for a couple of years' experience before splitting to open their own practice, or move to Boulder, or whatever your grand plan might be. Shhhhh.

Resources

Check out the American Physical Therapy Association site, www.apta.org. There's loads of advice on how to get started, where schools are located, and the different kinds of requirements (science classes, etc.) they might each have. It's a great resource. Rehaboptions.com is much less in-depth, but does have job listings and information.

Three of the best physical therapy schools are the University of Southern California, Washington University in St. Louis, and the University of Pittsburgh. For further investigation, pick up *U.S. News & World Report*'s "America's Best Graduate Schools" issue; it ranks the top physical therapy schools as well.

Private Investigator
Corporate Investigator/General Investigator

These days, the ol' "private eye" job is not all dames and double crosses. In fact, the investigation industry has been pushing to use the words *professional investigator* as the modern career title, to try to get away from all the well-known film noir slang. Because honestly, who wants a job as, say, a *private dick?* Don't answer that.

There are many different kinds of investigations. Depending on the line you're in, you might do more searching of databases than drinking black coffee on stakeouts. Still, private investigators definitely have their fair share of excitement—some from videotaping illicit affairs, some from cracking a fraud case.

Another change from the macho Humphrey Bogart stereotype is that today there are a surprising number of female PIs.

Private Investigating Today

Private investigators, as opposed to the police or FBI, are paid by individuals, attorneys, or corporations to research and find out the answers to all kinds of "fishy things" they have questions about. Most work at firms, not on their own as individuals. Some investigative firms do a variety of work, including spousal infidelity, blackmail, and insurance fraud. Others specialize in one area, such as computer security, or "due diligence" in giant corporate mergers—for example, making sure there aren't any skeletons in the closet of the person to be appointed the next CEO.

The line of investigating you're in will affect what kind of hours you work and what you do each day, naturally. Let's simplify by saying there are two paths: strict "white-collar" or corporate investigators, who work at corporations and investigate individuals for other corporations, and general firms that will handle anything.

When I first started, it was a male-dominated industry, but that has really evolved over the years. It's actually a great business for women because we do a lot of our work online and from databases; as long as you have a laptop and a cell phone, you can do it from anywhere. And as a woman, you have a built-in cover. People seem to be more disarmed by women. We tend to have a slightly nicer demeanor we can play up; it can work well if you're trying to get information.
—Lisa Dane, senior manager, Deloitte & Touche

Corporate Investigators

Corporate investigators do a lot more research and analysis than tailing leads and digging through trash. Let's say a corporation comes to your company and says it's missing $80,000,000, and these are the five people who have access to cutting checks. Forensic accountants will dig into the suspects' banking records, while you will do detailed background checks via the Internet and LexusNexus, delving into what they've done in the past and what they are doing now. You'll be searching for irregularities, past crimes, possible motivations—really any clues you can find. And for items not available online, you'll go to the courthouse to look up federal and state records of the five suspects (or contract this task out to other firms). Such investigators get their kicks solving these types of crimes and bringing the guilty to justice (which may mean simply having them disciplined or fired, depending on whether the company wants to get the law, and the media, involved). Crimes like these affect all of our daily lives, because white-collar crime impacts the prices of goods and services—just look at your car insurance.

General Investigators

At a general firm, you'll get all kinds of cases. Investigating marital infidelity is a very common type, and a profitable one at that. Sadly, lots of people want to know if their spouse is cheating on them, and they're willing to pay a fair price to find out. In cases like these, you will actually tail people and videotape and photograph them. You won't tap phones or do anything illegal, naturally.

In this field, the standard equipment is a high-powered video camera with "night shot" capabilities. But all kinds of surveillance equipment is put to use: most companies have a cache of backpack cameras, glasses cameras, pen cameras, you name it. Many of these small firms "contract out" or hire freelance investigators, and they expect these people to have bland cars and bland clothing so they can easily blend in with their surroundings. (Minivans and Jeep Cherokees are considered types of cars that don't stand out, by the way. That must excite the folks at Jeep.)

As a general investigator, you'll go on stakeouts, you'll tail people, you may even hide in a Dumpster or two. However, you will avoid confrontation, for the most part. You're basically collecting evidence to show your client, which they can take to the police or their lawyers.

One final note: today, PIs are law-abiding citizens. They aren't running around the streets like maniacs waving guns. Every once in a while, you'll read

A client will come to us when they've lost $100,000 or $100,000,000 trying to figure out how all the money went missing. These are the cases I like most. Say somebody at X Macaroni Company is funneling money out the door, putting fake employees on the payroll. At the end of the day, you the consumer end up having to pay more for your box of macaroni and cheese, because X Macaroni Company lost fifty million bucks last year to this employee. If I can catch the person and help recover some of that money, if it can save people ten cents on a box of macaroni and cheese, I'm doing my job.
—Lisa Dane, senior manager, Deloitte & Touche

about some rogue investigator, but most stay on the right side of the law to a fault. There are just too many chances for lawsuits and troubles.

What Kind of Person Is Good at This?

In any investigative field, being tenacious is paramount. People who are successful peel back layer after layer and keep digging despite the obstacles. They don't just do one quick search online and say, "Oh, I didn't find anything. Who wants wings?"

If you are primarily investigating outside the corporate world, the most important quality required is street smarts. You have to be somewhat confident and adventurous, because you'll find yourself in some terrible neighborhoods—and in some pretty upsetting situations, like serving someone with papers or getting caught photographing a tryst. How will you handle it when a guy who's been cheating on his wife chases you into a dead end? Or takes a baseball bat to your car? Though it's rare, these kind of things can happen. And you don't want to do the wrong thing and end up in trouble with the law. Male or female, you'll need some cojones.

You also have to be able to write. At the end of the day, corporate or general, you'll give your client a written report detailing all of your findings. It has to be coherent, accurate, and well written.

Hours?

The hours vary from case to case, and type of investigation to type of investigation. In the corporate world, if you're doing something routine like due diligence, the hours will be the basic nine to five-ish. You'll do some searches online, write up a report, and deliver it in a few weeks. If you're working on a larger fraud investigation, there can be deadlines to make for court dates, and you might be pulling all-nighters. For the most part, the hours tend to be pretty manageable.

Now, in the general, anything-goes land, well, anything goes. If you are investigating infidelity, for example, you're probably going to be working nights—usually, Friday and Saturday nights. In fact, when it comes to any kind of personal investigations, there will be a lot of night and weekend work. Most people are in their offices from nine to five, so you can't really find out much during that time. These evening and off-hours investigations can make relationships and personal life difficult. You have to stay with whom you're investigating, even when their schedule starts at 4 AM. In terms of hours per week, although corporate investigators are on salary, many general investigators work by the hour, so the number of hours worked depends on how aggressive and ambitious each is.

This assumes you work at a firm that does both corporate and general investigations.

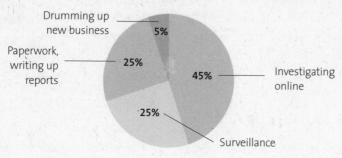

Drumming up new business — 5%

Paperwork, writing up reports — 25%

Investigating online — 45%

25% — Surveillance

Money?

Most investigators will tell you that "it's not about the money." Still, in the corporate world, at some firms, someone coming out of school with little or no experience can make between $30,000 and $40,000. There's a lot to learn, and as you do, you'll move up and get raises and bonuses. If you are one of the lucky few and become a partner and share the firm's profits, you can do very well, maybe a few hundred thousand. The Bureau of Labor Statistics reports the mean salary for investigators at management and technical consulting companies to be $73,390.

As far as general investigators go, the way to make the most money is to be a partner in the firm. Sharing of profits can lead to a fairly nice living, more than $100,000 if the firm is doing well. Outside that, the position pays far less than its corporate counterpart. The BLS reports a mean salary of $36,980, ranging from $19,230 to $61,520.

We work holidays all the time. Valentine's Day, for example, is a huge day for private investigators. The week before Valentine's Day is even busier, because often cheaters have to be with their loved one on Valentine's Day, so they'll go out with the "other person" the week before.
—Jonathan Gallant, partner, Investigative Solutions

Sometimes we sit there eight to ten hours waiting for someone. As soon as he comes out of the building, BANG he is in his car, he makes a left, an illegal left. Then he is on a busy street and you can't get by. You sat there eight hours and you are no better off than you were when you got there. It can be frustrating and extremely stressful.
—Jonathan Gallant, partner, Investigative Solutions

1   10

Stress-o-Meter: 7.5 (1 being a dog walker, 10 being an Olympic sprinter)

There's stress in any job where there can be confrontations. A large part of the high stress level comes from the fact that you have to get it right. You don't want to implicate the wrong person for committing fraud. Or adultery, for that matter. You can't screw up. If you do, you're gone, because you're ruining not only your own reputation, but your firm's. Plus, getting results is never easy. And paying clients are upset when they don't see results.

Pros

Working on amazing investigations, like solving a corporate fraud case that never even makes the paper.

The feeling of investigating someone who has no idea you are on to him.

Working with interesting people, from scum to CEOs.

Hours are flexible even when they are long.

Cons

Getting yelled at or threatened at times.

When you're junior, you'll be doing more mundane tasks than finding bad guys.

Clients are rarely happy; you may do a good job but the news isn't what they wanted to hear.

You Are a Private Investigator. You Wake Up And . . .

This daily schedule is for an investigator at a general firm who also gets some corporate cases, so it contains elements from both worlds.

8:00 AM: You arrive at work and jump on e-mail to see what's happened overnight, and whether any of the other offices or investigators need your help. You begin writing up a report on a fraud case you closed yesterday.

10:00 AM: You get a call from one of your associates that a guy who claimed he had whiplash from a car accident is playing tennis. You grab two cameras and race out to find him.

11:30 AM: You take the pictures out your car window. He has no idea, but he will, shortly. You note he has a terrible backhand, as well.

2:00 PM: Back at the office, you eat at your desk. You start doing some online research into an executive your client is about to hire. So far he's clean. The most interesting thing you find is that he has most definitely had a nose job.

3:00 PM: You get called to a meeting. A massive fraud case is coming up, and you'll be working on it. You get details on all the suspects whose backgrounds you'll need to dig into.

3:30 PM: You e-mail the tennis pics to the attorney who hired you in the fraud case. He sends you back a "THANKS!"

4:00 PM: You start doing research on the fraud case. This one will be on TV when it breaks; it's huge. You get so caught up in it you don't realize Miller Time has come and gone, it's almost seven. You log off your computer and head home.

I "Heart" Justice. How the Hell Do I Get This Job?

There isn't really any formal training required for this business. For a corporate job, a major in criminology, prelaw, or journalism is helpful in attaining the investigative skills firms look for in candidates. At the end of the day you're providing a report to a client, so any schooling that has taught you to write well is a huge plus. However, not having a degree in one of those fields isn't a deal breaker by any means; investigators come from many different backgrounds. When you start off as a junior person, you'll learn all of the online databases and become proficient in searching them. And really, the only way to learn these is to get the entry-level job, as the databases are offered only to companies who have the very expensive subscriptions; it's hard to get any sort of jump start.

That said, here's the exception: some of the more elite management consultation companies and professional security firms want people with a library science background, which means they already know how to search different kinds of databases. If you have this experience, you're going to be paid a far higher entry-level salary, around $60,000.

The best way to get an interview for a corporate job is by doing your homework and then approaching investigative firms. Remember, you're interviewing to be an investigator, so show these skills up front.

In the general world, you'll need to pass a required criminal background check, the requirements are different from state to state. Why? Well, you are out on the street in volatile situations, and the state wants to make sure you've been trained and aren't going to act like you are in a Vice City video game. With that in mind, one good way to get in the door of a general firm is to get part-time work in security. Many security guards are hired or contracted by investigative firms, and they sometimes ask the guards they like to join. Plus, in many states, it's the same license to be a guard as to be an investigator. While it may seem a less aspirational gig, it will give you a load of practical experience, and it's something you can do while you're in school, if you are working on a degree. Many general investigators have college degrees, but unlike the corporate job, this isn't a requirement.

When you interview at these firms, tell them flat-out that this is what you want to do. They get burned all the time by people who come and go; they aren't looking for yet another person who is going to quit to become a cop in six months. Tell them you are happy to sit in the office and answer the phone at first; show them how eager you are. Always remember, they are looking for people who seem smart and cunning, who are willing to learn from their superiors, and whom they can trust out on the streets.

Corporate or general, once you've obtained an entry-level position, you'll work assisting seasoned investigators while you learn the ropes. You'll be a sidekick. Once you've proven you know the ropes, you'll move on to greater responsibilities and your own cases.

Candidates should always ask questions in their interviews. "If I were to work here, what kind of cases would I be working on?" That sort of thing, at least. Be inquisitive. And you should know some background; research the place where you're interviewing. How good an investigator could you be, if you didn't even investigate us?
—Lisa Dane,
  senior manager,
  Deloitte & Touche

There is no schooling for it. The only actual way to do this is go out with an investigator and put in the hours. It's the only way you learn. A lot of the private detectives are former law enforcement, and they do a lot of the training. Different colleges—Boston University is probably the premier one—offer some sort of program that you can go through and become an investigator, but it's really an acquired skill you learn on the job.
—Jonathan Gallant,
  partner, Investigative
  Solutions

Resources

For more information, investigate some of these national and state associations:

National Council of Investigation & Security Services: nciss.org

National Association of Investigative Specialists: pimall.com/nais

Association of Certified Fraud Examiners: acfe.com (They offer a lot of courses, as well as an accreditation, which is not necessary to get a corporate job, but couldn't hurt. Some employers take it seriously; others don't.)

American Society for Industrial Security: asisonline.org

National Association of Legal Investigators: nali.com

A recommended book on a career in investigation is *The Complete Idiot's Guide to Private Investigating* by Steven Kerry Brown. And an industry journal you might want to flip through is the *Journal of Professional Investigators,* which is also online at pimagazine.com.

Psychologist

Are you a good listener? Do your friends come to you for help after a bad breakup? Do strangers on airplanes tell you their life stories? More important, do you enjoy hearing them? Perhaps the career of a psychologist might be for you.

A Note to Start

There are so many different career paths for psychologists that it would be hard to cover them all here. This chapter will focus on perhaps the most popular route, which is working with patients in therapy. But just so you know some of the other options, as a psychologist, you can do program development and manage a clinic; in a corporate setting, you can work for a company in its employee assistance program; you can have a career in sports psychology, working with athletes; you can work at an HMO and do behavioral health, or for the state or local government doing policy work, such as trying to get treatments integrated into schools; within schools, you can test and diagnose kids with learning disabilities, mental retardation, autism, Asperger's syndrome, and other developmental disabilities; or at a higher scholastic level, you can be a professor who both teaches and does research, or simply one who does research for the university. The choices are plentiful.

The Battle of the Consonants: PsyD vs. PhD

To become a psychologist, you need to have a doctorate degree. So before you even start thinking about all those different career options, you'll first have to decide between two kinds of doctorate degrees. You need to make this choice before applying to graduate school, so it's important to know the differences. However, if you are unsure after graduating college, you can always go for a master's in psychology before entering a doctorate program, and decide during that time.

The following may be a bit dry, so help yourself to a soda. A PsyD is a doctor of psychology. PsyDs work with people and do therapy. The big difference between PhDs and PsyDs is that PsyDs use research to help them in their work, but they don't actually do the research themselves. So as a PsyD, you'll

> What I do is help people who have problems, all sorts of problems. These are people who want to solve conflicts or dilemmas and figure out how to reach goals they have for themselves. I help people change behaviors that are getting in the way of reaching these goals.
> —Dr. Katie Gomperts, PsyD, clinical psychologist

> Lots of times people don't understand all the options for a clinical psychologist. They can take so many different career paths, even switch midcareer. It's very important to make connections, figure out what you like, and then seek out someone who is doing that. I recommend that grad students seek people outside the institution. Lots of people get stuck working for their mentor.
> —Dr. Fred Muench, PhD, clinical psychologist, director of clinical research and development

do a clinical (patient-based) dissertation rather than a research-based dissertation.

A PhD looks at behavioral principles from a scientific standpoint, using research and setting up scientifically validated tests to ask specific questions about behaviors. The emphasis is on combining science with practice. PhDs are trained to do both research and clinical work. Many PhDs want to teach and write books. They do therapy, but the main emphasis is on research. Look at it this way: in a PsyD, all professors are practicing psychologists, whereas in PhD programs, all professors are research scientists or scholars. PsyDs go to professional schools; PhDs go to universities. PhDs do loads of valuable research while they are graduate students, so many schools will actually pay for you to attend.

The PsyD degree used to have less clout than the PhD, but that's not really the case anymore. Presidents of the APA (American Psychological Association) have been PsyDs. Bottom line: if you think you want to do research, write books, and teach, PhD is probably a better bet. If you want to do more therapy, then PsyD might make more sense. But there are plenty of opinions on the matter, as you might guess, in the ever-conjecturing psychological world. Do your own homework.

But Wait, What about the MSW Degree?

MSW, or master's in social work, is a degree that allows you to do therapy, but you need to work for a few years before you are licensed. School time is shorter than for either doctorate, but you're not qualified to do psychological testing, and your study of pathology (depression, anxiety, psychosis, and so on) is far less comprehensive. Social workers do one-on-one and group therapy, but they also can do other things; for example, many child welfare workers are social workers. MSWs who want to do clinical work generally need to get some extra training on top of their degree. If you'd like to find out more, a good place to start is socialworkers.org, the official site of the National Association of Social Workers.

Back to PhDs and PsyDs. That's a Lot of Schooling. What's It All Like?

Again, this chapter is for a career based in therapy, which either degree can do. For a more academic career, you'd have to focus your graduate work on a lot more research, and a lot more publishing of papers.

Either of the two doctorate degrees takes at least four years, and often more, to obtain. There's four years of course work, plus your dissertation (this takes some people additional time). While you're taking classes, you also do externships (a minimum of two are mandatory), which are unpaid clinical rotations. Externships are mainly for you to get a clearer idea of what area you want to focus on in your career. Perhaps you'll do one where you work with children and realize "Hey, I can't stand kids. They are small and smell funny."

Doctorate Program Breakdown:

First year: Coursework.

Second year: Coursework and externship. By the end of your second year, you should really start thinking about what you'd like to specialize in.

Third year: Coursework and second externship.

Fourth year: Dissertation and internship. An internship is your first paid job before becoming a psychologist; you're not technically a psychologist until your dissertation is completed. You can apply anywhere for internships, so if you are in school in Chicago, you can do an internship in New York.

After that, you're *still* not licensed. Bummer. Now you need to accrue a number of *licensure hours,* in which you're practicing, but still under the supervision of a seasoned psychologist. It generally is about a year of work, after which you'll take a state licensing exam. When you pass that, you can finally (!) see clients independently.

Where Do You Do Your Psychologizing?

Psychologists who work with patients work in one of two basic settings. The first is a public place, like a hospital, school, or nursing home, where you'll see patients both one-on-one and in group settings. Hospitals and public places tend to be sterile, with a lot of doctors in lab coats walking around and the occasional houseplant. In these types of settings, you are generally an employee of the institution, and it pays you a salary.

The second setting is your own private office. In private practice, the décor and vibe are up to you. Most psychologists go for a sort of business-casual feel—light, airy, and comfortable. *Comfortable* is key, as patients need to feel that this is a "safe place." Picture a space with natural-fiber rugs, club chairs, and a bookcase or two. Basically, the Crate and Barrel catalog.

You'll apply to several internships in the hopes that you'll get your first choice. It's like a sorority rush; you apply to internships and rate your choices and hope that the internship you've chosen is the one that's also chosen you.
—Dr. Katie Gomperts, PsyD, clinical psychologist

Grad school is a long, arduous process. It's fun but very stressful. Externships can be done at a university or outside setting, and while doing this, you're writing a dissertation, and applying to internships, and doing your predoctoral clinical training. It's a lot.
—Dr. Fred Muench, PhD, clinical psychologist, director of clinical research and development

And What Are You Really Doing There?

Psychology can be somewhat of a thankless job, because the main goal is to make yourself superfluous, make someone confident enough so that they don't need you anymore.
—Dr. Fred Muench, PhD, clinical psychologist, director of clinical research and development

Talking, really. Or to be more accurate, listening. To be brief, in private practice you'll meet with patients on differing schedules; you may see one patient three times a week and another only once a month. And you'll use your schooling, training, and empathy to help them navigate their lives and come to realizations. You certainly don't spout advice, like on a bad TV show. Rather, you help them find their way by asking questions and hearing their answers. If you work in a public setting, the type of patients you see there will guide your day. If you are in a school, you may meet with some students daily, and some maybe just once, simply to give them a general mental health evaluation.

Who's Good at This?

There's a "Rogerian" perspective, based on the principles of Carl Rogers. You have to be the sort of person who believes that everyone is pretty much good, just misdirected. That's the key to psychology.
—Dr. Fred Muench, PhD, clinical psychologist, director of clinical research and development

Psychologists need to have empathy; it's the most important attribute. If you can't make a therapeutic alliance with someone, you really won't be able to help them. It takes patience, emotional stability, and curiosity about people and their issues. You have to be objective, as well as self-aware. Finally, you must be deeply responsible. You're dealing with people's mental well-being. If you are the kind of person who can't be held accountable for something that serious, this just isn't the gig for you.

What Are the Hours? Does It Take Over Your Life?

It could weigh heavily on your life, of course, but psychologists say you learn how not to let it. In terms of actual hours, it depends on whether you work in an institution or private practice. At institutions, the hours can be pretty grueling, fifty to sixty hours a week. That's because on top of seeing patients, tons of procedure and paperwork must be completed.

Private-practice hours are much more up to the individual. You can see as many or as few patients as you'd like in a day. Most psychologists in private practice tend to work about the "normal" amount, between thirty and forty hours a week. One thing that can add to those hours is whether you take insurance. Dealing with carriers is universally seen to be a major hassle and timesuck. Hooray American healthcare!

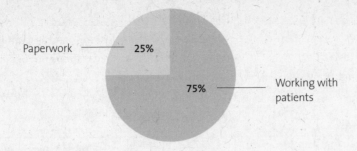

Paperwork — 25%

75% — Working with patients

How Much Cash for Your Wisdom?

Psychologists used to be upper middle class, but now most are middle class at best. You can't really bet on making a lot of money in therapy, but you'll probably do just fine. "Just fine" can be a little frustrating, though, since you go through all that schooling, rack up debt, and then . . . you don't make a killing.

The Bureau of Labor Statistics documents the mean salaries of clinical/counseling/school psychologists (most common) at $63,960, and industrial-organizational psychologists at $89,980. At a hospital or clinic setting, you really won't make more than $60,000 until you are in a director position (supervising other psychologists), and then you can make around $100,000. In a private practice, dealing with higher-end clientele, you can make $120,000 or more, if you're lucky. Beyond clinical work, if you get a PhD and go the academic route, you'll start at around $50,000, and you can go as high as $110,000. And if you go the corporate route, according to salary.com, a director of research at a drug company can make anywhere from $150,000 to $300,000.

1   10

Stress-o-Meter: 7 (1 being a security guard in Tahiti, 10 being a security guard in Tel Aviv)

It's really probably higher than that, but psychologists are better at putting things into perspective than most. They tend not to think their jobs overtaxing as compared to what some of their patients are going through. Of course, the stress level does depend on your patients; if you have suicidal patients, it's off the charts.

Pros

In private practice, you make your own hours, choose your own clients, and create your own office.

You're always problem solving, thinking, being challenged.

You really get to help people.

Cons

There's some pretty major stress and accountability.

When you're working, you can't zone out or daydream, ever.

It's hard not to take people's problems home with you.

Sometimes people don't improve.

Okay, You're a Psychologist. You Wake Up And . . .

This assumes you work in a private practice.

7:00 AM: You brew some coffee and watch the *Today* show; that Al Roker is a hoot! You don't have patients until later in the day; you make your own schedule and you prefer to have them all in a row in the afternoon. Still, you're an early riser.

10:00 AM: You check your messages and e-mails. You don't have a receptionist; you do everything yourself. One patient called to cancel her 1 PM appointment tomorrow. You mark it in your calendar, head to the gym, and then meet some friends for an early lunch.

1:20 PM: You get to your office and make sure everything is in place and clean.

1:30 PM: Your first appointment comes in, very distraught. She is a brilliant sixteen-year-old girl who has been struggling with bulimia—and this week, it seems, her driver's test as well. You've been working with her for six months and have only slowly begun to make progress.

2:30 PM: You start seeing the rest of the day's patients, one after the other: forty-five-minute sessions, with fifteen-minute breaks between. Most of your patients are dealing with eating disorders and relationship issues. Sometimes one informs the other. During breaks you use the bathroom, check your e-mail, and snack.

8:00 PM: By the end of the day, after many emotional conversations, you are exhausted. You turn off the lights, empty the garbage, and head home.

I Want to Help People. How Do I Get This Job?

You have to go to school, just as described earlier. That's it; it's a clear and formal path with no shortcuts. Getting into graduate school is quite competitive, so you'll need good grades and test scores. One thing you can do to show grad schools you are serious is to seek out a researcher at a hospital, clinic, or academic institution, and offer to work for free—in other words, intern. Even getting these free gigs, however, can be somewhat competitive. You don't have to be a psych major to be qualified for these kinds of internships, but you do need a certain number of undergrad psych classes. The psych department at most universities will have information on undergrad-level internships and their requirements. Outside those, all you can really do is study hard. Good luck.

Resources

For grad school information, check with the American Psychological Association, apa.org. It has a wealth of other resource material as well as articles and advice from professionals. And just like for undergrad educations, many reference books and magazines (most famous, *U.S. News & World Report*) also rate grad schools and give you insight into each institution. You can find these at any bookstore.

Other resources to check out include *Psychology Today,* perhaps the most popular industry magazine, and these books: *Career Paths in Psychology: Where Your Degree Can Take You* by Robert J. Sternberg, *What Can You Do with a Major in Psychology? Real People, Real Jobs, Real Rewards,* by Shelley O'Hara, and *The Fifty-Minute Hour* by Robert Lindner.

Publicist/PR Executive

P ublicists spread the word. Or sometimes, they work feverishly to stop the word from spreading. A publicist is a middleman (or to be more politically correct, *middleperson*) between his or her clients, the people who seek publicity, and reporters and writers who are looking for interesting stories.

Publicists aim to get the right kind of attention for their clients. The right kind of attention means that sometimes a publicist does the opposite of pitching a story. They angle to keep their clients out of the press for something unfortunate that they've said or done, like telling an embarrassing lie or perhaps, inappropriately touching a pony. Hey, these things happen. At the end of the day, the publicist's job is to make the client look good to the world at large.

And just who are these publicity-seeking clients? Anyone and everyone who thinks they need PR: from musicians and celebrity actors, to activist groups and politicians, to Wal-Mart and Coca-Cola. Obviously, the exact day-to-day job you have as a publicist will depend on who your clients are. Some large PR firms are generalists; they have all different types of clients. Other firms specialize, for example, by focusing exclusively on the music industry. Oh, and by the way, PR, or public relations, is the same thing as publicity, and a publicist is someone who handles PR. Different firms use different terms; don't let them throw you.

So Like, Am I Lunching All Day with Madonna?

Sadly, the life of a publicist is not all martinis and booking massages.

A lot of the job is careful planning. You want the right angle on your client's story, and you want it in the right press. You don't want your client's story in just any magazine; you want *Vanity Fair*, because you know by doing research that this will somehow better affect their career than being in, say, *People*. It also requires a tremendous amount of work just to get a story placed. It's called *pitching* a story, and it's what you'll spend most of your time doing.

Pitching is trying to get a media outlet—a magazine/newspaper editor, TV show, or Web site—to do a story on your client, a piece that you have already pretty much prepared and are handing them. Reporters and editors are busy, so if you have a good, ready-made story for them, you are helping them out immensely. But you can't just chuck it out there. You have to tailor what you say to each specific person, both specific to your client and specific to who is hearing the pitch.

Say your client is an inventor who just came up with a healthy potato chip, one that actually makes you live longer. Dare to dream. You will now e-mail, call, maybe even send reporters a big, fun package with a bag of these new chips inside—whatever it takes to get them interested in doing a big piece on your chip inventor client. So to *Healthy Living* magazine, your pitch will be something like "Crunch Yourself Healthy." To *Cosmo*, it will be "Look Sexy and Still Snack."

Pitching is rarely a one-shot deal; you don't send one e-mail and boom, an editor bites. A pitch can take a long period of time. For example, trying to get an art publication to write about an artist you handle can take weeks or months. In that time, there will be constant e-mails, phone calls, text messages, smoke signals, whatever you can think of that helps your client's case. You have to keep the press abreast of all that he is doing until one day, huzzah, they decide they really want to write about him. And you have to do it all without being annoying. Perseverance without annoyance is a balancing act. It's like trying to persuade a girl to go with you to the prom: you want to show her you like her by being persistent, but you don't want to seem like a stalker.

What Happens When I'm Not Pitching?

All kinds of stuff, all in the interest of garnering more positive spin for your clients. You may be supporting them by going to an event of theirs. For someone in the entertainment field, perhaps you are attending a premiere; for a client who designs furniture, you may be attending a trade show. You may be galvanizing relationships with specific reporters by lunching with them, trying to find out what kind of stories and angles interest them. Your client might be interviewed on a radio show, and you will sit beside them, making sure there are no gaffes or misunderstandings, smoothing things over during the commercial breaks.

Prepare to Be Touchy and Feely

Publicity is about people. "People, people who need people . . ." Go ahead, you know the words. If schmoozing people all day makes you ill, you'll find yourself in need of a medic as a publicist. This is not a job for the shy; cultivating relationships is key, and giving good talk is the number one skill. There are the relationships with clients, of course. But just as important are befriending and

There are a few ways to pitch. Some publicists pitch by cold calling. Our industry is small; we know all of the reporters in it, and we have relationships with them. So when we call, it's not really a deliberate pitch. We check in with them, catch up, talk about the industry in general, and make sure that they know what our clients are up to.
—Samantha DiGennaro, founder and president, DiGennaro Communications

The events I attend with my clients are speaking engagements. I try to do three things for them there: One, make sure that they are fully prepared. Two, make sure there are no slips of the tongue, and if there are, that they're corrected. And three, I make sure to connect them with reporters after the event.
—Samantha DiGennaro, founder and president, DiGennaro Communications

really knowing the press. What do they like, what interests them, what annoys them? This all helps when pitching a story.

And there are all the other people you will interact with as you try to promote your client. As a publicist, you're the point person when it comes to managing their image. There may be photo shoots, where stylists and photographers will be influencing your client's look, and you will be there, making sure he or she doesn't come off looking like a clown or an aerobics instructor (unless of course you represent clowns or aerobics instructors). You'll be by their side at events like grand openings, signings, and interviews. There will be a lot of glad-handing. Buy some Purell.

What Kind of Person Is a Publicist Person?

To be successful in publicity, you have to be passionate, someone who can really believe (sometimes, of course, you'll have to act) in what you're pitching. And those pitches must be well written, so although being an English or journalism major certainly isn't required, good writing skills definitely help. You'll need to be patient and able to keep cool even when things are going awry. You have to be a good salesperson, since you are selling your clients and their stories to the press. Publicists tend to be the kind of people who can take a call from the press while IMing a client while eating lunch with chopsticks, so multitasking is a key skill. You must have chutzpah; you need the ability to never feel guilty about calling or bothering anybody. Ever.

I Start as What and Become Who?

More often than not, the first job you'll get, and the way in, is as an assistant, doing all the things assistants do—phonin', faxin', gettin' stuff. Also, you will be pasting up clips (basically, gathering all the press the firm has garnered for a client so they can show what they've accomplished; these days it's more likely to be a PDF than actual pasted clippings). Once you prove your ability at these tasks, you'll probably get some small assignments pitching stories to, perhaps, local newspapers and the like. From there you'll work your way up, getting weightier titles and bigger and more important stories to pitch.

The Office Looks and Feels Like . . .

Office vibes are quite different from firm to firm. A good rule is, as the clients' offices go, so you go. So if your firm handles bands, music will probably be playing in the office, and you'll pretty much wear whatever you want. A small, general firm in a typical office setting might be casual most days, dressing up only when clients come in. However, if you work in a large, corporate PR environment, well, it will probably still feel like most large, corporate office environments. While you won't have to wear a Chanel suit every day, you probably won't be wearing sweatpants either.

As mentioned earlier, you won't be in the office all day, either. Depending on the client, you may be at their offices or at an event or opening, making sure all is going as smoothly as it can. Or at least helping to create that illusion.

> We do PR primarily for the music industry, so our office is very laid back. There's a poster of Bob Marley smoking a joint hanging right near my desk.
> —Rachel Reynolds, Gorgeous PR

Hours?

They're often long, but again, it all depends on your clients. Publicists need to be fairly accessible, especially in the entertainment world. Many own more than one cell phone battery, let's leave it at that. Still, there are jobs in PR that allow one to have a balanced life. If, for example, you do PR for the accounting industry, unless there is a scandal, you are pretty much working normal business hours. If you are Britney Spears's publicist, you probably sleep with a phone taped to your head. You should figure that on average there will be a few late nights a month, minimum; some weekend work; and the occasional crisis that could startle you from your sleep.

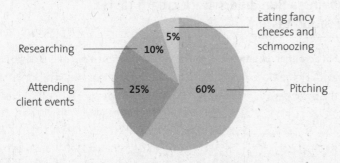

> As a publicist, you won't work 24/7, but you need to be accessible 24/7. You just never know when a reporter is going to call for a quote or come looking for an expert opinion from one of your clients. It's not the old days when magazines came out weekly or monthly; news is being constantly updated online. If you aren't available, your clients could miss a good opportunity for press.
> —Samantha DiGennaro, founder and president, DiGennaro Communications

How Many Pieces of Green Paper for Your Trouble?

No surprise here—starting salaries are low, especially in the hotter fields like entertainment publicity. As you grow and take on additional responsibilities, the best way to increase money is to jump around; publicists change jobs often.

If you are successful and are garnering PR for big accounts, you can make a ton. Get a great reputation and you may even start your own firm. But keep in mind that at first, you'll be eyeing the value menu at Taco Bell over the king crab roll at Nobu. However, in these sexy fields, there are perks that take the edge off. Free tickets, free CDs, and free DVDs, commensurate with the kind of clients you are working on, often come with the business cards.

Here's what the Bureau of Labor Statistics has to say, in a sampling of mean salaries for manager (senior) level PR executives across different possible industries:

Advertising and related services: $115,090

Management of companies and enterprises: $101,530

Colleges and universities: $77,790

Professional and similar organizations: $85,640

Local government: $65,500

According to the 2006 *PRWeek*-Korn/Ferry Salary Survey (prweek.com), the average starting salary in New York is $33,000 to $35,000, while the overall median is $92,000. The survey states that the top (meaning executive-vice-president-level) PR execs at *Fortune* 200 companies make an average of $580,000, including bonus. Nice.

> If you can bring a new client to your agency, that's usually rewarded through a bonus or a percentage of their billings. It's a good way to increase your earnings.
> —Alicia Kalish, publicist

 Stress-o-Meter: 7 (1 being a Ben & Jerry's ice cream taster, 10 being Kim Jong Il's food taster)

If your client is a young musician or actor, her dreams are in your hands. Other times you might be putting out huge fires—say, if your client has a bawdy home video released on the Web, *and* he looks fat in it. Something is always happening, and again, you are the point person. If you screw up, you screw up in public—in the press.

Pros	Cons
Seeing a story you came up with in the paper.	Having to be passionate about a client you don't believe in—or like.
Having a job you can be passionate about (when you believe in your clients).	Being on call 24/7.
Your winning personality and persuasiveness are the keys to your success.	Unrealistic expectations ("I wrote a poem, why aren't I on *Entertainment Tonight?*").
Working with interesting people.	Low money for long hours sometimes breeds bitterness.

Okay, You Are a Publicist. You Wake Up And . . .

Every day as a publicist is different. You could be at a shoot for an entire day or attending a conference all week. That said, here is a somewhat typical day.

9:00 AM: You roll over and check your pal, Mr. Blackberry. You have tons of e-mails but all seems well, so you get out of bed and flip through the papers. *Times, Post, News, USA Today, WWD, WSJ*—you need to know the latest.

10:00 AM: At the office, you call and remind a client you've nicknamed "Sir Sleeps-a-Lot" about an interview he has with a college newspaper. You then join a phone interview between one of your new clients and a reporter, listening intently to make sure there are no gaffes.

11:00 AM: Pitching time. (The rest of the day you will be in and out of pitch mode.) You make a barrage of calls for a new band you represent, whose album is about to drop. You e-mail an MP3 to a freelance magazine writer you know who'll love it.

1:00 PM: Lunch with a client, an actor. He complains that he hasn't seen himself in the papers lately. You explain you've been doing everything you can to keep him out, what with the affair and all.

2:00 PM: You Google clients, downloading every bit of press on them you can find. This press goes into a book or PDF, so you can wow them at the end of the month.

5:00 PM: You spend more time on the new band pitch, working with an assistant to put together a bunch of packages to mail, complete with the new CD and a poster of the band.

7:00 PM: You go to the opening of a new club, owned by some of your clients. You say hi and have a quick drink, then rush home to the comfort of your couch. And Mr. Blackberry. You try to knock off some e-mails so tomorrow morning maybe you can make an appearance at Pilates.

I Like the Public and I Adore Relations. How the Hell Do I Become a Publicist?

The best way into a PR firm is to intern. Get in the door and then do what publicists do—network, show your personality and your positive spirit. Everyone loves free labor, so check the college listing boards and local PR agencies' Web sites. PR firms frequently have interns, so there should be postings. Some might even pay an itty bit—but don't count on it. There's no precise major or background they are looking for, just a person with the right personality who's up for whatever the day throws at them. Be that person.

When you interview for an internship or an assistant job, the number one thing you'll need to show is enthusiasm. Being a publicist requires a lot of energy, so stifle the yawns and the cool, indifferent looks. Be excited about the job, about the firm's clients (make sure you know who they are, duh; try to note a piece of press you've recently seen), even about the weather. Be someone they want to meet, someone they think a reporter is going to enjoy getting a phone call from. Know what's happening on the media landscape, know who was on the *Today* show or *Good Morning America* that morning, and be ready to talk talk talk about it.

Resources

To prepare for an interview and even a job in publicity, one of the best things you can do is read every magazine that covers the field of publicity you are interested in. For example, want to be in music publicity? Know every page of every music magazine, every sidebar, every little place you could maybe get press for a client. Know all the influential Web sites and TV shows, and talk about them in the interview. Okay, you don't have to know *every* single one, but you get the point. Obviously, it's imperative to be up-to-date on these when you actually have the job, but showing in an interview how immersed you are is more impressive than any degree, and better than having read any big ol' publicity biography. However, it is worth your time to flip through the last few issues of *PRWeek* magazine, which you can also check out online at prweek.com. This way you'll be up on all the latest happenings or big PR campaigns that might be the current talk of the publicist world.

Here are a few associations that can give you more information and perhaps, most important, leads on available internships:

National Council for Marketing & Public Relations: ncmpr.org

Public Relations Society of America: prsa.org

Public Relations Student Society of America: prssa.org, where a *Student's Guide to Public Relations Education* is available

Real Estate Broker

Finding a place to live is usually a giant pain in the bottom. Although the prospect of a new home is always exciting, the open houses, the credit checks, the shady landlords, and of course, the actual moving day often combine into a perfect storm of stress and unpleasantness. If you've ever looked for an apartment or home by yourself or tried to rent or sell one on your own, then you probably sport the bruises of the real estate market.

A real estate broker's job is to make this process a lot less difficult. They are the sherpas who lead you through the urban or suburban jungles and match you with the right seller or buyer so that each of you can, after negotiations, get what you want. And that's no simple task: buying or selling a home is an emotional issue; it's not a stock or bond, but a place where you live, sleep, and eat. The best real estate brokers look beyond the dollars and the local crime and school statistics to find the right fit for each individual or family. The career can be quite a ride, with highs and lows, big deals and lost deals, and savant-level Blackberrying and cell phone dialing. Successful real estate brokers will tell you that the satisfaction of selling a home, of scoring a fat commission on a single sale, and of having a job that allows for flexible hours more than makes up for any downsides.

There are also commercial real estate brokers, who find "homes" for corporations. This job is much less touchy-feely and far more of a dollars-and-cents game. This chapter will focus on residential real estate.

> We do pretty much everything from finding that perfect apartment for someone, to selling a client's house, to acting as a mediator with couples arguing over what they see as the perfect home. You follow the process from start to finish, going on a little journey with either a buyer or a seller.
> —Samantha Brown, associate broker

Brokering, Soup to Nuts

Real estate brokers usually work at real estate agencies, but they can also be self-employed. They join their clients on the journey to buy or sell (or rent) a home, from the very beginning until the very end. Of course, first you need to get this client, a seller (or landlord) or a buyer (or renter). How do you find them? Much like dentistry, for the most part, brokering is a business built on referrals. Someone's friend Joey employed you to sell his condo, you kicked butt, and now one of Joey's friends—Jimmy—has come to you to help him sell his property. Or, if you work for a firm with a good reputation, people may come in based on the firm's strengths, not knowing any broker in particular, and get assigned to you. Either way, it's all based on past customer interaction.

It's something to keep in mind every step of the process, as every client can potentially yield, or not yield, more clients down the line. So be nice.

Okay, so Joey said good things, and now you're helping Jimmy sell his property. You'll go over to his house and inspect it—see what he's got and what you can do with it. Two things happen here, both incredibly important to the overall success of your mission, which is getting Jimmy the highest price for his home and selling it in a reasonable amount of time. First, you will start to strategize what the correct pricing should be for the property. This is a difficult task, because although as a broker you'll understand the price per square foot in the neighborhood, what similar condos nearby have sold for, and the general state of the market, some guesswork and psychology still apply.

Second, you will look around the property and tell Jimmy what he might do to help his cause. Maybe a fresh coat of paint is needed, a new refrigerator, or, in some cases, a battalion of cleaning people. These small touches really help a place "show" better—and thus get the higher price.

Once the property is priced correctly and spruced up, marketing begins. You will take photos of the kitchen, the deck, and the double-wide Jacuzzi tub, looking for the most flattering angles. These days, some brokers even shoot videos. Web sites have become quite important in the promotion of real estate, and these images draw in potential buyers far better than mere descriptive words (although you'll tailor those as well). Other than putting the property up on your agency's Web site, you'll also put ads in local newspapers and on sites like craigslist.com. You'll open up the listing to other brokers at your company so they can bring in their own clients. You may even open it up to brokers at other real estate agencies, listing it on the MLS (Multiple Listing Service), a site where licensed brokers can see every property on the market. Or you may keep the property as an "exclusive," meaning you'll find both buyer and seller. More work, but exclusives guarantee you the largest possible commission on a sale. If you *co-broker,* you share the commission with the other broker who brings in the buyer.

You'll organize, promote, and host *open houses,* which are times when anyone can stop in and look at the property. Generally these fall on weekends or after work, when buyers have more time to browse.

Then you cross your fingers a bit and hope—hope it doesn't rain on the day of an open house, hope the flowers you stuck in a vase make the old bathroom seem prettier, even hope the stock market doesn't crash. You'll usher buyers around the property and tell them all the positives—and, well, the negatives too. It pays to be honest (remember that referral thing), although at the end of the day, your loyalty is to the seller.

The most crucial part of selling a property is to price it effectively, where it's going to move fast but at the highest amount the market will bear. You don't want to be too aggressive and end up having the property sit around. And that's a difficult balancing act. Because if you come along and say, "I'd price this at a million dollars," and the broker down the street says, "One and a half million"—even if that's not realistic—chances are the client will go with the higher number. And then the property might not move, and three to six months later those people will come back and say, "I've made a terrible mistake."
—Mike McGrath, associate broker, Brooklyn Properties

Then, if luck is with you, you'll get a bid. Let's say you and Jimmy decide to ask a million dollars for his place. A prospective buyer offers $950,000. You tell this to Jimmy and advise him what to do. In this case, you think he should go down to $975,000, have the buyer meet him there, and walk away with a tidy sum. Jimmy could be stubborn and not be willing to go down a penny. Or the buyer may not be willing to go up. Here is where you negotiate, and where things can get stressful and emotional. A lot of money is on the table, and the deal is oh so close. Your job is to make it happen.

Now, let's say Jimmy is looking to buy, not sell. First, you'll talk about neighborhoods, what he likes and doesn't, what he can afford, what kind of life he lives, whether he needs a chef's kitchen or is more of a delivery pizza kind of guy. Then you will search all of the appropriate listings, ones exclusive to your firm as well as the MLS, looking for those that best suit him. Once you find some promising ones, you will (after sending him all available information online and narrowing down the list) take him around and show him said properties. And odds are, you won't find one he wants to buy on your first time out. You will be continually keeping your eyes peeled for Jimmy's perfect match. You will be on the computer, looking, then e-mailing, then taking Jimmy around, again and again. This process can take a long time. Buying or selling a piece of property is one of the largest investment decisions a person will make, and very rarely do they impulse buy. Except for, like, Jay-Z.

What Kind of Person Is a Broker Person?

Being a broker requires you to be a bit of a risk taker. The pay is 100 percent commission, meaning if you don't close any deals, you don't get any cash. That's a pretty big gamble right there. You need to be the kind of person who can roll with the downtimes and plan ahead during the good.

The job is a sales job, of course, but you are selling items with strong emotional attachments. So you need to be a people person, able to empathize with and cajole all types, as opposed to getting annoyed and wanting to hang up on them.

As mentioned, referrals are how you get clients. A lot of referrals come from friends, family, and former clients, but many will come from hard-core networking. If you live in New York City, that might mean going out to clubs and meeting people at the gym. In the Midwest, it might mean joining the Rotary Club and coaching Little League. Wherever they are located, real estate brokers tend to be social animals.

Finally, you simply have to love real estate. Diamonds in the rough, huge

You are dealing with so many different personality types—there's the person who wants to feel like they're negotiating, and there's the person that just wants to go in there and get it done. So you really have to be able to feel out your client and know whom you're working with.

—Samantha Brown, associate broker

penthouses, fixer-uppers—all of these should make your pulse race. When you walk into someone's house for the first time, do you always want to go on a tour? Are you overly concerned with closet space and acreage? These are good signs.

Where Do You Broker?

You can broker here, you can broker there, you can broker pretty much anywhere there are properties that need to be bought or sold. Yes, you'll have a desk at your real estate agency, but the truth is, with a cell phone and an Internet connection, you can do your job from any location. And you will. You'll be on the phone on a busy street, and on your Blackberry over lunch. Some brokers like the structure of going to the office, but since there's so much running around to open houses, many find it's easier to do some work from home, and some from the road, with the rare pop in to the firm. Yes, you'll be in your car a lot, traveling from property to property. Or if you live in a major city, on the subway or in a cab.

Wherever you are, how do you have to look? Professional. If you are selling properties in the hip part of town, you don't have to wear a formal business suit, but you won't be dressed like Keith Richards either. Most other places you will wear a suit. Real estate is expensive, and you need to look the trustworthy, professional part.

Hours

The hours are quite flexible. This is both a positive and a negative. Most people look for real estate after work or on the weekends, so daytime can be quite slow (with the exception of lunch hour), while evenings and weekends can be crazy. On the plus side, you can run errands or go to the gym on a Monday at 2:30. But brokering is time consuming, and you can do it seven days a week. After a Sunday spent at open houses, for instance, you might spend the evening online searching the MLS or other databases for properties for your clients. Brokers get caught up in the rush of sales and sometimes have trouble forcing themselves to go on vacation. If the market is hot, two weeks out of town might mean a significant loss of income.

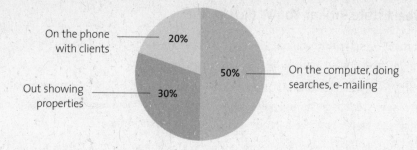

On the phone with clients — 20%

On the computer, doing searches, e-mailing — 50%

Out showing properties — 30%

Money

Brokers can do well. They can also make zero. It's a 100 percent commission job, with no safety nets. Yes, even though you "work" at a real estate agency, the only money you make is from deals you close. Real estate agencies take a commission on sales, generally around 6 percent of the sales price. As a broker, you will get a percentage of that percentage, which you will have to share if it's a co-broker situation. In markets with high real estate values, the money can add up fast. You may have to make only a few deals a year to have a healthy salary. And some years can be bumper, while others are bone dry. The mean annual income for brokers, according to the Bureau of Labor Statistics, is $80,230. But of course, in the case of real estate, location is everything. The BLS reports that in Nevada, the mean annual salary for a real estate broker is $147,120, while in North Carolina it's $42,030. Quite a difference.

In terms of benefits, well, often there are none. No health, life, dental, nothing. Some firms offer these, but many times, it's just you and your hopefully healthy commission.

You have to have savings—especially when you're first starting. And you need to know how to save throughout the year, because it's a roller-coaster ride. You might have a client selling a home who accepts an offer and the contract is signed, but you still don't get any money until the closing—and the closing might not happen for three months. So you have to be really good about planning ahead.

—Samantha Brown, associate broker

Stress-o-Meter: 7 (1 being a bargain hunter, 10 being a big-game hunter)

Any job where your pay is 100 percent commission is bound to be stressful. A few months without pay will up the acid level in the ol' stomach. Plus, you're dealing with often highly emotional buyers and sellers, who, for them at least, are making deals that are the equivalent of their life's savings.

Pros

Your schedule is flexible.

You can make a nice living if you hustle.

It's quite satisfying to find people their dream home.

Cons

Clients who are "just looking" waste your unpaid time.

Not having a steady salary can be unsettling.

You can find yourself just constantly working.

You, My Friend, Are a Real Estate Broker. You Wake Up And . . .

7:30 AM: Before you toast that English muffin, you check your Blackberry to see if any clients have written. You return one e-mail, rescheduling an appointment for later in the week.

8:30 AM: Now showered and dressed professionally, you go online and start doing searches for some of your buyer clients. After some serious pointing and clicking—huzzah!—you find a few new listings that might suit a family searching for a three-bedroom. You fire off an e-mail to them.

11:00 AM: You head out to show a property to a client who's looking to buy; afterward you'll take him to two others nearby. Hopefully one will be up his alley. While you are showing him the homes, you frequently sneak off to field phone calls from other clients. It's a constant struggle to be accessible but also not seem rude.

1:00 PM: You stuff a wrap down your throat while driving over to an exclusive condo property you are selling. You have three different couples coming to meet you there, spread out over the next two and a half hours.

6:00 PM: You go grab a drink with some friends, a fresh wad of business cards in your pocket. You never know whom you might meet who's "looking."

8:30 PM: Back home, you go online and do some more searches to see if any new properties were listed today that might fit your clients' needs. Then it's TV time.

Real Estate Seems Really Great. So How the Hell Do I Get This Job?

Let's start with the educational requirements: there are none. You don't even need a college degree, although these days, at the more established firms, most younger agents have them. Some schools offer majors in real estate, but again, it's not necessary. All that is required is a real estate sales license, which you get by taking a course. These differ in length from state to state, but you are looking at about forty-five hours—basically a week's commitment. To find out your state's requirements (and where you can take courses), simply Google your state's name plus "real estate license commission." Yay, technology. Once you have your license, you can work for a real estate agency and make commissions. After a year, if you have enough points (basically, if you've sold enough properties at a certain dollar amount) you can get another license, called a *broker's license*. The major advantage of this broker's license is that you can start your own firm if you wish, or work independently outside a licensed agency.

But back to the beginning. Once you've passed the course and have obtained your sales license, you need to become part of an agency. You do this the same way you get any other job: you make phone calls, send e-mails, get interviews, and then nail those interviews. Since you will be paid only by commission, finding a firm isn't always that difficult. But you want to make sure you go to one where you will actually have the opportunity to sell properties and thus make some money. Make sure you ask questions in the interview as well. An important one to ask is, "Will I start with rentals?" Rentals in certain cities can be lucrative, but they are generally looked down on. It's just a sketchier business; both landlords and tenants alike tend to be less reliable. If you are going to start in rentals, hey, it's a great way to learn. But you'll want to know that there is a career path where, after you prove yourself, you can move up. Real estate brokers say it's good to also sniff around on these subjects: Will you get any training? Will you work with someone more experienced, a mentor-like situation? Or will you be sitting there with no leads and no income?

What the agency will be looking for in you is sales ability. Did you work in retail? What did you sell, and how? This type of experience is good to flaunt. You will be asked why you want to get into real estate; your answer should not just be about money, but about your passion for all things home and garden. You should be up-to-date on the overall market and the local area where you want to operate. Be ready to talk about good streets and bad streets; show off your knowledge of your local 'hood. How can you sell a home if you don't know where the best pizza place in the area is?

Real estate brokers often don't start straight out of school; many come to the field from other jobs. They may have been in fashion or computing, and decided, maybe through even buying or renting their own place, that real estate was their future. A big advantage to this is that they've been part of the working world and have made a lot of contacts in their industry. Being a real estate broker is all about having that big Rolodex of people who know and trust you, and working in another industry is one way to build this up. Also, let's say you are fresh out of college. It's fairly difficult for a twenty-two-year-old to sell a million-dollar home to a father of four. But someone just a few years older with some life experience under his or her belt? Definitely doable.

Not to mention, if you are fresh out of school, a 100 percent commission job might be a tough first gig. However, there is another way to go straight from school to a job at a real estate agency: get a job as a broker's assistant.

What you might do is get your license and work as an assistant to a broker. You're not actually a broker—you're an assistant. If you're really interested in real estate I'd recommend that, because (a) you'll learn the business and (b) you're getting some money. Just make your boss aware that eventually you want to be a broker. And while you're proving yourself, you're learning from someone who's been in the business.
—Samantha Brown, associate broker

Resources

It's important to read your local papers and keep up on the market: the general economy, how homes are being priced, trends in the marketplace (the loft look is in—the ranch look is out). As well, search for local real estate blogs that cover your area. For example, New York City alone has hundreds of such blogs, such as curbed.com, therealdeal.net, and brownstoner.com. Nationally, make sure to read the real estate sections in *Crain's, The New York Times, The Wall Street Journal,* and the site realtytimes.com.

Some links to check out:

National Association of Realtors: realtor.org (Realtor.org/realtororg.nsf/pages/careers will take you directly to information on careers, including practical advice and links on getting started.)

Council of Residential Specialists: crs.com

Society of Industrial and Office Realtors: sior.com

National Association of Real Estate Brokers: nareb.com

And . . . the largest online real estate bookstore (they claim): dearborn.com/recampus/home.asp?pin_id=700000

Reporter
TV Correspondent/Print Journalist

News reporters seek the truth. Well, they seek the important, or at least interesting, truth, the truth that makes for a story the public needs or wants to know about. For although it may be truthful that you ate one too many meatballs at dinner last evening, it is hardly "news." Unless you happen to be Britney Spears. Of course, if you are Britney Spears, the fact that you are reading this book (or any book for that matter) is also news. But let's not get off track.

News reporters investigate stories, gather facts, and then present their findings to the public. They can do this in any medium, be it TV, print, radio, or the Web. They could be reporting on a new movie, or they could be following a political scandal; either way, their aim is to inform and educate, in a digestible and sometimes even highly entertaining way. Which is perhaps why some local news weathermen wear absurd toupées.

More Digestible Information, Please

News reporters are passionate about facts. What separates them from other magazine writers (and why this chapter is separate from the chapter on magazine writers) or TV or radio personalities is their strict reporting of news, their adherence to the facts, and their objectivity in presenting them. However, news reporters do at times, at least subtly, put their point of view into a story. For example, perhaps you've heard the term *liberal media* in reference to left-leaning newspapers or *conservative* to Fox News.

So how do reporters decide what stories to report on? Two main ways. One, they *pitch* an idea to their superiors. This means they say something like, "Hey, I've got a great idea for a story. I know this guy at the Pentagon who claims everyone there is addicted to Frappuccinos. It's a story of caffeine and killing power." Or, if you work at a local newspaper, "A source tells me there's drag racing going on behind the Carvel." If the superior likes it, they can give the reporter the green light (and funds) to go ahead and investigate and turn it into a piece for broadcast or publication.

I report and write stories for the National Affairs section of *Newsweek*. I'm part of a team, so when there's a big story like Katrina, I'm one of the people who gets sent to cover it. Plus, on off weeks, I'll do my own stories, for National Affairs or for other sections of the magazine. I've done the 2004 presidential campaign, the Duke rape case, and the real heavy-hitting stuff like new trends in sideburns.
—Susannah Meadows, senior writer, *Newsweek*

The other way is to be assigned a story, and especially for more junior reporters, it's the main way. Who gives you the assignment differs by medium. In TV, the *assignment desk* manages every reporter's time and doles out the story assignments. In print, that duty falls on your editor. The story might be due in a few hours, or it may be a longer-term investigative piece. You may have to hop on the next flight or you may be able to do a lot of the legwork from your desk. The field is fast-paced and stressful. Most times you will be hustling off somewhere while trying to figure out what you're exactly supposed to be doing as you go. Which is to say, it's damn exciting.

Reporting itself is simply the act of attaining information. But to be good at it, you have to be creative about where and from whom you're getting this info. As you become more seasoned, you'll learn that by calling the press secretary to some politician, you're only going to hear the party line. To find the juicy bits you must work along the edges, talking to the people who are looser lipped and more gossipy. Then you work your way in and confirm these rumors by confronting the main players with them.

What Makes for a Good Reporter?

Are you a stubborn, unrelenting type? Good. Because to be a decent news reporter, you have to be incredibly persistent. It sounds simple, but in practice it's very difficult to get people to give you information and get sources to go on the record. Are you willing to wait in an office all day until the person you need to talk with finally arrives? Or will you sit outside his or her home for hours in your car? Even if you have to go to the bathroom, really, really badly? It takes some stick-to-itiveness, if that's a word. Either way, you'll also need to be resourceful, because although you may not break any laws to gather the facts, you have to be willing to walk around fences. And maybe climb some trees. Crawl under some barricades. You get the idea.

It's important to be able to make people comfortable and to be able to develop trust. Journalists forge relationships with sources that last many years and can be helpful to their careers. These people have to trust that what they tell you, you'll represent fairly. Otherwise, they won't ever give you information again. If people tell you the inside scoop off the record, and you never print it, trust grows. But if you're a beat reporter and you print something that was supposed to be off the record, boom, you lost trust, and your source, just for that one story.

Reporters need to be extra sensitive because many times, sadly, they are dealing with stories of human tragedy. The callous reporters are the reason people love to hate the media—you know, the ones shoving microphones

I think being kind is really important. Plus, being unkind is counterproductive. Who's going to talk to you if you are gross like that? After the Amish school shooting, there was a rumor going around about a reporter who had barged into an Amish home while the family was eating dinner. Even if she got a story, that wouldn't be worth it for me.
—Susannah Meadows, senior writer, *Newsweek*

in the victims' faces asking, "So when they shot your son in the face, were you sad?"

Most reporters are good writers. However, many will tell you that without the reporting, the writing is just fluff. And sometimes, reporters won't even write their own stories. If they are on the road, they may phone in the details to a colleague or their editor at the office, who will take the story down and put it into proper form.

Finally, you have to be a hard worker. With all the doggedness and persistence come long hours and late nights. Being a journalist means going all out for the story, twenty-four hours a day. Oh, and how do you feel about airports?

Platinum-Level Frequent-Flyer Miles

Yes, the odds are that you'll travel quite a bit. Now, if you are a reporter for a local paper or TV station in Vermont, you will probably just be in your car, following stories locally or around the state. But if you cover national events for any large newspaper, magazine, or TV news show, you'll be on the road as much as a hippie jam band.

And you won't just travel, you'll travel often *without notice*. Many reporters and correspondents keep a "to-go" bag stuffed with toiletries and clothes on standby at all times. It's just part of the game.

As you can imagine, travel has its pros and cons. You'll get to see the world and meet some incredible people in exotic places. Although you're not really jet-setting; you'll spend many nights in unglamorous small towns in Iowa or Pennsylvania. All that travel means your life will constantly be in tumult. You have to get a real thrill from reporting in order to keep going. Because it can be hard on family and relationships.

News Hours?

Many. You're looking at sixty-to-seventy-hour weeks if you're working at one of the top national news outlets. Local ones tend to be a bit less. If you're an editor at a newspaper or magazine, as opposed to a reporter, the hours also tend to be more livable. As a reporter, you may well not have a traditional "weekend" off. The news happens every day, so you may get Sunday and Monday, or Tuesday and Wednesday. Also, TV news and newspapers are everyday affairs with deadlines each day, whereas magazines are weeklies or monthlies. For all, as the deadline approaches, the hours and stress increase exponentially, as you can well imagine.

When there's a big breaking news story, they may call me in the middle of the night and say, "A tornado has touched down in the middle of Kansas. Get a move on." Most of the time I'm in New York now, but directly after 9/11, for three or four years, I was on the road for about six to eight months a year. I spent, at one point, five or six months in Iraq, you know, pretty much straight through, and I've made monthlong trips to Pakistan, Afghanistan, Israel, and the Palestinian Territories.
—Dan Harris, anchor and correspondent, ABC News

You have a certain period of time to get a story. There's always sort of a panic, because you don't know if you are going to get anything, even though you have to. So it ends up being just work as much as you can, until you hit the deadline.
—Susannah Meadows, senior writer, *Newsweek*

Since news stories happen every day and at all hours, you'll have to work on them at all hours. You aren't always on call, but if you are in the middle of a big story or following a lead, you won't be able to stop to go meet your buddies for nachos or your husband for dinner.

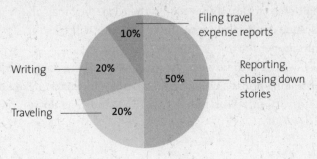

What's the Office Like?

Generally any organization that reports the news is super fast-paced, but also fun. There's lots of gallows humor as deadlines approach and everyone sprints (literally at times, à la *Broadcast News)* to get their stories in, although the vibe in TV is a bit different from newspaper, which is a bit different from magazine. For example, in terms of wardrobe, TV is a bit dressier than the others, especially if you are going to be on camera—although even as a print reporter, you'll probably keep a suit of some sort in your office, in case you have to run to court or to interview a politician at a moment's notice.

Depending on your level and company, you may have an actual office with a couch and a TV, or you may have a cube. Regardless of what piece of real estate you are bestowed, you'll probably spend a lot of your time outside the office. You'll be doing a lot of your communicating with colleagues, friends, and family via smartphone and laptop. Sometimes you'll be out there on your own; other times you'll have with you a fellow reporter, a camera operator if you are in TV, or a photographer. It depends on the piece.

Money?

While a few well-known journalists make gobs of money, most don't. It's just not a career for those looking to get rich. Remember, this is the kind of job people would do for free; note the low end of the salary range that follows.

If you're an established reporter, you could make anywhere from the high five figures to the low six. If you're an anchor in a small local market, you could make in the low six figures, and in a major one, the high sevens. Those jobs are few and far between, of course, and you'll need "anchor hair." There's

Unfortunately, you'll constantly be canceling dinner plans or vacations with friends or significant others because at the last minute you get an assignment. It happens frequently.
—Dan Harris, anchor and correspondent, ABC News

one way to make additional money: you might write a book or even a screen-play based on a story you unearthed. Bottom line: you'll do fine, and you'll love your job. But that's about it.

The Bureau of Labor Statistics reports the mean salary for all journalists as $40,370, ranging from $18,300 to $71,220. The mean for newspaper reporters is $36,770, and for radio and TV, $49,990.

Stress-o-Meter: 8 (1 being a bong engineer, 10 being a bomb engineer)

If you report on breaking stories, life is pretty stressful. The deadlines, competition, long hours, and constant travel can be fairly brutal. Plus, once you close the story, you worry about whether you got it right. You may wake up at night wondering whether you quadruple-checked a fact. It kind of never stops.

If you're a local reporter on a mellow beat, say traffic and weather, the stress is of course far lower.

Pros	Cons
Breaking a story is a thrill, a rush.	The travel is constant.
You'll see the world.	You have to bother people who have just been in a tragedy.
You're learning something new every day.	
You may garner a modest amount of fame.	You'll miss loved ones and events because of the long hours.

News Flash! You Are a Journalist. You Wake Up And . . .

This assumes you work for a news magazine.

8:00 AM: You find yourself on a plane. You are going to cover a story in the Midwest about a group of teenage bank robbers. You flip through some notes you took at 5:00 AM when you got the call from the office.

11:00 AM: You land and deal with getting a rental car and a map. You know that every journalist is going to be at the teenagers' high school, so you try a different tack and head to the mall, hoping to find some truants.

12:30 PM: Your stomach saves you. After being lured to the food court by the savory smell of chimichangas, you see a few teens sitting in a corner. Turns out they knew the suspects. You whip out your pad.

2:00 PM: You've bought eight Cokes and have scored some great info, which you call in to the office so everyone is up to speed.

3:30 PM: You tried to get interviews with the thieves' parents, but no luck. You drive to the school and watch football practice from the bleachers, where you meet and interview some more students.

5:00 PM: You try to get the parents again. Still no luck. Then you have a thought—grandparents. You do some research and find out they live just one town over.

6:30 PM: After some daredevil driving, you ring the grandparents' doorbell. They yell, "No comment!" at first but then soften when you act nice. They invite you in and tell you what a good boy their grandson is. Obviously no one has talked with them yet. They let you have a picture of their grandson as a Cub Scout. Jackpot.

9:00 PM: You FedEx the photo to the office and then head back to the hotel, where you try to craft the story. Tomorrow you'll try the parents one more time, and then fly back home.

I Want to Report the News. How the Hell Do I Get This Job?

There are more than a few different paths. The most straightforward one is to graduate from college, go to journalism school, and take several unpaid internships, one of which hopefully turns into a paying job.

However, many reporters never went to journalism school. And some don't believe it's really necessary; it seems a debate is always afoot on the subject. And it's not that school isn't helpful; the argument is that on-the-job training may be more practical than the academic. Of course, while you are in journalism school, you'll also be trying to attain this through internships. But do you need to go to school, or can you save time and money and just do the internships?

However, keep this in mind: let's say you eschew grad school and go for an internship. And you are up against another candidate who is in journalism school. This could leave you at a disadvantage, obviously. Also, beyond internships, you can't get an actual job if you don't have clips (articles you've written and published) or, for positions in the TV world, the equivalent, "a tape." Journalism school will help you get those, so for that reason alone, it may make sense—especially if you are coming to this career decision and are already finished with your undergrad education.

But if you are a freshman, sophomore, or junior in college, you have time to try to get an internship, which may be a less costly way to break in before committing to journalism school. Or at the least, you can apply for internships and journalism school at the same time. Whichever direction you choose, you'll probably want to do more than one internship.

Okay, so journalism school or not, you get an internship. Now what do you do? Be proactive. Sure, like any intern, you are going to have to do some crap, like transcribe interviews, get coffee, and answer phones. But if you're friendly and show interest about the interviews you're transcribing, if you ask questions and show you want to learn (without being "the annoying intern"), you

I recommend that you study everything but journalism, but that you do an internship. I think you should be as smart as possible on as many topics as possible; you never know what you're going to cover. Journalism school has a lot to offer, but journalism is not a classic profession where you need credentials, like medical school or law school. I think it's more of a craft—you just need to learn the basics. And I think the best way to learn the basics is on the job.
—**Dan Harris, anchor and correspondent, ABC News**

will get more responsibility. Reporters are overworked; they always need help. Try to get taken under someone's wing.

But what if you've interned, and damnit, it didn't turn into an actual job? Sadly, one thing you'll find about the world of journalism is that it seems as if no one is ever hiring for entry level. But don't fret; you just need to be persistent. And when you finally get a job interview, show off your can-do attitude. Many people applying for journalism jobs (and internships, for that matter) have major senses of entitlement. This comes from the fact that many of them are intensely qualified—Harvard grads and such. But a good attitude and a willingness to do whatever it takes can go further than these qualifications at times, because credentials don't get the story out in the real world.

And when you've landed that first job, you better keep up the same "I'll do anything" approach. Be happy just to write captions or to hold the camera. It's cliché, but being a team player and pitching in will gain you trust, and trust breeds better assignments. And then soon, you'll get your big chance, and hopefully you'll shine. That's the way it happens.

Resources

The best way to find a job in journalism, as in most other fields, is word of mouth. Talk to anyone and everyone. Short of that, you can look on sites like mediabistro.com and journalismjobs.com.

Editor & Publisher has compiled a list of the leading journalism schools in the good ol' U.S. of A., complete with links to each, at editorandpublisher .com/eandp/resources/journalism_schools.jsp.

Here are some organizations whose sites have articles, information on jobs, and forums where reporters can "share." The sites of the Poynter Institute and the Society of Professional Journalists are probably the best places to start:

The Poynter Institute: poynter.org

Society of Professional Journalists: spj.org

American Society of Journalists and Authors: asja.org

The Newspaper Guild: newsguild.org

Finally, a great book for budding reporters: *The Elements of Journalism: What Newspeople Should Know and the Public Should Expect* by Bill Kovach and Tom Rosenstiel.

The interns who very gently but persistently reached out to interesting people in the newsroom and said "I'll do anything for you—just give me something to do," ultimately, after they gained some trust, were able to do some pretty cool things. That's the trick. You just need the right attitude and approach.
—Dan Harris, anchor and correspondent, ABC News

I'll give you a good example of somebody who got a job. She's now covering the White House for *Newsweek* in Washington. There were a lot of people with big attitudes and egos, and her pitch was, "Hire me. I will work so hard for you and I promise I'll never complain and I won't have an attitude and I'll just be so grateful for whatever you give me." We hired her immediately.
—Susannah Meadows, senior writer, *Newsweek*

Screenwriter
TV Writer/Feature Writer

W riting for TV or films is, undeniably, a dream job. Whether you've penned a blockbuster movie or a B-level horror film, an episode of *My Name Is Earl*, or two jokes on *America's Funniest Home Videos*, making your living writing for the screen is pretty much as good as it gets. Not to mention, it's a fine living as well. So yes, screenwriting is a dream job. Of course, "dream job" is usually code for "It's hard to get, dude."

As great as it can be, it's not all sushi and starlets. There are talented screenwriters, ones with Emmys and even Oscars, who suddenly can't find a job on a TV show or even get a pitch meeting. Others make nice livings, but are terminally frustrated because they've never had any of their screenplays actually filmed. You see, kids, Hollywood provides lovingly with one hand, and then gives you an atomic-level wedgie with the other. As Woody Allen said, "Show business is dog-eat-dog. It's worse than dog-eat-dog. It's dog-doesn't-return-other-dog's-phone-calls." But enough with the negativity . . . Being a screenwriter is an amazing, exciting life, and those lucky enough to labor at it couldn't imagine themselves doing anything else.

> It's a great job. The worst day of writing is better than the best day of anything else; I really can't complain.
> —Nick Santora, writer, *The Sopranos*; co-executive producer, *Prison Break*

Feature Writing versus Television Writing

Although the skill set involved in writing an episode of *Law & Order* is very similar to that used in writing a dramatic legal feature film, the two jobs do have their differences. Over the course of their careers, many successful writers dip their toes into both fields, and so this chapter will aim to give an overview of each discipline.

Feature Writing 101

Features are the films shown in movie theaters. They are still considered the top artistic achievement in the world of film and video entertainment; everyone in the entertainment field looks on the act of writing a film and then having it actually produced with admiration. Feature screenplays are generally written by a single person (or occasionally a team). It is the stereotypical man-on-an-island existence, where you'll hole up alone somewhere and work on the script without collaboration, until your agent tries to sell it, or, if you've been hired to write it for a studio, present the work and get *notes* (feedback). Of course, there are meetings with your agents, managers, and lawyers, but most of the time, it's you and a computer.

Feature writers can work anywhere, be it at home, a coffee shop, or an office writing space. Any place they feel comfortable and can get work done. It's in many ways similar to the life of an author (see the chapter on authors).

Once you finish and sell a script, it may well be your last involvement with the project until you are invited to the premiere. Feature writers are not part of the production process on films; directors and producers are completely in charge. Sometimes writers are not even invited to the set.

Feature writers don't climb any corporate ladders. You're not on staff anywhere, and you don't get a salary. You simply write screenplays and try to sell them. But that doesn't mean that a sold script automatically gets turned into a movie. In fact, usually, they don't. Some successful feature screenwriters who make more than $1,000,000 a year have never heard an actor say one word of dialogue they've written, because none of their scripts has actually been produced.

And even if you write a screenplay that doesn't sell, but it impresses people as it makes its way around Hollywood, you could get paying work from it. Your script becomes a writing sample, and that alone may get you *rewrite work,* which is when a writer comes in and "rewrites" within another person's original screenplay. There tend to be a lot of rewrites in Hollywood, which has a very "cover-your-butt" management style. Sample dialogue at a studio: "The movie lost money. You put only one writer on it? You're fired." Rewrites can be very lucrative, although as a young writer you don't really get the same chance to shine as you would on an original work. For seasoned pros, there's a subset of rewrites known as *production rewrites,* meaning a script that is being rewritten while the movie is actually filming. Since money is being spent and the clock is ticking, production rewrites pay gobs of cash.

Selling Those Screenplays

A lot was just made of selling a screenplay. So how's it done? The first way is to *pitch* it. A pitch is simply a brief presentation of an idea for a film (or new TV show for that matter; pitching applies to the TV game as well). You pitch your idea to major studios and independent producers.

If someone likes your pitch, he or she will buy the idea and then hire you

As a feature writer, you don't control the outcome of the project you've conceived and written. You create a blueprint, and then others come in and interpret it. You'll have worked very hard to create something distinctive, but you have to be okay knowing that it probably won't come out exactly the way you intended. Because after you have gone away, the director, producer, and cast are all going to take your piece and bring it to life how they feel works best.
—**Mike Handleman and Dave Guion, screenwriters**

to write the script. If no one buys it, the upside is you haven't wasted several months writing something no one wants.

Which is the risk of the other way—actually writing a complete script before it's sold (this is called a *spec script*). In this case, you don't pitch it. Instead, your agents send it to studio executives and producers to read. And if you're lucky, someone buys it. Often scripts are sent out on Fridays so they can be read over the weekend, and hopefully there's a bidding war on Monday.

TV Writing 101

Writing for television is the opposite of the lone existence of the feature writer. TV shows have writing staffs; if you write for one, you will be part of this staff. There's a room, cleverly called "the writers' room" or often just "the room," where you spend your day with the other writers on the show. You sit around a conference table and work as a team to *break* stories—come up with structural plot lines for an episode. You'll bang your heads against the wall together when it's not going well, and jump up and down laughing and throwing awkward high-fives when the stories are flying. It's a team atmosphere, and generally a lot of free snacks and caffeinated beverages are lying around to keep it peppy.

Once the storyline is figured out, a single writer (or possibly a team of two) will write the actual script and dialogue on his or her own. It's a cycle; each writer has his or her turn at the plate, like a batting order. (You get paid extra when one of your scripts is made, thus the cycle to keep things somewhat fair.) If it's your turn to write that script, you go off (much like a feature writer) and bang it out. Once the script is written, you take it back into the room, where you and your team will dissect it, critique it, give notes on it, and sometimes tear it apart and put it back together. It's intense, yet inside a very casual, fun, freewheeling atmosphere that fosters creativity. Not that there aren't cliques and politics like at any other job.

The entry-level writing job on a television show is staff writer, although as a staff writer you'll spend more time helping come up with story ideas, and normally don't get to write any actual scripts. The next level is story editor. The level after that is executive story editor. Above that is co-producer, then producer, then supervising producer, co-executive producer, and finally executive producer, the highest level you get as a television writer. Lots o' titles.

As you can tell from those, in television the writers are also producers. Unlike feature writers, writers in television are part of each and every step in the process.

At the lower levels of TV writing, you are generally hired season to season.

So if the show you're on is canceled, suddenly you are looking for a new job. Or if the executive producer on your show didn't love you, well, he or she may not ask you back the next season. So just because you are part of a staff, being a television writer really isn't much more secure than writing features on your own. It's what magicians call "an illuuuuusion."

What Does It Take to Be Good?

Beyond the obvious—extreme creativity and writing skills—what does it take to make it as a screenwriter? First, as mentioned earlier, you have to be disciplined. You actually have to sit down and write and finish scripts. It's not easy. And you have to be somewhat of an optimistic person, because you are going to be rejected again and again until you finally make it.

Even though writing can be a lonely lot, your social skills are incredibly important. You are going to be pitching yourself, and your ideas, to agents, production companies, and studios, and you need to be likeable and convincing. You need to seem like the sort of person who isn't going to be a pain in the neck to work with. You'll have to pick your battles—decide which scenes to stand up for and when to throw in the towel.

In terms of computer or other job skills, scripts need to be in certain formats. There's the basic three-act structure of Hollywood film scripts that you can learn from any number of screenwriting books, but also there is the actual format of the words on the page. A lot of people in Hollywood won't read scripts unless they are formatted correctly. You could learn what font to use, where to double-space, and so on, and do them in any word-processing application. Or you could buy and learn Final Draft or Movie Magic Screenwriter, two software applications specifically designed for scriptwriting. Screenwriters swear by them; they are well worth the cost if you are serious about screenwriting as a career.

What else? Well, you need to be a good networker. As you'll see shortly, breaking into the business is very much determined by who you know, so you can't be scared to go out into the world and get to know people. You don't have to live in L.A. to be a feature writer, but in the beginning, it could help, just in terms of meeting people. As a TV writer, though, you'll probably need to be located in L.A. Most shows, although not all, are headquartered there.

Hours?

Both feature and television writers work hard, but they don't kill themselves—although the most ambitious ones come close. If you are lucky enough, you

In the feature world, the studio, director, producer, and cast can all demand creative changes and rewrites, and, it's kind of a joke, a lot of these will contradict each other. You have to know how to be diplomatic, when to fight and when not to fight.
—Mike Handleman and Dave Guion, screenwriters

There're a million people out there who want to do this, and everyone's fighting for an hour of someone's time to read their script. So meet people, use any connection you can, no matter how tangentially related to the business they are, and try to get them to read your stuff.
—Nick Santora, writer, *The Sopranos*; co-executive producer, *Prison Break*

can be working on several projects at once. You could be executive producer of a TV show and writing a feature on the side. In cases like these, when deadlines start to overlap, hundred-hour weeks are not unheard of. Those are the kinds of weeks when you just have to hook up the coffee IV drip and keep typing.

Feature writers work alone, so they work whatever hours best fit their schedules. Many try to have a "work day" to discipline themselves, going to their writing space from nine to five each day. Not that the current project isn't buzzing in their minds 24/7.

TV writers' days are more structured, as they meet at the show headquarters with the rest of the writing staff. They may put in a good fifty-five to sixty hours a week, depending on what part of the process they are in and what level position they hold. However, writers normally get the entire month of April off, and often May. Two months a year vacation, plus two more weeks off in the winter. It's pretty sweet. Of course, if you are an ambitious little bastard—and you kind of need to be—you'll be using some of that time to work on a feature screenplay or some new TV show ideas of your own you want to pitch.

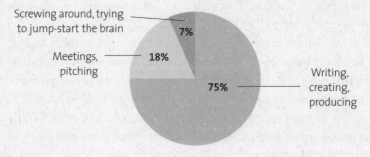

Screwing around, trying to jump-start the brain — 7%

Meetings, pitching — 18%

Writing, creating, producing — 75%

It's a youth-driven industry. I've mentally prepared myself that one day when I get older, the phone may stop ringing. It happens to everyone in this business, comedy writers more than drama, but still. The good news is that with the money, if you come into the business in your thirties and work through your forties, you won't need to work in your fifties. My biggest concern, though, is not financial security; I just don't want to have the fun taken away.
—Nick Santora, writer, *The Sopranos;* co-executive producer, *Prison Break*

Salary?

If you write feature films or TV shows, you will be a member of the Writers Guild, which is the writers' union. The Writers Guild has minimum salary guidelines for every level of job—not that you won't try to negotiate for more as you become super important, but there is a floor. And as you might guess, these are set on a lot of different criteria. Check wga.org, as contracts are renegotiated every few years. As an example, the minimum payment for a low-budget (under $5,000,000) feature screenplay and treatment is $56,500; for a high budget, it's $106,070.

Within the guild structure, feature writers can have scripts bought outright for negotiable sums, or they can be *optioned*, which means someone pays a certain amount of money to reserve the right to buy the film for a specified amount of time. So if your script is optioned for two years, and that time passes and the film hasn't been made, you can try to sell or option it again. Many people do get second and even third options.

TV writers get paid a base salary, plus they're paid a bonus for every script they write that's made into an episode. Royalties are paid to writers for DVD sales, syndication, foreign sales, and so on. Guild salary minimums start at around $5,000 a week, and those in the most senior writing positions can earn as much as $30,000 to $50,000 a week for a twenty-two-week season, not including the bonus script fees. It's a high-paying profession—you just have to keep working.

You could make eight figures a year or more if you have a hit film or TV show. You could make $200,000 a week—a goddamn week!—if you are one of the top production rewriters. The Bureau of Labor Statistics has a very broad listing for "writers and authors in the motion picture and video industries," where it reports the annual mean wage as $79,800.

Stress-o-Meter: 5 (1 being a carnival palm reader, 10 being a CIA profiler)

It's fun, but it's not easy. As feature writer, for example, trying to sell one idea that will pay for a whole year of your life is stressful. Deadlines are stressful. And just trying to break into the business is profoundly frustrating. But c'mon, once you're in and are writing thrillers or comedies and getting paid buckets of green paper? It's a blast.

Pros

Dude, you are writing movies and TV shows.

There's very good pay as you progress. Yacht money.

You could potentially be famous (if that is a pro for you).

You will be creating pop culture.

Cons

It's a very hard-to-break-into field.

For features, you are not in control of the final creative product.

Hard work helps, but you still need luck.

Hollywood likes 'em young, even for writers. It's hard to keep working as you pass fifty.

Cut to the Next Scene, Where Suddenly You Are a Screenwriter. You Wake Up And . . .

This assumes you are a feature writer.

9:00 AM: You head to the office, a small space you rent a few blocks from your home. You like to keep strict office hours, nine to five. You click around the Web, getting the brain started.

10:00 AM: You start to write. You are halfway through a new screenplay about a dog that knows how to golf. It's animated.

12:30 PM:	You grab some lunch at a diner around the corner. You sit at a table and read the paper. That's about as social as it's going to get today.
1:30 PM:	You're back at it.
3:00 PM:	You take a break and call your agent. You check in on the status of a couple of meetings you are hoping to get to pitch a different idea. Disney is set up for next week. Perfect.
5:00 PM:	You usually quit around five, but you are humming along. You keep going for another hour. You managed to stay off the Internet all day. A miracle.
6:00 PM:	You head home, daydreaming about what you can do with the money if Disney likes your pitch.

I Want In. How the Hell Do I Become a Rich and Famous Screenwriter?

The line forms over there, on the California border. A lot of people want in the movie business, and once you are inside Los Angeles proper, you can't spit without hitting someone who has a script. But don't spit. It's unhygienic.

First, hear this: You can become a screenwriter. It can be done. That's the most important thing you must keep telling yourself. Why them? Why not you?

The paths to break into TV writing and feature writing are similar. Here are the bold strokes: first write a great script, an amazing script, film or TV. Second, use that script to get an agent. Third, if you are lucky enough for the agent to sell that script (if it's a film) or to get an entry-level staff job (if TV), life gets a lot easier. Look at it this way; it's incredibly difficult to get into Harvard. But once you are in, well, it's not nearly as hard to pass.

If you want to get into writing television specifically, again, the first thing you'll need is a script that turns people's heads. You can do that in one of two ways. You can write a spec script for a show of your own invention. So it's your own voice, your own characters. Often Hollywood people love to read them because it's something they've never read before.

The other path is to write a script for a show that currently exists, that's currently on the air. You choose a show that people talk about, something popular, and write a great script that fits the premise and characters of the show.

Okay, so you wrote a script in one of those two ways. Now you must use every connection you have on this planet to get an agent to read it. And if you get an agent who believes in you, there's a good chance you may come out to L.A. for "staffing season." This is a feeding frenzy in April and May, where all

Don't pick some obscure show on basic cable that no one really watches, because no agent or Hollywood executive is going to want to read it. Pick a show that's hot, and write a script that fits that formula. So don't write an episode of *ER* where all the doctors become Apache helicopter pilots. Write an episode where there's a heartbreaking medical case that the doctors have to solve, that delves into personal relationships that grab the reader. If you can write the format of a show, the proper tone of a show, and do it in a way that turns heads, you can get an agent. And that's the first big step.
—Nick Santora, writer, *The Sopranos*; co-executive producer, *Prison Break*

the shows look to staff writers for the upcoming TV season. Hopefully, there will be a spot for you.

If you are trying to be a feature writer and have written a film script, you'll also aim to get an agent to read it. However, if you can't, there's another alternative. Trawl the Internet and bookstores for listings of all the major film festivals in the country and in Canada. Many of these festivals have screenplay competitions as well; a lot of people don't realize it. And you don't have to have a film made to enter; you just need a screenplay. There are entry fees, and some can be high, so make sure that the film festivals you choose are legitimate. If your script wins or places, or if the right person happens to be a judge and reads it and you garner some attention, that's a big score. Hollywood runs on attention, buzz. If one person likes your work, everyone wants to read it. A slang word for it is "heat." That a script is really getting some heat means that suddenly everyone is talking about it.

And . . . if you are lucky enough to have a finished film, definitely send the film to both agents and film festivals. It's easier to get agents and executives to watch your film than to read a script. Of course, if the film didn't come out the way you hoped and didn't properly reflect your writing, sigh, just send the script.

No two people get into the screenwriting game exactly the same way. Everyone has a Hollywood story. What will yours be?

Resources

You can go to school for screenwriting, but most screenwriters haven't. Film school is more for directors, cinematographers, and editors. But you should make sure to learn the lingo and conventions that are common in Hollywood, which you can learn in film school or in any number of available workshops and classes. There are also heaps of screenwriting books at any bookstore. It's recommended that you flip through them to learn the vernacular, but don't follow them as strict guides on how to write a script—that's an amateur move and won't show off your unique style. Some recommended ones: *Screenplay: The Foundations of Screenwriting* by Syd Field, *The Complete Book of Scriptwriting* by J. Michael Straczynski, *Hero with a Thousand Faces* by Joseph Campbell, *The Art of Dramatic Writing* by Lajos Egri, and *Making a Good Script Great* by Linda Seeger.

You are better off reading the teleplays and screenplays to great TV shows and films and seeing how they were put together. Check out script-o-rama.com, which has loads of screenplays you can download for free. Read as many as you can. Many other sites offer insight, advice, and group screenwrit-

Try to write something that will stand out when people read it. Don't try to write the next *Old School* just because you think that's what Hollywood is buying right now, hundreds of other writers will be doing that. Have a fresh, original voice that will make an impression on people.
—Mike Handleman and Dave Guion, screenwriters

I was a lawyer working eighty hours a week and I was miserable. Instead of going on vacation one year, I wrote a screenplay and on a whim, sent it to the New York International Independent Film Festival. Amazingly, it won best screenplay. The next thing I knew, I had an agent. Within a year, David Chase, the creator of *The Sopranos* had read the movie I'd written and asked my agent if I would write a freelance *Sopranos* script. I spoke to my wife about it and I said, "Look, I don't know anything about this business, but maybe we should give it a shot . . . how do you feel about moving to California?"
—Nick Santora, writer, *The Sopranos*; co-executive producer, *Prison Break*

ing hugs, such as creativescreenwriting.com, goasa.com (American Screenwriters Association), and wordplayer.com.

Another book, which isn't a how-to tome but more of a book on what it's like to be a screenwriter in Hollywood, is *Adventures in the Screen Trade* by William Goldman, as well as the follow-up, *Which Lie Did I Tell? More Adventures in the Screen Trade.* Both will give you a feel for what it's like to toil in the entertainment mines.

Teacher
Primary and Secondary School

You want a rewarding job? Teach. Teaching a child how to read, or how to climb the ropes in gym, is a far more heartwarming way to make money than, say, the fur trade. Of course, it's also far less lucrative than many jobs in the private sector, and the odds of your being called a butthead behind your back are increased. Still, teaching is a noble profession. A noble profession that happens to also have a little perk known as "summer vacation."

The Daily Job

If you're able to read this book, you've probably attended a school at some point in your life and have a pretty good idea what teachers do all day. They stand (there's a lot of standing) in front of classes that range in size from small and intimate to forty kids and unwieldy. And they teach. In lower grades, teachers handle a variety of subjects. In high school, they specialize; you could teach math, or history, or English.

How you teach is up to you. Some teachers are straight-from-the-textbook types. Others devise fascinating lesson plans that introduce students to dry material in a far more interesting way. Each teacher has his or her own style and level of commitment. You probably remember ones you've loved, ones you feared but respected, and ones that, well, sucked.

What you teach, however, is not up to you. School curriculum is decided by each state. Statewide student exams take place for each grade level, and teachers are supposed to ensure that their classes pass these tests. Schools are given overall grades based on how their students fare, and "failing" schools can be legally overhauled by the government. What books and supplies are used to prepare the kids for the tests are decided by local school boards, principals, and influential teachers (heads of departments).

You should not go into this because you think the hours are good, because they are really not especially. You work a lot at home, coming up with inventive lesson plans. Especially at the beginning, when you have none. Over the years, you start to build up a bank of them, but you still want to keep things fresh.
—Lauren Weinstein, teacher (various grade levels)

What Makes for a Good Teacher?

A lot of the drippy teachers took the job for the summers off and the flexible lifestyle, the number one lure of the career. But you'd be well advised to look

Every child has a different learning style, and I believe it's your job to figure out how that student is going to learn best. So you can't be a rigid person, because your way may not be the best way for all people. The worst teachers are the ones who think they know it all and don't have an open mind. You can always learn from others.
—Lauren Weinstein, teacher (various grade levels)

You need to be quick on your feet and decisive. There is a lot you have to manage in the moment. Things are constantly changing in the classroom, and you need to adjust on the fly.
—Rebecca E., elementary school teacher

A teacher who has tenure of, say, ten years has to do something really, really bad in order to get fired.
—Lauren Weinstein, teacher (various grade levels)

past these benefits; it's an important, demanding job; you don't want to do it and be miserable if it's not for you.

With that in mind, what makes for a good teacher? First off, you need to like kids. You need to enjoy being around them, and you need to know how to handle them without losing your cool.

You must be patient and flexible. The dynamics in a classroom are constantly shifting. The kids understand something you didn't expect them to, but can't grasp the concept of something you thought simple. Something happens in the news and they have questions. You are their teacher, but you are also an important adult in their life on whom they rely for all kinds of support and information.

Who's the Boss?

Tony Danza. Bad joke. No, technically, the principal of the school is "the boss." But it's a little more complicated than that, because teaching, at least in public schools, is a union gig. When you first get a job as a teacher, you join the teachers' union. The union has negotiated a contract for all the teachers in the area. This contract will detail exactly how much money you make, how many sick days you are allotted, how long after-school meetings are allowed to run, every job detail and benefit. So there's no going to your boss, the principal, and asking for a raise; everything has been prenegotiated and you know exactly where you stand.

Principals oversee their entire school. They maintain discipline and are to whom you turn for any kind of classroom or behavioral issue. They make sure the school is on course to achieve the educational goals set out by the state. One way they do this is by observing their teachers.

Being observed is a bit like being reviewed in a private company. A few times a year, the principal will sit in on one of your classes and observe you teaching a lesson. He'll take notes and write up a report of how he thinks you performed. If those observations go well for a certain number of years (depending on your local union's contract), you will be given tenure.

Tenure, basically, means it's very hard to fire you. This is an amazing thing or a horrible one. For teachers, it means they can feel comfortable that they have a pretty damn stable career. For students and parents, it sometimes means that they cannot get rid of an awful teacher, like the ones who have worn the same shirt every day for the last five years and can hardly keep their eyes open. Tenure is the reason they haven't been canned.

What Education Do You Need to Teach?

To become an elementary/middle/secondary school teacher, all you technically need is a degree in education. A master's degree is not required to start, although many states require that you get one within five years. Most teachers do, eventually, get their master's. This is not simply because they wish to be the best teachers they can be; no, there's money involved. Union contracts are set up in a way that the more education a teacher has, the more money he or she makes.

After you obtain your first job, you are given a certain amount of time until you must pass state testing in order to be a certified teacher. You need a license in order to teach—thank goodness. If you move to another state, you may have to become certified again in the new state, and take its tests.

Money?

As just mentioned, salary is contingent on the union contract and how much training you've received. There's a big jump in pay from an undergraduate degree to a master's, and then there are steps after that: master's plus fifteen graduate-level credits, master's plus thirty, and so on. This plus the number of years worked (plus anything new negotiated by the union) determines your salary.

Salaries are not as low as they are stereotyped (although not as high as they should be for such an important job). They vary from school district to school district, but starting salaries are generally in the $30,000 to $40,000 range. According to salary.com, an elementary school teacher's salary with one year's experience in New York is $38,869. With eight years' experience and some credits above an undergrad degree, that teacher could make around $75,000. And he or she can make over six figures with enough years and credits. Nationally, the Bureau of Labor Statistics reports the mean salary for teachers to be $46,990.

Teachers also get solid benefits, summers and holidays off, and great retirement packages (depending on how long they have taught). Public school teachers tend to make more than private school teachers. Private school teachers do generally have smaller class sizes and better infrastructure, though.

What's the Vibe?

In public schools (and most private ones), being a teacher is pretty casual. It all depends on the institution, but generally most teachers don't overdo it on school clothes. Sure they might wear a suit once a week, but they also might be able to get away with jeans on Fridays. Sadly, the fashion stereotype for teachers: wicked bad taste. They're on their feet all day, so that explains the orthopedic shoes. The rest, though . . .

As a teacher, you have to act grown-up, and you have to be able to discipline the kids. You may want to be the "cool" teacher, but you can't be that all the time. You can't grab a straw and get in on the spitball action; no, you have to stop the balls from being spit. It depends on where you teach, but discipline could be metal-detector-level serious or a minor irritation.

Teaching can be a solitary profession. Kids surround you all day, sure, but no one your own age. You don't hang out with colleagues (except on periods off in the fabled teachers' room—it's a plain little room usually, not the ultra pad of students' daydreams). You aren't able to field personal calls or be on IM like your friends with office jobs are, and you can really check e-mail only a few times a day. Plus there's not much intraoffice dating; the pool of teachers is pretty small.

Done by the 3 PM Bell?

Teachers' hours are considered fantastic. And they are pretty good, but people forget about the homework, which, for teachers, equals planning the next day's lessons and grading papers. Most teachers arrive at school between 7:00 and 7:30 in the morning, and their day is usually over (assuming they are not providing after-school tutoring or coaching the soccer team) by 3 PM. So although they still have work to get done by the next day, they do have some free time to shop or go to the gym while most of the rest of the world is stuck in office buildings. During the day, teachers generally get one period (generally forty-five minutes) off, plus another period for lunch.

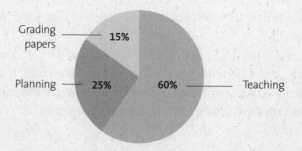

Stress-o-Meter: 6 (1 being a Civil War re-enactor, 10 being an Army Ranger)

It really all depends on the kids in your class. You could have kids you'll love forever, or you could have the "demon child." Your schedule could be easy, or the state could issue new standards that make it a nightmare. Overall, it's not too stressful, but you are "on" all day in front of your captive audience of students. You'll need good material to keep them awake.

However, if you work in a school that has gang, drug, or violence issues, the stress is much, much higher. A good rule of thumb is that if the school has metal detectors, the stress level will be increased.

Pros

You actually see children benefit and grow from your job.

You teach how you want to teach.

You have summers off.

Good retirement plan and benefits in general.

Pretty tough to get fired or laid off.

Cons

You're the lone adult a lot, so you don't have the opportunity to make many friends.

The community doesn't always appreciate how important a job you have.

Waking up early, every day.

You should make more money, considering how important your job is.

Boom, You're a Teacher. You Wake Up And . . .

This assumes you are an English teacher in a public high school.

5:30 AM: The alarm goes off and you slap it. It's still dark out, but this is your only chance to exercise. You put on some shorts and go for a jog.

7:00 AM: Showered and somewhat awake, you begin your commute. You get to school ten minutes before the bell and prepare for your class.

7:30 AM: The day begins for you with three classes back to back. It's a tough three hours of standing and being entertaining. The kids are all sleepy eyed as you begin your lesson; you're reading *The Old Man and the Sea*. You talk about different metaphors Hemingway uses throughout the book. At the end of each class, all but one of them turn in their papers, which are due. You give the lone one, whose parents you know just separated, an extra day.

11:30 AM: Lunch break. You head to the teachers' lounge; you brought your own lunch today and left it in the fridge. You chomp down your turkey sandwich as you listen to a beer-bellied gym teacher talk about how much he can bench.

12:05 PM: You go into the bathroom and into a cloud of smoke. Three students stand in front of you, shaking with fear. You direct them toward the principal's office, using your angry voice. Then you wash your hands, thinking, "What stupid kids; even teachers can't smoke inside anymore."

12:15 PM: You teach now until 2 PM; you have the coveted 2:00 to 3:00 period as your period off, which you use to check your e-mail and then photocopy material for tomorrow's classes.

3:00 PM: You are as excited as the students to leave, but you decide to start grading the papers in the classroom. It's easier to concentrate there than at home sometimes.

4:30 PM: You beat the traffic home, lie on your couch, and plan tomorrow's lesson. You wish you could just show the kids a video and relax, but you hunker down and plan.

8:30 PM: After dinner, you watch a little TV until 10:30, and then early to bed.

I Believe the Children Are Our Future. How Can I Become a Teacher?

My educational path was going to Hunter College to get a master's in childhood education 1–6. I was not an education major undergraduate. I was in advertising for five years and I decided I didn't want to do it anymore. I always had teaching in the back of my mind. It was a pretty big career change.
—Rebecca E., elementary school teacher

Well, if you know you want to teach early enough, the first thing you can do is major in education. But for many, teaching is a profession they come to after a few years in the private sector. They graduate from college, try a few things, and then realize, "Hey, I really want to teach." For these folks, the most common path is to go back to school and get a master's in education. This can be done full or part time while still keeping your day job.

You can specialize in one of many areas—concentrating, for example, on special education. Then, if you do a good job interviewing, you can teach. As mentioned earlier, there'll be tests to pass and extra credits to garner to increase your salary, but the path to becoming a teacher is fairly straightforward.

Before you make this decision, it's worth spending some time on the other side of the classroom to see if this is what you really want to do. There's no reason to put in the schooling commitment only to find out you hate the job. Look into internships and student-teacher possibilities, or even go down to your local school and see if you can observe someone. Many schools allow this for qualified graduates and undergraduates.

I would recommend going to public school and seeing if you can observe, or help out even. Say that you are trying to learn. I know a lot of people who have made relationships with people that way and even gotten jobs that way too.
—Rebecca E., elementary school teacher

Once you decide this is your future and manage to get an interview for a teaching position, make sure you don't come off as cocksure. You may think you have the key to teaching children, but a lot of times schools have a certain way they want new teachers to perform. Do more listening than talking, and show that you are open to their approach.

Resources

The American Federation of Teachers has a Just for Teachers page that has information on careers and lesson plans; aft.org/teachers/jft/index.htm. And the

National Council for Accreditation of Teacher Education site, ncate.org, claims to be "The Standard of Excellence in Teacher Preparation."

U.S. News & World Report ranks the best graduate education programs in its "America's Best Graduate Schools" issue. A listing of the top fifty schools is online (but without the necessary GPA and GRE scores you'll need to gain entry; for that you'll have to get the "premium" edition) at usnews.com/usnews/edu/grad/rankings/edu/brief/edurank_brief.php. The top three currently are Teacher's College at Columbia University, Stanford, and Harvard.

Here are some sites that can help you come up with innovative lesson plans:

School.discoveryeducation.com: From the Discovery channel, a site that offers teachers' tools, including lesson plan ideas and how to start your own school science fair.

Scholastic.com: The educational publisher's Web site offers tips for teachers, like "How to make the 100th day of school a math milestone."

Edhelper.com: Like its name, this site is helpful for those in the education field. It's filled with all sorts of advice and lesson plans.

Teacherplanet.com: Lots of links and resources available on this site.

In addition, there are some fun, well-designed educational sites that are built for kids, but that teachers may also find inspiring: brainpop.com, kids.nationalgeographic.com, and pbskids.org.

You just have to show that you are open and willing to try their ways of teaching. A lot of schools have a certain curriculum that they want you to follow and teach a certain way. You need to show that you are going to be a team player. There's a lot of pressure on the schools right now to perform up to the highest standards, because of No Child Left Behind.
—Lauren Weinstein, teacher (various grade levels)

Toy Designer/Toy Inventor

Let's clear up a few stereotypes about the toy game. First, to be a toy maker, you don't have to be an elf. The job, whose titles generally include *toy designer, designer,* and *toy inventor,* can be had by any person, large or small, with the ability to think like a child and design like an artist. Second, you don't have to live at the North Pole; there are toy companies throughout the country, although most are located on the coasts. However, one stereotype does hold true. There is a good chance your boss will be fairly jolly.

Working as a toy designer has pretty much been seen as the world's most fun job ever since the movie *Big,* starring America's sweetheart, the multidimensional Tom Hanks. Believe it or not, a lot of that film resembles the real world of toy making. Even the device of a twelve-year-old boy trapped in the body of an adult toy designer, although in a perhaps more metaphoric way, holds true. Like the fictional company in the film, large corporate toy companies make all sorts of toys, from conception to completion. There are also smaller upstarts that come up with ideas and prototypes and then sell them to the larger companies to build and distribute. At either, your job as a toy designer is to create something to play with, something challenging or just plain silly. It's the dream job of every preadolescent kid—well, up there with astronaut and princess, anyway.

Toys Two Ways

The toy market can probably be sliced into hundreds of segments, but here's a simple way to think about it: there are the completely new, never-seen-before toys, which could be defined as inventions, such as the Rubik's Cube; and then there are toys based on licensed properties, such as TV shows, movies, video games, you name it. A Spider-Man doll, based on the Marvel character and feature film, is an example of a licensed toy. Licensed properties are proven franchises; for example, before the film came out, you knew that the comic was an all-time classic and that the studios were going to pour marketing money into the movie release. So it was a solid bet that the action figure was probably going to sell to that already built fan base.

When not making licensed products, toy companies aim for other somewhat certain winners, like line extensions of top sellers, such as a new G.I.

Joe—now with nuclear-strength Kung Fu grip and a new sidekick, a Robot Ninja K9. These line extensions and licensed products are a reality that most folks don't think about when considering the career. You'll still get to come up with completely new toy ideas, but just how often depends on where you work.

How Does a Toy Become a Toy? Is Magic Involved?

Sadly, there's very little magic these days, just hard work. But you'll never be the one truly "making," or manufacturing the toy. That tends to happen with partners in Asia. Here's a basic breakdown of the process and the role of toy designer in it:

Let's start with how a licensed asset becomes a toy. The marketing department will come to you, the toy designer, and your team, and say, "Hey, we made a deal with the James Bond people, and we are going to make some Bond toys." In toy design, you generally work in teams of two or three people to begin, pulling in other folks along the way. You'll all talk about what will be in the Bond line—obviously a Bond action figure, a villain or two, a cool car, maybe some gadgets. Then you'll go back to your office and do some brainstorming.

You'll take around a week, could be more or less, and come up with some Bond toy concepts. Then you'll roughly sketch them out just to show your ideas, such as a Bond figure with a functional hand that can hold different items—a gun or a blonde or a dry martini. If you and your team think the idea has merit, then you will scan those sketches into Photoshop and begin to create a 2D rendering. This won't be perfect, of course, so you'll include some notes or other images to help get across what you intend, and then you'll regroup with marketing and some upper-management folks and present the functional-hand Bond concept. Generally, you won't present a single toy, but the whole Bond line and how this functional-hand Bond fits with the car, the villains, and other accessories.

After the usual back-and-forth, upper management will make some tweaks and then approve the idea. After that, a *control drawing*, which is a fairly technical drawing that depicts how the toy is physically going to work. There will be four views: front, back, top, and side. And then, using a kind of sculpting clay or foam putty, you will sculpt a small model of the toy, showing how you think it could look. These steps are important, as the actual execution and production of the toy will almost always be done overseas; and it's best to give them as tight a mock-up as possible to start. Trying to get a toy made with people in another country who may not have the greatest command of En-

We're solely an invention and design studio. We come up with new toy concepts, and then we pitch the idea to toy companies in person, or we send a prototype and video of the toy to clients like Hasbro, Fisher Price, Mattel, pretty much all the major players and some smaller ones too. We've done toys like the Regenerator (a remote-control car), which was Toy of the Year. You get to crash it and it regenerates itself.
—Rob Antonio,
  toy inventor and
  design director,
  KID Group

glish (nor you of their language) can be a struggle. And you want as little struggle as possible. Struggling is no fun.

It's hard to take a toy you've imagined and then create it physically in a mass-producible form, and thus you will spend a lot of time phoning and e-mailing manufacturers overseas. The fun part of the job, the brainstorming and making of the first models, happens more quickly, while the engineering and production stages tend to drag on. Ahh, the many complexities of life outside the imagination.

Now, to the creation of the invention-type toy. Creating these is similar, but it's a bit more of the Wild West. You don't have a final goal of "make it more like Bond!" in mind, although you may have a rough target to shoot for, a direction like, "Go for a board game," or, "Something for boys aged eight to eleven." Here you will, again in a team, think up ideas for toys. You will discuss them with your bosses and marketing people, and if everyone likes it, you will begin to create a prototype, along the same lines as before: Photoshop, sculpted models, and so on.

What happens next depends on whether you work for a larger toy maker like Mattel or a smaller studio. At a larger company with more resources, you may actually make a few toys—real working ones that can be tested in focus groups of moms and kids to see if they like them. Laughter or tears, which shall it be?

Smaller companies can't usually afford to manufacture small quantities of finished toys, so they'll build rough prototypes. This can be real "crazy guy in the garage with a blowtorch" work: gluing stuff together, making hand-hewn robotics. Then along with the prototype, they'll create sales and marketing materials that help sell the idea. Their goal is to get a Mattel or Hasbro to buy the idea from them and then manufacture and distribute it. Focus groups with moms and kids may be part of this process. For example, a video showing young Dicks and Janes freaking out over your new creation, Stanley the Starfish (in prototype form), can help convince the larger corporations that the toy is worthy of being bought and brought to market. If Stanley does get purchased by a larger company, the smaller company gets a commission, around 5 percent of sales, forever. So if Stanley's a huge hit, that can be good money.

What Kind of Person Is a Toy Person?

You have to have artistic chops; both computer design and hand skills are required. Photoshop, plus 3D modeling programs like AliasStudio, SolidWorks, or Rhino are going to be key tools that you can learn in school or training classes along the way. Other artistic skills you sort of need from birth, like the ability to sketch out your ideas or sculpt them. While these can be sharpened, they require a certain genetic code that not everyone has. By now, you probably know if you have an arty gene in your DNA. If you have great, wild ideas but can't draw a circle, it's pretty difficult to be a hands-on toy inventor or designer. However, you could work in marketing at a toy design firm and still be involved in coming up with toy and game ideas, but you will be more on the business side of things than the purely creative.

Toy designers are imaginative, of course, but they also need to be good at presenting their ideas and getting the business folks to understand their visions. Attention to detail and passion for the business of playthings are also a must.

Most toy designers have a BA in industrial design, which is graphic design, plus engineering, ergonomics, anything that makes the piece useable and functional. Toy designers and inventors are tinkerers by nature, fascinated by mechanisms. A lot of what you will do involves taking things apart and repurposing them, so if this was a childhood hobby of yours (to the eventual ulcers of your parents), it's a good sign.

Sometimes in order to get a model done you have to deal with hazardous chemicals, fumes, and power tools that can dismember you if you're not careful. If you're someone who doesn't like to get dirty then this might not be the job for you, because sometimes we'll go home covered in dust and paint.
—Rob Antonio,
toy inventor and
design director,
KID Group

Rumpus Room?

The offices of toy designers and inventors are, as you'd imagine, filled with fun stuff. Larger companies' offices may still have a corporate shell, and there may well be cubicles, but in the design section of the company these will be teeming with stuffed monkey arms. Radio-controlled cars will be zipping down the aisles. Inspiration is all around; you can't make fun toys if you are in a minimalist modern-design conference room or a mahogany-walled law office. You'll wear whatever you want; you'll play music and goof around. It's a fairly awesome place to work, as well it should be. Both large and small firms generally have a separate studio area where the carving, painting, and mounting, take place. Although these are an absolute candy store for people who like to make things, they're also more than a wee bit dangerous. You can't be fooling around near a table saw, or you'll end up like your shop class teacher Mr. Barnes, a.k.a. "Three-Fingered Barney."

Hours?

You'd think they'd be long and torturous, that there would be some kind of lame sentence here that read, "Being a toy designer or inventor is not all fun and games." C'mon, don't be so cynical. The hours actually aren't bad at all.

Most people work a standard forty-hour week; the occasional fifty- or fifty-five-hour ones come only during a crunch, under an approaching deadline, or if you can't keep yourself from working on some great opportunity. Few toy designers work weekends regularly. No, it's not too bad at all, especially compared to other jobs in design and industrial design.

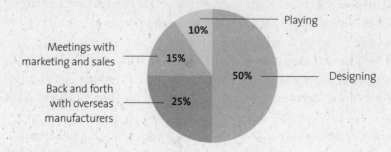

Play Dough

Exact salary numbers for toy designers are hard to come by. If you work for one of the larger toy companies, you can start at around $40,000, a bit more or less depending on the company and position. You will generally be hired with the title of *designer*. From there, the money goes up as you progress. As you rise into a management position, salaries rise to around $150,000 or $200,000.

Now if you are strictly an inventor at a small company that only sells its toy ideas to the larger toy manufacturers, you'll start around $30,000 to $35,000. Here, though, you will probably be given an incentive to invent; for example, you can receive 10 percent of the 5 percent your company makes from sales of your toy. It sounds like a small slice, but you get that with every toy you make, and it can add up. Either way, as a toy designer, you probably aren't going to make private-jet money, but you'll be able to send your kids to a private college.

The BLS lumps toy designers into the far broader category of "commercial and industrial designers," which may account for the numbers seeming low, compared to the anecdotals. It reports the mean salary as $56,780, with a range of $29,720 to $89,230.

1   10

Stress-o-Meter: 4 (1 being a singing telegram, 10 being a postal worker)

You're making toys. And though sure, there are deadlines, office politics, and the occasional screwup that sends everyone into a tizzy, you are making things of wonder. It's hard to create a cute, cuddly toy when you are chain-chewing Tums and nursing an ulcer.

Pros

You're working with toys.

The office is filled with fun, dynamic people.

Lots of new projects, so it doesn't get boring.

Hands-on creation, every day.

Cons

The back-and-forth with Asia during production can be a frustrating process.

Working with hazardous materials and tools.

Occasionally going home filthy.

Kerplooey! You're a Toy Designer. You Wake Up And . . .

This assumes you work at a large toy company and are currently working on a licensed toy.

7:30 AM: You eat breakfast and watch some cartoons to keep current with "the kids" before shoving off for work.

9:15 AM: You're at your desk, checking e-mails, seeing if the day will throw you any curveballs. The day doesn't, but suddenly a member of your design team yells, "Incoming!" and throws about fifteen balls of various sizes at your head.

10:00 AM: You attend a meeting with the marketing team, discussing a license they just acquired for a children's cartoon, *Dr. Blammo!* You bat around different toy ideas that might work: action figures, a board game, maybe a Remote Control Blammo-Mobile.

1:00 PM: You grab lunch with your design team and start to talk more deeply about ideas for Dr. Blammo. You really like the idea of turning the Dr. Blammo character into a doll you can speak to, which will then speak back to you. You start doing funny voices to further explain, eliciting stares from fellow diners.

2:30 PM: You and your design team gather around a computer and a speakerphone to talk with Hong Kong. You're in the fourth round of revisions on another project, sending JPGs marked up with comments back and forth. Since you are fussy about the tiniest of details, these calls can be frustrating.

5:00 PM: You drink an extra-large Coke and kick around a spongy soccer ball with another designer. You go over some other thoughts for Dr. Blammo. She has an idea to create a Dr. Blammo costume, complete with stethoscope ray gun and tongue depressor/nunchuks. Nice! You plan to sketch up all the thoughts tomorrow and see if they have any merit.

6:00 PM: Yabba dabba doo time. You head home.

I Am Childlike, Ask Anyone. How the Hell Do I Get This Job?

The most well-paved path is to go to school and get a bachelor's degree in industrial design. This will give you a solid base in designing all kinds of three-dimensional objects. If you aren't in industrial design school currently but want to go, know that you'll need decent grades, but also for many undergraduate schools, a high-school-level portfolio. This would show off your skills in drawing, sculpting, and so on; its purpose is to show basic proof of artistic aptitude. The schools want to make sure you have the ability to do what their classes require. A few industrial design programs have toy design majors; FIT in New York City and Otis in Los Angeles are two of the most famous.

When you leave industrial design school, you'll leave with the object that gets you your first, second, and tenth job—a portfolio. A portfolio, as you may have seen in other portfolio-requiring jobs across this book, is a compilation of your best work in book form. A beginning toy designer's portfolio should include sketches, renderings, and, where possible, photographs of actual prototypes of toys he or she has conceived. The portfolio should include between fifteen and twenty pieces, and as always, show only the best. Anything questionable might make your tastes and design sense seem uneven.

If you are already in school for something else, well, get thee down to the art school and talk your way into the industrial design classes. Sorry, but that's what you'll need to do, or else take some continuing education classes and try to learn and build a portfolio that way. An electrical engineer with design skills or an artist with industrial design skills could also break in. The basic idea is that you are capable of coming up with an idea in 2D, in a sketch, and then of bringing it to life in 3D, in a model or prototype. Still, eventually to get a job, you'll need the portfolio.

While still in school, you'll want to get an internship at a toy company. Internships can usually be found through your school, and their importance cannot be overemphasized. It's fairly competitive to become a toy designer, and having experience in the field will certainly help in any interview. Many times the place where you intern is the place where you'll get your first job. Toy companies want to make sure they are bringing in not only talented designers, but also folks who fit the personality of the place, and internships serve as tryouts. Smaller companies especially can't take any chances. As much as they may love your portfolio, they really want to see you in action before they commit.

And like in so many fields, you'll need to network. Whom you know is extremely important in the toy industry. It's a small world, after all. For that reason, if you can't get an internship at a toy company, then intern at an

> Your portfolio should show innovation, not just cool style or design. We need people who have really good ideas. We also look for someone who is versatile; if they have mechanical inclination or technical ability that is always a plus. You can also bring in prototypes or models that might showcase these skills.
> —Rob Antonio, toy inventor and design director, KID Group

industrial design shop. Someone there will know someone at a toy company, whether it's a former colleague or a friend from school. The same holds true for your first job. Don't hold out if you can't get into a toy company at first; go to a general industrial design place and keep sniffing around.

When you do get an interview, be it for an internship or a real job, remember to make that portfolio shine. You might consider bringing a sketchbook, which is just a book of different half-thought-out ideas and drafts, not nearly as finished as your portfolio. Especially for a first job or internship, the company will be really curious how your mind works, even beyond what's in your portfolio. A sketchbook can help get you over the hump. Keep it in your "back pocket," and present it if, and only if, you think it's needed.

Beyond that, just show them that you are an imaginative soul who'd be professionally fun around the office. Don't come in juggling or anything like that, but also don't be afraid to show your personality.

Resources

Core77.com and coroflot.com are two popular design Web sites. They both cover industrial and toy design as well as architecture package and interactive design. There's lots of information about schools, internships, and job listings. There's even a place where students can upload their portfolios so other students and companies can see them. And, it's worldwide, not just the United States.

The Toy and Game Inventor's Handbook by Richard Levy and Randy O. Weingartner highlights toys created by independent inventors and explains how you too can make your livelihood in this field.

Some magazines you may find inspiring: *Playthings* is a toy publication (also at playthings.com); *Wired* (wired.com) helps you stay on top of trends in technology; *MAKE* (makezine.com) is good for tinkering; *T3* (t3.co.uk) focuses on gadgets and *I.D.* (idonline.com) offers design inspiration.

Finally, two organizations that focus on the toy industry: the Industrial Designers Society of America, idsa.org, offers information, resources, and conferences and events where you can go and network with the ol' student discount. The Toy Industry Association, toyassociation.org, is more about the business of toys than toy design, but you may find it informative.

Veterinarian

Veterinarians are physicians for animals. And just like physicians for humans, there are all kinds, from general practitioners to specialists. There are vets who work with small animals, vets who work with exotic species, vets who work with wildlife and zoo animals, and even vets who are cardiologists or oncologists. Becoming any kind requires a lot of hard work and schooling, but still it's a job many people desire. Probably because animals are cute, cuddly, and, let's face it, far better patients than humans. Very few animals ever scream, "I am going to sue you, Dr. Quackenjerk!"

But it's not all a charming Dr. Doolittle story. For all the immense satisfaction that comes with healing animals, it's a very serious business with inherent sad moments. Animals get fatal illnesses, and as a vet you will have to euthanize many a beloved pet. Because it's a reality most prospective vets don't factor in, it's something that should be stated up front. Not to be a buzzkill.

What Do Vets Do All Day?

A lot. Exactly what will be defined by your specialty and/or the types of animals you treat, but regardless, most vets' days are pretty packed. Let's say you work in a private practice as a general practitioner, which is what most people think of when considering the career—the local vet where folks bring their dogs, cats, rabbits, and gerbils. When you work as a GP, your duties will be divided between medicine and surgeries. Medicine will be the majority of your day; it consists of such things as preventive care, vaccinations, and checkups. Just as parents bring their children to the doctor for all manners of aches and pains, the owners will bring their pets to you. There are animals with stomach viruses, flus, and all sorts of small ailments that are not major but need to be treated.

Though most of your day will be these less invasive appointments, unlike GPs for humans, you will also perform surgeries. So if you are open for nine hours, you'll probably have six hours of appointments, three in the morning, three in the afternoon. And the middle of the day will be set aside for surgeries and any "workups," such as blood work or X-rays. Surgical duties include births (C-sections too), dental (X-rays, teeth cleaning, extraction), orthopedics, emergency, exploratory, removing bladder stones, a lot of unblocking of urinary tracts, laser declawing, and pulling a sock out of a bottom (fairly common and yup, as disgusting as it sounds—it's not a sock you'll want to wear again). Anything more complex than these, you'll refer to a specialist.

What about the other kinds of vets? Well, specialists spend most of their day, naturally, working at their specialty. An oncologist, for example, examines tumors and surgically removes them, or prescribes courses of radiation or chemo. Vets who work with birds or exotics exclusively do pretty much the same things as regular vets, just on those animals.

And then there are the vets who work at the zoo. This, obviously, is a bit different from the normal vet office experience. For one thing, several animals at the zoo can kill and eat you. On the flip side, as a zoo vet, you don't ever deal with difficult pet owners, as all your "patients" are the zoo's. Here, you'll treat the smaller animals in an on-site hospital or examination room, while the larger ones, like the hippos, don't really fit through the doors. These get treated right in their cages or habitats. You'll make rounds and keep detailed records of all the different animals' health. And sometimes you'll perform in public. Yes, while grandparents show their grandkids the penguins, you might be in there doing an examination. It's part of working at the zoo. Plus, you also get to make this joke a lot: "Man, this place is a zoo today!"

What Does It Take to Be a Good Vet?

To be any kind of vet, you have to be a very motivated, dedicated individual. It's not the kind of career where you wake up and say, "Know what, I think I'm going to cure some ill animals!" It takes a long time to get to that phase.

How long? Well, first you get a four-year undergraduate degree, which can be any major, as long as you've taken all of the required premed classes. (Actually, you don't even need the degree, even though almost everyone gets it. Technically you just need the prerequisites, which, if you load up, you could get in two years of undergrad. It's possible to shave two years off your education this way, but again, very few do it.) Then it's off to vet school, typically a four-year program. Well, it's not as simple as "Hi-ho, off to vet school now." Getting in is pretty damn competitive; you'll need strong scores on the Veterinary Aptitude Test, MCAT, or GRE, plus good undergrad grades (3.0 or higher) to gain entry. Believe it or not, there are only twenty-seven vet schools in the United States, and only half of all applicants get accepted. Most of these schools are state funded, so it can be easier to get into your home state's school than into an out-of-state one.

Once you're in, it doesn't get any easier. Vet school is as intense as med school, filled with long hours of studying. You'll work in clinics and assist in

Many students don't get in on their first try. A lot of people advise that if you know this is what you want, you should start applying your first year of college, because most students get rejected a few times before finally being accepted. Persistence shows that you are serious about this as a career.
—Dr. Tamara Brennan, veterinarian

surgeries. Don't worry, you'll go out and have fun sometimes too, but you'd better not have too many nights of debauchery: at most vet schools, if you fail just one class, you'll be kicked out.

After you finish your four years, you are a doctor of veterinary medicine (DVM) and can practice as a general working vet. If you intend to specialize, you'll need to do internships and residencies; specialization requires these as additional training. Either way, fairly soon after you start practicing, you'll have to pass national and state board exams to become licensed. And even once you are, in order to renew your license every two years, the state requires you to complete a certain amount of yearly education. All in all, it's a pretty big commitment.

And it's an even bigger one if you wish to get into zoological medicine. Zoological medicine is a larger field than working at the zoo. Here is how the American College of Zoological Medicine defines it: "Zoological medicine is a discipline that integrates principles of ecology, conservation, and veterinary medicine and applies them to wild animals within natural and artificial environments." "Natural" means out in the wild; "artificial" means in zoos. There are two ways into this field, and neither of them is quick or painless. One is, after vet school, you can go through a residency program, around three years of nothing but zoological medicine. Then you'll have to publish five papers in zoo medicine, after which you're qualified to sit for an examination that tests all kinds of knowledge about zoo animal medicine and wildlife medicine. Pass, and yee-ha, you're considered an expert in zoo medicine, and you'll get additional initials behind your name besides the DVM. The other way you can qualify to sit for the boards is to get the DVM, then practice for six years in zoo or wildlife medicine exclusively, as well as publish five papers in that area. You skip the residency, but it takes longer.

Oh, one other thing about vet school—it ain't cheap. You can easily get out of school and be looking at $100,000 in debt. It's comparable to medical school in cost. It's enough to make you think about socialism.

So yeah, you really, really need to want to be a vet. In fact, as you can see, it's set up to weed out those who aren't passionate enough. On top of the passion and persistence, it takes a caring individual who loves animals and isn't squeamish. And if you work at a practice, you'll need to have a good "bedside manner" with pet owners. Owners of sick pets can be very upset, and not just that their pets are ill. They can be upset with what it costs to make their pets healthy again.

Is the Office Really a Zoo?

It depends what kind of vet you are, but the vibe at most practices is a professional one. You are dealing with the health of animals, and life and death, and you take it pretty seriously. Still, animals are fun, and everyone you work with loves them. It can be fairly jocular.

As far as dress code goes, at many practices, the vets wear scrubs; at others, it's usually some variation of business-casual, slacks or skirts. If you work in a zoo, you'll have a uniform. Zoos are pretty mellow, but since you are in public, you need to be recognized as a zoo employee. Otherwise people will think some drunk has gotten into the polar bear exhibit. Again.

Hours?

The hours aren't long, but they're usually wall-to-wall busy. You'll probably work a forty-hour week, but the actual hours will depend on how inundated your practice is. (If you work at a zoo, it's probably run by the city or state, so your hours will most likely be precise eight-hour days.) Most practices open around eight in the morning and close by six. However, you may not have a traditional weekend off; many vets are open Saturdays and/or Sundays. So your "weekend" could be a Sunday and a Tuesday; they may not even be consecutive days.

Like a physician, you may have "on-call" hours. Ninety percent of the time that just means answering questions on the phone, but every once in a while there will be an emergency to which you'll need to rush off. Those, luckily, are rare. Of course, if you work in an animal hospital, emergencies will affect your life more than if you were a general practitioner. For most vets, though, life is pretty well balanced. It's not overwhelming at all.

This assumes you are a general vet in a private practice:

> The people I work with have a team approach to everything; it's a professional but laid-back environment, and not high stress or fast-paced.
> —Dr. Tiffany Wolf, veterinarian, Minnesota Zoo

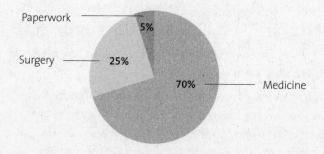

Paperwork — 5%
Surgery — 25%
70% — Medicine

Money?

Most vets who work in private practice make a base salary, plus they get a percentage of "production," which basically means a commission on how many patients they see.

Anecdotally, the numbers can be a bit higher (as is common) than what the Bureau of Labor Statistics reports; in this case it may be that the BLS didn't factor in the production profit sharing. Also, vet salaries are strongly affected by geographic location; large cities pay more than rural towns. According to the BLS, the national mean salary is $77,710, and the range runs from $40,960 to $127,050.

Stress-o-Meter: 6.5 (1 being a Zamboni driver, 10 being a NASCAR driver)

All in all, the lifestyle and the hours are not too intense. Still, the job can be emotional, and euthanasia, as mentioned pages back, is a very difficult and weekly reality. In the more specialized areas such as surgery, the stress is even more intense. Some animals, like birds, are very difficult to operate on, and some animals can of course be dangerous. For example, you never want to use a rectal thermometer on a lion, unless you are absolutely certain it's been anesthetized.

Pros

You work with animals, and you love animals.

Every day is different.

You really care about your job; it's a thrill to heal.

Cons

Some owners are simply difficult.

You will have to deal with some tragic cases, and even abuse cases.

It takes a lot of education—and debt—to become a vet.

The Years of Schooling Are behind You. You're a Vet. You Wake Up And . . .

This assumes you are a general vet in a private practice.

8:00 AM: Your first patient arrives: Harry, a Brussels griffon with some terrible halitosis. He's here for his annual shots and exam. It seems like all's well with Harry, except for the sour breath. You remind his owner to brush his teeth, and show her how.

8:45 AM: Next up is a cat named Lacey and an owner named Lacey. One of them is slightly insane, and it's not the one with paws. Human Lacey wants kitty Lacey to be given a battery of expensive blood tests you know aren't necessary. After twenty minutes of explaining that you couldn't possibly draw that much blood from the cat in one day, she agrees to just the most important ones.

9:45 AM:	You check a lump on a lovely Labrador. You see a look of relief on his owner's face when you tell him it's not a tumor, simply a fatty deposit, which this breed gets.
10:45 AM:	You take a fifteen-minute break and eat a Pop-Tart.
11:00 AM:	You anesthetize a dog and then begin to clean his teeth. This involves scraping the plaque off, something the dog would not allow if awake.
1:00 PM:	A woman comes in with her sixteen-year-old cat, which has gone blind. She asks about putting her down. The cat is very slow moving but does not seem in pain. It's probably not time yet, you advise her. But soon.
2:00 PM:	You take a half hour for lunch, with a sandwich and *Us Weekly* in the break room.
3:00 PM:	You see three more patients and then help close up the shop at 6:00.

I Want to Walk with the Animals, Talk with the Animals . . . How the Hell Do I Get This Job?

There are no real shortcuts. You ace the requirements and you go to vet school, as outlined earlier. One thing that's very good to do, though, is to work or volunteer in an animal clinic before you commit to vet school. It's quite a long path, and you should really make sure it's the path you want to travel before setting off. Plus, showing that you are experienced with and committed to helping animals doesn't hurt when applying to the competitive vet schools.

Once in school, definitely consider internships. Sometimes these turn into jobs for vets. So although they aren't necessary unless you wish to specialize, they can be helpful. When you do get interviews for an actual job at a practice, show your enthusiasm and your eagerness. You're the new kid, and there's a lot to learn. Just because you've been studying the last four years doesn't make you the hotshot vet.

General Resources

The following sites offer heaps of veterinary info:

Veterinary Information Network: vin.com

American Veterinary Medical Association: avma.org

Association of American Veterinary Medical Colleges: aavmc.org

U.S. News & World Report ranks the top veterinary schools in its "America's Best Graduate Schools" issue. The current top three (out of the twenty-seven that exist) are Cornell University, Colorado State University, and the University of Pennsylvania.

These journals are really more apt for practicing vets, but if you can get past some of the jargon, you may find them interesting nonetheless:

Journal of the AVMA

American Journal of Veterinary Research

Small Animal Research

Zoological Resources

A great resource for jobs and educational opportunities in the zoo world is the American Association of Zoo Veterinarians: aazv.org. Three others in the same vein are the Wildlife Disease Association, wildlifedisease.org; the American Association of Wildlife Veterinarians, aawv.net; and the American College of Zoological Medicine, aczm.org.

For zoo medicine residencies, Kansas State, the University of California at Davis, and the University of Georgia all produce strong candidates. Several zoos have good residency programs; the Bronx Zoo is probably the best known.

Video Game Developer

So you're like sitting on your futon in your boxers, playing PlayStation, when it hits you. "Brah, I so rule at video games. I am going to make awesome video games and become a game-rillionaire." Sure, it's a stoner dream. But it's also a real job, and a difficult and competitive one to get at that, in a growing industry filled with brilliant writers, designers, and programmers. If you're a gamer, it's an amazing way to make a living. Virtually amazing, that is.

What Exactly Is a Video Game Developer?

Video game developer can be a confusing title. Basically a VGD is a software developer (someone who "ideates," that is, creates software) for some sort of computer game. It could be an Xbox-type game, an arcade game, or an online or mobile game.

Video game development companies come in all shapes and sizes, but often they are quite small. The big firms you probably buy games from, like Electronic Arts or Activision, are really video game publishers. Within the publishers, are often video game development units, known as *in-house developers.* These developers come up with the games. They can also be assigned to work on games already conceived, for instance, the next Madden football. Think of it like this: publishers are like the Hollywood movie studios that put out films, and developers are the writers, directors, and crew who conceive and make them.

There are three types of developers: in-house developers as just mentioned; third-party developers, who are hired as independent contractors by video game publishers to develop games for them (perhaps their own department is overwhelmed, or they want to use a particular talent at an outside company); and independents, who basically are the same as third-party developers, but often will self-publish their own games.

Here's the part that's a bit muddled. Developers, whether they are individuals coming up with games or companies, have a staff of programmers, designers, artists, sound engineers, producers, and testers to help them physically produce the game, or they hire these people freelance. The thing is, any one of

> This is a fun, wild business, filled with outgoing artists and creative types. You don't normally find people going into game design who desire predictable, steady employment; those people go on to be lawyers and accountants.
> —**Scott Steinberg, CEO, Overload Entertainment**

these roles may be referred to as a "video game developer." You just had your mind blown, didn't you?

Don't be confused. All it means is that there are a lot of positions that help come up with a game. The developer described in this chapter is really at the top of this employment heap, the ones coming up with the games, leading the charge. Think of the other positions as ones that could lead up to it. Sorta.

What Do You, Like, Do Every Day, as Mr. Top-of-the-Heap Developer Guy?

Several things, naturally. First, come up with ideas for various video game titles; they could be original concepts, or many times, developers look for licenses—games they can create based on movies, bands, TV shows, and comic books. Then you oversee day-to-day development operations, which could include making sure a project is on schedule and that the game is fun to play, as well as managing the programmers, artists, and sound designers bringing the game to life. If you are an independent developer, since it's basically your own business, you can add all those business owner responsibilities to your plate as well.

But it's not like you walk in day one and they hand you $10,000,000 and ask, "So, what is your vision?" Big games these days cost as much as films to make, and entry-level jobs assisting developers, and in other positions, come first. It's a very competitive field to break into, as you shall see.

What Kind of Person Might Be Good at This?

First off, you probably consider yourself a gamer. If you don't, well, you probably don't know enough to get into this ultracompetitive field. Wanting to make games is like wanting to make movies. It's a dream. You need to be obsessed with it; your competition will be.

And just like people who make films, this gig of course requires a very creative person, a storyteller, a risk taker, and an artist. But not a solo artist. You have to be able to work in a team, as it takes more than one person to make a game. If it's a complex game like Vice City, sometimes teams of forty to sixty or even a hundred people may join forces to make it come to life.

If you want to be a programmer, then a degree in computer science certainly helps, but this is the sort of field where even in that most technical of positions, people with the love find their way in, regardless of background. It takes a lot of spirit and drive. You need to live games. And yeah, you will be

You need to be very flexible, because the entertainment business in general, especially entertainment software, is a hit-driven business. You have to be able to change stuff, be reactive. You need to know your subject matter, know games, and know the consumer. The more you know the consumer in this industry, the better off you'll be.
—Jay Cohen,
VP of publishing,
Ubisoft Entertainment

living them. As you'll see, you might be working seven days a week, fourteen hours a day in some stretches. It just happens. Welcome to the business.

What's the Office Like? People Playing Games All Day?

The sad thing is, people are too busy to play games—and when they get a free moment, the last thing they want to do is stare at a screen any longer. There are people who play games all day and get paid for it—QA people, or quality assurance. But it's not super fun or anything. Their job is to find flaws. So they will play every possible outcome of a game, spending days exploring a single level.

But hey, we were talking about the office. Which is almost always laid back and casual. People roll in around 10:00, 10:30. Well, that's how it is at the in-house developers and at the larger developers. Many others are small, just a few people in a room; sometimes people even work from home, wired up to all the other folks they need to create games. This way you can work with a programmer in Europe and an artist in Mexico. As you can imagine, in small or home offices the setting is even more "anything-goes" casual.

We are a jeans-wearing, open-layout kind of place. It's a young, fun environment. The average age is probably thirty.
—Jay Cohen,
VP of publishing,
Ubisoft Entertainment

Hours?

VGDs work hard. It's a business of deadlines; just like films, video games have release dates. And when deadlines loom, developers work very, very hard. They are known to sometimes sleep at the company. It's a labor of love, but it's labor. (In fact, in 2004, Electronic Arts was actually sued by some employees over the crazy hours—with no overtime pay, naturally—that they had to keep.) Is it always awful? No. Is it awful more than occasionally? Well, yeah.

Developers will tell you that long hours, though, are needed. You will gladly sacrifice nights and weekends going out with friends to make your game kick ass. It can be hard on relationships and even families when it's crunch time.

Here's where you'll spend those hours, assuming you have your own small company:

Everybody wants to be in the business, so what differentiates a real rock star from the average bear, I would say, is the drive and the willingness to put in the hours. You are certainly going to be in for a lot of work. It's like any creative medium; you have to have the will to succeed and you don't get to work normal nine-to-five hours. Despite what people think, it is not all fun and games.
—Scott Steinberg,
CEO, Overload
Entertainment

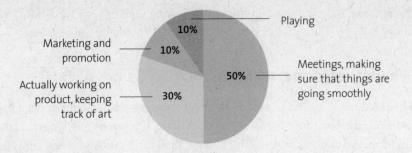

Playing — 10%

Marketing and promotion — 10%

Actually working on product, keeping track of art — 30%

Meetings, making sure that things are going smoothly — 50%

Mucho Dinero?

Well, you start fairly low, but not terribly low. An entry-level salary at a big developer is in the $30,000 range. You can be at that level for a long time, until you start to work your way up the ranks. Once you've been there four or five years and you start to produce, you're probably making in the fifties or sixties, and after you've done it for about ten years (keeping in mind that the video game business has been around only thirty years), it's possible to rise to creative head or studio head. At this point you could be making in the hundred thousands.

Game Developer magazine did an Industry Salary Survey in 2006. It found the industry-wide average salary for developers to be $70,000. The average for programmers with less than three years' experience was $52,989, while at the highest levels they averaged around $120,000.

If you want to make a killing, though, for the most part you have to do it on your own, not as an employee. (Or be an employee at a small company that gets bought by a big one, and you get a taste.) Although the large companies are great places to hone your skills, they own the games and reap the profits if they are huge hits. You just get a salary. So if you are ambitious and are ready, you have to start your own development company, and own your intellectual property—and a lot of people do.

 Stress-o-Meter: 8 (1 being a masseuse, 10 being a spinal surgeon)

That's right, it's almost as stressful to develop virtual lives as it is to save real ones. Well, let's hope not, let's hope that's just the VGD's adrenaline talking. (Gamers love to one-up people; you have to factor that in.) But the stress is high and here's why: this is a business where you never get the proper funding, or proper staff, to get things done. It's well known in the industry. It's also a reason why VGDs work the crazy hours. And long hours + not enough help + deadlines = stress.

Pros

You are getting paid to make video games.

It's exciting, rewarding, and pretty damn crazy that this is how you pay the bills.

Your friends will be blown away.

Cons

Stress.

Having to prove yourself every day and on every new game.

Getting things done is always a miracle.

Although your friends are impressed, it still probably won't get you laid.

Bam, You Are a Video Game Developer. You Wake Up And . . .

This assumes you are in the middle of developing a game, not coming up with one from scratch.

7:30 AM: You get out of bed, check your e-mail on your home computer, and begin to triage any problems that have come in from colleagues who worked later than you.

9:00 AM: You force yourself to go to the gym. You find weights much heavier in real life than in the virtual.

10:00 AM: You head to the office. You throw around a football with another developer and then sit down and figure out the day. One of the levels on the vampire game seems slow, a bit un-fun. You can't have that.

11:00 AM: You cram down an early lunch in a team meeting, brainstorming ways to improve the level. The deadline is approaching. And it's not the only thing you are working on; there's a new level that is still being tweaked.

12:00 PM: You spend the rest of your day keeping things moving, talking to teams, looking at different play experiences, thinking about improvements, thinking you really need a haircut. There is always a computer monitor in your face. It's hectic.

6:15 PM: Taking a break, you go grab dinner in a local coffee shop, alone, and read a chapter in a novel. It's like meditating, but with fries.

7:30 PM: You're back in the office, sucking down Diet Cokes and playing the new level the team has improved. It's very cool; you're psyched. But that other level still needs work. Shoot.

11:30 PM: You get home and dive into bed without even brushing your teeth.

I'm So Game. How the Hell Do I Get This Job?

Educationally, you don't have to do anything special. However, certain schools offer degrees in game design and programming, the more technical parts of development. More are offering them all the time. Among loads of others, check out the current course lists at MIT, USC, Stanford, Full Sail College of

Game Design, and Georgia Institute of Technology. Nintendo even has its own institute called Digiten.

If school isn't for you, the key is simply getting in the door. The first way in is through internships. Many of the larger development companies (and publishers with development departments) offer them. And these companies are not just American; don't be afraid to approach some of the foreign companies as well.

After those, the next way in is to get an entry-level job as a QA tester. These are the people who will play games for hours, days, weeks on end, looking for "bugs," or errors in the code. It's a low-level entry position, but it does give you a chance to influence how a game develops, and you will potentially be working with designers and producers, folks who are higher up in the food chain, and you'll be able to talk to them about possibly making improvements to the game. This gives you a chance to interface with the right people and try to make a move.

> A lot of people have great ideas for video games. The trick is bringing that idea to fruition, so you can show it off and build on it.
> —Scott Steinberg, CEO, Overload Entertainment

But truthfully, the best way to get a career in the game development and publishing business is to just get out there and do it. Make a game. It's just one of those fields where doing it yourself is the most impressive thing. And even if you don't have all the skills to build a game, it's still very possible to do so, thanks to the Internet. You can meet other people who are artists, who are programmers, who are just starting out, and you can assemble a small team and create sample demo projects. And when you have these, e-mail them out to different developers and show them who you are.

One of the fastest-growing trends is to create a game that is simple but fun and publish it online. You can sell your game online, cheap, say under $10, and be making a tiny bit of money while you build a reputation for yourself. Then you can go to a publisher and say, "Look I sold a thousand copies of this. Look how much fun it is to play and think about what I could do if you brought me on and I had a real team behind me."

If you do get an interview for a developer job, make sure you bring something to show. If you have a game, well that's the best, naturally. If not, show your art, show a soundtrack you've come up with, anything. Talk to them about what you've done on your own; show initiative, that you are a hard worker. And know about the company and what kinds of games it makes. They'll be looking for a temperament that fits theirs. Have it.

Resources

Online, check out gamasutra.com, ign.com, and the International Game Developers Association, igda.org. These are really good places to connect with peers and keep current. And you should also keep an eye on the latest games by visiting gaming sites, like gamespy.com, and all the main publisher sites, like Midway, Ubisoft, EA, and THQ. There is also an online trade publication for the gaming biz worth checking in on, next-gen.biz. And don't forget *Game Developer* magazine (gdmag.com), mentioned earlier. It has a *Game Career Guide* you can download for a small fee at gdmag.com/archive/cg06.htm.

As in every industry, networking is key. So if you can, try to hit the main trade shows and conventions, like E3, Electronic Entertainment Expo: e3expo.com. The Game Developers Conference, gdconf.com, is another wonderful place to go and get face-to-face time with industry people. Get your name out there, participate in forums, and talk to developers. A lot of them are looking for feedback, and they love connecting with the community. It is a very incestuous, small, and insular community—which, if you network, is to your benefit.

Wardrobe Stylist

Q: Who put Tom Cruise in a pink oxford and tighty whities in *Risky Business?*

A: A wardrobe stylist. (C'mon, it's the title of the chapter, after all.)

Wardrobe, or fashion stylists are the people who collaborate with photographers and directors to put models and actors in the right outfits for the photo or scene. Off the set, some are even personal stylists, traveling with the stars and making sure they look fashionable for the paparazzi, lest they end up in some magazine as "don'ts." As a stylist, you'll spend some seriously long hours shopping and schlepping. But if you love fashion and playing dress-up, there's no better way to pay the rent.

And it's probably best to mention it early. If you really want to be a stylist, you may have to move to one of the fashion capitals.

Before I Move, What Exactly Does a Stylist Do Every Day?

Stylists work with photographers or directors (see the chapters on photographers and film directors) to achieve a specific look for the models or actors. And these styling choices make a big impact on a scene. Audiences get an instant read into a character's psyche by how they look. Think about it: big black glasses on Woody Allen instantly read as intelligent, but also neurotic. Styling is even more important in a still photo; it's one of few clues as to who the models in it are and what their thoughts might be. If they have any thoughts. Oh, snap!

Stylists generally find a niche. You could be a crazy high-fashion stylist working on shoots for Karl Lagerfeld and Prada. You could be someone who works well with kids and ends up doing a lot of work styling children for advertisements. There are many paths, including, of course, the jack-of-all-trades one.

Regardless, here's the basic gig: once you are hired, you'll meet with the photographer or director and begin to collaborate on the look for the cast. After landing on an idea together, you'll go off and find some tangible resources that can be pointed to, evaluated, and agreed or disagreed on. You'll make a *style board*, usually just a piece of foam core with a bunch of photos and print-outs stuck on it. Like, if you're planning a shoot that's meant to be punk rock,

> If this is what you want to do, I hate to say it, but you need to go to one of the hubs of fashion or media, like New York, Los Angeles, Paris, Milan, or London. That's where the designers and photographers are based. If you want to learn, these are the places to do it.
> —Annabel Tollman, stylist, fashion director, *Interview* magazine

you'll look at old album art and rare early videos of the Ramones and the Sex Pistols, "pulling" any example images you think might work for the shot. Once everyone agrees that this is indeed the direction—late 1970s punk as opposed to early 1980s day-glo punk, you'll begin the process of sourcing the right items, everything from ripped shirts to beat-up Converses to safety pins for the punks' noses.

Of course, a lot of shoots call for styling that is more simplistic, a.k.a. duller. You might be doing the wardrobe on a Tidy Bowl commercial. The family in it should just look like contemporary suburbanites; their clothes really shouldn't stand out, just make sense for the scene. You'll still speak with the commercial director and dress the talent, but you won't have to hunt as hard for the right wardrobe, as, say, for a futuristic robot movie with fashionable droids. No, you'll be getting khakis and cardigans at the mall. You know, in the very chain stores that sell clothes to people who keep clean toilets.

Okay, so you and the director or photographer (and any one else who might have a say, like celebrity talent or the advertising agency) have come to an agreement on the look, and now it's time to go shopping. You'll get the sizes of all the members of the cast, and then you'll whip out your credit card (there will be a strict budget to adhere to) and hit the stores and wardrobe rental houses, as well as order items online. Prepare thyself for an immense amount of running around, and for lugging racks and racks of clothes. Watch any TV show or big-budget commercial and see how many different outfits the cast wears, including the people in the background. There are a lot, and the stylist outfitted all of them. On bigger productions you may have a cast of twenty people to dress, and you will need more than a few assistants to help. On smaller productions, say a one-day print advertisement shoot for Tide that has only a single model, you can probably do it all yourself. Still, it's not like you just buy one outfit for each person. You will have several choices, two of each when possible, in case someone spills a smoothie on herself or an actor rips his pants. It happens.

After the controlled chaos of shopping and finding the necessary items, you pack up all the clothes, jewelry, and shoes and haul them to the set—where you then go about unpacking them, carefully putting each character's wardrobe on separate racks. Now, a day or so before the shoot, it's time for the "fitting." The models or actors will try on each of the different outfits, and you and the director or photographer will make some final wardrobe decisions. You'll take Polaroids and label them, so on the day of the shoot there will be no question what each actor or model should be wearing. And during a fitting, you may have to do some refitting as well. This might be as simple as pin-

I am traveling every day, all day. It's an on-the-go, relying on your Blackberry profession. There's never enough time to get everything done and you are hustling to find the pieces you need before the production begins. You really have to like being active.
—Petra Flannery, stylist

ning a jacket in the back (if we never see the character's back), or you might need to call a tailor in to do last-minute alterations. Or you may still need more items, and have to make one last shopping dash.

The hardest part of your work is behind you. At last, the shoot day (or days) is here. Now your job is to make sure all the outfits look perfect. You will steam them and have them on hangers, ready to go. After the models or actors are dressed, you'll stand on the side of the set, ready to run in with a lint brush or an alternate hat at a moment's notice.

Once the shoot wraps, you are in charge of taking care of your purchases. Perhaps you'll keep an item or two for yourself. But most you will return to the stores or rental houses. And then it's on to the next job.

What Makes for a Good Stylist?

It goes without saying that you have to love fashion. You have be able to dress stick-thin models so that they look ultrachic, or be able to dress stick-thin models so that they look authentically homeless, depending on the concept. You have to immerse yourself in the world of fashion and trends and be competitive about knowing more about it than any one else in the room—because when you're around clients, you want to be able to come up with fresh, new ideas.

Other than having an addiction to fashion, you need to be very organized, able to find a single scarf in the heat of the moment on set. Also, it helps to be someone who is thick-skinned and can handle criticism, because in the subjective world of fashion, there's going to be plenty of it. You have to be a hustler and a treasure hunter, able to source that elusive Rolling Stones patch from the 1989 Steel Wheels tour when the photographer's dying for it. Maybe it's on eBay. Maybe the guy at the vintage guitar store knows someone you can borrow it from. You have to want to be the hero, to find the impossible.

Finally, you should be fun to be around. On the set, you spend long, stressful days in close quarters with the photographer and director. No one wants to work with a cranky little baby. And that personality of yours will not only help you get more jobs with him or her, but it will also help you network and meet other folks with whom to work. This is especially true when you start out as an assistant to a stylist. You'll be doing lots of lugging and grunt work, but you need to do it all with a smile, meet people, and network.

Do I Need a Degree?

To be a stylist, there are no educational requirements. And though it can be quite helpful, you needn't attend fashion school. If you wanted to become a costumer or a costume designer, a person who actually makes all the clothes or costumes for big-budget movies, the skills of sewing, pattern making, and so on would be necessary; here they are only helpful.

The one thing you must have in order to get paid work as a stylist is, as in other visual professions, a portfolio. This is simply a compilation of photos of your best styling. The pieces can be actual advertisements or editorial spreads that you styled, or they could be spec work you did with photographer friends. In fact, that's how you will make your first book. You'll hook up with a photography student or a photo assistant, and, using your own clothes and your attractive friends as models, you'll do some shoots purely for the portfolio. The photographer will get to use the shots for his or her book as well; it's a symbiotic portfolio-building relationship. If you do film and video work, you'll have either still shots of the actors in wardrobe or a *reel* with footage from different shoots. When a job is available, photographers and directors will call in some books and judge whose style they think might be right for the project. The portfolio is your calling card and your meal ticket. It needs to be constantly updated, exciting, and professional.

Stylish Office?

There are a few different places you could call your office. The first is a home office or small rental office space, where you make calls, invoice, do research online, and look for more work. The next is your car. You'll be spending enormous amounts of time in it, shopping and hauling your loot back to the set. You'll want to get a kickin' radio. Finally, there's each set you work on, which changes from job to job.

Sets are exciting places. There is a team atmosphere; everyone wants to make the shot or scene the best it can be. It's a cool, arty vibe. You may be in a studio, or you may travel to an exotic (or not so exotic) location. Often music's playing (not when you are recording sound, naturally) and snacks are being passed. Of course, when things aren't going well, that casual atmosphere goes south in a heartbeat.

The first big question stylists are asked is "what do *you* wear to work?" The answer is, clothes you can hustle in. You can't wear stilettos and run around all day.

Hours?

The hours can be both long and crazy, kind of like a Fellini film. You will be paid by the day, and the production will aim to hire you for the fewest days

Your portfolio has to be beautiful. Editorial work allows you to get beautiful images for your book, but it pays nothing. But those great images will help get you higher-paying, but less exciting, advertising work. One feeds the other.
—**Annabel Tollman, stylist, fashion director,** *Interview* **magazine**

If I'm going to a lunch or something or meeting a new client, I'll get dressed, and what I wear all depends on what I'm into at the moment. To a degree, you are your best advertisement. But you have to walk the line between looking fashionable and trying too hard. It's very amateur to go all out. But on days that you're working, you're schlepping. You need to be dressed comfortably.
—**Annabel Tollman, stylist, fashion director,** *Interview* **magazine**

possible. Because you want everything to look amazing, when you are prepping, you'll be using every minute. The actual shoot days can be more relaxed as described earlier, but most shoot days are still ten to twelve hours long. On the flip side, as a freelancer, you may not be working every day. And even if you are in such demand that you can work every day, you get to decide which projects to take and which to skip.

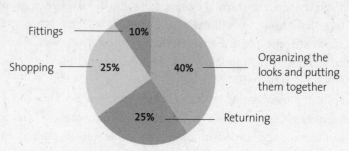

Money?

After several years, you can make quite a nice living. But to start, you won't make diddly. Assisting pays very little. You may make $100 for the day. And it takes a while before you move up to be a full-fledged stylist, and some time after that until you are being booked regularly. And as in any freelance job, there are no medical benefits or 401(k)s.

When you work in editorial, except on the highest-end shoots, you'll make around $500 for the production. That's not per day, that's for all the days: the shopping, the fittings, the shoot itself, and then all the wrap. It isn't much.

Working on commercials pays a healthier amount. On a fancy, big-budget commercial where the stylist is an important player, you could make between $2,000 and $10,000 a week.

If you become really successful, yes, you can expect to make a lot of scratch as a stylist. For people who keep busy, $100,000 a year is probably a bottom-range figure; some high-end stylists make $500,000 a year.

According to careerbuilder.com, stylists make between $1,000 and $10,000 a week, a wide range that depends on experience and the type of production.

The second big question stylists get asked is "as a perk, do you get to keep the clothes?" Yes, many times you do, although they may not always be your size.

Stress-o-Meter: 5 (1 being a weatherman, 10 being a war correspondent)

Being a stylist has its stresses; there are deadlines to make, clients to please, and occasionally crazy directors or photographers who enjoy yelling until their blood vessels burst like overfilled water balloons, but in the end it's fashion, and you'll live. More stressful is the freelance lifestyle, always wondering where the next project will come from.

Pros

If you love it, you really, really love it and you can't do anything else.

You get to meet a ton of fantastic, creative people.

You may be working in amazing locations.

You get things before they are out in stores, and you know the trends for next season.

Cons

It runs your life; it can be all consuming.

Sometimes the long hours make you miss out on social activities.

The money is rough to start; it can take five to ten years to make a decent wage.

Voilà. You Are a Wardrobe Stylist. You Wake Up And . . .

7:00 AM: Today is going to be hairy. You have some last-minute shopping to do before a fitting at 3:00. You're working on a music video for a rapper; it's set in the "boogie-down Bronx" circa 1981. You need to find some retro hip-hop clothes, early eighties stuff.

8:00 AM: Before the stores open, you search online. You want to maximize your time.

10:00 AM: You're in your car, hitting the rental showrooms first. You'll get some stuff here, and other things you can find at regular ol' stores. Like, you don't need to rent undershirts. Armed with a list of sizes for the actors, you skip lunch, hunting, right up to your meeting.

2:30 PM: You arrive at the production company; you're doing the fitting in one of the conference rooms. You and your assistant organize the last-minute purchases. Kangols to the left, gold rope chains to the right.

3:15 PM: Everyone but the rapper has arrived. You dress the cast and then call the director in. You and he discuss the merits of fat shoelaces on shell-top Adidas. You mix and match and finalize for the next couple of hours, taking pictures of every approved outfit.

6:00 PM: The rapper isn't coming. So you haven't dressed the star, and the shoot starts at 7 AM tomorrow. You just have to roll with it. You put five different outfits aside for him, then carefully put the other actors' clothes on hangers and label them.

8:00 PM: Tomorrow morning will be stressful until the star is properly outfitted. You lace up a pair of shell-tops to wear for yourself, so you can be in the spirit of the shoot. Then you crawl into bed and set the alarm for 6 AM. Ouch.

I Am Addicted to Fashion. How the Hell Do I Get This Job?

The way in is to assist a stylist. To do this, as mentioned, you may have to move. Although local TV stations and small magazines are scattered throughout the country, the main places to be a wardrobe stylist are in the media and fashion capitals: New York, Los Angeles, Paris, Milan, London. And to a lesser extent, San Francisco, Toronto, and Vancouver, where there's also considerable production (although these pale in comparison to the first list of towns). If it's not too late, it may make sense to go to school in one of these cities (whether in a fashion program or not) or even spend a semester or summer there.

So once you are in the right city, go find a stylist who you think is reputable, from whom you think you could learn, and try to get a crappy-paying but highly educational assistant job with him or her. Well, it's not so easy to just "go find one"! A lot of this business is based on who you know, so try to know people. Don't be shy, ask all your family and friends and their family and friends if they know anyone in the business, and use those connections. Also checkout newyork411.com and la411.com; these sites list all of the different people and suppliers who work in film and photography production. You can find stylists and stylist agencies (who help stylists book jobs) there, and you could cold-call. It's not as good as a personal connection, but it might be worth a shot. Lastly, go out where the fashion people go out and be charming. Even consider working in high-end boutiques, or stores like Barney's, where you'll not only be on the cutting edge of fashion, but be in places where stylists shop.

When you finally do get the interview, let them know this is what you really want to do, and that you will work incredibly hard for them. Some people may ask to see a beginner portfolio; some won't. If you have anything, no matter how raw, it won't hurt to bring it and explain that you are just beginning.

If it turns out you have to work for free or—you guessed it—intern to start, do it. Once you are in and on the set, you will start meeting people in the game. People such as the photographer's assistant or the prop people's assistant who, like you, need a killer portfolio to make the leap to the next level. You will form bonds and collaborate on days off to make these amazing portfolio pieces. And when one of you gets a job, hopefully they will be in a position to bring on the others. It's very typical for working cliques to start this way. Getting this first "in" cannot be overemphasized. One day years later you'll all be out and someone will make a toast and say, "Remember when we were all assistants?"

Then you simply keep working hard, meeting people, and improving your portfolio. Eventually you will get small jobs where you are actually the stylist;

you may even be referred by stylists you assist to jobs that are too low-budget for them to take on. And then one fine day, you'll spread your wings and no longer assist but be a full-fledged stylist. Bravo.

Resources

The main thing to do is keep up with fashion. You probably already know how to do this, but be sure to read all the American fashion magazines, and even French and Italian *Vogue*. Stay abreast of the latest fashion shows and trends on style.com. Basically, keep your finger on the thin-wristed pulse of fashion.

To find stylists already working, or if you are a beginning stylist and are looking for resources, anything from furriers to dry cleaners, check out the amazing newyork411.com and la411.com sites. They have everything imaginable. You might find that instead of actual stylists, they have agents or agencies listed. These "handle" or represent multiple stylists, which means they help them book jobs. If you get a reasonable person on the phone, he or she may point you in the right direction, or know of a stylist in need of an assistant.

Acknowledgments

The author would like to buy the following people a steak sandwich:

The brilliant Becky Cole, my first editor, who brought me in from the cold, Hallie Falquet, Brianne Ramagosa, Anne Watters, Rachel Rokicki, Songhee Kim, and everyone at Broadway for their Herculean efforts; Emilie Stewart, agent/sherpa; Matt Friedman, Mandy Vadnai, Melissa Weinberger, and Lisa Selin Davis, my excellent editorial assistants; my parents, Karen and Fred Rosen, as well as the rest of family: Lauren, Chad, Eli, Nera, Marilyn, Lauren, David, Alexander, and Billy the dog; and of course, the lovely Rachel Kash.

And most important, all the people documented on these pages who were kind enough to donate their precious time and talk candidly about their careers. Plus, all the folks who helped introduce me to the people who were kind enough to talk about their careers. Without them, there'd be no book at all.

About the Author

DAVID J. ROSEN has held many, many jobs. He is currently the author of the novel *I Just Want My Pants Back*, as well as a writer and director for television. In the past, he's worked as an advertising creative director, a camp counselor, an assembly-line worker, and a beer vendor for the St. Louis Cardinals. He lives in New York City.

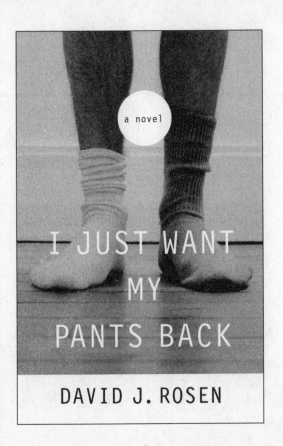

WHOLE LEARNING IN THE MIDDLE SCHOOL: EVOLUTION AND TRANSITION

Edited by

Glennellen Pace
Lewis & Clark College

Christopher-Gordon Publishers, Inc.

Norwood, MA

Credits

Every effort has been made to contact copyright holders for permission to reproduce borrowed material where necessary. We apologize for any oversights and would be happy to rectify them in future printings.

Chapter 4

Shannon Knepper's essay is used with permission.

Chapter 5

All student work included in the chapter used with permission.

Chapter 6

Journal entries by Kelly Conner, Martha Lampman, Mandy Pierce, Jesse Robisin, and Sara Shields used with permission.

Poems by Angela Duhrkop, Crystal Hunsaker, and Monica Smith used with permission.

Chapter 7

Journal responses by Jay Aaseng and Aaron Dalton used with permission.

Chapter 11

"Air Pollution" used with permission of Marissa French. "A Day in the Life of an Atom" used with permission of Kara Hohenshil. "Drip Drop" used with permission of Sandra Horan. "Band Waves" used with permission of Xiao-Wei Wang.

Chapter 12

Student work by Tammy Burnett, Cheryl Johnson, Reid Ditto, Dawn MacDonald, Celine Moreau, Barbara Pendlebury, Lucas Powesland, Candice Schultz, Bill Walker, Jacob Whatley, and Brenda Winger all used with permission

Christopher-Gordon Publishers, Inc.
480 Washington Street
Norwood, MA 02062

Printed in the United States of America

10 9 8 7 6 5 4 3 2 1   99 98 97 96 95

ISBN: 0-926842-44-7

Table of Contents

Foreword   ix
James Beane

Introduction   1

Chapter 1. Origin and Development of the Book   3
Glennellen Pace
>   Background of the Project   3
>   Finding the Authors   4
>   Rationale for the Book   4
>   Organization of the Book   6
>   Our Wish for Our Readers   10

**Chapter 2. Whole Learning and A Holistic Vision of the
Middle School: Principles That Guide Practice** 11
Glennellen Pace
>   The Link Between Whole Learning and the Middle School   11
>   The Language of Whole Learning   13
>   Challenging the Transmission Model of Education   13
>   The Middle School and the Transactional Model of Education   14
>   Principles of a Whole Learning Philosophy   15
>   A Current Vision of the Middle School Curriculum   21
>   The Vision and the Promise   22

Part I. Reflecting on Teaching as Learning   27

Chapter 3. On the Joys and Strains of Becoming   29
Tim Gillespie
>   Grounded—in Theory   29
>   Smelling the Chalkdust   29
>   Negotiating the Curriculum   32
>   Integrating the Curriculum   42

Cultivating Better Teaching   44
Wrapping Things Up   45

**Chapter 4. Making It Your Own: Whole Language in the
            Middle School   47**
Mary Burke-Hengen

A New Way to Teach Language Arts   47
Designing for Change   49
Skill Teaching   51
Teaching Essay Writing to Middle School Students   52
Students and Use of Time   55
Effectiveness of Writing Groups   55
Involving Parents   59
Other Paths to Learning   64
Assessment and Learning   67
Bringing It All Together   71
Looking Ahead   72

**Chapter 5. "Tracks in the Snow": Learning From Response
            Logs in Reading and Writing Workshops   75**
Scott Christian

My Vision as Teacher in a Multi-Cultural Community   75
Beginning the Workshops   76
Teacher Research as a Vehicle for Learning   77
Where Did the Teacher Research Vehicle Take Me?   89
Sharing Progress Toward the Vision with New Colleagues   90

**PART II. ORGANIZING CLASSROOMS FOR WHOLE LEARNING: THE
           LINK BETWEEN TEACHER INNOVATION AND ADMINISTRA-
           TIVE SUPPORT   91**

**Chapter 6. Hooked on History: A Cooperative Approach to
            Integrating History and Language Arts at the
            Middle School Level   93**
Shirlee Jellum

Opening the Door to Change   94
The Lure of Literature   95
From Process to Product   101
Making the Grade   103
One Step At a Time   104

**Chapter 7. Middle School English Classes: Workshop
Revisited**   107

Connie Russell

    Beginning the Process   108
    Planning for Curricular Change   109
    Merging the New with the Old   112
    Problems and Issues   117
    Coping   121
    Seeing the Results   123
    Next Steps   124

**Chapter 8. Integrating Curriculum in a Self-Contained
Middle School Classroom: Teacher Innovation
and the Impact of Adminstrative Support**   127

Sally Wells

    Laying the Groundwork   127
    Joining a Team   129
    Building a Program   131
    Struggling with Assessment   135
    Looking to the Future   138

**Chapter 9. Pushing the Boundaries in a Traditional Middle
School Environment: A School-within-a-School**   141

Lynn Moss

    Getting Started with a Democratic Classroom   141
    Events That Led to This Democratic Classroom   143
    A New Direction   145
    A Catalyst for Real Change   146
    Collaborative Curriculum Planning   147
    A Stumbling Block   149
    A Teaching-Learning Partnership Begins   150
    Assessment and Evaluation   154
    A Learning Community   156

**PART III. LEARNING TOGETHER: MIDDLE SCHOOL/UNIVERSITY
PARTNERSHIPS**   159

**Chapter 10. A Learning Journey: Exploring Teaching and
Learning in the Middle School Language Arts
Classroom**   161

Patricia Tefft Cousin **and** *Ellen Aragon*

A Learning Journey   161
The Context   163
The Curriculum   164
Case Study of David 169
Reflections and Plans   178

**Chapter 11. Looking Back, Looking Forward: A Science
        Teacher Incorporates Whole Language   183**
Suzan W. Mauney, Rosary V. Lalik, **and** *George E. Glasson*

My Participation in the Reading to Learn in Science Education Project   184
Changes at My Middle School   187
From Theory to Practice in a Newly Defined Middle School 188
Student-Centered Learning   188
Meeting Students' Needs in a Mixed-Ability Classroom 191
Interdisciplinary Teaching   193
The Value of Writing for Student Learning and Assessment 196
Future Challenges   198

**Chapter 12. Above the Tree Line: Collaborative Curriculum
        Construction   205**
Kenneth L. Bergstrom, Chris Mattson, Anne Reid, **and**
Dierdre Garner

Introduction: The Idea for a Collaborative Climb   205
Choosing a Trail: Discovering the Theme   207
Setting the Pace: "Handsitting" and Sharing the Lead   217
Knowing When We Get There: Repositioning Skills and
Transposing Content   229
Trusting and Cooperating: Important Lessons as We Climb 237
Preparing for the Next Climb: Looking Ahead   240

**Chapter 13. Reforming Middle School Mathematics Con-
        structively   243**
Charles R. Ault, Jr. **and** *Anne McEnerny-Ogle*
Background   243
Governance and Community Values: Anne Starts Her Story 245
The "Courtyard Project" as a Curriculum Demonstration   248

Textbook Realities and Assuming Leadership   250
The Inadequacy of the "Manipulative Concept"   254
From Rectangular Arrays to Quilts   259
Banking on Success   265
Conclusion   268

**Chapter 14. Embarking on Adventure: An Invitation to
Middle School Science**   273
Charles R. Ault, Jr. and *Neil Maine*

The Lure of Adventure   273
A School for Fish   274
Lawnmowers Across the Solar System   276
Bulldozing the Schoolyard   278
Counting Dead Birds   282
Advice to Science Adventure Guides   284
Who Will Speak for the Adventure?   287

CONCLUSION   291

**Chapter 15. Taking the Leap: An Analysis of the Joys and
Strains**   293
Kenneth L. Bergstrom and Glennellen Pace

The Decision to Move Toward Holistic Teaching and Learning 293
Strains: The Inhibiting Factors of Whole Learning   295
Joys: The Motivating Factors of Whole Learning   303
Weighing the Strains and Joys   309

INDEX   313

Foreword

James A. Beane

For more than a century the dominant trend in curriculum design
has been toward fragmentation. The legacy of that trend lives on
in separate subject/skill classes, teacher identities based on particular subject certifications, down-to-the-minute regulations about
seat time, separate programs for academic and affective purposes,
strict segregation of young people by age-groups, mutual exclu-
sion of school and community life, and an array of other disinte-
grating and disassembling arrangements. As I have described
elsewhere (Beane 1993a), this fracturing of knowledge, people,
time, and space has been all the more powerful because the interest in specialization it involves appeals to both high-culture aca-
demicians and social-industrial efficiency experts. For those who
love the trivial and abstract in the curriculum, who are more interested in the parts of ideas than the whole, the alliance between
these two interest groups has been a match made in heaven. It is
no wonder that the fragmented curriculum has held sway for so
long.

   Central as that story is to curriculum in this century, it has not
been the only story. As Kliebard (1986) reminds us, the history of
curriculum is really about the continuous struggle of various positions and viewpoints. For this reason we may recount a continuing
and simultaneous story—a long line of work—that has sought unity,
coherence, and connectedness in the organization and design of
curriculum. The Herbartians, for example, worked at the idea of
multi-disciplinary correlations during the 1890s. Progressives of
many stripes have promoted the integrated "project" approach since
the 1920s. And social reconstructionists have advocated for a problem-centered core curriculum since the 1930s.

   Now, in our own time, there is renewed interest in creating
curriculum arrangements along the lines of this second story.
Though support for this new movement can be found in several
places, its major progress has been located in two areas. One is the
language-arts based whole language movement that has virtually
transformed so many classrooms over the past decade. The other
is the middle school movement with its record of multi-disciplinary curriculum projects and, more recently, its push into work on
problem-centered, integrative approaches. I have wondered what
would happen when the two met as the whole language idea worked
its way up through the elementary school and converged with the

x

middle school reform movement (Beane, 1993b).

Now we have an answer and, as I suspected, it is one that offers real hope. It comes by way of this important new book, *Whole Learning in the Middle School: Evolution and Transition.* There are several important aspects to this book. One is the use of the term "whole learning" to designate curriculum projects that would otherwise go by names like interdisciplinary, multi-disciplinary, integrated, or transdisciplinary. With that term we are reminded at once of the need to think about *whole* ideas rather than simply their parts and to focus clearly on what and how young people are *learning* rather than simply on teaching methods.

Another important aspect is the whole language background of almost all of its authors. Just as we emphasize multiple paths to common learning so can we now recognize multiple paths to common curriculum reform efforts. In doing so, we may also build a stronger movement. For example, I believe that those with a whole language background have a great deal to teach the rest of us about the faith and patience that are a part of constructivist learning. On the other hand, those of us who advocate for a social problems approach might help interest-centered proponents to place more emphasis on socially significant themes. From this kind of conversation, there can only come more compelling curriculum possibilities for young people.

Yet another important aspect of this book is the interaction of theoretical reflection and actual classroom practice. In this sense, *Whole Learning in the Middle School: Evolution and Transition* stands firmly amidst the growing collection of powerful works that center on teachers' own stories of their craft, works like *Finding Our Own Way* (Newman, 1990) and *Seeing for Ourselves* (Bissex and Bullock, 1987) from the whole language field and *Integrative Studies in the Middle Grades: Dan Through Walls* (Stevenson and Carr, 1993), *Toward an Integrative Middle School Curriculum* (Brazee and Capelluti, 1995), and *Beyond Separate Subjects: Middle School Curriculum for the 21st Century* (Siu-Runyan and Faircloth, 1995) from the middle school field. There is no question that this body of literature will go down as a significant breakthrough in education. After all the in-service conferences, all the lectures, all the workshops, all the staff development activities, it is stories like these, as Glennellen Pace says, that "hold the greatest promise for enriching and improving our own learning and that of our students."

As we read this book, however, we will want to remember that there is still much work to be done. In some ways, we are still on the front end of the kind of curriculum reform described so eloquently here. For example, there are many educators who are showing sincere interest in whole learning but who have yet to catch on that it is not simply about making correlations across the existing subjects. How can we help them to see the implications for the genuine democratic communities described by several of the authors here? And as curriculum history suggests, once again, this is not the only curriculum movement on the scene. What can we do to consolidate our gains and push on amidst the growing clamor about national curriculum, national standards, and national tests? Surely no one believes our own bottom-up, democratic curriculum work can peacefully co-exist with standardized, top-down mandates. If we are overpowered in this way, will we have to wait another thirty or forty years for an opportunity to revive our vision?

These are hard questions and they cannot be ignored. But even as we fret about them, we should also recognize that they could not be asked without the prior efforts of people like those we meet in this book. Before we move ahead to those questions, then, it is important that we first savor the stories of these people. There is much to be learned here about classroom practice. There is also much to be learned about how we have gotten as far as we have. And, too, there is plenty to inspire us in the days ahead.

References

Beane, J. A. (1993a). *A middle school curriculum: From rhetoric to Reality,* 2nd ed. Columbus, OH: National Middle School Association.

Beane, J. A. (1993b). Pentimento, Judi! Pentimento. In Tom Dickinson (ed.), *Readings in Middle School Curriculum.* Columbus, OH: National Middle School Association.

Bissex, G. L. & Bullock, R. H. (eds.). (1987). *Seeing for Ourselves.* Portsmouth, NH: Heinemann.

Brazee, E. & Capelluti, J. (1995). *Toward an integrative middle school curriculum.* Columbus, OH: National Middle School Association.

Kliebard, H. M. (1986). *The struggle for the American curriculum: 1893-1958.* Boston: Routledge and Kegan Paul.

Newman, J. M. (1990). *Finding our own way.* Portsmouth, NH: Heinemann.

Siu-Runyan, Y. & Faircloth, V. (eds.). (1995). *Beyond separate subjects: Middle school curriculum for the 21st century.* Norwood, MA: Christopher-Gordon.

Stevenson, C. & Carr, J. F. (eds.) (1993). *Integrative studies in the middle grades: Dancing through walls.* New York: Teachers College Press.

INTRODUCTION

Chapter 1

Origin and Development of the Book

Glennellen Pace

Background of the Project

The seeds for this book were sown when middle school teachers Sally Wells and Lynn Moss joined me in proposing a conference session on whole language practices in the middle grades. They were former graduate students of mine in the Lewis and Clark College Master of Arts in Teaching Program based in whole language philosophy. They had brought with them to their classrooms a belief that knowledge is constructed by each of us as we interact with others and events in our environment. They had resisted teaching practices that cast the teacher in the role of expert who *gives* knowledge to learners; they had resisted practices that fragment students' learning (for example, memorizing rules of grammar, computational algorithms, or the Periodic Table of Elements divorced from the *real* experiences of writing a paper for a particular purpose and audience, or solving a problem requiring mathematical or scientific thought processes). Although each had experienced constraints, they continually strove to create learner-centered, integrated, thematic learning environments in their classrooms. We knew many middle school teachers who were interested in moving toward a curriculum with these features and wanted help with this process.

Joined by colleagues of Sally, we presented our session initially at a spring conference and again at a conference the following fall. Both the attendance at our sessions and the tremendous interest teachers expressed about this topic overwhelmed us. However, participants also shared their frustration over the paucity of literature on holistic approaches available specifically for middle school teachers, and many wondered how they could fundamentally change or improve on what they were doing in the face of organizational structures and policies in their schools, as well as state and district curriculum mandates. Thus, we saw the need for a book that would recognize the varying school cultures teachers experience and support teachers as learners engaged in changing their practice through *evolution* rather than *revolution*. We also wanted to hold evolving practice up to scrutiny against professed ideals as a way to nurture further change and to promote dialogue about the relationships of theory to practice.

Finding the Authors

So we began to talk with middle school teachers who were attempting to understand whole learning theory and to translate that theory to their own classroom practices, and who were also willing to share their stories. We looked for teachers working with varying populations, and from different geographical areas. Readers will find stories set in rural and urban districts, in small and large districts, and in districts with culturally similar to culturally diverse populations. Locations are widespread: Oregon, Washington, Virginia, Vermont, Wisconsin, Ontario (Canada), Alaska, California. The varying contexts provide stories of change under differing conditions. But taken together they also highlight issues and processes that all middle school teachers face in their evolution toward practices grounded in a whole learning philosophy.

Rationale for the Book

Over the past decade the whole language movement has gathered momentum in elementary schools across the country. Though whole language classrooms still represent a small minority, widespread changes are occurring as more teachers begin to consider the socially constructed nature of learning and the power of thematic, inquiry-centered, integrated curricula. Students in some districts now come into middle schools with elementary school experiences that make them openly question traditional methods. Whether urged by students, by their own disenchantment with the status quo, or by current middle school literature, middle grade teachers are showing a growing interest in curriculum integration, collaborative learning, teacher and student efficacy, and the importance of process as well as product in learning. Elementary teachers enjoy an excellent array of theoretical and practical literature to help them change traditional teacher-centered classrooms[1] to learner-centered workshops.[2] However, books are scarce that address junior high and middle school teachers' interests in changing traditional teaching approaches or classroom and school structures. Those that do exist focus largely on the language arts. We heard our colleagues express frustration about the shortage of materials written specifically for middle school teachers in transition; the constraints middle school teachers face in making these changes differ from those of elementary school teachers.

Thus, we wrote this book to address many of the specific issues middle school teachers face. Some of these issues created problems for us as we began planning this book.

First, whole language philosophy encompasses the entire curriculum, not just language arts; therefore, we wanted contributors to represent a wide variety of disciplines. On the other hand, since this kind of curriculum is integrated, school organizational schemes that represent traditional separation of subjects pose problems for the expression of an integrative philosophy. Nonetheless, a majority of middle schools today remain organized along subject area lines. We wanted the book to be useful to teachers in these more prevalent settings. For this reason, the authors represent a range of situations, from self-contained classrooms to those focused on specific disciplines. We hope the subject-area teachers' stories will help teachers still rigidly bound by subject divisions to move toward inquiry-centered, integrative practices in their own classrooms. And we hope the stories of those who have broken down subject-area barriers will help others to change curriculum organization in their schools. We are not arguing for elimination of discipline-specific ways of thinking. Teachers who are experts within the disciplines make important contributions as they demonstrate "thinking like an anthropologist," "thinking like a writer," or "thinking like a mathematician." But we do believe young people are more likely to develop these ways of thinking when they are immersed in "activities that clearly involve the integration of knowledge and skill from a broad range of sources—what [James Beane calls] 'big bang' projects."[3]

Second, the teachers contributing to this book range from those with years of commitment to a learner-centered, integrative model, to others whose theory and practice is evolving from a traditional model. So the practices they describe vary in differing ways from practices congruent with *idealized* principles from the literature on whole language or integrative studies. In all cases, though, these middle school teachers' stories show how they confront questions and issues that arise as they seek to put a whole learning philosophy—and the theory and research behind it—into practice.

In a six-year longitudinal study of whole language-motivated, teacher-initiated changes in classroom instruction, I identified several factors that may affect the extent to which teachers' classroom practices are congruent with principles of whole learning: (1) the teacher's current personally constructed philosophy and awareness of theoretical assumptions underlying specific practices, (2) school organization and administrative policies and support with respect to curriculum and instructional practices, and (3) the teacher's relationship with other teachers in the building.[4] The goal of this book is to promote successful whole learning practices while also recognizing these constraints and the doubts and confusions teachers experience in their own learning and development.

Organization of the Book

I asked the contributors to reflect on the middle school curriculum vision and learning principles presented in Chapter 2 as they told their stories and described their practice. I asked them to address their reasons for the curricular decisions they made and to say something about their own directions for future change. In their stories you will see examples of how each factor I identified—teacher knowledge, administrative support, relationships with colleagues— affected the success of their change efforts.

Three-Part Organization

The book is organized in three parts along with an Introduction and Conclusion. I recommend that the readers turn to the elaborated Table of Contents to gain an advanced sense of the contents of each chapter. In addition, I include the following information about the three-part structure, a brief summary of each chapter, and a discussion of several issues that cut across the book's three parts.

While in this chapter I provide background on the origin of the book and the purposes that evolved as the book took shape, in Chpater 2 I lay out the theoretical underpinnings behind the philosophy of learning and teaching that contribuors to this book hold, and connect these to a corresponding vision of middle schoool curriculum and organization.

Part I consists of three chapters, each of which reflects in some way on teaching itself as a learning process. Tim Gillespie, a long-time teacher educator, returns to the classroom for a year, a "rookie" in the middle school setting. He learns a lot about the differences between knowing the theory and putting it into practice. Mary Burke-Hengen shares with us her journey from teacher-controlled to learner-empowered approaches, first through writing, next through reading, and finally including the area of social studies. Scott Christian shows us what he learned about his students, and about teaching and learning, from a teacher-research project in his culturally diverse classroom focused on the use of response logs in reading and writing workshops. He underscores the importance to his continuing growth as a teacher of finding ways to continually study and reflect upon what happens in the classroom.

Part II consists of four chapters that show clearly how innovative teachers can create whole learning environments in a variety of organizational structures, but at the same time how important it is to have administrative support. Shirlee Jellum tells us about developing a whole language curriculum within her language arts classroom, then moving toward a partnership with a history teacher that resulted in an integrated curriculum within the constraints of a departmentalized structure. Connie Russell describes how four language arts teachers in middle schools, still functioning with departmentalized structures and five teaching periods, successfully moved away from a traditional text-book curriculum to reading and writing workshops. Sally Wells gives us a glimpse of an integrated, learner-centered self-contained middle school classroom. She then describes how her innovative goals led to a blended-grade, team organization that maintains the close social relationships possible in self-contained classrooms along with the strengths of an integrative curriculum, while at the same time maximizing students' access to expert guidance in the disciplines. And Lynn Moss takes us inside her classroom for a year of innovative risk-taking as she practices an authentic negotiation of classroom expectations and curriculum with her students. Four quite different stories, but all born out of a belief that learners must be invested in their learning and must ultimately construct knowledge first socially and then within themselves; and all the stories are quite clear about the importance of administrative support.

Part III consists of five chapters, each coauthored by middle school teachers and college or university teacher educators working in some sort of partnership. I believe such partnerships are critical to innovation in education: first, because educators in these differing roles have such rich insights to share with one another and, second, because if educators at the colleges and universities are to have a positive impact on the preparation of teachers entering the field, they must remain closely linked to professionals practicing in the field. Each of these chapters is testimony to the power of learning together—for educators as well as for middle school students. Pat Tefft Cousin and Ellen Aragon give us an account of their development of a successful writing workshop with a population of students who present some extra challenges. Suzan Mauney, Rosary Lalik, and George Glasson show the evolution of a science teacher toward student-centered learning and integration with language arts in ways that empower students and enrich their learning of science content and development of thought and language. Ken Bergstrom, Chris Mattson, Anne Reid, and Dierdre Garner, with their detailed account of collaborating with students to build curriculum based on students' issues and concerns, give us an up-close example of the type of curriculum negotiation Lynn Moss addresses in more general terms in Part II. Charles Ault and

Anne McEnerny-Ogle give us a view of a problem-centered approach to mathematics in the middle school, and of the constraints teachers face as they seek to put this approach into practice. Finally, Charles Ault and Neil Maine take us back again to science in the middle school with examples and a charge to turn science learning into an adventure.

We conclude the book with a chapter that asks, "Considering all the constraints and challenges involved, what motivates a teacher to teach this way?" Ken Bergstrom and I explore this question and discuss the reasons we find in the stories of the teachers who contributed to this volume.

Issues That Cut Across the Three-Part Organization

Although the three-part organization illuminates central themes within chapter clusters, several issues and tensions appear in chapters across categories.

Past Practices, Holding On or Letting Go

Mary Burke-Hengen, in Part I, Connie Russell and Sally Wells, in Part II, and Pat Tefft Cousin, in Part III, write about holding on to some past practices at the same time as they move into new territory. We see how individual teachers approach changing practice in different ways and at different rates.

Varied Experiences With Reading and Writing Workshops

All of the chapters in Parts I and II, and two in Part III (Tefft Cousin and Mauney) reveal some type of experience with reading and writing workshops. Though this topic has generated a noticeable volume of literature over the past decade, these authors contribute a variety of new perspectives and insights, demonstrating different ways these work for different teachers and students in varying school settings. For instance, Mary Burke-Hengen, Scott Christian, Shirlee Jellum, Connie Russell, Lynn Moss, and Suzan Mauney—across language arts, social studies, history, and science—show us the variety of ways they have used journals or learning logs. They also let us see how journals help them get to know their students better as individuals. Another example is the different approaches to student conferencing—Mary, for instance, makes a case for small groups where group membership remains constant over time, while Scott tells us conferencing in pairs works best in his experience.

The Teacher's Role in a Learner-Centered Classroom

Questions about the teacher's role in a learner-centered classroom surface in a number of chapters in all three sections, and remind us of the need to actively pursue serious dialogue about this issue. When does the teacher take the lead? How do we know when, as Ken Bergstrom puts it, to "sit on our hands"? In negotiating curriculum with students, where and how do curriculum mandates fit in? or the teacher's sense of need for some "common cultural literacy" (Tim Gillespie)? or the disciplinary knowledge and ways of thinking that have accrued over thousands of years? or topics about which teachers have special interest and expertise, and therefore want to share with their students? Is the teacher a *facilitator*, or does that suggest too passive a role? What does it mean for the teacher to be a *co-learner*? Charles Ault suggests the metaphor of the teacher as *host*, in a classroom where students construct knowledge in collaboration with their peers and the teacher, but where the teacher actively puts students in contact with a body of disciplinary and cultural knowledge and insights. I believe this metaphor captures the notion of the teacher as *mediator*, serving as an intermediary to bridge between where a student is and where he or she both *wants* to go (serving interests), and *needs* to go to (*hosting* access to expert knowledge with the goal of "shared meaning for concepts").

If we buy the notion of the teacher as host, how might that look? For instance, Tim Gillespie wonders about his "lectures" on the Civil War, a topic "dear to his heart." Did this, as he hoped, serve as a basis for his students to find their own personal "attachments" to history? What about Shirlee Jellum's account of students' study of war and the personal attachments they developed? How about the question of student and teacher choice in relation to the reading of novels? For example, Tim Gillespie and Connie Russell both write about experiences in assigning a novel to the entire class, but with very different results. And Pat Tefft Cousin and Tim Gillespie each draw different conclusions about time they had students spend specifically preparing for state writing assessments.

Charles Ault (Chapter 13) has this to say:

> Our discussion appears to have stumbled upon a paradox: granting to disciplined ways of knowing priority in contexts where, nonetheless, interdisciplinary themes of interest have primacy. . . . At one and the same moment, the teacher is both an ambassador of a discipline (constructions past) and an advocate of the child's interests (constructions future). The teacher's most dif-

ficult challenge in curriculum construction is to negotiate between these twin legitimate stakeholders, public heritage (the disciplines) and personal meaning (the
basis of interest). The paradox is real and should not be
resolved. The tension is healthy.

Our Wish for Our Readers

We have benefited from sharing with one another our stories and
dreams for the future. We firmly believe our relationships with
other teachers—our sharing, our stories—hold the greatest promise for enriching and improving our own learning and that of our
students. We hope these reflections and discussions—full of the
joys and strains of becoming learner- and inquiry-centered teachers—will inspire similar story-telling and dialogue between you
and your colleagues.

End Notes

1. Traditional, teacher-centered classrooms are characterized by
    clearly separated subject areas and by skill-and-drill student
    work.
2. Learner-centered workshops are characterized by student-de-
    fined questions and problems, and by thematic studies that cut
    across the disciplines and promote learning in a more holistic
    fashion.
3. James A. Beane, *A Middle School Curriculum: From Rheto-
    ric to Reality*, 2nd Edition, (Columbus, OH: National Middle
    School Association, 1993), 96.
4. Glennellen Pace, "Stories of Teacher-Initiated Change from
    Traditional to Whole-Language Literacy Instruction." *The El-
    ementary School Journal* 92.4 (March 1992): 461–476.

Chapter 2

*Whole Learning and a Holistic Vision of the
Middle School: Principles That Guide Practice*

Glennellen Pace

The Link Between Whole Learning and the Middle School

Whole Learning Within the Middle School Movement

The link between middle schools and *student-centered* education
has a long history. Since 1913, when "the Committee on Economy
of Time in Education . . . made the first specific mention of a separate junior division of secondary education,"[1] the rhetoric surrounding effective programs for students between the elementary and
high school years has repeatedly emphasized a curriculum tailored
to developmental characteristics of early adolescents and rooted
in the child-centered, exploratory, active learning theories of John
Dewey,[2] and later of Piaget.[3] Unfortunately, for a variety of reasons, the rhetoric has never matched the reality of middle level
education on any widespread basis.[4]

Continued, though spotty, attempts to create schools consistent with student-centered views have marked the middle school
movement since it appeared around 1960. Perhaps in the current
climate of reform the realities of schooling for a majority of early
adolescents will finally cohere with visions of an appropriate middle
level education. George, Stevenson, Thomason, and Beane in their
book *The Middle School—And Beyond*[5] suggest that two national
surveys[6] and the Task Force on Education of Young Adolescents
(the Carnegie Council on Adolescent Development)[7] provide evidence of substantive, positive changes in middle school organization and programs, though "the majority of schools in the middle
remain, programmatically, far from achieving the goals of the
Carnegie recommendations."

Whole Learning and the Whole Language Movement

The whole language movement that began in the early 1980s also has roots in the theories of John Dewey and Jean Piaget, as well as others such as Lev Vygotsky,[8] M.A.K. Halliday,[9] and Paulo Freire.[10] Yetta Goodman in *Questions and Answers About Whole Language* points to a long history of people, movements, and innovations promoting a student-centered, relevant curriculum and a learning environment "organized in keeping with democratic principles."[11] Although my own knowledge of schools and attendance at meetings of the major whole language organization, The Whole Language Umbrella, suggest elementary school teachers have been in the forefront of this grass-roots movement, whole language educators teach at all levels, preschool through graduate school, and middle school teachers in rapidly growing numbers are joining their ranks. Ken Goodman has called whole language "today's agenda in education."[12]

Recently, some educators have sought to find a term to replace *whole language* that they believe would better represent the cross-disciplinary nature of this philosophy, and at the same time make explicit its recognition and celebration of alternative communication systems (for example, mathematics, dance, music, art, drama) noted by Harste, Woodward, and Burke,[13] and of multiple intelligences as proposed by Howard Gardner.[14]

To those who view language as a separate subject area—a view that is easily understood, considering the prevailing curricular organization in our schools—*whole language* seems to refer only to the language arts curriculum. In fact, in reference to language, the term encompasses the entire curriculum and stems from the view that language is a vehicle for thought and learning within all content areas, across all disciplines, and is, at the same time, developed through use in connection with content. As Ken Goodman puts it, "Cognitive and linguistic development are totally interdependent . . . For learners it's a single curriculum focusing on what is being learned, what language is being used for. But for teachers there is always a double agenda: to maximize opportunities for pupils to engage in authentic speech and literacy events while they study their community, do a literature unit . . . , carry out a scientific study . . . , or develop a sense of fractions and decimals."[15] But whole language philosophy is not *just* about linguistic intelligence. It is also about valuing other ways of knowing, the use of alternatives to language for constructing and representing meaning, and the ways in which these alternative symbol systems create bridges between the multiple ways we make sense of our experiences and our communication with others.

In spite of a large body of literature protesting a language-arts-only conception of the term, contributors to this volume recognize that *whole language* may still suggest *language arts* to many of our readers. Recently, we are hearing the term *whole learning* in place of whole language, and have decided to use that term interchangeably with whole language. But this still leaves readers in need of a definition.

The Language of Whole Learning

Recent efforts to create schools and classrooms that better prepare individuals to be successful contributors to an increasingly complex, diverse, global community have, not surprisingly, resulted in new language—or new shades of meaning for "old" language—with which to communicate new knowledge and changed conceptions of schooling, and of teaching and learning.

However, as we generate new language for changing ideas, it is easy to forget that labels representing complex, abstract notions do not in and of themselves communicate the meanings underlying them. In the field of education today, at conferences and throughout the literature, we are bombarded with terms that are relatively new to the field or have evolved new meanings. For example, the literature and talk linked to a view of teaching and learning—often called whole language or whole learning—that challenges traditional, fragmented, skill-and-drill, pitcher-into-vessel transmission approaches includes words and phrases such as the following: social constructivism, student- or learner-centered approaches; integrated, integrative, interdisiplinary, multi-disciplinary, holistic, or thematic curriculum; a transactional model of education, transformational teaching and learning. Sometimes educators use these terms without definition; where they are defined, explicitly or implicitly, we find them used in different ways. Yet, from the literature on whole language, and the undergirding theory and research, we can glean a list of defining characteristics and principles to guide practice.

In the balance of this chapter, I will seek to provide a common understanding—for contributors to this volume and for readers—of what whole learning and the terms associated with it mean. At the same time, I will address the link between this philosophy of learning and teaching, as well as the current middle school vision that is embedded within this philosophy.

Challenging the Transmission Model of Education

The traditional model of education, largely influenced by behaviorist psychology, views the process of learning as habit formation, and the content as bits and pieces—each mastered according to predetermined standards—that, once learned, *add up* to some sort of whole. For example, learning handwriting, spelling, and grammar is thought to "add up to" writing; memorizing mathematical algorithms is expected to "add up to" mathematical problem solving. Someone outside the learner (a teacher) determines what will be learned, and provides an exact model that the learner is to reproduce correctly (a stance that discourages risk-taking and mitigates against errors). Once the learner has shown correct reproduction, *mastery* is achieved and the learner may move on to the next step.

In contrast, what Constance Weaver calls a transactional model of education[16] (and Ken Bergstrom, Chapters 11 and 14, terms *transformational teaching*) is influenced by cognitive psychology and by a view of the development of language and thought as socially constructed (grounded in the work of Piaget, Vygotsky, and Halliday). In this view, the learning of "parts" occurs within the context of meaningful "whole" experiences. For example, as language learners create written messages for specific and "real" purposes, they gradually gain control of handwriting, spelling, and grammar (and at the same time are likely to gain control of more abstract concepts such as relationships between audience, purpose, and voice). While the teacher plays a crucial and active role as *supporter* and *mediator* of learning, and provides important *demonstrations*[17] of complex, *holistic* processes (for example, writing letters, messages, stories, poems), s/he does not directly *control* learning. Instead, learners, supported by interactions with teachers and peers, have a good deal of control and responsibility for learning. This view takes into account individual differences and different rates of learning among learners; it honors the essential nature of risk-taking, of experiencing the inevitable "errors" that accompany reaching beyond what is already "known" in order to grow. The goal of learning is an ability to apply knowledge, "to think in novel ways [and] to use general strategies across a wide range of tasks and contexts."[18]

The Middle School and the Transactional Model of Education

The middle school movement that has developed over the past three decades, and the whole language movement of the past decade and a half, converge in this transactional model of education. Many educators recognize the clear connections to Dewey's work, and wonder if this is simply a third "go-around" of the progressive education movement of the 1930s and the open education movement of the 1960s. But it is not. Most of the information we have about language and learning did not exist three decades ago, so educators today can base practices on a far more extensive and powerful body of research and theory than ever before, drawn from many fields of inquiry and cutting across all the disciplines.[19] Furthermore, whole language visions include a political agenda that shifts power over curriculum to teachers and students and away from publishers of textbooks and standardized tests, and an agenda that seeks to promote a more democratic, just, and equitable society for all members of an increasingly diverse population. The new middle school vision, powerfully articulated by James Beane,[20] likewise is grounded in new understandings of thought and language development and the same democratic political agenda "to open the hearts and minds of young people to the possibilities for a more just and humane world—a world in which human dignity, the democratic way of life, and the prizing of diversity are more widely shared and experienced."[21] George, Stevenson, Thomason, and Beane decry the development of curriculum based on students' characteristics for the purpose of "get(ting) them to do what we want them to," likening this approach to "a fishing expedition: it amounts to finding the right bait to put on the hook."[22] In my experience, the fishing expedition metaphor is applicable to what happened in many open education classrooms of the 1960s. The new middle school curriculum vision, consistent with a transactional model of education and with whole language views, "is an expedition with early adolescents in which we explore possibilities and help them construct meanings."[23]

Today we see widespread agreement among educational scholars and national educational organizations about the power of the transactional model. Its principles appear in resolutions and policy statements from an array of organizations such as the National Council of Teachers of Mathematics, the National Association for the Education of Young Children, the National Council of Teachers of English, the Whole Language Umbrella, the Association for Supervision and Curriculum Development, the National Middle School Association, and the National Association of Secondary School Principals. This model, says Connie Weaver, quite simply represents "good education."[24] In the following two sections of this chapter, I'll first present principles of a whole learning philosophy that undergird a transactional model; then I'll summarize the features of the new curriculum vision promoted by James Beane and others, features that clearly reflect a whole learning philosophy.

Principles of a Whole Learning Philosophy

Whole language, says Ken Goodman, "is a complete curricular philosophy. It brings back into the foreground the progressive view of curriculum as integrative and inquiry centered. Furthermore, it integrates development of language, thinking, and content into a dual curriculum in which knowledge is built at the same time as thought and language are built."[25] Such a curriculum, though never "prepackaged," does have a number of guiding key features. I'll briefly discuss key features that suggest implications for whole learning practices in middle school classrooms. These ideas form the backdrop against which contributors to this book present and discuss their current classroom practices and directions for the future.

Curriculum is Meaning-Centered

In whole learning classrooms, learning experiences reflect and build upon students' concerns and world views, and favor authentic contexts over contrived experiences. Students acquire and develop knowledge and skills through purposeful use as they pursue problems and questions they pose together with their teachers. We call this kind of curriculum *holistic* because learning proceeds more from whole to part than from part to whole. This occurs when learners focus first on function (reporting news in the classroom newsletter), not form (spelling all the words correctly). In other words, conventions and adult-like competence develop slowly as students engage in complex, authentic activities rather than contrived exercises to practice discreet skills.

For example, if the district curriculum mandates a study of communities, students become involved in studying real questions, problems, and issues in the local, regional, national, and global communities of which they are members. They use language— reading, writing, speaking, and listening—as well as other communication systems—mathematics, scientific investigations, visual arts, music, drama, dance—to construct, represent, and communicate what they learn. Skills develop in the service of purposeful construction and communication of knowledge.

Classrooms Represent a Social Constructivist View of Learning

Drawing on the views of Jean Piaget and Margaret Donaldson, constructivists today cite the importance of teaching practices that encourage student invention, initiation, autonomy, inquiry, theory-building, and prediction.[26] Constructivist teachers know students learn complex processes through active engagement, trust students as meaning-makers trying to make sense of their world, and support and mediate but do not try to control learning.[27]

For example, as students pursue their study of communities, the teacher offers guidance without taking over. Rather than prescribing a list of predetermined questions, she trusts students through interactions with her and with other students to formulate questions and problems for study. The teacher may lead the class in generating a list of potential resources the students could locate within and outside of the school, but he allows them plenty of latitude to find and use their own resources. Students get better at posing problems and at using resources as they seek solutions, not through following rigid steps prescribed by the teacher.

While Piaget's constructivist views recognize learners must ultimately make sense of the world for themselves, learning is nonetheless "a fundamentally social event."[28] Vygotsky's social learning theories emphasize the critical role of social interaction in learning.[29] An interactive, collaborative environment allows learners to work in Vygotsky's "zone of proximal development," that area in which a learner cannot yet act alone but can function successfully with support from an adult or a more knowledgeable peer (what Bruner calls a "loan of consciousness"[30]). Since thought and language processes that begin interpersonally (through dialogue with others) later become intrapersonal (transformed to inner speech), mediation on the part of others promotes cognitive development. Language is central to this mediation process (a contrast with Piaget's view that language reflects but does not determine thought).

For instance, in a learning environment where the students and the teacher pursue their study of communities in an interactive manner, members of the class bring varying areas of expertise and varying "intelligences"[31] to bear on the problems being studied. Together, they are able to be far more successful than they would be on their own. An idea shared by one student sparks a new hypothesis from another student. A well-formed question from the teacher opens new avenues of speculation that students might not have thought about on their own. The teacher or a peer offers timely assistance as a student struggles to use cross-references in the encyclopaedia.

Integrated Curriculum

An authentically integrated curriculum is organized around problems or issues rather than according to traditional separate subject areas. Cognitive and affective activities are viewed as interrelated, not separate. Authentic integration differs from the contrived integration that accompanies some theme-oriented units of study in which students read, write, speak, listen, do math problems, complete an art project, sing a song, and otherwise "connect" with the theme across the disciplines in ways that remain superficial and artificial. True integration attends to and promotes the dynamic interrelationships among ways of knowing, and between students' language development (oral language and literacy) and knowledge acquisition.

For example, in a problem- or inquiry-centered curriculum, integration of mathematics, science, reading, writing, visual arts, and speech occurs when a study group interested in preserving water quality prepares and presents an illustrated report on the dumping of raw sewage into their local community's river. Students use this variety of communication systems for the purpose of constructing, representing, and communicating a specific body of knowledge. This is very different from integrating art by requiring everyone to create a diorama, math by making up hypothetical problems about waste disposal in some generic community, or persuasive writing through an assignment to take on the role of a houseboat owner writing a letter to the editor of a fictional newspaper.

This notion of integration grounded in authentic, problem-centered experiences is not an easy one to grasp. As individual teachers or teams or entire schools begin to move away from traditional approaches, they frequently decide to adopt *integrated* or *interdisciplinary* approaches. Unfortunately, the importance of authenticity and of inquiry- or problem-centeredness is not always understood. James Beane[32] discusses the problem of language in relation to this issue. Integrated, integrative, interdisciplinary, multidisciplinary, cross-disciplinary, thematic—all are used to describe a variety of attempts to move beyond traditional, departmentalized instructional *delivery* systems. But too often, regardless of the term used, the *real* issues are lost. As teachers move toward whole learning, it is important to ask hard questions about plans to *integrate*, and to be very clear about the *fit* of those plans with all aspects of a whole learning philosophy.

A Negotiated, Empowering Curriculum

Negotiation and sharing, with adults and peers, are important to the individual's learning process.[33] When teachers and students together make choices and take responsibility for curriculum, engagement in learning increases. Empowerment, or a sense of efficacy, develops when people make decisions, take risks, recognize and choose from alternative possibilities, and take responsibility for their learning. The concept of negotiation and the role of the teacher as a member of the learning community are critical elements.

Atwell, discussing misconceptions about the notion of student ownership in writing workshops, stresses the importance of teacher input and intervention in students' learning processes. She cautions that use of the term *ownership* may leave teachers wondering about their role in improving students' writing. Atwell suggests the terms *engagement* and *responsibility* may be more appropriate.[34] A whole learning philosophy supports classrooms characterized by, in Calkins' words, "high student input *and* high teacher input . . . (where both) bring all of their skills, wisdom, and energy to the teaching-learning transaction."[35]

For example, the district may mandate that all seventh-grade students will study communities, a mandate that may very well include some specific process and knowledge goals. The teacher may have process goals and concepts about communities that she believes are important for students to address. Whole learning is not a laissez-faire, anything-goes philosophy. The teacher works as a knowledgeable partner, perhaps sharing a reading with the whole class, or working with a group to expand on the questions they are asking, or assisting a student to reorganize a draft of a report.

A Learner-Centered Environment

Although it is often referred to as a student-centered environment, I prefer the term learner-centered, first because I believe it better represents a situation in which the teacher is also a learner and the students are also teachers, and second because I believe it better captures the importance of the teacher as an active contributor to and mediator of students' learning. In such an environment, students "are treated as capable and developing, not as incapable and deficient."[36] Teachers act as mediators of learning, supporting learning, helping students to work in their own individual zones of proximal development, offering invitations to learn rather than wresting control from the learner.[37]

For example, while the teacher may require that all students in the classroom share with other class members the results of their inquiries about communities, for this unit of study he allows students to decide *how* they will share. Some students struggle to express themselves in writing, but are truly gifted in their ability to stand up and talk about what they have learned, or to create and present a mural or a dance or a skit. Given a chance to use their gifts, the consequent increase in students' self-esteem and positive recognition by peers gives them renewed energy and success as they tackle ways of communicating that come to them less easily. This is not to suggest that written communication is unimportant for these students. Rather, because they are allowed to use their strengths in some situations, these students develop these strengths as well as ultimately the ability to reach beyond their comfort zones to communicate in ways that are more challenging for them.

In a learner-centered environment, teachers are viewed as learners, too. Whole learning teachers learn *with* their students, *from* their students, and *about* their students. They also engage in professional development that gives them direct knowledge of the research base undergirding whole learning practices so that they can make informed, contextualized decisions about their pedagogy. (This view stands in sharp contrast to teaching based on following a pre-determined method, or a prescribed and rigid set of procedures.)[38] Thus, whole learning teachers' commitment to continued development of professional knowledge underlies the evolving nature of instructional practices in these classrooms.

A Knowledge-Rich Environment

Whole learning classrooms, in the same way George, Stevenson, Thomason, and Beane describe their vision of middle school classrooms, "are not anti-intellectual; they do not retreat from either knowledge or skill."[39]

These classrooms include a wide range of print and non-print materials moving into and out of the classroom as many and varied projects and activities develop throughout the year. They draw upon many kinds of resources, including people within and outside of the classroom and school. Everyone is enriched in a learning environment that values the interests and experiences of individual students, promotes sharing of individual knowledge and insights, and encourages a wide variety of pursuits. A whole learning philosophy includes a stance that truly honors and celebrates the diverse cultural and individual heritages represented throughout the school and surrounding community. As students pursue questions and interests they have identified, they reach beyond the classroom doors into the community—local, national, even international. Learning occurs and results are shared in a variety of social configurations, too, sometimes individual, more often in collaboration with one or several others, and sometimes in a whole-class gathering. Variety is a hallmark of the materials, resources, and processes students use, and of their products, demonstrations, or other ways of sharing what they learn.

Ongoing, Authentic Assessment

While state- and district-mandated and standardized tests are still required in many schools, educators with a whole learning perspective know these tests do little to support the specific learning endeavors of students and teachers.[40] Long-term goals, a focus on learners' capabilities rather than deficiencies, and assessment interwoven with and evolving from daily learning characterize whole learning classrooms.

As members of a community, students construct shared knowledge. Conventions are not ignored, but personal invention and individual growth are supported as well. Self-reflection and self-evaluation stimulate development of a positive sense of self, and lead to creative, independent thinking and learning. Thus, students as well as the teacher participate in documenting learning through recording observations about products and processes integral to a project or learning endeavor, selecting and collecting samples of work, reflecting in learning logs or dialogue journals, analyzing data, and describing growth. Appropriate assessment includes a wide range of data-gathering techniques, represents the complexity of learning, and positively influences students' continued learning.

A Current Vision of the Middle School Curriculum

George, Stevenson, Thomason, and Beane tell us the new middle school curriculum vision is "rooted in general curriculum theory, rather than in specialized discussions about the middle school."[41] Indeed, key features of the new middle school curriculum vision proposed by James Beane[42] are all consistent with a whole learning philosophy. For instance, Beane raises questions about block-time core programs which, though they may represent a positive step forward by providing longer class periods, are nonetheless scheduled "alongside traditional subject courses." He maintains "a curriculum that facilitates integration and is person-centered, constructivist, and thematic makes sense and, therefore, ought to be the whole curriculum."[43]

George, Stevenson, Thomason, and Beane lay out the characteristics of this vision of middle school curriculum. In sum, they tell us it should include:

1. A learner-centered environment. This means:
   —curriculum is derived from students' questions and concerns, and negotiated by the teacher and students, not tightly controlled by specifications and mandates from outside the classroom;
   —curriculum is constructivist, "enabling young people to construct their own meanings rather than simply accept those of others"; and
   —teachers and other adults in the school are also viewed as learners.
2. An integrative curriculum. This means:
   —doing away with traditional separate subject boundaries;
   —viewing cognitive and affective activities as interrelated, not separate; and
   —developing knowledge and skills through purposeful use in the process of pursuing meaningful, worthwhile questions and issues.

3. Appropriate evaluation processes. This means aban-
    doning narrowly defined performance objectives for
    learning goals that:
    —address "self and social questions";
    —identify significant themes, activities, knowledge,
    and the finding of resources; and
    —respect the fact that while students "engage com-
    mon questions and concerns," they do not all "learn
    the same particular information."[44]

The elements of this vision, thoroughly familiar to whole language advocates, indeed suggest strong support for whole learning as "good education."

The Vision and the Promise

The middle school curriculum vision proposed here—continuous
with and consistent with goals, ideals, and practices associated
with a transactional or transformational model—is gaining attention at all levels of education. The whole learning principles presented are congruent with current views held by many educational
leaders and scholars about the importance of inquiry-oriented, constructive and integrative processes in learning. These principles,
and the middle school vision, hold promise for substantive, positive, and lasting changes in middle schools.

But classroom teachers are the only ones who can turn the
vision into reality. And it won't be easy. A federal education agenda
that includes a national curriculum; federal-, state-, and district-
mandated testing; and school organizational policies that perpetuate a fragmented curriculum and school day threaten the promise
of good education. Jacqueline Grennon Brooks and Martin Brooks,
in their excellent book *In Search of Understanding: The Case for
Constructivist Classrooms*, warn:

> Meaningful victories require bold actions. Many
> recent school reform initiatives are built on the time-
> honored but terribly flawed test-teach-test model of
> instruction. . . . Ironically, these initiatives are yoked to
> the very approaches that have brought about the need
> for school reform in the first place. . . . Meaningful
> school reform must address the central unit of the en-
> tire enterprise, the classroom, and must seek to alter the
> ways teaching and learning have traditionally been
> thought to interact in that unit.[45]

As George and his coauthors remind us, "The grounds for the struggle are not just pedagogical, but political as well."[46] Carole Edelsky eloquently presents the potential of whole language as a perspective to embody the kind of political stance needed in classrooms throughout schools (at all levels) "in favor of an equitable, democratic society. . . . (E)ducators with a whole language perspective (must) find ways to connect their theory-in-practice and their public pronouncements more directly to a fundamental political position" promoting justice and democracy.[47] While achieving appropriate middle school practices depends upon administrative policies and support for appropriate organizational patterns as well as upon the classroom practices of individual teachers, it is educators, in their own classrooms and in collaboration with one another, who hold in their hands the promise of good education for all students.

End Notes

1. Paul S. George, Chris Stevenson, Julia Thomason, and James Beane, *The Middle School—And Beyond* (Alexandria, VA: Association for Supervision and Curriculum Development, 1992), 3.
2. See, for example, John Dewey, *The Child and the Curriculum* (Chicago: University of Chicago Press, 1902); and "The Relationship of Theory to Practice in Education," *The Relation of Theory to Practice in the Education of Teachers, Third Yearbook of the National Society for the Scientific Study of Education, Part I*, ed. C. McMurry (Chicago: University of Chicago Press, 1904), 9–30.
3. See, for example, Jean Piaget and B. Inhelder, *The Psychology of the Child* (New York: Basic Books, 1969).
4. See George et al., 1–14, for a history of the middle school.
5. George et al., 10–13.
6. W. Alexander and C. K. McEwin, *Earmarks of Schools in the Middle: A Research Report* (Boone, NC: Appalachian State University, 1989); and Gordon Cawelti, "Middle Schools a Better Match with Early Adolescent Needs, ASCD Survey Finds," *ASCD Curriculum Update,* Nov. 1988: 1–12.
7. Carnegie Council on Adolescent Development, *Turning Points: Preparing Youth for the 21st Century* (New York: Carnegie Corporation, 1989). Recommendations included creation of small learning communities within schools, a core academic program, cooperative learning without tracking, shared decision-making for teachers and administrators, teacher preparation for teaching early adolescents, a focus on health and fitness, meaningful roles for families in adolescent education, and

reconnection with the community.

8. See Lev S.Vygotsky, *Thought and Language* (Cambridge, MA: MIT Press, 1962), and *Mind in Society* (Cambridge, MA: Harvard University Press, 1978).

9. See M.A.K. Halliday, *Learning How to Mean: Explorations in the Development of Language* (London: Edward Arnold, 1975).

10. See, for example, Paulo Freire, *Pedagogy of the Oppressed* (New York: Seabury, 1970).

11. Yetta Goodman, "A Question About the Past," *Questions and Answers About Whole Language*, ed. O. Cochrane (Katonah, NY: Richard C. Owen, Pub., Inc., 1992).

12. Ken Goodman, "Why Whole Language Is Today's Agenda in Education," *Language Arts* 69.5 (1992): 354–363.

13. Jerome C. Harste, Virginia A. Woodward, & Carolyn L. Burke, *Language Stories and Literacy Lessons* (Portsmouth, NH: Heinemann, 1984), 216.

14. Howard Gardner, *Frames of Mind: The Theory of Multiple Intelligences* (New York: Basic Books, Inc., 1985).

15. Ken Goodman, *What's Whole in Whole Language?* (Portsmouth, NH: Heinemann, 1986), 26 and 30.

16. Constance Weaver, *Understanding Whole Language: From Principles to Practice* (Portsmouth, NH: Heinemann, 1990). See page 9 for a useful chart contrasting transmission and transactional models of education. The term *transaction* comes from Louise Rosenblatt, *Literature as Exploration* (New York: Noble and Noble, 1938). To Rosenblatt, "the literary work exists in the *transaction* between the reader and the text . . mutually acting on each other to evoke an experience, a meaning, for the particular reader of the text" (N.J. Karolides, Ed., *Reader Response in the Classroom* [New York: Longman, 1992], 22). The meaning created must remain true to the text and true to the reader, but the precise meaning—with all its nuances and connections to the reader's past experiences—is unique. Applying the term to a model of education suggests the same type of relationship between "text"—i.e., experiences or events as well as print—and learners. In this relationship, both learner and "text" are *transformed* in relation to one another.

17. Whole language educators prefer the term *demonstration* to *model*. Traditional approaches use modeling; the goal is for the learner to "copy" the model. Demonstration better captures the complexity of holistic, authentic "modeling." The learner is not expected to produce an exact replica. Consider, for example, how children learn to speak. They are surrounded by demonstrations of language in use; we expect them to learn to use language, but not to speak the exact sentences they hear. See Brian Cambourne, *The Whole Story*, (New York: Ashton

Scholastic, 1988) for a more thorough discussion of this issue.

18. Weaver, 1:9.
19. See Diane Stephens, *Research on Whole Language: Support for a New Curriculum* (Katonah, NY: Richard C. Owen Publishers, Inc.,1991), 7–9.
20. James A. Beane,*A Middle School Curriculum: From Rhetoric to Reality*, 2nd ed. (Columbus, OH: National Middle School Association, 1993).
21. Beane, Epilogue: 106.
22. George et al., 82.
23. George et al., 83.
24. Constance Weaver, "Whole Language as Good Education," *The Whole Language Umbrella* 2.2 (1991), 1 and 9.
25. K. Goodman, 1992: 360.
26. For discussion of Piaget's influence see J. G. Brooks, "Teachers and Students: Constructivists Forging New Connections," *Educational Leadership* 47.5 (1990): 68–71. See also work by Margaret Donaldson, *Children's Minds* (Glasgow: Fontana, 1978).
27. For an excellent and thorough discussion of descriptors of constructivist teaching behaviors—descriptors that present teachers as mediators—see Jacqueline Grennon Brooks and Martin G. Brooks, *In Search of Understanding: The Case For Constructivist Classrooms*, (Alexandria, VA: Association for Supervision and Curriculum Development, 1993), 103–118.
28. M. Amarel, "Research Currents: The Classroom Collective— We, Them, or It?" *Language Arts* 64 (1987): 532–539.
29. Lev S.Vygotsky, *Thought and Language* (Cambridge, MA: MIT Press, 1962).
30. Jerome Bruner, *Actual Minds, Possible Worlds*, (Cambridge, MA: Harvard University Press, 1986).
31. Gardner.
32. Beane, Preface, xiv–xv.
33. See, for example, Jerome Bruner, *Actual Minds, Possible Worlds,* (Cambridge, MA: Harvard University Press, 1986), and G.A. Hull, "Research on Writing: Building a Cognitive and Social Understanding of Composing," *Toward the Thinking Curriculum: Current Cognitive Research*, (Alexandria, VA: Association of Supervision and Curriculum Development, 1989).
34. Nancy Atwell, *Side By Side: Essays on Teaching to Learn* (Portsmouth, NH: Heinemann, 1991), 149.
35. Lucy M. Calkins, *The Art of Teaching Writing* (Portsmouth, NH: Heinemann,1986), 165.
36. Weaver, 1990, 25.
37. Some educators suggest the term *learning* centered. Ken Bergstrom, for example, in a personal communication, May

26, 1994, explains:
One of the most notable characteristics of integrated study . . . is that it "takes on a life of its own." It becomes engaging to so many people in so many ways that, for a teacher, it is like trying to herd cats, or as Sergiovanni says about administration "like trying to carry a giant amoeba from one side of the road to the other." Learning centered captures this best for me.

38. See Stephens, 10.
39. George et al., 97.
40. See Weaver, 1990, 182–261 for a thorough discussion of the detriments of standardized tests and testing, and a presentation of more appropriate approaches to assessment and evaluation.
41. George et al., 102.
42. James Beane, "The Middle School: The Natural Home of Integrated Curriculum," *Educational Leadership* 49.2 (1991): 9–13.
43. J. Beane, 9–13.
44. George et al., 96–97.
45. Brooks and Brooks, 10: 120.
46. George et al., 102–103.
47. Carole Edelsky, *With Literacy and Justice for All: Rethinking the Social in Language and Education* (New York: The Falmer Press, 1991), 166 and 168.

PART I

Reflecting on Teaching as Learning

Chapter 3

On the Joys and Strains of Becoming

Tim Gillespie

Grounded—in Theory

One day, half a minute before the lunch bell was to ring, I was standing near my teacher's desk in a swirl of end-of-the-period activity. I felt like a circus ringmaster; three of my eighth grade students wanted me to sign library passes, two wanted to check out computer disks, another wanted to know a due date, and another wanted to see if all his assignments had been turned in. I was in fast-forward teacher mode: signing slips, checking the roster, collecting work, and entertaining for a fleeting moment the thought that I hadn't organized the classroom well enough for student self-sufficiency. It was an insight worth reflecting on, if I'd had the time or powers of concentration to do so; I didn't. Fifteen seconds to the bell.

In the midst of all the busyness, I spotted Kari gathering up her gear, and one more pressing detail occurred to me. "Kari," I said, "don't forget that 'About the Author' piece you were going to turn in for the class literary magazine."

"Mr. Gillespie," she said, rolling her eyeballs heavenward in dramatic exasperation. "I just gave it to you two minutes ago. Look, there it is in your hand."

Sure enough, I was holding her paper. I smiled sheepishly. The bell blatted and students began to pour out the door.

"Mr. Gillespie," Kari said, with good humor, on her way out, "I think you need to wake up and smell the chalkdust!"

Smelling the Chalkdust

For me, that school year was about waking up and smelling the chalkdust. It was particularly instructive since I began the year as a

29

20-year veteran rookie teacher.

Since 1971, when I started teaching, I have worked with elementary school children in inner-city Oakland, California, and high schoolers in Portland, Oregon. I've had a blended 5th-6th grade group in a tidy suburban grade school and run an alternative program for at-risk adolescents. I've taught humanities to "gifted" students and reading skills to "basic" students, and I've given demonstration lessons in hundreds of classrooms as a teacher educator.

Yet somehow in all this ranging around in the educational field, I had never taught in a middle school. When my own oldest son was in seventh grade, I decided I wanted to learn more about working with young people his age—so fascinating, complex, and full of the joys and the strains of becoming. Furthermore, I had been out of the classroom for a number of years, working as the language arts specialist at the local county education office, and I felt a need to knock off the rust.

So, in the fall of 1991, I joined the faculty at Beaumont Middle School, an old two-story brick building in Portland serving a diverse urban population of 700 students. On the first day of school that September, as I waited for my new class of eighth graders to stream through the doors, I was jittery with anticipation, a veteran with a long teaching history, but also a rookie—new to middle school, new to this particular school, and back in the classroom after some years away, years largely spent giving advice to other teachers.

I came back to the classroom with firm opinions, a backlog of experience, and, I thought, a clear philosophical and theoretical base for my work, which I generally labeled with words such as *process-oriented, whole language,* and *learner-centered.* With all this working for me, my classroom should have been—theoretically, anyway—a wonderful place to learn. Happily, on many days it was. At least my students told me so, in their ways, and I saw learning occur often enough. On some days, though, the classroom felt stale and resistant, a place where learning came haltingly. It was those other days I had forgotten about in my years away from the classroom.

On one of those less-successful days, I was sharing with my colleague Mary Burke-Hengen my frustrations about putting some of my beliefs into practice in the classroom. She said, with a wry look, "You can walk through the classroom door with a great theory, but that's no necessary guarantee it's going to be a great day." We both laughed.

I don't intend to demean the idea of having a theory of teaching. We *must* walk into our classrooms clear about our beliefs. I'm a firm believer in the old adage that if we don't stand for something, it's too easy for us to fall for anything (especially, in teaching, the disconnected, gimmicky activities and glitzy programs that so surround us). It's just that teaching is never a simple matter; we must have educational principles we live by, but we also must recognize that they don't always offer us apparent answers to every classroom issue we face. As Thomas Newkirk has pointed out, "... in practice, working with students is never so simple as applying basic rules."[1] On the second floor of Beaumont Middle School, in my small room packed with 28 lively eighth graders, my educational philosophies had to be matched to students' names and faces. In the classroom, we are not dealing with abstractions; we have to smell the chalkdust.

Luckily, I had some means for reflecting on my classroom struggles and successes, and on what they could teach me. I kept a journal, for one thing. Even better, I made a vow with my Beaumont teaching friend Mary Burke-Hengen to eat lunch and talk about our work every Tuesday and Thursday all year. Come hell or high water, field trip or fire drill, we'd work to preserve whatever we could of those precious twice-weekly 25-minute respites when we would grab a bite of lunch and chat. Sadly, schools are seldom set up to encourage sustained collegial discussion such as this, or much of any kind of ongoing teacher-to-teacher professional study, reflection, or support. For me, wrestling with the uncertainties and challenges of trying to move toward a more learner-centered teaching style, this running conversation with a valued colleague was essential. My ceaseless dialogue with Mary was my second most important source of learning that year; my primary source was, of course, the students themselves, with all their extraordinary demands, desires, delights, and questions.

As I struggled with translating my beliefs into actions in my classroom, in fact, I was struck with how similar my quest was to that of my middle school students. We were *all* in transition, all on the way to becoming something better and more fully-formed, all asking questions and trying to figure out what we were supposed to be doing. Maybe to be a good teacher, then, is to be in a state somewhat like perpetual early adolescence—one moment sure, one moment uncertain, one moment eager with anticipation, one moment fraught with anxiety—full of all the same joys and strains of becoming.

So, during this year of transition for me as a teacher, my theories and my practices danced around with each other but didn't always seem to step to the same tune. Nonetheless, in step or not, and always with the institutional drumbeat of a large school system in the background, I still had to make hundreds of instructional decisions every day, as all teachers do. Many of those decisions forced me to confront teaching issues rife with paradox. I particularly found myself wrestling during my rookie year at Beaumont Middle School with the two big issues of *negotiating the curriculum* and *integrating the curriculum*. My accounts of how I tried to deal with these two concerns will constitute most of the rest of this chapter.

Negotiating the Curriculum

Planning and Big Questions

My teaching circumstance at Beaumont seemed ideal for a learner-centered, integrated curriculum. Two years prior to my starting there, the school had gone to a "Core" class set-up, a three-period block dedicated to the study of language arts and social studies. The rest of the day, students had to rush around for 42-minute snippets of other subjects, but in Core class, we had a luxurious amount of time (126 minutes!) for the integrative, exploratory, and student-driven curriculum I imagined.

As soon as I got my new eighth grade teaching assignment, my planning questions began: What is the official curriculum? How much room is there in the curriculum for the students to do some of the designing? How much control can and should learners have over what, when, and how they learn? How do we fairly address and negotiate the interests of the school district (representing the local community), the interests of the students, and my interests as the teacher?

That August before school began, I considered these questions in my teaching journal, my thinking, and my conversations with Mary Burke-Hengen. I started by looking at the conditions under which I would have to negotiate curriculum. My first stop was the shelf full of official district curriculum documents.

The school district's language arts curriculum listed some broad goals for students in the areas of reading, writing, speaking, and listening. ("Students will be able to write for a variety of purposes and audiences" is an example.) No techniques, particular instructional materials, or textbooks were mandated. I thought the goals were generally sound and promoted the practice of authentic literary acts. I appreciated not having specific materials or techniques mandated and being given the professional responsibility to design the best curriculum for helping my students meet these goals, as well as the freedom to let students participate in that design. However, I was also supposed to help students do well on the annual high-stakes, multiple choice district reading achievement tests and on the state writing assessment, which required students to write a composition over three days on a given topic (such as, "Explain to a friend why he or she should eat vegetables").

As far as the social studies curriculum was concerned, the school district dictated the eighth grade course of study: U.S. history—specifically, the span of time from the Revolutionary War to the Civil War, no more and no less. A new, expensive U.S. history textbook was to be provided to each student.

These, I was reminded, are the sorts of conditions under which most of us teach. We may have room to maneuver in some places in the curriculum but have tightly-centralized control in others. Thus, part of our job in making our classroom curriculum sensible may often have to be working outside of the classroom, participating at a building or district level in the development of curriculum and reasonable assessment tools. At the moment, however, all I could do was write that thought in my teaching notebook. I had to deal with the documents in front of me.

It was clear what the district wanted. I didn't know yet what the students would want and need. One broad notion I have about curriculum is that the classroom should be more learner-centered than information-centered, that students should negotiate the curriculum with the teacher and choose many of their own projects. This approach asks students to take more responsibility for their schooling, to be active agents rather than passive recipients of learning, creators of knowledge as well as consumers of it.

However, one typical concern about some measure of student control over the curriculum is that certain essential information might be missed, some common cultural literacy overlooked. None of us wants our students to be ignorant, after all.

I had plenty of arguments to make to myself to assuage these concerns, starting with John Dewey's pronouncement that learning to learn is more important than learning any particular body of information. This idea is particularly relevant to our time, characterized as it is by such rapid changes. New knowledge is created at a fierce rate and old knowledge is continually revised. Thus, learning any specific body of information may well be less important than cultivating the ability to find, create, and use information. Furthermore, the contemporary curriculum in many school systems has become so crammed with so much essential information from so many disciplines on so many subjects that it would be impossible to cover it all anyway. (This also assumes the dubious proposition that just *covering* curriculum ensures that it will be learned.) Subject matter knowledge should not be an end, but a means or occasion for learning to think, read, write, and inquire, I told myself. Any content will suffice for this inquiry, so students should have great latitude in designing their own curriculum and pursuing their own interests.

Yet, on the other hand, I had to admit to myself that I have my own sense of an essential canon of content. In the U.S. history curriculum, in particular, there are certain ideas and data of such great importance, in my opinion, that I decided I was going to expose my students to them, no matter what. In the time period I was to cover with my eighth graders, this non-negotiable content included the development of the Constitution and the Bill of Rights, multi-cultural contributions to the American fabric, the settlement of the West from the point of view of Native Americans as well as pioneers, and so forth. I did not want students to have the choice whether or not to study these topics. So, I wondered, how did this square with the democratic principles of curriculum I hoped to let students exercise in my classroom? How was I to maintain interest, democratic ownership, choice, and involvement within a fairly pre-programmed curriculum?

These were the sorts of questions about the issue of negotiating curriculum that I carried around with me and discussed with Mary Burke-Hengen. But when September rolled close, I had to stop batting my questions around and figure out how and what to teach.

Negotiating Social Studies

In fact, the most difficult subject area for me to bring students into the planning and designing did prove to be social studies. For the most part, my U.S. history curriculum ended up being more given than negotiated.

My first dilemma was how to organize the material. The advice of many contemporary theorists is to organize curriculum into thematic units, particularly ones based on students' questions and concerns. However, the district curriculum and the textbook were organized chronologically, and I didn't really understand how to build thematic units around the district-stipulated time span in U.S. history. What would the themes be? Conflict? Justice? These seem such large and vague concepts, and I wondered in what ways they would serve to better organize what to me is the most compelling part of well-written history: its specificity of detail about human lives and dilemmas of the past. What would happen to any sense of additive history, of chronological progress, of event building on event, of the past being prologue to the future? And what if something I thought was important was left out of the themes? Ultimately, because I did not have the commitment or skill, I did not try to reorganize with students this slice of U.S. history into thematic units. Instead, we marched in traditional form from the Revolutionary War to the Civil War, September to June.

During the journey, however, I did everything I could think of to cultivate investment, to allow the negotiation of smaller chunks of curriculum, to help students construct their own meanings instead of just accepting the received wisdom of others.

For example, we began our study of history at the start of the year with the first kinds of questions that had popped up in some of the students' learning logs: Why should we study history, anyway? Who cares? What's the point? I asked students to write responses to these questions and interview their parents and other family members about them. From those data, the class constructed its own rationale that we put on the wall: "We study history so we don't make the mistakes of the past." This eighth-grade version of Santayana's maxim that those who don't know history are condemned to repeat it was our touchstone concept.

At the start of many of our large areas of study (for example, the Revolutionary War or the making of the Constitution), I had the students brainstorm a list of questions about that topic, questions to guide our inquiry. It was my hope that the students would see that historical understanding begins with our real questions, with intellectual curiosity, not with the phony recall-level questions of somebody else in the textbook and certainly not just with a bunch of facts. Then I would try to make sure that we figured out ways to answer all our brainstormed questions before our study of the unit was completed.

Early in the year, I put students into groups of four. Since I couldn't see launching into a study of the Revolutionary War without some review of prior historical events, I defined some background topics (such as Native American cultures prior to the coming of the Europeans, explorers, and early settlers). Next I asked each group to take one topic, learn all they could about it, then think of a way to teach what they had found out to the whole class. In response, one group produced a videotape, complete with costumes and artifacts, on colonial life. One group wrote and conducted a Jeopardy-type trivia game on the early explorers. On the whole, I thought these presentations were successful. However, the group that reported on Spanish settlement faltered—their information was sparse, their videotape presentation largely inaudible. Thus, my students had a hole in their knowledge of early Hispanic influence in the development of America. Should I have stepped in to fill the gap and re-taught the material? Should I have made the students re-do their presentation while others went on? What theory of learner-centered education would help me puzzle out what to do in this case? The determining factor was time; we moved on. I had caught myself in the trap of covering the curriculum.

For the rest of the year, groups had many opportunities to make presentations to one another in many forms—from newspapers to posters to plays—about topics being studied. Usually for these projects, I assigned the general content, but the students came up with the way the information was to be learned in the group and the way it was to be shared with others. None of this seemed like a very radical form of negotiating the curriculum, or the kind of open inquiry of which some theorists have painted a portrait, but the students were generally active and involved, so I was generally satisfied.

During our ongoing lunchtime conversations, Mary Burke-Hengen reminded me of the importance of keeping the history we were studying close to the world the students inhabited. So, when we came to the Constitution, students wrote their own. (In fact, after studying the First Amendment, the students petitioned me for the right to chew gum in class and to have a class party. The former was denied, the latter granted; I felt a bit like King George III must have, trying to negotiate between my sense of authority and the demands of my citizenry!) Students moderated debates on contemporary issues raised by the Bill of Rights, such as handgun control, protection of hate speech, and freedom of the student press. The debate on gun control was particularly heated in our city neighborhood, where some students strongly felt their families needed firearms for protection.

When we studied the judicial system, we took a trip to the county courthouse to view real trials. Later we role-played the historical trial of Cayuse Indians charged with murdering the Whitman missionaries in the early years of the Oregon Territory, and we compared the pressure and bias of that trial to the contemporary controversy surrounding the trial of police officers accused of beating Rodney King.

I had the students write frequently in social studies—in class, for homework, on exams. I strove for complex questions that asked for personalized response: "If you lived in Missouri in 1848, would you have travelled west on the Oregon Trail? What potential risks and benefits would you have considered?" This was intended to allow the students inside the material—as respondents doing the kind of analysis in the light of current understandings that real historians do.

At the end of the year, when my time, energy and imagination were waning, I fell back into some old bad habits. When we talked about the Civil War, I did most of the talking. (The Civil War is an interest of mine. My great-grandfather was a participant, and my family still has his diary and battle sword. I have read lots of Civil War history and visited many battlefields. It's an interest I wanted to bring into the classroom, but it was hard for me to figure out a form for the sharing of my knowledge other than discoursing. At times I felt, ironically, that my expertise was a burden. Rather than engage the students in inquiry and investigation, I was asking them to mostly just listen to what I knew.) As the school year waned, I was pressured to "get through the Civil War," as I found myself telling my students one day. As I got more tired and rushed, I was less learner-centered, more book-oriented, and more prone to teacher recitations. I was disconcerted through most of the month of May, feeling like the most conventional, me-centered teacher imaginable. Yet a couple of students told me how much better they liked my lecturing, since it seemed more like "real" social studies!

We finished the year with an activity where I asked the students to examine their own personal places in the ongoing history of the United States. What things had happened in *their* lives that were significant history, I asked, that they'd want to make sure their own grandchildren were exposed to in school? The answers ranged widely, from one student's experience of losing a relative in a drunk driving accident to students talking about current events they felt were important: the Clarence Thomas Supreme Court confirmation hearings and Anita Hill's allegations of sexual harassment, the L.A. riots, the breakdown of the ozone layer, and so forth. Through this question, I hoped that students would find some personal investment, an eyepiece through which they could see their own lives and times as part of the kaleidoscope of U.S. history.

So, I ask myself, was this a learner-centered, student-negotiated social studies curriculum? Not much, I fear.

Negotiating Language Arts

The issue of negotiating curriculum in the language arts was not as tricky for me as it was in social studies.

Three times a week, for a full period, we had a reading workshop, set up much like the workshop Nancie Atwell describes in her book *In the Middle*.[2] This was, by student acclamation, the best-liked aspect of our weekly schedule. Every Tuesday, Wednesday, and Thursday morning our day would begin with a 42-minute period of quiet reading. Students chose what they would read, and read they did, from Jane Austen to Stephen King. (We kept for a few months a tally of the total number of books read by all the students in class, just for fun; when the tally sheet got lost, we were up in the 600's.) I had students keep reading logs in which they had to write letters about their books at least twice a week, to be exchanged with me and their classmates for responses. We had informal five-minute talks about books a couple of times a week, usually initiated by my question, "Anyone reading a good one you'd like to recommend to the class?" The primary activity of reading workshop, however, was spending long periods of time sunk in books. This was the students' curriculum to the extent that they chose all their own reading matter.

Yet, even in the face of the success and popularity of reading workshop in my class, twice during the year I summarily stopped it for a month—to much complaining. The first time was in October when I wanted the class to have the experience of reading a book together. This was not negotiated; this was an assignment. We had a classroom set of copies of the novel *My Brother Sam is*

Dead by James and Christopher Collier[3] which I passed out. My reasoning was that the novel fit with the historic topic under discussion, the Revolutionary War, and offered another way to think about history—through historical fiction. Also, I figured if we worked our way through a whole book together, I could offer some whole-class reading instruction. The reading workshop was providing the wide and regular reading and good book-chat that I believe are the keys to cultivating comprehension and vocabulary skills, but I began to get a bit nervous about the lack of reading instruction. If we read a book together, I figured, we could at least discuss together some traditional literary elements as well as some reading and thinking strategies: What do you do if you don't know a word, or can't understand a passage? Did anyone have trouble with this certain section, where I got confused? How did you work through this difficulty?

I also hoped this reading assignment might have some carry-over into writing and that perhaps some students might try their hand at historical fiction. Happily, a number did, including Cameron, who wrote one of the most well-received pieces produced during the year, a nicely-imagined story of a Taino Indian seeing Columbus sail into his island harbor.

During our read-together of *My Brother Sam is Dead,* I set deadlines ("By Thursday, have read to the end of chapter three," for example), and we would discuss the book in a whole-class circle. My first question was always, "What did you think about today's chapter?" I also asked students to keep a log of responses to the reading, writing at least twice a week about something they liked or something they didn't like, any questions that arose, or anything else that struck them in the section. I gave an essay test at the end of the book with questions such as, "If *you* had been old enough to join the army, which side in the Revolutionary War would you have chosen, and why? Give reasons, including some that relate to incidents in the book."

The majority of my eighth-grade students did not generally enjoy this month-long community book reading. On an end-of-the-experience evaluation, many told me loudly and clearly that they did not like having reading workshop disrupted. Thus, for most of the rest of the year, we stuck to our independent, quiet reading workshop time. Whatever reading instruction I offered from then on was individual and conveyed through the reading logs or teacher-student conferences I would occasionally initiate.

In the spring, however, I stopped independent reading workshop once more for three weeks so we could try literature study groups, an idea I had been inspired to try through my lunchtime talks with Mary Burke-Hengen. (Literature study groups and independent reading are not mutually exclusive, of course; many teachers do both kinds of activities simultaneously, devoting part of reading time each week to a workshop and part to some group experience. I just wasn't adept enough to do this yet.) I had about a half dozen copies of 6 or 7 different titles, all relating in some way to what we were studying by then in social studies, which was life in the frontier American West. (The titles included books such as Louis L'Amour's *Comstock Lode*,[4] Dee Brown's *Bury My Heart at Wounded Knee*,[5] and Patricia Calvert's *The Snowbird*[6].) The groups, formed by their mutual interest in a certain title, met to discuss their books twice a week. Again, I hoped to make reading more of a community event, a shared experience. Unfortunately, the groups, with one exception, were not very engaged or enthusiastic. As soon as each group had finished its book, all returned, with relief, to their individual reading. Certainly I saw in retrospect how I could have set up the literature study groups for more success—with better training in group process skills, better modeling, better questions. But their resistance was mostly, the students told me, based on having to read a required book on someone else's timetable. So, we finished the year with reading workshop.

What lesson did I learn from this experience? Should we always have only an individualized reading program? Should students read only what they want? I still think there is some value in community reading projects and in learning to read in response to an assignment, which, after all, most adults must do in the workaday world. I still think, however, that a middle school reading program must have students' choices of reading material at its heart. I'm still trying to work out the balance in my classroom; teaching does feel at times like walking a tightrope.

In the writing curriculum, as in reading, it was easier for me to plan for student decision-making than it was in the social studies curriculum. Three times a week, we had a full-period writing workshop constructed along the lines of the sort of workshop recommended by Donald Graves in *Writing: Teachers and Children at Work*.[7] In such a workshop, the primary activity is writing—not studying about it, but actual pencil-to-the-paper time engaged in the act of composition. During these three periods a week, my students had complete control over what they would write about. For the first couple of weeks of school, we did a lot of brainstorming, listing, and talking about possible topics and ways to generate future topics. After that, decisions about topics and literary genres to experiment with were theirs alone. I saw my main responsibility as the cultivation of a classroom response community, so students could receive from each other and from me ongoing feedback to their work-in-progress. I saw my main opportunity for instruction to be during individual conferences with individual students on specific pieces of writing.

Once every six weeks or thereabouts, we would publish an all-class literary magazine, with a contribution required from each student. These magazines had publishing deadlines, so students could experience the high standards of final drafting as well as the ongoing process-work of the workshop. Students chose which piece of writing they would submit to the magazine and were responsible for putting it together in final-edited, camera-ready form. To support their manuscript preparation, we visited the school's computer lab once a week for word processing. Students drew the covers, wrote introductions and author notes, and illustrated the class magazines. Collating and binding each magazine was an in-class assembly-line type affair. When we each finally had our own copy of the publication in our hands, we would circle up the chairs, push back the desks, and celebrate with a literary reading, complete with applause and cookies. Each student would read his or her composition in the magazine to the group.

The writing curriculum had another component, too, on the two days a week we weren't having writing workshop. On these two days, students wrote in response to assignments I designed. My rationale was two-fold. First, I figured students should learn to write in response to assignments, since they will have to do so all their lives in many forms, from college "blue books" to workplace correspondence to insurance report forms to thank-you letters. Second, I wanted students to try their hands at a wide variety of forms and genres of writing. I wanted the science fiction enthusiasts to try their hands at poetry, the poets to experiment with a bit of sci fi, and so forth. So, during the course of the year, the eighth graders in my Core class tried their hands at poetry, fiction, "how-to" expository prose, letters to the editor, descriptive passages, consumer letters, persuasive pieces, and more—all required by me.

In addition, I succumbed to the pressure to get my students ready for the mandated state writing assessment in February. We spent two days a week for six weeks practicing writing in response to prompts similar to those used on the state exam. In retrospect, this was a ridiculous use of classroom time. The state exam topics were stilted and artificial, and after my students spent the required three days writing their state exam compositions, we didn't hear back about the results till June. By that time most of the students had forgotten about the experience altogether, so the feedback was not useful. We did pretty well as a class on the test, but I think the students would have done just as well without the test-focused preparation; the best preparation would have been just more writing in workshop and in a variety of genres.

The second half of the year, I began to have students construct rudimentary writing portfolios, my first classroom experiment with this activity. They were in charge of the collection and self-assessment of their work in the portfolio, which served as the main part of their final evaluation in the course. I set up some rough guidelines, such as that the portfolio had to have at least two final pieces that had been published in the class magazine and at least one social studies-focused writing. Students could put in anything else they wanted. I also asked them to describe why they had chosen what they did for their portfolio, and to tell how these works expressed their strengths as a writer. A closer analysis of a couple of pieces of writing was also required, centered on questions such as, "What did you learn as a writer from this piece?"

To sum up, some of my writing curriculum was student-chosen, some teacher-dictated. I suppose I can claim this added up to a balanced composition diet in my classroom. However, in Room 220 at Beaumont Middle School, I believe the centerpiece of the writing curriculum was the workshop, where students wrote and wrote and wrote—at their pace, in their style, and on their topics.

Negotiating Students

I have to mention one more thing on this subject of negotiating the curriculum. All year long, I *talked* with my students about it. I tried to draw them into my dilemmas and to continually ask their opinions about the curriculum. They were clear about what they liked (reading workshop) and what they didn't (films on Andrew Jackson), and appreciated being asked. I polled them occasionally on what they would change about Core class, and got input that helped direct the curriculum. Most interesting was when I asked them to write on the topic, "What do you think eighth graders need to know?" I got many useful answers ("I want to learn more about women on the Oregon Trail") and others not as useful ("You tell me. You're the teacher.") I wanted the tension in my own thinking—the need for students to design their own curriculum set against the need for students to be exposed to what the district wants them to know and what I think is essential—to be part of the classroom conversation. I always enjoyed bringing the students into my teacherly thinking, letting them have opportunities to have their say. After one of these talks, when I was basking in the student interchange and the frank and helpful input, Kyen veered by my desk on the way out of class and said, "Mr. G., you worry too much. Just keep doing what you're doing. You're a professional!" I had to laugh.

So, as I reflect back on my year and on the notion of negotiating curriculum with students, I have to ask myself if my Core class was student-driven or teacher-driven. Perhaps it was most like one of those driver-training cars with two sets of steering wheels, accelerators, and brakes. In reading and writing workshop, which together constituted about half of our total time as a class, the students were definitely the drivers. At other times, especially in the social studies curriculum, I held a stronger grip on the wheel. I had the override instruments and thus, overall, more control.

This teacher-weighted balance of control was probably inevitable, given my beginner's skills with transferring responsibility to students and the demands of the district's stipulated curriculum. In retrospect, however, I believe I could have let my students exercise more independence, autonomy, and negotiating power. I'm trying to learn to take my foot off the pedals and trust the students more.

Integrating the Curriculum

A truism of contemporary thinking about language arts instruction is the value of integrating curriculum, of erasing the traditionally drawn line between reading instruction and writing instruction, and between these language arts and other curriculum areas. I started the year with a vision of a classroom that would be interdisciplinary, flexible, and open, a seamless time span of ever-changing inquiry ranging across subject matters. Though such a vision is hardly possible in many middle schools, most high schools, and most colleges, with their clearly-delineated disciplines taught during brief, clearly-defined blocks of time, I figured I had at least a chance of doing some curriculum integration with my three-period Core class.

Plenty of subject matter integration did happen, in fact. We wrote about reading and read about writing, we surrounded the social studies with reading and writing, and we talked incessantly about it all. The subjects reinforced each other. My students became better readers because of their reading into U.S. history and better students of history because of the exploratory writing they did. All this is nothing new or innovative, of course. It is difficult to avoid curriculum integration at this level, since reading and writing are ways of thinking and tools of inquiry for any discipline.

However, in terms of the way time was organized and used in the classroom, my fuzzy notion of three open periods with students all working on different aspects of the curriculum in different ways never quite came into clear focus. Many times, especially as small groups worked on their social studies projects, the class did appear to be a three-ring circus of varied activities. Yet, more often than not, we worked as a class on one content area at a time. For most of the year, in fact, my class had separate periods for reading, for writing, and for social studies. In other words, what I seem to have created, with plenty of support from my students, was a dis-integrated classroom. The main reason for this happening was that the disciplines of reading and writing kept demanding time of their own.

Let me explain.

As reading workshop evolved, it turned out that the majority of my students preferred the classroom to be quiet during reading. Too many could not engage in extended involvement with a book if the noise of project work was swirling around them. Also, my students let me know that they preferred regularly scheduled days when they knew they would need to bring their personal reading books to class, to help them organize the variables of passing times and books and locker visits they all had to juggle. So, we set three mornings a week—Tuesday through Thursday—for the quiet, independent work of our reading workshop.

Writing also made claims of its own. I am convinced of the value of using writing as a tool of learning in all curriculum areas, and I am convinced that writing skill is gained through the use of writing in many contexts and for many purposes. However, as a writer myself, I also know that writing is a craft and that writers need some time just to study that craft. As Donald Graves and other writing scholars have pointed out, setting up predictable writing times and routines in the classroom is one of the best ways to support young writers.[8] Furthermore, as Graves has noted, allowing students to choose their own topics during writing workshop offers them the control over content that allows them more freedom to focus on and experiment with the writing craft.[9] So, with all this in mind, I decided to set aside at least three predictable, regularly scheduled periods of time a week for writing workshop, when the focus would not be social studies content or literature or any other subject matter, just the craft of writing. During workshop, the students decided what their own individual content matter would be.

Thus, by the third week of the school year, my eighth graders and I had settled into a routine we would continue till June. Almost half our time was set aside for the regularly scheduled study of discrete curriculum areas—in the form of reading and writing workshops. Most of the rest of the time was devoted to the U.S. history curriculum. So, on the majority of days in Room 220, we would have one long period of reading time, one long period of writing time, and one long period of social studies time. The schedule was predictable, and each discipline was given its due in turn. The structure worked well, the students supported it, and onward we marched.

So, was my curriculum interdisciplinary and integrated? No, not in the way I originally envisioned it. But I wouldn't want to have given up the successful literacy workshops. So I'm left with a conundrum: In my classroom, how can I honor the craft work of separate disciplines and also honor the idea of interdisciplinary thinking? Hmmm . . . I'm still thinking about it.

Cultivating Better Teaching

About three weeks into the school year, I woke up exhausted one morning with this not-so-remarkable thought: "Teaching isn't a sprint; it's a marathon." I had forgotten this important fact in my years away from the classroom.

Teaching is often talked about as a profession or a calling, but it is also an incredibly challenging *job* with some monumental expectations. It calls on all our wit, intelligence, energy, patience, and personality; it requires prodigious intellectual, emotional, and physical skills; it challenges our most deeply held values as we face every day the palpable manifestations of society's problems—poverty, hunger, child abuse, violence. Add to this all the institutional requirements, large student loads, and society's increasing expectations of schools, not to mention whatever outside-of-school lives and family commitments we may have. Teaching's demands are heavy and relentless: a nine-month marathon.

What this meant for me at Beaumont Middle School is what it means for most of us. The time and energy available for long-range planning, for carefully considering our classroom observations, for reading professional literature, for writing, for self-examination and reflection, is not sufficient. Luckily for me, I had my twice-weekly lunchtime discussion with my teaching colleague, Mary Burke-Hengen, and I did keep a journal. Though I was happy with the generally well-working, learner-centered workshops, I felt that at other times I was too often doing things in class that were unexamined—seat-of-the-pants curriculum, in other words. I know I was under the pressure of being in a new school and teaching a new subject matter and grade level, and that the work usually comes along more smoothly when we have a couple years under our belt. But this year at Beaumont, scrambling as I was to do a good job, I found myself at times relying on old habits and routines and activities which were not always necessarily connected to any well-reasoned educational philosophy or theory. And no matter what the quality of the thinking I had done, I knew that 28 students were going to come walking through the door every morning at 8:15. (The only saving grace in my instance was that the first student in the class was usually Iyabo, whose habit it was to sing gospel music to herself in a beautiful voice till the others began to arrive. Thank goodness for small gifts.)

Yet, I did feel a general sense of progress in my class. Regardless of my uncertainty and my stumbling around with my many educational questions, I believe most of my students were learning, and were learning to value and take charge of their own learning. Successes happened, even though I didn't always know why or how. The broad principles of whole language or learner-centered thinking did serve me well in much of my planning and decision-making; most of the time I thought we were engaged in purposeful, meaningful, authentic work in the classroom. But it wasn't always easy or smooth sailing; seldom so, in fact.

In a splendid example of the transmission of informal teacher lore, a colleague told me one day that "a study has proved that it doesn't matter what the teaching technique is, the key factor in students' success is the teacher's commitment." Well, this assertion left me with plenty more questions, starting with the properly skeptical one of who did this study and where and how. But I did find myself thinking of Sondra Perl and Nancy Wilson's book *Through Teachers' Eyes,* and its tentative conclusion that there may be factors more important to effective teaching than any particular pedagogical approach, and that the primary factor may be the teacher's faith that students can learn.[10]

Is this, then, perhaps the core truth of whole language or learner-centered thinking: If we keep our students at the center of our thinking, and if we believe our students can learn, we are permitted to flounder in our classroom execution, to be frequently unsure, often inconsistent, sometimes at odds with our own theories? No, that seems a bit glib, and too easy an answer to settle for. I *must* keep asking myself: What is most important to me? How will I improve my teaching? What are the principles by which I will live my teaching life? I must commit myself to living the questions.

Wrapping Things Up

To sum up, my veteran rookie eyes were re-opened to the tensions inherent in teaching and the challenges in trying to move toward a new model of teaching. All I can conclusively say is that I haven't reached any conclusions yet. I guess that's a good thing, to realize again that teaching and learning do not have conclusions, that they are unceasing processes of growth. As my students continually learn and grow, so must I. It is, for all of us, teacher and students, a painful and wonderful process—a strain, sometimes, but also a joy.

We will wake up and smell the chalkdust together.

End Notes

1. Thomas Newkirk, "Silences in Our Teaching Stories: What Do We Leave Out and Why?" *Workshop 4: The Teacher as Researcher*, ed. Thomas Newkirk (Portsmouth, NH: Heinemann, 1992), 27.

2. Nancie Atwell, *In the Middle: Writing, Reading, and Learning with Adolescents* (Portsmouth, NH: Heinemann, 1987), 149.

3. James Collier and Christopher Collier, *My Brother Sam is Dead* (New York: Scholastic, Inc., 1974).

4. Louis L'Amour, *Comstock Lode* (New York: Bantam Books, 1981).

5. Dee Brown, *Bury My Heart at Wounded Knee* (New York: Holt, Rinehart & Winston, 1970).

6. Patricia Calvert, *The Snowbird* (New York: New American Library, 1982).

7. Donald Graves, *Writing: Teachers and Children at Work* (Portsmouth, NH: Heinemann, 1983).

8. Graves, 268.

9. Graves, 21–31.

10. Sondra Perl and Nancy Wilson, *Through Teachers' Eyes: Portraits of Writing Teachers at Work* (Portsmouth, NH: Heinemann, 1986), 258–259.

Chapter 4

Making It Your Own:Whole Language in the Middle School

Mary Burke-Hengen

A New Way to Teach Language Arts

I shall never forget my first reading of *Teacher*,[1] the story of Sylvia
Ashton Warner living in New Zealand and teaching her Maori students to read and write using the "organic" method. It seemed like
creative common sense to me—children learning to read with the
help of a teacher who first recorded their thoughts in their own
language and isolated words of greatest personal meaning for study.
At the time I read this now-famous book, my students were twelve
boys living in a residential children's facility for emotionally-dis-
turbed children. They were often angry and aggressive as a result
of family abuse and neglect and the lack of school success which
had brought them into residential care. I felt lonely in my teaching
and was looking for ways to be more effective and to be connected
with other teachers, researchers, and scholars.

Although I mixed my efforts with these early ideas of what
was to become the whole-language movement with a continuation
of the conventional skill-teaching texts and programs provided by
the school district, the results I achieved encouraged me. I began
to see more effective ways to teach these students than taking apart
the components of reading and trusting that students would reas-
semble them in some sort of reconstitution of meaning, like a recipe
for orange juice.

By the time I read Donald Murray's *Learning by Teaching*,[2] I
had returned to the teaching mainstream and was teaching a class
called "Core" to two groups of middle schoolers. "Core" consisted
of studying grammar and the mechanics of writing and reading

from a basal text and novels, and answering comprehension questions. This language study was alternated with study of a social studies textbook, films, and worksheets. My class seemed a chore more than a core to teach, and I had a vision that one of the Core designers had shared with me: we should use themes and topics as a center for curriculum design. None too confident about what I was doing, but dissatisfied with the current results, I began to encourage students to finish their week's work a day early so that we could "have some fun on Fridays." The fun I had in mind was writing, something I'd once loved and thought students might enjoy. I felt sure the students would respond creatively to the freedom of thought possible in work where they could make choices about topic and mode of expression. I was correct. I took some time off that first spring and went to hear Don Murray speak. I was happy to see he looked old enough for me to believe he had substantiated his radical thoughts about the teaching of English over an extensive period of time. I continued with my experimentations.

Sometime after I'd read further and "discovered" the other Donald, Donald Graves,[3] I renewed my own love of writing by beginning to write short books and stories about my life and thoughts on education. The work took me back to my own adolescence and to youthful dreams. I shared some of this work with my students the next year so that they could see I didn't just ask them to write—I wrote, too. The students rewarded me with greater and greater participation. Friday now extended to include Thursday, giving us two days of home-grown curriculum. I began to think perhaps student achievement scores might also improve due to our "extra efforts." I kept a record of improvements that demonstrated students were benefiting in skill development as well as classroom attitudes.

Then came Nancie Atwell's *In the Middle*.[4] I loved her ideas for student folders and other organizational devices. I loaned the book to other teachers (I have now purchased it three times in order to keep a copy available for myself) because I believed her to be an expert who thought it was not only okay but desirable for students to choose for themselves books they wanted to read and topics they wanted to write about. I didn't see myself then as any kind of an expert on my students' learning. It was much later before I connected student empowerment with my own empowerment. Then, I simply knew that I could learn from—but not implement in totality—someone else's work that they had developed slowly over a period of several years. Reading and following some of the ideas in Nancie's Atwell's book in my mind helped me to let go of a lot of nonproductive control over student learning. But I wasn't Nancie Atwell. I knew I needed to construct a map for myself of where I was in my teaching, where I wanted to go based on the students I had, and what I knew and was comfortable with teaching. The changes I made became more directed.

Designing for Change

One night, I stayed late after school and sat down at the computer I'd asked to have in my classroom. I constructed a list. Starting at the bottom with descriptions of teaching practices I had discarded, I worked upwards in my descriptions toward the goals I hoped to achieve. "Teacher makes assignments and selects completion date" was close to the bottom, with "Teacher plans films and discussions as prewriting" towards the middle. Close to the top were "Teacher regularly writes with students and shares her writing," and "Writings are published regularly as a group and individually." When I had about twenty items, I began to understand—I was well on the way to describing a classroom based on a whole-language philosophy. It was uniquely mine, and I felt more sure I could and would be successful in what I hoped to accomplish. Not expecting quick results—allowing time and patience with myself—helped me to mesh observations of my students with theory. From this list, I designed a writing skills list for student folders similar to what Nancie Atwell then used, but one that encompassed my students' needs and my preparedness to teach to those needs. I have continued to change the list periodically to reflect more accurately student needs and my teaching practices (see next page).

The writing skills list began to serve as an outline for the year's writing curriculum. It helped to provide a focus for improvement in student writing without group teaching of the items as isolated and disconnected skills. It served as a list of goals. It was a tool to use in student conferences and in parent conferences. Finally, the list helped me to articulate skill expectations for writing so that it was clear that while we were learning the art of writing—the composing of stories, poems, and essays—we were also learning the craft of being a writer—correct grammar and spelling, the mechanics of punctuation, capitalization, sentencing, paragraphing, and the use of a wide vocabulary.

Discussing with students what makes good writing produced items for the writers' list also. Putting the lists we generated on butcher paper and hanging them up for a while gave my students a chance to internalize and use the ideas. Brainstorming together all the ways to say "He said" and "She said" without using "said" was fun, and we posted our results for reference during writing times. Thinking of as many descriptors as possible for assorted words—such as "girl," "water," "school"—subtly taught the idea of variety in description. All of these activities were a part of our prewriting, where I could most effectively teach them.

Date _____ _____*'s Writing*		
Skills		
Check and date. (Check midway to indicate if more work is needed.)	**Need**	**Mastered**
Uses periods correctly.	_____	_____
Uses capitals correctly.	_____	_____
Writes in sentences.	_____	_____
Uses question marks correctly.	_____	_____
Spells chosen words correctly.	_____	_____
Grammatical usage is correct.	_____	_____
Uses commas correctly.	_____	_____
Writes essays:		
Personal	_____	_____
Persuasive	_____	_____
Explanatory	_____	_____
Literary	_____	_____
Writes short stories:		
Uses dialogue.	_____	_____
Varies from "he said" and "she said."	_____	_____
Writing is descriptive.	_____	_____
Uses possessives correctly.	_____	_____
Uses colons and semi-colons.	_____	_____
Writes in ink neatly or type.	_____	_____
Formulates own topics.	_____	_____
Writes as many drafts as needed.	_____	_____
Keeps a list of future topics.	_____	_____
Publishes completed pieces.	_____	_____
Revises for sentence variety.	_____	_____
Revises to make meaning clear.	_____	_____
Revises for lead (hooking the reader).	_____	_____
Uses a varied and correct vocabulary.	_____	_____
Develops own editors and proofreaders.	_____	_____
Composes on the word processor.	_____	_____
Uses hyphen and dash appropriately.	_____	_____
Contributes to the work of others in writing group.	_____	_____

Finally, the list helped to remind me to teach new forms of writing so that students' writing possibilities were constantly expanding. Reading and then writing forms of poetry or essays that were new to many of the students energized the writing program. Using the forms as models with which to begin our own writings was a fun way to expand our writing, although I once overdid it and asked students to do a whole book of poems as a sampler of about twenty poetry writing techniques. The exercise resulted for some students in a resentment of the tryanny of form over ideas; they ended up with a dislike for poetry rather than the attraction to it that I was trying to foster.

Skill Teaching

I continued to teach common skills I saw most students needed to improve. For example, I would put a question—What is truth? What is a lie? What is your favorite current movie and why?—on the top of a piece of paper, then compile students' answers on a list, duplicate the list or make an overhead from it, and ask the students to look for one or more specific items of mechanics and grammar. Sometimes, time and creativity was not so abundant; I would duplicate worksheets which came with a writers' reference manual I had selected for my students and ask them to complete the exercise. I tried to keep the time spent on these exercises short and found that, ten to fifteen minutes was the most effective amount. I varied skill work so that at times it was done alone, at times with a partner, and at times as a whole group. I tried to make students responsible for one another so that they would edit each other's work carefully. This was not as effective as I hoped, but did lead to my teaching my students to find the best editors for their writings and to be specific about what they needed from each of them. Mothers, for example, I often found to be great editors for spelling and mechanics, while other students would more often ask questions about a piece of writing which led—but did not dictate—an author's consideration of changes.

Although using computer spellchecks modified my concern with spelling, I continued to try to extend vocabulary awareness through the occasional use of common lists. Social Studies readings and any class literature readings, along with words from student papers, formed the basis for these lists. I also encouraged students to write vocabulary words new to them in their reading journals and to define them. Now, I honestly conclude that this is not the most effective way to learn vocabulary. I believe the time is better spent making sure students have word analysis tools. So I would simply write words and their meanings on large charts or on a handout; or, better yet, post a few prefixes, suffixes, and roots from time to time and assess their use by students orally and in their writings.

Teaching Essay Writing to Middle School Students

I have tried each year to develop and to revise several lesson plans. One of the most helpful and successful of these plans is on essay writing. The following is a copy of a plan I developed for myself and for other teachers, followed by the one I gave out to students and their parents, sometimes including it with a parent letter.

ESSAY WRITING IN THE MIDDLE SCHOOL

1.   Duplicate a variety of essays written on different top-ics and in different styles. (For a class of 28 to 30 students, include six or seven titles with four or five copies per title.)

2.   Introduce essays in a general way by reading one of your personal favorites and inviting reactions to its content. Ask students to consider the author's pur-pose in writing the essay. Discuss student statements. End the discussion with a brief explanation of how essays can and often do defy description; they can be humorous, full of facts, often contain personal experiences, sometimes attempt to persuade, and are related to an old word, "theme," meaning *to explain, to make a statement about the essence; to tell the "So What?"*

        (Optional extension: discuss writing as think-ing and, that essays are an opportunity for us to find out what we ourselves think on a topic while we are presenting it to someone else.)

3.   Divide the class into small working groups of four or five.

4.   Explain briefly the essays that are available. You will probably want to post their choices of titles on the overhead or blackboard. Ask groups to decide on

their first, second, and third choices for reading and presentation to the class.

5. Allow time for groups to collect their copies and prepare a presentation of their essay to the class. They may all read a section, divide it into parts, alternate sentences, and so forth. Tell them they are teaching the essay to the rest of the class and, when they have presented it, students should understand the essay form a little better as well as understand the content of the essay presented.

      (Optional: students take evaluative notes on presentations.)

6. When all of the essays have been presented to the class, ask each student to write a definition of an essay, to name and describe two of the essays they particularly liked and tell why, and to name one they did not have a favorable response to. Finally, ask students to list several topics about which they could write an essay.

7. Assign the writing of several rough-draft essays: for instance, *two or three on topics and style of own choosing; at least one on a book, play, or event being studied by the class; one in a teaching mode, telling or instructing others on a "how to . . ."; one that entertains or persuades or does both; at least one that gives an opinion on a topic of personal importance.*

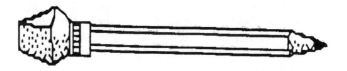

HOW TO WRITE AN ESSAY

1. Spend a lot of time thinking about what you want to write. As you are walking, doing the dishes, watching TV, listening to music, or reading your textbook, novels, newspapers, and so forth, think about topics that really suit you personally. Then, develop your ideas through a variety of techniques: clustering, brainstorming, matrix, freewriting, journal writing, reading, and discussion.

2. Then, WRITE:
    Introduction
    sets the mood
    one to five sentences
    > one very general sentence about the subject
    > several sentences stating EXACTLY the topic

    Body
    three paragraphs (at least)
    paragraphs of about five sentences
    > each paragraph has a TOPIC sentence, support-
    > ing details or examples, and a transition to the
    > next paragraph

    Conclusion
    one to five sentences
    > repeat, in other words, the topic of the paper
    > add comments about the future.

3. When you have several essays in your working writ-
    ing folder to choose from, select one to read to your
    writing group or to the whole class.

    LET THE ESSAY SIT FOR A DAY OR TWO, THEN SELF-REVISE
    BEFORE BRINGING TO YOUR WRITING GROUP FOR APPRE-
    CIATION AND SUGGESTIONS. *Remember: humor, anec-
    dotes, illustrations, and honesty add "Voice" to
    essays, yet the theme of the piece should come
    through clearly.*

4. Read your essay to your writing group or to the class
    and ask for comments about effectiveness of mate-
    rial. You may want to have a supply of file cards or
    small note papers so that other students can respond
    to each essay in writing. Ask them to address two or
    three specific items, and to note any questions they
    have that are not answered in your piece.
    Suggested items to include:

    Was the piece interesting to you as a listener?
    Did I convince you of anything? How?
    Was the topic well developed?
    Did I give enough examples and details for my ideas?
    Did I interest you enough in the topic? How?
    What was missing in the essay that you would include?
    Was the conclusion effective? Did it leave you want-
    ing to know more?

5. The essay you select to share in the class will be
    posted on the bulletin board, put into our classbook,
    and used as part of your evaluation for this term.

EVALUATION will be based upon the following:
number of drafts; evidence of revision; careful editing; development of original ideas; use of supporting evidence and details; neatness; promptness;
participation in writing groups and attention to the
writing of others; honesty and originality of ideas;
evidence of hard work; vocabulary; spelling and
punctuation; use of illustrations; use of interesting
language. (Add any specific requests for items that
you'd like me to look at in your paper.)

Students and Use of Time

Although I hoped that the kind of work I did with students on
essays and other types of writing would help students take responsibility for their work in class, it would be a lie to say I didn't or
that I don't get nervous about student use of time. In my efforts to
implement a whole language philosophy that would best serve my
students, I was sometimes disappointed at what I took to be student apathy about learning progress. I was excited about what we
were doing and I worried about the students who didn't seem to
invest much of themselves in their writings or their reading responses. In the middle of classroom activities, I sometimes didn't
remember my former classes and how many more students made
much less investment in class work in a teacher-dominated curriculum. I was discouraged at many points and needed to write
through the discouragement in my classroom journal. Sometimes,
I'd simply write what I observed, and then later try to generalize
about those observations.

As I moved from one to two to three days of individual work
in reading and writing workshops in my classroom, I frequently
evaluated students' work habits. I rated the students 1 to 5 in my
gradebook on the basis of whether they came prepared to work
and sustained their efforts over the time available. I encouraged
them to alternate activities so that part of the time was spent reading and part working on different pieces of writing. The intervals
of time between ratings became longer and longer as the classes
improved in their use of time. Days of joy for me occurred when I
became too busy to attend to rating schemes because of involvement with students in discussion and making suggestions rather
than in nagging supervision.

Effectiveness of Writing Groups

When I incorporated writing groups into writing workshop, I experienced some resistance from students. I had read about them, and I had had a good experience in a writing group myself through the Portland Writing Project (a local variation of the Bay Writing Project and a real help to teachers getting comfortable with writing themselves). Writing Project leaders assigned participants to groups, and I had realized after a few weeks working in my group that our diversity of backgrounds both as teachers and as writers was a tremendous strength. So when I decided to introduce writing groups into my classroom, I waited until we had been in school for two or three weeks and I had information about individual student characteristics and writing interests. Then I placed students together in groups that represented diverse abilities and interests. Once formed, I resisted making any changes for the first quarter. I put myself in a writing group, and encouraged group bonding (and oral storytelling and presentation) through activities like the following before we began to listen to and comment on our writing pieces. I found the small group bonding over a year's time results in an improved spirit of community and respect in the classroom.

TOTEMS FOR OUR TIMES
GOALS:

To promote cooperation in small groups, help forge group identity, foster a sense of connection with the earth and with other animals, learn about the ways of some Northwest Coast natives and gain an appreciation of their artistic and spiritual wealth, provide an opportunity for hands on and oral learning, and promote the exercise of creativity.

TIME AND MATERIALS:

This activity will take about three to five 45–60-minute periods. You will need medium to large pieces of white paper (18" by 24" seems to work the best), black and red marking pens, books of Northwest Coast artwork and stories, especially those with the forms commonly used by native people. (Provide rulers, scissors, and glue as needed.)

ACTIVITIES:

1.   Read and tell a variety of Northwest Coast native stories to students.
2.   Provide opportunities for viewing books, pictures, and films ("Our Totem is the Raven" is an excellent one to use) that provide visual examples of totems and also explain their meanings.
3.   Discuss with students the meaning of totems and have them consider what their totem(s) might be.

Discuss how Natives acquired their totems through inheritance, fasting, and prayer and then affirmed them over and over through dance, storytelling, and potlatching.

4. It is a good idea to have students write a summary statement or short essay describing their understanding of totems, how they are obtained, and how this concept applies to them. (See student example below.) Another optional but potentially helpful preparation is to have students read some Northwest Coast mythology using a reader's theatre technique. Have them prepare in small groups, the very same small groups in which they will be working later.

5. Explain that groups will build their own totems with each member of each small group contributing one piece of the totem and telling a story that explains its meaning and how it was achieved (if inherited, how did the ancestor achieve?). An example is helpful but not necessary. Decide whether you want all parts to be standard on each of the totems. Provide paper of that size if you do. Place materials/books at each table. Old and modern native music playing in the background while students are working would set a special mood for the work.

6. While students are working on the artistic part of their totems, they discuss and plan their stories. Encourage them to put visual clues on their pictures that they can use as cues while telling their stories. Another helpful devise is the use of file cards to list key beginnings of parts. Students should practice their stories several times within their small groups. *REVIEW AND DISCUSS ELEMENTS OF STORIES AS NEEDED.* Encourage the nervous ones to practice with you.

7. When groups are ready, have them mount totems on bulletin or chalk board and tell their stories. Be sure to tell one yourself, either as part of your writing group or on your own.

8. Encourage everyone to enjoy and show appreciation for one another. If you have anything that you could potlatch, like treats or even prizes like books, bookmarks, and writing utensils, do so, explaining that giving gifts was the function of the partygiver. Most Northwest native tribal people did not clap for each other's performances, but might have said, "E-So," or simply smiled warmly all around.

EVALUATION:

Teacher observation of group and individual functioning and attitudes. This task needs to be approached with respect for the stories of native people and for class members. Given the amount of preparation time, the quality of the stories and artwork should be high. If the stories are not of the quality you think they should be, consider bringing a storyteller, especially a native person, into class to help groups and individuals in their preparations. This unit should be fun and should help begin the process of sharing thoughts and feelings with one another.

The Totem

by Shannon Knepper

A totem is an outward symbol of something unseen and private within a person, family or tribe. It was part of the heritage of many North American Indians. The symbol was usually an animal or other natural object, not an individual; and it was treated with a great deal of respect.

A totem pole is a group of symbols, mainly animals, carved and painted on tall cedar trees. The crests and genealogy, history, traditions and legends of tribal people are preserved on these trees. Cedar trees were usually preferred because they do not have many knots (which are often a problem when carving,) and they do not split. On the Northwest coast where totem poles were most common, cedar trees are abundant and are able to absorb a great deal of water without rotting.

The totem in the film, "Our Totem is the Raven," is a raven. The raven was swift and clever and was chosen by the tribe as their symbol because the men in the tribe were swift and clever about catching salmon. The film told the story of an old man who challenges his modern grandson to catch one salmon using his own ingenuity and to go without food for a day and a night while staying in the woods alone. He said that if the boy was able to do this, he would prove his manhood. Becoming a man was very important to the grandfather, although at first, the boy could not see that this was worthwhile.

My totem is the Dragon Fly. I chose this animal especially because dragon flies are long, slender, and graceful. The Dragon Fly is an emblem of some of the inland Wolf Clans of North American Indians.

Some of my students seemed not to get enough help with their writing through writing groups. Thus, my students and I eventually decided that after meeting with writing group members, students could seek further advice from others outside their group. This approach had many long-term benefits, one of which was the development of editors who would be available over a longer period of time than our class. Second, it put students in a position of asking for my help rather than seeing me as a critical red pen. I thought it frequently led to more objectivity, since the editor for a piece was often hearing or reading it "cold," with no prior knowledge to fill in any missing gaps in the paper. Finally, when students chose parents as editors—and they often did—closer working relationships between parents and school resulted.

Involving Parents

How can a teacher gain parental support for a changed curriculum? What kind of support might a teacher want from parents? What vital part do parents play in the life of the child as regards the school? These were questions I wanted to answer.

The open houses most schools hold in the fall often give a teacher a ten-minute opportunity to explain the year's program, while parents assess whether the teacher will be able to meet the individual needs of their child. Not a good time to communicate more than the basics of classroom behavior expectations, homework expectations, and school routines. I decided it would be wiser to explain those expectations in a letter so I could use the open house for face-to-face communication to learn more about the parents and their expectations of the class and of me as teacher.

After that first letter describing general expectations, I continued the letter format throughout the year. I experimented with frequency and content for a couple of years, finally settling on four letters a year (at least one a quarter) and keeping the letters at two to three pages. I mixed explanations of whole language philosophy, and how I was using it as a base for our curriculum, with news about class activities and suggestions for how parents could involve themselves with their child (and with the class as I relied on parent volunteer help) to improve student learning. Following are some sample excerpts from letters written over the last several years.

The Letters

A Fall Introduction to the Class and Program

This school year started differently for me than most other school years. What was new this year was that most students started the year saying they love to read and write. From the first time we had a workshop period in class where students made their own choices for what they would read and write, they were ready to work and to learn. Now, we're getting to the tougher parts: spending class and outside class time learning more about how to revise and how to edit, working in small groups where sharing writing with other students and listening to their writing is expected, preparing interesting presentations for the class on books read, writing in journals about current reading, and being accountable for a sizeable amount of work given as a chunk rather than being broken up into small parts.

On the Writing Program

Students will be choosing their own topics for writing, and they will be writing every day. These topics will come from personal experience, classroom and home discussions, films, literature readings, current events, historical events, and writing response group discussions. Students will keep their writing in a writing folder in the classroom and will select only a few of their pieces of writing for revision and editing. This means that everything students write will not be corrected by me, although students will receive credit towards a grade for rough draft work.

Writing skill tends to improve through a combination of frequent practice and thorough concentration on one or two goals at a time. What I want is for students to realize their writing is truly theirs, and so they need to set goals they hope to achieve and to let you and me know what we can do to help in the achievement of those goals. I have suggested to students that they be as specific as possible when they share their writing with parents and others as to what they need and want from their readers and listeners: questions about what is unclear, organizational suggestions, proofreading of spelling, punctuation, grammatical usage, and other mechanical errors.

On Praise Regarding Writings

Remember the need to give praise for lines you like or thoughts you find stated in an honest voice. Sometimes I think we each have a ratio of praise to constructive suggestions which will most help us improve our writing, and we know what it is if someone asks. At this point, my ratio is three positive comments to one critical one. As a beginning writer, it was closer to nine positive comments needed in order to hear one criticism for me to be comfortable and to be able to use outside help to improve my writing.

Praise is a tricky business, most especially with young adolescents. If you give unqualified praise, you run the risk of not being helpful; say nothing and you may appear uncaring. When your child brings some writing to you, you may want to use some of the following responses: try to draw out what your child was doing, attempting, and thinking about in the piece of writing. Be specific about what you find attractive in the writing; for example, descriptions that delight, emotional power, unique ideas, details that make a point or enrich, precise word choice, neatness, honesty of voice, use of irony, sentence simplicity (or complexity).

On the Writing Process

Most of us need considerable time doing what is known as prewriting—getting ready to write—which as a process is as individual as the number of people in the room. As a class we explore a variety of ideas through viewing, talking, reading, and questioning; but individual differences show up after whole-class explorations. After a period of time—15 minutes, several hours, several days—we settle down and begin to clarify what we think by putting our ideas on paper. This is usually a rough draft. If we're fortunate, ideas come out fairly clearly; after letting the paper sit a bit before rereading it, we're ready for some revision. During this time, we'll probably do some rewriting before sharing the paper with others in order to get their ideas. In our classroom, students meet in preassigned writing response groups to share drafts, but I also encourage them to solicit editors among their family and friends. Any feedback is useful, but specific comments and suggestions are the most useful. Changes can still easily be made at this point, but may be hard to contemplate if criticism from others isn't accompanied by lots of praise and appreciation. It is often helpful if the writer reads a paper to others—rather than giving others the paper to read themselves—so *ideas* receive the attention they need and merit without a focus on mechanical errors (that comes later).

After time for additions, deletions, and rearrangements of content, which may involve one, two, or more successive drafts, we're ready for proofreading. Now it's time to look for spelling, punctuation, and grammatical errors. It's fair to have as many "skilled editors" as is possible and practical go over one's paper. After the writer believes the paper is as good as it's going to be at this point in history, it's time for a neat copy to be produced. Writing in dark ink on one side of the paper only is preferable. Typing or word processing produces even better results. A final reread before handing in is advised.

On Grading Students' Writings

Every piece of writing has a purpose for its existence. To satisfy the requirements of a class or a teacher is not really a purpose. Some form of publication is a purpose. Another purpose is to bring about a change in someone else's behavior or your own. To explore your own thoughts is a purpose. To become a better writer is a purpose. Evaluation of the essay, then, is not really done by the grade earned, but by the accomplishment of a goal. I ask students to provide all drafts of their essays. We talk about the grades that I assign to their papers. Whenever possible, I have them provide a cover sheet to their work and write a note to me about what they would like me to comment on in a particular paper. Sometimes we agree as a group that an assignment will receive a content and organization grade, sometimes a mechanics and spelling grade.

On the Writing of Essays

In each of these letters, I've been covering some aspect of our reading and writing program in addition to providing information about our other class activities. This time, I'm going to address a much-maligned form of writing, the essay. Just the word seems to connote nineteenth-century orators who often seemed to possess more hot air than good sense. Yet, an essay should do exactly that: make good sense. When done well, it is a thing of beauty in its logically constructed ideas and blending of intellect, experience and feeling. Some writers start with three to five topic sentences and develop them into individual paragraphs with supporting arguments, examples, and informative data; add a polished introduction and a cohesive conclusion; and check for smooth transitions between paragraphs. Many writers are simply not that *tidy*. They are far more likely to have an idea—rough or not yet defined at all—and to use the act of writing as a chance to remember and to think, so that by the time they draft the essay they *do* have a clear idea of what they're trying to say.

Meanings Contained in the Letters

Looking back over these accumulated letters of the last several years, I am reminded of the issues I was struggling with at the times I wrote each letter. I am reminded of my doubts, progress, successes. I can see more clearly now that I was optimistic in my presentation of a new philosophy of school learning, yet honest in my reporting of difficulties and places where I needed assistance. The letters changed slowly from year to year, and I reused only the specific portions that continued to apply. I used the letters as opportunities to articulate to myself, as well as to the parents of my students, the goals that related to what the students and I were doing. Slowly, I built support for a changing curriculum. The letters have been one of the most valuable investments of time I have made as a teacher.

Parents have mostly been supportive and even appreciative and complimentary of change towards a whole language approach. Often, they have experienced increased enthusiasm about school through their child. It's enjoyable to be with young people who are eager to read to you the latest song, poem, or story they have written. It is intellectually engaging to hear of the latest findings in the search for information on a particular topic and to be asked for your help. Parents become excited about their child's progress and also enjoy the opportunities to share their own literature favorites, including the pieces which affected their own development. Often, they connect the progress they see their own child make at home with the techniques and style of teaching used at school.

The letters are a reflection of my learning and change as a teacher. I became more transparent, more vulnerable, more open with the students. For me, the letters reflect my move away from using mainly teacher authority and teacher decision making in the classroom toward an increasingly shared authority where consensus was often sought—and sometimes achieved. I ceased to think of students, and their work and actions, as "cooperative" or "cute"; more often I found what I observed infinitely interesting, something I wanted to understand, not control. I became willing to acknowledge how much I learned from students and to respect them even more than I had in the past.

Other Paths to Learning

Visual Discovery and Interpretation

One avenue of learning I think middle school teachers may often neglect is the visual. I became interested in this path to learning through Ruth Hubbard's work, *Authors of Pictures, Draughtsmen of Words*.[5] She believes that drawing can be a path to awareness, a kind of rehearsal for writing. Through her work and by experimenting in my classes, I became convinced that visual representations can do more than help students express ideas in a different way. For a very small percentage of students, I found that drawing is the *main* path to their thoughts, and often the single best way students have to express their thoughts. As a prewriting strategy, drawing serves as self-guided imagery. The following story attests to the power of the visual to evoke feelings and moods.

Andrew's Story

Andrew was a sullen boy-man. He was six feet tall and in slight need of a shave when he was sent to my room, transferred to me because he had made threats to another teacher. If he didn't conform to school behavioral expectations in my classroom, there would not be a place for him in our school . He was thirteen years of age.

Those first weeks in my room he was quiet. Nonworking quiet. Sad and angry, he sat and did as close to nothing as a student can do. He resisted most of the efforts the other students and I made to involve him in our projects and small group activities. His attitude seemed to be "Deal with me at your own peril" (as his former teacher had reported). Yet I wondered, "Why is he here?" Students such as Andrew could and did find many reasons not to be in school if they truly didn't want to be. I continued to observe him and to try to involve him in the classwork.

Shortly after Andrew came into the class, I began to read *Walkabout*[6] to the students. Set in Australia, the book tells the story of two American kids, a girl and her younger brother, wandering about lost in the desert until an aboriginal boy finds, feeds, and directs them to safety. The girl is the same age as the aboriginal boy, just at puberty, and she is uncomfortable with their mutual nakedness and his dark skin, a problem that eventually results in the boy's death. Perfect plot for a mixed racial group of young adolescents, I thought; but some of my students objected loudly to the stereotyped white viewpoints the book represented. Yet, other students were busy studying the books I'd brought in about the Australian desert and about the plant and animal life talked about in the book. I decided to try to find a way into the book and trust that our discussions about stereotyping and bias would make the reading worthwhile.

Before the next reading time, I placed drawing papers and colored pencils and crayons on the students' desks. I asked them to draw while I read to them, but first to think about what the word "walkabout" meant. I reread the section in the book that explains the idea. We talked a bit about American "walkabouts." Then I read and they drew. It was a wonderful difference in atmosphere, and the drawings were interesting—Andrew's drawing most of all. I was pleased and surprised when he was willing to explain it. He had drawn a picture of one of Portland's famous bridges, the Burnside bridge, and underneath it—where many homeless often live—he had drawn some of these people around a campfire. There was one prominent figure, Bobby, the Burnside Bum.

What a curious thing it seemed to me that day: a homeless person as an example of an American walkabout. James Vance Marshall, the author, certainly would be surprised, I thought. Truth surprises in art, just as it does in writing, when the unexpected vision is articulated. Later, I found out that Andrew had spent time under the bridge when he and his mother were put out of their home, but then they got to arguing and were unable to live together out of her car. Andrew now lived with friends where and when he could, and had put together an existence which—though hostile and unenviable—was better than his life as Bobby, the Burnside Bum.

What We Need and Want to Know

As the Burnside Bum, Bobby knew some very important things about contemporary life. And what he needed to know may seem to bear little relationship to a language arts curriculum. Yet, Bobby helped the class, including me, to understand a part of the world we are concerned with and connected to. The creative expression through his drawing and his explanations did more than "use the language" or "develop thinking skills." What he did was to introduce into the class the realities of his own life and the lives of many Americans. What he learned was that his life and his experiences were relevant to others.

Gang membership, the carrying of weapons to school, racism, divorce, homosexuality—all of these became curriculum topics over time as my students identified and explored their lives, their interests and their concerns. The mysteries of how to develop "core" themes, an early vision for me, became clearer and clearer as I realized what some of the themes of adolescence might be. What different classes wanted to know varied somewhat. Friendships, peer pressure, drugs and alcohol, and sexuality were constant points of interest, but environmental concerns were high one year and gangs and racism the next. Over time, I developed a wide knowledge of resources for the classroom that I would never have predicted a few years ago. Students brought their own books for me to read, and I shared my books with them. Together, we constructed meaning about our world amd shared our understandings of its joys and its problems.

Literature Study Groups

Using literature study groups is a way for students to compare reactions and to discuss understandings of theme in small group discussions. The major hurdles I experienced with literature groups were organizing books available, handling students' choices, and scheduling. When a colleague and I wanted our students to read a book about the westward movement, we hoped some overall meaning about the immigration to the West might emerge. It seemed a perfect curricular integration with social studies. Further, we wanted to experiment with a variety of genres and writing styles. Student choices included nonfiction history books, typical western lore, a novel written from a female point of view, and a novel featuring the life of a Native American. I used book talks to introduce the selections, and journal writes and small group meetings during the course of the reading. For presentation and evaluation of their work, groups could select from several choices I devised, or could come up with their own design subject to my approval.

The group meetings were quite successful. At first, students organized the reading so everyone was at approximately the same place in the book for weekly discussions. They met once a week, usually right after an individual journal write, and discussed their reading. Sometimes I would give a focus topic, such as "What are your favorite parts of the book from this week's reading?" Often, I did not provide a topic, but asked to have a brief report of each meeting. I found the reports interesting, especially when conclusions related to specifics in the books. Overall, class participation increased, though some students still did not read with as much interest and attention, nor write journal entries as descriptive and responsive, as I had hoped. Nonetheless, everyone was in a group and participated at some level of interest; students who read more slowly or experienced difficulties with understanding what they read benefited as other students supported them.

Assessment and Learning

Assessing Change

The changes resulting from adopting a whole-language philosophy can be quite dramatic. When we as teachers see even small changes with our students, we become more and more interested in making further changes. We want to be successful as much as our students do. Some teachers will work from theory: once they're convinced of a right direction of thinking, they'll deduct what they need to do to align their classroom practices with their thinking and make big changes rapidly. Others—and I count myself as one of these people—work in an organic style: we have ideas about what we want to accomplish with our students and how to get started in that direction, and then we move toward those goals at our own pace, adjusting our curriculum and our classroom practices as needed. We incorporate responses, alter directions, check to make sure our students are with us and making observable progress. We need to evolve as we understand, as we are ready to see value in new directions.

Some statements about whole language sound so simple: teach to meaning and understanding, teach to the whole rather than the parts. But the meanings behind these statements may be misconstrued. For example, "teach to meaning and understanding" does not mean each student must work alone at his or her "level." It does mean taking into account each student's prior knowledge, honoring and drawing upon that knowledge to construct new meanings and understandings within the learning community. "Teach to the whole" does not mean whole-class instruction. It does mean addressing "parts"—for instance, root words, prefixes, and suffixes—in context; it does mean developing in students an understanding of bias in children's books through reading real books rather than memorizing some decontextualized list of characteristics. Teaching this way takes planning time and effort, whether you proceed from activities or theory. You still need a guide for your work, one that outlines all you wish to address in the course. Ideally, you will be free to plan how to do so without being restricted to a particular set of materials.

The worst possible thing I think we could do is to not teach, to abdicate from providing some structure to learners. Students will not be served by us if we do nothing. If we allow classroom chaos, they will lose valuable learning time, develop unrealistic expectations for education and jobs, and fail to acquire habits that will lead to personal success.

Whole language is a way of educating based on a respect for all learners, rather than a statement of what content should be used. It is grounded in my understanding of gestalt psychology (the whole is greater than the sum of the parts): namely, people make connections between present and past learnings and are able to comprehend, synthesize, predict, and formulate questions from a study of whole pieces of meaning rather than from parts of a whole isolated for study. When subject areas are integrated, the opportunities for multiplying connections of understanding vastly increase.

Curiosity: Prime Tool of Assessment and Understanding

As teachers, we can choose to be lifelong learners, curious listeners and observers, and aware influencers. It is profoundly useful to be curious about our students. These are just some of the things I have wanted to know about my students: Who are they as individuals as well as within their group? How do they feel about and approach new learning? What kinds of lives do they lead? What experiences helped to form them into the people they are now? What motivates them? What do they want to know? What do they already know? Do they demonstrate awareness as individuals of their own learning processes? Finally, how can we engage in constant mutual evaluation of class activities as well as individual learning?

Journal Writes as Assessment

Journal writings are among the best ways to have ongoing dialogue about a wide variety of subjects, including assessment of class activities. At the end of one of the first years of using a whole language philosophy as the basis for my teaching, I asked students to comment on what they believed they'd learned in our class that year and what they wanted to try next in their reading and writing. The following are excerpts from their journal writings:

> I learned how to organize my thoughts on paper more. I found that I liked writing essays and poems more. I would like to write a book about myself and make some of it up. I liked how we mixed learning with art. It made doing things that aren't usually fun, fun.

> I learned I could write stories because I never felt like I could write before. This summer I am planning on writing the beginning of a book, and I'm determined to finish it this time. I started to write a book in sixth grade but my brother laughed at it so I threw it away.

> I learned that others enjoy your writing more if you just let your thoughts flow on paper instead of trying to copy others and writing only something that you think others are going to like. Next I will try to develop my reading skill. I'm not at the point quite yet where I can just sit down and read a good book.

> The only thing I learned is that if you read, you forget where you are and you feel like you're part of the story. One interest I developed is reading more often without my mom telling me to. I like that you give us time to read. I write more. I learned a lot about clustering before you write.

> I really don't think I've changed that much. I think I've always known this stuff but had to find a way to use it. I believe that I'm a better writer than before. I am more interested in it than I used to be.

> I never used to like writing stories that much. Until I started writing about experiences I'd had or things that really interested me. I find all of us in this class so energetic and full of ideas. It could never get boring. This summer I plan to write 12–15 short stories with one set of main characters.

> The thing I will try next in writing is to write a love story. I learned to speak my mind, be creative, and not to judge a person on what they look like.
>
> The only thing I do know now is that I can read and write faster and better. Now I like to write stories and some poems. Next I'm going to start a novel and read the book, *Gone With the Wind.*
>
> Some skills I learned were how to set up a plot and how to just begin writing without much to write about. I think I'm going to try to perfect one of my past papers.

At other times, I asked students to respond to a more specific prompt, such as, What did you learn about your writing from this piece? After a prompt that included drawing a picture or a favorite part of our house, then writing about it, Fred said this about his piece on his bedroom:

> I surprised myself on how imaginative I can be. I never really thought of myself in his way. I found that I really enjoyed writing this piece. It was hard to stop writing after I got started. I didn't know that writing certain kinds of pieces is really fun. I also learned that I am O.K. at writing. That helps me to write. I found this descriptive writing fun, and I think we should do more with it.

This was at the end of the first semester. Fred went on to write many descriptive pieces, and without a prompt. He began a novel, wrote several poems and essays, and completed an exceptionally fine research report.

Asking Questions: A Strategy for Assessment and Learning

In whole language classrooms, questioning for assessment and questioning for learning are intricately intertwined. Asking students for their questions rather than for their answers helps me find out what students know, what they want to know, and what they are learning. I look for clues to what they wonder about, what they want to know about a specific topic, what questions they have after reading or viewing, and what questions they have about aspects of the curriculum they have studied in past years.

Besides giving me a window on students' learning, helping students learn to ask questions also extends their learning and their self-evaluation of their learning. One way to establish questioning as a strategy for learning is to start the year with interviews for which students design the questions they will ask one another in pairs, followed by interviews of friends, family members, and neighbors. Students learn how to construct an initial set of interview questions, how to conduct both personal and telephone interviews, and what questions they might take to librarians or expert sources as they pursue information for reports, or seek background information to bring plausibility to their fiction writing. (This often leads students to learn oral history about their families.) Questioning is one of the primary paths to learning for teachers and for students, whether the questions are asked of self, classmates, friends, family, teacher, or experts on a particular topic or in a field of study. On at least one occasion, however, I worried that I might have overemphasized the value of questions.

Jake asked so many questions during small- and large-group discussions, I feared the other students would notice his lack of commonly held information and begin to make intimidating comments that might short circuit his active approach to learning. One day a student in Jake's class who was staying late to work on one of her writing projects commented, "Jake must really be smart. He asks so many questions." From her perspective, questions were a mark of intelligence. Later in the year, when one of the girls in the class did snicker after Jake asked a fifth question for the period, no one else laughed or responded. Looking back, I think Jake verbalized questions other students might have wanted to ask but wouldn't because of their fears about not sounding smart.

An important classroom ritual is the asking of questions. Joining with the class in writing questions helps the students to understand that you are a learner, too. I keep small file cards or note papers handy in order to write down and post questions that occur to me or to students. We tape these questions above the chalkboard and leave them there as a reminder of what we'd like to know. Periodically we return to these, noting which we have answered in the normal course of class activities and readings, which still interest us, and which we'd like to take down.

Bringing It All Together

Whole language philosophy is grounded in a belief that each of us can achieve our potential as a learned and literate person. This is as true for adults as it is for young students. Learning constructed together transforms the disciplined drudgery of skills-based programs into a shared adventure. I found myself wanting to apply the approach to subjects beyond my language arts classes.

Writing to reading to social studies was the progression in my classes. Once I'd experienced success with the workshop model for writing, I found it easy to extend the model to reading. Social studies was a good deal harder, and it was not until I had read a lot, and worked with media specialists and other teachers, that my knowledge of resources expanded enough to truly integrate social studies. From my experience, I think teachers adopting a whole language philosophy should think in terms of *years* for implementation. It offers teachers as much as it does students in the way of learning and growth, but this doesn't mean you have to reject everything you have previously done; some things you may not want to give up. The most sound changes probably come in small degrees that slowly increase and likely do not involve all subject areas at the same time. As to how change occurs—through social studies, language arts, or some other means—I think that depends on individual teachers and schools.

Looking Ahead

Integration of subjects is at the heart of the restructuring of middle schools. Thematic organization offers great promise as a way of accomplishing this goal. When students participate in the choosing and the development of themes for study, the program becomes progressively stronger. Themes chosen by students relate most to the issues of their lives.

Learning and managing the content material for a flexible program based on topic or theme study has become for me as important an issue as changing learning strategies and deciding how available money should be spent. Along with most whole language teachers, I favor the purchase of trade books—books in which a novel is printed in its entirety—or poetry books, rather than anthologies of many genres.

As we seek to integrate subject matters, especially social studies and literature, using the computer as a bank in which to deposit materials relevant to a topic or theme offers another promising way to organize and to access content. The computer easily replaces file drawers and book shelves. Whereas in the past I would use an expanding folder to house a growing collection of resources, now I can use a scanner to put primary source documents, maps, essays, poems, biographies, and original diaries and journals in a computer folder, and put it all on a disk that I can hold in one hand. Furthermore, not only is the computer easy to use, it enables real scholarship. Students can add their essays on a theme or topic to a computer collection. Teachers can use many sources for content and can utilize a research approach. Students can use graphics and music along with their oral presentations. Both teachers and students can easily create multi-media presentations for individuals, small groups or the whole class.

Probably we won't see all of this very soon, and not just because of the expense, which is not all that great. Looking at and using a whole set of encyclopedias, which can now be fit on one laser disk, is a big change. Many of us love books: we love the smell, the feel, and the visual delight of them. We may be the same people who used to love a particular pen, or particular grade and feel of paper, or a particular kind of typewriter. We learned to use a word processor because we experienced the improvements it helped most of us make in our writing. Eventually, though, I think our use of computers for writing will lead to our use of computers for reading, viewing, listening, and creating. Perhaps it is true that the one thing that doesn't change is change. Today we move toward whole learning approaches to better meet the needs of our students. As our teaching and learning, and that of our students, continues to evolve, perhaps the computer will offer us the next set of questions to ask and solutions to discover.

End Notes

1. Sylvia Ashton-Warner, *Teacher* (New York, NY: Bantam, 1971).
2. Donald Murray, *Learning by Teaching* (Portsmouth, NH: Heinemann, 1982).
3. Donald Graves, *Writing: Teachers and Children At Work* (Portsmouth, NH: Heinemann, 1983).
4. Atwell, Nancie, *In the Middle: Writing, Reading, and Learning With Adolescents* (Portsmouth, NH: Heinemann, 1987).
5. Ruth Hubbard, *Authors of Pictures, Draughtsmen of Words* (Portsmouth, NH: Heinemann, 1989).
6. James Vance Marshall, *Walkabout* (Garden City, NY: Doubleday, 1961).

Additional Recommended Readings

Andrasick, Kathleen Dudden. *Opening Texts*. Heinemann, 1990.

Atwell, Nancie. *Workshop 1*. Heinemann, 1989.

Benson, Peter, Dorothy Williams, and Arthur Johnson. *The Quicksilver Years*. Harper & Row, 1987.

Burleson, Derek L. (ed.). *Reflections: Personal Essays by 33 Distinguished Educators*. Phi Delta Kappa Educational Foundation, 1991.

Calkins, Lucy. *Lessons from a Child*. Heinemann, 1983.

_____. *The Art of Teaching Writing*. Heinemann, 1985.

Graves, Donald. *Build a Literate Classroom*. Heinemann, 1991.

_____. *A Researcher Learns to Write*. Heinemann, 1984.

Journal of Reading: Special Issue on Vocabulary. International Reading Association, April 1986.

Koch, Kenneth. *I Never Told Anybody: Teaching Poetry Writing in a Nursing Home*. Vintage, 1978.

Macrorie, Ken. *20 Teachers*. Oxford University Press, 1984.

_____. *Writing to Be Read*. Boynton/Cook, 1984.

Nelms, Ben F. (ed.). *Literature in the Classroom*. National Council of Teachers of English, 1988.

Perl, Sondra and Nancy Wilson. *Through Teacher's Eyes*. Heinemann, 1986.

Power, Brenda Miller and Ruth Hubbard. *Literacy in Process*. Heinemann, 1991.

Probst, Robert E. *Response and Analysis: Teaching Literature in Junior and Senior High School*. Boynton/Cook, 1988.

Reif, Linda. *Seeking Diversity*. Heinemann, 1992.

Rhodes, Lynn K. and Curt Dudley-Marling. *Readers and Writers with a Difference*. Heinemann, 1988.

Romano, Tom. *Clearing the Way*. Heinemann, 1987.

Routman, Regie. *Invitations*. Heinemann, 1991.

Shapiro, Jon E. (ed.). *Using Literature and Poetry Affectively*. International Reading Association, 1978.

Simons, Elizabeth Radin. *Student Worlds, Student Words*. Boynton/Cook, 1990.

Chapter 5

"Tracks in the Snow": Learning From Response Logs in Reading and Writing Workshops

Scott Christian

My Vision as Teacher in a Multi-Cultural Community

Several years ago I taught in a junior high school in Bethel, a small town in rural Alaska. It was a traditional junior high school where students traveled from room to room and content areas were taught in isolation. My teaching assignment was three two-hour blocks of seventh-grade language arts, with an average of 24 students in each class. I taught in a portable classroom in the parking lot behind the school building where 340 students attended junior high and high school classes. The faculty had begun to discuss moving toward a middle school curriculum and had experimented with integration on a very limited scale, but I was aware that our overall instructional model was not appropriate for our students. I envisioned instead a dynamic, student-centered language arts program, where students were excited about learning and were producing quality written publications.

Bethel is truly a multi-cultural community. Students in my classrooms represented at least five distinct cultures. Approximately ten percent were English-as-a-Second-Language speakers, their primary language being Yup'ik. The presence of such diversity was a compelling reason for me to develop a language arts program that involved individual conferencing with the students and materials for a wide range of abilities and interests. I knew that if I wanted this vision to become a reality I had to lead by example. Successfully changing what happened in my classroom, I thought, might lay a foundation for future changes throughout the school.

Beginning the Workshops

I began implementing an adaptation of Nancie Atwell's readers' and writers' workshops.[1] Although I felt the changes were successful, by the end of the first year I identified areas where the program needed improvement. One area that concerned me was the reading log assignment. That first year students had used logs exclusively in response to their reading, and the logs did provide me with a valuable tool for assessing their progress. However, while many students used the logs to establish a dialogue about independent reading selections between students and with me, several students never moved beyond plot summaries in their logs, despite my detailed responses and examples of how they might reflect on their reading and record their reading experiences. Furthermore, the logs—tied as they were exclusively to reading workshop—gave me no insights regarding the students' writing processes. I frequently discovered during end-of-the-quarter conferences that students were experiencing frustrations, successes, and insights during writing workshop that I had been unaware of and that they did not express within the structures of the daily workshop.

I recognized that seventh grade students are very concerned about their relationships and status with their peers. For this reason they often feel pressured to keep their true opinions and emotions in check, while "blending in" with the class at large. I found this to be particularly evident in their reactions to whole-class reading selections and to group share[2] meetings focused on the students' writings. For example, if the popular students declared that a reading selection was "cheap," then a majority of others would make comments that supported this opinion. Yet, when I read their reading logs I discovered that in reality reactions to a piece varied widely. These logs showed me that some of the most critical (or positive) voices within the class had opinions that directly contradicted what they had said out loud in response to a reading. I saw this "gang mentality" toward other students' writing, too, particularly at the beginning of the year before we established group share guidelines to address this problem. On numerous occasions throughout that first year, I had heard students say things like: "I hate my story" or "My piece is stupid" or "You'll never do this one for group share." Then I would discover during a private teacher conference that the student really liked the piece, was indeed proud of it. It occurred to me that logs provided a confidential medium where the students could be sincere and not have to worry about their peers' reactions to their opinions and ideas. So why not open up the assignment to reflections on writing as well as reading? Thus, in my second year of implementing reading and writing workshops, I changed the reading log to a response log.

Teacher Research as a Vehicle for Learning

I decided for that second year to take a systematic approach to my own learning about teaching by conducting a study of my students' use of response logs. Based on my experiences during the first year of workshop implementation, I hypothesized that having students keep a response log in which they could reflect on their writing processes as well as their reading might provide me with important insights about their work as writers.

The Study

As I designed the study I determined I was interested in answers to two questions:

1.   Are response logs a valuable tool for learning about the students' experiences in writing workshop?
2.   What can I learn about student writing processes through the use of response logs?

The Assignment

In order to encourage the students to write about writing, a task I felt would be difficult, I dev eloped a page of questions to attach to their logs. I included this along with a help sheet for reading responses that I had created the previous year. I had developed this sheet for several reasons. Some of my students had a strong revulsion to ambiguity and responded negatively to a completely open log format. They wanted explicit instructions about what they should write. I also found I was continually repeating myself in my responses to students' entries, asking the same sorts of questions over and over. And, finally, when students would come to me to say, "I have nothing to say about this book. I liked it, but I don't know why and I just can't write anything about it," I often asked open-ended questions about the book that helped them to discover what they had to say. It seemed reasonable to provide these questions for students to refer to when they felt they needed that kind of help. Of course, I worried that providing a list of questions would encourage students to go down the list for each entry, resulting in dry, structured responses that would reveal little of substance about the students' reading experiences. But in students' responses to surveys I used, and in the content of the logs, I found that most students used the help sheet on a fairly regular basis only until they developed their own style and method for responding to reading. For others, a gentle nudge away from the help sheet encouraged them to use it more sparingly and thoughtfully. So the help sheets, a page about reading and a page about writing, were stapled into the back of every response log.

Another key component of the response log assignment was the homework log, a weekly sheet filled out by the student and signed by a parent. The previous year, several parents had contacted me expressing concern that I was not requiring homework. When I had responded that I expected students to read and write at home, these parents felt this was not sufficient. They wanted assignments from a grammar book and workbook, compositions about literature—the kind of work they had to do when they were in school. So, in order to satisfy the parents, and to create a record of the time students spent reading and writing outside of school, I instituted the homework log, which provided a record of the amount of time each student spent on language arts at home. I sent a letter to parents at the beginning of the year explaining the program. I also called several parents during the semester to encourage them to participate, and I reviewed this assignment in detail during a parent meeting. I was very pleased with the results. During the third week of school, approximately two-thirds of the homework logs (48 of 72) came back with a parent's signature. These reflected an average of 2.3 hours a week of reading and writing at home. At the end of the semester the return rate was over ninety percent, with an average of 3.6 hours per week of reading and writing reflected on the sheets. I think the homework log has been the single most important factor in the success of the response logs. It is much easier for the students to write thoughtfully about reading and writing in the response logs when they are in the routine of reading and writing at home.

My evaluation of the response log assignment was both formative and summative. The formative evaluations occurred weekly. Each class turned in logs on a different day of the week so that I wouldn't have to read a stack of 75 logs in one evening. I read and responded to each student's work and used a simple set of evaluation criteria. If the student had made a sincere effort to respond thoughtfully to individual and whole-class reading selections and to their experiences as writers (a minimum of three quality entries per week), had included a signed homework log reflecting a minimum of 2.5 hours of reading/writing at home, and the log was neat and turned in on time, it was worth ten points. If the student made an effort, but the log fell short in some way, it was worth five points, and I provided an explanation of how to improve the log. If the log was not turned in on time, or was obviously scribbled out at the last minute, the student received no points. The summative evaluation occurred at the end of the semester by way of individual conferences. I recorded the results of these conferences on a summative evaluation sheet. These end-of-semester conferences—where we looked through the log and reviewed interesting entries and the overall commitment to the log—provided insights and learning opportunities for the students and for me.

As I expected, the assignment went through a progression from chaos to order during the first semester. There was mass confusion during the first few weeks. Students copied pages out of their books. Some students were writing detailed plot summaries of their books. Some students were not bringing their logs to class. I then did three things that I believe were instrumental in turning the assignment around. First, I received permission from a student who had done a wonderful job on her log to make transparencies of a portion of it to share with the classes. I decided it was worth sharing as a demonstration, though I did worry that I might then see seventy-five duplicates of her form and style. This didn't happen, and the opportunities to discuss examples of thoughtful entries proved helpful to other students. Next, I instituted the Logging Festival. Students whose logs were not up to par, for whatever reason, were invited to attend a special logging session after school on Mondays. At first, I used this time to further explain the assignment. Later, it became a time for the students to read and work on their logs. At the beginning, I had a classroom full of students who for one reason or another had not completed their logs. By December, I had only five regular "loggers" who needed to come in every Monday after school for additional "logging" time. Finally, I arranged my schedule so that I would have at least an hour and a half on Tuesday, Wednesday and Thursday mornings—free from distractions and with a hot cup of coffee and soft music—to provide quality, thoughtful responses to the students' logs.

Toward the end of the first semester, after months of students' writing in them, carrying them around, and stuffing them into lockers, the logs were falling apart. I noticed that the physical deterioration seemed to perpetuate a spiritual deterioration. For example, I began to see a reappearance of the dreaded plot summaries, an indication that the students were losing interest in the assignment and were merely "getting it done." So, I went to PriceSavers in Anchorage and bought new spiral notebooks in a variety of colors for students to choose from. Preferring that students not use precious workshop time for clerical procedures, with my wife's help I stapled in new help sheets and sheets for recording the title/author/genre of independent reading selections. I did have the students number all of the pages in the log for easy reference to their entries. Then we revisited the purposes of the assignment and each student wrote a brief contract on the first page of the new log. The students were thrilled with these shiny new notebooks. Two weeks into the second semester the quality of the entries was better than ever before.

Data Collection

In order to answer my questions about the value of students using logs for reflections on their writing, I decided to systematically collect data from their logs during the first semester. I focused on collecting entries regarding writing. My procedure was simple. Each week I read the logs, put a paper clip on the pages with substantive entries regarding writing, and photocopied the tagged pages before returning the logs to students. Each week I sat down to read and reflect on these photocopied entries. I also had students respond to surveys at the end of each quarter and tabulated those results.

Discussion of Findings

At the end of the first semester, I examined the data for answers to my questions. I found the logs were valuable for learning about my students' writing processes in the following areas:

- How students find topics.
- Students' attitudes toward writing.
- Students' questions about writing.
- Variation in individual writing processes.
- How students feel about publishing.
- What students *really* think about their own and other students' writing.
- What happens during peer conferences.

In the following presentation and discussion of data, all student names are pseudonyms. Occasionally I have added punctuation where it was necessary to convey meaning. Otherwise, the entries appear exactly as they were written in the response logs.

How students find topics. Since it is often the place where writers begin with a piece, I'll focus first on reflections about selecting a topic. Although I occasionally had discussed with students where they found their topics, generally the discussions in the workshop were about what had happened after the topic was selected. However, several log entries during the course of the semester dealt with topic selection.

Anne was very shy and our conversations were limited in class. Generally she replied to a question with a yes, or a no, or a shrug. Although she began to open up more as the year progressed, her log helped me to see what was happening with her writing. Here is an excerpt from one of her entries.

> I'm writing a story about a boy getting a brain tumor. I got the idea from *Death Be Not Proud*.

I knew that she was reading *Death Be Not Proud,* but I hadn't realized she had made this connection between her reading and writing. During our status-of-the-class conferences,[3] which occurred at the beginning of each workshop, the students told me what genre they were working on, the draft number, whether they needed a peer conference or a teacher conference, and whether they needed a computer. Although I circulated through the room during the workshop, it was often several days from the time they began a piece to the time we first talked about it in any substantive fashion. After I read this entry and others like it that revealed that students were making a connection between their reading and writing, I was encouraged to talk with other students about this strategy for finding a topic.

Students' attitudes toward writing. Some of the entries revealed students' attitudes toward writing. For example, Beth used a voice in her log that was utterly distinct. She was at various times combative, reflective, sarcastic, whimsical and always a pleasure to read. I usually pulled her log from the stack to read when I needed a boost or a laugh. However, an observer in the class would have been hard pressed to select her from the group. She was generally very serious, shy, and busy as she went about her work. Her entries are examples of the "alternative voice" that sometimes emerges in a log, and further evidence of the value of logs in helping me to know my students. In log writing they can be themselves; in the classroom they have to be someone who "fits in." The following entry is from August, when I was first encouraging the students to reflect on how they write.

A NOTE ON WRITING

I think it's FUN!!! Except I'm going to be a chef, not a writer. My parents like to write. Last year I was into sad and depressing writing but this year I'm into poems and funny stuff and stories where everything rhymes. Things come to me easier if people don't tell me what to write like if they say write about trees I'll start out writing about trees but end up writing about exploding trees. Wait, no I mean exploding BRAINS! Sometimes my thoughts spill out my eyes but sometimes I have to scrounge the ground for ideas. I don't like to write a long page about what I don't like or things that drive me crazy. Because then I would go crazy and get funny feelings up and down my back.. Two things I would not write about or I mean two things that make my skin crawl like snakes. I hate snakes. More than any-

> thing in the world, I hate snakes! They're terrible! Hor-
> rible and Vile! Or caterpillars going up your nose! But I
> like to write about things I like. But if I write about
> chocolate, sometimes I crave it. I HAVE TO HAVE IT!
> Then I go berserk! So its hard to write about that.

I think this is a good example of an entry where I can see a little more of what is going on behind the scenes. It also reinforces my reasons for having a writers' workshop in the first place. Reading the research in support of writers' workshop is fine, but it is always more convincing to me to see the value in the words of a student: "I mean exploding BRAINS!"

Students' questions about writing. I also found entries that sought answers to questions students had about writing. Students asked questions regarding workshop concepts and procedures (drafting, pre-writing, revision, editing), as well as specific questions regarding a piece in progress. Again, the actual workshop period is a very busy time for everyone involved. Shy students in particular are reluctant to come to me with questions they fear might not seem pertinent. Being assigned to write about their writing in their logs meant students had time built into the writing program for reflection and for their questions to surface. As students became accustomed to this kind of thinking and writing, it seemed to me more questions emerged. The following example is also by Beth.

> I think for my next topic I'll do a Biography. Can you
> do that? And what exactly is it? Just wondering. I think
> a Biography would be SOOOOO neat!

When I wrote back I explained that it was more than all right to write a biography, noted the difference between a biography and an autobiography, and gave Beth some suggestions for starting out.

Variation in individual writing processes. We all know that writing processes vary from person to person and for any given writer at different times. Yet, the kind of information gathered on status-of-the-class sheets suggested to me that the vast majority of students used the elements of the writing process introduced at the beginning of the year in linear fashion:

1. Select a topic.
2. Pre-write.
3. Write draft one.
4. Confer with another student.
5. Write draft two.
6. Confer with the teacher.

7. Write the final draft or continue revision if needed.
8. Confer if necessary.
9. Publish.

True, students sometimes took a piece through as many as six or seven revisions, and other times did far fewer, but generally it was difficult to see exactly *how* a given student was progressing from selecting a topic to publication. Teacher-student conferences gave me some insights, as did monitoring the student response conferences, but the focus in conferences was usually on the writing itself, so I didn't have time to ask students about their process. Cassie is a talented writer. Early in the semester she wrote and shared a fiction piece in group share that was very well received. She subsequently submitted the piece to a national student publication. I was curious as to how she drafted her fiction. A response log entry gave me insight into her method.

> When I write, I just think up things as I go. First, I get the story in my mind. I write down the important things so I don't forget them. Next, I write the story. Sometimes as I go along I think of new things, and sometimes they're better than my other idea, so, I take out my first idea and put in the new way. I just keep doing that until my story's done.

From what I had observed during the workshop, I thought Cassie had the story all sketched out in her mind before she began. Her drafting took place at a fairly rapid speed. I knew from our conferences that she revised as she wrote draft one. But it was interesting to hear that she often wrote down "the important things," her own way of pre-writing, and that she continued the process of revising as her stories unfolded. After reading this entry, I was better equipped to discuss a piece in progress with her, because I understood more about the way she approached the stories she created. I knew that she would probably not have an ending in mind until she reached that point in her writing, and that everything in the draft was tentative because she was always considering "new ways."

Deborah grew tremendously as a writer during the first semester. Her first fiction piece was a struggle for her. The following series of entries provided valuable insights regarding the frustrations she was experiencing.

9/9/90

> Today I was thinking about how my story in writing was going to end. I think my story will end with a surprise party. I think the stories are easier to write then poems, because stories are more me. Poems are nice but I have a hard time writing about specific things. I don't like to write them.

At this point she is well into her first draft and feels good about it.

9/11/90

> In writing I've finished my first draft of "The Big Surprise." Mr. C read it during group share today. He gave me suggestions to make my piece better for my second draft. I think my story is a very good one. I think I'm going to write a story again after I'm done with this story.

So far so good. The class responded well to the piece and we all offered suggestions for revision. I was pleased that she had volunteered for group share because many of the students were reluctant to share early in the quarter.

9/17/90

> Today in writing I hardly did anything. The story that I'm revising is very stupid. The story totally doesn't make sense in the end. I want to ditch the whole story and start a new one. This is just one big frustrating story. I can't get it the way I want to.

During the workshop on this day, I had noticed Deborah sitting at the computer staring at the monitor a great deal of the time. But I had no idea she was having this kind of trouble. At the end of the workshop, she closed her file and went back to her seat. She didn't give me any indication that she was frustrated with the piece. After reading this entry in her log, I scheduled a conference with her. I encouraged her to try one last time, giving her suggestions for revising her ending, which was confusing. She left the conference willing to tackle it again, but I could see she was still obviously frustrated. We talked again, and she decided to put the piece away for awhile and to begin something new. As she worked on her next piece of fiction, she managed to avoid similar frustration by doing more preplanning of her story. I suspect that if I had not understood from her log her level of frustration with the first piece, I might have pushed her inappropriately to continue working on it.

Especially during the first quarter of the workshop, I find students abandon much of their work. Although this is reasonable at times, I try to encourage students to work through their problems so they can learn how to deal with difficult questions in revision. I don't want students to become hooked on first draft writing and to find it easier to abandon a piece than to struggle through the process. At the same time, I don't want students to become so frustrated that they are inhibited in the workshop. Thanks to these log entries about what Deborah was experiencing with her writing, I was able to offer the support she needed to move on to something else at this time.

How students feel about publishing. As I have noted, most seventh graders experience two "selves." There is the public self, desperate to fit into the group; and there is the private self, where the individual is groping for an identity and where a great deal more honesty and risk-taking is possible.

Ed was upset after the first issue of our quarterly magazine came out. He complained fairly loudly, perhaps for the benefit of others, that his piece was the worst one in the issue and that he would not publish again until he was sure he had written something "really good."

I told him that I felt the piece was a good start for so early in the school year, and pointed out several positive aspects to his piece. He said, "You say things like that to everyone." (No one ever said that teaching seventh graders would be a life affirming, affectionate journey into the warmth of the human heart.) I thought he just needed a little public positive reinforcement and didn't think of it again until his log came in two days later.

> The Seventh Sun cover looks a lot better than last year's. I feel sort of proud of myself that I published a story. Its not like a big book or something but its pretty good. I think the Seventh Sun is good thing to do. I also like to read storys and things that I haven't heard of and places that I haven't seen.

This is the kind of commentary that seldom occurs "in public." It truly is a risk for students to publish their work in our publication. The magazine is read by the entire junior high student body, and there is always the possibility that authors will receive negative comments about their work from their classmates. However, I've found that despite frequent public put-downs of their own work, students tend to enjoy seeing their work published and feel a sense of accomplishment, as this last entry suggests.

What students really think about their own and other students' writing. I have referred often to the public and private "selves" of seventh graders. Nowhere is this more evident than during group share. I can almost predict how the response will go based on the "status" of the writer in the community. There are surprises, but generally students do not criticize the work of the more popular students, while praise can be somewhat sparse for the students who are not part of the "in group." For this reason I look closely at what the students write in their logs concerning other students' writing, and I frequently share positive information with the writers. The log is also a place for the personal, more reflective responses that don't happen as easily in the context of group share.

Felicia seldom spoke during group share. Although a good writer, she either didn't feel comfortable offering responses or didn't trust her responses to be helpful to other writers. The same was true when we discussed pieces published in our magazine. In her log I found she did have ideas to share with others. The following entry reveals a connection she made with the writer of a piece of fiction.

> I like all of the stories in the Seventh Sun. I especially like Susan's piece. It showed how she felt in the story and she was also kind of like telling us how dogs seem to act when they are pregnant and ready to have the puppies. I liked the names that she gave the puppies. My favorites were Mercury, She-Ra, Wonder Woman and Zeus.

Susan had not been especially happy with the piece, but reluctantly had agreed to publish it. With the permission of Felicia, I shared her log entry with Susan, who was very pleased. So, the logs provided another avenue for response to authors.

Besides the insights they have provided regarding students' responses to other students' writing, logs have proven particularly useful for determining students' attitudes toward their own works in progress. For example, Gail spent the entire first quarter on a mini-novella. She was continually revising as she wrote the first draft, and although I was certain the rest of the students would enjoy reading the piece, and that it was a moving, quality piece of fiction, Gail's own attitude toward the piece was very critical. In this entry she discusses her frustration.

> Writing hasn't been that great lately. I really don't want to write this story. I think my story's stupid because I keep dragging on and on and I really don't know how to write it since I don't have the experience of parents dying, so I really don't know how it'd feel. I think I want to write an article for the Tundra Drums about the Jr. High Basketball Team in Atmauthluk. I think that will be better.

After reading this entry, I spoke with Gail and we discussed her reasons for abandoning the piece. I pointed out some specific strengths of the piece and encouraged her to continue. She replied that she didn't want to "waste time" on something that wasn't going to turn out "right." Through my own writing experience, I know that it is sometimes worthwhile to put a piece away for awhile and then to come back with a fresh perspective. We decided she should put the piece away for a few weeks, but should consider returning to it during the second quarter. She did, and after two more weeks of intense writing and revision, she finished a first draft. Because she had been revising so heavily during this first-draft writing, I felt the draft was ready to share. During an evening session in the computer lab, I asked her if we could bring it to group share.

Reluctantly she agreed, but insisted she be allowed to leave the room while we were reading and discussing the piece. Since it was a long piece (ten single-spaced, typed pages with a small font), I photocopied a class set so that students could read along as I read orally. After we read the piece and discussed it, I asked the students to write a short response to the writer on a 3 by 5 card. The responses were overwhelmingly positive. Students wrote that they had tears in their eyes while reading the ending, that it reminded them of a death in their family, that they felt like "they were really there." After the meeting, when the writer returned from her self-imposed exile, I reviewed some of the responses with her and asked if I could repeat the process with my other classes. She agreed, and the other classes had similarly positive responses. We did discover some incongruities in the ending, and she decided to take the students' advice and clarify the resolution. She was truly amazed by the positive responses and agreed to publish the piece as an entry in our Serious Fiction contest. Considering the fact that at one point she felt that her story was "stupid" and that she wanted to abandon it, I was thrilled to see the evolution of this piece to a point where we could publish it. Gail's log entry following this experience reflects her newly found confidence.

> Writing has been really good this week. Mr. C read my story to all three seventh grade classes and they wrote some pretty good responses. I didn't really realize people thought my story was THAT good. I guess it was a good first experience. I think I'll be more willing to share my stories in the future. I hope I get my story done by the end of the first semester.   Thanks Mr. C.!

Seeing students grow as they expand their sphere of comfort and confidence makes writers' workshop for me an exciting way to teach writing. The response logs helped me to understand more clearly the successes these students experienced.

What happens during peer conferences. Finally, the logs provided information for me about how students benefited from peer conferences. During our workshops, students could ask to confer with a peer after completing a first draft, or if they got stuck while writing a first draft. In my experience, conferencing seemed to be most effective when students worked in pairs. I found that when more than two students joined a conference group, they had difficulty focusing on responses to the author's writing.

When a student requested a peer conference, I tried to select a conference partner who was compatible with the writer but was not at the time deeply engrossed in a writing project. A small entryway leading to my room provided an ideal place for conferring. Furnished with a table and chairs, and with a door to shut it off from the classroom, students could talk without disturbing other writers. Students used a conference form to record the highlights of the meeting, handing it to me when they returned to the classroom from the conference. Although I felt certain that quality responses were frequent in the conferences, my only sense of what happened during these conversations came from the notes on the conference form. During my conferences with students and during informal conversations I discussed ways of responding, but the logs provided valuable additional insights regarding these student-to-student meetings.

Hilary had just finished her first draft of a very good poem. She asked during a status-of-the-class meeting if she could confer with a friend of hers. Because they were close friends, and because I had found it is most difficult for students to offer substantive responses to poetry, I feared they might use the opportunity to catch up on gossip. Nonetheless, I agreed to the conference. The meeting was relatively short, lasting about ten minutes. On her return, Hilary immediately asked to use a computer. The following day she had a conference with me about her piece and I was impressed at how the piece had changed from draft one to draft two. She said that her friend had "given her some good ideas." When I read her log the next week, I gained a more detailed picture of what had transpired.

> Today Amy read my poem. She liked it. she said that it ran smoothly. The only part that she didn't like was the part where it says something like the layer of freshly fallen snow tracked with car tires. She said that it made it stumble a bit. So, I changed it to birds feet. Does it sound better this way? Or do you think car tires is better?

The poem, written from the point of view of a narrator staring out of a window, had a very tranquil, somber mood. The "car tires" did disrupt the flow and mood of the poem. The student hadn't mentioned her reason for changing the line during our conference, and I hadn't known that she still felt unsure about the change. The poem turned out well, and we published it in our magazine. But if I hadn't seen her log entry I would not have understood the importance of what happened during the conference with her friend. After that, the two frequently responded successfully to each other's work. I also asked Amy to respond to other students' poetry because I saw she had a knack for it.

Conclusions

Are response logs a valuable tool for learning about students' experiences in writing workshop? Do log entries provide information about students' writing processes? My answer to both questions is a definite yes. Several dialogues occurred within the logs that I am confident would not have occurred otherwise. These provided a window for me to view students' writing processes in ways that don't otherwise happen in a class of twenty-five seventh graders. The students and I were able to establish a rapport independent of their concern about the opinions and reactions of their peers. The logs showed me where students had been during their writing journeys and helped me to improve the ways the workshop supported their individual growth as writers. I guess you might call these entries "tracks in the snow."

Where Did the Teacher Research Vehicle Take Me?

I spent two years developing reading and writing workshops. I learned a lot that changed my classroom and my teaching. I looked forward to the discussions my experiences might foster about change in the traditional structures within that junior high school; but the discussions never took place because I packed up and moved to a school that was well on its way to becoming a "true" middle school. My teaching assignment since then has precluded further reading and writing workshop development. However, I have gained additional insights about middle level students.

The most important idea that is continually reinforced for me is one discussed in the Introduction to this book: "Learning has both personal and social dimensions." I see this continuously in learner-centered classrooms where students are grappling with fundamental issues that affect their lives. Not only must we be *aware* of these characteristics of learning, but we must make a concerted effort to learn how these dimensions function for each student. The workshops and the response log assignment I used helped me to tap into both the personal and the social dimensions of learning. When students began to write about writing, it opened my eyes to a world that I could only guess about before.

A second idea appearing in the Introduction that is reinforced for me—also grounded in the literature about teaching and learning and in my continuing experiences as a learner and a teacher—is: "When teachers and students make choices and take responsibility for curriculum, engagement in learning increases." Nowhere in education is this more true than in the middle school. Our students are experiencing radical changes in their world view and in their personal development: emotional, physical, and psychological. It takes a concentrated effort on the part of teachers to recognize areas of interest and strength among the students so that they become engaged. Student empowerment is not a trivial concept to embellish our practice; it is a matter of survival.

Sharing Progress Toward the Vision with New Colleagues

The middle school where I am teaching now is making progress toward the kind of middle school vision promoted in this book and in the work of educators such as James Beane[4] and Stevenson and Carr.[5] We haven't arrived yet, but like my workshop students we are all pursuing the illusory goal of excellence. Once we reach what appears to be a pinnacle, we find that it flattens out to a plateau with another ridge just beyond.

End Notes

1. Nancie Atwell, *In the Middle: Writing, Reading, and Learning with Adolescents* (Portsmouth, NH: Heinemann, 1987).
2. Atwell, 84–86.
3. Atwell, 89–92.
4. James A. Beane, *A Middle School Curriculum: From Rhetoric to Reality*, Second Edition (Columbus, OH: National Middle School Association, 1993).
5. Chris Stevenson and Judy F. Carr, Integrated Studies in the Middle Grades: "Dancing Through Walls" (New York: Teachers College Press, 1993).

PART II

Organizing Classrooms for Whole Learning:
The Link Between Teacher Innovation and
Administrative Support

Chapter 6

Hooked on History: A Cooperative Approach to Integrating History and Language Arts at the Middle School Level

Shirlee Jellum

It all started in the middle of a spelling test. You know the one: 20 unrelated words, each letter slowly articulated as it's pronounced—*vaaaacuuuum*—then punctuated in Dick and Jane sentences for complete understanding: "Will you please *va cuum* the floor?" and finally repeated for emphasis: *VACUUM*.

Anyway, halfway through the next sentence I felt stupid, so stupid, in fact, that I began laughing—each word felt foreign, each sentence felt forced, even my voice felt phony. A few kids looked up, anticipating a joke, but they couldn't see anything funny about the singsong sentence that followed. Fortunately, I did, and between chuckles I announced the test was over (a couple of cheers), we'd no longer be taking spelling tests (several more whoops and hollers), and by the way, pass your spelling books forward, we're not using them anymore (footstomping and applause).

"Why?" the one perfect speller asked, eyeing me suspiciously.

"Who cares?" someone else shot back.

"That's why," I answered, pointing to the smart aleck. "Because nobody cares about spelling lists, and no one really learns from them."

Now was my chance to condense, organize, and explain what I'd learned during the previous five days spent at my first International Reading Association conference. For the remainder of the class period I enthusiastically shared my newfound knowledge of whole language in terms my middle school students could understand and appreciate: no more writing workbooks, no more grammar textbooks, no more literature anthologies and, yes, no more spelling tests.

"But how are we going to learn without any textbooks?" the

studious one asked.

"By reading and writing and discussing *real* literature," I answered.

Opening the Door to Change

It's not often we can pinpoint the exact moment of change. Usually it is a gradual process, carefully examined and evaluated either before it is implemented or after it has occurred. Yet, in a matter of seconds, I changed from tyrannical, textbook-toting teacher to dedicated whole language learner.

What led up to such a drastic decision? It wasn't the compelling testimonies of classroom teachers-in-transition, nor the spellbinding speeches of renowned researchers; it wasn't the words of famous writers, nor the wisdom of enlightened college professors. It was the voices of young children—their humorous to heartwrenching stories written in pictures and poems and prose, punctuated with dots and dashes and squiggles, and *spelled just the way the words sounded.* For five days I had listened to teachers translate the invented spelling of their primary students, but it wasn't until I was back in my eighth grade classroom, dutifully finishing a spelling unit begun by my substitute, that I learned *my* lesson: I'd been too dependent on the forces of tradition—especially the textbook.

I'd been trained to believe that the textbook was the backbone of education; in fact it has often been *the* curriculum. No wonder my students cheered when I collected their spelling books! Plagued with piles of textbooks—I was using an embarrassing *four* in my language arts class!—my students suffered from textbook overload. Not even the flashy photographs or eye-catching cartoons in the updated editions could entice them to read. So I did what many sympathetic teachers in the same dilemma would like to do: I opened new doors to authentic learning experiences based on whole language principles.

Not bound by state law, school policy, or even professional guilt to use textbooks, I easily moved from a traditional skills and drills mentality to a holistic, process-oriented philosophy. Using Nancie Atwell's *In the Middle*[1] as a guide, my students and I explored the richness and diversity of reading genuine literature and writing from personal experience. Freed from the constraints of the textbooks, we collectively took risks, made decisions, and set goals. Every day we eagerly read the classics—from Shakespeare, Poe and Cather to the contemporary favorites of Anthony, Hinton and L'Amour. Every day we wrote letters, poetry, biographies, stories, essays and plays. We had finally become owners of opportunities to read, write, explore, discover and grow. And it was this atmosphere, rich with relevancy, that prompted Kirk, the history teacher, to ask questions.

Confronted with outdated history textbooks, he asked what he could do to liven up the study of names, dates and lists. He wondered what he could do to generate interest and enthusiasm among classes of unmotivated middle schoolers.

Don't ask what *you* can do; ask what *we* can do," I responded. Then I shared with him what I'd shared with my students after their short-circuited spelling test; I talked with him about the principles underlying whole language theory and instruction. I described our successful, year-long transition from a traditional, textbook-driven curriculum to a holistic, literature-based study of language arts. Encouraged by his interest and enthusiasm, I suggested that we *truly* put whole language theory into practice by moving from a strictly departmentalized curriculum to an interdisciplinary approach to learning. I explained that, by combining history and language study through collaborative efforts, we could provide authentic learning experiences, basic to whole language philosophy. He wholeheartedly agreed. Over the next three years we pooled our resources and combined our energy, ideas, and expertise. We sought to provide meaningful opportunities for our middle schoolers to develop a love for learning.

The Lure of Literature

Along the road to becoming a whole language teacher, I learned the value of using literature as an avenue for learning. Textbook-driven instruction often focuses on memorization of facts. I pursued a literature-based approach that assumed readers would process information according to personal interest, prior knowledge, and a passion for learning. My own experience of assigning a multitude of textbook activities for each separate unit of study, amidst a cacophony of complaints, told me that approach was limiting. So I banished the textbooks to the backshelf and brought literature into the language arts classroom, starting with personal copies of paperback novels and books scrounged from garage sales and eventually adding young adult fiction purchased through student book clubs and school catalogues. Convincing Kirk to do the same was easy.

We both knew from experience that textbooks couldn't always provide the multi-dimensional learning opportunities we wanted our students to experience. We knew from our students' grimaces and groans that overuse of textbooks often precipitated pessimism toward learning. Kirk was acutely aware of student antagonism toward history and was ready for a change. So together we imagined humdrum historical facts springing to life through the body, heart, and soul of literature. We envisioned the lackluster lives of Puritans and politicians becoming animated accounts in biographies. We visualized irrelevant events on timelines becoming action-packed adventures in historical novels. Integrating literature into the history curriculum was our first collaborative challenge. Finding literary works suitable for all levels of interest and ability was our first step.

In a little over a year, I had accumulated hundreds of books in my classroom library, including dozens of classic and contemporary historical novels and biographies. With generous administrative support and help from our school librarian, we added a small but diverse library to the history class. Students now had access to historical books in both classes, a small but significant first step toward integrating the two courses.

Our next collaborative step was deciding how we'd incorporate historical literature into both our classes without overwhelming the students or overtaxing ourselves. Students already read self-selected literature an hour a day in my class; we needed to carefully think through how to frame the requirement to read historical books for credit in both classes without usurping their newfound freedom of choice. So, to create interest and spark curiosity, we decided to read stories *to* them.

We began by reading personal favorites, usually short, fast-action novels, biographies, and even some humorous poetry. I began with *Trouble River* by Betsy Byars,[2] an action-packed story about a young boy and his grandmother's wild raft ride down a river to safety. Kirk read a series of short, high-interest biographies, *Woman Chief* by Sobol[3] being a class favorite. By the time we'd each read aloud our first novels, they were hooked! But we didn't stop there. We continued reading aloud, knowing increased interest, knowledge, and relevancy weren't the only advantages of listening to literature. Students who were auditory learners and those who were reluctant, poor, or nonreaders especially benefited from being read to. They learned along with the more capable students and, as a result, everyone gained an awareness and appreciation of history unparalled in my previous experience. "I like read alouds," one student wrote, "because they give you ideas." Another added, "When somebody reads me something, I can understand it more and get a feel for the book." New ideas, better understanding, increased interest, improved skills—whatever the value of reading aloud might be—the lure of literature was the bait needed to get our students hooked on history.

Fishing for ideas on how to further integrate whole language principles into our classes, Kirk surveyed his students. Using current events and the history text for ideas, small groups brainstormed areas of interest ranging from historical events to contemporary social concerns. Then, as classes, they compiled, categorized, and discussed all options before casting ballots. *World Conflict: Wars from Past to Present* was our first unit of study for both history and language arts.

Next we co-planned the unit, combining our resources and sharing the responsibility of teaching and learning about war. Four major components emerged. Two were students' requests: a letter-writing campaign to soldiers in the Persian Gulf, and a formal debate on the pros and cons of the Vietnam War. Two were teacher-selected: an analysis of current events and the study of historical literature. Kirk and I felt all four components were valuable for three reasons. First, students had ownership in helping design the curriculum. Second, all four units represented the integration of reading, writing, listening, and speaking. Finally, along with their study of the history of world conflict, students would study current issues, making the curriculum more relevant.

We gave students time in both classes to discuss current events, practice debate, write letters, and read books. For the remaining classtime, we divided the instructional responsibilities into areas of expertise. Kirk selected current events and debate, while I focused on letter writing and literature. Though separated by walls and limited by the time constraints resulting from different prep periods, we still managed to collaborate in each phase of the planning process from instruction to evaluation. The two most integrated elements—debate and literature—deserve elaboration.

The current conflict in the Persian Gulf sparked informal, yet intense, discussions over the value of war. Several of our students had friends or family either stationed in Saudi Arabia or on standby. Emotions ran high. Unsubstantiated arguments about our involvement eventually led to speculation about the Vietnam War. (Similarly, many students had relatives or acquaintances who had served in Southeast Asia.) Through mutual interest and agreement, students decided to formally debate the pros and cons of U.S. involvement in the Vietnam War.

To introduce the concept of debate, my colleague and I videotaped ourselves debating the pros and cons of wearing hats in the classroom, a hotly-disputed topic at the middle school. Changing from hats to wigs to sunglasses to depict alternating panelists, we demonstrated the process of debate in an entertaining manner.

Following our introduction, Kirk helped develop students' debating skills while I helped refine their research skills in mini-lessons. For the next few weeks, our students simultaneously studied subjects ranging from logic and locution to paraphrasing and parenthetical citations. By debate deadline, our students were well-equipped to enthusiastically and effectively argue their points of view. We videotaped the final debate, using it not only as a model for future units involving debate, but also as a self-evaluation tool. Students critiqued their own as well as their peers' performances on a simple rating scale of poor to excellent in areas including preparedness, persuasion, and public speaking skills.

Creating curriculum from our students' interests and expertise in combination with our own judgment as teachers provided meaningful, authentic learning opportunities. Following the debate, our collaborative efforts continued throughout the semester with the study of historical fiction.

Once we had exposed students to the richness and diversity of historical fiction through read alouds, we began to require that each student read and respond to one historical book per month. By now they were eager to select their own novels from the wide array available in our classroom and school libraries. To meet the varied interests and abilities of all students, we expanded the options to include thematically related nonfiction and even some science fiction ("what-if" books such as *Z for Zachariah* by Robert O'Brien,[4] *After the Bomb* by Gloria Micklowitz,[5] and *The Children's Story* by James Clavell[6]).

During our study of the Vietnam War, students devoured books like *Young Man in Vietnam* by Charles Coe,[7] and *Fallen Angels* by Walter Dean Myers,[8] debating their social and literary merits in dialogue journals. Similarly, novels of conflict ranging from the French and Indian War (*Fawn* by Robert Newton Peck[9] was a favorite) through World War II (books on the Holocaust were in high demand, with *Night* by Elie Wiesel[10] and *Diary of a Young Girl* by Anne Frank[11] frequently on reserve) lined their lockers and bulged from bookbags. Historical literature had become the hot topic, fueling their imaginations with fact-based, fast-paced accounts of real people fighting in real wars.

To record their reading progress, each student kept a dialogue journal, a collection of personal responses written in letter format to friends, teachers, and in some cases, parents. We expected students to write at least one letter a week, focusing on a different element of literature in each response. Again, Kirk and I shared instructional responsibilities: while I introduced the elements of literature in mini-lessons (plot, character, conflict, setting, theme), he led discussions about the social, political and economic significance of war. Together, we provided the broad knowledge-base needed for a wide range of student responses. As a result, many literature letters were not only informative, demonstrating what they *learned*, but also insightful, revealing how they *felt*.

In response to *The Vicksburg Veteran*, a nonfiction book by Monjo,[12] one student wrote:

3-11

Mrs. Jellum,

I wouldn't be afraid to die at fourteen if I believed in what I was fighting for. Also the main character, Fred, is U.S. Grant's son. And U.S. Grant was one of the best generals in history. If I was fighting alongside my dad I wouldn't be afraid at all. And I think Fred felt that way too.

This book is true. The fight at and to get to Vicksburg is all true. The characters actually existed. This book was knarlly.

Jesse

Students, curious about their novels' historical accuracy, began reading introductions, gaining valuable insight concerning authenticity, as reflected in this student's response:

Mon. Feb. 25

Dear Mrs. Jellum,

For my history book I am reading the book, *The Last Silk Dress* by Ann Rinaldi.[13] Today in Social Studies I started to read it. In the beginning she has an author note. In it she says that some of the characters are real people and some of them are made up like some of the cernals in the war.

It takes place in the Civil War. It's about a 14 year old girl who comes up with the idea of collecting everybody's silk dresses and making a hot air baloon to use to spy on the Yankee's.

If there ever was a silk baloon nobody really knows. Some people say there was and some people say no way. Ann Rinaldi believes there was so she decided to write a book on it.

Sara

In response to character believability in *The Last Mission* by Henry Mazer,[14] another student writes:

March 6

Dear Mrs. Jellem,

His disquise was very believable. He was very big, or tall, and muscular for his age. He got away with it because of his size. It was volenteer work. He was so committed because he hated Hitler, because he was a Jew. He can't write his friends or his family because he's afraid of being caught.

Anyway's, he was on a mission when his plane went down. Now he is a P.O.W. for the Germans. He's not sure if he's going to be killed or not.

Mandy

With war raging in the Persian Gulf, the lure of historical literature about war was strong. In the comfort and safety of the classroom, students could experience the atrocities of war, often from a teenage protagonist's point of view. Many student responses expressed concern for a main character:

3-4-91

Shirlee,

I finally got the book *My Brother Sam is Dead.*[15] It was worth the wait! I love it! I've never read a book like this before. Like old time fashion, back in the war days.

I think Sam's father is mean. For example, when Sam came home from college, the whole family hadn't seen him since Christmas and the father doesn't even greet him, instead he gives an order. I think that was rude myself. I wouldn't want to be greeted like that!

This is taking place in the Revolutionary War. And the father doesn't want his son to fight! Sam wants to fight though in the war against the British which they call the "Lobsterbacks."

Kelly

Frequently, students made connections between historical conflicts and the current Gulf War:

March 18, 91

Dear Mrs. Jellum,

Yesterday I read 100 pages in my war book. I found out the South during the war had a lack of supplies. One lady had to buy new shoes, but she couldn't find any in town, so she remade the soles. Rosemary made the soles out of an old coat.

It was a good book in the begging but then it got boring. Now it is good and I can relate how the Civil War is different from the Gulf.

The Gulf was not as bad, as far as the lack of supplies. But they are the same in just plain war. Understand?

Well gotta read, Happy reading and writing.

Sincerly,

Martha

Yes, I understood. From poignant to provocative, analytic to evaluative, their fears and fantasies about war became relevant opportunities to read and respond to literature. Had Kirk and I merely required students to memorize facts, we never would have uncovered their curiosity, compassion, or concern for real characters facing real conflicts in past and present wars.

From Process to Product

Traditionally, at the end of each unit, we had both given our students final tests, requiring them to demonstrate their knowledge and comprehension (or lack of it, in many cases) of teacher-assigned topics of study. Because we both strongly believed in a student-centered, integrated approach to learning *and* evaluation, we gave our students the opportunity to apply their knowledge and understanding of war through a student-designed "affective project." We gave them a few guidelines to get started: students had the option of working individually or in small groups; each project had to include a reading, writing, speaking, and artistic component; students had to show the development of their written work, from prewriting to final draft. Our emphasis on the *process* as well as the *product* led students to value their learning as an ongoing endeavor, not just as a final outcome.

We provided time in both classes for students to work individually and in teams. After a semester of reading, writing, researching, debating, and discussing the pros and cons of war, our students collectively produced some of the finest works of art we'd witnessed in all our years at the middle school.

Culminating projects ranging from songwriting and soap carving to pen sketches and poetry lined our bulletin boards and bookshelves. Collages decorated doorways, historical newspapers hung in hallways, and videotaped docudramas demonstrated the humor and hellishness of war. On tape we witnessed examples of women's roles in the Civil War, from the grieving mother who lost both sons, to the heroic nurses on the battlefield. We eavesdropped on an interview with Hitler, Hussein, and Bush. We felt the agony of a family torn apart by the Revolutionary War. We read letters from frightened young men on the front line and desperate diary entries by a dead soldier's sister. We saw pages of discussion notes transformed into a narrative poem about the Civil War; two students collaborated to produce a poem about the current Gulf Crisis.

The Gulf War

People murdered
Families apart
Cities destroyed
The Gulf War starts

Oil in oceans
Protest in D.C.
Shortage of food
Scattered missile debris

Prisoners of War
American flags high
Gas masks in Isreal
Soldiers saying good bye

Massacre in Kuwait
Trouble in Baghdad
Taxes for war
Saddam going mad

Cease fire is called
Peace on the way
Negotiations made
End of war some say

News is spread
Soldiers come back
Families together
Both white and black

War no more
Countries at peace
Iraq is questionable
Saddam doesn't cease

Civilians protesting
Soldiers commanded
To kill the innocent
Peace is not granted

No freedom
No consideration
Saddam still a madman
A separated nation

by Angela and Crystal

Kirk and I encouraged students to explore their own attitudes toward war and to express their understanding of its complexities. They made personal connections with their learning that we rarely saw when we had simply required students to memorize and re-gurgitate a list of facts and figures. Monica's poignant tribute to her uncle eloquently illustrates this point:

Lies

They load up the airplanes,
waving their good byes.
Not knowing the government
had told them many lies.
Lined up in the jungles,
praying for their lives,
It's sad to think how many
had gone and left their wives.
They never came home heroes,
as though it was in vain.
And now to the government,
"Remember all their pain."
They wake up close to midnight,
hearing sounds of war,
Wishing it was all behind
a tightly locked door.
Walking through the jungle,
holding to their guns,
Hoping that one day
they'd have a couple sons.
Looking at the T.V.,
hearing dad is dead,
Mom looks up at heaven,
"Remember what you said."
So people were out there dying,
and the government still lying.
Her little kids are sighing,
not knowing why she's crying.
While over in that country,
their big brave daddy's dying.

by Monica

Making the Grade

Kirk and I also shared grading responsibilities. Because our sub-jects remained departmentalized and our report card system con-ventional, we were required to assign grades for our individual courses. To make our curricular integration more meaningful for students and more satisfying to us, students received the same grades on assignments and projects in both classes. For example, students who received an A for the historical literature component in language arts received the equivalent grade in history. Similarly, grades in history for the final debate had equal value in language arts. Final projects received identical grades in both classes.

The first year we began our interdisciplinary program, joint evaluation was relatively simple: after we developed evaluation criteria for collaborative assignments and projects, we graded work assigned and completed in our own classes, then made photocopies of the students' final grades for each other. The following year, when we received a common prep period, we continued grading collaborative assignments in our separate classes but communicated about our students' progress on a daily basis. Then, as we became more knowledgeable and comfortable with nontraditional grading procedures, we maintained student portfolios and elicited self-evaluations as part of our assessment process.

Assigning the same grade in both classes simplified our grading responsibilities and increased student motivation and success. Because students were working on integrated projects in both classes, they experienced half the normal number of assignments; thus learning efficiency increased. As a result, we witnessed a dramatic improvement in the overall quality of students' work. And when they began to self-evaluate their projects, justifying the grades they thought they deserved based on the effort and improvement evident in their portfolios, the *process* as well as the *product* became equally important in assessing their academic growth and success.

Empowering our students with decision-making abilities from project selection to final evaluation gave them a sense of ownership in their learning. "I like it because it gives you a choice," Brandon said. "I like it too," Karina stated. "It makes you more willing to work when you know it's what you chose." Amber added, "I like it better. I want to make my own decisions." Every step of the way students decided which units to study, which books to read, which topics to debate, and eventually which projects to grade. We provided the guidance, structure, and resources.

One Step At a Time

Moving from a traditional, departmentalized curriculum toward a transactional, interdisciplinary model took time: five years to be exact. Even though our *decision* to integrate occurred during a conversation, the transition itself was often a slow, painstaking process of trial and error. Not everything we tried worked. We had our moments of frustration, dissatisfaction and disillusionment. What worked for one class didn't always work for another, from day to day or year to year. What *did* work, however, was our willingness to take risks and, in the process, to learn from our mistakes.

One mistake I made in my transition from a textbook- to literature-based classroom was changing too much too quickly. I found out (the hard way) what it feels like to dive in head first before learning how to swim. During the weeks following the spelling test incident, I barely kept my head above water, but with patience and perseverance I was able to move into summer making plans for fall.

"One step at a time" was my motto that first fall. Kirk and I began to integrate a year later. We began slowly, introducing each component separately, beginning with the two of us simply reading aloud until students were comfortable with the concept of integration. After each new step, Kirk and I analyzed, discussed, and revised everything from instructional strategies to evaluation procedures. Because integration made sense, it didn't take long for the students to accept this new way of learning and ultimately *expect* it in their other classes. Predictably, not all teachers felt the same way we did.

For interdisciplinary instruction to succeed, not only do teachers have to mutually *decide they want it*, but the administrators have to *support their decision*. Our move to an integrated curriculum evolved out of personal desire, *not* administrative edict. We were ready for an integrated curriculum, and our administrators provided the financial and moral support we needed. Though they publicly promoted the district's move toward whole language, our administrators remained sensitive to the needs of *all* teachers, especially to those who felt threatened or intimidated by any kind of change. As a result of their leadership, we maintained our positive professional relationships with other teachers despite some philosophical differences.

It's been eight years since I stopped giving spelling tests. Seven years since I started writing workshop. Six years since I read aloud my first historical novel. In all that time I haven't heard one demand for a textbook, one complaint about reading, one groan about writing . . . until now. I'm currently teaching English at the high school level, where a departmentalized curriculum is standard procedure and textbook assignments are a daily expectation. Again, I'm fortunate to have a supportive administration, one that encourages innovation and experimentation, one that is willing to take risks. With their help, I'm hoping to connect once again with a history teacher who wants to create a relevant, inquiry-centered, interdisciplinary learning environment for students. In the meantime, within the context of the English classroom, I continue to offer students opportunities to explore and appreciate the richness and diversity of literature. But even more important, my students are developing a love affair with learning, by making connections, making choices, and making meaning out of their lives.

End Notes

1. Nancie Atwell, *In the Middle: Writing, Reading, and Learning with Adolescents* (Portsmouth, NH: Heinemann, 1987).
2. Betsy Byars, *Trouble River* (New York: Viking Press, 1969).
3. Rose Sobol, *Woman Chief* (New York: Dial Press, 1976).
4. Robert O'Brien, *Z for Zachariah* (New York: Atheneum, 1975).
5. Gloria Micklowitz, *After the Bomb* (New York: Delacorte Press, 1987).
6. James Clavell, *The Children's Story* (New York: Delacorte Press, 1981).
7. Charles Coe, *Young Man in Vietnam* (New York: Four Winds Press, 1968).
8. Walter Dean Myers, *Fallen Angels* (New York: Scholastic, Inc., 1988).
9. Robert Newton Peck, *Fawn* (Boston: Little Brown, 1975).
10. Elie Wiesel, *Night* (New York: Bantam, 1982).
11. Anne Frank, *Diary of a Young Girl* (Garden City, NY: Pocket Books, 1952).
12. F. N. Monjo, *The Vicksburg Veteran* (New York: Simon and Schuster, 1971).
13. Ann Rinaldi, *The Last Silk Dress* (New York: Holiday House, 1988).
14. Henry Mazer, *The Last Mission* (New York: Delacorte Press, 1979).
15. James Collier and Christopher Collier, *My Brother Sam is Dead* (New York: Four Winds Press, 1974).

Chapter 7

Middle School English Classes: Workshop Revisited

Connie Russell

This story began with Rozie, Kathie, Marie, Karen, and me, the district language arts coordinator, discussing the pros and cons of Nancie Atwell's *In the Middle*.[1] Kathie and Rozie had initiated readers' and writers' workshops on a limited basis in their middle school in the previous year. Now Marie and Karen from the other district middle school were interested. Reality set in. An established curriculum prevailed, each of their five classes had 25 to 30 students, and no one had enough paperbacks to establish a working classroom library.

Besides, there were doubts. They worried that research supporting readers' and writers' workshops left in question the impact on students over longer periods of time. In fact, they had many questions:

- Would students tire of the workshops like they tire of traditional middle school fare?
- What happens to the district curriculum guide?
- Would students learn what they needed to learn?
- Were there certain works of literature so important that every student should read them?
- Was class discussion of the same book important so that students could benefit from the insights of others?
- Would students pay for this trial-and-error year, going into the next grade with an inadequate background?
- How would progress be assessed?
- Would parents support this change?
- Would teachers be able to keep up with one 45-minute preparation period each day?

Beginning the Process

One must ask why these teachers, whose current program was respected by students, peers, administrators, and parents, wanted to change what they did. One of the reasons was their growing knowledge of current research and theory in language and learning. Theories of reader response criticism began more than fifty years ago with Louise Rosenblatt's work.[2] But teachers continued to see the text as the center of reading, and literary analysis as the only way to read literature. In the past 10 to 15 years, however, Rosenblatt's work has been back in the mainstream as researchers describe the act of reading as a transaction among reader, text, and context. No one has written more clearly than Nicholas Karolides in *Reader Response in the Classroom,*[3]

> However, a text, once removed, once published, is no longer in the author's control. In a very real sense, the author is outside the immediate, intimate reading circle. A body of words exists, the author's intentions threaded within them, waiting for a reader to respond to them, to enliven them. The words, in effect, have no symbolic meaning—are only marks on the page—until the reading event occurs, until the literary work has been lived through by the reader. To what extent this is a replication of the author's intention cannot be established. Even if authors have identified their intention, we cannot be sure that the text fulfills it, that there are, further, no unbidden, unconscious elements reflected in the text.

On the other hand, the text is not ignored in the transactional theory of literature. Students must be able to support their responses in valid transactions with the text. This is far from the theory of literary analysis, however, where the teacher stands as the authority and the text has one meaning.

Nancie Atwell made the link between research and practical classroom application for middle school teachers, but recognized that circumstances differ among districts and teachers, saying, "If you take my book and try to do everything the same way, you will fail."[4] So, while Marie, Karen, Rozie, and Kathie could find many worthwhile sources of information, they knew it was up to them and their students to create a program that would work.

Perhaps even more important to these four middle school teachers than the reports of classroom research were their experiences in the classroom. They knew that many of their students reluctantly read assigned text and that few read anything other than what was assigned. They knew that, in traditional classrooms, students were often "spectators trying to decide the meaning of the text, knowing the teacher is the ultimate authority."[5] In this type of classroom, the students' prior knowledge and opinions are of little importance. These teachers knew that still fewer students liked to write and, when they did, the writing had little voice because the teacher chose the topics. Again, the students were spectators in the classroom, feeling little ownership of their writing.

Finally, Rozie, Kathie, Karen, and Marie wanted the opportunity to experiment with ways they could improve learning within their classrooms. They knew skills and strategies taught in an isolated fashion showed little transfer to "real" writing tasks; but they also knew students needed to learn conventions.

So these teachers were ready to make changes; yet they felt any new program was doomed to be weak or even to fail without administrative support, without planning time, and without monies for adequate resources.

As language arts coordinator for the district, I requested support from their principals and from Central Office administrators to launch a pilot program that would differ from the current approved district curriculum.

Planning for Curricular Change

In the spring, the four teachers and I began to plan for the following year. As Atwell suggested, students would select their own books for reading. The teachers wanted to purchase classroom libraries. Each ordered 100 titles with five copies of each, except for books they knew challenged even the best readers. Usually, they ordered only two copies of these for each classroom. For the most part, the two grade levels purchased different sets of titles so students would have access to as many different books as possible. However, one example of a book ordered for both seventh and eighth grade rooms was Tolkien's Trilogy.[6] Students also had access to well-stocked media centers.

Next we sought to set up the structure of the workshops and to create organizational tools to help the teachers. Most people walking into a classroom that functions as a workshop see many activities going on at once. At first glance, they might think the classroom is unstructured or even chaotic. But the truth is that this kind of classroom takes far more "structuring" than a traditional classroom where the teacher is the authority, delivering wisdom to students. In a workshop, students have to know what is expected of them, what responsibility they have for setting and meeting their own goals. We recognized the importance of the teacher's role in making that happen. We also knew we had to conform to a school-wide daily schedule and to district expectations of monitoring and assessing student learning.

The teachers began by setting up the structure of the workshops. Marie and Karen decided to have readers' workshop two days a week with writers' workshop three days a week, while Rozie and Kathie had the reverse schedule. Believing it would lighten the paperload, each teacher balanced five class periods so that approximately one-half of the students had readers' workshop while the other half had writers' workshop. They also decided to alternate readers' and writers' workshops with thematic units already in the curriculum. All four had helped to write the district curriculum guide for language arts and they wanted to draw on the strengths of that curriculum. They had written thematic units that included speech and drama activities, classroom discussions based on a common novel, and expository writing. Besides, they believed alternating between the workshops and the district curriculum would be a good transition for students as well as for themselves. (Later, their experiences with the new program led them to retain this alternating pattern.)

Prior to the start of school in August, the four created schedules for their 45-minute class periods (see Figure 7.1). (As you will see, they later ended up modifying this schedule.)

A brainstorming session helped the teachers identify minilessons[7] they could access for both readers' and writers' workshops. For example, during the first two weeks of class, these mini-lessons would focus on classroom procedures since a workshop approach would be new to the students. From that point, minilessons were geared to the needs of the students or based on curriculum objectives. These mini-lessons covered everything from focus to descriptive writing. At times, the mini-lesson might be reading some poetry to encourage more students to try that form. At other times, teachers introduced authors by using information our team had collected. Students often had practice following a mini-lesson; however, students might not apply the mini-lesson to their own work if it wasn't appropriate at the time. Teachers revisited some of these lessons again later in the year, or asked students to recall a lesson when needed. While the schedule originally called for a mini-lesson each day, the teachers soon cut back to two or three a week, realizing that in a 45-minute class period the students needed fewer mini-lessons so they'd have more time to read and write.

Because students had never been exposed to readers' or writers' workshops before, the teachers created some rules and forms to make their work easier and help the students function comfortably. These teachers defined their expectations and set standards for their students; they also asked students to establish personal goals for reading and writing. They designed a sheet on which

	5	5	5	5	5	5	5	5	WEEKLY SCHEDULE

MONDAY	MINI LESSON	WRITING	CONFERENCING/ WRITER RESPONSE	SHARING
TUESDAY	WRITING	CONFERENCING/ WRITER RESPONSE		SHARING
WEDNESDAY	MINI LESSON	READING	READING OR	SHARING
THURSDAY	MINI LESSON	READING	READER RESPONSE	SHARING
FRIDAY	MINI LESSON	READING	→ →	SHARING

Figure 7.1 Readers'/Writers' workshop weekly schedule

students could write goals, and later self-evaluate their progress on those goals (see Figure 7.2). In addition, Rules for Workshop eased the transition from a traditional class setting (see Figures 7.3 and 7.4).

The teachers also knew that students needed to know from the beginning how they would be evaluated. District progress reports require letter grades. Yet readers' and writers' workshops place far more responsibility on students than is the case in a traditional classroom. The teachers agreed on an evaluation process they would share with the students during the first week of school. This information, along with clearly communicated expectations, helped students feel more at ease in the new environment (see Figure 7.5).

Besides meeting workshop standards, students could earn extra credit for creative projects related to workshop books. For instance, some students enjoyed creating games or artwork at home. To maintain continuity, during the weeks when classes turned their attention to district curriculum units, the breakdown for evaluation was much the same: a student's grade reflected reading and reading projects, writing assignments, and participation.

The teachers also wanted to make sure parents understood the new classroom procedures and expectations. They wrote letters at the beginning of the year to inform parents of children placed in one of these classrooms (see Figure 7.6)—approximately a third of the students at each grade level. Teachers gave a brief rationale for readers' and writers' workshops, and explained evaluation criteria and grading processes. During the fall open house, teachers provided more information to parents about the changes.

At the end of the first quarter, some students had lower grades than they had anticipated. Students of all abilities who hadn't taken responsibility for requirements and their own learning came to realize readers' and writers' workshops placed this responsibility squarely on their shoulders. Because the teachers had so clearly defined their expectations and evaluation system, most parents as well as the students accepted their grades; the majority of these students improved their grades the second quarter. In contrast, other students achieved higher first-quarter grades than they normally received because they responded well to having choices for reading and writing.

Merging the New with the Old

The district's published middle school English curriculum consisted of thematic units that integrated the language arts strands (reading, writing, speaking, and listening). As the school year began, Marie, Karen, Rozie, and Kathie had not made final deci-

Student _____   Period _____

Goals for Quarter   1   2   3   4

Readers' Workshop:

  1. _____

     _____

  2. _____

     _____

  3. _____

     _____

Writers' Workshop:

  1. _____

     _____

  2. _____

     _____

  3. _____

     _____

Evaluation:

Figure 7.2 Goals Form

1. Bring your daily writing envelope to each meeting of writing lab.

2. Write every day and finish pieces each quarter.

3. Find topics you care about.

4. Take risks as a writer, trying new techniques, topics, skills, and forms of writing.

5. Make decisions about what's working and what needs more work in your writing.

6. Listen to and question other writers' drafts, giving thoughtful, helpful responses in conferences.

7. Revise each piece; number and date the drafts.

8. Take responsibility for editing final drafts and show your editing in a contrasting color. As a final step, check all lessons listed on your mastery skill sheet.

9. Submit all drafts and conference sheets with those writing pieces that you plan to publish. The final draft should be legible and correct with decent margins.

10. Take care of your writing materials and resources provided. Your grade will be based on the entire writing process.

11. Keep on task and do not disturb or distract me or other writers. There will be no talking during the first ten minutes of writers' workshop.

Figure 7.3 Rules for using writers' workshop time

sions about which curriculum units they would use. They thought they would alternate readers' and writers' workshops with specific units in response to students' needs; needs did, indeed, emerge. For instance, as the year progressed, they found that most students did not choose non-fiction, poetry, or mythology on their own; in fact, these genres were underrepresented in the classroom libraries. Moreover, the workshop format gave students few or no opportunities to use creative dramatics. These teachers believed that students would benefit from relating through drama to the characters in certain classic or landmark books. They believed, too, as does Linda Rief,[8] that students need to be aware of prejudice in its many forms. They wanted to be active participants in the classroom, bringing out books that students might not choose themselves but that teachers thought students would learn from and would enjoy.

Ultimately, all four teachers agreed on four units at each grade

---

1. Students must read for the first ten minutes of reading workshop.

2. They must read or respond to reading for the entire workshop period. They may not do homework or read any material for another course. Reading workshop is not a study period.

3. They must read a book (no magazines or newspapers where text competes with pictures), preferably one that tells a story (e.g., novels, histories, and biographies rather than books of lists or facts where readers can't sustain attention, build up speed and fluency, or grow to love good stories.)

4. They must have a book in their possession when the bell rings; this is the main responsibility involved in coming prepared to this class. Students without materials will read assigned selections and write responses.

5. They may not talk to or disturb others.

6. They may sit or recline wherever they'd like as long as feet don't go up over furniture and rule #5 is maintained.

7. A student who is absent can make up time and receive points by reading at home, during home base (with a note from a parent or home base teacher), or after school.

Figure 7.4 Rules for using readers' workshop time

level that they would teach. For example, in eighth grade they would use "A Classic Study." Students would read *A Christmas Carol*[9] in one school and *The Diary of Anne Frank*[10] in the other school, both examples of prejudice. Students dramatized these selections. Furthermore, those who read *A Christmas Carol* attended the play at the Guthrie Theater in Minneapolis as a culminating activity. The seventh grade teachers retained a unit on non-fiction and one on mythology. Teachers found that units centered around more contemporary novels could be left out; unit objectives were met during readers' and writers' workshops.

A cycle emerged, with units running for three or four weeks, followed by workshops for the same number of weeks. Students liked alternating thematic units with readers' and writers' workshops, declaring that they looked forward to changes every three or four weeks. Actually, workshops influenced the way these curricular units looked. The teachers found themselves encouraging readers' response techniques in conjuction with thematic units. Journal responses and discussion groups replaced the use of study guides. Often, students chose their own projects for assignments. The teachers' writing assignments included student choices. For teachers and students, this unit-workshop balance seemed appropriate. Those feelings haven't changed. One student wrote, "I think it works quite well and gives readers' and writers' workshops variety." Another said simply, "I like the change."

```
40%  READING
          -Reading Record     Minimum:  75 pages/week=C
                                       100 pages/week=B
                                       125 pages/week=A

          -Response Journal   Minimum:  1 response per book
                -Quality
                -Quantity


40%  WRITING
          -Mini Lessons  (guided practice)
          -Use of Process
                -Drafts (quality, quantity)
                -Conferencing techniques
          -Final Drafts


20%  PARTICIPATION
          -Reading/Writing Log  (out-of-class work)
          -Sharing  (reading, writing)
          -Workshop Habits  (in-class work)


     UNIT STUDY
          -Daily Assignments
          -Tests/Quizzes
          -Projects
          -Writing


* Additional points can be earned for creative projects
related to workshop books.
```

Figure 7.5 Evaluation standards

Problems and Issues

Did the teachers find workshops a panacea for all ills? No! While students liked interacting with each other and having choices about what they read, reluctant and/or disabled readers and writers didn't magically disappear. The different levels of trade books in the room helped these students have more success than they otherwise would have had, but some still had difficulty meeting the minimum requirements because they were not used to being responsible for setting aside time to read and write. In most cases, these problems disappeared as parents helped, and as students realized the commitment they had to make at home each night to reading or writing.

In addition, some students were at first reluctant to write to each other rather than to the teacher. This problem undoubtedly stemmed from their view of the teacher as the evaluator and sole audience; they saw little merit in writing to another student. Besides, most students coveted the teachers' responses to them as individuals. In time, however, students became as interested in other students' responses as in those of the teachers.

Students Writing to Students

The schedule permitted students fifteen minutes daily to respond to their own reading or to another student's reading responses. Teachers encouraged students to respond to any other student's writing; though their close monitoring of students' work often led them to suggest that two students who were reading the same book might enjoy sharing responses with one another. Teachers' roles expanded as they became delivery persons, delivering a response from a student in one period to a student in another period. Often, two students reading the same book[11] would correspond.

> Aaron,
>
> So you're at the part where they're staying at the Prancing Pony Inn. The Black Riders are on their trail again, and I think it is more suspenseful now. Have they met Strider yet? They will soon if they haven't yet. He (Strider) plays a *major* role in the book. I thought the part with Tom Bombadil was funny—how he's always singing and dancing and needs about a total of three hours of sleep a night. I also thought that the Barrow-wight part was weird and confusing. It gets really scary right about now with the Black Riders on their trail, and the reading goes fast. Tell me when you finish and get into *The Black Cauldron*,[12] which I'm reading right now.
>
> Sincerely,
>
> Jay
>
> P. S. I wonder when Gandalf will find them?

Dear Parents:

This year your son/daughter will be involved in a pilot program in English class. The program is based on several years of research on how students best learn and think critically through their reading and writing activities. Through this program students take greater responsibility for their learning. Students will set goals in reading and writing and learn the skills needed to achieve them.

While we will continue teaching some of our more important units, much of the year will be a Readers'/ Writers' Workshop. Students will spend two periods a week writing on self-selected topics and three periods a week reading from a selection of carefully chosen books.

The students will be evaluated by the following criteria:

READING
> READING RECORD (Students must read a minimum of 75 pages a week for a C, 100 pages for a B, 125 pages for an A.)

> RESPONSE JOURNAL (Students must write a minimum of one response per book; the responses will be graded based on quality as well as quantity.)

WRITING
> WRITING MINI LESSONS (Students must write a minimum of one response per book; the responses will be graded based on quality as well as quantity.)

WRITING
> WRITING MINI LESSONS (Students will be judged on their application of lessons that teach writing or literary techniques.)

> USE OF WRITING PROCESS (Students will be judged on the quality and quantity of their drafts and on their conferencing techniques.)

> FINAL DRAFTS (Students will be judged on the quality of their final drafts—minimum of three per quarter— including content and mechanics.)

Figure 7.6 Parent Letter page 1 of 2

PARTICIPATION

 READING/WRITING LOG (Students are expected to read
 or write a minimum of one hour a week outside of the
 English class. Parents are to sign their son/
 daughter's personal log weekly.

 SHARING (Students are expected to share their ideas
 and works orally with the class.)

 WORKSHOP HABITS (Students will be evaluated on their
 cooperation, involvement, and effort in class.)

 GOALS (Students will be expected to set and work
 toward individual goals.)

UNIT STUDY

 DAILY ASSIGNMENTS
 TESTS/QUIZZES
 PROJECTS
 WRITING ASSIGNMENTS

 Our curriculum objectives will be met through the
combination of Readers'/Writers' Workshop and units. You
are invited to visit our classes to see our workshop in
action. We believe your son/daughter will be excited
about English this year and grow in acquisition of
communications skills.

                        Sincerely,

_____

I have read the letter about the pilot program in English
and will help monitor reading and writing at home by
initialing the Reading/Writing Log.

                         _____
                         Parent/Guardian Signature

Comments:

Figure 7.6 Parent Letter page 2 of 2

Jay,

I've just passed the part when the party got caught
in the snow, and they just decided to take the way through
Moria. Yes, they have met Strider, and I find that he
plays an interesting role in this story. I also think that
Baromir distrusts Strider. I am very fond of Gimli and
his courage and strength. I also think that Gandalf is the
only thing that keeps that group together. I am really
enjoying this book.

Aaron

Responses went beyond the walls of the classroom. One student wrote a response to her father following her reading of a book
that examined family relationships. She wondered about her own
great grandparents. Her father responded in writing, giving her
information about the family ancestry.

In writers' workshop, some students used to having topics
assigned had difficulty finding their own topics and their own
voices. Teachers conducted mini-lessons to help students find what
they had to say. For example, one teacher helped students realize
that small, everyday events could be interesting topics. Another
mini-lesson taught students to generate topics based on the books
they were reading—for example, a book about an adolescent's problem with a little sister might make the reader think about a problem with her own siblings.

Conferencing did not pose as many problems as finding topics. Most of these students come from elementary classrooms where
conferencing is used, and they are comfortable with the process
(although not all experienced it in sixth or seventh grade). Never-
theless, these four teachers demonstrated conferencing and structured mini-lessons on how to conference. Students would volunteer
to read their drafts to the class; teachers would then invite all students to participate in the conference. They would stop after questions or comments and talk about how these questions or comments
might help the writer. For example, a question that can be answered
by a simple "yes" or "no" is not going to help the writer generate
more thoughts.

As the year progressed, problems with the workshops dimin-
ished, although they didn't disappear. Students grew to appreciate
the value of conferencing in order to revise. One eighth grader
wrote in a survey near the end of the first year, "We get a lot more
stories done than last year when we did sentence structure and
things like that. It teaches us the same thing with real writing experience." Another noted, "Last year we didn't conference with
anyone." This year students conferenced with one another and with

the teacher. When students conferenced with the teacher, they were prepared to discuss the revisions they had made. Often, during their conferences, students or the teacher drew upon the content of mini-lessons. One student followed up a lesson on "showing" setting with this description of the Mall of America:

> Loud, mixing together, babbling-noise and jumbled words are all you hear. You have to shout over the commotion to hear yourself. Fragrances range from the spicy and garlicky smells of Italian restaurants and the smell of greasy hamburgers from fast food places to the sweet smells of perfumes drifting out of the department stores. In the distance you can faintly hear the merry-go-round music from over in Camp Snoopy. You can hear the rushing water from the flume and the sounds of terrified screams from the rollercoaster. Everyone is packed tightly together. You cannot see over tall people's heads. You feel a mixture of excitement and claustrophobia in you. You spot all the different shopping bags and wish you could find the store they came from.

Coping

As the students wrote more and better drafts, Rozie, Kathie, Marie, and Karen found themselves buried beneath piles of journals needing responses and papers ready for a conference or final assessment. Little by little, they revised their expectations for themselves in order to survive. Sometimes the solutions seemed simple. For example, while it made sense to have students respond to reading in journals, teachers could not cope with the bulk of these materials when they had to take them home. Marie and Rozie began using a response form so they could carry *sheets* rather than whole journals (see Figure 7.7). All four teachers stopped responding to every journal entry, though they continued to read most of them, finding the responses "windows into the students' learning processes and feelings." Teachers discarded other forms and practices as they realized these made more work than they saved, or failed to help students or teachers. Marie checked on students' progress once or twice a week rather than daily. Mini-lesson logs kept in student folders disappeared.

Writers' workshop also contributed to the problem of overload for teachers. They found they had to set deadlines for the three completed pieces of writing required each quarter (submitted along with all earlier drafts) in order to avoid receiving too many final drafts at the end of the quarter. Gradually, the teachers realized they could only conference on parts of drafts. Teachers and students learned

Name _____

Period_____ Quarter_____

READERS' STUDIO 211

Title _____

Author _____ Studio Dates _____

(Starting)   (Ending)

Difficulty Level of Book   5 = Very Difficult (50), 4 = Difficult (75), 3 = Average (125),
2 = Below Average (175), 1 = Easy (225)

TOTAL NUMBER OF PAGES FOR THE WEEK _____

SUMMARY (at least five sentences)_____

_____

_____

_____

_____

_____

_____

_____

PERSONAL RESPONSE (at least five sentences)_____

_____

_____

_____

_____

_____

_____

_____

Figure 7.7 Response Form

to negotiate. For instance, some students wrote several chapters and each chapter could be counted as one piece; in this case, teachers realized students would need to go on with the story before doing final editing on previous chapters. Nonetheless, even though they could not read everything, these teachers found that they knew more about their students' writing than ever before; they knew more because they no longer stood in the front of the room lecturing. Instead, they moved about the room, "listening in" and conferring.

Even with the problems that arose for Rozie, Kathie, Marie, and Karen, the positives outweighed the negatives. They saw students responding to literature in more positive ways. In January, prompted by her reading an article in *Language Arts*,[13] Kathie discussed the variety of responses she was seeing in her room. Students interacted with characters, questioned and predicted, linked events to their personal lives, and talked about authors. They "sold" books to each other and to their teachers. On a visit to Marie's room, I found four books piled on the edge of her desk that students insisted that she read. As students realized their responses, not just the teacher's, were acceptable, their self esteem and confidence grew. Students wrote more than they had ever written before—in their response journals and in their writing on self-selected topics. The writing grew in quality as well as in quantity as students learned to trust their thoughts, feelings, and reactions within a heterogeneous classroom setting. Following a visit by author Gordon Korman, several students launched into writing modeled after the humorous writing of this author.

The teachers met students' needs through the variety of reading materials available. Teachers saw students of all abilities thinking critically as they sought to explain what they thought about their reading and to express their ideas in writing. Critical thinking happened naturally as students created responses, revised drafts, and responded to others' writing.

Seeing the Results

What were the results of the first year's pilot program? Rozie, Kathie, Marie, and Karen felt they had provided a wide range of experiences for students. Students had drawn upon a broad spectrum of adolescent literature that they could relate to and enjoy. They had written with their own voices, feeling the freedom and learning the responsibility of taking risks, because process was as important as product.

At the same time the decision to continue using certain thematic units allowed teachers to address areas that might otherwise be lost (such as poetry, mythology, nonfiction, and drama) because students didn't choose these genres. Often interdisciplinary in nature, thematic units fostered connections with social studies or science. Classics could continue to be part of the curriculum, though the students learned to value different responses to the same book. An occasional whole-class reading of the same book taught students to listen to one another as well as to question and support varying responses and rationales. This was a real change from classrooms where students were spectators, passive recipients of the one "correct" interpretation of a book. Finally, these teachers retained some assigned writing in conjunction with thematic units, but more often students had choices for projects and responses.

Parents were positive about the program, too. One parent wrote, "I wish we had this when I was in school. I might have liked English." Many parents claimed their children had never read so much.

Next Steps

With these successes came plans for the next steps. The district provided release time for these teachers to discuss their successes as well as ways to further improve their learning environments. For example, all of them felt they had to facilitate more small group discussion. They planned new lessons for readers' workshop that might result in small groups discussing a common literary question, even though students were reading different books—for example, discussions about the protagonist-antagonist relationship or the use of figurative language and its impact on the reader. The teacher could choose three or four discussion questions based on identified student needs, but students could decide the group in which they would participate.

These teachers also knew they needed to spend more time demonstrating their own writing. While students often saw their teachers reading, they didn't always see the teachers' attempts at writing. Teachers missed opportunities to show how they had worked on parent letters or department memos. These demonstrations could also encourage the students to move away from the narrative mode, a very safe one for these young people. To meet the demands of a democratic society, students need to see that writing is a tool to change, persuade, inform. They need to take risks, attempting other forms. By discussing needs and shortcomings with each other, the teachers were reminded of how they might improve these areas during the second year.

In preparation for the second year of their program, Rozie, Kathie, Marie, and Karen planned a half day spring presentation for other seventh and eighth grade teachers who were interested in pursuing readers' and writers' workshops. As district language arts coordinator, I have seen that significant changes come from the ranks of teachers rather than from administrative mandates. Others at these two schools now expressed their willingness to try readers' and writers' workshops, at least on a limited basis. The middle school principals and Central Administration continued to support the program and were interested in learning more about it. The pilot team also shared their experiences at the Wisconsin Council of Teachers of English and National Council of Teachers of English conventions where their sessions were warmly received.

With the beginning of the second year, all eight seventh and eighth grade language arts teachers in one middle school began using the workshop approach. At the other middle school, teachers showed interest but also hesitation. Not everyone adopted readers' and writers' workshops right away; some confessed they didn't have the theoretical background they needed. However, all these teachers during a half-day release time voiced a desire to continue working together, to inch ahead in their endeavors. In my role as a coordinator, I know how crucial it is that these teachers have the time to dialogue about the interrelationships of theory and practice; fortunately, a supportive administrative staff has continued giving the participants this important release time.

The learning environments continued to evolve in the classrooms of the four original pilot program teachers. During the second year, Rozie, Kathie, Marie, and Karen found the lines between readers' and writers' workshops disappearing. This gave students opportunities to finish books they couldn't put down or to continue writing drafts that were important to them.·

Small group discussions in these original four classrooms improved. Teachers used impromptu groups or scheduled a half hour a week for small group discussions. They applied previously acquired knowledge about cooperative learning, using these techniques more skillfully to improve the quality of the interaction among students.

These teachers look forward to new challenges as interdisciplinary and integrated approaches to curriculum gain favor. They wonder how to connect readers' and writers' workshops with other subjects. They wonder how students' choices about their reading and writing topics might better correlate with the topics of other disciplines. As the paperload increases, teachers are looking for new and better ways to evaluate students' progress, acknowledging the fact that they can't evaluate or grade everything that students write. Teachers at one of the middle schools are beginning to use portfolios as methods to evaluate fairly. Students share responsibility as self-evaluation and peer evaluation become integral components of the workshops. Teachers have designated certain contents for portfolios, such as writing that shows all stages of the process, reading responses, and a reading log. Students make choices about which writing and which responses they will include for evaluation by the teacher. They include their goals and self-evaluation. The students, in quarterly conferences, discuss their growth with the teachers.

Yes, these teachers will continue to be learners along with

their students, seeking ways to make language arts more meaningful and purposeful for students as well as for themselves. In the meantime, they are satisfied that readers' and writers' workshops are a reality rather than a dream. Their classrooms are not places where students spend less than three percent of their time reading.[14] A comment from a social studies teacher at one of the middle schools reflects the changes he sees in the students: "I want to compliment the English Department; I have never seen students read as much as they are reading this year. They get done with their work in my class, and they get out a novel. I don't have to say a word."

My sincere thanks to the dedicated professionals who made the writing of this story possible: Rozanna Bejin and Kathie Trzecinski, DeLong Middle School, and Marie Leonard and Karen Mittag, South Middle School, Eau Claire, Wisconsin.

End Notes

1. Nancie Atwell, *In the Middle* (Portsmouth, NH: Heinemann Educational Books, Inc., 1987).
2. Louise M. Rosenblatt, *Literature as Exploration*, 4th Ed. (NY: Modern Language Association, 1983).
3. Nicholas J. Karolides, ed., *Reader Response in the Classroom: Evoking and Interpreting Meaning in Literature* (New York: Longman, 1992), 24, 25.
4. Nancie Atwell (Speech at National Council of Teachers of English Convention, Baltimore 1989).
5. Richard Beach and James Marshall, *Teaching Literature in the Secondary School* (San Diego: Harcourt Brace Jovanovich, 1990), 3–12.
6. J.R.R. Tolkien, *Lord of the Rings* (Boston: Houghton Mifflin, 1988).
7. Lucy Calkins, *The Art of Teaching Writing* (Portsmouth, NH: Heinemann Educational Books, Inc., 1986), 167–172.
8. Linda Rief, *Seeking Diversity: Language Arts With Adolescents* (Portsmouth, NH: Heinemann Educational Books, Inc., 1992), 101–112.
9. Charles Dickens, *A Christmas Carol* (Boston: Houghton Mifflin, 1991).
10. Albert Hackett, *The Diary of Anne Frank* (NY: Dramatists Play Service, Inc., 1990).
11. J.R.R. Tolkien, *The Fellowship of the Ring* (New York: Ballantine Books, 1965).
12. Lloyd Allexander, *The Black Cauldron* (New York: Dell Publishing, 1965).
13. Carole Cox and Joyce E. Many, "Toward an Understanding of Aesthetic Response to Literature," *Language Arts* 69 (1992): 28–33.
14. John Goodlad, *A Place Called School* (NY: McGraw-Hill, 1984), 107.

Chapter 8

Integrating Curriculum in a Self-Contained Middle School Classroom: Teacher Innovation and the Impact of Administrative Support

Sally Wells

Laying the Groundwork

My new principal, Doug Miller, was coming to observe my self-contained sixth-grade classroom for the first time. As I was mentally preparing for his visit, I wondered if I was a bit crazy to have him observe my class on their first day of doing independent research. I had planned only a ten-minute mini-lesson to review the procedures the students were to use in collecting data on their individually chosen research topics. I was hoping that the students' enthusiasm for their topics would result in a class full of eager researchers.

Doug had asked me what I wanted him to look for in my class. I told him that I was hoping my students would be engaged in their work, and asked him to look for "on-task" behaviors. What I really wanted to know was whether my students were excited about their work, but I wasn't quite sure how to ask Doug to look for this.

The time whizzed by. I hardly noticed Doug's presence as students were let loose to begin their research. My teaching partner and I had gathered a wide variety of trade books from three public libraries, our school library, and our own classroom resources. The portable library cart was filled with some two hundred resource books on the ancient civilizations of Egypt, China, and India. I was unaware of when Doug left my room.

When I met with him later for a follow-up conference, Doug started by asking me, "How did you do it?"

"Do what?" I responded a little awkwardly.

"How did you get so many kids excited about doing research?"

"Well . . . ," I stammered as I tried to put my thoughts together, "they are each studying something they want to know more about. They are trying to become experts on some aspect of ancient civilizations. Each student chose his or her own topic and I think the element of ownership is important. I didn't assign a specific topic to anyone."

Doug went on to tell me that he had done several timed interval observations to check "on-task" behavior. The results of his observation were impressive, 16 out of 17, 22 out of 24, 20 out of 20 "on-task." I was excited by this information. I had been so busy helping students find the right books to start their research that I hadn't looked up very often to see the big picture of my class while Doug was in there.

Doug asked how I had prepared the kids for their first day of independent research. The preparation had taken a couple of weeks and involved mini-lessons in writers' workshop on using reference materials, indexes, tables of content, and card catalogs. The students had practiced summarizing information in the form of a question with an answer. They read information from a book, covered up the page, then asked a question which they could answer based on the reading just completed. This seemed to work well as a way to encourage summarization skills while discouraging plagiarism.

We had seen several films on different ancient civilizations and had had a parent come in to speak about a recent trip to China, during which she had seen The Great Wall and the Terra Cotta warriors. Another teacher had shown slides of Egypt. We had even pulled the social studies texts out of the cupboard, blown the dust off them, and read a bit to give everyone some background on these civilizations. Then each student chose a very specific aspect of one of these civilizations on which to become an expert. Students would eventually be turning their research into board games similar to Trivial Pursuit®.

Doug asked how I handled having more than one student wanting to do research on the same topic. I acknowleged that two topics, King Tut and the Great Wall of China, had indeed interested several students. This worked well since I used it as an opportunity to encourage collaborative research. This allowed a couple of less able readers to work with stronger students. When it came time to create board games, only one King Tut researcher would be on a given team. Teams designing a board game together would revise and edit the information gathered by students. In this way, collaboration would not only help in the editing of information, but each of the students in a group would learn about the others' research. For example, one Egypt group might combine information about King Tut, mummies, pyramid building, and religion.

As Doug and I continued to talk, I knew that in identifying

the qualities that made this research unit work so well I was listing principles of whole language instruction:

- The students gathered information from trade books rather than a text book.
- Students chose their own topics.
- I was learning along with my students—I felt excited about the information they shared with me.
- The unit bridged several curricular areas—reading, writing, social studies.
- The students worked collaboratively.

This was turning out to be the most unusual observation conference I had ever had, but it set the tone for the way in which I work with my principal. Doug wanted to know what theoretical understanding I had for the way I was teaching. He was very supportive of what he saw and encouraged my beliefs in whole language education: in integrated curriculum, in blended-grade classrooms, in collaborative learning and teaching.

Joining a Team

During the past couple of years since that initial experience in a self-contained classroom, my teaching situation at Henkle Middle School in White Salmon, Washington, has continued to evolve. I am now teaching a fifth-sixth grade blended class. I would not have been able to develop the kind of curriculum I have without tremendous support from Doug, my principal, and the support of our district superintendent, Dr. Rich Carter. We are not a district with much money. While it would be nice to have more funding for some of the dreams I have, I feel very fortunate to work in a district with administrative support for innovative program planning.

Several weeks after my conference with Doug, a district-wide in-service was held on the topic of restructuring. The in-service was good, but I left wondering what would really happen. Would there be change? Where would the change come from—from teachers or administrators? Our superintendent emphasized that in order for restructuring to be effective, leadership needed to come from teachers.

Following the day-long in-service, administration encouraged staff to examine their current paradigms. Where were we stuck and where did we want to go? Each employee was to list three things he or she felt should be addressed or changed in restructuring programs throughout the school district. I gave my list to my principal and wondered what would happen from there. Within a week, Doug asked me to drop in for a brief conference. He had my list in front of him when I walked into his office.

"Are you ready to do all of these things on this list—mix age groups, integrate curriculum, and go to an ungraded progress report?" he asked.

I must have gulped before I answered. I didn't really think he would be willing to address all of those things at once. I must have sounded a little hesitant as I answered, "Uh, I think so. What do you have in mind?"

That meeting was the beginning of an exciting, definitely challenging process that resulted in a team of three of us starting a blended fourth-fifth-sixth grade program less than one year after our in-service on restructuring. The team grew to four teachers the second year. We are not the only "different" program in the school district, either. The administration is committed to offering parents and students a number of choices even though we are a small district. Some of the options that first year included a teacher remaining with a class for two years, a couple of fourth-fifth and fifth-sixth grade blended classes, a fourth-fifth-sixth grade blended program, and traditional same-aged classes. At the same time, the high school moved to a four period day.

I'm not sure how each of the programs evolved from vision to reality, but I know our fourth-fifth-sixth blend couldn't have come together as well as it did without a tremendous amount of administrative support. First, Doug told me that another person had expressed interests similar to mine. It didn't surprise me that the other person was Amy Taylor. Amy and I had taught sixth grade together for two years, though Amy was teaching fifth grade that year. We had similar philosophies about many educational issues and had done quite a bit of team planning in the past. Doug knew that Amy and I worked well together, so he started throwing ideas at us for ways in which we could move toward the reality of a fourth-fifth-sixth grade program. It wasn't long before a third person, Chuck Dorsey, started working with us. We didn't know Chuck well because he had just joined the staff, but the three of us became wonderful collaborators as we planned and implemented our program. A fourth teacher, Phil Brady, joined the staff at Henkle the first year of our blended grades program. Though his schedule didn't allow him to do everything with us, he joined us during planning sessions and included his class in a number of projects.

The second year, Phil joined the team in all respects. We lost our fourth graders to the elementary school, so we are now a fifth-sixth grade blend. The number of grades in the program is not as important as is our philosophy—our recognition that our students' abilities are diverse and our belief that we can honor that diversity to the advantage of all.

Building a Program

Learning About Other Programs

From the outset, the administration played an active role in supporting our team. Both Doug and the principal at the elementary school, Dale Palmer, showed an interest in learning more about existing blended-age programs. Dale put together a thick notebook of pertinent research articles. It was wonderful to have someone else gather these articles; I certainly wouldn't have had time to do as thorough a search myself.

But we did more than read the literature. Over the first couple of months following the decision to become a team, several teachers from our elementary and middle schools observed blended-grade classes at schools in Washington and Oregon. I went to Emily Dickinson Elementary School in the Kent School District near Seattle, Washington. As a former Montessori teacher, I had taught a blended-age class for a number of years; but it was important for me to see public school programs in operation. Emily Dickinson is accustomed to having observers. A couple of teachers and the building principal greeted us, and gave us an overview of their program—complete with a video presentation[1]—before we actually visited classrooms.

The five-hour drive back to White Salmon went more quickly than I'd experienced in a long while. Everyone in the van had interesting comments, both positive and negative, about the things we had seen at Emily Dickinson. The interchange of ideas among colleagues was stimulating. I was excited about this upcoming project, but I also felt overwhelmed by the amount of work required to pull it all together into a new program by September. We had repeatedly heard from the Emily Dickinson staff that teaching blended-grade classes required more work than anything any of them had done in the past; at the same time, they assured us it was more rewarding than anything they had previously done as educators. I was concerned about the thought of working harder than I already was. In the past, I had often worked at school until 5:00 or 6:00, but now I was pregnant with my first child and knew that I wanted to get home earlier, not later than that. Amy and Chuck both have families and shared my view.

Planning Our Program

We approached Doug with our concerns about the amount of work required to put this program together. The teachers at Emily Dickinson received paid planning time during the summer. We knew this would be difficult for our district to afford, but we decided to ask for it anyway. In place of this, Doug offered to get substitutes during the coming school year so we could have a couple of days for planning. He also sent Amy and me to a conference on non-graded programs, and Chuck to observe another example of blended-age programs at Willamette Primary School, West Linn, near Portland, Oregon.

Our first planning day was amazing; it helped us from the beginning to identify personal characteristics that helped define our separate roles. As we have grown to a team of four, we have found we compliment each other well. Chuck is the "random-abstract thinker." Amy is the organized one. Phil is philosophical, and I'm somewhere in between.

At the first blended-grades meeting, we didn't start with an agenda. Rather, we allowed ourselves to ramble a bit, to express concerns and feelings about getting into this blended program, and to let the agenda evolve. Being able to ramble was, and still is, important. Having started on that note makes it comfortable now to bring up concerns; we know our partners are receptive to discussing issues as they arise—we don't require an issue to be on an agenda before it can be discussed.

Our period of rambling at that first meeting generated an agenda for the rest of the day. We began by identifying our concerns and questions about this new program. The second item on the agenda was to develop a "wish list." Finally, we spent the rest of the day looking at the existing fourth-, fifth-, and sixth-grade curricula to decide how we might include portions of these in new and more integrated ways. By the end of the day, I felt exhausted but intellectually stimulated from this work with my future teaching partners.

Ongoing planning time is important in establishing and building a program of this nature. It takes a great deal of coordination to keep the pace of change moving at roughly the same speed in three or four different classes. Finding a way to have some common prep times during the school day headed our "needs list." Achieving this took a lot of schedule juggling on Doug's part, and the willingness of our P.E. and Music specialists to take larger than normal class sizes. The first year we had two or three common prep periods each week. We didn't always use these to plan jointly, but the time was available so that we could meet during the regular day. Now, in the second year of our blended-grade program, we don't have a common planning period. Consequently, we end up meeting during lunches and after school. This puts stress and strain on the program because it does take additional time to stay "in synch" with one another and to plan jointly.

Often we meet each other in the halls to share little snatches of information. We have had to meet outside the normal day, too, one afternoon each week. Each of us comes with a notepad of issues or concerns. These lists help us to focus when we get too random in our thoughts, too caught up in diversions. I keep a small notepad on my desk so that during the week I can jot down things I want to discuss as I discover them. We are sensitive to the potential for becoming overwhelmed by this program, so we have become efficient with our use of time and are usually finished by 4:00.

We have also approached Doug in a minor panic when we needed a major block of planning time. He has been supportive and helpful. For example, when we started the first year we had the initial six weeks pretty well organized. As the end of that six-week period approached, we realized we had a lot of planning to do for the next block of time. We also needed to do long-range planning, to develop the "big picture" for the rest of the year now that we had a better feel for what worked and what didn't. Doug got subs for all of us for a day and we met at Chuck's home for another round of major planning.

As we looked ahead to our second year, we realized how much planning would be required, especially as a fourth person was joining our team. Our "pie-in-the-sky" hope was to get a week of paid planning time during the summer. I think we knew that was out of the question, considering our district's budget; and it was. However, once again Doug hired subs for a couple of days so we could plan for the coming year.

Developing Our Curriculum

Where did we start with curricular change that first year? After a fair bit of rambling, sharing philosophical concerns, and idealizing, we tried to set some guidelines for ourselves. We needed to define our philosophical goals before we could address specific curriculum plans. Some of our goals included:

- truly blending our age groups to create a sense of family within each homeroom, along with a group identity across the blended classes;
- involving students in all aspects of curriculum—from planning activities to considerations of assessment—so they would have ownership in the program;
- integrating subject areas;
- involving students in self assessment for individual projects and for permanent progress reports.

While we agreed on these goals, how to achieve them overwhelmed us. So we ended up with some compromises. We defined where we were now and where we wanted to be in three years. This helped us decide which areas we'd tackle first, and where we'd maintain the status-quo until we could adequately plan and prepare for more change.

We began by examining the existing fourth-, fifth-, and sixth-grade district curriculum guides. Especially in science and social studies we found we could easily reconfigure curriculum content to create thematic units. This reorganization resulted in a sequence that, in only two years, addressed all science and social studies topics assigned to the three grade levels. Therefore, we envisioned the third year in the sequence as an "open" one during which students would join us in identifying themes and topics they wished to study. (We might also have considered ways to spread the district curriculum topics across three years, providing some time for student-selected topics each year.)

Next we considered the language arts curriculum both as an entity of its own (specifically with respect to reading and writing) and as a logical interface with our thematic blocks. We would continue our writers' and readers' workshops, but would shift some mini-lessons[2] on topics such as research or non-fiction writing to our thematic block period of time. So, while we would dedicate separate periods to workshops and to sustained silent reading, teachers would also take an active role in assisting students with content area reading and other information access skills, including more effective use of our media resource center. (Our computer lab and library have merged to become one media center. Students have access to data bases, and pursue a lot of independent research there.)

We reorganized the math curriculum into several blocks of time throughout the year: one to include work with heterogeneous groups in which the emphasis was on cooperative learning and problem-solving strategies, another to teach computational skills to students grouped for instruction to meet individual needs, and a third to address applied math either as an elective or in homeroom groups. Finally, we looked at ways math cuts across other curricular areas. In spite of this reorganization, we tended to leave math "as is" more than any other area.

For the first month of the school year we kept our homerooms together most of the time to foster a sense of family. Students participated in our all-important daily class meeting, chaired by the class president. The ritual of the class meeting became a sacred time of day. Students also engaged in many cooperative learning activities; for example, math groups worked together on problem-solving strategies using the Lane County, Oregon, Problem Solving Materials.[3] To help us get to know our students, readers' workshop centered on silent reading, individual reading conferences, and journal writing. In writers' workshop, we worked explicitly with all aspects of the writing process to provide all students with a common language and common reference.

After the first month of school, students began switching class-rooms throughout the day. Initially, this caused some confusion for all, but it opened the door to the variety of learning experiences we wanted to offer. The students loved this structure once they got used to moving from one place to the next.

We grouped the students in math computation classes based on a diagnostic pre-test. While we had some mixed feelings about this grouping, we saw some advantages in providing for students' different learning rates. Grouping in this fashion also enabled us to more effectively utilize our special education staff and educational assistants.

For me, the most exciting changes occurred in writers' and readers' workshops. We polled students on their interests, and used this information to identify what we would teach. For example, in writing workshop, some students expressed an interest in learning more about writing fantasy. I was interested in fantasy, too, and agreed to offer a special writers' workshop on that genre (though I had never taught it before, so I had a bit of extra preparation to do). During these "special" workshop periods, each of my team members also offered workshops focusing on one particular genre (though we always maintained one "open" choice, or regular writers' workshop). It was a joy for me to teach "special" classes because students *chose* to be there. The writing that came out of my fantasy group that year was outstanding. Almost every student exerted more effort and gave more of themselves than they had generally done in the past. (See Figure 8.1 for an example of "special" class choices provided for students.)

Struggling with Assessment

"Do we really have to grade ourselves on our report cards??!!" groaned several students as I handed out the first-quarter progress reports.

"You've been doing self-assessments in writing and math and block all quarter," I responded.

"Yeah, but our parents are going to see these!" commented another student.

"Give it a try," I encouraged. "I think you'll be pleasantly surprised by how closely your marks and mine match each other."

My teaching team had spent many, many hours discussing student assessment, report cards, progress reports, and other topics related to evaluating and reporting children's progress and achievement. Several teachers in both blended- and single-grade classes wanted to develop an alternative progress report. Discussion about report cards brought up conflicting ideas, dissatisfaction with existing systems, and more questions than answers. Yet,

CHOOSE-YOUR-OWN-MATH

Name: _____

You will take two of the following classes in January, with each class lasting two weeks.

Please rank the classes from 1 to 4, with 1 being the class you most want to take, 2 for your second choice, etc. Please mark all four choices because it may not be possible to schedule you for your first two choices.

_____   *Visual Thinking and Patterns:* We will use a variety of materials—cubes, pattern blocks, and other "stuff"—to create visual images. These pictures will help solve mathematical puzzles and stories.

_____   *Geometrical Constructions:* We will design and build complex and beautiful shapes. These shapes can then be used to decorate our rooms and homes.

_____   *Measurement and Construction:* We will be using blueprints and wood to measure, cut, and construct a bird house.

_____   *Angles, Lines, and Designs:* We will use LOGO, a computer language that draws figures, to increase our knowledge of geometry and to learn how to write programs that will help us escape nasty mazes.

CHOOSE-YOUR-OWN-WRITING

Name: _____

You will be beginning a new writing topic in January. Please rank the following classes from 1 to 4, with 1 being the class you most want to take, 2 for your second choice, etc. Please mark all four choices because it may not be possible to schedule you for your first choice.

_____   *Pop-up Books:* [***First priority will be given to students who have not already done this project.]

_____   *Picture Books*

_____   *Individual Writing Projects:* For people who want to work on individual pieces of writing.

_____   *Poetry*

Figure 8.1 Example of "special" class choices

we began moving in the direction of positive change.

Prior to starting the blended program, our building used computerized report cards with a letter grade for each content area. The card included a list of 75 or so comments for teachers to select to go with assigned grades. We'd pick the appropriate comments and fill in the little bubbles on the grade sheet. I never seemed to find just the right way to say what I wanted with those canned comments, so I spent hours writing comments after the report cards had come back from the computer scanners.

At the same time, across the district we had begun to use portfolios to document growth in students' writing. The district intends that these portfolios will move with the child throughout all 12 years of schooling. A student and parents may examine the portfolio at any time. The goal is that, upon graduating from high school, each student will receive his or her portfolio representing twelve years of writing samples and reflections on the writing.

The focus on developmental growth, characteristic of these portfolios, was consistent with our goals for assessment in our classes. We wanted to move away from letter grades, to document and better represent individual growth. We also wanted to put an emphasis on developing social responsibilities and citizenship.

At first, we borrowed heavily from the progress report used at Emily Dickinson Elementary School. We organized the form in sections: Math, Language Arts, Social Studies, Science, and so forth. We also added sections called Social Responsibilities and Involved Citizens. Next, we listed descriptors under each section. Under Math, for example, we listed computational skills, problem solving, and projects; we further delineated "skills" in minute detail under each section, rating each on a four-point scale. Likewise, we listed descriptors rated on a four-point scale under all the other sections; for instance, Writing (under Language Arts) was rated for each writing process element along with "use of time," "goal setting," "grammar," and "spelling." (As we used the form during our first year, we found that reporting progress as "bits and pieces" was counterproductive and out of synch with our more integrated, holistic curriculum.)

The report forms, printed as multiple copies on NCR paper, went first to students, who marked their self-assessment in one column. Next, teachers added their marks, covering students' evaluations with a ruler while recording their own ratings.

Feedback from parents and students the first time we used these progress reports was interesting and mixed, to say the least. One parent wrote back that this was what she really wanted to know about her daughter. A number of parents wanted to know what the letter grade would be in a specific subject. Many people assumed that 1, 2, 3 corresponded to A, B, C. At conference time, parents asked more questions, but these individual conferences provided us with an important opportunity for communicating our goals. Most people liked the developmental reporting scale for social skills, but several still wanted letter grades in academic areas.

As teachers, we liked some aspects of the new progress reports, but knew we didn't yet have what we wanted. For example, while we found detailed descriptors counterproductive, some parents still wondered whether "mastery" in multiplication referred to one-, two-, or three-digit numerals. A progress report using a numeric or alphabetic scale is unlikely to please everyone or allow you to say as much as you might wish about a child's learning.

Now in our second year, we have modified the progress report again (see Figure 8.2). In the first section, listing Academic Content Areas, we report letter grades. We preserved the developmental (1–4) rating for the Social Responsibilities and Involved Citizen sections. We have added more narrative reporting through a letter cowritten by all teachers in our blended program. The letter describes the various themes, topics, and skills taught during the quarter. For example, a given student might have worked with me in math, with Amy in writers' workshop, and with all four of us for the thematic block. A student's narrative in this case would include a note from the homeroom teacher, a paragraph from me describing the student's progress in math, a paragraph from Amy describing the work in writers' workshop, and a paragraph from each of us about Thematic Block.

So far this year, we've received positive feedback, and we haven't felt overwhelmed by the new format. We will evaluate again at the end of the year to decide what further revisions we need to make. We continue to search for ways to do more narrative reporting and to utilize student portfolios more imaginatively and effectively. In our discussions, we continually ask questions that send us back to our philosophy: what do grades mean? what is assessment? how does assessment differ from evaluation? where do we want the emphasis to be—on the process of learning or on specific outcomes to be mastered, or some balance of these? how do we better interweave assessment with learning? These questions haunt me, and I'm glad they do because they keep me from becoming complacent. I need to continue questioning what assessment means to me, to parents, and—most important—to my students.

Looking to the Future

What happens next? Where do we go from here? We are looking ahead with excitement to our third year. We were right to acknowledge the need to change slowly; yet we are eager to be closer to the model we envisioned several years ago. We want to build on the

Henkle Middle School
1993 - 1994 School Year
Progress Report

Student Name _____ Homeroom Teacher _____

Content Areas	1st Quarter Teacher	Student	2nd Quarter Teacher	Student	3rd Quarter Teacher	Student	4th Quarter Teacher	Student
Math								
Reading								
Writing								
Vocabulary								
Spelling								
Science								
Social Studies								
_____								
_____								
Physical Education								

Comments:	1st Qtr	Comments:	2nd Qtr	Comments:	3rd Qtr	Comments:	4th Qtr

Music

Comments:	1st Qtr	Comments:	2nd Qtr	Comments:	3rd Qtr	Comments:	4th Qtr

Integrated Subject Areas

Evaluation Key: 1. *Area of Strength* 2. *Acceptable* 3. *Developing* 4. *Area of Concern*

Social Responsibilities	1st Quarter Teacher	Student	2nd Quarter Teacher	Student	3rd Quarter Teacher	Student	4th Quarter Teacher	Student
Self-Directed								
Displays positive attitude								
Demonstrates responsible behavior								
Completes work on time								
Keeps materials organized and available								
Works independently								
Actively listens								
Shows leadership								
Cooperates with classmates								
Uses time well								

Involved Citizens	1st Quarter Teacher	Student	2nd Quarter Teacher	Student	3rd Quarter Teacher	Student	4th Quarter Teacher	Student
Shows respect to classmates								
Demonstrates thoughtfulness								
Shares strengths with others								
Contributes to a clean environment								
Demonstrates sportsmanship								

....
Please tear off and return

Parent Signature _____ Teacher Signature _____

Date _____ Student Signature _____

Parent Comments / Observations: _____
_____
_____

Figure 8.2 Progress Report

most powerful elements of the program. For instance, I remember a sixth grader who told me last spring, "You know, Mrs. Wells, I'm worried about going to seventh grade next year because we've gotten to make so many choices about what we want to study and I just know there won't be as many choices next year"

Student choice is powerful. Students know what is important to them. When a student has a vested interest in what he or she is studying, intrinsic motivation is strong. This spring, as we look toward next year, we will include current students in planning the curriculum, especially the thematic units of study.

We envision taking topics the students choose and guiding them through a process of inquiry that will teach life-time skills. Being able to identify a topic, retrieve information, assimilate that information, and convey it to others empowers students, builds self-esteem, and prepares them to take their learning with them as they encounter a wide variety of situations.

End Notes

1. Joel Barker, "Business of Paradigms," *Discovering the Future Video Series* (Burnsville, MN: Chart House Learning Corporation, 1989).
2. Nancie Atwell, *In the Middle: Writing, Reading , and Learning With Adolescents* (Portsmouth, NH: Heinemann, 1987).
3. Lane County Education Service District, *Lane County Mathematics Project: Problem Solving in Mathematics* (Palo Alto, CA: Dale Seymour Publications, 1983).

Chapter 9

Pushing the Boundaries in a Traditional Middle School Environment: A School-within-a-School

Lynn Moss

Getting Started with a Democratic Classroom

"Hey! Whatcha 'sposed to do if you're not gonna sign this thing?" The young man defiantly stuck out his jaw, folded his arms, and waited. The class turned and stared, stunned into a thick silence.

The fifty seventh graders on my team had just spent four periods a day for the first sweaty week of a hot September in an intense effort to create a classroom constitution. We'd worked all together in what we called "general assembly," as well as in committees and sub-committees. We'd created lists of classroom rules from their past experience, as well as rules that they thought would work to make our life together run smoothly. We had also examined the actual U.S. Constitutional rights guaranteed to students as citizens of the United States. We looked, too, at the limits on those rights, the "compelling state interests" that affect schools. We then examined the rules that the student committees had proposed in light of U.S. Constitutional law, and debated the constitutionality of each proposed rule. To give an example of this discussion, the proposed rule of "No whining" was struck down after an emotional debate, where one young lady expressed her conviction that this rule would violate her right to freedom of expression.

I was having my first experience with seventh graders conducting this kind of classroom democratic process. Previously, I'd always reviewed the standard school rules at the beginning of the year, adding some stories and tidbits of advice gleaned from prior years. But after a workshop on the process of Judicious Discipline given by Dr. Forrest Gathercoal[1] of Oregon State University, I saw an opportunity for setting the structure and tone of a whole-language classroom for these students from the very first day. Our purpose would be to negotiate a set of agreed-upon standards and procedures to facilitate learning. The process would require interaction, which would also serve to help the students become acquainted with each other. The curriculum itself would be empowering, as students would learn about their rights as citizens, as well as participating in the responsibilities of a democratic group. Naively, with my adult need to create simplicity out of chaos, what I had envisioned was that the team would eventually arrive at three or four nice, simple, easily applied rules, such as "Respect one another." I discovered, instead, that this process unleashed an innate hidden potential of 12-year-olds: they are natural litigators, and our team lawbook ended up with 32 laws!

John, however, with his challenge, had stopped the entire process. What would we do if someone refused to sign the finished classroom constitution? The kids looked at me and at one another, and everyone waited to see what would happen next.

"Whatcha 'sposed to do if you aren't gonna sign it?" he repeated, staring at me. I would like to report that I quickly had a perfect response, a soothing phrase, a precise question to ask back. In fact, I was amazed at how unexpected I found this question. It's astonishing, I thought to myself, how often I assume that the students will just do whatever I ask of them.

"What an interesting question, John," I finally said.

John blurted out, "Hey, I've been talking about gum but you guys are up there and you're not writing it down. I mean, you guys are up there and you have the pen!"

In fact, John was right. My teaching partner and I had black markers and newsprint and we would take turns acting as scribe and discussion leader. At the moment of John's challenge, the class was working on creating a Preamble for our Constitution. Except for John, who was working on nursing a grudge from a few days back. Despite my efforts to make gum a non-issue, anyone who knows seventh graders knows that this is an area of passion. A few days back, the class had created a rule that said, "Gum is okay, but rude popping is not." However, unknown to me, John had subsequently been asked by an instructional assistant passing through the room to get rid of his gum. It was still the first week of school, and although things looked promising to the kids, trust is not established overnight. John had gotten rid of his gum, but had not known what to do with his frustration except to effectively step outside of what must have seemed to him as a grand charade. It took a little time to sort out the events behind the challenge—it seems to be in the nature of schools that emotional issues such as these erupt two minutes before some bell rings and everyone has to get up and leave. I was reminded that our classroom was but a subculture in a larger institution, and that we would have to develop ways of functioning within that institution. (There is no school-wide rule regarding gum, but apparently it is an area of passion for adults as well.)

Before school the next day, I approached John in the hallway and told him that I wanted to share with him a kind of personal vision. I told him that, for this day, what I would love to see is for him to take the pen. Although I didn't go into a description of this with him, I had understood that, for John (and probably others), the position and the pen represented power. I wanted to share this power with him and other students.

"Forget it. I can't write," he said.

I told him that the newsprint posters were a record of our ideas, not a spelling or penmanship test. And I told him that I had another dream, too. I told him that what I would most want to happen was that he would be the first person to sign the class Constitution.

"I don't care about that thing," he muttered, and walked away. An hour later, he came to me and said, "I'll take the pen."

He did; and he was also the first person to sign the document. All proposed rules were ratified, most of them by 90 percent or more of the team. "Respect your local teachers!" was the only rule ratified unanimously by the class. I accepted this as a gift from them in return for the respect we had shown to them by listening to their concerns and ideas about how the classroom should run.

Events That Led to This Democratic Classroom

I was teaching in a public intermediate school, grades seven through nine. Many of you would recognize it: the same bells, the same subjects, similar underlying assumptions, and probably familiar-looking kids in the hallways. I had been in the same school for all of the 6 years that I had been a classroom teacher, but much had changed. Teams, new learning theories and teaching strategies, a changing school neighborhood, new administration; all had their impact on the school. And I'd changed, too.

I arrived at this school after attending an elementary teacher-preparation program emphasizing a whole-language approach to educating children. This preparation confirmed what I had come to understand from my previous years as a pre-school teacher. I soon discovered that no one at my intermediate school spoke my particular dialect of pedagogy. Most of my colleagues had secondary, not elementary preparation. And so, like an exile in a foreign land, I left behind the language of my origins, but not the rhythms or the culture, which were too deeply embedded and central to my philosophy of education to abandon. I struggled to create a whole-language environment for my students, but I did not name it whole language, largely because my colleagues were not familiar with that term. "Can you get it at Learning World?" I was asked, during one attempt at communicating about whole language with a fellow teacher. Probably not!

On the other hand, I found it possible to change the structure of my own classroom rather significantly. Over time, I discovered that the kind of flexibility available to me as an educator within the school increased.

The process of change was incremental. Seven years ago I began as a social studies/language arts block teacher. I inherited a file cabinet of fill-in-the-blank worksheets and a curriculum of "subjects" that were disconnected from each other. It was also the first year of interdisciplinary teams in my building, and everyone was excited by the prospects and possibilities of teaming. As the year wore on, however, some of the difficulties of actually creating interdisciplinary "units" of study became more obvious. Every subject, of course, had traditional topics that needed to be "covered." And so, how did one actually connect such disparate topics as frog dissection and the study of Islam? What topics would veteran teachers "give up" to make time for some new interdisciplinary topic of study? That each team would create even one interdisciplinary unit became a stressful expectation. A few teams managed to do one, would spend a couple of weeks on it, and then, with a sigh of relief, would return to their separate scope and sequence of topics. More teams, however, discovered—as did my teammate and I—that the real strengths of teaming, at least initially, lay in the sharing of students. Instead of creating a topical unit of study, my teammate and I focused on creating a menu of student skills and learning strategies that we would both emphasize throughout the entire year: active listening, notetaking, using the library as a tool for learning, working cooperatively in groups, for example. This was actually an important first step for me away from seeing the exclusive focus of my efforts in the classroom as the teaching of content. Teaching students how to learn became the backbone of my efforts, the scaffolding upon which I hung the topical content of my class.

The next big step was two years later, when the administration reconfigured my team to include a math teacher and another social studies/language arts block teacher as a pilot project. We were highly influenced by the work of Sizer and the Essential Schools Coalition[2] when we sat down for three days together to brainstorm how we would organize our program. We maintained our content area specialist roles. I became the social studies teacher for the team. But we decided that, among the four of us, we had four periods of time in the bell schedule. We arranged for these periods to be blocked together, and then organized our time independent of the bell schedule for the building. We created flexible skill group "labs" for reading and math, then heterogeneously grouped the students for the rest of the subjects, including another math class emphasizing concepts. We all taught a math lab. We all taught a reading lab. We all taught study skills and strategies. And we all taught in our content areas. But an important bridge had been built for increased communication among the subject areas by the very structure of the program we had designed. We saw increased opportunities for some cross-discipline units of study. Reading groups read a novel about whales. The students studied whales in science class. And we all went whale-watching. The English teacher and I switched subject areas for a time so that she could teach about medieval Japan, which she knew a lot about, and I could teach poetry, which I loved. The "subject" lines began to blur. A student needing help in math, for instance, could ask any of the four teachers for guidance.

Within my classroom, I found myself including more drama and role playing, more art, more design technology.[3] "Design a system to move water from the Nile River to your crops." The classroom began to feel more like a laboratory. The textbooks sat on the shelf more of the year. As a result of the frustration of competing for the best media with all of the other seventh grade social studies teachers in the district, I decided one year to teach my history class backwards! The kids seemed to "learn about" the Middle Ages just as well in September as they had previously done in April.

Thus, I discovered that many of the boundaries which I had thought of as inflexible were, in fact, much more fluid. Risks taken, new strategies tried, bridges of communication that were built, structures that were bent, all had positive outcomes for the students. We tested, interviewed, polled opinions, and compared data to be sure of this! The administration supported our new proposals for change because the results of previous changes were positive

A New Direction

The teaching situation that I describe in the rest of this chapter is the outcome of one such recent change. I had become increasingly frustrated that much of what I did in my classroom still consisted of "learning about" history. I wanted to make more connections with other realms of knowledge. And so I joined with another teacher to design a team that consisted of 50 heterogeneously-grouped students and two teachers. We had two rooms with an opening wall that allowed us to be a big group for films, guest speakers, celebrations, and other special events. We had four periods of the school day, plus a homeroom period, which allowed us quite a bit of time within which we could flexibly schedule our own day. Our academic responsibilities required that my teaching partner and I provide instruction and assessment in four subjects: mathematics, science, language arts, and social studies. We did, however, have a great deal of flexibility in how we approached these responsibilities.

Before we began teaming together, my teammate and I met several times over the summer months to begin planning. What had drawn us together was our mututally held desire to create a truly integrated curriculum for our students. We spent the summer months trying to weave together our school's standard seventh grade curriculum into themes, such as "Migration" or "Adaptation." I saw our efforts to develop themes as an improvement on the discreet subject matter boundaries that were standard in my school, despite the "interdisciplinary teams" that had been functioning for five years. I remembered the previous year that one bright young man had muttered, "From frogs legs to Islam!" as he entered my social studies classroom after a science lab. Indeed, after a day of shadowing a student, one of my colleagues had commented that the experience reminded her of watching television when someone else has the remote control! Well, our thematic units would improve on that, we thought. One more step on the one-step-at-a-time path to change that I had been on for the past seven years.

A Catalyst for Real Change

Once in awhile, however, one takes a step and finds no solid ground underneath. It happened that, months before, I had written to James Beane,[4] who envisions a major revision of the middle school curriculum to better meet the needs of the adolescent. I had hoped that perhaps he might be able to help me connect with some other schools that who were creating adolescent-centered learning units.

A week before school started, he responded, saying that he would be in Portland on some other business and perhaps we could meet. And so, the week before school began, my teammate and I sat with Jim Beane for about five of the most exciting hours of my career and talked about his ideas, and how they were functioning in real classrooms. He convinced us that involving kids in the curriculum planning process was an essential ingredient and referred us to the article that he, Barbara Brodhagen, and Gary Weilbacher[5] had written about a curriculum experiment in a Madison, Wisconsin, public school where the students and their teachers had collaborated on creating their own curriculum. Jim Beane convincingly presents a strong case for a middle school classroom that addresses the real concerns of adolescents, that respects their dignity and individuality, and that provides young people with actual practice in the democratic processes upon which our nation is based. What could be a more powerful, more authentic curriculum than that which addresses the stated questions and concerns of the students in the class themselves?

And so, in late August, one week before school began, we threw out all our planning, all our units, and decided instead to base our learning for the year on the real issues raised by our students. Not, mind you, the issues that we thought in advance might be raised! No, we would wait and go through a process of inquiry with our students. We would begin the year with miles and miles of blank butcher paper. We would ask the students to voice the real questions and concerns they have about themselves and their own lives, and about the world and their place in the world. We would form our curriculum for the year around those questions and concerns. Imagine: one week before school, with no handouts to print, no textbooks, no labs planned. It took some courage. It also took support from our building principal. During a case of cold feet a day or two before school started, we told him that we felt a lot like we were in a kind of "free fall," but we did, after all, have those unit plans we had created earlier as a parachute, if we needed them. Our principal reminded us that committing to this process pretty much eliminated parachutes, or else we might end up sabotaging our own efforts. Quite true, as it turned out.

Collaborative Curriculum Planning

The September curriculum planning with our students was indeed an incredibly exciting process. After creating a class constitution, we spent almost two weeks examining the questions and concerns with which these young people arrived in seventh grade. The students listed these on butcher paper. The walls of our rooms became covered with the seeds for our inquiry for the year. Never would someone watching these students ever again think that adolescents "don't care." The questions and concerns raised by these students were thoughtful, important, sometimes poignant; they encompassed a broad range of issues, such as, Why do people make war? Will we all die of AIDS? and What happened to JFK's spirit in America? The students then grouped these concerns into broad themes, which became the curriculum for our year. At this point in the process, one of our primary roles as teachers was to help students see the intersections between their personal concerns and the issues of the larger world body. (For a more precise explanation of this curriculum planning process, see "Living in the Future: An Experiment with an Integrative Curriculum."[6])

Not unexpectedly, the themes students chose to explore did not completely overlap with the standard seventh grade curriculum for our school district. For example, *Conflict, Environment, Our Future, Space,* and *The Economy* were some of the themes my students chose to explore. The encouragement of our building principal, Fred Sutherland, to free ourselves from a narrow interpretation of district curriculum goals was critical during this process.

Since the curriculum planning process came on the heels of building a classroom constitution, the students on our team spent much of September getting to know one another through working in groups, brainstorming, presenting information to the larger class, and leading lively discussions. We established learning logs, too, as a place for students to reflect in writing; we set up a rotating schedule so we could dialogue in writing with each student once every two weeks. I had four learning logs to respond to each day for four days of every week. This was a manageable limit and allowed me to really reflect and comment upon the students' thinking and work. The students absolutely loved corresponding with their teachers, and shared thoughts and feelings about their work, their reading, the classroom process, and sometimes frustrations and problems they would not have shared in group discussion. Furthermore, the learning logs became tangible evidence of students' growth over time; like a diary, these became "precious" to many of our students. We were addressing issues important to them, and they responded from their hearts. There was nothing contrived about the curriculum of the first three weeks of school. How will we run our classroom? What direction will our learning take this year? The students had a real purpose and deep interest in the outcome. And thanks to a number of crises, such as when John pointed out the power of position and pen, I learned in many different ways to become more supportive and less controlling. I became a better listener, and learned to wait longer before I responded. I learned to ask better questions. I learned that the structure of a classroom and its processes can imply a lot about the balance of power within that classroom. I learned to trust in our group process—to trust that our process might be messy or ambiguous or even confrontational at times, but that if I waited, if I could sustain the tension of not having neat little conclusions at the end of every 45-minute lesson, something rich and real and solid might happen for us all.

Suddenly, I recognized that I was actually immersed in a whole-language environment! I hadn't asked, "What science questions do you have about the world today?" or "What are the critical mathematical problems you face?" And yet, in the process of eliciting the true concerns of these young people, every subject offered in the school and more was touched upon.

Instead of correcting worksheets, I spent my time trying to realize the potential for exploration lying within each question that the students had raised. I had not been a textbook-based teacher for several years. (The local libraries are used to seeing me appear with boxes to fill for my classroom.) But I realized that I was looking upon questions so exciting, so varied and, at times, so poignant, that print alone could never answer all of them. I saw opportunities to truly connect my classroom to the larger community. I knew we would need to approach knowledgable individuals to help us explore some of the issues raised. I saw questions that might best be explored through drama, creative writing, or art. I saw many opportunities for scientific exploration and experimentation. Students would need practical applied mathematical skills for the evaluation and presentation of many of the inquiries. Students would need to become comfortable with a wide range of skills and strategies as they grappled with the questions they themselves had raised.

A Stumbling Block

It was at this point, ripe with so many possibilities, that a problem developed. This often happens in the real world, and after all, my story is not a fairy tale. The panorama of possiblities had the effect of overwhelming my teaching partner. We tried a temporary compromise: we would buy some time for ourselves to become better adjusted. We would use our "parachute," one of the preplanned, interdisciplinary units that we had created over the summer. We told the students that we needed some time to get ready for their first selected academic theme. If the kids were suspicious of our intentions, they didn't show it. Probably they were used to teachers needing time to prepare. With the clear vision of hindsight, I now realize that this decision derailed us more than we could have known at the time. Not only had we done something of a double-shuffle with the kids, but we had also claimed the responsibility of "preparing the curriculum" for the students. The students sat back. Textbooks were passed out, lessons delivered. It was beginning to feel once again like school.

As it turned out, during this period of time, my teaching partner and I realized that we had quite different comfort zones in the face of the new classroom structure and curriculum we had unleashed. Not only that, but we had attempted at the same time to co-teach, with both of us present in the classroom at the same time, which is a process I now understand to be much like a form of improvisational dance. We realized that we were hearing very different music; we couldn't get our rythmns to synchronize. So that we could move forward, each of us doing what we are best at doing, we closed the doors between our rooms. One chapter ended. Another began.

I returned to the themes that the students had selected. The first theme they had decided to address was "The Environment." And yes, because I had told them it was to be "prepared," it was. Using the lists of questions and concerns they had created in September, I selected readings, and created labs, simulations, and hands-on activities that addressed their questions. It was an exciting six weeks, during which I experienced my first confrontations with a number of issues relating to integrated curriculum. The kids would at first ask, "Is this science or social studies?" (My teaching partner had assumed the official responsibility for teaching language arts, I "to ok" science and social studies, and we shared mathematics.) The discussion about "subjects" was one of our first issues and generated a number of interesting classroom discussions. For instance, would reading an article about the environmental impact of disposable vs. cotton diapers be classified as science or social studies? And what about the survey of their own families' diaper preferences, or the classroom graph of the results of the survey? Was that math or social studies? And was the paper they wrote on the topic, or the persuasive speech they gave about the issue, language arts or science? The students quickly became more comfortable with calling our integrated curriculum "Core," and seemed to have no problem with anything from poetry to math problems appearing on the day's agenda, as long as they related to the enviromental questions that we were addressing.

A Teaching-Learning Partnership Begins

It was with our second unit, *Conflict*, that I let go of the sole responsibility for "preparing" the curriculum for my students. We began by reviewing the key questions and concerns students had expressed at the beginning of the year that we had grouped under the theme, *Conflict*. We added, revised, or set aside questions in group brainstorming and discussion sessions. Each student chose a specific question to investigate, such as: Why do kids join gangs? Why did veterans feel bad after the Vietnam War? Why do people commit suicide? Some students picked a question that was primarily of individual interest to them and which they would pursue independently. Other students picked questions that were quite broad and encompassing, or of more common interest. These students formed small collaborative groups, each taking responsibility for one aspect of the question.

My initial responsibilities, as I saw it, included helping the students pose, clarify, and expand their questions. Throughout the brainstorming process I took every opportunity to prod for clarification and elaboration, and to help students extend beyond initial questions. Students need to learn how to formulate questions and how to learn by investigation and inquiry—seventh graders are not generally prepared to do much of this. Some students tended to try to reestablish their familiar comfort zones by quickly zooming in on a topic (such as

"War") rather than on a question. I asked questions such as, "What specifically intrigues you or concerns you about war?" With discussion, students generated a range of questions—for example: What was it really like to be a soldier in Vietnam? What do all those medals and ribbons that I've been collecting for years really mean? What kinds of tanks were in World War II and did they play a significant role? All of these, incidentally, were questions from what I secretly thought of as my "GI Joe" group. Initially, this group was my toughest personal challenge because it pushed some personal buttons for me. I am not a war buff, and I've never really enjoyed military history. I tended to doubt whether these questions posed by the students represented an authentic inquiry. Based on the outcomes of this experience, however, I now tend to trust more readily the child's internal processes and guidance. Eventually, all kinds of things came to light that might have been missed opportunities for growth if, because of my discomfort, I had steered this group away from the topic. For example, one young lady within this group had focused like a laser on Hitler's treatment of the Jews. She read a number of books, such as *The Diary of Anne Frank*[7] and *Number the Stars*.[8] Interestingly, however, she also read excerpts from *The Rise and Fall of the Third Reich*[9] and *Inside the Third Reich*.[10] It slowly became apparent that she, in fact, was searching for what had motivated people to follow Hitler. Why did they become Nazis? What she finally revealed to me was that she is a direct descendant of one of Hitler's closest associates. Her final line in her paper was a quote from this relative: "We are all guilty and we know it and try to deny it." For this young lady, the project on conflict held a deeply personal and powerful meaning, one of trying to come to terms with a difficult family inheritance.

After the students had all settled on their inquiry, the next step was for them to make a plan for how they might begin to find answers to their questions. For example, the student whose question dealt with what it was really like to be a soldier decided to network among family and friends to connect with veterans. She expanded her inquiry to include veterans of other wars in addition to the Vietnam war so that she might have a basis for comparison. She then interviewed these veterans.

Another of my responsibilities as teacher usually evolved once students' investigations were under way. How could they best present their learning? (For example, the young lady who was interviewing veterans decided to write a war diary for a fictional soldier who would be based on her interviews.) The entire classroom community, not just the teacher, was the audience for students' presentations. They would have to present their learning in a way that helped others to learn as well. Interestingly, the students' level of concern skyrocketed at this point. I pointed out that their presentations would be something like a piano recital, although these could take a wide variety of forms. At a piano recital, one would certainly not decide to play "Chopsticks"! The presentation, or exhibit, would have to be of "recital quality." The students and I conferenced individually to develop mutually agreed-upon contracts. These set the criteria for presentations and projects, as well as performance benchmarks and target dates along the way towards completion. The art of appropriate goal-setting is difficult for many students, and I learned that each student needed to be counseled individually in order to set a project goal that would be an achievable challenge. Furthermore, the fleshing out of an idea into reality and the breaking down of a large task into manageable steps—also difficult tasks for many of my students—kept them from feeling overwhelmed or tempted to do superficial work.

It was about this time that I revamped my gradebook. It became more of a notebook, with an entirely different kind of bookkeeping. I kept copies of the contracts with the benchmark dates, as well as notes taken during conferences with the students. I conferenced with them regularly, at their request (a sign-up clipboard) or mine. I kept notes on their goals, their progress, the target dates we set, and any problems they were encountering. This gave me a regular opportunity to suggest or help arrange for resources that might be helpful to students, as well as to monitor their progress toward meeting the agreed-upon criteria and standards for their work.

Our classroom became a "workshop," modeled somewhat along the lines of a writer's workshop.[11] I usually began the class with a brief mini-lesson, often skills related. For example, during the *Conflict* unit, I taught several mini-lessons on telephone skills, such as introducing yourself, explaining your purpose, making a clear request, what to do when you can't get through to the person you want, and how to use the telephone book. I also included lessons on how to order media from the media center, how to review a movie, how to write good interview questions, how to ask follow-up questions, and how to write an opinion survey. The content of the mini-lessons emerged from the actual work of the students and their real needs.

As the unit on conflict progressed, students also expressed interest in lessons on presentation skills, such as lettering, drawing maps, organizing data and making effective graphs, bookbinding, making transparencies, or operating a video camera. Sometimes I worked on a skill with a small interest group; at other times lessons were appropriate for the entire class.

Our learning "space" expanded, too. The front office staff at the school were very kind about letting my students use the telephone. Students watched filmstrips and videos in the hallways. The library functioned as a virtual extension of the classroom. Parents made arrangements to provide transportation for their offspring to conduct face-to-face interviews. Our classroom extended into the entire school community.

In process, the classroom often looked something like this:

"What's the difference between a thermonuclear and a nuclear bomb?" Khara asked me.

"Hmmm . . . , that's a good question," I replied. (This kind of statement seemed to come out of my mouth more often!) Right now, Khara was creating a peace quilt, with an accompanying booklet that described in detail her learning and the symbolism of the quilt. "Why don't you check with Michael and see if he can help you with your question? Then let me know what you find out!"

Michael was deeply involved in researching the engineering of nuclear weapons. When I looked up again a few minutes later, Khara and Michael were still talking and Michael was sketching out an answer on paper for her. An open dictionary was on the table. Later, Khara stopped by to summarize Michael's answer.

That morning, Ryan had stopped by before school to drop off a video that he had checked out of the library. "I think everybody should see this," he said. "Could you preview it and make some time for it?"

"I'll preview it this weekend, Ryan, and then we could summarize it and see if the class wants to give an hour to this topic; okay?" I responded.

Partway through this unit, I stopped and asked the students to write down some of the things they had learned so far that might apply to other learning situations. Some of their responses were:

- I learned how to get information out of a big book.
- The phone book has a lot of important numbers in the front.
- I learned how to call up people I don't know and talk with them.
- Don't start something you can't finish.
- There can be more to research than just reading a book, like interviewing somebody, or watching a movie.
- Sometimes there's a big difference between an idea and how it comes out.
- I learned how not to get stuck, and how to move on to a new goal.

As these comments demonstrate, some students obviously experienced frustrations during this process. "Just give me a worksheet," a student had muttered on one dark day. But the comments also reveal that students can overcome their frustrations, given sufficient time and support.

As in a writer's workshop, creating in our classroom was a multidimensional process. Students went through the processes of vision, revision, conferencing, and polishing. Students who sidestepped an element and prematurely announced themselves "Done!" were initially surprised by receiving a "Not Yet" in place of a grade. "It takes a lot of practice for a piano recital," I'd remind them. I overheard a group of students advising a newcomer to our team. "She's a tough grader," one young lady said, "but she wants you to do good."

In addition to providing skills lessons, I also felt I had the responsibility to build a common thread of learning throughout the unit that would tie it together. Since our unit was *Conflict*, I decided to share with the students a variety of types of non-violent ways of resolving conflict, as well as sharing profiles of some peacemakers in our history. And so, about once a week, I would show a movie, such as *Gandhi*, or a profile of Martin Luther King, Jr. Or we might make a play out of Dr. Seuss' *Sneetches*,[12] or perhaps a psychologist might come to talk with us about methods of resolving internal conflicts. Generally, Friday was "my day" to focus on something I felt was important and of general interest to the entire class.

The unit closed with students sharing their learning. This occurred in as many different ways as I had earlier anticipated. In some cases, a student had arranged to invite speakers to our classroom, such as a local sheriff, so that other kids could learn from them as well. Some students had videotaped or recorded interviews that they shared with the class as part of their learning. To illustrate a point, students showed portions of movies; a shared *Star Trek* episode illustrated the conflict between friendship and duty. Students presented data visually, read papers to the class, and did a reading of a play written about schoolyard bullies.

Assessment and Evaluation

The final step for us was a collaborative process of assessment and evaluation. Students considered various aspects of the process. What was the hardest part of their project? What turned out to be a part that they were particularly proud of? What new skills had they acquired during this project? What goals did they meet? exceed? miss? How well had they organized their notes? How well did they utilize classroom time? Since the students were working to meet clear criteria spelled out individually in our contracts, the evaluation process was not particularly difficult. In fact, I had seen the evolution of all the students' work multiple times, and so there were almost no surprises. In most cases, the class greeted presentations with spontaneous applause; students' pride in their work was evident. One student wrote me a note:

> I just wanted to take this space (on a self-assessment) to
> thank you for this opportunity. I have learned very much.
> I have done something I am proud of and that's a great
> feeling.

Another student wrote, "You showed me I can do something if I put my mind to it." And a third student, who had chosen to investigate the conflict between the pros and cons of the death penalty, told me: "I thought I knew what was right before I began investigating. I didn't realize how complicated it is. Now I'm not so sure."

Perhaps some people would take issue with regarding "not so sure" as a sign of this student's growth. But I knew the student had done a thorough job of investigating both sides of the issue; she now saw clearly its complexity. This was, in fact, a more mature point of view than her earlier position. Out of this experience I felt sure that, as she continues to grow, she will reflect on, and carefully formulate her positions on, controversial issues.

One final note on evaluation. I did have those report cards, don't forget! I found myself most comfortable with assigning target points for student work. For example, I might say that to achieve an "A" during the *Conflict* unit, a student needed to accumulate 500 points. Then, there would be a menu of somewhat flexible point values. Reading a historical novel relating to the issue might be worth 100 points if the student also connects it in some agreed-upon way to his or her inquiry. Interviewing an expert could earn 75 points if the student submitted the questions prepared in advance, as well as a transcript of the interview and a statement of conclusions drawn from it. Part of what we did during our conferencing sessions was to negotiate these target points. A student who submitted a poor interview write-up might receive a "Not Yet" in place of any points, and would have to revise it, in some cases having to telephone the interviewee for follow-up information. A student who did a deeply insightful interview and write-up might receive more than the target points. In fact, many of the students earned well over the 500 target points. The points became beside the point! The learning became the object of focus for most of the students.

I juggled the themes of inquiry so that in each grading quarter I addressed and was able to justify evaluation in both social studies and science. In addition to the mini-lessons I taught four days of the week, during units that lent themselves well to a science focus, I generally planned a lab for "my" day. During our unit on space, for example, we performed several simple physics labs to help us understand gravity, orbit, and so on. The science teachers in the school got used to my approaching them for lab equipment, as well as to pick their brains for more ways to build science into our classroom investigations.

A Learning Community

You would recognize the school that I taught in. It is probably in many, many ways a lot like your school. One of the most important things that I learned from this year is that many of the boundaries we place between us and the ideal are actually much more plastic and flexible than we may initially realize. What were some of the boundaries that we were able to stretch within our school? First of all, the content of our negotiated curriculum defied the subject-area boundaries and connected all the disciplines. Furthermore, the classroom became the entire community, and "teacher" became an expanded concept as students reached out to learn from one another and from experts outside of our classroom. On Saturdays, groups of students might get together to watch a movie that related to their inquiry; or as a class we might gather to visit a water treatment plant. (We called these "Independent Field Trips" because parents provided the transportation. That the parents became involved in this way in the learning community was a bonus.) We pushed the boundaries of who decided what kids should learn, and how much responsibility students had to take for their own learning. In fact, despite my initial discomfort in departing from the well-known path, all of this felt enormously natural; so much so that I was left wondering why we in schools developed the unnatural path of totally separate treatment of subjects.

Consider carefully the boundaries that limit you and keep you from connecting with the whole child. Could some of these boundaries be stretched a bit, here and there? A more fulfilling, meaningful path may be only a few important steps from where you now stand.

End Notes

1. Forrest Gathercoal, *Judicious Discipline* (Ann Arbor, MI: Caddo Gap Press, 1990).
2. Theodore R. Sizer, "Diverse Practice, Shared Ideas: The Essential School," in *Organizing for Learning: Toward the 21st Century*, ed. Herbert J. Walberg and John J. Lane (Reston, VA: National Association of Secondary School Principals, 1989), 1–8.
3. Susan Dunn and Rob Larson, *Design Technology: Children's Engineering* (New York: Falmer Press, 1990).
4. James A. Beane, National College of Education, National-Louis University, Madison, Wisconsin.
5. Barbara Brodhagen, Gary Weilbacher, and James Beane, "Living in the Future: An Experiment with an Integrative Curriculum," *Dissemination Services on the Middle Grades* 23 (June 1992): 1–7.
6. Brodhagen et al., 1–7.
7. Anne Frank, *Diary of a Young Girl* (New York: Pocket Books, 1952).
8. Lois Lowry, *Number the Stars* (Boston: Houghton Mifflin, 1979).
9. William Lawrence Shirer, *The Rise and Fall of the Third Reich* (New York: Simon and Schuster, 1960).
10. Albert Speer, *Inside the Third Reich* (New York: Macmillan, 1970).
11. Nancy Atwell, *In the Middle: Writing, Reading, and Learning With Adolescents* (Portsmouth, NH: Heinemann, 1987).
12. Dr. Seuss, *Sneetches and Other Stories* (New York: Random House, 1989).

PART III

Learning Together: Middle School/University Partnerships

Chapter 10

A Learning Journey: Exploring Teaching and Learning in the Middle School Language Arts Classroom

Patricia Tefft Cousin and Ellen Aragon

A Learning Journey

This is a story of a learning journey, a journey we have taken as we have collaborated, in our roles as a university teacher and public school teacher, on reading and writing curriculum in middle school classrooms. When we first began working together, we decided to initially focus on refining the writing process curriculum in Ellen's classroom. We each read curriculum books on writing like *In the Middle* by Nancie Atwell,[1] *Writers in Training* by Rebecca Kaplan,[2] and *Seeking Diversity* by Linda Rief.[3] We also talked to other teachers about holistic, process-oriented classrooms. We imagined that Ellen's classroom would be as equally well organized and run as those we read about in books and articles. Ellen's reflections chronicle that process:

> After reading several professional books about how to teach reading and writing to middle school students, I became inspired. I couldn't wait to get to my classroom and set it up in the way the books told me. I wanted my kids to come in and engage in meaningful reading and writing activities. I envisioned myself gliding around the room witnessing in-depth conversations about books; kids scrambling for paper to take notes about passages or looking for another book by the same author. I was ready. Reading and writing centers were organized and inviting.

However, we found that our reality looked very different from our expectations and dreams. Our ideas about what it meant to change to an effective, student-oriented language arts curriculum were challenged. Again, Ellen's reflections:

> The students did not know what to do, they did not understand and most importantly they did not care about my curriculum. In other words, it was meaningless to them. I went back to the books, knowing there was a piece I was missing. I looked longingly at the student samples included in these books and thought, "How can I make my kids do this?"

After several enlightening and challenging years working together in middle school classrooms, we can now look back and realize our first mistake was thinking we could *make* kids do anything. As we reflected on what we wanted our classroom to look like, we realized we had focused the change process *on the students*. But we have found that in order to enable and support the learning process for our students, we needed to first initiate change *in ourselves* and the way we viewed our roles as teachers in the classroom. As we began to shift our view from our world to theirs, numerous opportunities for learning for both the students and ourselves opened up.

From Experts to Learners

In this chapter, we chronicle our change as teachers who believed we were experts to teachers who viewed ourselves as learners. It is also a chronicle of what we have learned from collaborating with each other. We first discuss the contexts in which Ellen teaches, classrooms far different from those we had read about in books. Second, we discuss how the curriculum used in Ellen's class was developed based on the students' needs, focusing particularly on how the writing process was supported in this context. Third, we present a case study of one student to illustrate how reframing our role impacts what we do in the classroom. The case study demonstrates a process of critique and reflection for examining our work as teachers. We see the day-to-day work with our students as an ongoing process in which we move back and forth between the role of teacher and learner. The classroom of our dreams no longer governs our view of success; instead, we now focus on what we see every day in our classrooms.

The Context

The Community Environment

The middle school in which Ellen works is located in a district in the suburban area of Los Angeles. In a community formerly dependent on a steel mill, the school serves a diverse group of 1,300 students, many from families with low socioeconomic status. Unemployment is common. Of the parents who are employed, many have a daily three-hour commute to jobs in Los Angeles. Over 70 percent of the parents of our students have not graduated from high school. This school deals with many of the challenges encountered when working with students who have had few of the educational and social opportunities many consider "basic" for success in school.

The majority of students who attend this school have reading and writing competency levels that are far less sophisticated than we would expect for students this age. Eighty percent of the students are designated as Chapter 1 students, as determined by scores at the 30th percentile or less on standardized achievement tests. More than one-third of the student body changes during an academic year due to transiency. Many dislike reading and writing because they have had few experiences in which school activities have been connected with them personally.

The School Environment

A context like this certainly called for a school environment far different from the traditional middle school. And when the school, beginning its fifth year of operation, opened, it was with an innovative structure and curriculum based on *Caught in the Middle*,[4] *Middle School Quality Criteria*,[5] *Turning Points*,[6] and the *State of California Language Arts Framework*.[7] Seventh and eighth graders learn in integrated classes for math/science (one teacher), and social studies/language arts (one teacher), while sixth graders remain in self-contained classrooms. Most students with special needs participate in regular education classrooms in which specialists co-teach and collaborate with the classroom teacher. The curriculum is organized around an integrated thematic approach, with a heavy emphasis on the use of simulations, computers, manipulatives, and hands-on activity-oriented projects. This setting provided a ready and open-ended context to organize language arts instruction in new ways.

The Curriculum

Developing the Curriculum

The books we had read were excellent resources for our initial attempts at refining the writing process curriculum. However, we now know that we did not have a full understanding of *our role* as teachers in mediating the process with the students, particularly with the large group of students who had few successful experiences with writing. We had to learn how to guide and encourage students throughout all aspects of the writing process.

Through experimentation based on our knowledge of the writing process and observation of our students, we found that we had to create a curriculum that would personalize learning and provide support for the students we saw each day. Students had to learn that their experiences had value and could be used as the basis for their writing. When students had difficulty in generating ideas, we learned to recognize this as a sign that a particular topic might not be one with which the writer was well acquainted. We would then suggest choosing another topic that had more relevance to the writer's life. Over time the students came to trust their voices and experiences.

Developing Methods of Interaction

We also focused attention on developing specific methods of interacting with students that mediated the writing process for them. Examples of some of these methods follow:

Support and Feedback for Writing

We developed multiple methods to provide support and feedback for writing from peers. One of the most successful ways was to read student writing to the class on a regular basis. We usually asked the students to focus their comments on two or three elements, such as what got them interested in this piece, what types of elaboration or description were effective, or how dialogue was used. A heuristic we used was to ask students to divide a paper into six squares (one square for each piece read aloud). As an author read a piece, other students recorded specific comments to share as part of the large group discussion.

A second method involved teaching students to read and respond in pairs. We demonstrated this process to the entire class by reading a short piece. One of us then responded to it and wrote responses and questions about the piece on the overhead. Then another piece was read and we asked students to write an individual response. Volunteers then shared their responses with the class. After this was completed several times with the large group, we asked students to do this in pairs. This type of peer review became a regular part of our writing curriculum.

Encouraging Different Genres of Writing

We provided multiple opportunities to try out different genres of writing. Our primary method for this was to match literature selections and books exemplifying specific genres of writing with student exploration of that genre. For example, when students were engaged in reflective writing, we asked them to read the story, "The Pie," in a book of short stories by Gary Soto.[8] This story was a reflective piece about theft. After reading and discussing this piece and others like it, students developed new understandings about this style of writing.

Author study further extended these activities. For each genre, we read a series of pieces by an author who wrote in the genre. The entire class discussed the writing style and techniques the author used. After completion of this author's work, we suggested to students that they consider adapting some of this author's style and technique as they composed in the same genre.

Structures and Strategies to Support Initial Attempts at Writing

We provided supportive structures that boosted students' initial attempts at writing. We discussed the "typical" pattern or structure for specific types of writing, for example, the components of an argumentative piece. We also exposed students to the five-paragraph structure. While we did not require students to use these structures, we found they provided an example students might try out. Many of our less sophisticated students seemed to benefit from our discussions of possible writing structures and formats, seeming to have had little experience or exposure to this information. While some students relied on these formats when they first began to write, they moved away from them as their competency level increased.

We also planned and presented diverse types of pre-writing strategies—for example, mind mapping, outlining, semantic mapping, graphic organizers—to help students organize their ideas into paragraphs.[9] We asked them to choose the planning structure that seemed to best fit their style and employ it as they began a new piece.

Practice for the State Writing Assessment

We provided opportunities for students to analyze and practice the evaluation format used as part of the state assessment program. We planned time to teach students how to read writing prompts used in the state writing assessment program. We taught test-taking strategies, such as understanding how to underline the important words in both the Writing Situation and Directions for Writing, and to box any words that told them what to write. And we provided many experiences in writing to prompts.

Use of Writing Conventions: Revising and Editing

We taught and supported the use of writing conventions and revision as part of the writing process. We asked students to write rough drafts for several weeks before we introduced revision. They needed to have a series of drafts completed, to acquire some familiarity with the process, before we asked them to make first attempts at revision. We then allowed them to choose the draft that they wanted to revise.

Second, we taught students to use a consistent set of editing marks. One effective strategy to teach proofreading and editing was called "Fix-It." We took sentences or paragraphs out of the students' own work (with their permission) and put them on the overhead. We then asked students to come up to the overhead to "fix-it" for the class. We discussed corrections as a group.

Third, we asked that final copies reflect a standard of writing based on clearly communicated criteria. We generated rubrics with students after the drafting stage to help clarify standards. Students employed these rubrics as part of the self-evaluation process for both the draft and the final product (see Figures 10.1 and 10.2). The conversations that took place as the class developed rubrics were critical to students' understanding of effective writing.

Conferencing and the Mediation of Learning

We focused on effective interaction and conferencing skills. We particularly worked on new ways to interact with students and mediate their learning. Students often perceived traditional teacher interaction styles as overly harsh—for example, giving constructive ideas for revision. They often resisted when they were told they could do better, complaining or refusing to work. Their learning egos seemed like fine china, very delicate. We have learned that most needed a great deal of our attention, along with a recounting of what they were doing well for a longer period of time than we had expected. We had to develop balances between push-

Rubric-Criteria Checklist

Unit: _____Values Essay/Rough Draft_____ **Topic:** _____

Name: _____ **Peer:** _____

General Criteria	Self		Peer	
	Yes	No	Yes	No
Is at least 250 words				
Written in paragraph form (indent)				
Paragraphs are made up of complete sentences				
Periods at the end of each sentence				

Quality Check

Introduction 'hooks' the reader				
Introduction presents main idea of essay				
Paragraph 2 develops role of friends				
Paragraph 3 develops role of family				
Paragraph 4 develops role of strangers				
Conclusion gives a feeling of completness				
Conclusion gives a strong final impression				
Conclusion supports your purpose for writing				

Comments

Figure 10.1 Rubric Used to Evaluate Rough Drafts

Scoring Rubric for Values Essay

6

Goes beyond the requirements of the task
- Everything stated in 5 plus:
- Varied sentence structure to add interest; long and short sentences
- Conclusion leaves the reader feeling they have experienced a new perspective;leaves them thinking about the topic
- It flows beautifully between paragraphs without the standard abrupt paragraph transitions

5

Fully achieves the requirements of the task
- Fully explains the role of each; family, friends and strangers
- Uses descriptive examples to support opinions for each (showing)
- Ideas are presented logically and make sense to the reader
- There are no gaps; reader doesn't have to fill in for himself: "I think he means..."
- Vocabulary is descriptive and there are no unnecessary words such as: and, a or but
- Has a catchy lead that "hooks" the reader without giving away too much information in the intro paragraph

4

Adequate achievement of the task
- Is a complete well-written essay, but lacks pizazz
- The writers voice doen't seem as strong, may lack some descriptive examples
- Ideas are logical and make sense

3

Limited completion of the requirements
- May not have 5 complete paragraphs
- Limited description
- Vocabulary is repetitive; good, nice, etc.
- Opinions stated but may not be backed up with examples
- Ideas may be unclear or confusing to reader

2

Requirements of the task are not complete
- Incomplete paragraphs; may not be written in paragraph form
- May be brief
- Ideas make little sense to reader

1

Does not achieve any of the requirements
- Little attempt to complete the essay; illustrates little effort

Write a 50 word justification for the score you gave below:

Your score

Figure 10.2 Rubric Used to Evaluate Final Products

ing students to do better and supporting them in terms of what they had done, even if unsophisticated. It was a balance that we determined individually for each student. Ellen summarized this focus with the following reflection.

> I have learned to care about who my kids are, understand where they have been, and know where they are so I can take them to the next step. I believe that my kids give me a test when they turn in their first piece of written work. My response to them will determine if our future interactions will be risk-taking, productive experiences or resisting battles. I must be very careful to refrain from any sort of criticism during these first interactions. The first response has to be positive. I have to look for every strength and I have found that I should not make a suggestion at that point.

Some aspect of our curriculum is always in transition. We have found that no strategy, or activity, or format remains the same. It is our knowledge of the language learning process that provides the framework for curricular decision making.

Evaluating the Curriculum

The implementation of the writing process and the accumulation of student pieces led to the development of writing portfolios and a concurrent focus on how to evaluate their growth. We developed questions to use as a template to analyze student work, and our own teaching, as we looked at each sample of student work (see Figure 10.3). These questions also helped us consider new contexts to develop that would better support students' writing. We see curriculum and assessment as intricately tied together.[10] When a student is chosen for this type of evaluation, we fill out the form (Figure 9.3) as the student progresses through each stage of the writing process. We have found that it provides an effective format for teacher reflection and planning.

Case Study of David

In the following case study we demonstrate how we used the questions as an integral part of the writing process curriculum. We describe one student and his progression through one piece of writing to illustrate how the classroom structures, and teacher and peer interaction, supported his use of more sophisticated writing behaviors. We chose a student who constantly presented challenges,

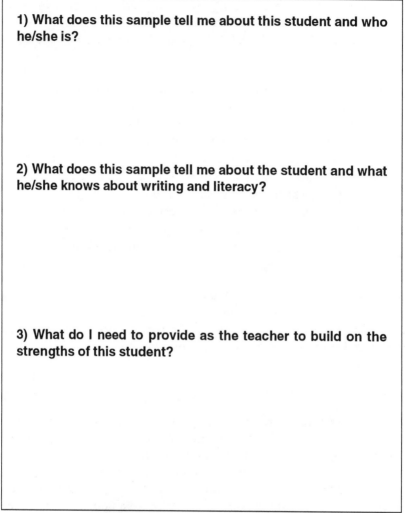

1) What does this sample tell me about this student and who he/she is?

2) What does this sample tell me about the student and what he/she knows about writing and literacy?

3) What do I need to provide as the teacher to build on the strengths of this student?

Figure 10.3 Writing evaluation form

an unsophisticated writer and one who also needed particular types of support from us. We show David's first draft, final draft, and his reflection about the pieces. Ellen's reflections about each part of the process follow. Then we highlight what we did curricularly and discuss the types of interactions we employed to support him.

The Student

David (a pseudonym) was an eighth grader with most of his attention focused on everything but school. David moved slowly through life. He walked slowly. He talked slowly. And, most frustrating for us, he slowly completed school work, often reluctant to become engaged in anything in the classroom. David's academic abilities were typical of many of the students in the class, not as well developed as we would have wished for an eighth grader. The writing process was very laborious for him, and he had often had difficulty completing his writing pieces, becoming frustrated and quitting, appearing not to care if he failed. He *did not appear* to be motivated to do well in school, often doing the minimum to survive in the classroom.

Yet, it seemed that these behaviors were ways to protect himself from failure. As we worked with him, we found that his learning ego was very immature; he was extremely sensitive to any criticism of his abilities. He would lash out if he perceived any criticism of what he was doing, saying, "See, no matter what I do, you don't think it's any good." Any request for more sophisticated work he perceived in this way. And any type of discussion of his work in front of his peers he interpreted as an occasion to create a power struggle. David presented a continual need for reflection on our part as we refused to support his low opinion of himself and his writing. We wanted him to tap his potential to become a more sophisticated writer.

Context for Writing for Case Study Samples

Many of our middle schoolers' writing reflected few of their experiences. It seemed that they had learned these were of little value in school. As a result, we noticed that many students infrequently used description and elaboration in their pieces since they chose to write about topics about which they had little knowledge. We planned a series of focused writing experiences to give students opportunities to "show, not tell." We wanted these focused activities to provide them with demonstrations regarding how description and elaboration are used in writing, devices used to express one's voice or views. Eventually students were asked to incorporate aspects of these focused activities into their longer pieces. These activities also provided some opportunities to practice writing to prompts since they would be expected to do this as part of eighth grade and high school competency assessments.

David wrote the following samples when we asked students to write a letter to a friend describing "A Beautiful Place." We asked that the description give the reader a picture of that beautiful place. Students began by writing a rough draft in a narrative letter form. This was a form that many students felt comfortable with and that we could later adapt to a more formal piece. After the rough draft, students exchanged papers and employed the partner reading and response strategy we had taught earlier. Partners read the piece and wrote down questions they still had about the beautiful place. Using these questions, writers rethought and revised their writing. Upon finishing the final revision, each student completed a self-evaluation (see example, next section).

David's Rough Draft

> One day I had a heat stroke and my mom woke me up. And all of a sudden I found out I wasn't home. I found out I was at a hospital and I looked out the window. And I saw a pretty green park and some pretty pink flowers. And the park was pretty. I wanted to go outside and play, but I couldn't because I was still sick from my heat stroke.
>
> Questions from Partner
>
> 1. How did you have a heat stroke?
> 2. What did it look like?
> 3. How was it designed?

Ellen's Reflections

Discussion

David's piece is unsophisticated for an eighth grade writer, possibly indicating more about his lack of interest in writing than about his competence in this area. He did use his own experiences as a basis for the text, a sign to us that he had begun to recognize a writer finds ideas for writing in his own experiences. In addition, the piece reflects his personality. His use of the heat stroke experience as the basis for his discussion of a beautiful place demonstrated his enjoyment of discussing unusual events.

David's Final Draft

> One day I was standing outside in the hot sun in front of my house. I started getting weaker and pale. All of a sudden, I fell down and hit the hard concrete floor. I felt myself waking up in a hospital with my mother on my side. I laid there and waited for the sickness to find its way out of my body. I was almost well but I didn't care. I got out of my cold hospital bed and found my way around to the window. As I opened the blinds to the window, I found a beautiful park with a crystal clear lake in the middle of the park. The park had pretty green grass all over and pretty pink blooming flowers. It was a beautiful day. The sky was the color of a blue crystal and the clouds were as white as the snow.

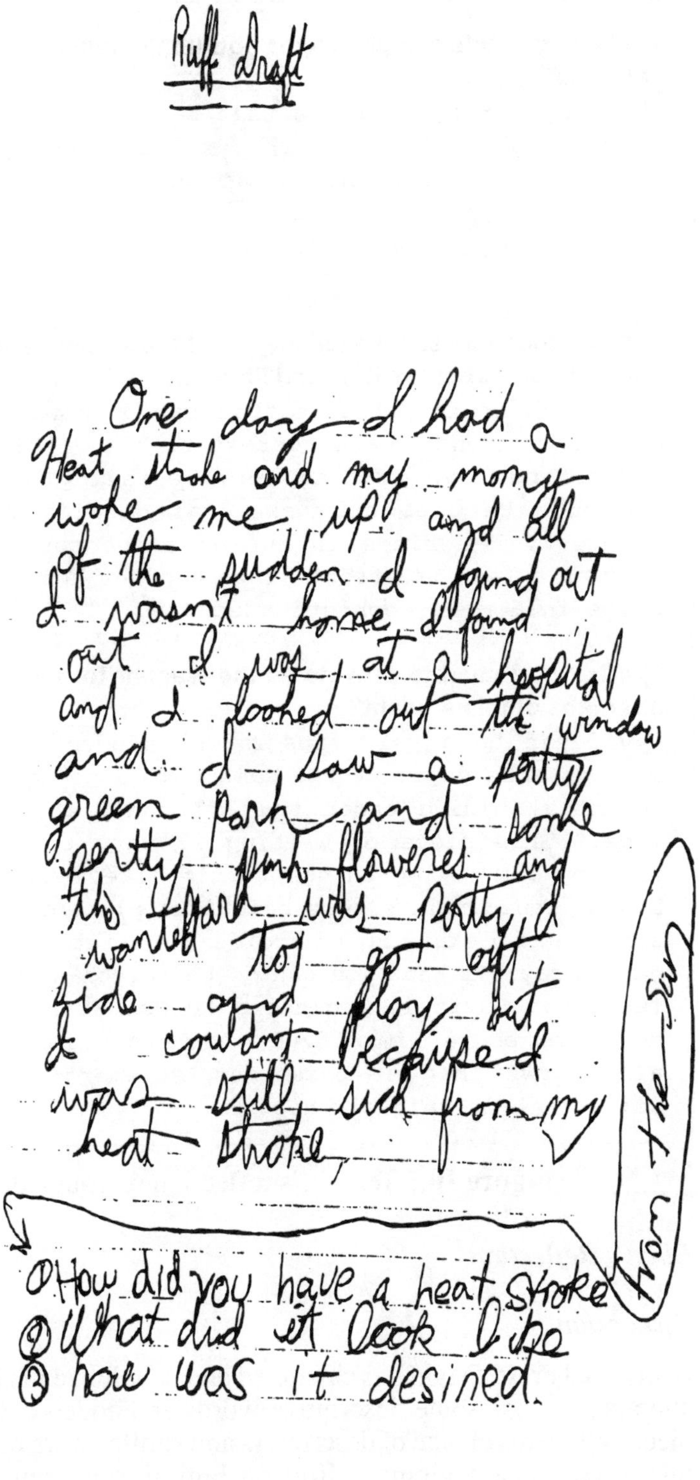

Ruff Draft

One day I had a Heat stroke and my mommy woke me up and all of the sudden I found out I wasn't home I found out I was at a hospital and I looked out the window and I saw a pretty green park and some pretty pink floweres and the park was pretty I wanted to go out side and play but I couldnt because I was still sick from my heat stroke,

from the sun

① How did you have a heat stroke
② What did it look like
③ how was it desined.

Figure 10.4 Rough draft

---

1) What does this sample tell me about this student and who he/she is?

The rough draft tells me that David is only putting enough effort into this writing to say that he did it. It shows his attitude toward life, "I did it so leave me alone." It also illustrates his strategy of partially participating.

2) What does this sample tell me about the student and what he/she knows about writing and literacy?

The rough draft tells me that David knows how to use an incident to add context to his writing. He understands that writing has a beginning, middle, and end. He uses only skeletal details to add interest. He writes in run-on sentences. I see this as a lack of effort since he does know how to write in a more sophisticated way.

3) What do I need to provide as the teacher to build on the strengths of this student?

David can be a very frustrating student to work with on some days. At the same time I see a lot of potential hiding under that "I don't care attitude." This piece of writing is very typical. I find myself saying things to him like, "Only you, David, could relate this beautiful place to a heat stroke and a skate board accident!" I remind myself not to say, "I know you can do better than this." I feel that David is beginning to use writing as a means to share himself with others. His writing also shows that he possesses an emerging comic voice that is uniquely his.

Figure 10.5 Teacher's reflection on rough draft

Ellen's Reflections

Discussion

In his final draft, David has expanded and developed his ideas. He attempted to use some descriptive words and added detail to his piece. While his choice of descriptors and similes were rather trite, this piece was a beginning effort for him in trying out these devices. We also became aware of how critical the peer sharing experiences were in helping David reframe what he had written.

<u>final Copy</u>

One day I was standing out side in the hot sun in front of my house. I started getting weaker and pail. All of the sudden I fell down and hit the hot concret floor. I felt my self waking up in a hospital with my mother on my side. I laid there and waited for the sikness to find its way out of my body. I was almost well but I didn't care I got out of my cold hospital bed and found my way around to the window. As I opened the blinds to the window I found a beatifull park with a crystal clear lake in the middle of the park. The park had pretty green grass all over and pretty pink blooming floweres it was a beutiful day the sky was the color of a blue crystal and the clouds were as white as snow

Figure 10.6 Final draft

Self-Evaluation

Why did you chose this rough draft to evaluate?

When I looked at my rough draft, I knew it had to be better. Why this rough draft stuck out is because it is no good. It needs to be improved.

How did you come up with your topic?

How I came up with my topic is because it is a true story and it really happened to me except the part of the heat stroke. It was really a skate board accident.

What improvement do you see between your rough draft and your final copy?

My final copy was hard to write because I had to put a lot of detail and showing. That's why it was hard to write.

How did your partner's questions help you in your writing?

My partner's questions helped me more because in my final copy it helped me with some more details so my final copy was perfect.

Ellen's Reflections

Discussion

We developed the self-evaluation questions to help students review what they had written, evaluate what they had done well, and define what areas they might work on in the future. We found that using these types of questions over time helped students to begin to evaluate their own pieces and created in them a sense of accomplishment and self-worth. These also provided a means for students to tell us what worked for them.

Through interactions with David, we found that certain elements had to be present to support his involvement in writing. We learned to give him time to produce his writing, to provide quiet, restrained encouragement, and to find something positive even in his most unsophisticated writing. Most importantly, we learned how to work with him to improve his writing, using such questions as, "What can you do with this part here?" and then jointly brainstorming possibilities of what he could do. We found the most effective questions or comments were those that asked David to take responsibility for his own work. If one type of support or intervention was not effective, we developed another.

Our interactions with David demonstrate the tenuous task of figuring out how to best support a challenging student, one who did not want to be identified as a "school boy." We have come to learn that each student is an individual, and that some generic strategies are usually successful. We find ourselves adapting and refin-

1) What does this sample tell me about this student and who he/she is?

This piece of writing tells me that David has the ability to produce higher quality writing as long as there is a structure in place for his success. I believe that the dialogue that he had with his revision partner helped support his writing. His partner asked him about missing details and questioned what he wrote.

2) What does this sample tell me about the student and what he/she knows about writing and literacy?

It is clear that when David takes his time and has been given support by other writers, he can be a capable writer. The number of run-on sentences decreased significantly, even though he had frequent spelling errors. It is also evident that David has internalized some understanding of description and elaboration.

3) What do I need to provide as the teacher to build on the strengths of this student?

I need to provide those structures for David in my classroom that guide him. These learning opportunities need to include positive dialogue about

Figure 10.7 Teacher' reflections on final draft

ing these strategies for each student in the class. For example, we found that David needed a set of concrete steps to take to revise his piece. We asked him to: (1) reread his piece, (2) find a peer to read the piece and write down questions regarding points of confusion, (3) discuss the comments with the peer, (4) decide what areas he would address, and (5) make revisions. We found that general directions to "revise your piece" were not helpful to the students like David.

It is the process of focusing our energies on questions, such as those listed on our reflection form, that allow us to keep focused on where we can effect change. Change occurs as a result of the interactions that we have each day with our students. The strategies, activities, and social contexts for writing that we establish in the class are our means to structure and guide these interactions.

Reflections and Plans

As we continue to work together, we focus on developing effective methods to support students in developing their voices along with the writing competencies needed for academic achievement and access to a variety of career options. Exposure to and opportunities to try out diverse styles of writing create students who feel comfortable with any writing task, whether personal or academic. Too often our curriculum has emphasized one goal at the expense of the other. We know both are necessary.

We feel constrained in working with 35 to 40 students in the class when so many need individual attention. Agendas about curriculum and class size need to be determined at the school and district level. We would like more dialogue and discussion about these issues.

We often turn to the writings of others to inform our practice. Rose reminds us of the importance of personal mentorship.[11] His story of his own academic challenges and those of students he has met at U.C.L.A. highlight the key role of individuals who take a personal interest in the life and achievement of students. Vygotsky's notion of the zone of proximal development allows us to see the need to support students first socially before we expect them to perform individually.[12] We see this construct played out as we observe students working together. Flores and Diaz help us see our role as cultural mediator; as teachers we need to mediate between the culture of the student and the culture of the academy so the student is not asked to sacrifice one for the other.[13] Our responsibility is to mediate the academic competencies so these students can succeed and become more proficient readers and writers, along with promoting their specific cultural "ways of knowing and doing." Ellen comments about these ideas:

> As a teacher of writing at the middle grades, I am fast concluding that my purpose is to tap potential in my students as writers and to give them meaningful experiences in which the process of producing a piece is as important as the product. As I look back I recognize that my most effective lessons were those that taught the students to be self and peer evaluators. The crucial piece to this is that kids must be able to ask themselves the key questions and be able to self-reflect on their learning. I plan to spend much more time on teaching this so the students will be able to direct more and more of their learning.
>
> I am also creating more authentic writing demonstrations and experiences like researching a career area or writing a letter to a significant adult. Building upon writ-

Reflection on Showing

When I looked at my ruff Draft I knew it had to be better why this ruff Draft stickes out is because it is no good it needs to be improved.

How I came up with my topic is because it is a true story and it really happened to me exept the part of the beat stroke it was really a shate board acedent,

My final Copy was hard to write because I had to put alot of detail and showing thats why it was hard to write,

My partners question help me more because in my final copy it helped me with some more Details so my final Copy was perfect.

Figure 10.8 David's reflection

1) What does this sample tell me about this student and who he/she is?

His reflection tells me that underneath that tough exterior David really does care about his writing. He also enjoys having some decision-making responsibility and writing about things that have really happened. It also shows me that he has a potential to develop a comic voice.

2) What does this sample tell me about the student and what he/she knows about writing and literacy?

David understands the importance of the writing process to improving his writing. My battles with him about the process itself were lessened as he saw his writing improve through the use of the process. He no longer finds the revision process pointless and is therefore more fully engaged. He understands that details make his writing come alive. He values his partners' support. The questions helped guide him to fill in the missing details.

3) What do I need to provide as the teacher to build on the strengths of this student?

I found his reflection very valuable in telling me about David as a writer. He identifies his weaknesses in his rough draft and what he needed to do to make it better. Although he doesn't identify his weaknesses in the areas of conventions, they become less and less significant through the process of revision. I know how to emphasize things at the appropriate stage and not overwhelm him with a zillion requirements right away. As he feels more confident, he is better able to handle new challenges and keep improving. My job is to not only see his writing improve, but to keep his confidence soaring. New battles are developing about final copy quality criteria since David still rejoices in being Done!! Again this is a critical balancing act. I feel I am succeeding with this balancing act when the student's expectations and standards for their writing rises.

Figure 10.9 Teacher's reflection on self-evaluation

ing topics they care about can only be done when you have taken the time to find out about the students as individuals and their goals for themselves. I am finding that I can link their future goals, which tell me a lot about them, to short-term goals that we can accomplish together in class. For example, students interested in sales or the legal profession recognize the importance of learning to make an effective presentation. Learning how to research, take notes and prepare audio-visual aids can be integrated into the eighth grade curriculum. Making the connection between becoming a proficient writer and their future goals isn't easy at first, but it is crucial.

As we move from goal-setting to identifying strengths, a portfolio of their writing is used to find evidence of strengths. From this we move to identifying areas to improve and these become tied to short-term goals. Once students set short-term goals based on what they believe they need to improve, it is my job to provide learning opportunities in these areas. The portfolios provide the basis for my instructional decision making.

While some journeys come to an end, our learning journey as teachers continues. As we meet each class, we again refine what we know about the reading and writing process. We seek to support students in becoming successful readers and writers. Middle schoolers are strange and wonderful beings. We believe their strongest memories of writing in middle school should be the experiences they had working with others to discover their potential as writers.

End Notes

1. Nancie Atwell, *In The Middle: Writing, Reading, and Learning With Adolescents* (Portsmouth, NH: Heinemann, 1987).
2. Rebecca Kaplan, *Writers in Training* (San Jose, CA: Dale Seymour Publications, 1988).
3. Linda Rief, *Seeking Diversity* (Portsmouth, NH: Heinemann, 1992).
4. California State Department of Education, *Caught in the Middle* (Sacramento: State of California, 1987).
5. Californina State Department of Education, *Middle School Quality Criteria* (Sacramento: State of California, 1988).
6. California State Department of Education, *Turning Points* (Sacramento: State of California, 1989).
7. California State Department of Education, *State of California Language Arts Framework* (Sacramento: State of California, 1987).
8. Gary Soto, *Summer Life* (New York: Dell, 1982).
9. C. Gilles, M. Bixby, P. Crowley, S. Crenshaw, M. Henrichs, F. Reynolds, and D. Pyle (Eds.), *Whole Language Strategies for Secondary Students* (New York: Richard Owen, 1988).
10. K. Short and C. Burke, *Creating Curriculum: Teachers and Students as a Community of Learners* (Portsmouth, NH: Heinemann, 1991).
11. M. Rose, *Lives on the Boundary* (New York: The Free Press, 1989).
12. L. Vygotsky, *Mind in Society* (Cambridge: Cambridge University Press, 1978).
13. B. Flores and E. Diaz, *Teacher as Cultural Mediator* (Presentation at Claremont Reading Conference, Claremont CA, 1989).

Chapter 11

Looking Back, Looking Forward: A Science Teacher Incorporates Whole Language

Suzan W. Mauney, Rosary V. Lalik, and George E. Glasson

Authors Note: *Although all three authors worked together to write this chapter, we chose to tell the story from Suzan Mauney's point of view.*

I teach in a middle school of approximately 800 students in grades six, seven and eight. We are organized into teams of four academic subjects: math, science, language arts and social studies. I am the science member of my team and also the team leader. In addition to my usual teaching duties, I am a sort of coordinator of student activities and events for my team. Our average teaching load is 120–140 students. My team members and I share a common planning period, which allows us to meet regularly to discuss students, share ideas, vent frustrations, plan activities, conference with parents, and meet with administration and support personnel. After our middle school restructured a few years ago, we eliminated ability-grouped classrooms and now group students heterogeneously in all subject areas except math. Our classrooms contain children from a variety of cultures, socioeconomic levels, and populations that include special education, remedial, average, above average and gifted ability students. Our school system supports the full-inclusion model for special needs students; this means we mainstream the majority of identified special needs students into regular classrooms for the entire school day. My team has a full-time special needs teacher who supports us by assisting in all classes with identified special needs students. Unfortunately, due to the large number of students in her case load, classroom teachers experience an additional burden in meeting these students' needs.

Families of children attending the school represent a variety of socioeconomic groups. Some are affiliated with a nearby university; others are employed in manufacturing or support services.

While our school is located in a university town, we draw students from the rural areas surrounding us as well. Small local farms are still a factor in the economy of the county in which I live and teach. Because of the university, we have a large international community and a fair number of transient families, here for a few years as a parent or parents complete a degree. Local industries provide jobs for a number of people; but the local economy has experienced some depression of late, and the number of unemployed and non-traditional family units increases yearly. In short, we teach a diverse group of youngsters with varied needs in classrooms with generally 30 or more students.

Over the past twelve years of teaching, I have seen many changes implemented at my school, some system-wide, others site-based, and still others within my own classroom. Though all linked in some way, the evolution of these changes took place separately. Our central office staff mandated county-wide changes that impacted every school in our system. These mandates included moving from self contained and special education resource classrooms to the full-inclusion model. Site-based changes came out of the restructuring of our middle school as we moved toward teaming and interdisciplinary teaching. My own personal changes came about as a result of my dissatisfaction with some of my teaching methods. But all these changes began to occur at roughly the same time. I am currently trying to find ways to make them converge within my own classroom as I struggle to adequately meet the needs of all my students. In order to elaborate on these changes, I must first reflect on the search I began a number of years ago to improve my own effectiveness as a teacher.

My Participation in the Reading to Learn in Science Education Project

Early in my career as a teacher I think I searched for new ideas, themes and activities primarily because I wanted to be good at what I chose to do. I resisted the dry, textbook approach to teaching science, but didn't really know how to make my subject more meaningful to my students. I knew I preferred more laboratory-based teaching and that my students enjoyed that, too, but I felt like I was just doing labs as an afterword rather than as a springboard for introducing a concept. I wanted my students to value science as a way of understanding and interpreting the world around them. I had a vision of science helping students to make connections, but I just wasn't informed and confident enough to make this happen.

When I first began teaching, our school had a departmentalized structure similar to a high school, with science classrooms clustered in one area of the building. In spite of our physical prox-imity, each science teacher did pretty much his or her own thing. When we first formed interdisciplinary teams, the physical arrange-ment was left unchanged. This made it nearly impossible to work as a team, especially across the disciplines. Days went by when I hardly saw my other academic teammates. I did confer occasion-ally with the other eighth grade science teacher; however, we didn't have a shared planning period and really only saw each other for brief moments. Besides that, over the first five years we had three different physical science teachers, so I never experienced the sup-port of having a consistent science colleague. I felt like a one-person team. I needed some support, but the system didn't lend itself to the sort of professional support I have come to value so much.

I came to an important realization about my teaching: although I had included many laboratory experiences in my classes, I hadn't really allowed my students the time or opportunity to discover much for themselves. I credit this realization to my involvement with the Reading to Learn in Science Education Project at a local uni-versity. My county science supervisor sent me a notice advertising a research project for science teachers. The project had a limited number of positions available; the application process included a required interview. Since I was already questioning my teaching, I saw the project as an opportunity to improve my effectiveness in the classroom. I applied and participated in an audio- and video-taped interview. When the two researchers involved in the project, a language arts educator and a science educator, started asking questions, I knew I was in the right place. They asked me how I taught, what I thought science was all about, how I thought it should be taught; they wanted to know about the role of language in my classroom, and most importantly, about my view of myself as a learner after five years of teaching. When I left the interview, I knew I wanted to get into the project and I prayed that my honest answers were the right ones! When I received notification of ac-ceptance into the program, I was thrilled. I felt I was finally going to get started on fixing things in my classroom. Involvement in the project was one of the most important factors in my evolution as a teacher.

The project focused on science education and how language arts could be more fully integrated into the science curriculum. I began working with six other teachers from elementary through high school as we explored the way we all taught, our successes and failures, and our desires to find new and better ways to be effective teachers and learners. This was my first real experience with the value of reflecting on my craft and collaborating with other professionals to help develop and implement some new strat-egies and methods in my classroom.

With the help of the two university researchers, project participants discussed our teaching in terms of what worked and what didn't. We read research on science methods and language use in the classroom and used these references and our discussions to frame a general philosophy. We discussed the learning cycle model of Atkin and Karplus[1] as it applies to the science classroom. The group revised the model to make it more relevant to our own experiences.[2] Our version of the cycle (see Figure 11. 1) includes an initial discovery or *exploration* component—most relevant to my teaching—in which students are allowed a great deal of freedom to observe and interpret without the constraints of teacher-provided information.

In most of my teaching, I had designed traditional teacher-directed activities primarily to reinforce material we'd already discussed in class. My students had experience with laboratory procedures, but weren't allowed to think about their own understandings beforehand. Much of the curiosity labs might have aroused never had a chance. Instead, curiosity took the form of student concern over whether an answer or solution was right or wrong. I was giving my students information and asking them to draw conclusions before they had figured out what questions they might like to ask, and without taking into account what they might already know.

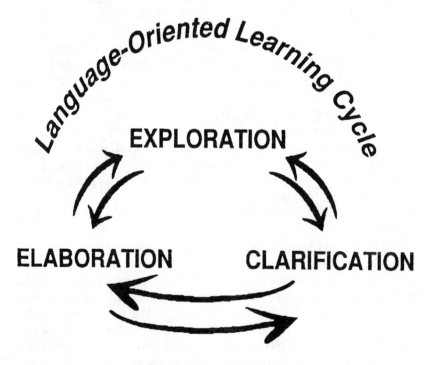

Figure 11.1 Phases of the language-oriented learning cycle

The second phase of the learning cycle involves *clarification* of initial explorations through student discussion, questioning, reading, and related activities designed to enlarge students' knowledge base. I found language-based activities were helpful in the clarification phase of the learning cycle. The third phase of the cycle involves *elaboration* of the knowledge gained through application, related research, and investigation. Providing students with opportunities to transfer their new-found knowledge to other activities helped me better understand the nature of their thinking and learning processes. Later, this provided a bridge for my collaborative work in developing interdisciplinary units with other teachers.

Changes at My Middle School

At this point, my story begins to converge with other changes that had an effect on my classroom and teaching. My middle school had completed a self-study. A visiting committee made recommendations for improving programs, among other things strongly advising that we change our ability-grouped structure. They cited current middle level research suggesting heterogeneity is the most effective way to meet the needs of adolescents. Our principal determined to make as many of the recommended changes as possible, including moving classrooms to put the focus on team proximity, providing a team as well as personal planning period, and eliminating ability grouping in classrooms. We implemented these changes over the course of a year despite much parental concern about heterogeneous grouping and the usual trauma for teachers in moving from one classroom to another.

For eight years I had taught ability-grouped classes; suddenly I was faced with the challenge of teaching to a mix of all abilities. However, the other changes implemented at the same time eased this transition. Rearranging classrooms so team members were physically near each other promoted the team spirit, for both teachers and students, previously missing in the building. Redesigning the master schedule to allow for a team planning period, in addition to a personal planning period, was crucial to the success of the entire venture. Suddenly my team colleagues were in sight and we all had a common time to meet each day. The time to dialogue with colleagues proved invaluable during this transition and helped us make the move to heterogeneity with more confidence. We had time to discuss individual student problems and to work toward solutions together. Parent conferences could now take place within the school day rather than before or after school. We regularly invited the guidance counselors in to discuss concerns. Once each grading period we got together with the other eighth grade team to talk about areas of joint interest, to coordinate field trips, and to just stay in touch. When we began creating our first interdisciplinary units, the time to plan together within the school day was critical to our success. In short, the common planning time made it possible to work together without having to juggle four different schedules. Thus, team members met the challenges of the new changes together rather than in isolation.

From Theory to Practice in a Newly Defined Middle School

The combination of my work with the project at the university and the changes going on at my school proved to be fortuitous. As I explored my teaching through work with the university, I was able to test, discard or implement some fairly substantial modifications within my newly defined classroom in my newly defined middle school. One of the first modified activities I tried, based on the learning cycle, involved working with solubility of several salt compounds. The initial exploration activity went very well; my students came up with a variety of alternative suggestions about how to get the salts to dissolve better. They wanted to heat the solutions, something I had not planned to do initially. Here was an example of the student-generated ideas I had hoped the activity would promote.

The process broke down, however, when I rushed students through clarification in order to get to the elaboration segment. I raced through an explanation of solubility curves before students had time to really understand how to use them. As a result, when they calculated the solubility of their salts, they had absolutely no idea how to apply their data to the solubility curves. I was still operating in my old mind set of only devoting two or three days at the most to any activity because, after all, I was responsible for being sure they covered enough "stuff" to be prepared for high school. The realization that knowledge building can't be rushed was critical for me. I had to learn that, painful as a slower pace might be to me as the teacher, students need *time* to construct their own understanding; this has more value than covering material in a cursory fashion.

Student-Centered learning

My search for new ways to teach led me to less self-centered approaches, geared more toward what my students needed to be successful learners and to ways I could support that process. Instead of prefacing an activity with lots of information about the topic, I allowed the students to generate their own understandings by pure observation, discussion, and reflection. For example, density is a concept that most eighth graders and, in fact, many adults find difficult to grasp. In the past I always gave a definition followed by the mathematical formula, density=mass/volume, and then moved straight into a lab where the density of some objects must be calculated. More often than not the only thing anyone learned was that you can find the mass of something, measure its volume and then come up with some meaningless number which is supposed to be its density.

Now I introduce the concept of density by organizing students into groups of four to six to examine and analyze a beaker containing a number of mystery liquids (exploration). The liquids arrange themselves into layers of different colors. This provides a springboard for all kinds of predictions and inferences. Prior to this activity, I simply instruct students to write down all observations group members make concerning the liquids in the beaker. I allow groups to struggle on their own, resisting the urge to bail them out when they ask me how many layers this "junk" really has, anyway? The tone in the classroom during these activities is lively. Free discussion is encouraged; it is not uncommon for students to move around the classroom to look at other groups' samples in order to help them form their own opinions. I enjoy watching students argue with one another about why there are five layers instead of eight or if the "junk" on the bottom is hair mousse or Vaseline. I encourage their attempts to use long spatulas to retrieve a sample of each layer; the "yucks" and "gross" comments that arise as they touch this "disgusting stuff" show me the kids are actively involved. Some of the insights and interpretations this activity engenders are amazingly creative.

This activity always generates controversy over whether there is really a thin, extra layer at the very top of the beaker. Usually more students believe it is a real layer rather than an optical illusion, but once in a while a brave soul insists that no layer exists. One of my inclusion students who functions at a low level in writing and reading, but has a remarkably perceptive streak, argued convincingly that the layer in question was a reflection of one of the colored layers below. He was able to present to other students a common sense and straightforward explanation that was, indeed, scientifically correct.

I have found that this no-pressure approach to problem solving frees some students who may be pegged as low ability or learning disabled to share ideas and interpretations they might otherwise have kept to themselves for fear of being "wrong." One of the biggest problems I've had as a teacher is worrying so much that the students are "getting" the science that I actually inhibit their thought processes by guiding them too much. Most of what we learn and remember is probably knowledge that we've had to seek, at least partially, on our own. Schooling that promotes the solitary pursuit of knowledge imposes artificial constraints on students. In the real world, we are more apt to work as part of a group in which each member's contributions are necessary to the final outcome.

The group nature of the exploration can be liberating; students can share ideas first with a small group and then decide whether they want to share with the entire class during a whole-group discussion. Small-group collaboration allows an individual to modify initial ideas before submitting them to the whole class for scrutiny. My eyes are opened to the often under-appreciated potential of all students as I listen to their contributions in small groups. (Many of their wonderful ideas would never be shared if I only permitted large-group discussions.) Traditionally, we reward the most vocal students with attention; but I've come to see that they are not the only ones who have something to say.

Most of us who teach enjoy the role of knowledge sharer, but how often do we give our students opportunities to explore some topic without first prefacing the "exploration" with some information that may influence the outcome of the activity? I believe now that a teacher has to be willing to turn over some autonomy to students. Doing so requires faith in students' abilities and enough self-confidence to give up a piece of the traditional teaching role. I can be an effective teacher even if my students don't need me all the time. They have the ability to reason through any number of problems on their own. Isn't independent thought one of the things American public schools are supposed to nurture? Teachers can support the efforts of their students without sacrificing their own importance in the classroom. Initially, the thought of giving up some of that control was frightening to me. I kept thinking, "What if they don't figure it out?" or, even worse, "What if they come up with the wrong answer?" I was still equating my effectiveness as a teacher with my students' ability immediately to give back the "scientifically correct" interpretation. As science educators we profess to believe in discovery, but we stubbornly hold on to our scientific "truths."

This issue of the "right" or "wrong" answer is a holdover from my own experiences as a student and a teacher trainee. I was taught the way I was teaching and, although it was once accepted practice, I'm not sure it was particularly effective. I have virtually no recollection of much of the science I was supposed to have learned in public school. Today, I can justify initial acceptance of a "wrong" answer from a student because I have learned to listen to what my students say. For a given task each child brings a certain amount of knowledge; this may be more or less than that of other students or even the teacher. If a student constructs an interpretation using the logic of observations tied to existing knowledge, that interpretation has value. It may not represent scientific "truth," but at that point and time for that student it represents valid learning. Eleanor Duckworth says, "Any wrong idea that is corrected provides far more depth than if one never had a wrong idea to begin with. You master the idea much more thoroughly if you have considered alternatives, tried to work it out in areas where it didn't work, and figured out why it was that it didn't work, all of which takes time."[3] I'm not suggesting that we as educators encourage our students to leave the classroom with a whole set of questionable notions. Instead, we should value what they bring to us and help them find ways to test their ideas, and decide through additional experiences and analyses if there is a need to revise their "truths."

I'm still working on trying to provide my students with more opportunities to truly explore on their own. In a unit on energy and motion, for example, we discuss the notion of friction and how it is both a positive and negative component of movement. I had several skateboarding enthusiasts one year who wanted to investigate friction as it relates to their hobby. I encouraged them to bring their boards in to class, where everyone then took part in testing this mode of transportation on various surfaces. We found the 50-year-old linoleum floors in our schools were actually pretty good surfaces for skate boarding. A few of the kids even taught a minilesson on how the different kinds of wheels and ball bearings affect their style of boarding. An unplanned activity such as this helps me because I see things through the eyes of my students instead of forcing my students to see through the eyes of someone who has been teaching about energy and motion for years. The learning that occurred as part of our unplanned skateboarding unit was considerably more meaningful to the students than anything I could have come up with because it connected to their experiences.

Input from my students helps me make better choices about the direction my instruction should take. Why re-teach things they already know just because the book or curriculum is set up that way? Use a child's natural curiosity to explore some aspect of a topic you've never explored, such as skateboarding, and see how much everyone (including the teacher) can learn. Generate some real scientific curiosity rather than the artificial curiosity that comes from more traditional prescribed investigations with little relation to students lives.

Meeting Students' Needs in a Mixed-Ability Classroom

Coincidentally, as I examined how to make changes in my instruction, I also tried to figure out what might work best in a mixed-ability classroom. I discovered the value of cooperative learning, partly as a result of my involvement in the university research project. My elementary teaching colleagues had been using cooperative strategies for years, but they were not as widely used in secondary settings. After listening to these colleagues talk about their classrooms and seeing them in action on videotapes, I decided it was time for me to make some changes. I had previously assigned two-person lab groups, but now I found I needed groups with enough students to insure authentic, varied discussions. By organizing the students into clusters of learners, I was able to help my students see the value of collaborative endeavors both for learning and for fostering an atmosphere of community and democracy in the classroom.

One great potential benefit of a heterogeneous classroom is that it can foster acceptance of others as individuals rather than as members of some special group. Students are no longer separated by perceived ability differences that often lead to social stratification as well. I found that many exploration activities lend themselves well to a group process that values the prior knowledge that each student brings to the task. Furthermore, as we moved from our exploration work into more focused activities, the integrity of the cooperative group continued to have a positive impact on learning.

As we moved from exploration into clarification activities, our small groups shared with the whole class and then moved back into their original arrangement to work on expanding their knowledge and refining their understandings. In the clarification portion of the layered liquid lab, for instance, each group was responsible for sharing with the entire class their observations and inferences about the liquids. During whole-class sharing we discussed areas of agreement as well as dissension and used findings to focus our search for more information.

As part of this search, each group did reading on the topics we had brainstormed from our initial activity. The textbook was used as a source for gathering further information. I encouraged trips to the library as well as discussions with family members (some of them former students of mine). We incorporated new terms—such as density, viscosity, weight, and thickness—into the search. The groups now had a more sophisticated basis for explaining why the liquids formed discrete layers.

To help them confirm their explanations, I gave each group four solid objects: a checker, a cork, a rubber stopper, and a copper penny. Each group made predictions about where they thought the objects would come to rest within the liquid layers. They sketched their predictions and then tested them by dropping the objects into the beaker. I asked students to revise their explanations about the densities of the layers if they observed that the objects did not behave as predicted.

When we reconvened as a class, we found our new knowledge clarified our inferences about the layers. The consensus was that the density of the liquids determined the position of the layers and that the objects must have lower densities than the layers they floated on. Further, students determined that, contrary to what many people think, solids are not heavier than liquids in all cases.

Now it was time for students to scientifically confirm their findings by actually measuring and calculating the densities of the layers. I provided a chart of liquids and their densities. With actual measured values in hand, groups matched their calculated densities to those on the chart. In this way they confirmed or adjusted their original predictions about what that "junk" in the beaker really was. I saw lots of surprised faces when students learned that Karo syrup instead of Vaseline formed the thick bottom layer and that tinted water was the reason for the "mystery" layer at the top. As part of our elaboration activity, we brainstormed and discussed situations in which knowing the density of a substance might be useful. Suggested situations ranged from flotation devices to the best metals to use in cars and airplanes. Density for these students had some relevance; it was something more than a useless number.

Interdisciplinary Teaching

While encouraging my students to value collaboration with peers, I, too, was experimenting with developing interdisciplinary units collaboratively with colleagues. My work with the university project helped me to view language as a valuable tool for teaching and learning science. I realized that reading science references and writing up reports was a very limited use of the written word in my classroom. I believed I had missed opportunities to use language—particularly writing—for years because I used writing primarily as an end-product exercise. We would do a lab and write about it or conduct research and write about it. Writing was used at the end of an activity as a summative evaluation rather than as a tool for use during all stages of learning. I knew that writing things down helps me learn, but I had not given my students the most beneficial kinds of writing tasks. They had not had much opportunity to put their understandings about science into their own words.

By this time I had begun work on a masters degree in curriculum and instruction and had also taken a content area reading course. Previously I had considered reading as a subject learned in elementary school. I knew that sometimes middle schoolers needed some help with it; but I never really considered all the possibilities for addressing reading in my science classroom. For instance, it had never occurred to me to use a science journal such as those kept in English classes. I know keeping a journal is a great way to reflect on something read or heard, or to record questions. So one of the first curriculum modifications I put into place was a science journal in which students would document their progress in science class. These journals became a place to record observations about discrepant events, such as *The Alien Balloon,* where I blow up a balloon and magically cause two plastic cups to adhere to the sides without the use of glue, tape, hidden strings or mirrors. It was a place where students wrote about what they knew before we started a new unit, or about what they had learned as we ended a unit. It also became a place where students wrote to me about personal concerns. This helped me to know my students better as individuals, and to better understand their reasoning processes.

My new awareness of the power of language as a tool for learning in a science classroom helped me to form an alliance with another teacher which, to this day, is an important part of my teaching. My colleague, Donna, is the language arts teacher on my team. As she and I began to dialogue, we realized how much we have in common philosophically and that we share a need to constantly experiment and change the ways we teach. Donna uses reading and writing workshops[4] in her language arts classroom. The flexibility in her program allowed us to develop our first interdisciplinary units. Donna and I worked together to find articles that students could read in conjunction with Earth Day and solicited input from our math and social studies colleagues on how we could best integrate their disciplines into the unit. I surveyed my students to find out what kinds of environmental problems they would like to know more about.

As part of our unit on the environment, my students used the information they had from reading various articles to create poems and collages. As part of their language arts curriculum, they wrote articles about the issues they had studied for magazines they created on these topics. They wrote, performed, and produced their own music videos about issues such as acid rain and global warming. You haven't experienced music until you hear groups of eighth graders sing(?) about toxic waste or air pollution.

Initially, students expressed uncertainty about this meshing of two, three, or more disciplines, but the more they experienced the freedom to choose their own topics and create their own music, the more satisfying it was. Many times students would say they weren't sure if they were doing English in science class or science in English class. As the boundaries between disciplines came down, our ability to learn and enjoy experiences increased dramatically.

Without the support of and collaboration with Donna, I doubt I ever would have tackled such a unit on the scale we eventually achieved. Teaming and collaborating are now so important to my teaching and creative endeavors that I wonder how I functioned in isolation for so many years. Our continuing lament is that we have so many ideas and so little time! Our latest unit , one on technology and invention, incorporates science fiction novels as part of our study of the importance of scientific progress.

```
                    AIR POLLUTION


           Air pollution destroys the air.
              don't you know it's every-
           where?
              In the city in the streets
           it's getting harder and harder
              to defeat.
           Our fate is in our hands
              if we stop it now
           we can save our lands.
              People are dyin' everyday
           So listen up to what we
              say.


           Factories, smoke, fuels and
              exhaust, because of these
           it's air we've lost.
              Recycle now, clear the
           air because in the future
              it won't be fair.
           One day we'll find a good
              solution come help fight
           air pollution .
```

by.
Angie Petersheim
Marissa French
Heather Early

Figure 11.2 Song lyrics

The Value of Writing for Student Learning and Assessment

I now try to include some type of writing whenever I begin a new lesson. I've learned about such things as anticipation guides, word associations, analogies, reading a related article in a group, or simply writing a story or poem about a topic such as atoms or waves or light. When used at the onset these tasks stimulate student curiosity, provide focus for important questions, and help students organize their thoughts. They also help me have a better conception of what students know before I jump into a lesson. I use writing activities to check for understanding at the middle or end point of a lesson or unit. My students have told me directly and in their science journals that they enjoy these opportunities for writing. Besides being an organizing tool, writing can provide an outlet for students' thoughts if the format is open ended enough to foster creativity.

Realizing how much I could learn about my students through their writing was an added benefit to my work with the university project. I found it was too easy to undervalue the thought processes of my students and overvalue my own. Not until I closely analyzed my students' work did I realize my assessment of their knowledge level was probably more a function of my own preselected, narrowly conceived criteria than of their actual approaches to a task.

For example, the notion of waves is an important concept that threads its way through the physics portion of my course. When I asked my students to write about waves I was initially discouraged to note that most of them only wrote about water waves like the ones they see at the beach. I was hoping for discussions of radio waves, photons of energy, and ultraviolet radiation. I was looking for terms that I was familiar with like crest, trough, wavelength and amplitude. On the other hand, I did get descriptions such as peak, valley, rise and fall. My initial reaction was that I'd have to teach everything from the beginning; but I realized I was wrong. These kids knew what they were talking about even if they didn't know my scientific terms. I had been focusing on finding examples of my own language and thought processes in their work rather than using the reflections of my students to understand how their minds were putting together information.

Now we begin our study of waves by going outside with a bunch of Slinkies and observing wave movement and relationships. Students still don't come up with many scientific terms, but their writing shows that they understand wave movements and characteristics (see Figures 11.3a and 11.3b). Instead of looking only at a finished product, I now see the importance of comprehending the manner in which young people put together the pieces of a scientific puzzle.

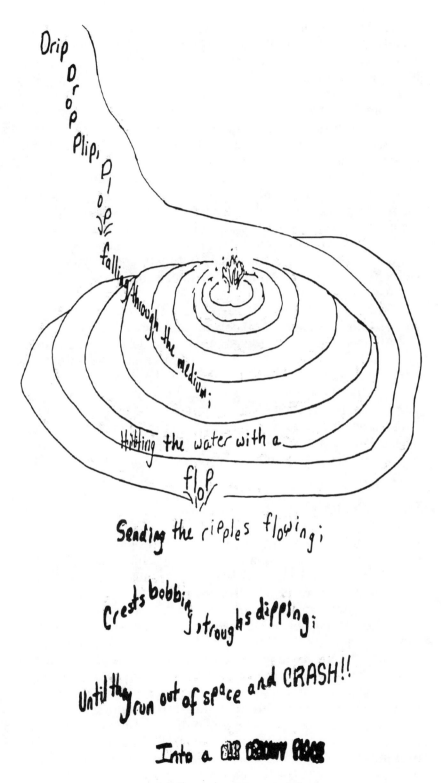

Drip

Drop

Plip, Plop

falling through the medium;

Hitting the water with a

flop

Sending the ripples flowing;

Crests bobbing, troughs dipping;

Until they run out of space and CRASH!!

Into a ▓▓ ▓▓▓▓ ▓▓▓▓

Figure 11.3a Student example

As part of an independent study called "Teacher as Researcher," I looked closely at some student work from an exploration activity. We were about to begin a study of atoms and chemical bonding; I wanted to know what concepts my students already had in place. I asked them to write a paper called "A Day in the Life of an Atom." The format was entirely of their own choosing; I gave no guidelines concerning length. I simply announced they were to generate some document that would help me better understand what they understood about atoms.

The variety of formats amazed me. Some students produced traditional narrative writing, but many others chose poetry, cartoons, and choose-your-own-adventure booklets. I learned that for a number of students the concept of an atom was fairly sketchy while others' notions went beyond what I expected, as they revealed in stories such as the one about hydrogen atoms bonding with oxygen atoms to fall as rain on a windshield, only to evaporate when the sun came out.

The student example in Figure 11.4 showed me that the student already had a fairly well developed notion of chemical bonding. Another student created imaginary towns where only the noble gases were allowed to live and outsiders like chlorine were ostracized. This student obviously understood the inert nature of some gases. A choose-your-adventure story included a choice about whether the reader wanted an atom of chlorine to remain alone as a dangerous gas or to find happiness in the arms of a cute atom named sodium. My students wrote more and less than I expected, which helped me to design instruction based on students' needs.

Future Challenges

I wish I could say I've travelled the road of teacher reflection and come out with a pure vision of what my teaching should be, but I haven't. The move in my school system to eliminate ability-grouped classrooms in favor of a full-inclusion model for special needs students presents many new challenges. Although I feel confident about the positive changes I've made in my classroom, I still feel I'm not doing all I need to be doing. I feel frustrated some days, knowing I am not meeting the needs of all my students. In a lesson on writing chemical formulas, I may have 10 students who understand the concept of outer electron exchange as it relates to bonding while 15 others are still trying to grasp the notion of invisible particles called electrons. The group of 10 are ready to move on but need some explanation, while the other 15 need me to go back over the parts of the atom. Every child's needs are legitimate and I feel an obligation to teach from where students are; but I often feel I must ask, "Who do I sacrifice today?" I don't want 10 students to

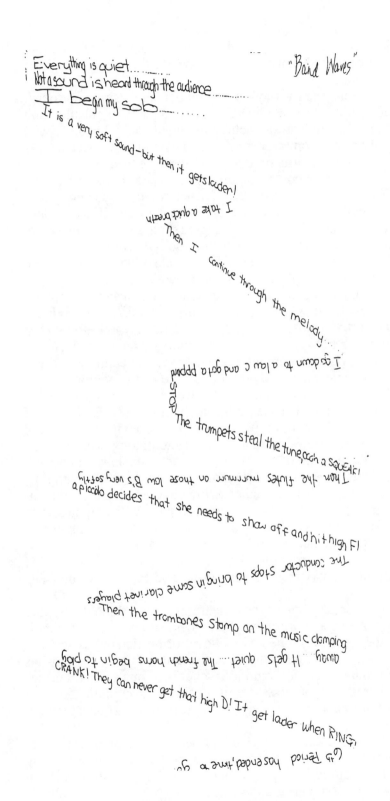

"Band Waves"

Everything is quiet............
Not a sound is heard through the audience............
I begin my solo.............

It is a very soft sound—but then it gets louder!

I take a quiet breath

Then I continue through the melody....

I go down to a low c and got a ppppp
STOP

The trumpets steal the tune, ooh a SQUEAK!

Then the flutes murmurm on those low B's very softly
a piccolo decides that she needs to show off and hit high F!

The conductor stops to bring in some clarinet players

Then the trombones stomp on the music clomping
away. It gets quiet.....The french horns begin to blare
CRANK! They can never get that high D! It get louder when RING,
(4th Period has ended, time a go.

Figure 11.3b Student example

languish in boredom, nor should I permit 15 to get more and more confused because I don't have time to help them understand the parts of the atom.

I am searching for ways to differentiate my instruction so that students can progress at an appropriate and suitably challenging rate. A smaller student-to-teacher ratio would help, but those who control the purse strings seem not to understand the impact of class size on quality of instruction. So teachers have to search for alternatives; these often come from totally unexpected places.

One such unexpected place for me is a computer programming tool called HyperCard.[5] I learned about it when I took a graduate course as part of my masters' degree program. I convinced my language arts colleague, Donna, to take the class with me. A former teaching colleague, Butch, had taken the class the summer before and assured me that HyperCard had potential as a teaching tool. After a traumatic beginning, during which Donna and I felt totally overwhelmed and out of place with this technology, we both became HyperCard junkies. We now incorporate HyperCard into our curriculum as both extension and enrichment. Our friend, Butch, as our supervisor of computer technology, has continued to encourage our interest and to provide technical and moral support.

We only have six computers, but we've scheduled our classes so that all of our students learn this technology over the course of a year in our classrooms. We were able to convince our school system that this is a valuable tool for differentiating instruction by showing them some of the programs our students have created. Our students have written programs that can be used as tutorials on a variety of topics. Instead of writing a research paper, our students can write a computer program, complete with graphics, text, sound, and animation. Students have written programs on everything from elements in the Periodic Table to the history of communication. The programming language is exceptionally user friendly and we have successfully instructed all our students in its use.

Just as in any other type of learning, some students become more interested and proficient than others. However, the technology is there for everyone and the level of proficiency is self-imposed rather than teacher directed. Currently, this technology has been introduced at all the middle schools in our county, and we have shared our successes with teachers throughout the state through presentations at state conferences and staff development sessions.

This year I am working in a project funded by our state department of education to promote collaboration and inquiry among teachers pursuing changes in their individual classrooms. I am hoping to get some ideas and strategies from the group to help me develop better means of fostering scientific literacy within my own

A Day in the Life of an Atom

One day Oscar the oxygen atom was very depressed. He felt he had no purpose in life. He just floated aimlessly around in the air, until he met Heidi and Hilda the hydrogen twins. They fell in love and decided to get hitched. They became one and turned into a raindrop. They began falling, falling, and SPLAT! The raindrop landed on the windshield of a car. All of a sudden the windshield wipers started to smear them all over the window. They were terrified, but reassured each other that everything would be all right. At that moment the sun suddenly appeared. Raindrops began evaporating all around them. They held on to each other with all their might, but before they knew what had happened, they were seperated. Now Oscar felt more alone and depressed than ever before. However, he finally came to the conclusion that it is better to have loved and evaporated, then never to have loved at all.

-Kara Hohenshil
11/11/89

Figure 11.4 Student example

classroom. I would like to develop some science kits on a variety of topics that I can use to provide students with more hands-on experiences, whether they are struggling or need to be challenged.

I have already begun work on a crime lab chemistry kit that will enable students to use chromatography to figure out which criminal wrote the ransom note. I'm not sure whether the individual learning kits will accomplish what I'm hoping for, but I do know that the answer to the problems of teaching in a heterogeneous classroom is not more whole group instruction. All children need as much individual attention and small group instruction as possible; we need to view them as individual learners, not assembly-line products.

I am ready to try a year of ungraded science teaching. I feel trapped by the pressure to assign a letter grade. My students are hung up on the grade, though they don't really care what it means or what it measures. I want to try to evaluate my students from a more process-oriented vantage point. I'd like to be able to assess where each student is "scientifically" at the beginning of a school year, and chart progress over the next nine months. I am interested in what they already know, what they would like to know, how they think they learn best, and what they want me to do to help them.

I would love to sit down with all my students at the beginning of the year and talk to them individually about their prior experiences with science. I love the way writers' workshops include regular teacher conferences with students where both determine goals and expectations for the year. It seems to me that a science classroom should and could work more like that. Letter grade evaluation doesn't provide the student with an opportunity to understand achievement or set appropriate directions for study. I want to evaluate progress and process, and help my students see learning as a continuum rather than a series of isolated experiences. I don't yet have concrete plans for making all this happen; but the vision is important enough to me to continue seeking answers to my questions.

I am not comfortable in the role of a teacher revolutionary, but I see many areas where I do not feel public schools are reaching all the children we could be reaching. I feel stymied by the fact that my average class size is still around 30 students, my classroom facilities are woefully inadequate for a well developed laboratory science experience, and the level of funding within my school system is barely maintained from one year to the next. In addition, I see an emerging activism among parents of our identified gifted students who are justified in feeling that their children are not getting the level of instruction they need to be challenged, to achieve their potential. Parents and teachers express concern that the full-inclusion model for special needs students was mandated and then forced on the schools without enough preparation. As a teacher, it is easy for me to feel that the more we are asked to do, the more we are criticized for not doing everything to everyone's satisfaction. It is easy to feel caught in the middle.

Yet, I believe most people who teach do it for the satisfaction that comes from interacting with a room full of students who are all special in their own way. We enjoy that give and take, and relish every little success even while we despair of the failures. The bottom line is that all kids deserve the best education we can furnish. It is that belief that keeps me constantly questioning my own teaching and looking for ways to make it better for all of us learners.

End Notes

1. J.M. Atkin and R. Karplus, "Discovery or Invention?" *Science Teacher* 29.5 (1962): 45.
2. George E. Glasson and Rosary V. Lalik, "Reinterpreting the Learning Cycle From a Social Constructivist Perspective: A Qualitative Study of Teachers' Beliefs and Practices," *Journal of Research in Science Teaching* 30.2 (1993): 187–207.
3. Eleanor Duckworth, *"The Having of Wonderful Ideas" and Other Essays on Teaching and Learning* (New York: Teachers College Press, 1987).
4. Nancie Atwell, *In The Middle: Writing, Reading, and Learning with Adolescents* (Portsmouth, NH: Heinemann, 1987).
5. Danny Goodman, *The Complete HyperCard 2.0 Handbook* (New York: Bantam Books, 1990).

Chapter 12

Above the Tree Line:
Collaborative Curriculum Construction

Kenneth L. Bergstrom, Chris Mattson, Anne Reid and Diedre Garner

Introduction: The Idea for a Collaborative Climb

We who climb mountains, hiking along forest trails, watching the trees shrink in size due to the inhibiting effects of the alpine climate, know the thrill of reaching that point in the journey when we scramble just high enough to be "above the tree line." On a clear day, as the view widens and deepens, the exhilaration enables us to see the world from a different perspective—more connected, more whole.

Even though this moment in the trip may be anticipated, each time the feeling is new and refreshingly real. Each climb has its own unique story: we may be hiking with a new collection of friends; the weather is certainly unique for each climb; it may be a completely different mountain or just a new trail to the summit. Yet, there is that feeling of breaking out above the tree line that excites our sensibilities. We realize that our steps have purpose and direction; we are making progress. We often get a second wind—we are refreshed and renewed; and we are spurred on by a glimpse of the summit.

Some fear and trepidation also come with this part of the journey. It feels less safe—less protected from the elements than when we strolled among the trees below. It is more precarious climbing here. Where vegetation struggles for a foothold, so do we. This moment tweaks the adventuring spirit in us. It is often a defining moment in the climb—a milestone. We are not yet at the peak, but we are clearer about whence we have come and excited about where we are heading.

For us, as educators on a journey toward learner-centered curriculum, the analogy is apt. This chapter represents a defining moment in all of our career paths. By working collaboratively with

young adolescents to generate themes from their personal and social concerns, and by facilitating learning which repositions skills
and transposes content in an integrative way, we have all broken
out "above the tree line." We have a sense of accomplishment, a
shift in perspective, a certain uneasiness, combined with a renewed
commitment to continue upward. We are excited to share with the
reader the joys and strains of our climb while collaboratively constructing curriculum with our students.

Early in 1993, Glennellen Pace called Ken Bergstrom, a
teacher educator at Goddard College. A conversation with Jim
Beane had led her to ask Ken to contribute to this work. Ken was
pursuing his interest in curriculum negotiation with young adolescents together with two of his students. Chris Mattson, a pre-ser-
vice teacher completing his Senior Study on campus, and Anne
Reid, a practicing teacher pursuing a master's degree in the off-
campus program, were both beginning action research projects on
the topic. Anne, with a class of her own, was well into the documentation of her study. Chris contacted Dee Garner, a cooperating
teacher in Goddard's teacher education program, to secure a site
for his investigation. With Chris leading, and Ken and Dee in supporting roles, the three worked with a group of eighth-grade students in Dee's Language Arts class at Spaulding Middle school in
Barre, Vermont. Anne, in Orangeville, Ontario, at Princess Margaret School, began documenting her project with seventh- and
eighth-grade students. Ken shared some of Anne's work with Chris,
which helped him to crystallize the story of his experiment.

As the four of us shared the emerging themes, the struggles
and successes of the two experiences were evident. Chris, as a
new teacher, was buoyed by Dee's support and heartened by Anne's
writing. Ken suggested that we all participate in the writing, as co-
authors, and this chapter was begun.

This collaboration was a natural phenomenon for us at
Goddard College. Based upon the ideas of John Dewey and other
progressive educators, the Goddard experience is, by design, student-centered and collaboratively constructed. Much like a strong
middle level program, Goddard students receive much teacher time
through advising. The curriculum arises from the concerns of faculty and students and is often integrated and evolving. Teachers
and students both serve as facilitators of learning and negotiate
different aspects of independent and group studies. A comprehensive period of evaluation requires that students and teachers alike
reflect on each semester's experience and document their learning
in narrative form. The experiments which Chris and Anne were to
lead in their respective sites are a reflection of their experiences in
different Goddard programs. As Chris reminded us, "Everything I
was to do with the kids at Spaulding, I had already practiced in my
Goddard education."

In this chapter we share our learning through the stories generated at each site. We offer a framework crafted from the ideas that guide our work, ground them in the actual tales from the classroom, and then share the insights we gained. We close with some advice for other hikers who wish to reach "above the tree line."

Choosing a Trail: Discovering the Theme

I want to argue that the middle school ought to be a general education school and that its version of general education ought to be of the kind based upon personal and social concerns.

James Beane[1]

In response to his question of what should be the middle level curriculum, James A. Beane proposes that a general, rather than a specialized education, is more developmentally responsive to the needs of young adolescents. Beane suggests that a general education is based on the common issues, problems, interests, and needs of young people and the society in which they live, whereas a specialized education is based on the particular concerns of some, but not all. Common concerns arise from two sources, the particular stage of life in which one finds oneself, and the interrelationship which exists among all who live on this planet.

For young adolescents this means that the concept of general education is placed within the context of the developmental concerns of their age group and within the reality of their being part of a whole society. It seems that early adolescence is a time when identity and values are being explored within a context that is not always, if ever, clear to the adult observer. It does not seem that specialized curriculum, designed around academic and exploratory subjects, which focus primarily on intellectual development, is responsive to the holistic needs of the kids.

In theory, it would seem that the personal and social concerns of young adolescents do reflect the collective culture of the age and could suggest a curriculum framework which would more closely match their developmental needs. In the array of literature about the nature of adolescence, the discreet categories of intellectual, social, physical, and emotional are often used as if they were independent functions and of equal concern to young adolescents. This is not the case. All are interrelated, but even intellectual and physical development are placed within the critical context of the social and personal world of each child. One student will stay home from school if she is having a "bad hair day"; another, in questioning the role of authority figures like parents and teachers and the value of institutions like school and the justice system, is moving from concrete to abstract thought within the context of his own experience.

So, in practice, how do we, as teachers, access the personal and social concerns of our students? While the process which Chris and Anne use is borrowed and adapted from one which Jim Beane and Barbara Brodhagen[2] have developed, the essence of it is to simply ask the kids. This requires a belief on the part of teachers that young adolescents do know and will articulate what is important to them, if they believe that those asking are genuinely listening. Chris's and Anne's experiences assure us that it works.

Anne's Story

I explained that for the next three months we were going to spend time on a theme or question that as a whole group we felt worthy of our time and effort. I said that I would not be choosing the theme, but would act as a guide, recorder, facilitator. I introduced the concept of constraints by talking about taking an airplane flight, in that one has to buy a ticket, go to the check-in counter, present a boarding pass, abide by the schedule, and so on. When asked what constraints they saw in terms of their current experience with schools, the students said they had to be in school until they were sixteen, had to have teachers and administrators, had to have entry and dismissal times, had to learn "stuff." When I told them that the "stuff" was called curriculum in educational terminology, Pamela said, "Oh, you mean everything that is on the timetable beside the door."

I asked everyone to think about this question: If we did not have subjects in school how could we find out about what we needed to learn and how could that be organized? This question was greeted with eloquent silence! Finally Beckie said, "Do you mean like the long discussion we had the other day?" The long discussion had resulted from an oral report on the history of women's rights in Canada as part of Tammie's final project. What was intended to be a three-minute report turned into a fifty-minute interaction in which every student participated and didn't want to have end at dismissal. When I said yes, that was one of the many possibilities, I heard Todd mutter to himself, "She can't be serious."

I was rather taken aback by this comment because I believe my program is quite flexible, with many opportunities for individual input, independent learning, natural groupings, wholesome food anytime, informal seating arrangements, and the list goes on. What I realized was that much of what happens in my classroom is window-dressing, well-intentioned and well-received, but none-theless not addressing the crux of the matter. If I read Todd's comment correctly, he was saying that the content, the vehicle for learning, was not meeting his needs, no matter how wonderful everything else was.

I asked each individual in the class to record some responses to this question: "What are the issues, problems, and concerns that you have as a young adolescent?" Everyone began writing at once. When this was completed, I invited everyone to find a friend or two or three, to compile a group list from their individual lists, and to record this list on chart paper so that the whole class could read the questions once they were posted on the walls (see Figure 12.1).

When the questions were completed, each group posted its list. I read each sheet aloud and asked each group if there were any additions or deletions they wished to make. This was the first time that I have read anything aloud to a class when every student was entirely absorbed by the material. At this point, I wanted to reflect on the process that had occurred in the development of these questions and I suggested that we all take out our journals and write about what had just happened. I immediately started to write and nearly everyone followed my lead; within five minutes we were all writing.

My observations revolved around the intensity and engagement of every student in the small-group compilation of questions. As I wandered around the room during this activity, I had listened to the strategies used to compile the group list. Some groups simply recorded every question individuals had written and then deleted similar questions. One group did this in advance by reading out each list separately, deleting similar questions, and finishing with an edited list. Another group passed around the chart paper and each person chose one question from the list to record on the large sheet. Students were eager to sign their names to the completed list and to see what the other groups had to say.

The range of questions was intriguing. Adolescents clearly are concerned with the personal issues of appearance and relationships, and with the global issue of violence and war. The search for a separate identity within or outside the familial and school structure seems to be a high priority. The theme of death and dying is a recurring one, which suggests that the concept of personal mortality is a real concern for the young adolescent. My sense is that questions were meaningful, relevant, and an honest expression of the common issues and purposes that Beane proposes as the framework for curriculum.

My only question was whether the issues and purposes identified by the students were in any way inhibited by my phrasing of the original question or by the use of questions as a means of expression. Maureen triggered the further exploration of this by her

From Lindsay, Beckie, and Maureen

Why do people have bad hair days?

Why is there an age limit on drinking and buying cigarettes?

Why is there an age limit on driving? Are they afraid we will take over the roads?

Why do we have to come to school?

Why can't we live alone at our age?

Why are parents always nagging at us?

Why do we have to die?

Why do we get zits?

Why do parents always have to know where we are?

Why are drugs against the law?

Will our world come to an end?

Why do people pick their noses?

Why do adults label teenagers?

Why do teachers cancel dances for no reasons?

Why don't we have more trips?

Why don't we have a junior high in Orangeville?

Why do kids have to listen to teachers when we know we're right?

Why don't we have recess?

Why is the opposite sex so hard to understand?

Why do we have to come to school so early?

Why aren't we allowed to hang out after school?

Why do we have to watch our parents drink and smoke, but they tell us we're not allowed?

Why can't we eat junk food in class?

Why do some people think they are so good?

From Mike, Bill, Spencer, Scot, and Todd

What does alcohol do to make you drunk?

Why can't kids drink?

Why doesn't Orangeville have a junior high?

Why do parents think they're the green giants?

Why do parents have control over us?

Why do we get detentions in art?

Who invented school?

Why do we have three English classes in one day?

Why do we have freckles?

Why is there a law about smoking?

Why can't we talk in class when we want?

Why did Billy the Kid die?

Why do we have gays?

Are there aliens?

From Richard and Jacob

Why is it that through your life you learn lots and lots but no matter how much you read or learn, all your knowledge will only be a grain of sand on a 300 acre beach?

Why is the sky blue?

Why do people try to prove themselves?

Why do we have subjects we don't need?

Why are there so many rules in the world today?

Why is there school and if there wasn't, what would we be doing? How would we live? Would we be living in caves like prehistoric man?

(continued on next page)

Figure 12.1 *List 1*: Personal concerns from young adolescents in Anne Reid's class

From Lucas, Reid, and Darryl

Why do we have to take French when we don't like it?

Why do teachers cancel dances?

Why are the things you usually have to do boring?

Why do we have to do assignments we don't like?

Why do people murder people?

Why do people die?

Why is the world so violent?

From Cheryl, Brenda, Tammie, and Raegen

Why do we have bad hair days?

Why are parents so strict?

Why do we have to stand outside and teachers don't?

Why are guys our age so annoying?

Why do kids our age act dumb but think they're so cool?

Why are parents so snoopy?

Why does lipstick get on your teeth?

Why do we get grounded when we don't do anything?

What's going on in the world?

Why do teachers always stare when you are working?

Why do good friends all of a sudden backstab?

Why do we lose things just when we need them?

Why do we put up with jerks?

From Celine, Sharon, Candice, and Dawn

Why do people abuse animals?

Why does the world try to solve its problems with wars?

Am I going to die today?

Do people find it pleasurable to watch oth-

ers suffer as they kill them?

Why are people psychos?

Are we going to get kidnapped today?

What is going to happen today?

Why do people have bad days?

Figure 12.1 continued *List 1*: Personal concerns from young adolescents in Anne Reid's class

response to my observation that her group had an extensive list. She laughed and said, "Oh, I have strong opinions about everything!" This prompted my next suggestion that the groups record the issues about which individuals in the group had strong opinions (see Figure 12.2).

When we added the opinion charts to the question charts around the room, Lucas looked at the result and said, "This is great, but what a mess!" My question to the class became, "How do we make it less messy?" The response from Mike was that we should look for questions in common; from Spencer, that we should look for similarities; from Lucas, that we should see if there were any big topics. The patterns identified were:

- rights: women's, men's, animals', children's, parents', and teachers';
- violence: playground, racial, rape, robbery;
- world issues: pollution, extinction, war;
- relationships: with parents, with friends, with teachers, between sexes, abusive, between the races.

At this point I asked for suggestions for a question that could frame the foundation of our investigation, fully expecting that this question would come from the "big" topics that the students had just identified. Wrong! Pamela said, "What this is really about is what it means to be an adolescent involved in all these issues." Heads everywhere nodded in agreement. I asked if the question could then be stated, "What does it mean to be an adolescent?" General buzzing filled the room. When silence finally returned, Bill said what we needed were two questions: what does it mean to be a male adolescent, and what does it mean to be a female adolescent. This received strong affirmation: our theme had been discovered, or—perhaps more accurately—uncovered.

As a collaborative group, we were able to arrive at a framework for investigation. I had absolutely no doubt that the two questions reflected the common purpose, intent, and concern of this particular group of young adolescents. It reaffirmed my belief that the world of young adolescents is rich with possibilities for learning. Reaching this point in the construction of our learning took approximately five hours over three days. There was never a perfect day with every student present and no interruptions, but we forged ahead anyway.

Chris's Story

After a few days in the classroom getting to know the kids and classroom procedures, I was ready to start the process of eliciting the personal and social concerns of this class of eighth graders. Because I didn't know the students well, I had little idea how accustomed they were to articulating their concerns and issues, and was worried that they might not be ready to begin listing them. I decided that I would take it slowly, warming up to the idea of creating questions.

On the first day of our work together, I spoke briefly about my research and my beliefs about student ownership of the curriculum. I asked them to become part of an experiment to help teachers better understand the way kids learn, and I told them that they were making an important contribution to my learning. Then I demonstrated some question making, sharing with them some of the things I puzzled over, including issues that were of a personal

From Brenda, Cheryl, Tammie, and Raegen

Death, animal rights, sex, racism, child abuse, living, sexism, divorce, jobs, pollution, women's rights, laws today, Canadian Army, homosexuals, all sports, health, human rights, schoolwork, smoking and drugs (only live once, make it a fun one), Canada, Scotland, slavery, possessive people, abortion, crossing guards, dances, homocides, any kind of abuse, my background, Americans, my age group, music, school, the age of drinking and getting a driver's license.

From Jessie, Bill, Mike, Scot, and Jacob

Be able to drink and drive, girls should stay in the kitchen, freedom, hash and pot should be allowed in Canada, should be able to smoke, girls should be Cinderellas, no age limit for drinking, girls should not be allowed to hit guys and the guys should not be allowed to hit back, the hippies, school should be optional, girls should loosen up.

From Pam and Shannon

Right to live, homeless kids, fighting, smoking, drinking, dating, dancing, sleeping around, birth control, parents, happiness, gays and lesbians, robbing, prostitution, getting in trouble, clothing, child abuse, drugs, sex under age, homophobic people, women's rights, aids, death, cancer, right to be who you want to be, family, teenagers, school, abortion, guys, rules, music, to be taught in the best possible way, to be brought up in a good environment, the right to state your point of view, friends, peace, happiness, peace, religion.

From Reid, Darryl, and Lucas

People should not have to do something they don't want to do, should have to go to school five days a week, no psychos, you should always get a break from work, you should always do your best, if you think bad things bad things will come to you, if you think good things good things will come to you, never let anybody ruin a good thing for you.

From Dawn, Celine, and Candace

Animal abuse, murderers, rapists, child abuse, strict parents, racism, sexism, environmental problems, world peace, talking behind people's backs, thinking of yourself, things happening in the world, teachers making us do things we don't want to do, peer pressure, our families, friends, school subjects we don't need.

Figure 12.2 *List 2:* Issues about which Anne's class held
strong opinions

and social nature. I adopted a prompt from a survey developed by participants in the Middle Level Curriculum Project,[3] and asked the class to finish the following sentences:

- I am . . .
- I wish I knew why . . .
- I wish I knew how . . .
- I wish I knew more about . . .

Then I asked them to freewrite in response to the following questions:

- What are the things that you daydream about?
- What are the things that you worry about?
- What is really important to you?

My intention was to stimulate their thinking about themselves, to try to draw out some of the issues that concerned them, and to show that their personal thoughts were a valid and important part of "writing class." The responses were wonderful and illustrated some of the concerns one would expect from early adolescents (see Figure 12.3).

After they had finished writing, I asked them to find a partner and share some of their responses. They reconvened into the large group, and everyone shared one item that they had in common. My purpose was to have them become more comfortable with the process we would be using: individual reflection, small group share, search for commonalities, large group share. I was both surprised and pleased by their response; they were more prepared than I had anticipated to articulate their personal and social concerns. Some of the patterns that emerged were concerns with relationships between friends and family members; concerns over the future, death, the earth's destruction; and the importance of friendship and pets. I compiled the responses and common themes on a large piece of newsprint and posted it prominently in the classroom.

The next day we had a double class period in which to develop and list the common concerns of the class. Because I was still unsure about their grasp of how to form questions, and because most of the theorists I read emphasized the need to demonstrate processes of negotiation and questioning, I decided to demonstrate the process of question-making with Dee and Ken. The three of us came to class armed with newsprint sheets listing *our* personal and social concerns as questions. We began with our lists of personal concerns, posting them, and then reading and explaining them briefly. Next we demonstrated the important process of deciding which were our "common" personal concerns. I instructed the class to list "the questions you have about yourself," then to get together with their group, share their questions, and list the questions they had in common on chart paper. We repeated the process, including our demonstration, for social concerns, in this case asking students to list "the questions they had about the world."

Having finished that, we spent the rest of the class dealing with the harder, more abstract task of making connections between the two lists in order to draw out possible themes for study. We asked, "What patterns, ideas, or themes emerge from the two lists; what connections can you make; what do they have in common?" Once groups completed this process, we went around the room sharing responses. We didn't have time to create a common list for the whole class, and I regret that I never followed through to create and post one. However, despite the time constraints and the fact that some students were still suspicious of this soliciting of real concerns, I was quite happy with how well they did with what we thought was going to be a particularly difficult, abstract task (see Figure 12.4).

I wish I knew why some people have to pick on others even when they aren't so perfect themselves. I wish I knew more about being a better friend. I wish I knew why humans are so dominant. Maybe if we were smaller we wouldn't be so powerful. I wish I knew more about my grandfather. I wish I knew why cars don't have screen windows. I wish I knew more about cars. I wish I knew how the Bermuda Triangle works. I wish I knew why people with Down's syndrome look alike. I wish I knew how the earth was created. I wish I knew more about the afterlife, if there is one. I wish I knew more about who my ancestors were.	I worry about my sister because I miss her so much. I always daydream about why God put us here. Maybe he's just testing out humans to see how well we treat our resources and our environment, and if it doesn't work he'll just wipe us all out and start all over again. I worry about getting blown up in a nuclear war. I slouch back in the blue plastic chair and wander into worry about the future. The things that are really important to me are my family and my friends. I daydream about my past with my mother and worry if I'll ever see her again. I think about my future: my husband, my children, lifestyle and all that stuff.

Figure 12.3 *List 3:* Response to warm-ups from Chris's students

Sam, Nick, Jon, and Erik

Common Personal Concerns

Will we pursue our career choices?

If we die, what will it be like?

Can we rewrite life's little script?

When we are older will we have as much fun as we do now?

Will we get married, stay married, and have kids?

Will we fulfill our dreams ($$, adventure, jobs)?

Common Social Concerns

What does crystal clear Pepsi taste like?

How many licks does it take to get to the center of a Tootsie Roll Pop?

What's the big deal about the future?

Will global warming affect the climate?

Will everything always be overpriced?

Common Themes

Future concerns and choices

Financial concerns

Death—fulfillment before death; are there good reasons for death (war)?

Kim, Myesha, Becky, Christina

Common Personal Concerns

Will I go to heaven or hell?

How will I die?

Who will I marry?

Is there really a heaven or hell?

If God created us, who created God?

How many kids will I have?

What college will I go to?

If heaven is up and hell is down, why are people buried underground?

If you die and your spirit goes to heaven, isn't it crowded there?

Is this real?

There are so many people around, why was I chosen to be me?

If you get to pick who you want to be in a next life, why do some people choose to be evil?

Am I gifted?

Common Social Concerns

How do people know what the interior of the earth looks like if no one has ever seen it?

Are there people on other planets?

Why are some people so hateful because of skin color?

How and when will the earth end?

Why does the government kick people out of their homes?

Common Themes

Equality

Prejudice, social justice

Death and dying

Michelle, M.J., Melissa, Liza, Nicole

Common Personal Concerns

Will I finish my education?

What will/who will my relationships be in the future?

What will my career be?

Will I get a license and a car?

Will I get to go to my favorite place?

How will I die? Will I be young or old?

Will we smoke in the future? Will we quit if we already do?

Common Social Concerns

Will there ever be a cure for incurable diseases?

Will the world come to an end?

Will prejudice and racism cease?

Will there ever be world peace?

Are there aliens?

Will our continents disappear?

Will pollution stop?

Will our seasons reverse?

(continued on next page)

Figure 12.4 *List 4*: Personal concerns, social concerns, and common themes

Common Themes

Pollution problems—smoke, seasons, diseases, end of the world, continents disappearing

Future—aliens, friends, marriage, kids

Death/Diseases—dying young or old, how, when, where, why, world ending.

Pat, Joe, Nick

Common Personal Concerns

What kind of education will I get?

What will our future jobs be like?

Will we ever commit homicide?

Why and how will we perish?

Common Social Concerns

Will there be a third world war?

How will the world end?

Are they coming for us?

How did dinosaurs die?

Will there ever be a crime- and hate-free world?

Are we ever going to travel through time?

Common Themes

What will happen to us and how will we end?

What makes people commit crimes?

Will humans become extinct from our own undoing?

What will future technology be like?

Are there other forms of life in the universe?

Figure 12.4 continued *List 4*: Personal concerns, social concerns, and common themes

All children need to construct their own meaning. It is presumptuous of us as adults to believe that our agenda for our students is more important, more necessary, or more engaging than the tasks of their developmental age group. Young adolescents, in particular, are experiencing a wondrous transition from child to adult. Their tasks are to seek an identity, develop a sense of autonomy, and explore the intimacy of different relationships. They are eager to know who they are and where they fit in the scheme of things. To them, personal and social concerns are one and the same. That world between childhood and adulthood is rich with themes for learning that are part of these young adolescents' lives. All we need to do is scratch the surface with a few genuine, well-articulated questions and the topics for study spew forth, making the regular curriculum look impoverished by comparison. These kids want to know about life. Would our schools not better serve them by responding with a collaboratively constructed curriculum of interest? Ultimately, they choose their own trail up the mountain. Why not engage them in the conversations which will help them choose wisely?

Setting the Pace: "Handsitting" and Sharing the Lead

> *Once students have become active participants in their own learning, the role of the teacher must change. No longer is the teacher able to be the One Who Knows, from whom students, in return for polite respect and good behavior, will (somehow) glean the Knowledge that*

the teacher deems important. When students are devis-
ing their own questions, the teacher's role finally be-
comes one of Educator, that of leading the students
further on their way of understanding.

G. Boomer[4]

The role of the teacher changes dramatically when we encourage adolescents to choose the path with us. How can teachers
direct students when they themselves are uncertain of the way to
go? When the traditional curriculum is set aside in favor of one
that is immediately and collaboratively created, the lines between
teachers and learners blur. The best teachers in this kind of classroom are usually the best learners. As a lead learner, the teacher
demonstrates the very best of a collaborative process, asking questions, clarifying concepts, facilitating discussions, bringing resources, creating appropriate dissonance, diagnosing issues, and
sharing enthusiasm. Planning becomes less linear and more organic. Teachers in this setting know that things will seldom, if
ever, go according to plan, so they open themselves to the possibilities of a shared classroom experience, prepared to hear new
ideas, change directions, shift gears, and to take their cues from
the students. These teachers are bold enough to be flexible, to risk
some confusion for a new insight or the chance of a student's success. And they know when to let the students lead. Perhaps the
most important aspect of this new way of teaching is to know when
to "sit on one's hands" and let the students take the lead. It certainly makes for a more interesting and successful hike.

Both Chris and Anne struggled with the question of when to
"sit on their hands" and watch the process evolve, and when to
intervene as the teacher/authority. This balancing act of who decides led Anne and her class to seek a common theme as a whole
class. For Chris, it played out as small groups within the class
investigating their own common themes. As Anne facilitated the
development of the theme to be studied with her class, soliciting
questions and opinions, she felt the need to hold herself back from
such teacher-centered interference.

Anne's Story

It seemed that the responses to the query about strong opinions
extended and enriched the original list of questions. These opinions confirm that young adolescents do care and think about a diverse range of topics, that significance is attached to the self and
to the society in which kids live. Already, my thoughts were churn-
ing about the rich possibilities for learning inherent in this information. It was quite difficult for me at this point to not take the

information, create a theme, design the learning activities, and decide upon the assessment strategies. I didn't because I wanted the whole process to be truly collaborative.

Through a process of interactive questioning and dialogue, we had arrived at the large issue that would form the nucleus of our investigation: What does it mean to be a male and a female young adolescent? The classroom walls were lined with sheets of chart paper filled with questions of every kind. When I asked what kind of organization could assist our learning, Billie Lynn said she could see questions that had the same theme as other questions, such as the relationships that adolescents have with each other, their parents, their teachers. Other students noted question themes about appearance, how males and females think differently, the wide and ever-changing feelings adolescents have. I introduced the categories of social, physical, intellectual, and emotional, and suggested these categories might be used to organize the similar themes within the questions.

The original set of questions included several about death. I told the students about a huge boulder that was in a ten-acre field on our family farm. I would go there to think about serious issues, such as whether Bernard was going to ask me to go steady, would my parents ever die, and did I have a soul? This sparked a discussion about organized religions, aliens, and ghosts. Sharon said that all these topics might be categorized as spiritual and could form our fifth category.

At lunch, Pam lingered behind and said she had another idea for a category even though there had not been many questions asked about her concern. The previous evening she and her Mom had had a big fight about a pair of designer jeans that Pam wanted. Her Mom said that all teenagers believe money grows on trees, and to wait until she had to pay for everything herself. Pam said she didn't want to admit it, but maybe her Mom was right. She looked around her room and saw a portable television, a compact disc player, lots of clothes, and stuffed animals. Could we investigate the financial side of being a young adolescent? I said that sounded like a worthwhile topic; so we added economic to our list of categories. We now had six organizers through which to investigate the theme "What does it mean to be a female and male adolescent, emotionally, socially, physically, intellectually, spiritually, and economically."

At this point I felt the need to recap what had happened in our collaborative process. I asked the students to reflect on what it felt like to be a part of this effort. Todd wrote, "I like being asked my opinion because I don't feel left out." Candace said, "I like doing this. I like giving my opinion, and I find it interesting to see what my friends want to know." Chauvin stated, "It feels great to have my opinions matter. Finally we have a teacher who really cares

A Sample of Categorized Questions from Anne's Students

Emotionally

What does emotionally mean?

Why do girls cry more than boys?

Why do girls seem more emotional?

Why don't boys express their emotions?

Why do both sexes tease each other?

Why do both sexes put each other down?

Why do girls complain about physical problems so much?

Why do girls complain about their appearance?

Why do girls seem to grow up emotionally before boys?

What do adolescents feel about their parents and what do parents feel about their own and other adolescents?

Why do parents put down kids?

Why can't fathers talk to their daughters and mothers talk to their sons?

Who can adolescents talk to about their feelings?

What are mood swings and why do we have them?

What can parents do to help?

Why can't teachers see us as people first?

Physically

What is physically?

Why are boys taller than girls?

Why are there differences in height?

Is there a relationship between height and weight?

Why do we get zits?

Is there a difference between stamina and endurance between male and female adolescents?

Do boys participate in more physical activities than girls?

Why are there growth spurts?

Why do we feel physically different from other kids our age?

Why do I sound differently now than I did two years ago?

Why do girls get broader hips and boys broader shoulders?

Why are there differences in appetites?

Why do girls worry about gaining weight and boys don't?

Why do girls worry so much about how they look and boys don't?

How can females help boys understand processes like menstruation and pregnancy?

Socially

How does the opposite sex feel when you are on a date?

Why do couples fight over nothing?

Why are some jobs only made for the opposite sex?

Why is there racism?

Why do friends fight over little things?

Why don't people respect others for who they are?

Why don't people do what they want instead of following the crowd?

Why do people judge others by their color?

Why do people hurt family members?

Why do adolescent girls have very little confidence in themselves?

Why don't parents trust their kids?

Why don't boys tell us how they are feeling?

Why do some girls think they are gods?

Why are some girls so snotty to boys in our school?

Why do some of our friends do drugs?

Why are relationships with the opposite sex so important to teens?

Why does the media have such an effect on teens?

Why are there so many stereotypes?

Why is sex such an important issue for teens?

Why after sex are guys "studs" and girls "sluts"?

Why don't some people trust other people?

(continued on next page)

Figure 12.5 *List 5:* What does it mean to be a male or female adolescent?

Why does it matter to my friends whom I am friends with?

Why is being different not such a good thing?

Why is fashion such a big issue today?

Why is money such a big issue?

Why do some guys think they can jump girls' bones?

Why do some guys put on a show for girls?

Why do we have enemies?

Intellectually

What is intellectually?

Why do girls feel feelings guys can't understand?

Are guys afraid to express their feelings because they think their friends are going to make fun of them?

Why do people think smoking is cool?

Why do some people think that Blacks and Indians don't have the rights that we do?

What is the difference between the way boys and girls think?

Do people of other races think differently from whites?

Could a person live with an artificial brain?

Would a person be able to think with a brain the size of a peanut?

Why do boys think the best way out is fighting?

Why do girls tend to talk things out?

Do girls think the same as boys when they are in trouble?

Why do girls talk behind other people's backs?

Why do guys think they can overpower us?

Why do girls think about their hair all the time?

Is one sex smarter than the other?

Why do parents expect their kids to be so smart?

Why do people act stupid when they are so smart?

Why do people think that girls are smarter than boys?

Do people think the same sexually?

Do people think the same about art?

Why do boys think they should have more power, but girls think they should be equal?

Why are boys' and girls' attitudes different toward school?

Economically

Why do adolescents like to spend money?

How much money do adolescents spend?

Do most adolescents get a job?

Where do adolescents get their money?

What do adolescents spend money on?

Why do people care about money more than other things?

Why are adolescent clothes so expensive?

Why do parents argue so much about money?

Why does money cause problems when it's just paper?

Why do some people have more money than they need?

Why do some people try to buy friends?

Why does it cost so much to attract the opposite sex?

How does the media affect what we buy?

If everything were free, would we be happy?

Why are things so expensive these days?

Why do we lack self confidence? Is it because of the media?

Why do teens spend so much money on stupid stuff?

Why are there taxes?

Why do girls' clothes cost more than boys'?

Why are some people rich and others poor?

How do advertisements suck people in?

Spiritually

What does spiritual mean?

Why do people fear death?

Why do people refuse to believe in ghosts?

Why do people take their own lives?

Why do people believe in Satanism?

Why do people join cults?

(continued on next page)

Figure 12.5 continued *List 5:* What does it mean to be a male or female adolescent?

Is there a God?

Is there reincarnation?

Can we really bring spirits into our house by holding a seance?

Is there a heaven?

What really happens when you die?

How long will the world be here?

Is there human life on other planets?

Will we turn into spirits when we die?

Is there a devil?

What does spirituality mean to different people?

What does spirituality mean to different religions?

Why do different cultures believe in different gods?

Why do people think there is more than one god?

Why does it matter what we believe?

Why are there arguments about religion?

What does religion mean to adolescents?

Do people really have souls?

Why do we have out-of-body experiences?

Why do spirits try to contact people?

Are ouija boards fake or real?

Do guys and girls have different spiritual thoughts?

Do teens think differently about spiritual things than do adults?

Do people's spiritual beliefs have anything to do with how they were brought up?

Figure 12.5 continued *List 5:* What does it mean to be a male or female adolescent?

about how we feel about school. Just being asked what we think is important enough for me." Ike and Scot were worried, "This is asking my opinion and I am confused." Brenda wrote, "As adolescents, finally, we get the chance to say what we feel about the subjects we think are important." Bill said, "I feel there were a lot of good questions. Some questions were stupid though and unrealistic."

My journal reflects my sense that these young people were both overwhelmed and delighted by the collaborative process. I saw an intensity and engagement in the construction of their questions, and a lively curiosity about the content of their classmates' work. From their comments, I knew they also recognized that I viewed them as important and heard what they said in a real way. Some students worried that the whole process would turn into a confrontation between the strongly held views of male and female adolescents in the class. This concerned me as well, and I tried to remain very open to the body language, the nuances, and the interchanges to sort out the bravado from the deeply held convictions. I was saddened and then angry about the feeling of so many students that having their voices actively sought and validated was a rare occasion in their school life. I was impressed with the variety and scope of their questions. Most were sincere and begging for investigation and answers.

I also wondered if the mere process of articulating the questions was in itself a learning experience. Perhaps as educators we have been so preoccupied with the answers that we have overlooked a critical component in the construction of knowledge and personalized meaning. What are the questions that we want and need to have answered if we are to be creative, collaborative, and caring individuals on this planet? I think these young adolescents are defining quite clearly what it is they want and need to know. This surely must be a first step in a meaningful, relevant, and transformative learning process.

Earlier I said that real learning can appear to be messy and fragmented. If only you could have seen Room 15 at this point: we had sheets of chart paper all over the place; desks were askew as they had been rearranged to accommodate the self-selected groupings; colored markers had fallen off desks; cushions were scattered all over the rug area. Even the plants were drooping because we had been so caught up in our discussions that no one had remembered to water them. My desk was strewn with notes to myself, notes to the principal, notes to my dentist, notes to the caretaker not to touch one part of this exciting, beautiful mess! Thank heavens it was the end of the day and we could all go home and regroup ourselves and our thoughts.

The next morning I suggested that we recap where we were and where we were going. We recalled our major question of what does it mean to be a female and male adolescent in our six categories. We decided to see if we could devise more questions now that we had the framework of the six categories. I would act as recorder on the overhead projector to compile the questions, and we would conduct this process as a brainstorming session, at this point accepting all ideas (see Figure 12.5).

When I read the class journals at the completion of this part, I found mixed reactions. Chauvin wrote, "I like this process because I can talk to my friends better than the whole class. I think this is the best method because people can get the more questions out. If you are shy in a large group, you don't always say what you want to say." Jacob said, "I'm ahead of the process. It is good working in groups even though our thoughts and questions have dried up." Scot stated, "The only thing I like about this is talking to our friends and getting free time." Dawn predicted, "I think this is going to be a very different kind of project. I think that there are going to be a lot of arguments about the opposite sex in our questions and answers. It is going to be very interesting." Lucas wrote, "I think that the process that we are taking is very good, because it is a lot easier to understand and we can find out everything. I think that I have put in a few good ideas for the research. If we had done this research any other way I think it would have been a lot more difficult." Todd agreed, "I like working this way because there is a lot more brain power in a group." Reid was cryptic, "It is boring and stupid!"

We posted all the charts in the room. I again read them aloud to the class. I wanted the students to see where their individual questions and concerns were similar, and where they were different. I asked them not to discuss any of the questions at this time; I would provide ample time for discussion later.

My reaction to the questions was that they were rich with intent and meaning. Students obviously had difficulty with the "intellectual" category, but I made no attempt to point out any errors with categorizing questions. I think in the initial stages of a collaborative process, honest attempts have to be honored, not devalued for what can easily be corrected at another time. I applied the same belief to the sexual, street language of some of the questions. My intuition also told me that if I made an issue of the real talk of adolescents expressing their sexual concerns, they might not be willing the next time to ask the questions they really wanted to have answered. This, I believe, would have been a serious loss. I could see clearly from this set of questions many common issues and concerns in this class of 24 young adolescents.

Because the sociological preference of this class was to work in small groups, I was not surprised at the response when I asked how our investigation should proceed. What pleased me was the unanimous request that the small groups be composed of both sexes. Given the provocative nature of the sexist issues raised in the questions, and the concerns expressed in their journals, I was quite astonished when everyone agreed that more could be accomplished with mixed groups. Reflecting on this later, I was glad I had not interferred with the initial forays into the perceived relationships between the males and females in this class. They were genuinely looking for some understanding of each other, I believe, although the language of the questions ostensibly defied that probability. I am slowly learning the value of a "wait and see" approach when interacting with young adolescents.

I asked the students to make a list of names of both males and females with whom they would like to work, and I would form the groups so that there would be at least one or two preferred choices in each group. I did not give students total free choice in selecting groups. I use various strategies to create groups within the class, although my bias is in favor of free selection. This time, however, I wanted to ensure mixed groups of equal numbers. Also, I realized there might be considerable reluctance to publicly select a member of the opposite sex to be a learning partner. I could remove that particular constraint by combining *some* elements of student choice with my knowledge of the individuals in the class.

First, I asked each group to decide on the categories of questions they would most like to investigate. Considering our timeline, I suggested one topic was too little and six too many; however, each group could prepare a proposal for study. As I walked around the room listening to the process of selection, I heard several strategies. One group voted after eliminating two categories by oral agreement. Each person in another group defended his or her choice in turn. One group broke into pairs and each pair selected a topic. Another group had each person prioritize the six categories and reached consensus that way.

The end results were interesting. Two of the groups chose three categories; four chose two categories. Each of the six groups selected the social category; five of the groups selected the spiritual category. The two groups with three choices added the emotional category to their list. Omitted from all groups were the intellectual and economic categories.

The priorities of this class were clear. The concept of relationships with each other and the world around them was what intrigued, dismayed, frightened, fascinated, and absorbed these young adolescents. This is not news to anyone who works with adolescents; what may be different with this process of collaboration is the articulate and compelling definition of the social issues these students made when given the opportunity. What may be even more surprising is that spiritual questions are so critical to young adolescents. The range of questions is very broad, but one can see the struggle felt by this age group with their own spirituality and the expressions of the spirituality of others in the world context.

Many times throughout this exploration of learning I felt the need to take deep gulps of air. There have been times when I needed to suspend judgment, to wait, to listen more intently than ever before, to realize that this is organic, moving from whole to part to whole—at incredible speed sometimes—that I am changing in still undefined ways, and that these amazing young people are changing, too. The word "transformation" keeps dancing in my head, but I can not quite pull in the words to explain what is happening. It is exhilarating and terrifying to explore the largely uncharted territory of negotiating curriculum with young adolescents.

Chris and Hand-Sitting

In Barre, Chris, along with Dee and Ken, first experienced the need to "sit on hands" during the development of topics to be studied. Chris relates two examples that show the facilitative role of the teacher in this kind of learning, and the importance of the teacher allowing the students to make their own choices.

Chris's Story

One group of four boys, working well collaboratively, successfully generated a list of their common concerns:

- Will we pursue our career choices?
- If we die, what will it be like?
- Can we rewrite life's little script?
- When we are older will we have as much fun as we do now?
- Will we get married, stay married, and have kids?
- Will we fulfill our dreams ($$, adventure, jobs)?

But when faced with thinking about their social concerns, they resisted, maintaining they didn't have any social concerns or questions about the world and relegating that kind of thinking to the world of adults (and, perhaps, girls). Their initial list read:

- What does crystal clear Pepsi taste like?
- How many licks does it take to get to the center of a Tootsie Roll Pop?
- What's the big deal about the future?
- Will global warming affect the climate?

After reading this list, Ken had an interesting conversation with the group, during which he tried to get at the underlying issues behind the first two questions. Instead of dismissing their responses as disrespectful, he took them seriously and challenged the boys to think further. In doing so, we uncovered some genuine concerns about teenagers' roles as consumers and questions about economics. While we had a good discussion that resulted in the question, "Will things always be overpriced?" they never fully bought into the idea of inquiry about market forces and adolescent consumerism. Their questions and concerns about death and personal fulfillment simply proved to be more attractive, and we honored their choice.

Ultimately, they generated significant and meaningful themes; they listed concerns about the future and choices they would make, financial concerns, and the idea of what it means to be fulfilled before death. This last idea was the one they chose to pursue. It seemed to meet their needs in terms of the general classroom fascination and curiosity about death, and their genuine quest for understanding the idea of personal fulfillment.

What is important here is that the teacher's role should not be to disallow or discourage seemingly frivolous or "wise" remarks, but to take them seriously, giving students the message that their work is important, and looking for the subtext of their responses to "tease out" the underlying issues. In this example, if the teacher's response had devalued the questions, opportunities to have a short but valuable conversation about a social issue, and to show students the importance of their questions, would have slipped away.

A parallel example involved another group of three boys whose questions showed a diversity of interests. Under "Comon Personal Concerns" they wrote:

- What kind of education will I get?
- What will our future jobs be like?
- Will we ever commit homicide?
- Why and how will we perish?

Their list of "Common Social Concerns" read:

- Will there be a third world war?
- How will the world end?
- Are they coming for us?
- How did dinosaurs die?
- Will there ever be a crime- and hate-free world?
- Are we ever going to travel through time?

The common themes they arrived at were:

- What will happen to us and how will we end?
- What makes people commit crimes?
- Will humans become extinct from our own undoing?
- What will future technology be like?
- Are there other forms of life in the universe?

A conversation with this group during the process demonstrated an important aspect of teaching in this kind of environment. Several of their initial questions were about themselves and violent crime. Instead of classifying these youths as potential criminals, we found an interesting underlying issue that was drawn out through conversation: deviant social behavior. Our discussion led to their question, "What creates crime and makes people commit crimes?"

As did the "fulfillment group," they eventually decided not to pursue this issue. Space aliens proved to be too interesting to pass up, and they had a good experience with it. The lesson here is one of "handsitting." One of the hardest things to do is nothing. So often I found myself wanting to dictate the kids' processes, knowing the rich opportunities of some of the avenues they passed up. The decision of when to intervene as a teacher is an important one. We want to be able to allow students the follow an inquiry that has personal significance for them, but we also need to help them expand their horizons past where they can already see. The balance is a tenuous one.

This theme of "handsitting" continued through the process of deciding what course our learning would take. With the topics selected, the next stage was to negotiate how we were to conduct our inquiries. I wanted to employ Cook's model:[5] what do we already know about our topic? what do we need to find out? how will we go about finding out? how will we know what we've learned? cycling from small group to large group as we answered each of the questions.

I began asking each of the small groups to brainstorm every-thing they knew about their topic. All groups except for one struggled with this. The "death/disease/afterlife" group was quite successful; they really enjoyed newsprint, markers, and making lists. The rest, however, had difficulty coming up with more than one or two items, even with the help of the adults present. Feeling frustrated, I asked the class what they thought the problem was, but they didn't seem to know, either. I suspected that they were a bit tired of all the "process stuff" and wanted to "do" something. So I moved on to "What do we want to find out about these top-ics?" This went better.

The next day, I began by trying to develop lists of activities the groups could engage in to investigate their topics by brain-storming in the large group. This was slightly more fruitful as they came up with a predictable list: read books, magazines, and news-papers; watch videos; and conduct surveys and interviews. I sent them back to small groups with the task of constructing a list of specific activities, hoping I could work out a research plan with each group and confer about the order of activities and matters of planning. In this way I thought I could address organizational and problem-solving skills.

While I was trying to work out activities, one group decided to conduct a survey. Another group saw this and followed suit with their own survey. I attempted to rein this in, asking each group what they wanted to discover from their survey, asking what they knew about the nature of surveys, but they resisted working with me. I wasn't getting through to them. They wanted to do surveys; that was all, and that was that. So I decided to abandon the process and just watch what was happening, let them go to it since they were so interested in it.

One of the groups conducting surveys became "stuck." The boys in the "fulfillment" group polled the eighth grade about what they wanted to accomplish before dying and the ways in which they wanted to die! Then, they came up with the idea of conduct-ing a similar survey at a local nursing home. A flu epidemic at the nursing home made that impossible, and despite my attempts to counsel them into giving up on this unfruitful avenue, they spent a lot of time calling and visiting and trying to collect these data.

The struggle with the surveys illustrates two important is-sues. One is the opportunity to teach important skills in a mean-ingful context, in this case the purpose of surveys, how to gather information from groups of people, and how to conduct effective surveys and tabulate their results. I was not able to do this as effec-tively as I would have liked due to time constraints, but the stu-dents did learn something about gathering opinions in this kind of research. The other point relates to "handsitting." I realized that the next time I would be more alert and perhaps insist that we negotiate a schedule of activities together prior to independent activity.

It takes a certain amount of faith in one's own abilities and a trust in the abilities of one's students for a teacher to proceed in this way. For many teachers, this discussion raises questions of "Who's in charge here anyway?" Teachers who share their power and responsibility with students remark that they and their students actually end up learning more than if they had not done so. In a classroom where learning becomes more important than teaching, all the participants share a bond created by learning together. Teachers, often with more experience, knowledge, and skills in some areas, become respected for that. They become more valued as they relinquish many decisions to students who need to exercise their abilities and responsibilities. The question becomes, at what point does the teacher intervene with important skills and resources for which students are ready? The teacher's role is much like the role of a trail guide: it is important to know the territory and the group on the expedition, but it is equally important to be ready for the fact that each trip will be a unique learning experience.

Knowing When We Get There: Repositioning Skills and Transposing Content

> *[T]he curriculum described here repositions "traditional" content within the context of personal and social themes where it becomes what is known and prized . . .*
>
> *In like manner, skills "traditionally" emphasized are also repositioned . . . Here though, they are not seen as isolated or self-justified skills, but rather as functional skills, developed and used in the context of important themes under consideration.*
>
> James Beane[6]

The knowledge and skills of traditional learning, often found in textbooks and those dust-covered curriculum guides, is not jettisoned in favor of a new collection of concepts and competencies. But neither are they the center around which the curriculum is built; they orbit and surround the themes that emerge from young adolescents, and are called forth—by teachers or students—at appropriate moments, to influence the course of the learning journey. Wise teachers, those who know their subjects well, know them as whole; good math teachers know where mathematics blends into philosophy and theology and where it blends into patterns and art. They look for opportunities to share skills from their stored repertoire to enhance the learning process of their students and to readapt important content concepts to expand their students' interests. The question becomes, at what point does the teacher intervene with important skills and resources for which students are ready? This requires that they remain alert and ready to intervene with useful, valuable ideas that can help students answer their own questions. Teachers also become aware of colleagues as vital resources for their students to draw upon, and become more comfortable crossing traditional subject-area boundaries.

When skills are repositioned around the interests of young adolescents, and important content is transposed to suit those interests thus changing the very nature of teaching, new ways to learn emerge. As Anne describes the inquiries her class carried out, she was able to pierce to the heart of what this kind of learning is about. It becomes transformative as process and content are fused, and the group—teachers and students—find their way, collaboratively constructing their learning.

Anne's Story

What I understand at this point is that for authentic learning to occur, content and process must fuse so that the lines between them become indistinguishable, and a new meaning is formed from that fusion. For the first time, I think I understand what it means when we say learning is the construction of meaning, and that once personal meaning is created, it is part of the individual forever. This amalgamation of content and process may be the essence of transformational learning, which reaches far beyond skill acquisition, regurgitation of detail, and even rearrangement of thought. This concept of learning is phoenix-like; something new is created from the old. I began this experiment to illustrate the negotiation of curriculum with young adolescents; I moved to the concept of collaborative construction of curriculum with young adolescents; now, I embrace transformational learning through the fusion of content and process within that curriculum. To see how all this is playing out in the investigation of what it means to be a female and male adolescent, and how meaning is being constructed through the process, I want to return to the groups and their explorations of the themes.

The first responsibility of the six study teams was to create from the social, spiritual, and emotional categories a process for finding answers. All groups returned to the lists of questions they had constructed earlier. As I listened to the discussion, most teams were sifting through the questions, eliminating those that did not seem relevant, keeping those that interested one or more in the group.

Group 1 consisted of two girls and two boys. Initially, the two boys decided to work on the spiritual questions and the girls on the social issues. After two sessions, the four decided to design questions together, but do the actual investigations in pairs. The boys categorized their areas of interest into four subtopics: religions, cults, death and after-life, and ghosts. For religion, this pair wanted to investigate whether their peers believed in God, what kinds of rituals and customs were evident in different religions, and what kinds of architecture the different religions have. They wanted to find out if cults have sacrifices or use brainwashing; and if cult members beg for money, have code names, kill people, and commit suicide. They were interested in whether or not humans have souls, and if there is life after death, or what really happens when we die. They wished to examine the question of ghosts, if they exist, if there are other forms of living or non-living entities. The boys decided that library research would be their primary method and they would record their findings in jot notes.

The girls used the question format to frame their investigation of social issues. Their seven questions related to self, peers, and family: why do adolescent girls have so little self-confidence? why are relationships with the opposite sex so important to teens? why is sex such an important issue? after sex, why are girls considered sluts and boys considered studs? why do adolescents fight with their families so much? and why don't parents trust their kids? They decided on two strategies for information-gathering—a survey and interviews with classmates.

Group 2 focused on researching social and spiritual issues, working in mixed pairs to bring both the female and male perspectives to their work. One pair chose questions related to three themes: relationships between adolescents of the same sex, relationships between adolescents of the opposite sex, and how adolescents feel about themselves. The other pair categorized the general areas of Satanism, ghosts and the supernatural, differences between adolescent and adult spiritual views, death and the after-life. They identified specific questions for each category. This group also chose their peers as the primary source for their study. One activity on the issue of Satanism led to the creation of a composite verbal picture of Satan as imagined by students in Room 15, based on a short survey designed to elicit this information.

Group 3 included the emotional along with the social and spiritual as their areas of investigation. Their plan for learning was very detailed and structured into topics, subtopics, and questions. The spiritual inquiry would include hell, death, reincarnation and the after-life, cults and Satanism, beliefs about God, the significance of dreams, and the supernatural. Under the emotional issues category, this group wanted to research girls' and boys' feelings, hostility between the sexes, adolescent feelings about adults, and adults' feelings about teens. The social issues would include relationships with peers, respect for others, feelings toward peers, adult expectations, independence, family relations, sex and sexuality, and stereotyping. Each member of the group chose an area of responsibility and methods to find answers to their questions. One chose library research, others decided to videotape interviews with ten classmates of both sexes.

Group 4 decided to work as a whole team and not divide into pairs. Their inquiry into spiritual questions would include ghosts and the supernatural, formal religions, the extraterrestial, death and the after-life, and cults. The social issues would include relationships, sex, stereotypes, media, substance abuse, child abuse, racism, and abortion. Their investigation of physical issues would concentrate on the differences between male and female development, and the effects of the physical changes upon the self-image of adolescents. The group decided to use movies and documentaries as their primary sources of information about the supernatural. They were going to choose four pieces, view them together, take notes, compare their findings, and prepare a report. This group also wanted to collect information by designing five survey questions from each of their three categories and giving this survey to the three intermediate classes.

Group 5 chose to work as a whole group on the framework of their investigation and then to work in same-sex pairs to carry out the inquiry. The girls chose to videotape interviews with 11 students and 6 teachers; the interview would solicit opinions about the sexual issues important to adolescents, and about relationships among adolescents. The boys wanted to gather information from an even wider audience. They would create an interview about emotional questions and do this interview with 10 intermediate females, 10 males, 7 teachers, and 4 adults outside the school.

Group 6 initially decided to work in same-sex pairs, and then reconfigured to work as a whole group. This group did not subdivide their categories, but selected 20 spiritual questions and 17 social questions to explore. They decided to prepare a questionnaire and to audiotape interviews with classmates.

What was I doing while this planning and designing was taking place? In the beginning, I spent time with each group each day. I asked questions to clarify for myself what each group was planning to accomplish, but I did not offer any opinions about the content of the proposed investigations. I asked questions about the responsibilities within the groups; I asked how I could help facilitate the surveys and interviews within the class, with other classes, and with teachers within the building. I asked that, before they conducted surveys or interviews, I see a draft copy of those documents. Most groups wanted to discuss how they were going to collect the information before they had decided what they were going to collect, but eventually were able to prepare a written proposal for investigation.

To facilitate communication between me and the groups, I asked that each group select a liaison person with whom I could meet regularly. That person would identify for me any concerns of the group or any problems that needed my attention. I, in turn, could pass on resources, observations about group dynamics, schedules for interviews, and concerns I might have. These meetings proved useful since I was able to see only two or three groups a day. The major concern of the liaisons was what to do with students who were not doing their share. I talked about my accountability as a teacher for what happens within the classroom, and that those expectations in part were defined by the Education Act of Ontario, partly by Dufferin County school policies, partly by Princess Margaret School regulations and staff decisions, and partly by my expectations of myself as a teacher. I suggested that the concept of accountability might be applied to individuals within groups. Billie Lynn said that in order for that to happen everyone would need to be very clear what the group expected of each individual. It would also give me a way of checking the accountability of each student. We made the decision to go back to the groups and make certain that this clarification and recording of responsibilities took place. At the next meeting, the liaisons reported that the problem seemed to have been worked out and everyone was feeling more comfortable with their group's functioning.

I spent much of my time with the groups creating surveys and interviews. They had little knowledge of this form of information gathering beyond that it involved questions, statements, and people. We worked on writing specific questions; designing scales, rating techniques, and systems of recording collected data; interpreting meaning; and reporting the results. Due to overlap in the populations they would survey, we worked out a massive schedule for times, places, and use of the video camera and tape recorders. Students who wished to survey other classes or teachers wrote letters or made visits to the teachers to determine appropriate times for their participation.

I was absorbed and intrigued by the first instinct of young adolescents to turn to each other for opinions and information. This, perhaps, should not have surprised me, but it did cause me to think about how often we give adolescents opportunities to confirm and validate who they are through each other. This process clearly was a priority for these young adolescents. It also provides another example of what I am choosing to call the fusion of content and process. If the content is authentic (as it was for these young people), and the process is authentic (as it is when selected by these young people), then I believe this greatly enhances the possibility for the creation of personal meaning, or learning.

As teachers we can facilitate learning by honoring the reality of the content and processes that young adolescents can indeed provide, if given the opportunity. We can facilitate learning by clarifying and extending the methods used to communicate that learning. We can facilitate learning through the richness of our practical experience, theoretical knowledge, and avid curiosity about our own personal meanings. We can acknowledge that learning is personal, unpredictable, and dynamic. We can recognize that inherent in students' questions is prior learning and direction for future growth. We can be certain that our students will know whether we honor their reality and authenticity.

The pursuit of meaning seems to be a uniquely human endeavor. Meaning may occur as an immediate and intuitive insight, but it is just as likely to accrue over time. The school setting should provide the context through which individuals can pursue their personal meanings or learning within a systematic framework. I believe that each of the individuals in this class of young adolescents had a sense of the wholeness of being an adolescent at the same time as the parts of that whole were being explored and examined. The role of the teacher is to mediate and guide the creation of personal meaning as the investigation of the parts proceeds.

And What About Chris's Story?

Chris's experience for the short amount of time he had to work—less than three weeks for the actual inquiry—produced rich results:

For two weeks the groups worked on their research, and as they researched, their topics became more and more focused. There were some problems, of course, among them group dynamics. Many had very little experience working in cooperative groups, and most had no experience working in groups of four or five. Another problem was absences. I don't think there were two days in a row that the entire class was present, and often groups had more than one member absent due to illness or in-school suspension. But despite the constraints of time, inexperience, absences, and lack of trust, some amazing work went on. What follows is a list of the activities in which each group participated:

Group 1. Fulfillment before death.
- Designed a survey and applied it to all eighth grade language arts classes, several adults in the school, and the residents of a local nursing home; then organized and interpreted the data.

- Read articles about experiences with death.
- Developed questions and conducted an interview with local paramedics about their experiences with lifesaving and death.
- Organized all of their information and findings and used the writing process to create a report that answered some of their questions about what people need to feel fulfilled before they die.

Group 2. Prejudice and discrimination.
- Developed a survey on personal prejudice, applied it to eighth grade language arts classes and some adults in the school, organized and tabulated their data, and presented it in both narrative and graphic form.
- Developed questions and interviewed a local member of the Abenaki Nation about her experiences with prejudice and discrimination.
- Read and wrote about racism, sexism, and homophobia.
- Organized their findings and used the writing process to create a report.

Group 3. Life after death.
- Read and wrote about death, disease, near-death experiences, and different cultural perspectives on life after death.
- Created individual reports about AIDs and the grieving process.
- Developed and executed an experiment with the Ouija Board to determine its authenticity and reliability, recording their questions, the board's answers, and their responses.
- Planned a seance.
- Visited the city clerk's office and obtained a recent death certificate and a sample of death records from the 19th century, discussed, compared and analyzed these records, focusing on causes of death, and wrote and illustrated a poem based on the imagined/reconstructed experience of a death record of a woman and her stillborn child.
- Developed and conducted a survey of eighth grade language arts classes about their feelings about death, compiled their data, and created a graphic representation.
- Used the writing process to compile their individual written pieces into a group report, and summarized each of the activities and the members' contributions.
- Collaboratively designed and taught a lesson, focused on feelings about death, to a sixth grade class using multiple activities including poetry analysis, questionnaires, small group discussions, and responding to children's art about death.

Group 4. Alien life in the universe.
- Read books and articles, and wrote about accounts of encounters with space aliens.
- Watched part of the *Nova* series about other life in the universe.
- Planned and conducted phone interviews with representatives from the State Police and the Vermont Air National Guard about reported alien sightings or abductions.
- Collaboratively planned and wrote a report summarizing their learnings.

Group 5. Drug use in sports.
- Conducted library research on the use of steroids in the sports world, and the use of steroids in high school athletics.
- Researched and read about the use of other drugs and alcohol among major sports figures.
- Used the writing process to collaboratively report on their learnings.

Some of the skills used in these group inquiries included:
- designing, conducting and interpreting both qualitative and quantitative aspects of surveys;
- developing interview questions;
- conducting interviews;
- telephone research;
- library research;
- accessing public records;
- historical research;
- identifying and analyzing patterns;
- defining sociological terms;
- using the writing process—including pre-writing, multiple drafts, peer response, and editing—and practicing various types of writing such as summary, narrative, exposition, poetry, questionnaire, lists, journals;
- extrapolation of data;
- representing data in graphic form;
- mathematical computations;
- lesson planning;
- teaching;
- organizing time;
- notetaking;
- problem-solving;
- conflict resolution;
- planning;
- evaluating self and others;
- and more.

What do kids learn from this? I think they learn confidence in themselves. They learn to take risks in a supportive environment that encourages growth. They learn to negotiate and to be up front with teachers about their needs as learners. They learn how to take responsibility for their own learning. They learn resourcefulness. They learn that schools can be engaging places where their thoughts, ideas, and concerns can be valued. They learn that questions are often more important than answers. What happens after you die? Really, who can answer that question? No one can, but the results of such an inquiry can be incredibly rich and fruitful. Finally, they learn the same skills we teachers have always believed are important, but they learn them *within the context of their own questions,* and *when they need to learn them.*

Viewed this way, it is easy to see the power and possibility of student inquiry and, importantly, the repositioning of teaching skills into a meaningful context within the interests and control of students. All of this happened in a two-and-one-half-week span of time with an average of five 40-minute class periods per week, not including one in-service day, and one snow day. All of this happened despite the inexperience of the teachers and the students, an unfamiliar teacher, group problems, time problems, behavior problems, and absences.

Finally, students learn something about what it really means to be human. In Beane's terms, they learn about democracy, dignity, and diversity. They learn about the importance of their own voices and the importance of the equality of all voices in the classroom. They learn that different people learn in different ways. They learn how to value and accept themselves and others. And they learn some of the skills they need to bring this knowledge out of the classroom and into the world that awaits them.

Trusting and Cooperating: Important Lessons as We Climb

> *The essence of teaching lies beyond surviving in the classroom, beyond classroom management concerns, beyond curriculum content and process, and even beyond the developmental needs of students. The best middle grades teaching results from simply understanding individual students with the mind and the heart—it is an act of love.*
>
> Ken Bergstrom in Stevenson & Carr[7]

It is silly to think that the most important things we might learn in school can be tested on nationally-normed achievement tests when we are surrounded by opposing evidence of our experience every day. The most valued lessons in life do have a deep connection to the affective realm of learning. Those special moments are etched in our every part. We learn what we feel deeply, almost always in a valued relationship with others.

As teachers, we are steeped in a people business. Whatever we do should have a clear connection to what it means to be human, not just the academic aspect, but all dimensions. Teaching in an integrative, holistic way values the affective learnings—as well as the physical, social, psychological, spiritual, and intellectual— because all are learned together in synergistic moments when each developmental aspect enhances the other. This is at the very heart of what makes life worth living. And while we may not do it very well each time, it is important to teach in a way that allows us to get to know our students and to touch each others' lives. A few comments from Anne's and Chris's writing reflect these moments.

From Anne

The highlight of the process for me happened the day the students recorded their strong opinions. Richard and Jacob always work together and are not included in freely formed groups. They do not socialize with anyone else in the class, but will participate in groups if I put them with other students. On this day, Richard was absent and Jacob was sitting by the table where I was distributing the chart paper. As I was asking Jacob if he wanted to work alone on his list or join a group, two things happened at once. He said, "Yes, I will work alone," and Scot, who is one of the most popular and powerful boys in the class, said, "Do you want to work with us, Jacob?" I could see the absolute wonder in Jacob's face about being asked to join that particular group. Jacob looked at me, then at Scot, and as casually as he could muster said, "Sure!" I want to believe that this inclusion happened because of the collaborative atmosphere that was being nurtured throughout this process of curriculum construction.

From Chris

I learned that the element of trust and relationship is the most important part of creating the "fertile ground" in which to sow the seeds of collaboratively constructed meaning. I learned that flexibility is crucial, that being open to all the possibilities for choice and direction that emerges from a room full of young adolescents suddenly in charge of their own learning is much more important than the merits of following any plan or curriculum development model. And if the relationship you have built with your students is a trusting and solid one, that flexibility becomes easier.

Students' Voices

The kids, too, are clear about the importance of this learning. Some of their selected voices reflect the empowering nature of the experience:

> I think we all learned how to express our feelings. At first I was afraid to express everything I thought because I had the feeling I would be laughed at. This changed in our group because we all said what we felt and we listened to each other. In class I felt safe because the teacher always says what she feels and she will always listen to our ideas. In our group listening was difficult, but we learned that, if we wanted to get anything done, we had to listen to each other.

> Before we had this theme I thought we were a bunch of troublemakers who like to hang out on street corners. Now I think Ms. Reid is right; we are special for all kinds of positive reasons. I think that gave everyone a new surge of self-confidence. We had lots of opportunities to find out for ourselves.

> I feel this project was a good way to answer our questions and make people think more about ourselves and others in our age group. I feel that interviewing girls has given me more knowledge of the way girls are. This project was not like most projects because it was personal and I dealt with my feelings and the feelings of other adolescents. This project has made a difference for me because it helped me to say everything I wanted to say. All I know is that things that really matter go into my soul; all the rest go into my mind. This theme did both.

> I learned that adolescents have very strong opinions about certain topics. I learned that I can stick up for what I believe to be right and true. I had strong opinions about sexism and racism before, but not as strong as now. I am not afraid to tell people my opinions.

> I think it was really neat that we could help the teacher on what we do at school instead of the teacher planning it all and the students having no choice at all. The only change I would make would be to make the groups larger. I learned that I can work in a group which is great because then I don't have to do everything by myself. I had fun doing this investigation; it would be a good experience for any adolescent.

I think this was a good process because students are more in control of what we want to learn. We asked the questions that we wanted and we spent time on what was important.

I feel closer to my friends because of the feelings we shared. I feel now that people's opinions are important. I learned that the kids in our class have a unique way of showing that everyone is special. Our opinions are more important than anything else in the world. Everyone made everyone else feel good by doing this theme.

After this theme study, I feel more comfortable speaking my mind, expressing my emotions, talking freely with teachers, and talking in front of the class. I was sometimes afraid that if I said something that a person didn't want to hear, I would get in trouble. It got to the point where I could say what I wanted to, wherever I wanted to, to whomever I wanted.

Our study on adolescents was a learning experience for me. I learned how to work with a group of males and females. I learned that adolescents have many different opinions on teen life and that males seem a little less serious about the adolescent war with life. I learned that being an adolescent is a tough job and that all teens do not have a normal adolescent life. I liked being able to research a topic that involved the way I feel and the way that many of the people around me act and communicate.

While some might want to wait until the weather conditions are just right before attempting this kind of climb, that is, until a trusting and cooperative bond has been established between students and teachers, it is exactly the risk of the unknown that enhances the possibility of such a caring atmosphere. We could delay indefinitely, for one reason or another: the kids aren't ready for this yet, I don't know the material well enough, what about the real curriculum? what will my colleagues say? However, the atmosphere must be created through the learning if it is to be real and more than a "nice" place to go to school. Authentic learning takes place in schools that are more than mere factories or social clubs. Trust and cooperation must be experienced and nurtured along with all the other aspects of the learning.

Preparing for the Next Climb: Looking Ahead

It is important for us to critique the journey and to determine whether it is worth the redefined effort and realignment of time that teaching and learning in this way demands. None of us will choose to return to the traditional classroom. This is far too exciting and exhilarating. The rewards of this adventure for all learners are clear. With surprises full of new learning around each turn, who would not want a return trip?

We need to refine some of the aspects of this process. Is there a better way to determine the questions kids have about the world and their place in it? Will the same themes always emerge from groups of young adolescents? How might we extend the learning over longer periods of time? How can we as teachers continue to resolve the struggle over the repositioning of skills and transposing of content? How do we ensure that this kind of classroom works for all kids? How can we better connect with the community resources available to us? How can we extend the learning so that kids have an opportunity to engage in worthwhile social action based upon their learning? How can we invite others—parents, colleagues, and community members—to join with us and our students in a collaborative evaluation process?

We will answer these questions only as we dare to greet each new class of young adolescents with "What are your questions about yourselves and the world?" Collaboratively seeking answers will require another trek "above the tree line."

End Notes

1. James A. Beane, *The Middle School Curriculum: From Rhetoric to Reality* (Columbus, OH: National Middle School Association, 1990), 36.
2. James A. Beane and Barbara Brodhagen, Speakers, *Vermont Middle Level School Development Institute* (Barre, VT, July, 1992).
3. L. McDonough, "Middle Level Curriculum: Search for Self and Social Meaning," *Middle School Journal* 23.2 (1991): 29–35.
4. G. Boomer, N. Lester, C. Onore, and J. Cook (Eds.), *Negotiating the Curriculum: Educating for the 21st Century* (Bristol, PA: Falmer Press, 1992), 117.
5. J. Cook, "Negotiating the Curriculum: Programming for Learning," in G. Boomer, N. Lester, C. Onore, and J. Cook (Eds.), *Negotiating the Curriculum: Educating for the 21st Century* (Bristol, PA: Falmer Press, 1992), 15–31.
6. James A. Beane, *The Middle School Curriculum: From Rhetoric to Reality* (Columbus, OH: National Middle School Association, 1990), 48–49.
7. Ken Bergstrom, in C. Stevenson and J. F. Carr (Eds.), *Integrated Studies in the Middle Grades: Dancing Through Walls* (New York: Teachers College Press, 1993), 1.

Chapter 13

Reforming Middle School Mathematics Constructively

Charles R. Ault, Jr. and Anne McEnerny-Ogle

Background

For many years, Anne McEnerny-Ogle—"Annie-Mac" to the children—taught in an elementary school. The pre-eminence of her reputation among parents, colleagues, and students for exemplary mathematics teaching propelled her into positions of responsibility within her district. She introduced the community to *Family Math*[1] and was chosen by the Oregon Department of Education to pilot new assessment instruments in elementary school mathematics. In addition, the Oregon Consortium for Quality Science and Mathematics Education (OCQSME), a regional collective of more than a dozen school districts that shares Eisenhower Mathematics and Science funds for staff development work,[2] called upon her expertise for several years in succession.

Though the changes in curriculum she brought to elementary mathematics were popular and remain in place, Anne tells us, "I decided to follow my love of math and teach at the junior high level." Her story of trying to innovate in ways that encouraged early adolescents to construct mathematical understanding in purposeful and enjoyable ways will reveal greater obstacles and deeper frustrations than she knew in the world of younger children.

This year, had I not moved my family from Oregon while on sabbatical leave, my oldest son might have known Anne as his teacher—for the second time. He first encountered her several years ago when he was pulled along by his parents to the new evening course in *Family Math*. We signed in on a blackboard laid out with Venn diagrams that captured salient and interesting attributes of the families enrolled. The math activities were problems—often puzzle types, but ones that illustrated an important concept or style of reasoning. There were brownies to bake (after measuring ingredients), detective mysteries to solve logically, a fascinating topological structure to reproduce from a single 3" x 5" card (cuts with scissors allowed, but no cutting the card into separate pieces), and a guest parent's occupation was referred to to show how the parent used mathematics at work. We also graphed body measurements for people in the class, an activity highlighted by the presence of at least one pregnant mother.

I asked Anne at the end of the very first class why the kinds of things we did together in *Family Math* did not have a higher priority for school math. I lamented that in my experience (including a few short years of teaching primary grades), most children have rather strong feelings—usually quite negative—about mathematics (i.e., "arithmetic") by age 7. They feel much more positive about baking brownies, puzzle-play, bellies that grow babies, tricky stories and, sometimes, using numbers to find patterns.

She answered with an impressive description of trends and practices in the school (introduction of *Math Their Way,*[3] for example) and the priorities she had for mathematical learning. Thus began our professional relationship.

A short time afterward, the final class of my course for prospective teachers, "Teaching Elementary School Mathematics," met in Anne's school library. First, her fourth-graders worked in pairs to solve a multi-digit, multiplication problem. They were instructed to use manipulative materials to represent the task and to prepare an algorithmic solution on a transparency to share with my students. Their reasoning in solving the problem (as exemplified by the use of the manipulative model) and their ability to communicate their thinking were as important as their competency with algorithmic methods. They were challenged to connect the steps of the algorithmic procedure with the operations of the manipulative model (interlocking cubes).

This exhibition of fourth-grade prowess illustrated practices for teaching arithmetic judged ideal by Lampert.[4] It stressed, in Lampert's words, "principled conceptual knowledge" as well as "procedural competence." The children knew why they did what they did. As one said, "It's easier to do when you know what it means."

Clearly, the adult students present that day felt humbled—by Anne's teaching talent as well as the capabilities of so many ten-year-olds. But the program for the day was only one-third complete! Next, the prospective teachers took the same test the fourth graders had piloted for the state. It consisted of a novel problem—not one with any readily apparent or arithmetic solution. Working in small teams, they struggled to represent the problem situation pictorially and logically. After a while, they convened with the fourth graders to communicate their reasoning and demonstrate their problem-solving accomplishments. The fourth graders scored the teachers' work using the same scale that was proposed for the state-wide assessment of mathematical learning and that had been developed to reflect the standards of the National Council of Teachers of Mathematics (NCTM).[5]

In the final phase of this day of the class's visit to a "real" school (but a rather "unreal" experience—unlike anything the prospective teachers remembered from their days as ten-year-olds), Anne led us outside, to the newly completed entryway for the school building. A long-term, school-wide "courtyard project" had influenced its design and construction, but this is another tale told by Anne herself later in this chapter.

Governance and Community Values: Anne Starts Her Story

After 15 years of teaching grades one through four, I decided to follow my love of math and teach at the junior high level. My mistake was thinking that what was possible at the elementary level was possible at this level as well.

Part of the dilemma is the transition from a junior high school to a middle school, a transition our district keeps planning to make. Our school remains very much a "junior" high school in name and practice, but includes only grades 7 and 8. Many of the teachers, however, would like to begin the work of building a true school "in the middle".[6]

Critical to the concept of a junior high school has been the departmentalization of subjects in alignment with secondary school structure. Often, junior high becomes "high school pre-school." Just as pre-school and Head Start prepare young children for the routines of elementary schooling, junior high supposedly prepares young adolescents for the departmental structure of the secondary school.

What's even more apparent, the goals for subject learning at the high school level shape the content taught in junior high. In mathematics, this goal means taking the initial step toward grade 12 calculus in grade 7 mathematics. Tracking begins in earnest in an effort to maximize the success in our district (a very prosperous community, 80 percent college-bound) of having as many students as possible learn calculus while still in public school—with many others being just about ready to do so.

Anne chose to move from elementary to middle school teaching because of her love of mathematics. What she first experienced was a fundamental change in control over the curriculum—a dramatic shift in the priorities of schooling and who had responsibility for those priorities. Neither the conception of mathematical thinking embodied in the concerns for communication and problem-solving of the NCTM standards, nor research about the nature of early adolescent development, dominated curriculum construction. Preparation for secondary school did, and the top-down governance structure made decisions in keeping with the most desired outcome for secondary school mathematics learning: the production of large numbers of graduates skilled in introductory calculus. The self-contained fourth-grade classroom, rich in themes of study connecting subjects and where Anne worked to craft experiences that made learning personal for students, seemed far away indeed.

The problem Anne is up against, in simplest terms, is that the schools are doing pretty much what the people want. In this case, it is getting ready for the competition of college admissions. The stakes are high: economic opportunity and social status. Hence, the willingness to take risks is low. Anne cannot yet demonstrate to her community constituency that the reforms she wishes to make will increase the success of the school in carrying out the will of the community.

Two principles of reform come to mind. One, to paraphrase Sarason,[7] is that for teachers to create in their classrooms the conditions for learning that they value for students, teachers must first experience these conditions as the environment in which they work. Schools are for teachers as well as for children. The second, after Gowin,[8] is that the control of meaning controls the effort. The evidence in support of this proposition can be found in the practice of politics at every level by the ways in which interest groups attempt to force changes in language. For example, the timber industry has begun to refer to "clearcuts" of the forest as "regeneration cuts." Opponents of "clearcutting" the forest refer to these same stands of trees as the last tracts of the "ancient forest." By describing parts of the forest as "old growth," the timber industry hopes to convey the idea that an undesirable condition exists. Clearcutting, goes the argument, allows the forest to "regenerate." The opponents of clearcutting counter that what grows back is a mere, and almost oxymoronic, "tree-farm"; not a majestic "ancient forest." These labels—old growth and ancient forest—compete in the effort to control meaning and thereby influence public opinion.

Following Sarason, implementing an ideology of student control over the responsibility for learning begins with a policy of teacher control over essential aspects of the curriculum. Following Gowin, support for or resistance to such efforts depends on what they mean to the membership of the school's constituency.

The task for Anne is to persuade her constituency—her colleagues, the community, and the governance structure—that her vision means higher levels of intellectual success in mathematics for an increased proportion of the general student population while, at the same time, restricting none of the opportunities for the most able students. At present a most eloquent and research-anchored exposition of this theme is Gardner's *The Unschooled Mind*.[9] Gardner reviews the extensive body of research concerning what forms everyday, intuitive knowledge may assume in students' minds and how these practical and reasonable ways of thinking may conflict with disciplined understanding. He argues for the reasonableness of "understanding," in ways representative of what disciplined thinkers in a variety of subjects respect, as *the* academic goal of schooling. He recognizes the difficulty of this objective and acknowledges the compromise schools tend to make: rewarding extraordinary feats of memorization that are only caricatures of disciplined understanding. For example, children learn very early in school that the Earth rotates about its axis daily and revolves around the Sun annually in a path called an "orbit." Later, they are taught that the Earth's orbital position combines with the "tilt" of its axis of rotation with respect to the plane of its orbit to cause seasonal variation in weather. Yet a very high proportion of middle school students (and Harvard graduates as well) believe that the seasons change because the distance between the Earth and the Sun changes through the year. They have dutifully memorized proper verbal knowledge without constructing a mental representation of the geometry of the Earth's movements in space. A lifetime of everyday-scale experience of a "flat-earth," where the sun "rises above" and the sun "sets below" the horizon persists as a form of intuitive knowledge that obstructs an understanding of the movements of the Earth in space scaled to its proper orbital parameters. We just don't speak of the the horizon turning to block our view of the sun in the evening.

Gardner further describes how students learning to do arithmetic may consistently follow procedures they believe logical, only to produce incorrect answers. Their errors—not random—reflect commitment to faulty understanding, "bugs" in their cognitive programs, as this tradition describes metaphorically. This interpretation suggests that a teacher should try to recognize a pattern in a student's arithmetic errors, then infer from this pattern what cognitive principle or misunderstood procedure generates the pattern. Instruction thus credits students with thinkiing and helps them realize why their errors are errors as well as how to solve the problems correctly. Says a student in such a situation, "Oh, now I understand what I was doing wrong!"

Anne left elementary teaching because of her love of mathematics. She wished to share the joy and satisfaction of mathematically disciplined thinking with her students and believed that the middle school held open the opportunity to explore the richness of mathematical structures as tools of inquiry. She has met opposition and found herself lacking control over vital decisions. If she can communicate that the changes she advocates mean higher levels of intellectual accomplishment, others may join her efforts, first establishing the conditions for teachers that she wishes to exist for the students. The ideology of a "seamless whole" of knowledge is less her ally than the disciplined habits of mathematical thinking, but the kind of mathematical thinking she aspires to teach requires a problem-solving context, with genuine problems and their characteristic demands shaping the contours of thought. Her community respects being "smarter," though many may have little idea of what smarter in mathematics truly means. Change in middle school curriculum must mean in this community of values the likely prospect of greatly enhanced intellectual accomplishment.

The "Courtyard Project" as a Curriculum Demonstration

As an elementary teacher, I frequently devised projects that crossed barriers of subject and grade level divisions. One such project was to create a courtyard in what was once a 2150-square-foot parking lot. The students worked with local businesses and parents to determined how to remove it, haul it, and dispose of it with environmental concerns answered.

They then planned the brick walkways, underground sprinkling systems and planting. Small groups worked on selling bricks, making planting schedules, writing letters soliciting funds and help. Curriculum integration was closely tied to mathematics.

My class of prospective elementary teachers encountered the fruits of this project when they visited Anne's school at the end of their course, "Teaching Elementary School Mathematics." Where once there was a drab, asphalted parking lot, there now lay a patio of bricks arranged in geometric designs, enhanced by attractive landscaping. We learned of the calculations with large numbers and the liaisons with the community needed to carry out the project. The courtyard entranceway to the school was a stunning achievement, describable only in superlative terms. There had been sketches and design proposals, blueprint drawing details to scale, estimates and measurements of bulk material (weight and volume) for disposal and purchase, innumerable efforts to calculate costs accurately, then solicitations of donations from community businesses.

The result was more than a courtyard. The children had built community as well, within the school across grade levels, and between the school and its adult patrons. They had learned pride and pursued quality for intrinsic reasons—having a wonderful courtyard that would favorably impress all who entered the school. The planning process gave children a genuine opportunity to make decisions and set priorities. They had control and responsibility over parts of the project and learned to negotiate the limits of their control with the teacher. Instruction braided together the skills of art, mathematics, cooperation, and communication. These elements suggest that the project was a model of constructivist learning—it even engaged the services of a construction company!

Keep in mind this "courtyard project" is an exemplar of the kind of curriculum demonstration Anne has hoped to import to the middle school. There are some key features to highlight: (1) the priority of the problem-solving context, (2) the pre-eminence of mathematical thinking in planning, (3) the application of skills from diverse fields, (4) the integration of experience with cognition, (5) the importance of quality accomplishments, (6) the linkage to the community of school activity, and (7) the cooperation and collaboration of diverse groups of children in the successful completion of the project.

The courtyard project did not begin with mandated topics for study and a presumably logical and sequential separation of these topics into lesson structures. Instead, from a general goal there emerged several specific problems to solve (for example, "How many trucks would be needed to carry away the old asphalt? Where would it go—would its disposal be environmentally sound?"). The project permitted children to wrestle with how to organize their efforts, direct their thinking, and define the problem.

Still, educational authority, judgment, and expertise were abundant, because the goal of improving children's mathematical thinking justified the project. The exercise was not a simplistic and idealistic exercise in child-directed learning with teacher as facilitator, but rather a complex, goal-directed operation, with the teacher as expert in shaping the parameters of problems. Reasoning, as found in the discipline of mathematics, had priority; though, of course, this priority did not exclude other fields. This priority accorded prominence to concepts of estimation and measurement, scale drawing and geometric design, meaningful calculation and manipulation of large numbers.

What came first was not basic skills but the context and purpose for problem solving set by the project. This context meant that basic skills were embedded in the process of answering important (and real) questions. Failure to answer questions might compromise the success of the project; hence, failure to achieve proficiency in solving specific types of problems could not be accepted.

To do mathematics is to work with symbolic abstractions whose relations are governed by a finite set of rules. To design and build a school courtyard is fun, challenging, and messy (it even involves real concrete). To merge the two is to wed cognition and experience, to join inseparably the emotions of art and artisanship with the rigors of thinking formally and quantitatively.

The courtyard project engaged children in work not only for themselves but for others. Some of them some day will enroll their own children in this school. No doubt, both generations will find satisfaction in the courtyard project. The point is that the project produced something useful, something of value to a real constituency. The project had an audience. Therein lies the reason for quality work, the need for thorough understanding of the subject. The courtyard project brought recognition (newspaper coverage, for example) and interaction with businesses and local government. The children learned school subjects while behaving as citizens concerned about improving their community. They were not pretend-citizens and make-believe members of town councils. There was no simulation of business contracts and tokens to stand for costs. They were not getting ready for a distant future in which real citizenship responsibility might be assumed. They were going about the business of being citizens in the present, doing the sorts of things citizens of their size and ability can do well.

Textbook Realities and Assuming Leadership

We now have an example of Anne's vision and have already begun to analyze what happened when she tried to import it to the middle school. Her story continues:

> I had hopes to use similar projects at the middle school level, but I was in for some surprises. Stepping into the eighth grade math class means starting with chapter 7 of a textbook selected by others. The book was "chosen" for the middle school by the high school and central office. Breaking away from the format means writing a proposal to be reviewed by the high school.
>
> Within this time called middle school, students have the strain of pre-adolescence and the subjects taught in different classrooms on a set schedule. The time and walls set up artificial barriers between the subjects. Often, in our effort to specialize the learning in the pre-high school setting, we lost the true middle-school student.

Here we find exactly what form Anne's collision with the governance structure has taken: the directive to begin with chapter 7 of the textbook others—at the high school and central office—have selected. This circumstance is most telling. There appears little leeway for professional discretion and judgment, for Anne's creative vision, for inspired leadership in curriculum construction. And if these conditions do not exist for the teacher, how can they be inherited by the classroom climate as encouragement of initiative, responsibility for one's own learning, and support to pursue meaningful interests? Prospects for courtyard projects "in the middle" indeed appear dim.

The barriers stem from the attempt to manage learning rationally, from outside and above the classroom. Demands for efficient management impose divisions of labor, separation of subjects, and fragmentation of faculty work. The school lacks a structure for finding problems, linking work to the community, working to embed disciplined understanding in personally meaningful contexts. There is little apparatus for addressing how interesting the curriculum might be and whether its outcomes include being good for the community in addition to preparation for future schooling. These are, however, precisely the kinds of things a teacher willing to assume risk and exercise leadership will do.

The goal of eighth grade math is to work efficiently through the assigned chapters of the textbook. The payoffs for dutifully and successfully accomplishing this goal are manifold, but deferred far into the future. The psyche of the "true middle school student" exists more in the present than in this nebulous future of economic opportunity and social status, though a few might take to mathematics no matter how encountered because of an intrinsic appreciation for the aesthetics of the subject.

Anne, in shock from the transition from elementary to middle school teaching, finds herself up against the twin demons of pre-high school structure and centralized authority. Her response is characteristic of teachers of her caliber: assume leadership and take risks. Tactfully, she acknowledges institutional constraints and the concerns of her constituencies and begins to scale back her expectations:

> When the other junior high math teachers and I started a manipulatives-based program we met with a variety of resistance. We were well prepared in Mind's Eye philosophy[10] and technique, but we forgot to bring four important collegial groups with us: students, parents, administrators, and other teachers.
>
> As I worked on the preparation of materials, laying out the flow of the lesson and developing the cooperative group activities, I didn't realize that these other

collegial groups would have a substantial effect on the lesson.

Many of my students had been taught using a text-book approach and enjoyed the simplicity of the routine. Parents enjoyed the textbook approach because they could read the material that lead to the answers and help their students. If students were absent, then work could be done at home by simply following the book. Parents had read the Japanese comparative studies[11] and were concerned about their own student's test scores. They saw mathematics as computation. They knew that the majority of the questions on the math achievement tests were arithmetic and wanted to be assured that those scores would be high. They didn't care about manipulative-based work and problem solving since they weren't on the test.

Administrators found the textbook a simple solution to difficult problems. A textbook can tell where a class is going and where it has been. The text's assessment guides the instruction and helps assure common instruction.

Anne intends to bring along her constituency. She understands that to do so she must acknowledge what values and expectations this constituency holds, as well as why they believe these expectations are reasonable. She has taken an important step in the direction of leadership and touched upon several issues emblematic of conflict.

What gives a teacher educational authority and the obligation to challenge the prejudices of the popular culture is his or her knowledge about the heritage of disciplinary structures, his or her understanding of how human inquiry in various fields has succeeded in solving its characteristic problems. Freedom of academic inquiry is a valued ideology and its fruits are a proper foundation for schooling. As curriculum, these fruits—or "restructured claims" in Gowin's words—provide a counterweight to the unschooled mind and its intuitive beliefs about the natural world, its prejudices about social reality.

Anne acknowledges the strengths of the text program, and she understands the nature of the testing and evaluation practices of the school system. Whether or not mathematics in school is good mathematics from the point of view of mathematical expertise is of less concern to parents and administrators than scores on instruments that suggest comparative advantage or disadvantage in securing economic opportunity and social status, either for individuals or nations. Worry over securing privilege (admission to a prestige college) or succumbing to oppression (serving in a low-wage position) dominate what scores mean.

A careful reading of international comparative studies in mathematics might add some interesting twists to community concern over the mathematics curriculum. Simple measures of achievement scores hide more informative claims. Argue Stigler/Siegler,[12] many of the practices in Japanese classrooms are precisely those that U. S. reformers find resisted strongly. Japanese teachers spend more time than American teachers in meeting with each other to share ways of helping students learn, and less time each day (at the secondary level) instructing large groups. The portrait of a successful Japanese classroom during a mathematics lesson, moreover, reveals that the class spends much time on seeking thorough conceptual understanding of the principles needed to solve a single type of problem. This several year study of mathematics teaching in three Asian and two U.S. school districts dispels myths and caricatures about mathematics learning on both sides of the Pacific. The authors describe, for example, how Japanese children may experience more recreational breaks during the schoolday than their American counterparts. Hence, school authority does not feel oppressive. Nor, at the sites studied in Japan, does rote memorization exert a harmful influence over conceptual thinking.

The "Asian" (a misleading word, given that the range of practices among Asian peoples and within Asian nations varies as widely as between Asian nations and communities in the U.S.) context for schooling and learning mathematics may often reflect "family values" found lacking in U.S. households. A member of the family has a duty to learn; fulfilling this duty may reflect on the honor of the family. Furthermore, the expectation in the school setting is that all children will learn their subjects thoroughly— though some may have to work extraordinarily hard to get there (counting on help from other members of the family). There seems less of an attitude that "some have it; some don't." And perhaps there are fewer parents who apologize for their children's poor performance by saying, "I was never any good at math in school either." Such a statement suggests implicit belief in a deterministic role of genetics, a position unfounded in science and less evident in Asian communities.

Test score concern is real and approaches a national mania. Efforts to reform "high stakes assessment" (scores used to make comparisons among schools and students) include restructuring what tests measure. In mathematics, this reform means movement toward tests that require communication and success in problem solving as well as computation. Of course, it is hard to accept mediocre achievement in computation and teachers ought to defend the need for practice until proficiency is obtained. Yet a person who can solve an equation and calculate an answer cannot compete in intellectually demanding contexts with one who can construct a mathematical expression that represents a problem situation. As everyone perhaps remembers from grade 6 arithmetic, it's one thing to know how to divide, and another to know when. (And, I might add, still another to figure out what to do instead of dividing that will yield the correct result, for example, as in the question, "How many times must I add the divisor in order to obtain the dividend?" (The answer will be the quotient.)

Our discussion appears to have stumbled upon a paradox: granting to disciplined ways of knowing priority in contexts where, nonetheless, interdisciplinary themes of interest have primacy. For the constructivist teacher, this paradox is reality. At one and the same moment, the teacher is both an ambassador of a discipline (constructions past) and an advocate of a child's interests (constructions future). The teacher's most difficult challenge in curriculum construction is to negotiate between these twin legitimate stakeholders, public heritage (the disciplines) and personal meaning (the basis of interest). The paradox is real and should not be resolved. The tension is healthy.

Teachers may find themselves working for a group of elected officials and their appointed administrators who hold neither of these concerns in high regard. Instead, those in power may worry more about issues such as securing operating funds, avoiding public controversy, establishing smooth institutional operations, achieving politically popular scores on narrowly focused measures of achievement, minimizing expense while maximizing average student performance, reducing misbehavior and controlling drug abuse, balancing the voices of curriculum censorship from right and left, keeping the buses running, increasing class-size, and maintaining athletic programs. What changes in curriculum might mean to each of these concerns controls the effort. In the next example of Anne's quest to invigorate middle school mathematics, her project confronts exactly this kind of a problem.

The Inadequacy of the "Manipulative Concept"

Other teachers, both in the junior high and high school, had only heard of the manipulative concept and didn't understand it. When they were asked questions by parents, or heard comments by students, they didn't know how to respond. When they served on budget committees with administrators, they were reluctant to approve money request-for lab materials that they didn't understand.

While many middle school teachers believe in collaborative learning, curriculum integration, and process/product importance, they don't think these concepts work in mathematics. They see math as two tracks, for "Them that have it, and them that don't."

Incorporating the manipulative and problem solving based lessons required students to think, experiment, summarize, write, develop conjectures, and validate those conjectures. Many students were reluctant to pursue their conjectures. They wanted to know the one "right" answer and they wanted to know the one "right" method.

In this passage we find how both the jargon of reform and the existence of deeply rooted beliefs about mathematical ability may become obstacles to change. Anne also introduces how the exploration of mathematical ideas begins to take on a disciplined form by making "conjecture" its starting point. Students, she finds, are reluctant to embrace conjecture as a method. Like the administration, they seek security and expect quick feedback.

First let us attend to the phrase, "the manipulative concept." This shorthand phrase may carry much meaning to those in-the-know, but it does not communicate well to the outside world. It greatly oversimplifies what constructing mathematical understanding entails and, unfortunately, it symbolizes early childhood development. As Anne realizes, teachers themselves often poorly understand "the manipulative concept." As a consequence, Anne was unable to secure funds to purchase materials for a middle school mathematics laboratory.

The notion that math is for those that "have it" is deeply rooted in the Western cultural mythology of schooling regarding intelligence, which includes, among other prejudices, preference for evidence of speed in doing arithmetic calculations rather than ability to explain arithmetic operations. Consider that the comment, "I never was any good at math," is a socially respectable statement even among the college educated. In contrast, imagine someone very learned saying seriously, "I've never been very good at understanding anything I read."

Anne makes progress by rightly focusing on a central concept of mathematical thinking: *conjecture*. Something about this notion of *conjecture* is essential to the approach she wants her students to take toward learning mathematics. In fact, the concept of *conjecture* unites constructivist principles of learning with the aims of disciplined understanding in mathematics. Mathematicians posit conjectures and ask if they are true; they use the tools of mathematical inquiry to find out and persuade others of the truth of these conjectures. When children are challenged to make conjectures, they too must use the tools of mathematics to find out whether their conjectures are true, then work to communicate and convince others of the validity of their conclusions. In doing so, the construction of the argument matters most; in the construction of the argument lies the proof of the conjecture's truth. There is no one "right" method to know in advance and no way to know the "right" answer without evaluating the structure of an argument.

Consider, for a moment, a simple example of conjecture in a primary grade mathematics class. Children have learned to count and are beginning to explore the basic operations with numbers. They learn to count by twos and threes. They learn to arrange sets of cubes into geometric shapes—a pattern for 3, 4, 5, and so forth. They realize that the number of cubes in the set is constant even if the shape of the arrangement changes (an instance of confirmed conjecture). Next, the children learn that numbers can be either "odd" or "even." They are learning not only how to do some arithmetic, but also concepts about the properties of numbers. Based on such properties, they can make conjectures.

For example, starting with "2" and counting by twos they can generate the set of even numbers. Starting at "1" and counting by twos they can generate the set of odd numbers. But what happens if you add two even numbers? Will the answer be odd or even? Will this result always be the same, regardless of which two even numbers are added? How can you prove that the result must logically be even for all possible combinations of two even numbers? Can you demonstrate this logic with objects, with pictures, and in symbolic form, accompanied by linguistic sophistication?

Of course, many other conjectures come to mind: "adding two odd numbers results in an odd number" (a false conjecture), "adding an even and an odd results in an odd number" (a true conjecture). The more sophisticated might wish to conjecture about the odd-even pattern effects of multiplying odd and even numbers. Dividing causes new problems, for the answers may not be included in the set of counting numbers (3/2, for example, is *rational* not *whole*). The odd and even concept seems applicable to whole numbers but has little meaning when applied to rational ones (the set of numbers used to express fractions).

Rather quickly this example demonstrates how conjecture might prompt exploration into the nature of number and how these explorations might lead to collaboration, interaction, communication—and enthusiasm. Of course, after several years of conditioning by traditional school instruction in arithmetic, children learn to eschew risk and win rewards. They expect quick feedback as to whether they are "doing it right" and "getting the right answer." Most likely, their parents felt the same way about school math. Yet *conjecture* has a trusted pedigree in the field of mathematics and presents an opportunity for Anne to educate her constituency away from addiction to "right answer" fixes and toward disciplined understanding.

Thus the "conjecture method" of teaching mathematics connotes greater sophistication than the "manipulative concept" alone. What Anne presents via manipulatives to students is multiple ways of exploring a conjecture and a variety of tools for determining whether it is "right." A broad conception of manipulatives includes symbols, charts and tables, graphs, computer simulations, drawings and diagrams, dramatization (yes, students can perform skits to try out mathematical ideas), as well as physical objects and sounds (music, of course, is pre-eminently a representation of mathematical patterns).

All, in effect, are "props" to assist logical reasoning. All provide means to represent the structure and operations of a mathematical proposition. Physical objects provide the most direct translation of the conjecture into actions and arrangements with the potential to reveal stable patterns—the truth of the conjecture. Anne's budget committee colleagues were "reluctant to approve money requests for lab materials that they didn't understand." What they failed to understand was the significance and power of the "conjecture method" to the teaching of mathematics, from both the perspectives of disciplined mathematical understanding and constructivist approaches to learning. Manipulatives in mathematics make conjectures easier to explore and, at the same time, prompt students to make increasingly sophisticated conjectures. In turn, mathematics helps us to do what is naturally rather difficult—represent problems in symbolic ways, then manipulate these symbols according to fixed rules, even when the solution path required by logic appears counter-intuitive.

The process of understanding mathematics often resides in the ability to "translate" a question or situation (the problem) into a mathematical representation—all else in solving a problem is manipulation of the representation according to algebraic and arithmetic rules. The representation may be one of many forms: physical model, drawing, dramatization, equation, or computer program. Multiple physical models and drawings, as the means of representing the same problem, are always possible and the ability to translate the problem among several such representations, cognizant of what abstract properties remain unvariant, comes very close to equaling what it means to understand mathematically.

Perhaps the most simple example of this point of view is a concept such as "threeness." Whether buttons, M&Ms, kittens, dots, lines, or pennies owed, "threeness" is an abstraction that remains the same across set after set of different objects, provided that each set maps onto the same counting number. The representation of counting numbers might include number lines, color-coded bars (each 1 cm longer than the preceding bar), dot patterns, objects to place in containers, beads on a string and, of course, numerals. When a child has succeeded in abstracting the concept of number, we might say that he or she has "a number line in the head" and, by inspection of this mental representation of number, is able to solve problems of joining and separating sets of whole numbers. The child comes to know what adding and subtracting mean in terms of what happens to sets of objects, lengths of strings, and positions on a number line. The child, through the challenge of translating among these representations, ultimately constructs a mental representation of the abstract concept, number.

Having the mental representation suggests that the child has achieved mathematical understanding—and there is no reason to believe that this process of construction through translation among representations applies only to young children. It is this belief that Anne stands ready to act upon in the middle school.

It takes time to construct understanding. Anne's middle school colleagues are in the midst of debating the value of taking the time to get there and, as she has observed, many believe that those destined to arrive already "have it." Those that don't, won't.

The use of manipulatives makes understanding deeper, not simply success easier, for manipulation of representations and translation among representations are the processes that lead to the mental construction of mathematical ideas. The experience of an idea well understood is a pleasant feeling, an intrinsic satisfaction, and the antidote to student frustration expressed as "Don't make me understand it; I just want to know if I got it correct."

A conservative approach to mathematics learning stresses the outcome of computational proficiency and acknowledges the need for extensive practice. What Anne's parent constituency rightly fears is that adherence to the rhetoric of the conjecture method, the frenetic search for relevant and interesting problem contexts, and the time to reflect upon multiple representations (and solution strategies) compromise the amount of practice needed to achieve computational proficiency. Constructivist reformers in mathematics teaching are well advised to consider this point. As Lampert synthesizes, the goal is understanding *and* proficiency—and the more routines that happen proficiently, the more time and mental energy there is to invest in learning new concepts.

Traditional middle school math curricula do not suffer from a lack of emphasis on practice, however. Regrettably, much too rarely are students challenged to do the most fundamental work of problem solving: compose an equation (or procedure) first in concrete, then in abstract form; then use it. Translating a real world situation into a mathematical expression is hard work and takes practice, just as does computational proficiency.

The tragic reality is that school math so rarely, if ever, challenges students to apply their mathematical thinking in this way.

When Anne teaches, the situation is very different, however. Her lessons derived from a "quilting project" prompted a variety of conjectures and sustained efforts to represent and solve interesting problems. Her story about "quilts" impresses us with the momentum of her effort to import the style of the "courtyard project" to the middle school, despite the opposition and constraints she has acknowledged.

From Rectangular Arrays to Quilts

One example of a non-routine, manipulative-based lesson was Quilts. In the initial lesson called Rectangular Arrays, students used tiles to determine all of the arrays possible. As the students worked in groups, they recorded the possibilities on grid paper. From those records they determined "square numbers," primes, composites, and factors. The visual model allowed them to see the actual "square" numbers and that prime numbers are those with just one rectangular array. Cooperative groups allowed students to check each other on the simplest of problems, such as using the wrong number of tiles and the mistake of recording the wrong factors. Using a large display encouraged the team to look for patterns in multiplication and dimensions.

After determining the patterns, the students were able to make a conjecture about the next number of factors a number might have and whether it might be an odd or even number. After looking at records for the numbers 1 to 27, students saw a pattern that even numbers always had 2 as a factor and that after the number 2 no even was ever a prime number. Therefore, they conjectured that the number 28 would not be a prime number. Also, they noticed the pattern the square numbers were following: 1 x 1, 2 x 2, 3 x 3 . . . The last square was a 5 x 5 and they conjectured that the next square number would be 6 x 6 and that 28 would not be a square. They validated those conjectures by using tiles and cutting out rectangular arrays.

In this example, Anne has used conjecturing as the means to help students construct, out of exploration and representation with a physical model, basic concepts about number. Moreover, this disciplined mathematical work was to become embedded (eventually) in the context of an engaging project and suggests how expert middle school math teachers can integrate disciplined knowing with interdisciplinary themes.

The nature of this project threatens a seldom-questioned assumption about mathematics learning: the need for rigid sequencing. It is possible that students will need some rudimentary algebra skills out of step with the text program in order to pursue their conjectures. They might begin to work with notions of translation, rotation, and reflection—concepts about spatial tessellations—as well. And here they are in middle school playing with the primary grade concept of odd and even numbers!

Sequential structure is not, of course, necessarily wrong—but "rigid" sequential thinking about math learning obstructs constructivist learning. The flight of a butterfly is a better analogy for the path of learning than the flight of an arrow toward its target. The butterfly is free to rest upon the flower of its fancy; if the target is missed, the arrow is lost.

When mathematics learning conforms to constructivist principles, rigid sequential (and extremely reductionist) practices recede. Teaching introduces algebraic principles of representation before grade three; middle elementary grade children solve simultaneous equations with graphical representations.[13] Development of proportional reasoning and probabilistic thinking, not to mention geometric design and geometric solid space concepts, proceed concurrently with training in arithmetic. Young children, with a "number line in the head," engage in work with all four basic arithmetic operations from the very beginning (not subtraction after memorizing certain addition facts). By middle school, the array of representations—algebraic, arithmetic, graphical, tabular, pictorial, physical, and computer models—at their disposal prepares them to work on difficult and rewarding problems. They can continue the fundamental work of constructing equations as representations of problems.

This revolution in the way mathematics is taught will come, in part because of the ways in which mathematics is done. Machines of computational prowess that only NASA could access during the Apollo mission days now cost the same as a ten-year-old, high-mileage, used Chevy sedan. People who do more than enter data must understand how to structure and represent problems in order to exploit the productivity of the tools of the information age. Having been fastest in the multiplication table drills of youth will not count for much.

Yet there is no guarantee that even the best mathematics will mean much to the typical middle school student. Abstract exploration of number properties, even in the context of aesthetically appealing physical model representations—the rectangular arrays—may fail to capture interest. The teaching of mathematics must often link to other subjects to make the subject personal, as told by Anne:

Despite the level of problem solving, reasoning and communication, all of which are the three main standards for the NCTM, the entire lesson lacked a very important element in middle school mathematics—connection. How does any of this connect to the student's life?

Part of the problem of "connecting" in mathematics is the dilemma of what to connect it to! In a middle school/junior high school it is wonderful if the social studies, language arts, science, and math teams can join forces. However, a number of different obstacles stand in the way. In an effort to reduce the blocks, we tried to start with small steps. Finding a purpose for the mathematics, not just getting ready for high school, is a major goal for the middle school math program.

A nice extension to the Rectangular Arrays lesson was making quilts. One of the student council representatives suggested that we give gifts to the organization that helps children with AIDS. The students were simply asked to prepare the quilt tops. They used the information that they'd learned and took it several more steps.

The students needed to determine how large twin-size blankets were. They needed to plan a layout with borders to fill out the total size. They drew scale drawings of their designs, taking into account the size of seams, array plan and individual patch sizes. Students needed to work as a team to discuss the mathematics and the artistic plan. One team member's responsibility was to keep a diary or *minutes* of the team's effort.

While many of the diary entries were simple lists of experiments, they were also meant to be reflections of the group's discoveries. One team reported:

> ". . . we started with a square top, but beds aren't square, so we had to change our entire layout. After we changed to a rectangle, we had to change our number of patches. Even though we used less patches, the outside strip (perimeter) was the same. That surprised us."

The discovery that many of the groups made concerned another lesson often taught at the same level: constant areas can have varying perimeter and constant perimeters can have varying areas. The fact that the students identified the relationship in their own work made the mathematics their own—and more interesting.

> The final collection of quilts showed a good variety of designs and solutions to the task. There was no one "right" answer.

This project, beginning with rectangular arrays and concluding with gifts of quilts to AIDS children, clearly illustrates constructivist learning in the mathematics classroom. There is the starting point of exploration and the security of generating questions that cannot have wrong answers. The teacher accepts lines of thought, clarifies challenges, and introduces alternatives helpful in pursuing inquiries.

Clearly, the students came to feel that the quilting project had a significant purpose. Anne's approach to teaching began with pattern-finding, then introduced number theory concepts. When applied to the problem of quilt design in the context of making gifts for AIDS children, the middle school mathematics curriculum had arrived at an interesting juncture. Making quilts in the present had ostensibly replaced the primary goal of preparing for future mathematics in high school. Consider, however, that students made discoveries about area and learned to express these discoveries with appropriate mathematical concepts. Through a circuitous pathway, they still found themselves progressing substantially in the kind of mathematical knowledge needed in preparing for high school.

Given greater responsibility for the topics and context of study, students felt highly motivated and this motivation caused learning to out-pace, in Anne's judgment, what reduction to a logical sequence of study, determined by expectations for future work, might achieve. From her vantage, efficient management of learning outcomes often has proven illusory; the messy work of wrestling with unanticipated initiatives and meaningful contexts has held many pleasant surprises.

With the step of embedding rectangular arrays in quilting, Anne has established continuity between personal experience, school categories of experience according to subjects, and concepts of the field of mathematics. She has connected the work of school to the good of the community. Moreover, the students have chosen a subject that promotes equity—the mathematics of textiles is a fascinating theme, one that crosses cultures, accords respect to women, and includes the invention of the modern conception of the computer. In the future, Anne plans to exploit the quilting theme with greater sophistication.

Constructivist teaching conceives of learning more as continuous development than as incremental accretion, more as complex differentiation than as simple assimilation. Without an approach to acquiring fundamental schemas in mathematics that exploits the social construction of knowledge and, at each juncture, the dependence of the learner on the useful availability of prior knowledge, the long-term prospects for learning in the natural and social sciences at a deep level of understanding are very dim. For the child who leaves elementary school frustrated by arithmetic only to encounter remediation in junior high school, these fundamental schema abort. To assign creative and enriching work in mathematics only to the track of students, whatever the age, who have demonstrated computational proficiency is to ensure that the gap with the rest will never close. These are the lessons of constuctivism consonant with the value Anne's community places on academic excellence and future opportunity.

Formal mathematics is the study of logical relations among symbols. These symbols harbor unobvious meaning, abstracted with difficulty in many cases. The logic governing how to configure them into patterns may clash with simple intuition. The task, then, of the student, is to grasp this unobvious meaning.

Fortunately, a student has an essential tool to apply toward this end: current knowledge. After all, one key premise of constructivist learning is to use what one already knows in order to secure new—and more sophisticated—knowledge.[14] Continuity of development counts highly. Deliberate reflection on meaning characterizes the successful student. The meaningful learner is committed to finding ways to put familiar conceptual apparatus to work on the task of new learning. But doing so alone, and in the absence of relevant subsuming concepts, often invites excessive frustration. Reflecting, for example, on what dividing by a fraction might mean risks just this sort of mind-knotting confusion. Let's see, three-fourths divided by two-thirds means . . . uh, well, you just invert and multiply to get the answer. But in what situation would you set up fractions in this way? Add a bit of imagery: you have three-fourths of a dollar. Two-thirds of a dollar equals 1 colaxni, a foreign currency. How much, in colaxnis, is your seventy-five cents worth? Or, restated, how many colaxnis are there in three quarters? Or, how many times can you subtract two-thirds of a dollar from three-fourths of a dollar? The last form of the question helps intuit an approximate answer: once and a fraction more, for starters, seems the obvious reply.

To make meaning less unobvious, to render the counter-intuitive logical, is a primary task for the teacher. So, too, is guiding the transfer of meaning to new contexts altogether. Leinhart[15] claims that experienced, "expert" teachers differ greatly from their "novice," beginning colleagues in large measure because novices do not grasp how to make the meaning of centrally organizing concepts obvious to their students. According to Leinhart, novice teachers tend to teach how to perform arithmetic operations with, for example, rational numbers (i.e., using fractions in calculations) as discrete, isolated skills for each type of calculation. Expert teachers, in contrast, help students grasp the principle of identity ("many ways to express the number one") and its fundamental role in deriving, justifying, and understanding the reasonableness of the algorithms for performing operations with fractions ("multiplying by 'one' does not change the amount"). When a child taught by a novice forgets how to do a calculation with fractions, the skill is truly gone. When a child taught by an expert forgets how, application of principled, conceptual understanding has the potential to reconstruct a valid procedure. According to Novak,[16] the ability to retain knowledge depends upon its meaningful connections and orderly structure; rote-learning rapidly fades. In short, it may take longer to teach for understanding, but the payoffs are worth waiting for.

Understanding mathematical constructions promises power. This power justifies intervening in students' lives with the expectation that they learn mathematics. Once again we return to the theme that disciplined understanding grants Anne the right to proselytize on behalf of a constructivist mathematics curriculum. Her wish—and every teacher's most legitimate responsibility—is to extend to her students the opportunity of liberating their thinking and gaining access to realms of understanding they would most unlikely construct on their own.

On the other hand, integration for the sake of integration is an insufficient principle to guide curriculum planning and teaching. Integration happens, and integration is promoted, when genuine problems are addressed. The focus on the problem takes precedence over glorifying integration, and the focus on the problem from a disciplined perspective accords prominence to some concepts over others. This process is exactly what transpired in the example of quilting.

This section began with a transition from the discussion of the concept of "conjecture" to the example of developing conjectures while working with rectangular arrays. We learned how Anne helped her students find personal satisfaction in learning by embedding their mathematical knowledge in a quilting project. The project connected school mathematics to community work in a courageous and socially responsible way—expressing care for children with AIDS. Together, the conjectures and the project disrupted rigidly sequential learning in mathematics and slowed the process of practicing skills to proficiency. The payoff—the benefit from taking this risk—came in the form of realizing what concepts truly mean.

The next example of Anne's continuation of project work in the middle school illustrates the problem of pursuing a constructivist agenda within the culture of traditional schooling. What begins with genuine purpose ends in simulation, corrupted by a reward system.

Banking on Success

> Connecting mathematics with a real-world purpose is a bit easier with a community bank that wants to help. A local bank had an idea of using the school as a branch for students to use for actual savings.
>
> Students handling other students' money was a bit of a problem for our school but we decided to use the techniques and project for something just as important as opening a savings branch at the school.
>
> Students opened savings accounts with their "achievements." Achievements were counted as grade point averages, positive progress reports, awards, "gold slip" achievement slips, tardy-free quarter certificates, and a variety of other schoolwide recognition programs.
>
> Students learned how to open savings accounts, make deposits and withdrawals. Other students in five math classes are taking turns being trained by the local bank in the proper banking techniques and use of computer software. They're trained in marketing, ethics, and accuracy in accounting, including computing interest.
>
> While it is still a bit early to determine the actual success, we're getting quite a bit of interest in the accounts since the students can make withdrawals for free lunch movies and various privileges.
>
> The curriculum integration involved banking history and extensive language arts with the passbook contract writing and marketing activities. Several students are taking strong leadership roles by serving on the bank's Board of Directors.

There may be no such thing a "free lunch," but at Anne's school, it seems, there is a "free lunch movie." You can bank on it. In fact, the bank promotes the deposit of "tardy-free quarters."

Prompted by a magnificent opportunity to take schooling into the community, courtesy of an invitation from a business, the school culture transmogrified the banking project into authoritarian practices, benevolent, of course, but still quite pernicious. The primary investment through the banking system is clearly in control of student behavior. Running amuck is the complete dominance of behavioral conditioning as the *sine qua non* of school psychology. Even the ancillary learning is classified as "training." The unquestioned assumptions of behaviorist ideology in this instance have completely subverted the aims of constructivism. The mentality of reward-and-conquer reigns supreme. The opportunity to do the real work of finance, while a student, was lost. Unlike the court-yard project demonstration and the quilting project in which children, as true citizens, worked to improve their community, these middle schoolers are the victims of sham-banking. They trade in tokens whose primary effect is to increase film-watching at school. The system has treated the students no better than rats trained even to recharge the batteries that run the reward dispenser they must learn to press in order to survive.

Is there an alternative? Let's hope so. Perhaps the local bank could help the school set up an account for managing special event funds in cooperation with a parent organization. Perhaps the students might persuade the school board to financially reward energy and resource efficiency at the school in some way that involved crediting and debiting accounts. Maybe real money is just too controversial an item to trust to middle school treatment—the culture could not withstand the shock of actual embezzlement by twelve year olds. More seriously, people's personal financial information is protected by privacy rights. In addition, community reluctance to give special customer access to a private concern is a well-founded ethic. After all, inviting private business transactions into school is a bit like a government granting protected monopolies.

If school sensibilities preclude real financial work, Anne and her colleagues can try to imagine other contexts where the same mathematical concepts might be explored and applied. Their responsibility is to exploit the tension between discipline-mandated objectives and student-directed learning, striving toward a resolution respectful of mathematical concepts and student interests. They should not permit the behavioral paradigm to subvert the aims of constructivist theory so often instantiated as project work and simulation.

Why is this subversion of aims so pervasive? The constructivist agenda rattles shibboleths down to the foundation of schooling. The easy compromise is to applaud interdisciplinary study, praise the involvement of students in choosing what to learn, and glorify the structure of a day centered upon activity other than listening. Evaded are the hard questions of whether students have constructed mental representations of complex phenomena and whether they can solve problems requiring disciplined understanding.

A challenge to constructivist reform is to change the culture of evaluation, not only at the level of high stakes tests but also at the level of daily feedback to students. In brief, evaluation ought to focus on what kinds of problems have been solved and according to which principles of reasoning. Too often we find that the scoring of appearance, accuracy, and completeness predominate over evaluation of conceptual understanding.

The banking system protocol assessed, in effect, comportment, not understanding. As with most assessment in the middle school context, awarding points rewarded dutiful behavior over meaningful understanding. As in the typical school culture, assessment served as a tool of management, particularly of motivation, by means of extrinsic reward (and punishment).

The first step on the pathway out of this extrinsic reward excess and inadvertent devaluation of conceptual understanding is to premise instruction—even student-directed project works—upon the goal of grasping the meaning of principles of mathematical reasoning made explicit. Students ought to know that they are working toward mastery, in context, of particular abstractions and problem-solving strategies. They should be able to express what understanding mathematics means. When these goals are articulated and prominent, they can compete for priority in assessment with measures of quality that score only accuracy, completeness, and appearance.

The banking project reveals not so much how reform must compromise with powerful opposition, but how powerful opposition gobbles up the reform and digests it according to its own constitution. Anne appreciates the concerns and anxieties of the opposition, though she might not recognize the extent to which they have already subverted her aims. Her narrative turns again to testing, the hungry predator of reform:

> The five–six day lessons are wonderful, the lengthy projects are great, but what about the rest of the learner-centered days? What about the district achievement tests? What about the state tests whose scores are published in the newspaper? What about the high school entrance exams?
>
> While these high publicity tests still have a high percentage of arithmetic, the balance of teacher-directed, student-directed study is a delicate one. I have not worked out the entire program. My colleagues and I are developing a middle school math program slowly. Since we have several components that need careful attention, we tend to work on the conservative side of change. We find it's easier to add or drop pieces of the program after researching and educating the parents, administrators, fellow teachers and community groups.

Tests lead to scrutiny and comparison of schools by the public. The results appear in newspapers as charts and graphs read in quick glances. This system of testing and media reporting was deliberately created by politicians to cause parents to exert more pressure on schools for "basic" achievement.

The high school entrance tests place individuals in risky positions—the gates of financial security and social status close somewhat or open wider depending on the results. Constructivist reformers seem to be riding on different rails—if not entirely derailed by such high stakes.

Anne and her colleagues have the balance about right—opting for conservative change, adding and dropping elements, and working to educate their constituency. The harsh criticism of banking must be tempered by considering this project in the context of all the examples presented and discussed. Anne's progress is real. By maintaining her concern that a robust conception of mathematical understanding is for all students, she can make progress in persuading others that the path to this conception must be a personal one. By keeping her confidence in "understanding" as a reinforcing feeling, she can explain to others the destructive power of overly pervasive, external reward schedules when persistent problem solving behaviors are expected.[17]

Conclusion

Anne concludes her narrative by itemizing local, state, and national agendas for change in mathematics teaching:

> The "traditional" math curriculum emphasis has been gradually shifting. During the early 1970s, math at the primary grades started to see some changes with *Math Their Way*. This manipulative-based math was not a first, but was certainly a leader in the changes that occurred in the classroom.
>
> As lessons in the elementary grades were evolving, secondary teachers were starting to see the use of problem solving as an important issue. The Lane County, Oregon, "Problem Solving Series" was the first, and still serves as the bible for teaching strategies in mathematics in our region.
>
> New approaches and techniques were being developed in all curriculum areas, as well. Among them were curriculum integration, collaborative learning, holistic lessons, learning styles and teaching styles, various assessment alternatives, and the ideas of portfolios.
>
> In 1980, the National Council of Teachers of Mathematics produced their first draft of the professional standards for teaching mathematics. This revolutionary document from a professional organization emphasized technology, including computers and calculators,

manipulatives, problem solving, heterogeneous classrooms, and cooperative learning.

In 1990, the Oregon legislature (HB3565—the Oregon 21st Century Schools Act) directed the schools to
assess mathematics in a variety of ways, the major one
of which is "outcome-based" performance tasks.

Applying new methods of teaching and assessment
presents some unique challenges at the middle school
level, given the state and national rhetoric of becoming
"first in the world in math and science."

From these reports, from her own experience, and from her
own disciplined study, Anne struggles to share with her constituencies the imagery of mathematical understanding. She shared this
imagery with me in Family Math class years ago.

It includes an "event-sense" of the subject—what doing math
feels like. It moves on to encompass conjecture and knowledge of
how to represent ideas, even translating among these multiple representations. The imagery of mathematical understanding respects
the semantics (what things mean) as well as the logic (how procedures work) of mathematical problems. It encompasses principled
conceptual knowledge as well as procedural proficiency and depends upon constructing mental models through activity, with symbols, talk, objects, sounds, and drawings.

The disciplines of human inquiry are very specialized languages for solving problems—science and mathematics included.
To construct the language for oneself, one must converse within a
community of shared purpose and use its concepts to order personal experience. Curriculum is a vehicle for carrying this conversation to the doorsteps of the experts. The teacher, as host, is
responsible for seeing that the talk is lively and respectful of the
personal experiences shared in these conversations.

This context is pre-eminently a social one, and matters of
self-interest, group identity, interpretation of authority, and power
abound. The analysis of the "banking on success" project exemplified the entanglement of power with curriculum. National agendas for reform are, in essence, the workings of power relations at
odds over what the understanding of mathematics means. The lens
of "power" illuminates how, throughout schooling, the sentiment
professed by many students as preference for "getting it right" over
"understanding" is the direct consequence of pursuing rational self-
interest. Unfortunately, the fruits of this rationality contrast starkly
with true intellectual achievement. Power relations ultimately rest
on the shoulders of those who control the conversation.

The phenomenological distance between student conceptual
development and the role of power in social relations is great, but
must be bridged if we are to get smart about school learning. The

center-span of this bridge is language, with its constructions of mind deliberately invented to solve problems, make sense of experience, and—through meaning—control effort. We share these symbols socially in meaningful systems, such as mathematics, yet grasp their unobvious meaning individually. Through our capacity to conceive, label, and share stable patterns in the flux of personal experience (counting, combinations, frequency), we work toward the social goal of having a common experience of the world (calculations, probabilities). Our ability to achieve shared meaning for concepts—the consummation of the act of teaching—makes possible shared experience.[18] Learning is private and social at the same time. No one can do our learning for us, but it turns out we need each other to figure out what things mean.

Mathematics is a unique, enlightening, empowering, enriching, and an altogether titillating way of experiencing the world; it is well worth sharing, in Anne's and my view. At least there is nothing inherent about the meaning of mathematical concepts that runs counter to this conclusion. Only the social and personal factors conditioned by schooling create the feelings of dread, tedium, incompetence, and hopeless confusion felt by too many students.

In the long term, some students will pursue mathematics for intrinsic pleasure. For others, the construction of mathematical ideas will present the opportunity to think thoughts otherwise closed to them. Many must pursue one or more aspects of mathematics until achieving useful proficiency (bankers, for instance). For all learners, mathematics demands discipline and practice. No one ought to experience mathematics as a mode of thinking that makes little sense.

The NCTM standards cited by Anne make the "big three"—problem solving, reasoning, and communication—national priorities for evaluating learning in mathematics. Thus, the future holds promise that high stakes testing may align with constructivist principles.

Whether for practice, in application, as a project, from conjecture, or just for fun (recreational puzzles), problems should permeate the mathematics curriculum. The concepts for working problems successfully are mental inventions, tools of thinking. The product of working on problems is not only a solution, but the construction of a mental model encompassing the operation of mathematical principles. The mathematics curriculum is a constructivist one to the degree that students comprehend its symbols as inventions with some purpose in mind—a sensible purpose, that makes thinking about hard problems easier. That's pretty much what happens in Anne McEnerny-Ogle's classroom.

End Notes

1. Jean Kerr Stenmark, Virginia Thompson, and Ruth Cossey, *Family Math* (Berkeley, CA: Regents of the University of California, 1986).
2. Charles R. Ault, Jr. and Phyllis Campbell Ault, "The Oregon Consortium for Quality Science and Mathematics Education (OCQSME): Five Years of Collaborative Staff Development," *Excellence in Science Teacher Education* (AETS Yearbook), eds. P. Rubba, L. Campbell, and T. Dana (Columbus, OH: ERIC/SMEAC, 1993).
3. Mary Barratta Lorton, *Math Their Way* (Menlo Park, CA: Addison-Wesley, 1976).
4. Lampert, Magdalene, "Knowing, Doing, and Teaching Multiplication," *Cognition and Instruction* 3 Fall, (1986): 305–342.
5. Commission on Standards for School Mathematics, *Curriculum and Evaluation Standards for School Mathematics*, (Reston, VA: National Council of Teachers of Mathematics, Inc., 1989).
6. Nancie Atwell, *In the Middle: Writing, Reading, and Learning With Adolescents* (Portsmouth, NH: Heinemann, 1987).
7. Seymore Sarason, *The Predictable Failure of School Reform* (San Francisco: Jossey-Bass, 1990).
8. D. Bob Gowin, *Educating* (Ithaca, NY: Cornell University Press, 1981).
9. Howard Gardner, *The Unschooled Mind* (New York: Basic Books, 1991).
10. Ted Nelson, Gene Maier, and Albert Bennett, *Math in the Mind's Eye* (Salem, OR: Math Learning Center, 1987–1993).
11. Harold W. Stevenson, "Learning from Asian Schools," *Scientific American* 267 (Dec. 1992): 70–76.
12. James W. Stigler and Michelle Perry, "Cross-Cultural Studies of Mathematics Teaching and Learning," *Perspectives on Research on Effective Mathematics Teaching, Volume 1*, eds. D. A. Grouws, T. J. Cooney, and D. Jones (Reston, VA: National Council of Teachers of Mathematics/Lawrence Erlbaum Associates, 1988), 194–223.
13. See Nathan Caplan, Marcella H. Choy, and John K. Whitmore, "Indochinese Refugee Families and Academic Achievement," *Scientific American* 266 (Feb. 1992): 36–42; and Lore Rasmussen, Robert Hightower, and Peter Rasmussen, *Lab Sheet Annotations: Miquon Math Lab Materials* (Berkeley, CA: Key Curriculum Project, 1985).
14. Ausubel, D., *The Psychology of Meaningful Verbal Learning* (New York: Grune and Stratton, 1963).
15. Gaia Leinhart, "Expertise in Instructional Lessons: An Example from Fractions," *Perspecitves on Research on Effective*

Mathematics Teaching, Volume 1, eds. D.A. Grouws, T. J. Cooney, and D. Jones (Reston, VA: National Council of Teachers of Mathematics/Lawrence Erlbaum Associates, 1988), 47–66.
16. J.D. Novak, *A Theory of Education* (Ithaca, NY: Cornell University Press, 1977).
17. See Mary Budd Rowe, *Teaching Science as Continuous Inquiry: A Basic* (New York: McGraw-Hill, 1978).
18. D. Bob Gowin

Chapter 14

Embarking on Adventure:
An Invitation to Middle School Science

Charles R. Ault, Jr. and Neil Maine

The Lure of Adventure

Somewhere between the childhood imagery of *The Wind in the Willows* and the emerging themes of adulthood in *The Adventures of Huckleberry Finn* resides the sense of adventure most appealing to the psyche of the middle schooler. In both stories, the lure of adventure is apparent, whether "just messing about" in a boat on a summer afternoon, attuned to the pleasing rhythms of nature, or embarking by raft down a mighty river upon a journey of self-discovery and social discovery. In one case a boat, and in the other, a raft, go where the currents of wind and water take them. Among the willows and cattails hovers the unfamiliar yet aesthetically appealing dragonfly. Along the banks of the Mississippi, Huck experiences the trials of self-discovery in the face of adversity. Adventure encompasses the delight of making the unfamiliar well known as well as the satisfaction of self-growth.

An adventure provides the context for making knowledge meaningful and knowledge, in turn, provides the means for successfully completing the adventure. Adventure is emotional, cognitive, social, and personal and it demands skilled adventurers. And no one invited along on the adventure is expected to be a passive passenger.

What are the features of adventure salient to a conception of science? First, adventure means travel through new and unusual territory and the experience of out-of-the-ordinary things. Second, going on an adventure means careful planning and preparation aimed at achieving some goal. Third, adventurers expect encounters with unanticipated problems and know they must learn to improvise solutions along the way. Finally, through teamwork, adventurers overcome obstacles and learn the values of trust and support while, at the same time, progressing in self-reliance. Picture a team of men and women struggling to ascend Mt. Everest. Each plays a role in support of the group, yet the accomplishment of reaching the summit is a deeply personal achievement. No ascent ever begins without extensive planning, and no journey up Mt. Everest's slopes fails to encounter unforeseen difficulties. And the reason for trying is less an intention to conquer the mountain than a desire to feel the exhilaration of the experience.

To do science is to join an adventure in solving problems. In recounting some of our adventures doing science with a variety of learners, we draw upon our combined half-century of experience in schooling, as primary and intermediate grade teachers middle and secondary school science teachers, and, presently, as district science specialist and college professor of science education. The best way to learn about an adventure is to go on one, of course, as Jack Hawkins discovered in *Treasure Island*. The second best way is to read a good story. From this point on, we let examples tell our story, drawing from each a bit of wisdom about embarking on science adventures with middle schoolers. Our narrative begins with grade 4 and ends with a story about continuing the adventure in secondary school.

A School for Fish

A small footbridge crossed the tiny creek between the school in Colorado and the rest of the grounds. At the edge of the playing field, the creek emptied into a quiet pool, formed by a small wall of concrete. Often at lunch break, children would watch caddis fly larvae crawling along the creek bed, searching for flotsam and jetsam to stick to their bodies as camouflage.

The storm began as the school day ended. Ominous clouds gripped the sides of the mountains. Imagining the heavy rainfall, and possible spring snowfall at higher elevations, was easy. Predicting what torrents would wash down the small creek on the school grounds was not.

The creek still ran high when school began the next day and the bridge, surprisingly, was secure. Never was recess so anxiously anticipated—everyone wanted to explore the storm damage. The quiet pool looked more like a newborn lake, with a delta of coarse sediments at the shallow end. And in the pool were a few new guests—large fish from far upstream, washed down by yesterday's storm.

So began "Fish at School." During recess Michael and Jeff ran back into the classroom. They had to have an empty tennis ball can. A few minutes later they were back, looking for something bigger. There were fish at school, trapped in the shallow, sediment-choked pond. And, of course, they would be much easier to study in the classroom, thought Michael and Jeff. They found in the kindergarten playhouse exactly what they were looking for: a "bass"-inet.

Four "lunkers" crowded together at the bottom of the bassinet sitting in the reading corner. The reading corner was about to experience significant remodeling. A pair of wooden doors, joined at their hinges and placed as a room divider, defined this cozy space. In this cozy space was the "reading tub," an ancient plumbing artifact lined with puffy pillows and perched upon four tub-feet.

No one could resist: "Let's put the fish in the bass-tub!" The tub answered the challenge of finding a better place to keep the fish than in the soon-to-shrink outdoor pool. Their care and feeding proved difficult—diet, water oxygenation, and temperature had to be properly maintained. (At the time, and influenced by punning, we thought we had a tubful of bass; later, we realized our prize catch must have been trout.) Luckily, Jennifer's family was in the appliance business—Maytag repair. Thanks to her, we secured a washing-machine pump to circulate water.

What to put on the menu (for the fish)? The answer was simple: several experienced hunters went back to the creek to harvest Rocky Mountain crawdads. To the evident satisfaction of our piscine guests, these were served as fresh as possible (live).

Full-grown crawdads were, unfortunately, too large for our school of fish to swallow. Each recess, hunters returned with the catch-of-the-day and added it to the menu. Popular entrees included grasshoppers, caddis fly nymphs, crickets and, throughout the winter, the nutritious earthworm. The refrigerator in the teachers' lunchroom, of course, played host to about a week's supply of living fish food.

The fish survived at school for a long time—past this author's tenure as a teacher there. Their most important educational legacy, aside from the thrill of watching an efficient predator in action ("He swallowed it whole!"), was prompting interest in stagnant versus moving (hence oxygenated) waters. One side of the science room became host to two large aquaria. In one, there was a pump and filter running at good speed. The other was kept perfectly still. Students placed water from the small pool in both. Their buckets of water also relocated a great number of pond denizens of diminutive to microscopic size. These were the colonizers.

Week by week, the class watched the tanks, removed samples of water, and recorded the type and abundance of organisms observed at micro and macro scales (hand lenses and microscopes were readily available). Drawings papered the wall, each framed with a circle (the view through a microscope). Critter sketches and critter counts accompanied the drawings. The children transformed one side of the room into a hands-on science museum.

The tanks, in effect, went their very separate ways. After a month, wiggly, reddish worms dominated the muds at the bottom of the stagnant one. The tank with the circulating, bubbling waters had a good number of zippy little water fleas scurrying about. The class had done much more than a "science lab." They had designed an investigation, and pursued it as an adventure.

Lawnmowers Across the Solar System

One year in Connecticut, the official fifth-grade science curriculum began with study of the sun and its planets. All too often children learn book wisdom about the sky, but fail to internalize the geometry of orbital motion and its consequences for us as observers in motion. Rarely do they know where to look in the sky to find planets and seldom do they perceive the extent to which the sun's apparent trajectory across the sky changes during a year.

This year would be different—maybe. At least we would learn about finding things in the sky, not just read about what was "up" there. A little bit of didactic teaching was used to convey the idea that the planets revolve about the sun in orbits that come close to defining a plane. When extended to the distant stars, this plane intersects a series of constellations. Another way to trace this sequence of constellations around the sky is to realize that our orbital motion around the sun makes the sun appear to journey in a great yearly loop through the sky centered on the earth. The constellations forming a backdrop to the sun, month by month, are the same ones that house the planets: the twelve zodiac constellations, Virgo, Leo, Taurus, Gemini, and so forth.

The text had students on the playground walking around with umbrellas in their hands, styrofoam balls affixed to the ends of stays representing planets. The activity works this way: one person stands still, observing as if from a motionless earth. The one with the umbrella walks around his or her stationary buddy, slowing twirling the umbrella while doing so. The earth-person describes which distant objects line up with the position of the styrofoam mars-ball attached to the umbrella. Even though the umbrella-holder walks continuously forward at a steady pace, the mars-ball appears to repeatedly stop moving forward, back up some, then resume its march in tandem with the walker.

In this manner the students learned to explain the "retrograde motion" of the outer planets according to the now discredited Ptolemaic, or earth-centered, cosmic model. Well, maybe. There is a bit of a jump from using playground umbrella models of an abandoned theory and interpreting real celestial observations in keeping with an application to present-day concepts. What we needed was a way to engage in authentic astronomy—some way of gathering experience to use as grist for the thinking in terms of an orbital model.

Accordingly, we embarked on a series of daytime astronomy adventures. The night has the advantage of looking out at space through the shadow of the earth, but daytime presents the opportunity of observing a star in brilliant close-up (never looked at directly, of course). Courtney headed to the janitor's closet to fetch a ladder. Samuel brought a fine pair of binoculars to school, and a few other students lined a large box with white paper. On a bright, sunny autumn day we began our search for sunspot activity, using the binoculars to project an image of the solar disk onto the white paper inside the box.

Within minutes we had an image. Within a few more minutes it was gone. The ladder and binoculars were repositioned and we could see the disk again. And, yes, one or two sunspots were easily detected. But why wouldn't the sun stay still? "It's the ladder that's moving!" several agreed.

From sunspots, we turned to watching shadows. We marked with chalk throughout the day where the shadow of a window corner fell. Outside we traced outlines of student shadows. Following the instructions from a daytime astronomy guidebook, students used large, wire-mesh vegetable strainers as "sky-domes." Beneath the dome they placed a piece of cardboard. Next, they tried to find the position on the wire screen where a head of a colorful pin would cast its shadow exactly on the centerpoint of the cardboard beneath the dome. They left the pin in the mesh, pointy-end dangling downward. Later in the day, they again placed the strainer and cardboard on the ground, maintaining its original location and orientation. Pins were added as before.

To the scale of the dome, the pinheads stood for the position of the sun in the observer's sky at successive intervals of time. With several points, the task of extrapolating the trace of the sun across the sky for that date became easy. By weaving a piece of colored thread or yarn along this path, we could preserve our model of the sun's daily traverse for that date.

The excitement comes much later—when daily traverses are compared. The angle of the sun above the southern horizon at midday (when the sun is directly above the south point or has completed exactly one-half of its march across the sky) changes through the year. But by how much? By a whopping 47 degrees! The lowest angle comes when winter starts; the highest on the first day of summer. There are only 90 degrees from horizon to zenith (the point directly overhead). Early in a July morning, the Connecticut sun has already climbed higher than it will by noon in December. The effect of comparing these observations by juxtaposing threaded vegetable strainers is stunning. And the sun, in Connecticut, never passes overhead, even at noon in June.

Our bit of celestial adventure with our daytime star in brilliant close-up was coming to an end. The children knew to look for planets in that bright swath of sky defined by the constellations of the zodiac. They realized that whether the planets were above the horizon depended on the time of day (or night). They all could find Jupiter in the western sky—prominent that autumn as soon as the sun had set. Retrograde motion (the east-west switch, with respect to the stars, of a planet's movement) remained as baffling as the umbrella demonstration.

So how does the lawnmower figure into this story? Many believed at the outset of doing daytime astronomy that "at noon the sun is directly overhead." Nearly all had refined this belief into the understanding that at "midday" shadows are shortest, and they point north. Using this insight into shadows and the confusion in meaning between midday and noon, students decided to design and investigate sundials. They were not sure how to position either the gnomon (the stick that casts the shadow) or the dial face where readings of the shadow would be made. (Resolving these problems requires a very good understanding of the role of latitude.)

We decided to control the experiment carefully and make use of popsicle sticks. The plan: mark shadows on the ground, use gnomons of equal length, and manipulate only the tilt and compass-bearing of the gnomon. Each student planned to use toothpicks or stones to record the tips of the gnomon's shadow through the day. The children set up research stations in the grass and made the first observations. The critical ones would come during lunch.

Just before lunch, the maintenance crew mowed the lawn. Not one gnomon survived.

Bulldozing the Schoolyard

Often the proper point of departure for an adventure in science is citizen involvement in solving problems—young citizen involvement, at an appropriate level of feasibility, for the sake of the community in which they reside. In searching for dragons to slay, these young citizens should not Winnie-the-Pooh their way along—"oh bother"—lamenting dire circumstances and worrying themselves to distraction, after the fashion of Pooh's pal Eeyore, about pollution, habitat degradation, and species extinction. Instead, they must, in the spirit of *Wind in the Willows*, gain, through attention to nature's astonishing intricacies, an appreciation for their surroundings—what Barry Lopez calls a sense of place or "querencia,"[1] in which honoring one's home becomes synonymous with discovering one's identity, and from which deeply satisfying commitments to community may follow. The goal of science adventure is understanding, and from this understanding, commitment.

Understanding begins with attention to and appreciation of details. As these connect, feelings merge with meanings. Instead of being a simple nuisance, the irritatingly abrasive stems of horsetails (*equisetum sp.*) become a story about how their rooting chemistry has unlocked silica from volcanic stone. In place of distraction, the noxious sting of windblown dust at a coastal saltworks transforms to a verse in an epic about the dissolution of salts from lava by sulfuric drizzle hundreds of miles away. Understanding must count on the opportunity to experience and appreciate directly the phenomena of interest. And few phenomena of life buzz with more intricate detail and productive capacity than wetland habitats.

The decline of wetlands habitat is a problem felt throughout the nation. Oregon boasts (or, in some minds, is plagued by) a far-reaching land use planning program administered by the Land Conservation and Development Commission (LCDC). The first goal for statewide planning is "citizen involvement."[2] For the purposes of planning, a citizen is defined as "any person within the planning area." Notably, age does not appear in this definition and we applaud the state for acknowledging that kids are citizens, too. In keeping with goal number one, "citizen involvement," the LCDC calls upon schools "to provide information on land-use education" and "to offer courses in land-use education." In a number of situations, we have found a way to reverse the sense of these objectives—in effect, asking not, "What information can society provide to students about land use?" but, rather, "What can students do to solve land use problems for society?" Of course they can learn about the decline of wetlands, but the more important issue is can they participate in defining this problem, in monitoring its severity, and in mitigating its extent?[3]

Science adventure is a quest that promises intrinsic rewards both from engaging in virtuous work and from appreciating astonishing experiences, understanding guiding the transformation of the latter into the former. As educators, we wish to find our students becoming neither ignorant altruists nor smart cynics; instead, we desire to cultivate among them an informed vision committed to solving problems. Doing so requires attention to good literature as much as good science and we acknowledge that the record of natural history writing, from Thoreau's *Walden*[4] to Leopold's *Sand County Almanac*,[5] has never hidden these moral and ethical perspectives (often aesthetical) beneath a cover of scientific objectivity. As Leopold puts it:

> Ecology is now teaching us to search in animal populations for analogies to our own problems. By learning how some small part of the biota ticks, we can guess

how the whole mechanism ticks. The ability to perceive
these deeper meanings, and to appraise them critically,
is the woodcraft of the future.[6]

We believe that middle schoolers are developing an acute
sense of right and wrong, of heroes and villains. They are engaged
in testing the meaning of authority, responsibility, and rules. Each
wishes to slay dragons in the course of an adventure. These students are on the verge of forming social stereotypes that may last a
lifetime. Separating the content of the academic curriculum from
these concerns of middle school youth is unwise, even
miseducative. Animating science by learning it in social contexts,
where questions of right and wrong are real—however intractable—
is essential.

The dragon in our story is the greedy land developer who,
assisted by many tons of earthy fill, converted a small but vibrant
freshwater wetland community into a solid foundation for constructing human habitation. Economic expediency had perturbed—
in fact, obliterated—the integrity of a biotic community whose value
to the larger community was expressed through the force of legal
protection, albeit too late. Fortunately, restoration of its beauty and
stability was possible in another location (tidal and estuarine wetlands are not as easily resuscitated).

Typically, such a story of villains and heroes unfolds in county
courthouses, city council work, and planning offices, not school
classrooms. But these meetings are quite often public ones open to
all interested citizens (such as school people). And so, using the
method of reading newspapers and keeping ears open, it came to
the attention of a school in Clatsop County, Oregon that local government officials were looking for a "mitigation site"—a place to
dig a hole, fill it with water, and let an area succeed ecologically to
the stage of a wetland of size, beauty, integrity, and stability equal
to what development had destroyed elsewhere. The bill, of course,
was to be paid according to legal mandates.

What better place to dig a very large pit and fill it with water
than behind a school? What better schoolyard project in ecological succession or "disturbance ecology" than monitoring succession from bare mud to cattail jungle? So the school worked out a
proposal that the local government accepted, and the class wrestled
for a short time with the issue of whether wetlands habitat had a
right to displace the flora and fauna already adjacent to their building. They found in favor of wetlands, the scent of adventure being
stronger than any desire to stay with the status quo.

Soon the bulldozer arrived. The natural water table and local
drainage pattern had to be studied beforehand, of course, to determine exactly where and what kind of excavation would be required
to create a sustainable wetland. The hole having been dug, it be-

gan to fill.

The students invited botanists to school as consultants. They needed to learn which seeds to sow and in what proportions. Students learned to discriminate among sedge and rush seeds and the sensitivity of different species to the degree of submergence they could tolerate. Picture five students huddled over a lab table carefully sorting miniscule seeds by species type, preparing packets for the time of planting, zone by zone, from open water to upper shore level.

They started to watch the bare earth for signs of the new shoots, keeping track of what insects and birds appeared first on the scene of their disturbance. They made inventories and monitored species change and abundance. Cattails grew tall. Sanderlings stopped by. A net and funnel trap over a cylinder sunk into the muck in the center of the pond captured thousands of newborn insects in just days. After scaling these findings to the surface area of the entire pond, expressions of astonishment occupied their faces. Bugs were hatching out, literally, by the barrel. The students kept careful photographic records of the site as well as numerical data—a seasonal census of plants and animals—to serve as baseline information in future years. From the outset, they planned a project with the interests of the next generation of students in mind.

Each year, the students add to their data to use in evaluating the effects of abnormally high rainfall or prolonged drought against long-term trends of succession. They have an endless host of new "neighbors" to meet. They can watch expectantly for the day that a rare migratory songbird stops to feed. And, year by year, the school can gather data for land-use planners on just how effective such mitigation projects are in terms of the health, diversity, and abundance of local fauna and flora. Most importantly, mucking about in hip-waders, net in hand, stalking dragonfly nymphs, is genuine adventure.

In many parts of the country, economic serendipity has equipped school sites with optimum conditions for wetland laboratories. Fortunately, hiring a bulldozer to get one going may be necessary only in extreme cases. Outside of densely populated urban areas, many schools are adjacent to restorable or investigable natural areas. We have invited students to trek through thicket and swamp, forest and field, tidal marsh and ravine ridge, in dozens of districts, with ecological explanation and resource conservation ever in mind. They have learned to use instruments as simple as string and as complex as underwater video to amplify their senses. Often, the most appreciated tool is a camera equipped with a macrolens, for a modestly magnified world in stunning close-up never fails to invite students on an adventure. No dragon has ever appeared more fierce than a dragonfly nymph or a tiger beetle larva encountered face-to-face.

Counting Dead Birds

One of our favorite anecdotes about science, community, and environmental monitoring is the tale of collecting dead Common Murres along the northern coast of Oregon. They nest (living ones, that is) off Chapman Point in dense colonies of hundreds of thousands of birds. Not all survive, and mortality is highest among the young.

The project started as an outgrowth of an interpretive program at Haystack Rock. There, during peak tourism weekends, teachers and their students have organized a program to educate the public about the natural history of the intertidal zone. Puffins nest atop Haystack; mussels cling in dense colonies to its base.

Each spring, the Seaside schools sponsor "Sea Week." Every grade level has a way to participate. Middle schoolers visit the estuary of the Necanicum River, slopping through mudflats with screens and shovels. High school biology students are there to help them interpret their findings. What at first glance looks like an expanse of lifeless mud and monotonous gray color, becomes, after a bit of straining, an entire universe of bizarre creatures tunneling beneath the goo.

From the muck they move to the marsh and begin to make measurements of slope and elevation above the mudflat. They discover the very sharp zonation produced by different tolerance ranges of sedges and grasses to living where brackish water rises and falls with the tide.

Students of many ages find ways of participating in the Haystack Rock interpretation program or other coastal habitat conservation efforts after Sea Week is over. One year a group of Biology Club students from the high school bid on a federal request for proposals. They received funding to conduct a census of the Snowy Plover. It nests in coastal dunes but is threatened by invasive species of grass, pet predators, and beach buggies. Working with a conservation biologist hired by the Biology Club, students found themselves featured on the evening news in Portland, Oregon. Their work was genuine, appreciated by professional scientists, and saddening. The Plovers were there, but in tragically low numbers.

One strategy for finding out what is going wrong in the environment is to compare suspected changes with past records of "normalcy." Of course, to make these comparisons and watch for perturbations, baseline data is a prerequisite. Gathering lots of observations about how ecosystems function when there is no problem is exactly the kind of information few public agencies have the funds to secure. Yet gathering this information helps students form very appropriate concepts in science.

Consider for a moment Tom Sawyer at work whitewashing his fence in Hannibal, Missouri. It's a long fence and he needs help. To each passerby, he speaks about the joy of this work. As help joins in, others wish to join.

The beach in Oregon is a long fence whose whitewashing can take an unusual form. For several years, Seaside, Oregon, students and teachers have conducted regular censuses of dead Common Murres on the beaches from Gearheart north to the Columbia River jetty. Picture a pick-up truck driving along the beach. The driver sights a bird. Out hop a couple of adolescents. They look at the bird. "It's a Murre!" They tag it (date and place) and throw it into the truck bed.

Every few yards this scene is repeated. Before long, curious tourists, busy at beachcombing, ask what's going on. "Want to help?" is the reply. Some join the patrol, scanning the high-tide line for dead birds. They are doing "Tom Sawyer science."

"Tom Sawyer science" does not mean cleaning the beach. These carcasses belong there. Removing them is a disturbance of natural material cycling. What is the justification? Where's the science? The answer: baseline data. Counting dead Murres and comparing adult versus juvenile mortality at regular intervals is an indirect way to monitor the conditions of the sea.

In the summer of 1991, a modest oil spill occurred in Puget Sound. Currents carried the spill to sea as well as onto Washington beaches. What Oregonians began to wonder was, would remainders of the Puget Sound plume reach the northern Oregon coast? Who would sound the alarm? Inferring from the dead bird count that this particular oil spill had arrived in Oregon's waters was not simple. Oily Murres are always present among the deceased and the total number of dead birds fluctuates greatly without oil spill perturbations. And this spill was not moving in with massive levels of destruction.

Watching for more dead oily birds would not do. And certainly fish and wildlife professionals—not to mention the U.S. Coast Guard—have better ways of finding and tracking oil slicks at sea than spending hours picking over avian carcasses. But by applying more than a little bit of mathematical sophistication and some genuine ecological savvy in the interpretation of dead bird data, Seaside school-folk were the first to find evidence of the effects of the Puget Sound spill off of Oregon's northern coast. What they compared was the present ratio of adult-to-juvenile mortality with the past average. Under normal circumstances, juvenile deaths greatly outnumber adult deaths. What they found was a "spike" in adult deaths. Hence, the ratio changed—adults were perishing in comparison to juveniles in suddenly and substantially increased proportions. That evening, using the dead bird data from "amateurs," local news programs alerted the community, yet professional scientists challenged the report's credibility. However, the "amateur" school-folk were right—oil from Puget

Sound had arrived.

Damage from this spill to Oregon's rookeries and beaches was not significant. More importantly, the credibility of school science research was greatly enhanced, both in the minds of the public and the students in the system. They had answered Aldo Leopold's call of nearly a half century ago to put into practice the great range of what is possible for "amateurs" in science. They had shown how to break the "professional monopoly on research,"[7] a monopoly more the product of schooling myths than machinations of fish and wildlife biologists. Lamented Leopold, "To the amateur are allotted only make-believe voyages of discovery, to verify what professional authority already knows. What the youth needs to be told is that a ship is a-building in his own mental dry dock, a ship with freedom of the seas."[8]

Advice to Science Adventure Guides

Make-believe voyages will not suffice as science adventures. For the voyage of discovery to succeed, youthful minds must depart dry dock and set sail. We have distilled our experiences into nine points of departure for those who wish to heed Leopold's call:

1. *Begin with the notion of "science as problem solving."* This notion requires identifying problems to solve. Defining the problem is the first—and educationally sound—step to take. In defining (and finding) a problem, teachers and students interact with the community beyond school. The degree to which students can be engaged in this step is a function of experience and resources. Never omit students entirely, nor conclude that students must only work on problems and curriculum entirely of their own choosing. However, no one should go on an adventure without first giving consent, and student participation in selecting and defining problems is a means of securing consent.

    Keep in mind that nothing is more important for middle school students to appreciate about science than its role as a way of solving problems. The progressive, cumulative nature of science—and hence its value to society—is based upon problem (and, often, "puzzle") solving. Problems, puzzles, and challenges fix the goal for learning. Without the context of a goal, learning quickly becomes burdensome and rote, no matter how creative and comprehensive the coverage. When students learn science as a way to try to solve problems, they learn that the answers cannot be looked up. Something must be done to find answers. This something is science.

2. *Embed mathematical reasoning in the problem.* Within the context of an inquiry, teach students how mathematical tools make sense of data. Ratio and proportional thinking, derivation of a function, symbolic deduction, probabilistic reasoning, charting or graphing, and geometric representation come to mind as domains science repeatedly calls upon. Students in science class need to understand the reasonableness of a technique and often try to invent a reasonable procedure, for keeping track of thinking when number, chance, logic and space are critical. Recall that interpreting the spike in the tally of dead Common Murres required substantial application of mathematical reasoning.

    Mathematics is a barrier for far too many children. How many of us appreciate mathematics as a tool for helping us to think more easily and clearly about problems? Math helps us to keep track of events or objects and their relations in a logical way while we work through complexities of reasoning that would otherwise defeat us. Uncommonly, school math asks students to invent mathematical representations— models and equations—of problem situations. Perhaps as much or more than any other subject, mathematics suffers from isolation. Science, however, provides an ideal context for integrating mathematical problem solving with content. No one will be able to think their way out of difficulty on the adventure without help from mathematics.

3. *"Simulate" to prepare.* In order to prepare for the complexities of investigating real phenomena, simulation is useful. Simulations not only amplify patterns and regularities in phenomena of interest, they provide structure for teaching specific skills. Simulation is a good start on the path toward context. Simulations can take the form of board games, role playing, or dramatization. They point to the kinds of understandings that will be useful on the adventure.

4. *Include community good as an outcome.* Schools are for kids, all would agree. More particularly, they are to help kids prepare for (and be prepared for) their future. But schools can do more: they can lead to good outcomes for the community now. In doing so, they transform the nature of school experience in very positive ways for the middle school learner. School

work becomes important work for immediate reasons and success means immediate feedback of value
to the learner. Working on a project with tangible
results for some audience beyond the classroom less-
ens the burden on selling students that they need to
learn things now because they will need them later.
Middle schoolers seems less than convinced of this
principle; hence, teachers impose various point systems to make reinforcement immediate. Community
good is a subtle goal often requiring cooperation and
collaboration throughout a school or district.

5. *Help younger children learn.* In meeting the needs
of the preadolescent, consider the importance of the
roles they can serve and the functions they can perform that benefit younger children. A distinct disadvantage of middle school structure is the isolation of
preadolescent youth from younger children. Seeking an outcome of "community good" often dove-
tails with the goal of helping younger children learn.

6. *Provide time for planning.* In solving problems, there
needs to be time to plan. This need is as true for the
teacher as for the students. One escape for the teacher
from the dilemma of integrating instruction but lacking time for planning is to collaborate with the students on planning. This collaboration begins with
defining the problem. It continues with designing the
investigations or project design. It concludes with
presenting findings to some audience, younger children or a government agency, for example. All of
these stages—defining, investigating, proposing solutions, acting to solve, communicating results—involve planning. Time for planning may be the key
change in how students and teachers spend time when
an integrated, problem-centered style of teaching and
learning predominates.

7. *Use diverse assessments.* Try to temper the momentum in school learning to have all students learn the
same things to similar levels of proficiency. Students
challenged equally may learn very different things
to very different levels of proficiency. Aptitudes in
engineering (or "shop work"), video-editing, artistic
display, expressive communication, artistic representation, social leadership, mathematical construction,
verbal persuasion differ widely. Opportunity to learn
meaningfully—and be assessed validly—honors this
diversity. Assessment can be used to validate and
communicate the diversity of outcomes in solving

problems rather than focus learning on a narrow set of objectives for all.

8. *Include planned social experiences.* Attention to the whole learner means planning for social interaction and development as a matter of course in a science course. An evening rocket launch by the full moon, with ample parents in attendance, can be a social as well as a culminating experience. Perhaps there can be a mock space shuttle launch in school with everyone involved. Student-planned health fairs, mural painting in a public location, or a community science festival can bring students and learning together and mark closure to an adventure in an atmosphere of celebration.

9. *Design and make things.* By middle school age, children can "make things" with remarkable success. Much important learning is still tied to manipulative creations—to pragmatic, utilitarian constructions. They are becoming, capable engineers with the capacity to design and produce video documents, computer programs, model rockets, bird-feeding stations, nutritious menus, solar-powered vehicle prototypes, and so forth. Many respond to "technical education challenges"—design a switch to light a sign when someone stands in front of a window, for example. Too often, schools overemphasize print media and abstract, verbal learning. Much in the way of good thinking skills develops best in the context of pragmatic, engineered solutions to specific problems and challenges. Clearly, attention to the "whole child" means providing ways to capitalize on middle schoolers' capacities to make things.

Who Will Speak for the Adventure?

Our narrative began with literary references intended to evoke the imagery of a metaphor for middle school science: adventure. Each example of investigation has illustrated the relevance of one or more of the features of this metaphor to a conception of science. Students who invited the bulldozers into their backyard had ventured into the world of authentic problems and civic conflict, a less-than-perfect world in need of idealistic resources. The Rocky Mountain thunderstorm set the stage for improvisation and students designed procedures for investigating aquatic life. The Connecticut sky replaced text drawings as children tried to interpret the sky using a model of motion obscured by the scale of everyday events. Throughout these examples, out-of-the-ordinary experiences were the rule. The dead bird story completed the adventure metaphor by yielding a model of science teaching framed by students in roles of responsible citizens practicing "amateur" science for the good of the community. They had the preparation and knowledge to monitor their own surroundings with tools of science, and the pluck of Tom Sawyer to draw others to the task.

Through our examples and quotations from Aldo Leopold, we have argued implicitly that the science most appropriate for everyone is ecology. Ecology is the right tool, but is, after all, only science, lacking within itself what to do with its understandings. For ecological insight to matter, students must not fall victim to "learning to see one thing by going blind to another"[9] —must not learn concepts of ecology without human context. A closing reference to a children's story aptly makes this point.

In Dr. Seuss's moral fable of the "Lorax,"[10] who spoke for the trees, the unscrupulous "Once-ler," destroyer of the Truffula tree forest and manufacturer of "thneeds, which everyone needs," pondered a pile of rocks. The Lorax had left this pile of rocks "here in this mess . . . with only one word, UNLESS." After recounting the history of the Truffula forest, its demise and the departure of the Barbaloots, Humming-Fish, and Swomee-Swans, the Once-ler realized the meaning of the Lorax's last words:

> UNLESS someone like you
> cares a whole awful lot,
> nothing is going to get better
> It's not.

Then the Once-ler entrusted to the young man "a Truffula Seed . . . the last one of all!" He placed the boy in charge of bringing back the forest. Ecology teaches that it takes more than a seed to grow a forest, but also that now a "forest" is what everyone needs (to paraphrase Seuss). We call upon the science teaching community to carry out "Lorax Projects" in schoolyards across the country, entrusting students with the responsibility to work to enhance life in their own communities. Better to plant a sweet viburnum berry bush for winter forage than to teach a student by rote the names of birds that migrate. Those who do the former, will no doubt learn the latter, while remaining anxious to embark again in pursuit of science adventure. They can always refresh their appreciation of the natural world by taking time to absorb the aesthetic beauty of viburnums and birds. With reason to care, they might commit themselves to the "integrity, stability, and beauty of the biotic community"[11] which is their home.

End Notes

1. Barry Lopez, *The Rediscovery of North America* (Lexington, KY: University Press of Kentucky, 1990). This work is also available as a reprint in the *Orion Nature Quarterly*, Summer 1992, pp. 10–16.
2. Oregon Department of Land Conservation and Development/ Commission, *Oregon's Statewide Planning Goals* (Salem, OR: Department of Land Conservation and Development, 1990).
3. See, for example, Steven Andrews, *Student Watershed Research Project (SWRP)*, Unpublished proposal to the National Science Foundation (Beaverton, OR: Saturday Academy, Oregon Graduate Institute, 1991).
4. David Pepi, *Thoreau's Method: A Handbook for Nature Study* (Englewood Cliffs, NJ: Prentice-Hall, 1985).
5. Aldo Leopold, *A Sand County Almanac and Sketches of Here and There*, Charles W. Schwartz, illustrator (New York: Oxford University Press, 1949).
6. Leopold, 187.
7. Leopold, 185.
8. Leopold, 185–186.
9. Leopold, 158.
10. Theodore S. Geisel and Audrey S. Geisel, *The Lorax by Dr. Seuss* (New York: Random House, 1971).
11. Leopold, 225.

CONCLUSION

Chapter 15

Taking the Leap:
An Analysis of the Joys and Strains

Kenneth L. Bergstrom and Glennellen Pace

The Decision to Move Toward Holistic Teaching and Learning

Why do the teachers who share their stories in this book embrace the risks inherent in this kind of teaching? What is it that motivates them to change and to grow? What are the obstacles that they identify and work to overcome in their quest to find a better way? Is this a path that all teachers should pursue?

Any call to transformational, or constructivist, teaching and learning requires an honest examination of the motivators and inhibitors—in the cases presented here, the joys and strains—a kind of personal and professional force-field analysis. Few publications have clearly addressed this analysis. Susan Drake explores reasons teachers initiate curriculum integration in her monograph, *Planning Integrated Curriculum: The Call to Adventure.*[1] Stevenson and Carr also address the issue of teacher willingness to change in their book, *Integrated Studies in the Middle Grades: Dancing Through Walls.*[2] If teaching is to change from isolated classroom successes to a more sweeping professional metamorphosis of schooling, then we must encourage all teachers to address their own concerns and the issues raised by others about this kind of teaching and learning. Weighing the strains and joys must be pursued by individuals alone, and in the company of colleagues and members of the greater learning community. It is through these collegial exchanges that a wider transformation will occur.

In this chapter we analyze data from numerous conversations with teachers—including those who have contributed to this book—in an effort to delineate the motivators and inhibitors to integrated study, the joys and strains of whole learning. Some teachers, strongly driven by a need to find a better way to reach more children, seldom consider the inhibiting factors until they come

face to face with them. Their will to succeed is enough to overcome the apparent obstacles. Others carefully consider and plan
how to deal with constraints to this kind of teaching. Still others
focus on the obstacles and feel unwilling to weigh the benefits
until someone else addresses the obvious problems.

This uneven distribution of willingness and readiness to innovate in schools is normal. Everett Rogers[3] found five distinct
groups among teachers who were considering the adoption of any
innovation like whole learning: *Innovators*, comprising 8 percent
of the population, are eager to try new ideas, willing to take risks,
and open to change; *Leaders*, about 17 percent, are also open to
change, but are more trusted by colleagues and thus better integrated into the culture of the school; *Early Majority* is that 29 percent who follow these other groups in a cautious, yet deliberate
path toward change; *Late Majority*, another 29 percent, is a group
set in their ways, but who will respond to collegial pressure; and
Resisters are those (17 percent) who are opposed to new ideas, yet
not highly influential with colleagues because of their relative isolation from mainstream ideas. Others have found similar distribu-
tions among teachers facing change. Powell also describes five
categories of response to innovation: *Innovators* and *Adopters*
welcome change, *Susceptibles* express feelings of dissonance and
resentment toward current practices, *Nonsusceptibles* believe no
change is needed, and *Resisters* sabotage efforts to change.[4] Hall
and Hord in their book *Change in Schools: Facilitating the Process* take a dynamic view.[5] They suggest that change in individuals is related to six stages of concern about, and levels of use of, an
innovation, from little concern toward increasing involvement, and
from nonuse through increasingly complex and sophisticated use.

It is significant that Rogers looked at people's readiness to
change within the context of their collegial influence. Glennellen
Pace found this had a powerful effect on teacher-initiated innovation.[6] Throughout this book, we have heard about issues around
collegial connections. In the next section of this chapter, we will
consider examples of this factor from these stories.

In many cases, among teachers we have talked with over the
years, we hear about colleagues who drag their feet because of the
problems they see with moving toward transformational teaching.
It would be unwise to ignore entirely the complaints of these colleagues who cannot see beyond the obstacles. While some of us
may not consider them good enough reasons for not changing our
ways of teaching, we cannot deny that they are valid concerns and
deserve to be acknowledged.

At the same time, the convictions of those who do dare to
innovate need to be heard by everyone. Most often, it is these voices
that recapture the essence of the call to teach. This can reinvigo-
rate the purpose of the profession and move us toward a fuller

realization of success for all children.

Ultimately, however, each individual educator makes a choice. Taking the leap into the experience of whole learning can be simultaneously scary and thrilling. In a safe, respectful, encouraging environment, teachers feel assured of support even in the face of failure. In an isolated, suspicious environment, risks are harder to take. Yet, even in these latter situations, sometimes because of them, teachers are stretching themselves and taking a leap into a new way of learning.

Strains: The Inhibiting Factors of Whole Learning

What would prevent someone from attempting to teach in an integrated way? From a series of inquiries over the last few years, we have collected many responses from hundreds of middle school educators. Some have been long-time advocates and practitioners of whole learning; others were only considering the territory and weighing the benefits and pitfalls. Interestingly, advocates and opponents articulate similar issues. This creates a common ground for further discussion. The following deterrents are mentioned most often.

Lack of Support

Community and Administration

Lack of support and cooperation for a non-traditional undertaking is a great deterrent for many teachers. In an age when the word *accountability* is heard at every turn, many feel the critical gaze from the watchful eyes of the community. Educators may *assume* that the community will not back this kind of learning, and hesitate to seek support. Administrators, not wishing to risk the questioning glare of the community, may create obstacles to whole learning. These leaders may not support risk-taking behavior, or may impose restrictions on teachers who wish to innovate.

It is significant that one entire section of this book addresses the importance of *having* administrative support; and we see the implication, at least, of administrator support in the stories throughout the book. For example, Charles Ault and Anne McEnerny-Ogle show us how Anne, in her effort to create a math lab, encountered difficulties with administration (as well as other colleagues, and parents). On the positive side, Connie Russell's story of change couldn't have happened without agreements with building principals and central office administration in a district with fairly heavy curriculum mandates. And Sally Wells asserts strongly that her journey from a self-contained whole learning classroom to a multi-age team organization depended upon the blessing of the central administration, and the very concrete efforts of her principal to provide visits to other schools, and time for planning.

Students

Some teachers tell us students themselves are unsupportive of new approaches. Often students reach the middle grades feeling disillusioned and unmotivated. Disinterested in school in general, these students may resist a teacher's authentic attempt to reinstill meaning and fun into the curriculum. Stories from Mary Burke-Hengen, Lynn Moss, and Patricia Tefft Cousin and Ellen Aragon show us examples of this phenomenon and how they successfully reached this kind of student.

Colleagues

Often cited by teachers as the most powerful source of non-support is fellow teachers—colleagues. The suspicions of the teacher next door or down the hall can make teachers think twice about whether to risk teaching an integrated unit of study. Critical innuendo from other teachers creates tremendous strain on experimenting with one's teaching. Whether it is the isolated context of schools, which can breed jealousies, or the striving of teachers to belong to more than a quasi-profession, teachers have been slow to support one another's professional risk taking. However, when teachers *have* collegial support, the quality of teaching and learning can improve dramatically. None of the contributors to this book were actively shunned by colleagues, as is the case for innovators in many schools. But they did experience different kinds of colleague support, with differing results.

- Tim Gillespie found his twice-a-week lunchtime chats with colleague Mary Burke-Hengen invaluable as he struggled to turn whole learning theory into practice.
- Scott Christian, after two years of trying to lead innovative efforts at his school, moved on to a school where the faculty were more committed to becoming a "true" middle school.
- Shirlee Jellum's innovations in language arts went far beyond what they otherwise could have once she began working with a colleague who taught history. Now at the high school, she appreciates the importance of a supportive administration, but finds herself still without a colleague who shares her interests.
- Connie Russell's story is, first and foremost, a story of collegial collaboration. It also shows us how teachers who are

willing to work together for change can, at the same time, be sensitive to the threat they may pose to other teachers. In this story, we see teachers staying on good terms with their more traditional colleagues, inviting them to join in, but allowing others to change in their own time.

- Sally Wells' innovations within her self-contained classroom, appreciated by her administrator and colleagues, led to an innovative mixed-age team organization.
- Lynn Moss and her colleague had to abandon their teaching partnership. "We realized that we were hearing very different music; we couldn't get our rhythms to synchronize." So they closed the doors between their rooms, and went back to teaching alone.

Some collegial support difficulties have to do, as in Lynn's case, with "hearing very different music"; others, such as Shirlee's case now that she is at the high school, with entrenched notions of "territory" (departmental boundaries). But the flip side, the power of successful collaborative ventures, is clear, too, in stories such as Sally's. If we are to become a profession with a strong ethos, we must stop feeling suspicious of and second guessing our colleagues and learn to support the risk-taking of one and all.

We believe educators today must refuse to buy into accusations that schools are to blame for everything from increased drug abuse to economic non-competitiveness. Feeling "under the gun" inhibits reflective innovation in one's profession; it can sap the desire to find a better way. Educators need to encourage, celebrate, and showcase exciting examples of learning and teaching, like those shared here. Whether we all agree about the benefits of whole learning, it is important to encourage the risks of those who seek better ways, to discuss our reservations with them, and to come together as professionals willing to learn from one another.

Lack of Planning Time

Another big obstacle to teaching in an integrated way is the perceived lack of planning time. Learning to teach in a new way requires extra time to plan creatively and collaboratively around a particular venture. Whole learning requires a more dynamic kind of planning than does a conventional unit of study. For every successful unit, teachers plan parameters that provide the security to be open to a range of specific possibilities. But an important key to whole learning is the imagining of different scenarios. Too much up-front planning can inhibit the flexibility required by the twists and turns that integrated studies take. Thus, subsequent, ongoing preparation distinguishes planning for whole learning from planning for traditional teaching. Teachers who focus on students' needs around a learning adventure know that what actually happens in the classroom never matches a preconceived plan. An inquiry takes on a life of its own, and that means ongoing planning, in the middle of class as well as before and after.

For the teacher, this requires a constantly expanding knowledge of resources: people, places, and materials—a special challenge for whole learning teachers working alone. Working with a partner or a member of a team greatly enhances the expansion of knowledge and resources, but requires more time for planning together. A lack of team planning time is a serious drawback, as Suzan Mauney shows us. Sally Wells also addresses this issue very clearly, giving us a glimpse of the ways her team solved the collaborative planning problem.

We recognize, however, that adjusting to the needs of whole learning requires more than additional planning time. Teachers need to practice a different kind of planning; they need to learn to think differently about planning. Spending time planning and sharing together as a team helps But other ways to learn to think differently include visiting other schools—as Sally's team did—or becoming involved in a university project—as Suzan did. As teachers develop a wider range of resources, enabling them to support varying student interests and to be "quick on their feet," and as they share the ongoing planning tasks with others (such as students, colleagues, and community members), teachers move toward the kind of planning required for whole learning classrooms.

Too Difficult

For many, transformational teaching is simply too hard. Its demands are significant: identifying a theme, learning new teaching techniques, negotiating with students, documenting learning in new ways, and relating well to the greater learning community. If teachers are to take on extra load, they need to be convinced of the additional benefits of this approach. It requires much more work to organize learning when students are producing knowledge than when they are simply consuming it in the form of prepackaged materials and textbooks. Teachers ask: Why take on the aggravation of extra planning and after-school work contacting resources? Why expend more effort when much of what I already do goes unrewarded? Why work this hard at a job that is underappreciated?

This internal personal obstacle is perhaps one of the toughest to address. It is refreshing to see it honestly brought into conversations, albeit most often by those teachers who are already taking the leap and anxiously awaiting their colleagues to join them. For those who still look at teaching as a job rather than a profession, whole learning—where the boundaries are unclear—is a threat to their attempt to do the job and head for the peace and quiet of home. They are unwilling to extend themselves beyond their perceived limits.

The shared stories of teachers who have made the leap may be the best way to answer the questions about difficulty. As Sally told us, teachers at Emily Dickinson Elementary School told her team that integrative teaching required more work than anything they had ever done before; but it also produced more rewards.

Lack of Resources

Many teachers seem to be on the brink of this new kind of teaching, but cannot find the resources to make it happen. Time, discussed above, appears to be the most significant resource, but teachers perceive that whole learning requires a number of other commodities as well. Money would, no doubt, solve most of these problems. Teachers cite the need to finance field trips, to bring in outside resources, and to purchase supplementary materials. Teachers readily admit that they could raise the money to buy the resources, if they indeed had the time, or if it weren't too difficult. One can see the circular, dead-end reasoning that can result from a discussion of inhibitors.

One of the greatest overlooked financial resources in schools is the budget line item of textbooks. Imagine what $25 or $30 per student could buy for resources in an integrated inquiry. Think how students could use that kind of money to produce a presentable documentation of their learning for the community. How much longer will we allow textbooks, unconnected as they are to the needs and interests of any particular group of students, to dictate the content of our classrooms? It is time for teachers to learn to manage the budgeting process of schools in such a way that they can use funds to support the way they intend to teach. Shirlee Jellum, Connie Russell, Sally Wells, and Lynn Moss all show us ways in which they used funds to purchase materials appropriate for their use.

Whole learning teachers find other ways to work around the resource problem. Consider, for example, Lynn Moss's Saturday field trips. These proved to be a wonderful way to get around the lack of field trip budgets, and to enlist the involvement—and consequent support—of parents at the same time.

Inflexible Scheduling

When asked, teachers always list scheduling problems, expressed as time as well as space concerns, as an inhibitor to whole learning. Blocks of time are not always available for extended classes (as we saw in Connie Russell's story). Integrated study requires some in-depth work by students, and a 45-minute period is a distinct deterrent to that kind of in-depth work. Other teachers are not always willing to release students for extended periods. Arranging special field trips becomes a headache, which also causes resentments among colleagues. Besides, a place to work for more than one period is often unavailable. Teachers mention the lack of adequate space in which to create an ongoing project. Sharing rooms during different parts of the day is a problem for many teachers.

Fortunately, many schools are now making the move to block scheduling, which is more accommodating to whole learning initiatives. In a number of cases, this only allows some teachers to lecture their students for twice as long. But for teachers of this more active approach, it has been a blessing. They can proceed with integrated learning without stepping on the toes of colleagues. They are also making temporary arrangements to use alternate spaces and to negotiate special arrangements with colleagues so that they can have students for longer blocks of time.

Predominant Curriculum

Some teachers mention the pre-determined, pre-established curriculum as a reason not to consider whole learning. If there is already a formal scope and sequence to follow, they argue, there will not be enough time to pursue something above and beyond that. Whole learning would be another addition to the already crowded school year. When would one find time to complete the required curriculum? Besides, students take standardized tests that measure the standardized curriculum. Therefore, they must teach to that formal curriculum.

Several contributors to this volume address this issue. For example, Tim Gillespie takes time away from writing workshop activities to "prepare" students for state writing assessment tests. He concludes this was a waste of time, believing students would have done as well with writing workshop alone. Pat Tefft Cousin and Ellen Aragon, on the other hand, believe that test preparation activities that are included along with other aspects of writing workshop assisted their students. Connie Russell and the teachers she worked with looked at ways in which workshops could replace the formal curriculum, and also made the decision to keep part of the district curriculum. Sally Wells' team started with the district curriculum, gleaning from it some general topics and guidelines that could be addressed in more student-centered ways, and looking, too, at how to include student-generated topics and respond to student interests. Lynn Moss notes the importance of "freeing" oneself from narrow interpretations of curriculum mandates.

To see holistic teaching and learning as the antithesis of teaching content and skills is misguided. Both chapters by Charles Ault and his coauthors present especially strong portraits of cognitive development in holistic learning environments. Advocates have never argued that whole learning is devoid of skill and content learning. As James Beane[7] points out, the difference in whole learning is that knowledge and skills are usually repositioned around student interest or transposed to answer kids' questions. Content and skill are present in a more meaningful way. Whole learning makes the scope and sequence charts come alive. Teachers cannot rely on the formal curriculum guides to organize learning, because the interests of children have not yet been heard. They *can* use the guides to help students document their progress.

In some states, it is true that curriculum dictates preclude engaging in very much experimentation. However, in most cases, it is also true that it was teachers, sitting on those curriculum committees, who originally determined the scope and sequence. What is preventing the emerging breed of teacher from volunteering for a committee to revise the curriculum process? They can lead the charge against standardized curricula and standardized tests. They can help put into place assessment procedures that document not only content and skill knowledge, but also the resourcefulness, creativity, cooperation, initiative and social responsibility learned by students in the whole learning classroom.

Too Risky

Another internal deterrent mentioned by many teachers is that constructivist teaching is just too full of unknowns—it is too frightening. The fear of failure, concern about one's abilities, ostracism by colleagues, and possible pressures from parents and the community prevent many from taking the risk inherent in whole learning. Fear can paralyze. Pressure to change without adequate support and understanding can be overwhelming.

To change not only means trying something new, which in itself can make the palms sweat, it also requires letting go of the familiar, which can create internal havoc. As Mary Burke-Hengen reminds us, each teacher must take on the new and let go of the old, in ways consistent with his or her own style. Some are able to handle sweeping changes in short periods of time; others, as Mary tells us, "work in an organic style . . . need to evolve as we understand, as we are ready to see value in new directions."

It is important for those of us who enjoy the thrill of new learning to be sensitive to the enormity of the barriers perceived by others, even while we invite and encourage them to take the risk. We cannot change other teachers, but we can modulate the professional ambience to applaud innovations that improve the quality of education. Most teachers change their belief systems when they see that it makes a difference in the lives of their students.

Need to Re-address Evaluation

A growing number of teachers recognize that transformational teaching does not lend itself well to the traditional teach-and-test techniques; that it calls for a new way to think about assessment. The need to learn new documentation, assessment, and evaluation strategies worries many practitioners. Tests that come with the book become useless when the book is no longer integral to the study at hand. Holistic learning requires teachers to decide what the learning outcomes are at all phases of the venture: before, during, and after. How does one plan to assess an outcome that only became evident at the end of the inquiry? Teachers who are unwilling or unable to craft and recraft goals and objectives while the study proceeds become disillusioned because the learning is not measured in a standardized way.

Fortunately, the topic of assessment is finally getting the attention it deserves in educational reform. The results of ongoing research and networking will offer teachers new ways to consider student learning. Teachers attuned to students' learning processes are not at a loss in whole learning situations. They know how to design assessments that are integral to the learning activities themselves. They have students recording and discussing their learning daily, applying the skills they are acquiring in necessary tasks, creating artifacts to share with the community, and planning exhibitions to teach others.

Classroom Control Issues

Some teachers note that teaching in an integrated way might create some control problems. Because whole learning can often take on a life of its own, planning is ongoing and changing. It means that students need to assume some of the responsibility for the ongoing tasks. Teachers can't and ought not do it all. This necessarily means letting go of some of the control that teachers traditionally have held. It requires a shift of perspective to see that increased student accountability can be a benefit of this kind of learning. An unwillingness to reconsider the power arrangements in traditional classrooms holds many teachers back from exploring better ways to teach. Everyone loses when teachers regard students as developmentally inferior—as younger and less experienced—rather than as people with different perspectives, and different kinds of expertise, who are valuable and significant contributors to the learning community.

But the issue of classroom control goes beyond questions of content and process. The dynamics in a constructivist environment are, indeed, very different from those in a traditional classroom setting. Remember Lynn's student asking, "Whatcha 'sposed to do if you're not gonna sign this thing?" at the end of a full week of work on a classroom constitution. Offering students a chance to practice democracy rather than to simply hear it touted, requires a teacher who can respond to the unexpected and guide the course of a study, not totally dictate it. To succeed, teachers must see students as the capable individuals they are, and trust that with support and challenge they can come to love and feel successful about their learning. Teachers must invite students to become partners in their own learning, ready to experience the adventures yet to unfold.

Joys: The Motivating Factors of Whole Learning

The teachers who have told their stories in this book have overcome many of the obstacles. Some have had a supportive environment, with fewer constraints, in which to work; others have found creative ways to deal with constraints. What is it that has motivated them so strongly that they have dared to deal successfully with these challenges? Why is it important for them to learn to teach in a way that they were not taught? What is it that supports their sense of confidence and fuels their risk-taking? The following list of joys elaborates the forces behind whole learning.

To Ensure Developmental Appropriateness

An integrated approach offers more opportunities for richer kinds of learning. Because it is learner-centered, it is more natural, interesting, and developmentally appropriate. As Scott Christian tells us, "I was aware that our overall instructional model was not appropriate for our students. I envisioned instead a dynamic, student-centered language arts program . . . "

Whole learning can accommodate a variety of students' needs, learning styles, and intelligences. Everyone does not need to be on the same page at the same time. Having students study different aspects of a topic at the same time has advantages. More students become involved at their own level with more chances for successful growth. And students become teachers of one another.

Teachers who study early adolescence know that active, hands-on, creative learning activities help students build abstract concepts. Learning is more sound and is retained longer if it is applied in a meaningful way to real problems in kids' lives. Whole learning promotes real problem solving and critical thinking about issues students believe are worth exploring.

Many teachers of young adolescents *choose* to teach this age group. They like the energy and excitement of this critical developmental transition. They have a deep empathy for their students, often because they clearly recall their own developmental successes and struggles when they were this age. Because they often identify with these students, teachers sometimes rage against the powerlessness our culture inflicts upon youngsters. They work to liberate young adolescents from the constraints against which they struggled in their own youth.

It is indeed heartening that teachers who are learning to teach in an integrated way offer developmental appropriateness as the primary reason for their efforts. After all, it is the kids who draw us to this work in the first place. And when it is all completed, it will still be the children who are the most powerful statement of how well we have succeeded.

To Promote Collaboration

Many teachers are seeking the opportunity to learn to collaborate well. All of the contributors to Part II of this volume tell stories of attempts to work collaboratively with colleagues. And all of the contributions to Part III represent collaborative efforts between middle school and college or university educators. Working closely and creatively with others on a worthwhile project promotes growth and brings rewards. Teachers need to learn how to become colleagues. And while it is not necessary to like all of one's colleagues, we do need to learn how to work with each other collaboratively. This means sharing ideas, watching each other teach, reflecting together on our practice, and discovering that working together we can find better solutions to problems than any one of us could have created alone. Whole learning works with colleagues, too, teaching a multitude of lessons through socially constructed, collaborative experience.

Such teachers also value the chance to join with their students in creating a community of learners. While it is important for teachers to know their subject well, in a whole learning situation teachers will not always be experts on everything students seek to pursue. But students are capable of becoming experts in areas teachers may not know well. Lynn Moss, Ken Bergstrom, and Charles Ault give us especially good examples of this. The potential of students teaching their teachers can deepen the mutual respect in a classroom. It is also valuable for students to watch their teachers approach a topic about which they know little. This demonstration in the role of lead learner helps students learn how to learn, and creates a camaraderie and spirit within a class that can add much to the success of an inquiry. Whole learning in a collaborative setting intends to develop the social along with the cognitive abilities of each learner in a mutually enhancing way.

To Reflect the Real World

Many teachers are glad to discover whole learning because integrated inquiry is a reflection of the real world. Students become interested in and motivated by their own learning when it is about something real that they want to understand. Kids have numerous questions about themselves and their place in the world. Although challenging, this kind of meaningful, relevant learning involves and engages kids thoroughly and positively. They clearly see the need to learn a skill when it is critical to the next step in their learning. When they have authentic problems to solve, students exhibit a perseverance that is often lacking in contrived situations; they develop and use skills strategically in the course of their study. The stories Ken Bergstrom and his co-authors share with us paint clear portraits of the power of student-identified themes to engage these learners.

One of the most important lessons for young adolescents to learn is that they can affect the real world in a positive way. Learning about real-world issues gives students a chance to apply what they have learned, to contribute meaningfully to their classroom or larger community. The power of young adolescents making a positive contribution to their corner of the planet is transformative. Consider, for example, Charles Ault's and Neil Maine's accounts of the wetlands project, and the counting of dead Murres. These lessons in social responsibility rarely occur in classrooms centered around teacher lectures and textbooks.

Teachers who are themselves fascinated with real issues are eager to get their students involved in whole learning. They know that reconnecting schools to life beyond those walls is crucial. It is how children develop a life-long love of learning.

To Renew Self

Many teachers find that teaching in a new and different way is exciting. Teaching an open-ended inquiry is as interesting for them as it is for their students. A sense of purpose, not present in teacher-centered, teacher-controlled classrooms, can permeate a whole learning adventure. As is the case on a journey to new places, the thrill of exploring the unknown is exhilarating.

When we asked teachers what motivated them to move toward constructivist teaching, they identified the importance of disequilibrium and dissonance in their own learning. They felt their best asset as a teacher was to be a good learner. To pursue their own learning meant to stretch for new ideas in their practice, to seek worthy challenges, and to take calculated risks. We see this in the stories of every single contributor to this book. For instance, Tim Gillespie took a leave from his job as a coordinator and spent a year in the classroom to stretch for new ideas about practice. Connie Russell and four middle school teachers sought to learn more about reading and writing workshops and to put what they learned into practice in spite of a departmentalized structure and district curriculum requirements. Lynn Moss kept "pushing the boundaries," taking risks in spite of feeling at times as though she were in a "free fall" because she believed she could stretch herself and learn to better meet the cognitive and affective needs of her students. In every story this willingness to learn, to stretch, to risk comes through.

Teachers tell us they see in whole learning an opportunity to renew themselves. Teachers such as Mary Burke-Hengen affirm that the purpose of education is growth—for everyone; they understand the importance of being lead learners, and demonstrating engaged learning for their students. Embracing whole learning is simply a matter of personal and professional fulfillment. As one teacher told Ken, "it shakes things up and keeps us all moving and growing."

To Connect School Subjects

Teachers of whole learning are waging a battle against the disconnectedness of learning in school. Because real learning does not happen in 45-minute periods designed to fit separate subjects, a school's often artificial categories or disciplines seem disconnected and make little sense to students and to many teachers. (Remember Lynn's student muttering, "From frog legs to Islam"?) Discovering disciplines as lenses through which to examine a problem or interest area is a more natural approach for human beings.

We do see resistance to whole learning in today's schools. Most of it stems from teachers being uncomfortable about teaching in ways so different from their own experiences as students. Identifying oneself as a teacher of a subject rather than a teacher of kids is a factor as well. An increased level of collegiality—as we see in Shirlee Jellum's work with her colleague in history—helps teachers become more comfortable about asking questions about another's field of study. Collaborative ventures around themes will lessen the anxiety about infringing on another's subject "turf."

As Sally Wells' team discovered, this whole topic approach can actually cover more in greater depth, as well as fill in the gaps between subjects. An in-depth study allows for more and richer learning experiences than does a cursory overview of an entire single subject. It seems very inappropriate to ask young adolescents to conceptualize the span of an entire discipline, when they have yet to explore the depths of their own learning potential. Teachers of whole learning have learned to repress that "ghost" of subject coverage. The flow of an inquiry that provides meaningful continuity through an unlimited number of ongoing activities creates opportunities for area specialists to become important leaders at different moments.

Teachers who are inclined toward whole learning are naturally holistic thinkers, or have learned to think holistically. They see all of the subject areas represented in any topic. They refuse to be categorized as belonging to any one area because they have so many general interests. They know that their specialized knowledge in a particular area is important, because it can help students learn important skills when the time comes. But they also recognize that being a generalist is important if they are to help students see the connections in this world.

To Have Fun

Where along the way, in the development of schools, did we forget that learning ought to be fun? All of the great teachers that we can remember knew how to enjoy life and to appreciate the humor in the world. Some teachers believe that "to have fun" is a good motivator for teaching an integrated study.

A sense of humor is apparent in many teachers who strive toward integrated study. They see the humor in many situations and take the time to share it. Laughing together is not only a builder of morale, it also helps create a relaxed learning atmosphere, conducive to better learning. When teachers believe it is important to learn from their own mistakes, they try to instill in their classrooms an appreciation of "failure" as a tool for learning. Whole learning, like any adventure into the unknown, is fraught with the potential for miscalculations and mistakes. By not taking themselves too seriously and showing that mistakes are a valuable part of their growth, teachers help students value their own learning struggles.

One of the most attractive attributes of whole learning is the obvious opportunity for celebration. The risk inherent in developing a theme, following it through multiple curious twists, and arriving at a successful culmination is indeed cause for enjoyment and celebration of that experience. Celebration regenerates enthusiasm for learning. Having fun is a great motivator for all.

To Involve the Community

The opportunity to garner community support also encourages some teachers to pursue integrated learning. By involving community resources with the school in a special learning project, positive public relations can result for both. Teachers may begin with small steps in this direction: Scott's involvement of parents in his students' reading and writing; Lynn's arrangements with parents for Saturday field trips. But we see the full richness and power possible through community involvement in stories such as those told by Charles Ault and Anne McEnerny-Ogle, and Charles Ault and Neil Maine.

In an age when schools are often under the scrutiny of a disassociated community, whole learning presents many opportunities for the school and its community to become reunited. The community is full of resources that can add a meaningful, real-life connection to student learning. Field trips take on added importance when students need the information for their inquiry. They learn to make their own arrangements and prepare other class members for visits. They locate people in the community to come to school. Most teachers, after an initial timidity, are amazed at the collection of people at their fingertips who are eager to share their knowledge, skills, and experience with school children.

Whole learning is a means for reconnecting schools and their larger community settings. By inviting parents and community members to the celebrations of learning in which they participated, strong new bonds of mutual support are built. The community comes to see the school as a place that involves kids in meaningful learning. The school comes to see the community as an indispensable resource for real learning. There is no more vibrant public relations program than young adolescents busily learning in their community and sharing that learning with those around them.

To Respond to Collegial and Administrative Support

As whole learning becomes a more acceptable practice in schools, a few practitioners recognize that their teaching situations already offer collegial support for integrated teaching and learning. To respond positively to that encouragement is a worthy reason to pursue this approach.

Many teachers are eager to explore new ways of learning and teaching when they feel supported to do so. We see in this volume schools where administrators have worked diligently with their staff to eliminate the external obstacles mentioned earlier: lack of support, lack of planning time, scheduling problems, lack of resources, curriculum rigidity, no preparation in alternative assessment. Colleagues are available to help teachers overcome the fears and difficulties of learning to teach as they were not taught.

When an entire school or district takes the leap together into whole learning, and teachers are supported professionally and personally, instead of isolated instances of classroom experimentation we see a more institutionalized approach where students learn holistically throughout their school careers. Imagine the transformative power of that educational experience with a cadre of teachers who have integrated their practice with their lives, and know how to work collaboratively, how to build a curriculum around the interests of students, how to have fun, and how to revitalize themselves through their work.

Weighing the Strains and Joys

If we look at the lists of strains and joys, side by side, we see a qualitative difference between the two that goes beyond one being optimistically positive and the other pragmatically negative. While the strains address practical teaching concerns—resources, the need for support, and teachers' perceived lack of abilities—the joys speak to a higher vision of learning focused on students, collaboration, community involvement, authentic and connected experiences, fun and excitement. One side of the list focuses on the limits; the other on the possibilities. While some teachers see only the technical aspects of their role, others see the full range of professional responsibilities. Jack Miller noted that we all have both dimensions within us—one is the "small self," the other is the "larger self."[8]

When we teach from the small self, it is easy to see the obstacles and to get stuck in our own problems. When we choose to operate from the larger self, there is an inherent statement of our faith in students as capable learners. We see that problems have solutions, and our view of educational possibilities expands. Carl Glickman's research on teacher development supports this perspective about those who choose whole learning.[9] Teachers at the high end of Glickman's continuum exhibit a high concern for others, expend extra time and energy, and express a strong desire to serve others. All these qualities are important for teachers of integrated learning. He also finds that high levels of abstract thinking and altruistic motivation characterize the most capable and competent teachers. Those teachers who can conceptualize, tolerate some ambiguity, and respond flexibly to the developmental needs of students are the most likely to teach in an integrated way. Successful teaching, Glickman argues, is adaptive, flexible, thoughtful, and exploratory. Good teachers reflect upon what they are doing, re-evaluate the results of their practice, and continually search for new ways to connect with their students. Certainly the challenges of whole learning require teachers who are more technically oriented to develop these traits of the "larger self." Whether or not all teachers can achieve this level of development, we ought to encourage this direction and point to successful examples for them to follow.

As teachers become more developmentally ready to assume this new teaching role, we may be witnessing an indication of an evolutionary change in education. Marilyn Ferguson devotes Chapter 9 of her landmark book, *The Aquarian Conspiracy*,[10] to educational matters: "Flying and Seeing: New Ways to Learn." She explains the need for connection and innovation within the new curriculum to take learning beyond schools. Such is the goal of whole learning. She tells of teachers who are spontaneous and supportive; who search for meaning beyond the facts, reflect on the process of teaching, and are learners themselves; who encourage cooperation; who involve students in joint planning and demonstrate self-respect; and who go beyond everyday routines to meet the needs of their students. These are the teachers, she believes, to whom the future belongs. If this is true, whole learning teachers will surely find a place in tomorrow's schools.

Ed Clark, Jr., notes that integrated learning seeks to make teaching and learning more whole (*integrare*, Latin, meaning "to make whole").[11] It intends to value context as well as content; concepts as well as facts; questions as well as answers; imagination as well as knowledge; developmental intent as well as grade content; process of learning as well as product of learning; and quality of information as well as quantity of information. In short, learning as well as teaching. Teaching that is grounded in the whole learning of students has more integrity than teaching that is based on the facts and figures of a disconnected collection of subject matter.

Within that search, teachers themselves seek integrity. Stephen Covey[12] reminds us that integrity is a bonding of humility and courage: the humility to understand the world as whole and to see kids as powerful directors of their own learning; the courage to remain whole in a world that tries to disconnect us from one another and from our own understanding of the world. It is the integrity of the teachers who share their work here that we celebrate. They have dared to take the leap and offered to their students, and to us, the lessons of humility and courage.

End Notes

1. Susan M. Drake, *Planning Integrated Study: The Call to Adventure* (Alexandria, VA: Association for Supervision and Curriculum Development, 1993).
2. Chris Stevenson and Judy F. Carr (Eds.), *Integrated Studies in the Middle Grades: Dancing Through Walls* (New York: Teachers College Press, 1993).
3. Everett Rogers, *Diffusion of Innovations* (New York: The Free Press, 1971).
4. D. Powell, "Barriers to Change in the U.S.A.: Texts, Tests, and Other Pressures." Paper presented at the meeting of the International Reading Association, Toronto, Canada, May 1988.
5. G. E. Hall and S. M. Hord, *Change in Schools: Facilitating the Process* (Albany: State University of New York Press, 1987).
6. Glennellen Pace, "Stories of Teacher-Initiated Change from Traditional to Whole-Language Literacy Instruction," *Elementary School Journal* 92.4 (March 1992): 461–476.
7. James A. Beane, *The Middle School Curriculum: From Rhetoric to Reality* (Columbus, OH: National Middle School Association, 1990).
8. Jack Miller and Susan Drake, "Integrated Study Using the Story Model" Presentation at the "What's All This Talk About Curriculum Integration?" Conference, Scottsdale, AZ, (January 1994.
9. Carl D. Glickman, *Supervision of Instruction: A Developmental Approach* (Boston, MA: Allyn and Bacon, 1985).
10. Marilyn Ferguson, "Flying and Seeing: New Ways to Learn," in *The Aquarian Conspiracy* (Los Angeles, CA: J.P. Tarcher, 1980), 279–321.
11. Edward T. Clark, Jr., Workshop Handout. Goddard Institute for Teaching and Learning (Plainfield, VT: By the Author, 1993).
12. Stephen R. Covey. Keynote Presentation at the Meeting of The National Staff Development Council, Dallas, TX, 1993.

Contributors

Glennellen Pace is Associate Professor of Language and Literacy, and Elementary Program Coordinator at Lewis & Clark College in Portland, Oregon. She spent ten years as a multi-grades teacher, four of them in blended grade classrooms. Prior to coming to Lewis & Clark College, she was an instructor of reading and writing courses and visiting professor in charge of field placement and supervision for teacher preparation programs at the University of Oregon, Eugene, and Assistant Professor of Reading and Language Arts at the University of Wisconsin, Eaur Claire.

Ellen Aragon currently teaches 'critically' at-risk students in the morning and works in an administrative capacity afternoons at Almeria Middle School in Fontana, California. Additionally, she is in her second year as portfolio mentor for the Fontana Unified School District. She has an M. A. from California State University, San Bernardino.

Charles R. Ault, Jr. is Associate Professor of Education at Lewis & Clark College, Portland, Oregon. He received his Ph.D. from Cornell University. At Lewis & Clark, he has been active in developing programs for science teachers while also teaching courses in elementary school science and mathematics. He often works in collaboration with the Oregon Museum of Science and Industry (OMSI) to help classroom teachers understand principles of museum education.

Kenneth Bergstrom, a core faculty member at Goddard College, received his Ed.D. from the University of Vermont. In addition, he has worked in Vermont classrooms for 13 years at the elementary, middle, and (briefly) secondary levels. His strong interest in professionalizing teaching led him to serve as initial staff for Vermont's Standards Board for Professional Educators.

Mary Burke-Hengen, after a decade at the middle school level, now teaches at Jefferson High School in Portland, Oregon, where she was given an opportunity to integrate global studies and world literature into one course. She also teaches an integrated government, economics, and literature course. She holds an M. S. from State Cloud State University, Minnesota in social science and an M. S. from Portland State University in special education/learning disabilities.

Scott Christian currently teaches eighth grade language arts as part of an interdisciplinary team at Nikiski Middle School, Alaska. He began teaching at the secondary level in a remote Eskimo village near the Bering Sea, then taught at the primary level before moving to the middle grade. He is currently a Dewitt Wallace/Reader's Digest Fellow and is part of the Bread Loaf School of English where he is pursuing an M. A.

Patricia Tefft-Cousin received her Ph.D. in Reading from Indiana University. She is currently Associate Professor at California State University, San Bernardino. A former classroom teacher in both regular and special education, she currently teaches course in special education and literacy She has published a number of chapters and articles. She is currently involved in a long-term curriculum change project in a district in Southern California with three other university colleagues.

Deirdre Garner, a graduate of the University of Rhode Island, worked for five years at Spaulding Graded Middle School in Barre, Vermont. There she was involved with the Vermont Writing Project and worked with student teachers from Goddard College. She is currently teaching English on a ninth grade team at Copperas Cove High School, Texas.

Tim Gillespie is the Language Arts Specialist at the Multnomah County Education Service District in Portland. Oregon. He has taught fifth grade through high school, most recently in an eighth grade classroom at Beaumont Middle School in an urban Portland neighborhood. In addition, he co-directs the Oregon Writing Project at Lewis & Clark College and is a Past President of the Oregon Council of Teachers of English. He holds an M.A.T. from Lewis & Clark College and an M.A. from the University of New Hampshire.

George Glasson, Associate Professor at Virginia Polytechnic Institute and State University, specializes in middle and elementary school science education. He is currently involved in the statewide V-QUEST Project, a collaborative effort that is part of the National Science Foundation's systemic reform initiative for improving science and mathematics teaching and learning. A former middle school science teacher, he received his Ph.D. from the University of North Carolina at Chapel Hill.

Shirlee Jellum received her Master's Degree in Reading and Language Arts from Seattle Pacific University. She currently teaches English in a small, rural high school in the heart of the Columbia River Gorge. She began teaching middle school language arts in the mid-80s and became an enthusiastic whole language educator. With help from a like-minded colleague, they developed an integrated curriculum to bring relevance to the study of history and language arts.

Rosary Lalik is an Associate Professor of Reading and Language Arts Education at Virginia Polytechnic Institute and State University and holds her Ed.D. from Syracuse University. She has also worked as a classroom teacher and reading specialist at the elementary level and she has assisted high school and college students to learn strategies for academic success. For the last 10 years, she has been Director at the Virginia Tech site of the Virginia Reading to Learn project, which is designed to help teachers support active, inquiry based learning at the middle and secondary levels.

Neal Maine retired in 1993 from elementary and secondary teaching, his district's teacher support program, and leadership of a consortium of high schools working to author a "natural resources curriculum" as part of the statewide effort to implement the Oregon 21st Century Schools Act. Now incorporated at "Pacific Educational Consultants, he continues to work as a consulting ecologist on wetland preservation projects while making contributions to the Portland State University Center for Science Education.

Chris Mattson, a graduate of Goddard College, currently teaches eighth grade Language Arts/Social Studies at Spaulding Middle School, Barre, Vermont. Part of a two-person team with another teacher who specializes in Math/Science, he and his colleague work with 40 eighth grade students in an integrated program.

Suzan Mauney has been teaching science at Blacksburg Middle School, Virginia for 12 years. She holds a B.S. degree from Georgia State University and an M.A. in Curriculum and Instruction with a concentration in science education. She is active in the Virginia Middle School Association, Virginia Association of Teachers of English, and Virginia Society for Technology Education.

Anne McEnerny-Ogle has taught for 21 years at the elementary and middle school levels. Currently she chairs the Mathematics Department at Waluga Junior High School in Lake Oswego, Oregon. She serves as the editor of The Oregon Mathematics Teacher and as an adjunct faculty member for Portland State University. In 1993 she received a Milken Foundation National Teacher Award, and the state of Oregon has awarded her a Kyotaru Fellowship to Japan to study practices of mathematics instruction.

Lynn Moss received her Master of Arts in Teaching from Lewis & Clark College in Portland, Oregon. She is currently teaching 9-, 10-, and 11-year-olds in a multi-age classroom at Hazeldale Elementary School in Beaverton, Oregon. Prior to that she spent several years teaching seventh grade.

Anne Reid was educated in a one-room school where the concept of a community of learners was organic. She received a B.A. from Queen's University, Kingston, Ontario, and her M.A. from Goddard College, Vermont. She has taught people from the ages of 3 to 73, but because of the past nine years, have become an active advocate for young adolescents. She currently teaches at the Princess Margaret Public School in Orangeville, Ontario.

Connie Russell is the K-12 Reading/Language Arts Coordinator for the Eau Claire Area School District. Prior to this position, she served as an elementary reading resource teacher, a sixth grade teacher, and a fourth grade teacher. She is a Past President of the Wisconsin Council of Teachers of English and received the Chisholm Award in 1994 for meritorios service to the language arts.

Sally Ann Wells teaches fifth and sixth grades at Henkle Middle School in White Salmon, Washington. Her early years as an educator took place in Oregon teaching environmental education at residential outdoor schools and in Colorado as a teacher at Jarrow Montessori School. She received her Master of Arts in Teaching from Lewis & Clark College in Portland, Oregon.